Pre-Calculus 11

Authors

Bruce McAskill, B.Sc., B.Ed., M.Ed., Ph.D.
Mathematics Consultant, Victoria, British
Columbia

Wayne Watt, B.Sc., B.Ed., M.Ed.
Mathematics Consultant, Winnipeg, Manitoba

Eric Balzarini, B.Sc., B.Ed., M.Ed.
School District 35 (Langley), British Columbia

Len Bonifacio, B.Ed.
Edmonton Catholic Separate School District
No. 7, Alberta

Scott Carlson, B.Ed., B.Sc.
Golden Hills School Division No. 75, Alberta

Blaise Johnson, B.Sc., B.Ed.
School District 45 (West Vancouver), British
Columbia

Ron Kennedy, B.Ed.
Mathematics Consultant, Edmonton, Alberta

Harold Wardrop, B.Sc.
Brentwood College School, Mill Bay
(Independent), British Columbia

Contributing Author

Stephanie Mackay
Edmonton Catholic Separate School District
No. 7, Alberta

Senior Program Consultants

Bruce McAskill, B.Sc., B.Ed., M.Ed., Ph.D.
Mathematics Consultant, Victoria, British
Columbia

Wayne Watt, B.Sc., B.Ed., M.Ed.
Mathematics Consultant, Winnipeg, Manitoba

Assessment Consultant

Chris Zarski, B.Ed., M.Ed.
Wetaskiwin Regional Division No. 11,
Alberta

Pedagogical Consultant

Terry Melnyk, B.Ed.
Edmonton Public Schools, Alberta

Aboriginal Consultant

Chun Ong, B.A., B.Ed.
Manitoba First Nations Education Resource
Centre, Manitoba

Differentiated Instruction Consultant

Heather Granger
Prairie South School Division No. 210,
Saskatchewan

Gifted and Career Consultant

Rick Wunderlich
School District 83 (North Okanagan/
Shuswap), British Columbia

Math Processes Consultant

Reg Fogarty
School District 83 (North Okanagan/
Shuswap), British Columbia

Technology Consultants

Ron Kennedy
Mathematics Consultant, Edmonton, Alberta

Ron Coleborn
School District 41 (Burnaby), British
Columbia

Advisors

John Agnew, School District 63 (Saanich),
British Columbia

Katharine Borgen, School District 39
(Vancouver) and University of British
Columbia, British Columbia

Barb Gajdos, Calgary Roman Catholic
Separate School District No. 1, Alberta

Sandra Harazny, Regina Roman Catholic
Separate School Division No. 81,
Saskatchewan

Renée Jackson, University of Alberta, Alberta

Gerald Krabbe, Calgary Board of Education,
Alberta

Gail Poshtar, Calgary Catholic School
District, Alberta

Francophone Advisor

Mario Chaput, Pembina Trails School
Division Manitoba

Luc Lerminiaux, Regina School Division
No. 4, Saskatchewan

Inuit Advisor

Christine Purse, Mathematics Consultant,
British Columbia

Métis Advisor

Greg King, Northern Lights School Division
No. 69, Alberta

Technical Advisor

Darren Kuropatwa, Winnipeg School
Division #1, Manitoba

McGraw-Hill Ryerson

Toronto   Montréal   Boston   Burr Ridge, IL   Dubuque, IA   Madison, WI   New York
San Francisco   St. Louis   Bangkok   Bogotá   Caracas   Kuala Lumpur   Lisbon   London
Madrid   Mexico City   Milan   New Delhi   Santiago   Seoul   Singapore   Sydney   Taipei

McGraw-Hill Ryerson
Pre-Calculus 11

Copyright © 2011, McGraw-Hill Ryerson Limited, a Subsidiary of The McGraw-Hill Companies. All rights reserved. No part of this publication may be reproduced or transmitted in any form or by any means, or stored in a data base or retrieval system, without the prior written permission of McGraw-Hill Ryerson Limited, or, in the case of photocopying or other reprographic copying, a licence from The Canadian Copyright Licensing Agency (Access Copyright). For an Access Copyright licence, visit *www.accesscopyright.ca* or call toll free to 1-800-893-5777.

ISBN-13: 978-0-07-073873-7
ISBN-10: 0-07-073873-4

http://www.mcgrawhill.ca

2 3 4 5 6 7 8 9 10   TCP   1 9 8 7 6 5 4 3 2 1

Printed and bound in Canada

Care has been taken to trace ownership of copyright material contained in this text. The publishers will gladly accept any information that will enable them to rectify any reference or credit in subsequent printings.

Microsoft® Excel is either a registered trademark or trademarks of Microsoft Corporation in the United States and/or other countries.

TI-84™ and TI-Nspire™ are registered trademarks of Texas Instruments.

The Geometer's Sketchpad®, Key Curriculum Press, 1150 65th Street, Emeryville, CA 94608, 1-800-995-MATH.

VICE-PRESIDENT, EDITORIAL AND PUBLISHER: Beverley Buxton
ASSOCIATE PUBLISHER AND CONTENT MANAGER: Jean Ford
PROJECT MANAGER: Janice Dyer
DEVELOPMENTAL EDITORS: Maggie Cheverie, Jackie Lacoursiere, Jodi Rauch
MANAGER, EDITORIAL SERVICES: Crystal Shortt
SUPERVISING EDITOR: Janie Deneau
COPY EDITOR: Julie Cochrane
PHOTO RESEARCH & PERMISSIONS: Linda Tanaka
EDITORIAL ASSISTANT: Erin Hartley
EDITORIAL COORDINATION: Jennifer Keay, Janie Reeson, Alexandra Savage-Ferr
MANAGER, PRODUCTION SERVICES: Yolanda Pigden
PRODUCTION COORDINATOR: Jennifer Hall
INDEXER: Natalie Boon
INTERIOR DESIGN: Pronk & Associates
COVER DESIGN: Michelle Losier
ART DIRECTION: Tom Dart, First Folio Resource Group Inc.
ELECTRONIC PAGE MAKE-UP: Tom Dart, Kim Hutchinson,
                                        First Folio Resource Group Inc.
COVER IMAGE: Courtesy of Ocean/Corbis

Acknowledgements

There are many students, teachers, and administrators who the publisher, authors, and consultants of *Pre-Calculus 11* wish to thank for their thoughtful comments and creative suggestions about what would work best in their classrooms. Their input and assistance have been invaluable in making sure that the Student Resource and its related Teacher's Resource meet the needs of students and teachers who work within the Western and Northern Canadian Protocol Common Curriculum Framework.

Reviewers

Stella Ablett
Mulgrave School, West
   Vancouver (Independent)
British Columbia

Kristi Allen
Wetaskiwin Regional Public
   Schools
Alberta

Karen Bedard
School District No. 22
   (Vernon)
British Columbia

Gordon Bramfield
Grasslands Regional
   Division No. 6
Alberta

Yvonne Chow
Strathcona-Tweedsmur
   School (Independent)
Alberta

Lindsay Collins
South East Cornerstone
   School Division No. 209
Saskatchewan

Julie Cordova
St. Jamies-Assiniboia School
   Division
Manitoba

Janis Crighton
Lethbridge School District
   No. 51
Alberta

Steven Daniel
Department of Education,
   Culture and Employment
Northwest Territories

Ashley Dupont
St. Maurice School Board
Manitoba

Dee Elder
Edmonton Public Schools
Alberta

Janet Ferdorvich
Alexis Board of Education
Alberta

Carol Funk
Nanaimo/Ladysmith School
   District No. 68
British Columbia

Howard Gamble
Horizon School Division #67
Alberta

Jessika Girard
Conseil Scolaire
   Francophone No. 93
British Columbia

Pauline Gleimius
B.C. Christian Academy
   (Private)
British Columbia

Marge Hallonquist
Elk Island Catholic Schools
Alberta

Jeni Halowski
Lethbridge School District
   No. 51
Alberta

Jason Harbor
North East School Division
   No. 200
Saskatchewan

Dale Hawken
St. Albert Protestant
   Separate School District
   No. 6
Alberta

Murray D. Henry
Prince Albert Catholic
   School Division #6
Saskatchewan

Barbara Holzer
Prairie South School
   Division
Saskatchewan

Larry Irla
Aspen View Regional
   Division No. 19
Alberta

Betty Johns
University of Manitoba
   (retired)
Manitoba

Andrew Jones
St. George's School (Private
   School)
British Columbia

Jenny Kim
Concordia High School
   (Private)
Alberta

Janine Klevgaard
Clearview School Division
   No. 71
Alberta

Ana Lahnert
Surrey School District
   No. 36
British Columbia

Carey Lehner
Saskatchewan Rivers School
   Division No. 119
Saskatchewan

Debbie Loo
Burnaby School District #41
British Columbia

Jay Lorenzen
Horizon School District #205
Sakatchewan

Teréza Malmstrom
Calgary Board of Education
Alberta

Rodney Marseille
School District No. 62
British Columbia

Darren McDonald
Parkland School Division
   No. 70
Alberta

Dick McDougall
Calgary Catholic School
   District
Alberta

Georgina Mercer
Fort Nelson School District
   No. 81
British Columbia

Kim Mucheson
Comox Valley School
   District #71
British Columbia

Yasuko Nitta
Richmond Christian School
   (Private)
British Columbia

Vince Ogrodnick
Kelsey School Division
Manitoba

Crystal Ozment
Nipisihkopahk Education
   Authority
Alberta

Curtis Rey
Hannover School Division
Manitoba

Oreste Rimaldi
School District No. 34
   (Abbotsford)
British Columbia

Wade Sambrook
Western School Division
Manitoba

James Schmidt
Pembina Trails School
   Division
Manitoba

Sonya Semail
School District 39
   (Vancouver)
British Columbia

Dixie Sillito
Prairie Rose School Division
Alberta

Clint Surry
School District 63 (Saanich)
British Columbia

Debbie Terceros
Peace Wapiti School
   Division #76
Alberta

John Verhagen
Livingstone Range School
   Division
Alberta

Contents

A Tour of Your Textbook

Unit Opener

Each unit begins with a two-page spread. The first page of the **Unit Opener** introduces what you will learn in the unit. The **Unit Project** is introduced on the second page. Each Unit Project helps you connect the math in the unit to real life using experiences that may interest you.

Project Corner boxes throughout the chapters help you gather information for your project. Some **Project Corner** boxes include questions to help you to begin thinking about and discussing your project.

The **Unit Projects** in Units 1 and 4 are designed for you to complete in pieces, chapter by chapter, throughout the unit. At the end of the unit, a **Project Wrap-Up** allows you to consolidate your work in a meaningful presentation.

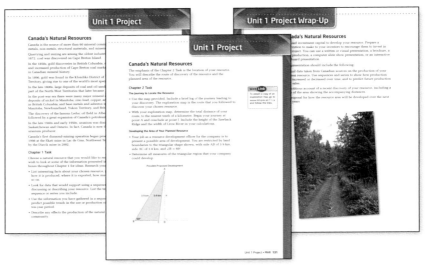

The **Unit Projects** in Units 2 and 3 provide an opportunity for you to choose a single **Project Wrap-Up** at the end of the unit.

Chapter Opener

Each chapter begins with a two-page spread that introduces you to what you will learn in the chapter.

The opener includes information about a career that uses the skills covered in the chapter. A Web Link allows you to learn more about this career and how it involves the mathematics you are learning.

Visuals on the chapter opener spread show other ways the skills and concepts from the chapter are used in daily life.

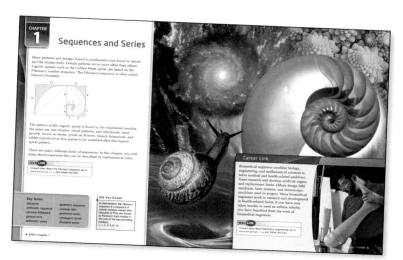

Numbered Sections

The numbered sections in each chapter start with a visual to connect the topic to a real setting. The purpose of this introduction is to help you make connections between the math in the section and in the real world, or to make connections to what you already know or may be studying in other classes.

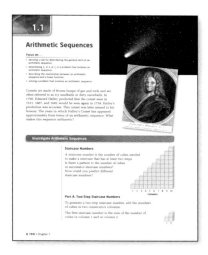

Three-Part Lesson

Each section is organized in a three-part lesson: Investigate, Link the Ideas, and Check Your Understanding.

Investigate

- The **Investigate** consists of short steps often accompanied by illustrations. It is designed to help you build your own understanding of the new concept.

- The **Reflect and Respond** questions help you to analyse and communicate what you are learning and draw conclusions.

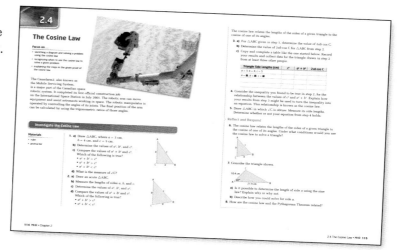

Link the Ideas

- The explanations in this section help you connect the concepts explored in the **Investigate** to the **Examples**.

- The **Examples** and worked **Solutions** show how to use the concepts. The Examples include several tools to help you understand the work.
  - Words in green font help you think through the steps.
  - Different methods of solving the same problem are sometimes shown. One method may make more sense to you than the others. Or, you may develop another method that means more to you.

- Each Example is followed by a **Your Turn**. The Your Turn allows you to explore your understanding of the skills covered in the Example.

- After all the Examples are presented, the **Key Ideas** summarize the main new concepts.

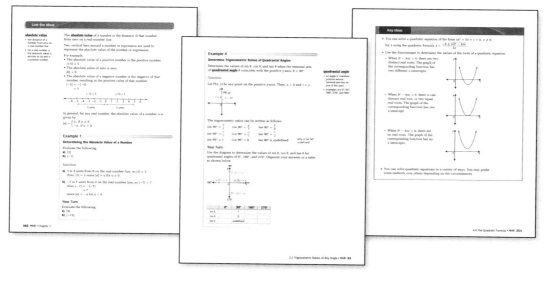

Check Your Understanding

- **Practise:** These questions allow you to check your understanding of the concepts. You can often do the first few questions by checking the Link the Ideas notes or by following one of the worked Examples.

- **Apply:** These questions ask you to apply what you have learned to solve problems. You can choose your own methods of solving a variety of problem types.

- **Extend:** These questions may be more challenging. Many connect to other concepts or lessons. They also allow you to choose your own methods of solving a variety of problem types.

- **Create Connections:** These questions focus your thinking on the Key Ideas and also encourage communication. Many of these questions also connect to other subject areas or other topics within mathematics.

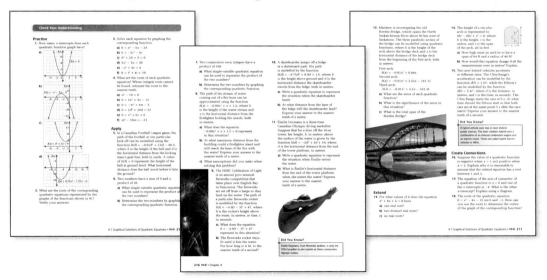

- **Mini-Labs:** These questions provide hands-on activities that encourage you to further explore the concept you are learning.

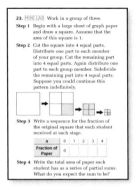

Other Features

Key Terms are listed on the Chapter Opener pages. You may already know the meaning of some of them. If not, watch for these terms the first time they are used in the chapter. The meaning is given in the margin. Many definitions include visuals that help clarify the term.

Key Terms
rational expression
non-permissible value
rational equation

Some **Did You Know?** boxes provide additional information about the meaning of words that are not Key Terms. Other boxes contain interesting facts related to the math you are learning.

Did You Know?

In mathematics, the *Fibonacci sequence* is a sequence of natural numbers named after Leonardo of Pisa, also known as Fibonacci. Each number is the sum of the two preceding numbers.
1, 1, 2, 3, 5, 8, 13, ...

Did You Know?

The first Ferris wheel was built for the 1853 World's Fair in Chicago. The wheel was designed by George Washington Gale Ferris. It had 36 gondola seats and reached a height of 80 m.

Opportunities are provided to use a variety of **Technology** tools. You can use technology to explore patterns and relationships, test predictions, and solve problems. A technology approach is usually provided as only one of a variety of approaches and tools to be used to help you develop your understanding.

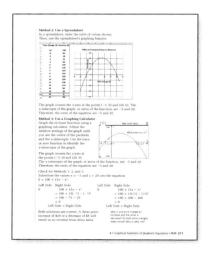

Web Links provide Internet information related to some topics. Log on to www.mhrprecalc11.ca and you will be able to link to recommended Web sites.

Web Link

To learn more about the Fibonacci sequence, go to www.mhrprecalc11.ca and follow the links.

A **Chapter Review** and a **Practice Test** appear at the end of each chapter. The review is organized by section number so you can look back if you need help with a question. The test includes multiple choice, short answer, and extended response questions.

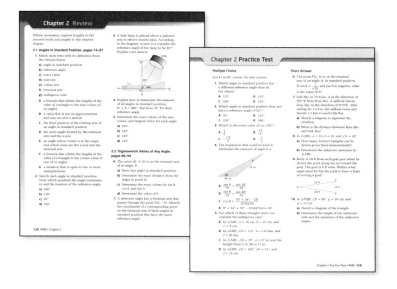

A **Cumulative Review** and a **Unit Test** appear at the end of each unit. The review is organized by chapter. The test includes multiple choice, numerical response, and written response questions.

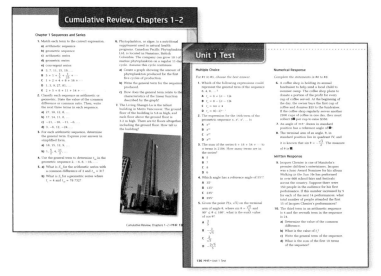

Answers are provided for the Practise, Apply, Extend, Create Connections, Chapter Review, Practice Test, Cumulative Review, and Unit Test questions. Sample answers are provided for questions that have a variety of possible answers or that involve communication. If you need help with a question like this, read the sample and then try to give an alternative response.

Refer to the illustrated **Glossary** at the back of the student resource if you need to check the exact meaning of mathematical terms.

If you want to find a particular math topic in *Pre-Calculus 11*, look it up in the **Index**, which is at the back of the student resource. The index provides page references that may help you review that topic.

Unit 1

Patterns

Many problems are solved using patterns. Economic and resource trends may be based on sequences and series. Seismic exploration identifies underground phenomena, such as caves, oil pockets, and rock layers, by transmitting sound into the earth and timing the echo of the vibration. Surveyors use triangulation and the laws of trigonometry to determine distances between inaccessible points. All of these activities use patterns and aspects of the mathematics you will encounter in this unit.

Looking Ahead

In this unit, you will solve problems involving...

- arithmetic sequences and series
- geometric sequences and series
- infinite geometric series
- sine and cosine laws

Unit 1 Project　Canada's Natural Resources

Canada is a country rich with natural resources. Petroleum, minerals, and forests are found in abundance in the Canadian landscape. Canada is one of the world's leading exporters of minerals, mineral products, and forest products. Resource development has been a mainstay of Canada's economy for many years.

In this project, you will explore one of Canada's natural resources from the categories of petroleum, minerals, or forestry. You will collect and present data related to your chosen resource to meet the following criteria:
- Include a log of the journey leading to the discovery of your resource.
- In Chapter 1, you will provide data on the production of your natural resource. Here you will apply your knowledge of sequences and series to show how production has increased or decreased over time, and make predictions about future development of your chosen resource.
- In Chapter 2, you will use skills developed with trigonometry, including the sine law and the cosine law to explore the area where your resource was discovered. You will then explore the proposed site of your natural resource.

At the end of your project, you will encourage potential investors to participate in the development of your resource. Your final project may take many forms. It may be a written or visual presentation, a brochure, a video production, or a computer slide show. Or, you could use the interactive features of a whiteboard.

In the Project Corner box at the end of most sections, you will find information and notes about Canada's natural resources. You can use this information to help gather data and facts about your chosen resource.

Sequences and Series

Many patterns and designs linked to mathematics are found in nature and the human body. Certain patterns occur more often than others. Logistic spirals, such as the Golden Mean spiral, are based on the Fibonacci number sequence. The Fibonacci sequence is often called Nature's Numbers.

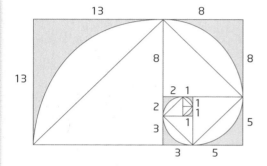

The pattern of this logistic spiral is found in the chambered nautilus, the inner ear, star clusters, cloud patterns, and whirlpools. Seed growth, leaves on stems, petals on flowers, branch formations, and rabbit reproduction also appear to be modelled after this logistic spiral pattern.

There are many different kinds of sequences. In this chapter, you will learn about sequences that can be described by mathematical rules.

Web Link

To learn more about the Fibonacci sequence, go to www.mhrprecalc11.ca and follow the links.

Key Terms

sequence	geometric sequence
arithmetic sequence	common ratio
common difference	geometric series
general term	convergent series
arithmetic series	divergent series

Did You Know?

In mathematics, the *Fibonacci sequence* is a sequence of natural numbers named after Leonardo of Pisa, also known as Fibonacci. Each number is the sum of the two preceding numbers.
1, 1, 2, 3, 5, 8, 13, ...

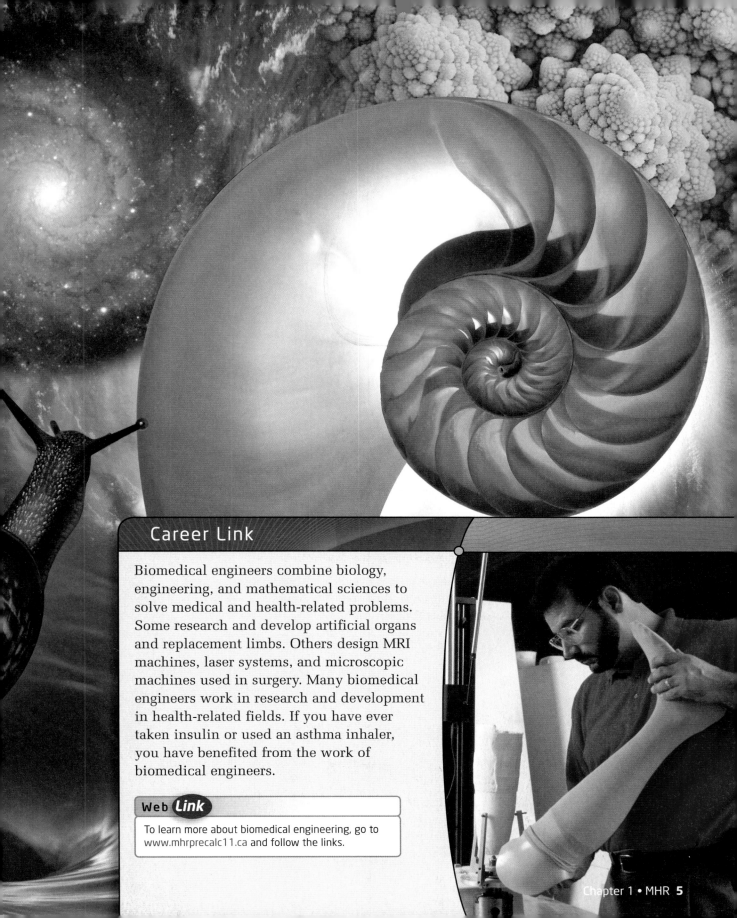

Career Link

Biomedical engineers combine biology, engineering, and mathematical sciences to solve medical and health-related problems. Some research and develop artificial organs and replacement limbs. Others design MRI machines, laser systems, and microscopic machines used in surgery. Many biomedical engineers work in research and development in health-related fields. If you have ever taken insulin or used an asthma inhaler, you have benefited from the work of biomedical engineers.

Web Link

To learn more about biomedical engineering, go to www.mhrprecalc11.ca and follow the links.

Arithmetic Sequences

Focus on...

- deriving a rule for determining the general term of an arithmetic sequence
- determining t_1, d, n, or t_n in a problem that involves an arithmetic sequence
- describing the relationship between an arithmetic sequence and a linear function
- solving a problem that involves an arithmetic sequence

Comets are made of frozen lumps of gas and rock and are often referred to as icy mudballs or dirty snowballs. In 1705, Edmond Halley predicted that the comet seen in 1531, 1607, and 1682 would be seen again in 1758. Halley's prediction was accurate. This comet was later named in his honour. The years in which Halley's Comet has appeared approximately form terms of an arithmetic sequence. What makes this sequence arithmetic?

Investigate Arithmetic Sequences

Staircase Numbers

A *staircase number* is the number of cubes needed to make a staircase that has at least two steps. Is there a pattern to the number of cubes in successive staircase numbers? How could you predict different staircase numbers?

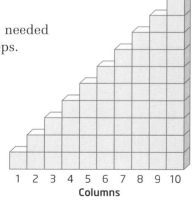

Part A: Two-Step Staircase Numbers

To generate a two-step staircase number, add the numbers of cubes in two consecutive columns.

The first staircase number is the sum of the number of cubes in column 1 and in column 2.

For the second staircase number, add the number of cubes in columns 2 and 3.

2 3

For the third staircase number, add the number of cubes in columns in 3 and 4.

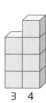

3 4

1. Copy and complete the table for the number of cubes required for each staircase number of a two-step staircase.

Term	1	2	3	4	5	6	7	8	9	10
Staircase Number (Number of Cubes Required)	3	5								

Part B: Three-Step Staircase Numbers

To generate a three-step staircase number, add the numbers of cubes in three consecutive columns.

The first staircase number is the sum of the number of cubes in column 1, column 2, and column 3.

For the second staircase number, add the number of cubes in columns 2, 3, and 4.

For the third staircase number, add the number of cubes in columns 3, 4, and 5.

2. Copy and complete the table for the number of cubes required for each step of a three-step staircase.

Term	1	2	3	4	5	6	7	8	9	10
Staircase Number (Number of Cubes Required)	6	9								

3. The same process may be used for staircase numbers with more than three steps. Copy and complete the following table for the number cubes required for staircase numbers up to six steps.

Term	Number of Steps in the Staircase				
	2	3	4	5	6
1	3	6			
2	5	9			
3					
4					
5					
6					

4. Describe the pattern for the number of cubes in a two-step staircase.

5. How could you find the number of cubes in the 11th and 12th terms of the two-step staircase?

6. Describe your strategy for determining the number of cubes required for staircases with three, four, five, or six steps.

Reflect and Respond

7. a) Would you describe the terms of the number of cubes as a **sequence**?

b) Describe the pattern that you observed.

8. a) In the sequences generated for staircases with more than two steps, how is each term generated from the previous term?

b) Is this difference the same throughout the entire sequence?

9. a) How would you find the number of cubes required if you were asked for the 100th term in a two-step staircase?

b) Derive a formula from your observations of the patterns that would allow you to calculate the 100th term.

c) Derive a general formula that would allow you to calculate the nth term.

sequence

• an ordered list of elements

Link the Ideas

Sequences

A *sequence* is an ordered list of objects. It contains elements or terms that follow a pattern or rule to determine the next term in the sequence. The terms of a sequence are labelled according to their position in the sequence.

The *first term* of the sequence is t_1.
The *number of terms* in the sequence is n.
The *general term* of the sequence is t_n. This term is dependent on the value of n.

The first term of a sequence is sometimes referred to as a. In this resource, the first term will be referred to as t_1.

t_n is read as "t subscript n" or "t sub n."

Finite and Infinite Sequences

A *finite sequence* always has a finite number of terms.
Examples: 2, 5, 8, 11, 14
 5, 10, 15, 20, ..., 100

An *infinite sequence* has an infinite number of terms. Every term is followed by a new term.
Example: 5, 10, 15, 20, ...

Arithmetic Sequences

An **arithmetic sequence** is an ordered list of terms in which the difference between consecutive terms is constant. In other words, the same value or variable is added to each term to create the next term. This constant is called the **common difference**. If you subtract the first term from the second term for any two consecutive terms of the sequence, you will arrive at the common difference.

The formula for the **general term** helps you find the terms of a sequence. This formula is a rule that shows how the value of t_n depends on n.

Consider the sequence 10, 16, 22, 28, ...

Terms	t_1	t_2	t_3	t_4
Sequence	10	16	22	28
Sequence Expressed Using First Term and Common Difference	10	10 + (6)	10 + (6) + (6)	10 + (6) + (6) + (6)
General Sequence	t_1	$t_1 + d$	$t_1 + d + d$ $= t_1 + 2d$	$t_1 + d + d + d$ $= t_1 + 3d$

The general arithmetic sequence is t_1, $t_1 + d$, $t_1 + 2d$, $t_1 + 3d$, ..., where t_1 is the first term and d is the common difference.

$t_1 = t_1$
$t_2 = t_1 + d$
$t_3 = t_1 + 2d$
$\vdots$
$t_n = t_1 + (n - 1)d$

> The *general term* of an arithmetic sequence is
> $t_n = t_1 + (n - 1)d$
> where t_1 is the first term of the sequence
> n is the number of terms
> d is the common difference
> t_n is the general term or nth term

arithmetic sequence

- a sequence in which the difference between consecutive terms is constant

common difference

- the difference between successive terms in an arithmetic sequence, $d = t_n - t_{n-1}$
- the difference may be positive or negative
- for example, in the sequence 10, 16, 22, 28, ..., the common difference is 6

general term

- an expression for directly determining any term of a sequence
- symbol is t_n
- for example, $t_n = 3n + 2$

Example 1

Determine a Particular Term

A visual and performing arts group wants to hire a community events leader. The person will be paid $12 for the first hour of work, $19 for two hours of work, $26 for three hours of work, and so on.

a) Write the general term that you could use to determine the pay for any number of hours worked.

b) What will the person get paid for 6 h of work?

Solution

State the sequence given in the problem.

$t_1 = 12$
$t_2 = 19$
$t_3 = 26$
$\vdots$

The common difference of the sequence may be found by subtracting any two consecutive terms. The common difference for this sequence is 7.
$19 - 12 = 7$
$26 - 19 = 7$

The sequence is arithmetic with a common difference equal to 7. Subtracting any two consecutive terms will result in 7.

Did You Know?

The relation $t_n = 7n + 5$ may also be written using function notation: $f(n) = 7n + 5$.

a) For the given sequence, $t_1 = 12$ and $d = 7$.
Use the formula for the general term of an arithmetic sequence.
$t_n = t_1 + (n - 1)d$
$t_n = 12 + (n - 1)7$ Substitute known values.
$t_n = 12 + 7n - 7$
$t_n = 7n + 5$
The general term of the sequence is $t_n = 7n + 5$.

b) For 6 h of work, the amount is the sixth term in the sequence. Determine t_6.

Method 1: Use an Equation

$t_n = t_1 + (n - 1)d$ or $t_n = 7n + 5$
$t_6 = 12 + (6 - 1)7$ $t_6 = 7(6) + 5$
$t_6 = 12 + (5)(7)$ $t_6 = 42 + 5$
$t_6 = 12 + 35$ $t_6 = 47$
$t_6 = 47$

The value of the sixth term is 47.
For 6 h of work, the person will be paid $47.

Method 2: Use Technology

You can use a calculator or spreadsheet to determine the sixth term of the sequence.

Use a table.

You can generate a table of values and a graph to represent the sequence.

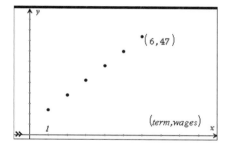

The value of the sixth term is 47.

For 6 h of work, the person will be paid $47.

Your Turn

Many factors affect the growth of a child. Medical and health officials encourage parents to keep track of their child's growth. The general guideline for the growth in height of a child between the ages of 3 years and 10 years is an average increase of 5 cm per year. Suppose a child was 70 cm tall at age 3.

a) Write the general term that you could use to estimate what the child's height will be at any age between 3 and 10.

b) How tall is the child expected to be at age 10?

Example 2

Determine the Number of Terms

The musk-ox and the caribou of northern Canada are hoofed mammals that survived the Pleistocene Era, which ended 10 000 years ago. In 1955, the Banks Island musk-ox population was approximately 9250 animals. Suppose that in subsequent years, the growth of the musk-ox population generated an arithmetic sequence, in which the number of musk-ox increased by approximately 1650 each year. How many years would it take for the musk-ox population to reach 100 000?

Solution

The sequence 9250, 10 900, 12 550, 14 200, ..., 100 000 is arithmetic.

For the given sequence,
First term $t_1 = 9250$
Common difference $d = 1650$
nth term $t_n = 100\ 000$

To determine the number of terms in the sequence, substitute the known values into the formula for the general term of an arithmetic sequence.

$$t_n = t_1 + (n - 1)d$$
$$100\ 000 = 9250 + (n - 1)1650$$
$$100\ 000 = 9250 + 1650n - 1650$$
$$100\ 000 = 1650n + 7600$$
$$92\ 400 = 1650n$$
$$56 = n$$

There are 56 terms in the sequence.
It would take 56 years for the musk-ox population to reach 100 000.

Your Turn

Carpenter ants are large, usually black ants that make their colonies in wood. Although often considered to be pests around the home, carpenter ants play a significant role in a forested ecosystem. Carpenter ants begin with a parent colony. When this colony is well established, they form satellite colonies consisting of only the workers. An established colony may have as many as 3000 ants. Suppose that the growth of the colony produces an arithmetic sequence in which the number of ants increases by approximately 80 ants each month. Beginning with 40 ants, how many months would it take for the ant population to reach 3000?

Example 3

Determine t_1, t_n, and n

Jonathon has a part-time job at the local grocery store. He has been asked to create a display of cereal boxes. The top six rows of his display are shown. The numbers of boxes in the rows produce an arithmetic sequence. There are 16 boxes in the third row from the bottom, and 6 boxes in the eighth row from the bottom.

a) How many boxes are in the bottom row?

b) Determine the general term, t_n, for the sequence.

c) What is the number of rows of boxes in his display?

Solution

a) Method 1: Use Logical Reasoning

The diagram shows the top six rows. From the diagram, you can see that the number of boxes per row decreases by 2 from bottom to top. Therefore, $d = -2$.

What is the value of d if you go from top to bottom?

You could also consider the fact that there are 16 boxes in the 3rd row from the bottom and 6 boxes in the 8th row from the bottom. This results in a difference of 10 boxes in 5 rows. Since the values are decreasing, $d = -2$.

Substitute known values into the formula for the general term.
$$t_n = t_1 + (n - 1)d$$
$$16 = t_1 + (3 - 1)(-2)$$
$$16 = t_1 - 4$$
$$20 = t_1$$
The number of boxes in the bottom row is 20.

Method 2: Use Algebra

Since t_1 and d are both unknown, you can use two equations to determine them. Write an equation for t_3 and an equation for t_8 using the formula for the general term of an arithmetic sequence.
$$t_n = t_1 + (n - 1)d$$

For $n = 3$ $16 = t_1 + (3 - 1)d$
$$16 = t_1 + 2d$$

For $n = 8$ $6 = t_1 + (8 - 1)d$
$$6 = t_1 + 7d$$

Subtract the two equations.
$$16 = t_1 + 2d$$
$$\underline{6 = t_1 + 7d}$$
$$10 = -5d$$
$$-2 = d$$

Substitute the value of d into the first equation.

$16 = t_1 + 2d$
$16 = t_1 + 2(-2)$
$16 = t_1 - 4$
$20 = t_1$

Is there another way to solve this problem? Work with a partner to discuss possible alternate methods.

The sequence for the stacking of the boxes is 20, 18, 16, ...
The number of boxes in the bottom row is 20.

b) Use the formula for the general term of the sequence.
$t_n = t_1 + (n - 1)d$
$t_n = 20 + (n - 1)(-2)$
$t_n = -2n + 22$
The general term of the sequence is $t_n = -2n + 22$.

c) The top row of the stack contains two boxes.
Use the general term to find the number of rows.
$$t_n = -2n + 22$$
$$2 = -2n + 22$$
$$-20 = -2n$$
$$10 = n$$

The number of rows of boxes is 10.

Your Turn

Jonathon has been given the job of stacking cans in a similar design to that of the cereal boxes. The numbers of cans in the rows produces an arithmetic sequence. The top three rows are shown. There are 14 cans in the 8th row from the bottom and 10 cans in the 12th row from the bottom. Determine t_1, d, and t_n for the arithmetic sequence.

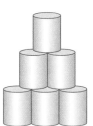

Example 4

Generate a Sequence

A furnace technician charges $65 for making a house call, plus $42 per hour or portion of an hour.

a) Generate the possible charges (excluding parts) for the first 4 h of time.

b) What is the charge for 10 h of time?

Solution

a) Write the sequence for the first four hours.

Terms of the Sequence	1	2	3	4
Number of Hours Worked	1	2	3	4
Charges ($)	107	149	191	233

How do you determine the charge for the first hour?

The charges for the first 4 h are $107, $149, $191, and $233.

b) The charge for the first hour is $107. This is the first term.
The common difference is $42.
$t_1 = 107$
$d = 42$

Substitute known values into the formula to determine the general term.
$t_n = t_1 + (n - 1)d$
$t_n = 107 + (n - 1)42$
$t_n = 107 + 42n - 42$
$t_n = 42n + 65$

Method 1: Use the General Term
The 10th term of the sequence may be generated by substituting 10 for n in the general term.
$t_n = 42n + 65$
$t_{10} = 42(10) + 65$
$t_{10} = 485$
The charge for 10 h of work is $485.

Method 2: Use a Graph
The general term
$t_n = 42n + 65$ is a function
that relates the charge to
the number of hours
worked. This equation
$f(x) = 42x + 65$ could be
graphed. The slope of 42 is
the common difference of
the sequence. The
y-intercept of 65 is the
initial charge for making a house call.

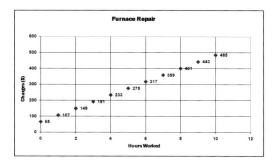

The terms may now be generated by either
tracing on the graph or accessing the table of values.

The charge for 10 h of work is $485.

Hours Worked	Charges ($)
0	65
1	107
2	149
3	191
4	233
5	275
6	317
7	359
8	401
9	443
10	485

Your Turn
What is the charge for 10 h if the furnace technician charges $45 for the
house call plus $46 per hour?

- A sequence is an ordered list of elements.

- Elements within the range of the sequence are called terms of the sequence.

- To describe any term of a sequence, an expression is used for t_n, where $n \in$ N. This term is called the general term.

- In an arithmetic sequence, each successive term is formed by adding a constant. This constant is called the common difference.

- The general term of an arithmetic sequence is
  $t_n = t_1 + (n - 1)d$
  where t_1 is the first term
  $\quad n$ is the number of terms $(n \in$ N)
  $\quad d$ is the common difference
  $\quad t_n$ is the general term or nth term

Check Your Understanding

Practise

1. Identify the arithmetic sequences from the following sequences. For each arithmetic sequence, state the value of t_1, the value of d, and the next three terms.

   a) 16, 32, 48, 64, 80, …

   b) 2, 4, 8, 16, 32, …

   c) −4, −7, −10, −13, −16, …

   d) 3, 0, −3, −6, −9, …

2. Write the first four terms of each arithmetic sequence for the given values of t_1 and d.

   a) $t_1 = 5$, $d = 3$

   b) $t_1 = -1$, $d = -4$

   c) $t_1 = 4$, $d = \dfrac{1}{5}$

   d) $t_1 = 1.25$, $d = -0.25$

3. For the sequence defined by $t_n = 3n + 8$, find each indicated term.

   a) t_1 b) t_7 c) t_{14}

4. For each arithmetic sequence determine the values of t_1 and d. State the missing terms of the sequence.

   a) ■, ■, ■, 19, 23

   b) ■, ■, 3, $\dfrac{3}{2}$

   c) ■, 4, ■, ■, 10

5. Determine the position of the given term to complete the following statements.

   a) 170 is the ■th term of −4, 2, 8, …

   b) −14 is the ■th term of $2\dfrac{1}{5}$, 2, $1\dfrac{4}{5}$, …

   c) 97 is the ■th term of −3, 1, 5, …

   d) −10 is the ■th term of 14, 12.5, 11, …

6. Determine the second and third terms of an arithmetic sequence if

   a) the first term is 6 and the fourth term is 33

   b) the first term is 8 and the fourth term is 41

   c) the first term is 42 and the fourth term is 27

7. The graph of an arithmetic sequence is shown.

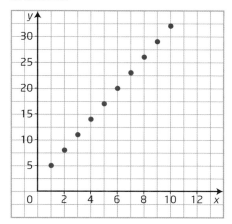

a) What are the first five terms of the sequence?

b) Write the general term of this sequence.

c) What is t_{50}? t_{200}?

d) Describe the relationship between the slope of the graph and your formula from part b).

e) Describe the relationship between the y-intercept and your formula from part b).

Apply

8. Which arithmetic sequence(s) contain the term 34? Justify your conclusions.

A $t_n = 6 + (n - 1)4$ $\quad 34 = 2 \cdot 4n$
$\qquad\qquad\qquad\qquad 32 = 0$

B $t_n = 3n - 1$

C $t_1 = 12, d = 5.5$

D 3, 7, 11, …

9. Determine the first term of the arithmetic sequence in which the 16th term is 110 and the common difference is 7.

10. The first term of an arithmetic sequence is $5y$ and the common difference is $-3y$. Write the equations for t_n and t_{15}.

11. The terms $5x + 2$, $7x - 4$, and $10x + 6$ are consecutive terms of an arithmetic sequence. Determine the value of x and state the three terms.

12. The numbers represented by x, y, and z are the first three terms of an arithmetic sequence. Express z in terms of x and y.

13. Each square in this pattern has a side length of 1 unit. Assume the pattern continues.

Figure 1   Figure 2   Figure 3   Figure 4

a) Write an equation in which the perimeter is a function of the figure number.

b) Determine the perimeter of Figure 9.

c) Which figure has a perimeter of 76 units?

14. The Wolf Creek Golf Course, located near Ponoka, Alberta, has been the site of the Canadian Tour Alberta Open Golf Championship. This tournament has a maximum entry of 132 players. The tee-off times begin at 8:00 and are 8 min apart.

a) The tee-off times generate an arithmetic sequence. Write the first four terms of the arithmetic sequence, if the first tee-off time of 8:00 is considered to be at time 0.

b) Following this schedule, how many players will be on the course after 1 h, if the tee-off times are for groups of four?

c) Write the general term for the sequence of tee-off times.

d) At what time will the last group tee-off?

e) What factors might affect the prearranged tee-off time?

Did You Know?

The first championship at Wolf Creek was held in 1987 and has attracted PGA professionals, including Mike Weir and Dave Barr.

15. Lucy Ango'yuaq, from Baker Lake, Nunavut, is a prominent wall hanging artist. This wall hanging is called *Geese and Ulus*. It is 22 inches wide and 27 inches long and was completed in 27 days. Suppose on the first day she completed 48 square inches of the wall hanging, and in the subsequent days the sequence of cumulative areas completed by the end of each day produces an arithmetic sequence. How much of the wall hanging did Lucy complete on each subsequent day? Express your answer in square inches.

The Inuktitut syllabics appearing at the bottom of this wall hanging spell the artist's name. For example, the first two syllabics spell out Lu-Si.

16. Susan joined a fitness class at her local gym. Into her workout, she incorporated a sit-up routine that followed an arithmetic sequence. On the 6th day of the program, Susan performed 11 sit-ups. On the 15th day she did 29 sit-ups.

a) Write the general term that relates the number of sit-ups to the number of days.

b) If Susan's goal is to be able to do 100 sit-ups, on which day of her program will she accomplish this?

c) What assumptions did you make to answer part b)?

17. Hydrocarbons are the starting points in the formation of thousands of products, including fuels, plastics, and synthetic fibres. Some hydrocarbon compounds contain only carbon and hydrogen atoms. Alkanes are saturated hydrocarbons that have single carbon-to-carbon bonds. The diagrams below show the first three alkanes.

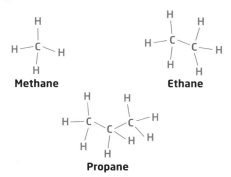

Methane   Ethane

Propane

a) The number of hydrogen atoms compared to number of carbon atoms produces an arithmetic sequence. Copy and complete the following chart to show this sequence.

Carbon Atoms	1	2	3	4
Hydrogen Atoms	4			

b) Write the general term that relates the number of hydrogen atoms to the number of carbon atoms.

c) Hectane contains 202 hydrogen atoms. How many carbon atoms are required to support 202 hydrogen atoms?

18. The multiples of 5 between 0 and 50 produces the arithmetic sequence 5, 10, 15, …, 45. Copy and complete the following table for the multiples of various numbers.

Multiples of	28	7	15
Between	1 and 1000	500 and 600	50 and 500
First Term, t_1			
Common Difference, d			
nth Term, t_n			
General Term			
Number of Terms			

19. The beluga whale is one of the major attractions of the Vancouver Aquarium. The beluga whale typically forages for food at a depth of 1000 ft, but will dive to at least twice that depth. To build the aquarium for the whales, engineers had to understand the pressure of the water at such depths. At sea level the pressure is 14.7 psi (pounds per square inch). Water pressure increases at a rate of 14.7 psi for every 30 ft of descent.

  a) Write the first four terms of the sequence that relates water pressure to feet of descent. Write the general term of this sequence.

  b) What is the water pressure at a depth of 1000 ft? 2000 ft?

  c) Sketch a graph of the water pressure versus 30-ft water depth charges.

  d) What is the y-intercept of the graph?

  e) What is the slope of the graph?

  f) How do the y-intercept and the slope relate to the formula you wrote in part a)?

Did You Know?

In 2008, the beluga was listed on the near-threatened list by the International Union for the Conservation of Nature.

20. The side lengths of a quadrilateral produce an arithmetic sequence. If the longest side has a length of 24 cm and the perimeter is 60 cm, what are the other side lengths? Explain your reasoning.

21. Earth has a daily rotation of 360°. One degree of rotation requires 4 min.

  a) Write the sequence of the first five terms relating the number of minutes to the number of degrees of rotation.

  b) Write an equation that describes this sequence.

  c) Determine the time taken for a rotation of 80°.

22. Canadian honey is recognized around the world for its superior taste and quality. In Saskatchewan in 1986, there were 1657 beekeepers operating 105 000 colonies. Each colony produced approximately 70 kg of honey. In 2007, the number of beekeepers was reduced to 1048. Assume that the decline in the number of beekeepers generates an arithmetic sequence. Determine the change in the number of beekeepers each year from 1986 to 2007.

23. The Diavik Diamond Mine is located on East Island in Lac de Gras East, Northwest Territories. The diamonds that are extracted from the mine were brought to surface when the kimberlite rock erupted 55 million years ago. In 2003, the first production year of the mine, 3.8 million carats were produced. Suppose the life expectancy of the mine is 20 years, and the number of diamond carats expected to be extracted from the mine in the 20th year is 113.2 million carats. If the extraction of diamonds produces an arithmetic sequence, determine the common difference. What does this value represent?

Extend

24. Farmers near Raymond, Alberta, use a wheel line irrigation system to provide water to their crops. A pipe and sprinkler system is attached to a motor-driven wheel that moves the system in a circle over a field. The first wheel is attached 50 m from the pivot point, and all the other wheels are attached at 20-m intervals further along the pipe. Determine the circumference of the circle traversed by wheel 12.

25. A solar eclipse is considered to be one of the most awe-inspiring spectacles in all of nature. The total phase of a solar eclipse is very brief and rarely lasts more than several minutes. The diagram below shows a series of pictures taken of a solar eclipse similar to the one that passed over Nunavut on August 1, 2008.

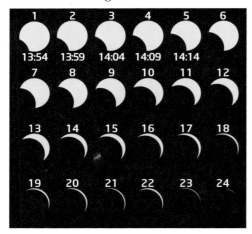

a) Write the first five terms of the sequence that relates the time to the picture number. State the values of t_1 and d.

b) Write the general term that defines this sequence.

c) What assumptions did you make for your calculation in part b)?

d) At what time was the sun completely eclipsed by the moon?

Web Link

To learn more about a solar eclipse, go to www.mhrprecalc11.ca and follow the links.

Create Connections

26. Copy and complete the following sentences using your own words. Then, choose symbols from the box below to create true statements. The boxes to the right of each sentence indicate how many symbols are needed for that sentence.

| t_1 | n | t_n | $<$ | d | $\leq$ | $\geq$ | $>$ | $\neq$ | 0 | 1 | $=$ |

a) An arithmetic sequence is an increasing sequence if and only if ■ ■ ■.

b) An arithmetic sequence is a decreasing sequence if and only if ■ ■ ■.

c) An arithmetic sequence is constant if and only if ■ ■ ■.

d) The first term of a sequence is ■.

e) The symbol for the general term of a sequence is ■.

27. Copy and complete the following graphic organizer by recording the observations you made about an arithmetic sequence. For example, include such things as the common difference and how the sequence relates to a function. Compare your graphic organizer with that of a classmate.

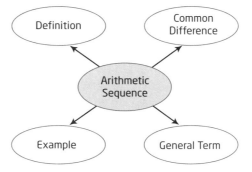

28. MINI LAB

Step 1 Create or use a spreadsheet as shown below.

What is the shape of the graph that models the arithmetic sequence? Could an arithmetic sequence graph have any other shape? Explain.

Step 2 Explore the effect that the first term has on the terms of the sequence by changing the value in Cell C2.

a) As the value of the first term increases, what is the effect on the graph? What happens as the value of the first term decreases?

b) Does the graph keep its shape? What characteristics of the graph stay the same?

Step 3 Investigate the effect of the common difference on an arithmetic sequence by changing the values in Cell D2.

a) What effect does changing this value have on the graph?

b) How does an increase in the common difference affect the shape of the graph? What happens as the common difference decreases?

Step 4 If a line were drawn through the data values, what would be its slope?

Step 5 What relationship does the slope of the line have to the equation for the general term of the sequence?

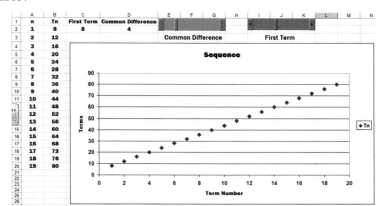

Project Corner　　Minerals

- A telephone contains over 40 different minerals, a television set has about 35, and an automobile about 15.

- Of the approximately 193 000 metric tonnes of gold discovered, 62% is found in just four countries on Earth. All the gold discovered so far would fit in a cube of side length 22 m.

- Of the approximately 1 740 000 metric tonnes of silver discovered, 55% is found in just four countries on Earth. All the silver discovered so far would fit in a cube of side length 55 m.

- In the average 1360-kg car there are approximately 110 kg of aluminum, 20 kg of copper, 10 kg of zinc, 113 kg of plastics, and 64 kg of rubber.

- Canada is the world's largest potash producer.

Arithmetic Series

Focus on...

- deriving a rule for determining the sum of an arithmetic series
- determining the values of t_1, d, n, or S_n in an arithmetic series
- solving a problem that involves an arithmetic series

Carl Friedrich Gauss was a mathematician born in Braunschweig, Germany, in 1777. He is noted for his significant contributions in fields such as number theory, statistics, astronomy, and differential geometry. When Gauss was 10, his mathematics teacher challenged the class to find the sum of the numbers from 1 to 100. Believing that this task would take some time, the teacher was astounded when Gauss responded with the correct answer of 5050 within minutes.

Gauss used a faster method than adding each individual term.

First, he wrote the sum twice, once in ascending order and the other in a descending order. Gauss then took the sum of the two rows.

Web Link

To learn more about Carl Gauss, go to www.mhrprecalc11.ca and follow the links.

$$
\begin{array}{cccccccc}
1 + & 2 + & 3 + 4 + & \cdots + & 99 + 100 \\
100 + & 99 + & \cdots + 4 + 3 + & 2 + & 1 \\
\hline
101 + & 101 + & \cdots & + 101 + 101
\end{array}
$$

What do you think Gauss did next?

Investigate Arithmetic Series

Materials

- 30 counting disks
- grid paper

In the following investigation, work with a partner to discuss your findings.

Part A: Explore Gauss's Method

1. a) Consider the sequence of positive integers 1, 2, 3, 4, 5. Represent each number by a small counting disk and arrange them in a triangular table in which the number of disks in each column represents the integer.

b) What is the sum of the numbers in the sequence?

c) How is the sum related to the total number of disks used?

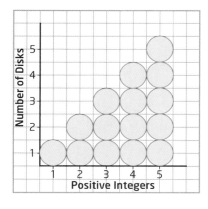

2. a) Duplicate the triangle of disks.

   b) Rotate your new triangle 180°. Join the two triangles together to form a rectangle.

   c) How many disks form the length of the rectangle? the width?

   d) How many disks are in the area of the rectangle?

   e) How is the area of the rectangle related to the sum of the sequence 1, 2, 3, 4, 5?

Reflect and Respond

3. Explain how you could use the results from steps 1 and 2 to find the sum of n consecutive integers. Use the idea of the area of the rectangle to develop a formula that would find the sum of n consecutive integers.

4. Explain how this method is related to the method Gauss used.

Part B: Construct a Squared Spiral

5. Start from the centre of the grid.

   a) Draw a segment of length 1 unit, vertically up.

   b) From the end of that segment, draw a new segment that is 1 unit longer than the previous segment, to the right.

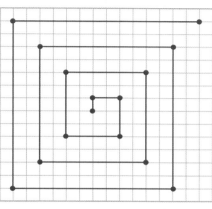

   c) From the end of this segment, draw a new segment that is 1 unit longer than the previous segment, vertically down.

   d) Continue this through 14 segments.

6. a) Record the lengths of the segments as an arithmetic sequence.

   b) What is the total length of the spiral?

   c) Explain how you calculated the total length of the spiral.

Reflect and Respond

7. a) Use Gauss's method to calculate the sum of the first 14 terms of your sequence. Is the sum the same as your sum from step 6?

   b) In using Gauss's method, what sum did you find for each pair of numbers? How many terms were there?

8. Derive a formula that you could use to find the total length if there were 20 segments for the spiral.

arithmetic series

- a sum of terms that form an arithmetic sequence

- for the arithmetic sequence 2, 4, 6, 8, the arithmetic series is represented by 2 + 4 + 6 + 8.

In determining the sum of the numbers from 1 to 100, Gauss had discovered the underlying principles of an **arithmetic series**.

S_n represents the sum of the first n terms of a series.

S_n is read as "S subscript n" or "S sub n."

In the series $2 + 4 + 6 + 8 + \cdots$, S_4 is the sum of the first four terms.

You can use Gauss's method to derive a formula for the sum of the general arithmetic series.

The general arithmetic series may be written as
$$t_1 + (t_1 + d) + (t_1 + 2d) + \cdots + [(t_1 + (n-3)d] + [(t_1 + (n-2)d] + [(t_1 + (n-1)d]$$

For this series, t_1 is the first term
$\qquad\qquad n$ is the number of terms
$\qquad\qquad d$ is the common difference

Use Gauss's method.
Write the series twice, once in ascending order and the other in descending order. Then, sum the two series.

$$
\begin{aligned}
S_n &= \quad t_1 \quad + \quad (t_1 + d) \quad + \cdots + \; [t_1 + (n-2)d] \; + \; [t_1 + (n-1)d] \\
S_n &= [t_1 + (n-1)d] + [t_1 + (n-2)d] + \cdots + \quad (t_1 + d) \quad + \quad t_1 \\
\hline
2S_n &= [2t_1 + (n-1)d] + [2t_1 + (n-1)d] + \cdots + [2t_1 + (n-1)d] + [2t_1 + (n-1)d] \\
2S_n &= n[2t_1 + (n-1)d] \\
S_n &= \tfrac{n}{2}[2t_1 + (n-1)d]
\end{aligned}
$$

The *sum* of an arithmetic series can be determined using the formula
$$S_n = \frac{n}{2}[2t_1 + (n-1)d]$$
where t_1 is the first term
$\qquad n$ is the number of terms
$\qquad d$ is the common difference
$\qquad S_n$ is the sum of the first n terms

A variation of this general formula can be derived by substituting t_n for the formula for the general term of an arithmetic sequence.

$$S_n = \frac{n}{2}[2t_1 + (n-1)d]$$

$$S_n = \frac{n}{2}[t_1 + t_1 + (n-1)d] \qquad \text{Since } t_n = t_1 + (n-1)d.$$

$$S_n = \frac{n}{2}(t_1 + t_n)$$

The *sum* of an arithmetic series can be determined using the formula
$$S_n = \frac{n}{2}(t_1 + t_n)$$
where t_1 is the first term
$\qquad n$ is the number of terms
$\qquad t_n$ is the nth term
$\qquad S_n$ is the sum of the first n terms

How would you need to express the last terms of the general arithmetic series in order to directly derive this formula using Gauss's method?

Example 1

Determine the Sum of an Arithmetic Series

Male fireflies flash in various patterns to signal location or to ward off predators. Different species of fireflies have different flash characteristics, such as the intensity of the flash, the rate of the flash, and the shape of the flash. Suppose that under certain circumstances, a particular firefly flashes twice in the first minute, four times in the second minute, and six times in the third minute.

a) If this pattern continues, what is the number of flashes in the 30th minute?

b) What is the total number of flashes in 30 min?

Solution

a) Method 1: Use Logical Reasoning

The firefly flashes twice in the first minute, four times in the second minute, six times in the third minute, and so on. The arithmetic sequence produced by the number of flashes is 2, 4, 6, … Since the common difference in this sequence is 2, the number of flashes in the 30th minute is the 30th multiple of 2.

$30 \times 2 = 60$

The number of flashes in the 30th minute is 60.

Method 2: Use the General Term

For this arithmetic sequence,

First term $\quad\quad\quad t_1 = 2$
Common difference $\quad d = 2$
Number of terms $\quad\; n = 30$

Substitute these values into the formula for the general term.

$t_n = t_1 + (n - 1)d$
$t_{30} = 2 + (30 - 1)2$
$t_{30} = 2 + (29)2$
$t_{30} = 60$

The number of flashes in the 30th minute is 60.

b) Method 1: Use the Formula $S_n = \dfrac{n}{2}(t_1 + t_n)$

$S_n = \dfrac{n}{2}(t_1 + t_n)$

$S_{30} = \dfrac{30}{2}(2 + 60)$ Substitute the values of n, t_1, and t_n.

$S_{30} = 15(62)$
$S_{30} = 930$

What information do you need to use this formula?

Method 2: Use the Formula $S_n = \dfrac{n}{2}[2t_1 + (n - 1)d]$

$S_n = \dfrac{n}{2}[2t_1 + (n - 1)d]$

$S_{30} = \dfrac{30}{2}[2(2) + (30 - 1)(2)]$ Substitute the values of n, t_1, and d.

$S_{30} = 15(62)$
$S_{30} = 930$

What information do you need to use this formula?

The total number of flashes for the male firefly in 30 min is 930.

Which formula is most effective in this case? Why?

Your Turn

Determine the total number of flashes for the male firefly in 42 min.

Example 2

Determine the Terms of an Arithmetic Series

The sum of the first two terms of an arithmetic series is 13 and the sum of the first four terms is 46. Determine the first six terms of the series and the sum to six terms.

Solution

For this series,
$S_2 = 13$
$S_4 = 46$

Substitute into the formula $S_n = \frac{n}{2}[2t_1 + (n-1)d]$ for both sums.

For S_2:

$S_n = \frac{n}{2}[2t_1 + (n-1)d]$

$S_2 = \frac{2}{2}[2t_1 + (2-1)d]$

$13 = 1[2t_1 + (1)d]$

$13 = 2t_1 + d$

For S_4:

$S_n = \frac{n}{2}[2t_1 + (n-1)d]$

$S_4 = \frac{4}{2}[2t_1 + (4-1)d]$

$46 = 2[2t_1 + (3)d]$

$23 = 2t_1 + 3d$

Solve the system of two equations.

$\begin{aligned} 13 &= 2t_1 + d &&① \\ 23 &= 2t_1 + 3d &&② \\ \hline -10 &= -2d &&①-② \\ 5 &= d \end{aligned}$

Substitute $d = 5$ into one of the equations.
$13 = 2t_1 + d$
$13 = 2t_1 + 5$
$8 = 2t_1$
$4 = t_1$

With $t_1 = 4$ and $d = 5$, the first six terms of the series are
$4 + 9 + 14 + 19 + 24 + 29$.

The sum of the first six terms is

$S_n = \frac{n}{2}[2t_1 + (n-1)d]$ or $S_n = \frac{n}{2}(t_1 + t_n)$

$S_6 = \frac{6}{2}[2(4) + (6-1)5]$ $S_6 = \frac{6}{2}(4 + 29)$

$S_6 = 3(8 + 25)$ $S_6 = 3(33)$

$S_6 = 99$ $S_6 = 99$

Which formula do you prefer to use? Why?

Your Turn

The sum of the first two terms of an arithmetic series is 19 and the sum of the first four terms is 50. What are the first six terms of the series and the sum to 20 terms?

Key Ideas

- Given the sequence $t_1, t_2, t_3, t_4, \ldots, t_n$ the associated series is $S_n = t_1 + t_2 + t_3 + t_4 + \cdots + t_n$.
- For the general arithmetic series,
  $$t_1 + (t_1 + d) + (t_1 + 2d) + \cdots + (t_1 + [n-1]d) \quad \text{or}$$
  $$t_1 + (t_1 + d) + (t_1 + 2d) + \cdots + (t_n - d) + t_n,$$
  the sum of the first n terms is
  $$S_n = \frac{n}{2}[2t_1 + (n-1)d] \quad \text{or} \quad S_n = \frac{n}{2}(t_1 + t_n),$$
  where t_1 is the first term
  $\qquad n$ is number of terms
  $\qquad d$ is the common difference
  $\qquad t_n$ is the nth term
  $\qquad S_n$ is the sum to n terms

Check Your Understanding

Practise

1. Determine the sum of each arithmetic series.

a) $5 + 8 + 11 + \cdots + 53$

b) $7 + 14 + 21 + \cdots + 98$

c) $8 + 3 + (-2) + \cdots + (-102)$

d) $\dfrac{2}{3} + \dfrac{5}{3} + \dfrac{8}{3} + \cdots + \dfrac{41}{3}$

2. For each of the following arithmetic series, determine the values of t_1 and d, and the value of S_n to the indicated sum.

a) $1 + 3 + 5 + \cdots \ (S_8)$

b) $40 + 35 + 30 + \cdots \ (S_{11})$

c) $\dfrac{1}{2} + \dfrac{3}{2} + \dfrac{5}{2} + \cdots \ (S_7)$

d) $(-3.5) + (-1.25) + 1 + \cdots \ (S_6)$

3. Determine the sum, S_n, for each arithmetic sequence described.

a) $t_1 = 7$, $t_n = 79$, $n = 8$

b) $t_1 = 58$, $t_n = -7$, $n = 26$

c) $t_1 = -12$, $t_n = 51$, $n = 10$

d) $t_1 = 12$, $d = 8$, $n = 9$

e) $t_1 = 42$, $d = -5$, $n = 14$

4. Determine the value of the first term, t_1, for each arithmetic series described.

a) $d = 6$, $S_n = 574$, $n = 14$

b) $d = -6$, $S_n = 32$, $n = 13$

c) $d = 0.5$, $S_n = 218.5$, $n = 23$

d) $d = -3$, $S_n = 279$, $n = 18$

5. For the arithmetic series, determine the value of n.

a) $t_1 = 8$, $t_n = 68$, $S_n = 608$

b) $t_1 = -6$, $t_n = 21$, $S_n = 75$

6. For each series find t_{10} and S_{10}.

a) $5 + 10 + 15 + \cdots$

b) $10 + 7 + 4 + \cdots$

c) $(-10) + (-14) + (-18) + \cdots$

d) $2.5 + 3 + 3.5 + \cdots$

Apply

7. a) Determine the sum of all the multiples of 4 between 1 and 999.

b) What is the sum of the multiples of 6 between 6 and 999?

8. It's About Time, in Langley, British Columbia, is Canada's largest custom clock manufacturer. They have a grandfather clock that, on the hours, chimes the number of times that corresponds to the time of day. For example, at 4:00 p.m., it chimes 4 times. How many times does the clock chime in a 24-h period?

9. A training program requires a pilot to fly circuits of an airfield. Each day, the pilot flies three more circuits than the previous day. On the fifth day, the pilot flew 14 circuits. How many circuits did the pilot fly

   a) on the first day?

   b) in total by the end of the fifth day?

   c) in total by the end of the nth day?

10. The second and fifth terms of an arithmetic series are 40 and 121, respectively. Determine the sum of the first 25 terms of the series.

11. The sum of the first five terms of an arithmetic series is 85. The sum of the first six terms is 123. What are the first four terms of the series?

12. Galileo noticed a relationship between the distance travelled by a falling object and time. Suppose data show that when an object is dropped from a particular height it moves approximately 5 m during the first second of its fall, 15 m during the second second, 25 m during the third second, 35 during the fourth second, and so on. The formula describing the approximate distance, d, the object is from its starting position n seconds after it has been dropped is $d(n) = 5n^2$.

   a) Using the general formula for the sum of a series, derive the formula $d(n) = 5n^2$.

   b) Demonstrate algebraically, using $n = 100$, that the sum of the series $5 + 15 + 25 + \cdots$ is equivalent to $d(n) = 5n^2$.

13. At the sixth annual Vancouver Canstruction® Competition, architects and engineers competed to see whose team could build the most spectacular structure using little more than cans of food.

A Breach in Hunger

The UnBEARable Truth

Stores often stack cans for display purposes, although their designs are not usually as elaborate as the ones shown above. To calculate the number of cans in a display, an arithmetic series may be used. Suppose a store wishes to stack the cans in a pattern similar to the one shown. This display has one can at the top and each row thereafter adds one can. If there are 18 rows, how many cans in total are there in the display?

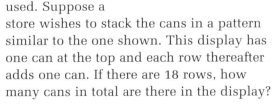

Did You Know?

The Vancouver Canstruction® Competition aids in the fight against hunger. At the end of the competition, all canned food is donated to food banks.

14. The number of handshakes between 6 people where everyone shakes hands with everyone else only once may be modelled using a hexagon. If you join each of the 6 vertices in the hexagon to every other point in the hexagon, there are $1 + 2 + 3 + 4 + 5$ lines. Therefore, there are 15 lines.

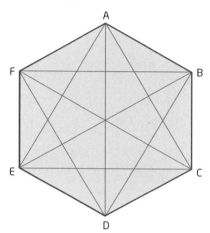

a) What does the series $1 + 2 + 3 + 4 + 5$ represent?

b) Write the series if there are 10 people in the room and everyone shakes hands with everyone else in the room once.

c) How many handshakes occur in a room of 30 people?

d) Describe a similar situation in which this method of determining the number of handshakes may apply.

15. The first three terms of an arithmetic sequence are given by $x, (2x - 5), 8.6$.

a) Determine the first term and the common difference for the sequence.

b) Determine the 20th term of the sequence.

c) Determine the sum of the first 20 terms of the series.

Extend

16. A number of interlocking rings each 1 cm thick are hanging from a peg. The top ring has an outside diameter of 20 cm. The outside diameter of each of the outer rings is 1 cm less than that of the ring above it. The bottom ring has an outside diameter of 3 cm. What is the distance from the top of the top ring to the bottom of the bottom ring?

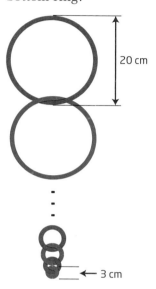

20 cm

3 cm

17. Answer the following as either true or false. Justify your answers.

a) Doubling each term in an arithmetic series will double the sum of the series.

b) Keeping the first term constant and doubling the number of terms will double the sum of the series.

c) If each term of an arithmetic sequence is multiplied by a fixed number, the resulting sequence will always be an arithmetic sequence.

$$_n - 2n^2 + 5n.$$

...ne the first three terms of this series.

b) Determine the sum of the first 10 terms of the series using the arithmetic sum formula.

c) Determine the sum of the first 10 terms of the series using the given formula.

d) Using the general formula for the sum of an arithmetic series, show how the formulas in parts b) and c) are equal.

19. Nathan Gerelus is a Manitoba farmer preparing to harvest his field of wheat. Nathan begins harvesting the crop at 11:00 a.m., after the morning dew has evaporated. By the end of the first hour he harvests 240 bushels of wheat. Nathan challenges himself to increase the number of bushels harvested by the end of each hour. Suppose that this increase produces an arithmetic series where Nathan harvests 250 bushels in the second hour, 260 bushels in the third hour, and so on.

a) Write the series that would illustrate the amount of wheat that Nathan has harvested by the end of the seventh hour.

b) Write the general sum formula that represents the number of bushels of wheat that Nathan took off the field by the end of the nth hour.

c) Determine the total number of bushels harvested by the end of the seventh hour.

d) State any assumptions that you made.

20. The 15th term in an arithmetic sequence is 43 and the sum of the first 15 terms of the series is 120. Determine the first three terms of the series.

Create Connections

21. An arithmetic series was defined where $t_1 = 12$, $n = 16$, $d = 6$, and $t_n = 102$. Two students were asked to determine the sum of the series. Their solutions are shown below.

Pierre's solution:

$$S_n = \frac{n}{2}(t_1 + t_n)$$

$$S_{16} = \frac{16}{2}(12 + 102)$$

$$S_{16} = 8(114)$$

$$S_{16} = 912$$

Jeanette's solution:

$$S_n = \frac{n}{2}[2t_1 + (n - 1)d]$$

$$S_{16} = \frac{16}{2}[2(12) + (16 - 1)6]$$

$$S_{16} = 8(24 + 90)$$

$$S_{16} = 912$$

Both students arrived at a correct answer. Explain how both formulas lead to the correct answer.

22. The triangular arrangement shown consists of a number of unit triangles. A unit triangle has side lengths equal to 1. The series for the total number of unit triangles in the diagram is $1 + 3 + 5 + 7$.

a) How many unit triangles are there if there are 10 rows in the triangular arrangement?

b) Using the sum of a series, show how the sum of the blue unit triangles plus the sum of the green unit triangles results in your answer from part a).

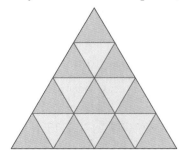

23. Bowling pins and snooker balls are often arranged in a triangular formation. A triangular number is a number that can be represented by a triangular array of dots. Each triangular number is an arithmetic series. The sequence 1, (1 + 2), (1 + 2 + 3), (1 + 2 + 3 + 4), … gives the first four triangular numbers as 1, 3, 6, and 10.

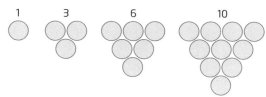

a) What is the tenth triangular number?

b) Use the general formula for the sum of an arithmetic series to show that the nth triangular number is $\frac{n}{2}(n + 1)$.

Project Corner | Diamond Mining

- In 1991, the first economic diamond deposit was discovered in the Lac de Gras area of the Northwest Territories. In October 1998, Ekati diamond mine opened about 300 km northeast of Yellowknife.

- By April 1999, the mine had produced one million carats. Ekati's average production over its projected 20-year life is expected to be 3 to 5 million carats per year.

- Diavik, Canada's second diamond mine, began production in January 2003. During its projected 20-year life, average diamond production from this mine is expected to be about 8 million carats per year, which represents about 6% of the world's total supply.

A polar bear diamond is a certified Canadian diamond mined, cut, and polished in Yellowknife.

Geometric Sequences

Focus on...

- providing and justifying an example of a geometric sequence
- deriving a rule for determining the general term of a geometric sequence
- solving a problem that involves a geometric sequence

Many types of sequences can be found in nature. The Fibonacci sequence, frequently found in flowers, seeds, and trees, is one example. A **geometric sequence** can be approximated by the orb web of the common garden spider. A spider's orb web is an impressive architectural feat. The web can capture the beauty of the morning dew, as well as the insects that the spider may feed upon. The following graphic was created to represent an approximation of the geometric sequence formed by the orb web.

geometric sequence

- a sequence in which the ratio of consecutive terms is constant

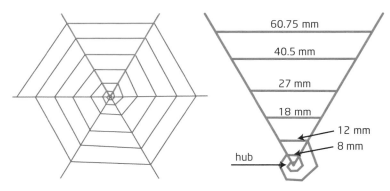

The capture spiral is constructed by the spider starting on the outside edge of the web frame, and winding inward toward the hub. The lengths of the sections of the silk between the radii for this section of the spiral produce a geometric sequence. What makes this sequence geometric?

Did You Know?

An orb web is a round spider web with a pattern of lines in a spiral formation.

Coin Toss Outcomes

Work with a partner for the following activity.

Materials
• 3 coins

1. a) Toss a single coin. How many possible outcomes are there?

   b) Toss two coins. How many possible outcomes are there?

   c) Create a tree diagram to show the possible outcomes for three coins.

2. Copy the table. Continue the pattern to complete the table.

Number of Coins, n	Number of Outcomes, t_n	Expanded Form	Using Exponents
1	2	(2)	2^1
2	4	(2)(2)	2^2
3			
4			
⋮	⋮	⋮	⋮
n			

3. a) As the number of coins increases, a sequence is formed by the number of outcomes. What are the first four terms of this sequence?

   b) Describe how the terms of the sequence are related. Is this relationship different from an arithmetic sequence? Explain.

   c) Predict the next two terms of the sequence. Describe the method you used to make your prediction.

   d) Describe a method you could use to generate one term from the previous term.

4. a) For several pairs of consecutive terms in the sequence, divide the second term by the preceding term.

   b) What observation can you make about your predictions in step 3c)?

Reflect and Respond

5. a) Is the sequence generated a geometric sequence? How do you know?

   b) Write a general term that relates the number of outcomes to the number of coins tossed.

   c) Show how to use your formula to determine the value of the 20th term of the sequence.

common ratio

• the ratio of successive terms in a geometric sequence,
$$r = \frac{t_n}{t_{n-1}}$$

• the ratio may be positive or negative

• for example, in the sequence 2, 4, 8, 16, ..., the common ratio is 2

In a geometric sequence, the ratio of consecutive terms is constant. The **common ratio**, r, can be found by taking any term, except the first, and dividing that term by the preceding term.

The general geometric sequence is t_1, $t_1 r$, $t_1 r^2$, $t_1 r^3$, ..., where t_1 is the first term and r is the common ratio.

$$t_1 = t_1$$
$$t_2 = t_1 r$$
$$t_3 = t_1 r^2$$
$$t_4 = t_1 r^3$$
$$\vdots$$
$$t_n = t_1 r^{n-1}$$

> The *general term* of a geometric sequence where n is a positive integer is
> $$t_n = t_1 r^{n-1}$$
> where t_1 is the first term of the sequence
> n is the number of terms
> r is the common ratio
> t_n is the general term or nth term

Example 1

Determine t_1, r, and t_n

Did You Know?

One of the most common bacteria on Earth, Shewanella oneidensis MR-1, uses oxygen as an energy source for respiration. This bacterium is generally associated with the removal of metal pollutants in aquatic and marine environments.

In nature, many single-celled organisms, such as bacteria, reproduce by splitting in two so that one cell gives rise to 2, then 4, then 8 cells, and so on, producing a geometric sequence. Suppose there were 10 bacteria originally present in a bacteria sample. Determine the general term that relates the number of bacteria to the doubling period of the bacteria. State the values for t_1 and r in the geometric sequence produced.

Solution

State the sequence generated by the doubling of the bacteria.
$$t_1 = 10$$
$$t_2 = 20$$
$$t_3 = 40$$
$$t_4 = 80$$
$$t_5 = 160$$
$$\vdots$$

The common ratio, r, may be found by dividing any two consecutive terms, $r = \dfrac{t_n}{t_{n-1}}$.

$$\frac{20}{10} = 2 \quad \frac{40}{20} = 2 \quad \frac{80}{40} = 2 \quad \frac{160}{80} = 2$$

The common ratio is 2.

For the given sequence, $t_1 = 10$ and $r = 2$. Use the general term of a geometric sequence.

$t_n = t_1 r^{n-1}$

$t_n = (10)(2)^{n-1}$ Substitute known values.

The general term of the sequence is $t_n = 10(2)^{n-1}$.

Your Turn

Suppose there were three bacteria originally present in a sample. Determine the general term that relates the number of bacteria to the doubling period of the bacteria. State the values of t_1 and r in the geometric sequence formed.

Example 2

Determine a Particular Term

Sometimes you use a photocopier to create enlargements or reductions. Suppose the actual length of a photograph is 25 cm and the smallest size that a copier can make is 67% of the original. What is the shortest possible length of the photograph after 5 reductions? Express your answer to the nearest tenth of a centimetre.

Solution

This situation can be modelled by a geometric sequence.

For this sequence,
First term $t_1 = 25$
Common ratio $r = 0.67$
Number of terms $n = 6$ Why is the number of terms 6 in this case?

You need to find the sixth term of the sequence.

Use the general term, $t_n = t_1 r^{n-1}$.

$t_n = t_1 r^{n-1}$

$t_6 = 25(0.67)^{6-1}$ Substitute known values.

$t_6 = 25(0.67)^5$

$t_6 = 3.375...$

After five reductions, the shortest possible length of the photograph is approximately 3.4 cm.

Your Turn

Suppose the smallest reduction a photocopier could make is 60% of the original. What is the shortest possible length after 8 reductions of a photograph that is originally 42 cm long?

Example 3

Determine t_1 and r

In a geometric sequence, the third term is 54 and the sixth term is -1458. Determine the values of t_1 and r, and list the first three terms of the sequence.

Solution

Method 1: Use Logical Reasoning
The third term of the sequence is 54 and the sixth term is -1458.
$$t_3 = 54$$
$$t_6 = -1458$$

Since the sequence is geometric,

$$t_4 = t_3(r)$$
$$t_5 = t_3(r)(r)$$
$$t_6 = t_3(r)(r)(r) \qquad \text{Substitute known values.}$$
$$-1458 = 54r^3$$
$$\frac{-1458}{54} = r^3$$
$$-27 = r^3$$
$$\sqrt[3]{-27} = r$$
$$-3 = r$$

You can use the general term of a geometric sequence to determine the value for t_1.
$$t_n = t_1 r^{n-1}$$
$$t_3 = t_1 r^{3-1}$$
$$t_3 = t_1 r^2$$
$$54 = t_1(-3)^2 \qquad \text{Substitute known values.}$$
$$54 = 9t_1$$
$$6 = t_1$$

The first term of the sequence is 6 and the common ratio is -3.
The first three terms of the sequence are 6, -18, 54.

Method 2: Use the General Term
You can write an equation for t_3 and an equation for t_6 using the general term of a geometric sequence.
$$t_n = t_1 r^{n-1}$$

For the third term, $n = 3$.
$$t_n = t_1 r^{n-1}$$
$$54 = t_1 r^{3-1}$$
$$54 = t_1 r^2$$

For the sixth term, $n = 6$.
$$t_n = t_1 r^{n-1}$$
$$-1458 = t_1 r^{6-1}$$
$$-1458 = t_1 r^5$$

Solve one of the equations for the variable t_1.

$54 = t_1 r^2$

$\dfrac{54}{r^2} = t_1$

Substitute this expression for t_1 in the other equation. Solve for the variable r.

$-1458 = t_1 r^5$

$-1458 = \left(\dfrac{54}{r^2}\right) r^5$

$-1458 = 54 r^3$

$\dfrac{-1458}{54} = \dfrac{54 r^3}{54}$

$-27 = r^3$

$\sqrt[3]{-27} = r$

$-3 = r$

Substitute the common ratio of -3 in one of the equations to solve for the first term, t_1.

Substitute $r = -3$

$54 = t_1 r^2$

$54 = t_1 (-3)^2$

$54 = 9 t_1$

$6 = t_1$

The first term of the sequence is 6 and the common ratio is -3.
The first three terms of the sequence are $6, -18, 54$.

Your Turn

In a geometric sequence, the second term is 28 and the fifth term is 1792. Determine the values of t_1 and r, and list the first three terms of the sequence.

Example 4

Apply Geometric Sequences

The modern piano has 88 keys. The frequency of the notes ranges from A_0, the lowest note, at 27.5 Hz, to C_8, the highest note on the piano, at 4186.009 Hz. The frequencies of these notes approximate a geometric sequence as you move up the keyboard.

a) Determine the common ratio of the geometric sequence produced from the lowest key, A_0, to the fourth key, C_1, at 32.7 Hz.

b) Use the lowest and highest frequencies to verify the common ratio found in part a).

Did You Know?

A sound has two characteristics, pitch and volume. The pitch corresponds to the frequency of the sound wave. High notes have high frequencies. Low notes have low frequencies. Frequency is measured in Hertz (Hz), which is the number of waves per second.

Solution

a) The situation may be modelled by a geometric sequence.
For this sequence,

First term	$t_1 = 27.5$
Number of terms	$n = 4$
nth term	$t_n = 32.7$

Use the general term of a geometric sequence.

$$t_n = t_1 r^{n-1}$$
$$32.7 = (27.5)(r^{4-1}) \quad \text{Substitute known values.}$$
$$\frac{32.7}{27.5} = \frac{27.5r^3}{27.5}$$
$$\frac{32.7}{27.5} = r^3$$
$$\sqrt[3]{\frac{32.7}{27.5}} = r \quad \text{Take the cube root of both sides.}$$
$$1.0594\ldots = r$$

The common ratio for this sequence is approximately 1.06.

b) For this sequence,

First term	$t_1 = 27.5$
Number of terms	$n = 88$
nth term	$t_n = 4186.009$

Use the general term of a geometric sequence.

$$t_n = t_1 r^{n-1}$$
$$4186.009 = (27.5)(r^{88-1}) \quad \text{Substitute known values.}$$
$$\frac{4186.009}{27.5} = \frac{27.5r^{87}}{27.5}$$
$$\frac{4186.009}{27.5} = r^{87}$$
$$\sqrt[87]{\frac{4186.009}{27.5}} = r \quad \text{Take the 87th root of both sides.}$$
$$1.0594\ldots = r$$

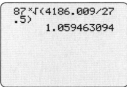

```
87×√(4186.009/27
.5)
        1.059463094
```

The common ratio of this sequence is approximately 1.06.

Your Turn

In 1990 the population of Canada was approximately 26.6 million. The population projection for 2025 is approximately 38.4 million. If this projection were based on a geometric sequence, what would be the annual growth rate? Given that this is a geometric sequence what assumptions would you have to make?

- A geometric sequence is a sequence in which each term, after the first term, is found by multiplying the previous term by a non-zero constant, r, called the common ratio.

- The common ratio of successive terms of a geometric sequence can be found by dividing any two consecutive terms, $r = \dfrac{t_n}{t_{n-1}}$.

- The general term of a geometric sequence is
$t_n = t_1 r^{n-1}$
where t_1 is the first term
  n is the number of terms
  r is the common ratio
  t_n is the general term or nth term

Check Your Understanding

Practise

1. Determine if the sequence is geometric. If it is, state the common ratio and the general term in the form $t_n = t_1 r^{n-1}$.

a) 1, 2, 4, 8, …

b) 2, 4, 6, 8, …

c) 3, −9, 27, −81, …

d) 1, 1, 2, 4, 8, …

e) 10, 15, 22.5, 33.75, …

f) −1, −5, −25, −125, …

2. Copy and complete the following table for the given geometric sequences.

	Geometric Sequence	Common Ratio	6th Term	10th Term
a)	6, 18, 54, …			
b)	1.28, 0.64, 0.32, …			
c)	$\frac{1}{5}, \frac{3}{5}, \frac{9}{5}, \ldots$			

3. Determine the first four terms of each geometric sequence.

a) $t_1 = 2, r = 3$ **b)** $t_1 = -3, r = -4$

c) $t_1 = 4, r = -3$ **d)** $t_1 = 2, r = 0.5$

4. Determine the missing terms, t_2, t_3, and t_4, in the geometric sequence in which $t_1 = 8.1$ and $t_5 = 240.1$.

5. Determine a formula for the nth term of each geometric sequence.

a) $r = 2, t_1 = 3$

b) 192, −48, 12, −3, …

c) $t_3 = 5, t_6 = 135$

d) $t_1 = 4, t_{13} = 16\ 384$

Apply

6. Given the following geometric sequences, determine the number of terms, n.

Table A			
First Term, t_1	Common Ratio, r	nth Term, t_n	Number of Terms, n
a) 5	3	135	
b) −2	−3	−1458	
c) $\frac{1}{3}$	$\frac{1}{2}$	$\frac{1}{48}$	
d) 4	4	4096	
e) $-\frac{1}{6}$	2	$-\frac{128}{3}$	
f) $\frac{p^2}{2}$	$\frac{p}{2}$	$\frac{p^9}{256}$	

7. The following sequence is geometric. What is the value of y?

3, 12, 48, $5y + 7$, ...

8. The following graph illustrates a geometric sequence. List the first three terms for the sequence and state the general term that describes the sequence.

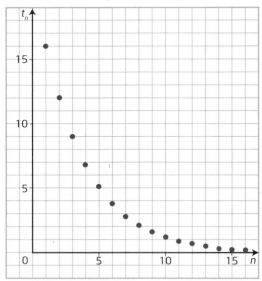

9. A ball is dropped from a height of 3.0 m. After each bounce it rises to 75% of its previous height.

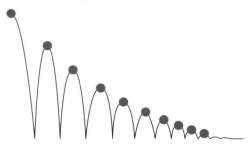

a) Write the first term and the common ratio of the geometric sequence.

b) Write the general term for the sequence in part a).

c) What height does the ball reach after the 6th bounce?

d) After how many bounces will the ball reach a height of approximately 40 cm?

10. The colour of some clothing fades over time when washed. Suppose a pair of jeans fades by 5% with each washing.

a) What percent of the colour remains after one washing?

b) If $t_1 = 100$, what are the first four terms of the sequence?

c) What is the value of r for your geometric sequence?

d) What percent of the colour remains after 10 washings?

e) How many washings would it take so that only 25% of the original colour remains in the jeans? What assumptions did you make?

11. Pincher Creek, in the foothills of the Rocky Mountains in southern Alberta, is an ideal location to harness the wind power of the chinook winds that blow through the mountain passes. Kinetic energy from the moving air is converted to electricity by wind turbines. In 2004, the turbines generated 326 MW of wind energy, and it is projected that the amount will be 10 000 MW per year by 2010. If this growth were modelled by a geometric sequence, determine the value of the annual growth rate from 2004 to 2010.

Did You Know?

In an average year, a single 660-kW wind turbine produces 2000 MW of electricity, enough power for over 250 Canadian homes. Using wind to produce electricity rather than burning coal will leave 900 000 kg of coal in the ground and emit 2000 tonnes fewer greenhouse gases annually. This has the same positive impact as taking 417 cars off the road or planting 10 000 trees.

12. The following excerpt is taken from the book *One Grain of Rice* by Demi.

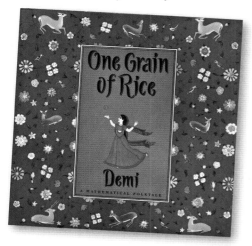

Long ago in India, there lived a raja who believed that he was wise and fair. But every year he kept nearly all of the people's rice for himself. Then when famine came, the raja refused to share the rice, and the people went hungry. Then a village girl named Rani devises a clever plan. She does a good deed for the raja, and in return, the raja lets her choose her reward. Rani asks for just one grain of rice, doubled every day for thirty days.

a) Write the sequence of terms for the first five days that Rani would receive the rice.

b) Write the general term that relates the number of grains of rice to the number of days.

c) Use the general term to determine the number of grains of rice that Rani would receive on the 30th day.

13. The Franco-Manitoban community of St-Pierre-Jolys celebrates Les Folies Grenouilles annually in August. Some of the featured activities include a slow pitch tournament, a parade, fireworks, and the Canadian National Frog Jumping Championships. During the competition, competitor's frogs have five chances to reach their maximum jump. One year, a frog by the name of Georges, achieved the winning jump in his 5th try. Georges' first jump was 191.41 cm, his second jump was 197.34 cm, and his third was 203.46 cm. The pattern of Georges' jumps approximated a geometric sequence.

a) By what ratio did Georges improve his performance with each jump? Express your answer to three decimal places.

b) How far was Georges' winning jump? Express your answer to the nearest tenth of a centimetre.

c) The world record frog jump is held by a frog named Santjie of South Africa. Santjie jumped approximately 10.2 m. If Georges, from St-Pierre-Jolys, had continued to increase his jumps following this same geometric sequence, how many jumps would Georges have needed to complete to beat Santjie's world record jump?

14. Bread and bread products have been part of our diet for centuries. To help bread rise, yeast is added to the dough. Yeast is a living unicellular micro-organism about one hundredth of a millimetre in size. Yeast multiplies by a biochemical process called budding. After mitosis and cell division, one cell results in two cells with exactly the same characteristics.

a) Write a sequence for the first six terms that describes the cell growth of yeast, beginning with a single cell.

b) Write the general term for the growth of yeast.

c) How many cells would there be after 25 doublings?

d) What assumptions would you make for the number of cells after 25 doubling periods?

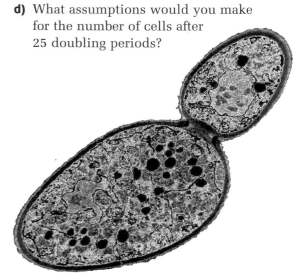

15. The Arctic Winter Games is a high profile sports competition for northern and arctic athletes. The premier sports are the Dene and Inuit games, which include the arm pull, the one foot high kick, the two foot high kick, and the Dene hand games. The games are held every two years. The first Arctic Winter Games, held in 1970, drew 700 competitors. In 2008, the games were held in Yellowknife and drew 2000 competitors. If the number of competitors grew geometrically from 1970 to 2008, determine the annual rate of growth in the number of competitors from one Arctic Winter Games to the next. Express your answer to the nearest tenth of a percent.

Did You Know?

Sledge jump starts from a standing position. The athlete jumps consecutively over 10 sledges placed in a row, turns around using one jumping movement, and then jumps back over the 10 sledges. This process is repeated until the athlete misses a jump or touches a sledge.

16. Jason Annahatak entered the Russian sledge jump competition at the Arctic Winter Games, held in Yellowknife. Suppose that to prepare for this event, Jason started training by jumping 2 sledges each day for the first week, 4 sledges each day for the second week, 8 sledges each day for the third week, and so on. During the competition, Jason jumped 142 sledges. Assuming he continued his training pattern, how many weeks did it take him to reach his competition number of 142 sledges?

17. At Galaxyland in the West Edmonton Mall, a boat swing ride has been modelled after a basic pendulum design. When the boat first reaches the top of the swing, this is considered to be the beginning of the first swing. A swing is completed when the boat changes direction. On each successive completed swing, the boat travels 96% as far as on the previous swing. The ride finishes when the arc length through which the boat travels is 30 m. If it takes 20 swings for the boat to reach this arc length, determine the arc length through which the boat travels on the first swing. Express your answer to the nearest tenth of a metre.

18. The Russian nesting doll or Matryoshka had its beginnings in 1890. The dolls are made so that the smallest doll fits inside a larger one, which fits inside a larger one, and so on, until all the dolls are hidden inside the largest doll. In a set of 50 dolls, the tallest doll is 60 cm and the smallest is 1 cm. If the decrease in doll size approximates a geometric sequence, determine the common ratio. Express your answer to three decimal places.

19. The primary function for our kidneys is to filter our blood to remove any impurities. Doctors take this into account when prescribing the dosage and frequency of medicine. A person's kidneys filter out 18% of a particular medicine every two hours.

a) How much of the medicine remains after 12 h if the initial dosage was 250 mL? Express your answer to the nearest tenth of a millilitre.

b) When there is less than 20 mL left in the body, the medicine becomes ineffective and another dosage is needed. After how many hours would this happen?

Did You Know?

Every day, a person's kidneys process about 190 L of blood to remove about 1.9 L of waste products and extra water.

20. The charge in a car battery, when the car is left to sit, decreases by about 2% per day and can be modelled by the formula $C = 100(0.98)^d$, where d is the time, in days, and C is the approximate level of charge, as a percent.

a) Copy and complete the chart to show the percent of charge remaining in relation to the time passed.

Time, d (days)	Charge Level, C (%)
0	100
1	
2	
3	

b) Write the general term of this geometric sequence.

c) Explain how this formula is different from the formula $C = 100(0.98)^d$.

d) How much charge is left after 10 days?

21. A coiled basket is made using dried pine needles and sinew. The basket is started from the centre using a small twist and spirals outward and upward to shape the basket. The circular coiling of the basket approximates a geometric sequence, where the radius of the first coil is 6 mm.

a) If the ratio of consecutive coils is 1.22, calculate the radius for the 8th coil.

b) If there are 18 coils, what is the circumference of the top coil of the basket?

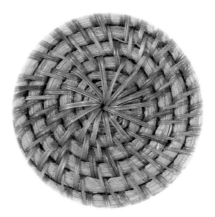

Extend

22. Demonstrate that 6^a, 6^b, 6^c, ... forms a geometric sequence when a, b, c, ... forms an arithmetic sequence.

23. If $x + 2$, $2x + 1$, and $4x - 3$ are three consecutive terms of a geometric sequence, determine the value of the common ratio and the three given terms.

24. On a six-string guitar, the distance from the nut to the bridge is 38 cm. The distance from the first fret to the bridge is 35.87 cm, and the distance from the second fret to the bridge is 33.86 cm. This pattern approximates a geometric sequence.

a) What is the distance from the 8th fret to the bridge?

b) What is the distance from the 12th fret to the bridge?

c) Determine the distance from the nut to the first fret.

d) Determine the distance from the first fret to the second fret.

e) Write the sequence for the first three terms of the distances between the frets. Is this sequence geometric or arithmetic? What is the common ratio or common difference?

Create Connections

25. Alex, Mala, and Paul were given the following problem to solve in class.

An aquarium that originally contains 40 L of water loses 8% of its water to evaporation every day. Determine how much water will be in the aquarium at the beginning of the 7th day.

The three students' solutions are shown below. Which approach to the solution is correct? Justify your reasoning.

Alex's solution:
Alex believed that the sequence was geometric, where $t_1 = 40$, $r = 0.08$, and $n = 7$. He used the general formula $t_n = t_1 r^{n-1}$.
$t_n = t_1 r^{n-1}$
$t_n = 40(0.08)^{n-1}$
$t_7 = 40(0.08)^{7-1}$
$t_7 = 40(0.08)^6$
$t_7 = 0.000\ 01$
There will be 0.000 01 L of water in the tank at the beginning of the 7th day.

Mala's solution:
Mala believed that the sequence was geometric, where $t_1 = 40$, $r = 0.92$, and $n = 7$. She used the general formula $t_n = t_1 r^{n-1}$.
$t_n = t_1 r^{n-1}$
$t_n = 40(0.92)^{n-1}$
$t_7 = 40(0.92)^{7-1}$
$t_7 = 40(0.92)^6$
$t_7 = 24.25$
There will be 24.25 L of water in the tank at the beginning of the 7th day.

Paul's solution:
Paul believed that the sequence was arithmetic, where $t_1 = 40$ and $n = 7$. To calculate the value of d, Paul took 8% of $40 = 3.2$. He reasoned that this would be a negative constant since the water was gradually disappearing. He used the general formula $t_n = t_1 + (n - 1)d$.
$t_n = t_1 + (n - 1)d$
$t_n = 40 + (n - 1)(-3.2)$
$t_7 = 40 + (7 - 1)(-3.2)$
$t_7 = 40 + (6)(-3.2)$
$t_7 = 20.8$
There will be 20.8 L of water in the tank at the beginning of the 7th day.

26. Copy the puzzle. Fill in the empty boxes with positive numbers so that each row and column forms a geometric sequence.

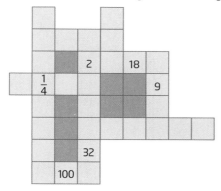

27. A square has an inscribed circle of radius 1 cm.

a) What is the area of the red portion of the square, to the nearest hundredth of a square centimetre?

b) If another square with an inscribed circle is drawn around the original, what is the area of the blue region, to the nearest hundredth of a square centimetre?

c) If another square with an inscribed circle is drawn around the squares, what is the area of the orange region, to the nearest hundredth of a square centimetre?

d) If this pattern were to continue, what would be the area of the newly coloured region for the 8th square, to the nearest hundredth of a square centimetre?

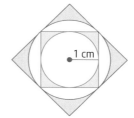

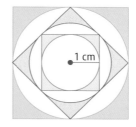

Project Corner   Forestry

- Canada has 402.1 million hectares (ha) of forest and other wooded lands. This value represents 41.1% of Canada's total surface area of 979.1 million hectares.

- Annually, Canada harvests 0.3% of its commercial forest area. In 2007, 0.9 million hectares were harvested.

- In 2008, British Columbia planted its 6 billionth tree seedling since the 1930s, as part of its reforestation programs.

Geometric Series

Focus on...

- deriving a rule for determining the sum of *n* terms of a geometric series
- determining t_1, r, n, or S_n involving a geometric series
- solving a problem that involves a geometric series
- identifying any assumptions made when identifying a geometric series

If you take the time to look closely at nature, chances are you have seen a fractal. Fractal geometry is the *geometry of nature*. The study of fractals is, mathematically, relatively new. A fractal is a geometric figure that is generated by starting with a very simple pattern and repeating that pattern over and over an infinite number of times. The basic concept of a fractal is that it contains a large degree of self-similarity. This means that a fractal usually contains small copies of itself buried within the original. Where do you see fractals in the images shown?

Investigate Fractals

Materials

- paper
- ruler

Fractal Tree

A *fractal tree* is a fractal pattern that results in a realistic looking tree.

You can build your own fractal tree:

1. a) Begin with a sheet of paper. Near the bottom of the paper and centred on the page, draw a vertical line segment approximately 3 cm to 4 cm in length.

b) At the top of the segment, draw two line segments, splitting away from each other as shown in Stage 2. These segments form the branches of the tree. Each new branch formed is a smaller version of the main trunk of the tree.

c) At the top of each new line segment, draw another two branches, as shown in Stage 3.

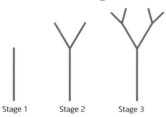

Stage 1   Stage 2   Stage 3

d) Continue this process to complete five stages of the fractal tree.

2. Copy and complete the following table.

Stage	1	2	3	4	5
Number of New Branches	1	2			

3. Decide whether a geometric sequence has been generated for the number of new branches formed at each stage. If a geometric sequence has been generated, state the first term, the common ratio, and the general term.

Reflect and Respond

4. a) Would a geometric sequence be generated if there were three new branches formed from the end of each previous branch?

b) Would a geometric sequence be generated if there were four new branches formed?

5. Describe a strategy you could use to determine the total number of branches that would be formed by the end of stage 5.

6. Would this be a suitable strategy to use if you wanted to determine the total number of branches up to stage 100? Explain.

Web Link

The complex mathematical equations of fractals are used in the creation of many works of art and computer generated fractals. To learn more about art and fractals, go to www.mhrprecalc11.ca and follow the links.

Image rendered by Anton Bakker based on a fractal tree design by Koos Verhoeff. Used with permission of the Foundation MathArt Koos Verhoeff.

geometric series

- the terms of a geometric sequence expressed as a sum
- for example, $3 + 6 + 12 + 24$ is a geometric series

A **geometric series** is the expression for the sum of the terms of a geometric sequence.

A school district emergency *fan-out* system is designed to enable important information to reach the entire staff of the district very quickly. At the first level, the superintendent calls two assistant superintendents. The two assistant superintendents each call two area superintendents. They in turn, each call two principals. The pattern continues with each person calling two other people.

At every level, the total number of people contacted is twice the number of people contacted in the previous level. The pattern can be modelled by a geometric series where the first term is 1 and the common ratio is 2. The series for the fan-out system would be $1 + 2 + 4 + 8$, which gives a sum of 15 people contacted after 4 levels.

To extend this series to 15 or 20 or 100 levels, you need to determine a way to calculate the sum of the series other than just adding the terms.

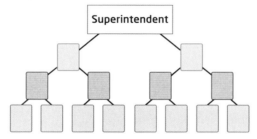

One way to calculate the sum of the series is to use a formula.

To develop a formula for the sum of a series,

List the original series.
$S_4 = 1 + 2 + 4 + 8$ ①

Multiply each term in the series by the common ratio.
$2(S_4 = 1 + 2 + 4 + 8)$
$2S_4 = 2 + 4 + 8 + 16$ ②   The number of staff contacted in the 5th level is 16.

Subtract equation ① from equation ②.

$$\begin{aligned} 2S_4 &= \quad\;\; 2 + 4 + 8 + 16 \\ -\;S_4 &= \;\, 1 + 2 + 4 + 8 \\ \hline (2 - 1)S_4 &= -1 + 0 + 0 + 0 + 16 \end{aligned}$$

Why are the two equations aligned as shown?

Isolate S_4 by dividing by $(2 - 1)$.
$$S_4 = \frac{16 - 1}{2 - 1}$$
$$S_4 = 15$$

You can use the above method to derive a general formula for the sum of a geometric series.

The general geometric series may be represented by the following series.

$$S_n = t_1 + t_1r + t_1r^2 + t_1r^3 + \cdots + t_1r^{n-1}$$

Multiply every term in the series by the common ratio, r.

$$rS_n = t_1r + t_1r(r) + t_1r^2(r) + t_1r^3(r) + \cdots + t_1r^{n-1}(r)$$
$$rS_n = t_1r + t_1r^2 + t_1r^3 + t_1r^4 + \cdots + t_1r^n$$

Subtract the two equations.

$$\begin{aligned} rS_n &= \quad\quad t_1r + t_1r^2 + t_1r^3 + t_1r^4 + \cdots + t_1r^{n-1} + t_1r^n \\ S_n &= \quad t_1 + t_1r + t_1r^2 + t_1r^3 + \cdots \quad\quad\quad + t_1r^{n-1} \\ \hline (r-1)S_n &= -t_1 + \; 0 + \; 0 + 0 \; + \cdots + \; 0 \; + \quad 0 \quad + t_1r^n \end{aligned}$$

Isolate S_n by dividing by $r - 1$.

$$S_n = \frac{t_1r^n - t_1}{r - 1} \text{ or } S_n = \frac{t_1(r^n - 1)}{r - 1}, r \neq 1$$

Why can *r* not be equal to 1?

> The *sum* of a geometric series can be determined using the formula
>
> $$S_n = \frac{t_1(r^n - 1)}{r - 1}, r \neq 1$$
>
> where t_1 is the first term of the series
> n is the number of terms
> r is the common ratio
> S_n is the sum of the first n terms

Example 1

Determine the Sum of a Geometric Series

Determine the sum of the first 10 terms of each geometric series.

a) $4 + 12 + 36 + \cdots$

b) $t_1 = 5, r = \dfrac{1}{2}$

Solution

a) In the series, $t_1 = 4$, $r = 3$, and $n = 10$.

$$S_n = \frac{t_1(r^n - 1)}{r - 1}$$
$$S_{10} = \frac{4(3^{10} - 1)}{3 - 1}$$
$$S_{10} = \frac{4(59\ 048)}{2}$$
$$S_{10} = 118\ 096$$

The sum of the first 10 terms of the geometric series is 118 096.

b) In the series, $t_1 = 5$, $r = \frac{1}{2}$, $n = 10$

$$S_n = \frac{t_1(r^n - 1)}{r - 1}$$

$$S_{10} = \frac{5\left[\left(\frac{1}{2}\right)^{10} - 1\right]}{\frac{1}{2} - 1}$$

$$S_{10} = \frac{5\left(\frac{1}{1024} - 1\right)}{-\frac{1}{2}}$$

$$S_{10} = -10\left(\frac{-1023}{1024}\right)$$

$$S_{10} = \frac{5115}{512}$$

The sum of the first 10 terms of the geometric series is $\frac{5115}{512}$ or $9\frac{507}{512}$.

Your Turn

Determine the sum of the first 8 terms of the following geometric series.

a) $5 + 15 + 45 + \cdots$

b) $t_1 = 64$, $r = \frac{1}{4}$

Example 2

Determine the Sum of a Geometric Series for an Unspecified Number of Terms

Determine the sum of each geometric series.

a) $\frac{1}{27} + \frac{1}{9} + \frac{1}{3} + \cdots + 729$

b) $4 - 16 + 64 - \cdots - 65\ 536$

Solution

a) Method 1: Determine the Number of Terms

$t_n = t_1 r^{n-1}$	Use the general term.
$729 = \frac{1}{27}(3)^{n-1}$	Substitute known values.
$(27)(729) = \left[\frac{1}{27}(3)^{n-1}\right](27)$	Multiply both sides by 27.
$(27)(729) = (3)^{n-1}$	
$(3^3)(3^6) = (3)^{n-1}$	Write as powers with a base of 3.
$(3)^9 = (3)^{n-1}$	
$9 = n - 1$	Since the bases are the same, the exponents
$10 = n$	must be equal.

There are 10 terms in the series.

Use the general formula for the sum of a geometric series where $n = 10$, $t_1 = \frac{1}{27}$, and $r = 3$.

$$S_n = \frac{t_1(r^n - 1)}{r - 1}$$

$$S_{10} = \frac{\left(\frac{1}{27}\right)[(3)^{10} - 1]}{3 - 1}$$

$$S_{10} = \frac{29\ 524}{27}$$

The sum of the series is $\frac{29\ 524}{27}$ or $1093\frac{13}{27}$.

Method 2: Use an Alternate Formula

Begin with the formula for the general term of a geometric sequence, $t_n = t_1 r^{n-1}$.

Multiply both sides by r.

$rt_n = (t_1 r^{n-1})(r)$

Simplify the right-hand side of the equation.

$rt_n = t_1 r^n$

From the previous work, you know that the general formula for the sum of a geometric series may be written as

$$S_n = \frac{t_1 r^n - t_1}{r - 1}$$

Substitute rt_n for $t_1 r^n$.

$$S_n = \frac{rt_n - t_1}{r - 1} \text{ where } r \neq 1.$$

This results in a general formula for the sum of a geometric series when the first term, the nth term, and the common ratio are known.

Determine the sum where $r = 3$, $t_n = 729$, and $t_1 = \frac{1}{27}$.

$$S_n = \frac{rt_n - t_1}{r - 1}$$

$$S_n = \frac{(3)(729) - \frac{1}{27}}{3 - 1}$$

$$S_n = \frac{29\ 524}{27}$$

The sum of the series is $\frac{29\ 524}{27}$ or approximately 1093.48.

b) Use the alternate formula $S_n = \frac{rt_n - t_1}{r - 1}$, where $t_1 = 4$, $r = -4$, and $t_n = -65\ 536$.

$$S_n = \frac{rt_n - t_1}{r - 1}$$

$$S_n = \frac{(-4)(-65\ 536) - 4}{-4 - 1}$$

$$S_n = -52\ 428$$

The sum of the series is $-52\ 428$.

Your Turn

Determine the sum of the following geometric series.

a) $\frac{1}{64} + \frac{1}{16} + \frac{1}{4} + \cdots + 1024$ **b)** $-2 + 4 - 8 + \cdots - 8192$

Example 3

Apply Geometric Series

The Western Scrabble™ Network is an organization whose goal is to promote the game of Scrabble™. It offers Internet tournaments throughout the year that WSN members participate in. The format of these tournaments is such that the losers of each round are eliminated from the next round. The winners continue to play until a final match determines the champion. If there are 256 entries in an Internet Scrabble™ tournament, what is the total number of matches that will be played in the tournament?

Solution

The number of matches played at each stage of the tournament models the terms of a geometric sequence. There are two players per match, so the first term, t_1, is $\frac{256}{2} = 128$ matches. After the first round, half of the players are eliminated due to a loss. The common ratio, r, is $\frac{1}{2}$.

A single match is played at the end of the tournament to decide the winner. The nth term of the series, t_n, is 1 final match.

Use the formula $S_n = \dfrac{rt_n - t_1}{r - 1}$ for the sum of a geometric series where $t_1 = 128$, $r = \dfrac{1}{2}$, and $t_n = 1$.

$$S_n = \frac{rt_n - t_1}{r - 1}$$

$$S_n = \frac{\left(\frac{1}{2}\right)(1) - 128}{\left(\frac{1}{2}\right) - 1}$$

$$S_n = \frac{\frac{-255}{2}}{-\frac{1}{2}}$$

$$S_n = \left(\frac{-255}{2}\right)\left(-\frac{2}{1}\right)$$

$$S_n = 255$$

There will be 255 matches played in the tournament

Your Turn

If a tournament has 512 participants, how many matches will be played?

Key Ideas

- A geometric series is the expression for the sum of the terms of a geometric sequence.
  For example, $5 + 10 + 20 + 40 + \cdots$ is a geometric series.

- The general formula for the sum of the first n terms of a geometric series with the first term, t_1, and the common ratio, r, is
  $$S_n = \frac{t_1(r^n - 1)}{r - 1}, r \neq 1$$

- A variation of this formula may be used when the first term, t_1, the common ratio, r, and the nth term, t_n, are known, but the number of terms, n, is not known.
  $$S_n = \frac{rt_n - t_1}{r - 1}, r \neq 1$$

Check Your Understanding

Practise

1. Determine whether each series is geometric. Justify your answer.

   a) $4 + 24 + 144 + 864 + \cdots$

   b) $-40 + 20 - 10 + 5 - \cdots$

   c) $3 + 9 + 18 + 54 + \cdots$

   d) $10 + 11 + 12.1 + 13.31 + \cdots$

2. For each geometric series, state the values of t_1 and r. Then determine each indicated sum. Express your answers as exact values in fraction form and to the nearest hundredth.

   a) $6 + 9 + 13.5 + \cdots \ (S_{10})$

   b) $18 - 9 + 4.5 + \cdots \ (S_{12})$

   c) $2.1 + 4.2 + 8.4 + \cdots \ (S_9)$

   d) $0.3 + 0.003 + 0.000\,03 + \cdots \ (S_{12})$

3. What is S_n for each geometric series described? Express your answers as exact values in fraction form.

   a) $t_1 = 12, r = 2, n = 10$

   b) $t_1 = 27, r = \frac{1}{3}, n = 8$

   c) $t_1 = \frac{1}{256}, r = -4, n = 10$

   d) $t_1 = 72, r = \frac{1}{2}, n = 12$

4. Determine S_n for each geometric series. Express your answers to the nearest hundredth, if necessary.

   a) $27 + 9 + 3 + \cdots + \frac{1}{243}$

   b) $\frac{1}{3} + \frac{2}{9} + \frac{4}{27} + \cdots + \frac{128}{6561}$

   c) $t_1 = 5, t_n = 81\,920, r = 4$

   d) $t_1 = 3, t_n = 46\,875, r = -5$

5. What is the value of the first term for each geometric series described? Express your answers to the nearest tenth, if necessary.

a) $S_n = 33$, $t_n = 48$, $r = -2$

b) $S_n = 443$, $n = 6$, $r = \dfrac{1}{3}$

6. The sum of $4 + 12 + 36 + 108 + \cdots + t_n$ is 4372. How many terms are in the series?

7. The common ratio of a geometric series is $\dfrac{1}{3}$ and the sum of the first 5 terms is 121.

a) What is the value of the first term?

b) Write the first 5 terms of the series.

8. What is the second term of a geometric series in which the third term is $\dfrac{9}{4}$ and the sixth term is $-\dfrac{16}{81}$? Determine the sum of the first 6 terms. Express your answer to the nearest tenth.

Apply

9. A fan-out system is used to contact a large group of people. The person in charge of the contact committee relays the information to four people. Each of these four people notifies four more people, who in turn each notify four more people, and so on.

a) Write the corresponding series for the number of people contacted.

b) How many people are notified after 10 levels of this system?

10. A tennis ball dropped from a height of 20 m bounces to 40% of its previous height on each bounce. The total vertical distance travelled is made up of upward bounces and downward drops. Draw a diagram to represent this situation. What is the total vertical distance the ball has travelled when it hits the floor for the sixth time? Express your answer to the nearest tenth of a metre.

11. Celia is training to run a marathon. In the first week she runs 25 km and increases this distance by 10% each week. This situation may be modelled by the series $25 + 25(1.1) + 25(1.1)^2 + \cdots$. She wishes to continue this pattern for 15 weeks. How far will she have run in total when she completes the 15th week? Express your answer to the nearest tenth of a kilometre.

12. Building the Koch snowflake is a step-by-step process.

• Start with an equilateral triangle. (Stage 1)

• In the middle of each line segment forming the sides of the triangle, construct an equilateral triangle with side length equal to $\dfrac{1}{3}$ of the length of the line segment.

• Delete the base of this new triangle. (Stage 2)

• For each line segment in Stage 2, construct an equilateral triangle, deleting its base. (Stage 3)

• Repeat this process for each line segment, as you move from one stage to the next.

Stage 1   Stage 2

Stage 3   Stage 4

a) Work with a partner. Use dot paper to draw three stages of the Koch snowflake.

b) Copy and complete the following table.

Stage Number	Length of Each Line Segment	Number of Line Segments	Perimeter of Snowflake
1	1	3	3
2	$\frac{1}{3}$	12	4
3	$\frac{1}{9}$		
4			
5			

c) Determine the general term for the length of each line segment, the number of line segments, and the perimeter of the snowflake.

d) What is the total perimeter of the snowflake up to Stage 6?

13. An advertising company designs a campaign to introduce a new product to a metropolitan area. The company determines that 1000 people are aware of the product at the beginning of the campaign. The number of new people aware increases by 40% every 10 days during the advertising campaign. Determine the total number of people who will be aware of the product after 100 days.

14. Bead working has a long history among Canada's Indigenous peoples. Floral designs are the predominate patterns found among people of the boreal forests and northern plains. Geometric patterns are found predominately in the Great Plains. As bead work continues to be popular, traditional patterns are being exchanged among people in all regions. Suppose a set of 10 beads were laid in a line where each successive bead had a diameter that was $\frac{3}{4}$ of the diameter of the previous bead. If the first bead had a diameter of 24 mm, determine the total length of the line of beads. Express your answer to the nearest millimetre.

Did You Know?

Wampum belts consist of rows of beads woven together. Weaving traditionally involves stringing the beads onto twisted plant fibres, and then securing them to animal sinew.

Wanuskewin Native Heritage Park, Cree Nation, Saskatchewan

15. When doctors prescribe medicine at equally spaced time intervals, they are aware that the body metabolizes the drug gradually. After some period of time, only a certain percent of the original amount remains. After each dose, the amount of the drug in the body is equal to the amount of the given dose plus the amount remaining from the previous doses. The amount of the drug present in the body after the nth dose is modelled by a geometric series where t_1 is the prescribed dosage and r is the previous dose remaining in the body.

Suppose a person with an ear infection takes a 200-mg ampicillin tablet every 4 h. About 12% of the drug in the body at the start of a four-hour period is still present at the end of that period. What amount of ampicillin is in the body, to the nearest tenth of a milligram,

a) after taking the third tablet?

b) after taking the sixth tablet?

Extend

16. Determine the number of terms, n, if $3 + 3^2 + 3^3 + \cdots + 3^n = 9840$.

17. The third term of a geometric series is 24 and the fourth term is 36. Determine the sum of the first 10 terms. Express your answer as an exact fraction.

18. Three numbers, a, b, and c, form a geometric series so that $a + b + c = 35$ and $abc = 1000$. What are the values of a, b, and c?

19. The sum of the first 7 terms of a geometric series is 89, and the sum of the first 8 terms is 104. What is the value of the eighth term?

Create Connections

20. A fractal is created as follows: A circle is drawn with radius 8 cm. Another circle is drawn with half the radius of the previous circle. The new circle is tangent to the previous circle at point T as shown. Suppose this pattern continues through five steps. What is the sum of the areas of the circles? Express your answer as an exact fraction.

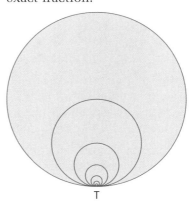

21. Copy the following flowcharts. In the appropriate segment of each chart, give a definition, a general term or sum, or an example, as required.

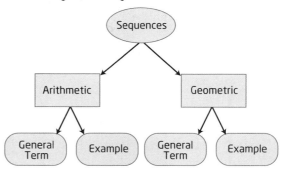

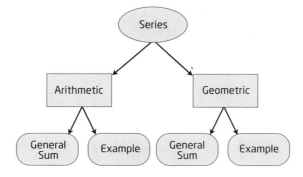

22. Tom learned that the monarch butterfly lays an average of 400 eggs. He decided to calculate the growth of the butterfly population from a single butterfly by using the logic that the first butterfly produced 400 butterflies. Each of those butterflies would produce 400 butterflies, and this pattern would continue. Tom wanted to estimate how many butterflies there would be in total in the fifth generation following this pattern. His calculation is shown below.

$$S_n = \frac{t_1(r^n - 1)}{r - 1}$$

$$S_5 = \frac{1(400^5 - 1)}{400 - 1}$$

$$S_5 \approx 2.566 \times 10^{10}$$

Tom calculated that there would be approximately 2.566×10^{10} monarch butterflies in the fifth generation.

a) What assumptions did Tom make in his calculations?

b) Do you agree with the method Tom used to arrive at the number of butterflies? Explain.

c) Would this be a reasonable estimate of the total number of butterflies in the fifth generation? Explain.

d) Explain a method you would use to calculate the number of butterflies in the fifth generation.

Did You Know?

According to the American Indian Butterfly Legend:

If anyone desires a wish to come true they must first capture a butterfly and whisper that wish to it.

Since a butterfly can make no sound, the butterfly cannot reveal the wish to anyone but the Great Spirit who hears and sees all.

In gratitude for giving the beautiful butterfly its freedom, the Great Spirit always grants the wish.

So, according to legend, by making a wish and giving the butterfly its freedom, the wish will be taken to the heavens and be granted.

Project Corner — Oil Discovery

- The first oil well in Canada was discovered by James Miller Williams in 1858 near Oil Springs, Ontario. The oil was taken to Hamilton, Ontario, where it was refined into lamp oil. This well produced 37 barrels a day. By 1861 there were 400 wells in the area.

- In 1941, Alberta's population was approximately 800 000. By 1961, it was about 1.3 million.

- In February 1947, oil was struck in Leduc, Alberta. Leduc was the largest discovery in Canada in 33 years. By the end of 1947, 147 more wells were drilled in the Leduc-Woodbend oilfield.

- With these oil discoveries came accelerated population growth. In 1941, Leduc was inhabited by 871 people. By 1951, its population had grown to 1842.

- Leduc #1 was capped in 1974, after producing 300 000 barrels of oil and 9 million cubic metres of natural gas.

Infinite Geometric Series

Зепо.
(Visconti, Icon. greca.)

Focus on...

- generalizing a rule for determining the sum of an infinite geometric series
- explaining why a geometric series is convergent or divergent
- solving a problem that involves a geometric sequence or series

In the fifth century B.C.E., the Greek philosopher Zeno of Elea posed four problems, now known as Zeno's paradoxes. These problems were intended to challenge some of the ideas that were held in his day. His paradox of motion states that a person standing in a room cannot walk to the wall. In order to do so, the person would first have to go half the distance, then half the remaining distance, and then half of what still remains. This process can always be continued and can never end.

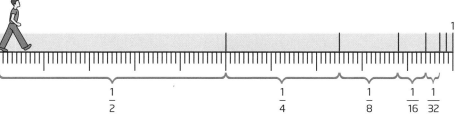

Did You Know?

The word *paradox* comes from the Greek *para doxa*, meaning something contrary to opinion.

Zeno's argument is that there is no motion, because that which is moved must arrive at the middle before it arrives at the end, and so on to infinity.

Where does the argument break down? Why?

Investigate an Infinite Series

Materials

- square piece of paper
- ruler

1. Start with a square piece of paper.

    a) Draw a line dividing it in half.

    b) Shade one of the halves.

    c) In the unshaded half of the square, draw a line to divide it in half. Shade one of the halves.

    d) Repeat part c) at least six more times.

2. Write a sequence of terms indicating the area of each newly shaded region as a fraction of the entire page. List the first five terms.

3. Predict the next two terms for the sequence.

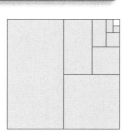

4. Is the sequence arithmetic, geometric, or neither? Justify your answer.

5. Write the rule for the *n*th term of the sequence.

6. Ignoring physical limitations, could this sequence continue indefinitely? In other words, would this be an infinite sequence? Explain your answer.

7. What conclusion can you make about the area of the square that would remain unshaded as the number of terms in the sequence approaches infinity?

Reflect and Respond

8. Using a graphing calculator, input the function $y = \left(\frac{1}{2}\right)^x$.

    a) Using the table of values from the calculator, what happens to the value of $y = \left(\frac{1}{2}\right)^x$ as *x* gets larger and larger?

    b) Can the value of $\left(\frac{1}{2}\right)^x$ ever equal zero?

9. The geometric series $\frac{1}{2} + \frac{1}{4} + \frac{1}{8} + \frac{1}{16} + \cdots$ can be written as
$$\frac{1}{2} + \left(\frac{1}{2}\right)^2 + \left(\frac{1}{2}\right)^3 + \left(\frac{1}{2}\right)^4 + \cdots + \left(\frac{1}{2}\right)^x.$$
You can use the general formula to determine the sum of the series.

$$S_x = \frac{t_1(1 - r^x)}{(1 - r)}$$

$$S_x = \frac{\frac{1}{2}\left(1 - \left(\frac{1}{2}\right)^x\right)}{1 - \frac{1}{2}}$$

$$S_x = 1 - \left(\frac{1}{2}\right)^x$$

> For values of *r* < 1, the general formula $S_x = \frac{t_1(r^x - 1)}{(r - 1)}$ can be written for convenience as $S_x = \frac{t_1(1 - r^x)}{(1 - r)}$. Why do you think this is true?

Enter the function into your calculator and use the table feature to find the sum, S_x, as *x* gets larger.

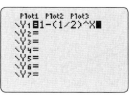 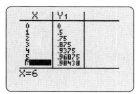

    a) What happens to the sum, S_x, as *x* gets larger?

    b) Will the sum increase without limit? Explain your reasoning.

10. a) As the value of *x* gets very large, what value can you assume that r^x becomes close to?

    b) Use your answer from part a) to modify the formula for the sum of a geometric series to determine the sum of an infinite geometric series.

    c) Use your formula from part b) to determine the sum of the infinite geometric series $\frac{1}{2} + \left(\frac{1}{2}\right)^2 + \left(\frac{1}{2}\right)^3 + \left(\frac{1}{2}\right)^4 + \cdots$.

Convergent Series

Consider the series $4 + 2 + 1 + 0.5 + 0.25 + \cdots$

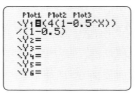 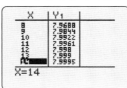 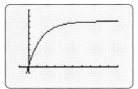

$S_5 = 7.75$
$S_7 = 7.9375$
$S_9 = 7.9844$
$S_{11} = 7.9961$
$S_{13} = 7.999$
$S_{15} = 7.9998$
$S_{17} = 7.9999$

As the number of terms increases, the sequence of partial sums approaches a fixed value of 8. Therefore, the sum of this series is 8. This series is said to be a **convergent series**.

convergent series

- a series with an infinite number of terms, in which the sequence of partial sums approaches a fixed value
- for example,
  $1 + \dfrac{1}{2} + \dfrac{1}{4} + \dfrac{1}{8} + \cdots$

Divergent Series

Consider the series $4 + 8 + 16 + 32 + \cdots$

$S_1 = 4$
$S_2 = 12$
$S_3 = 28$
$S_4 = 60$
$S_5 = 124$

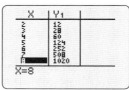 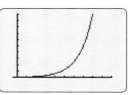

As the number of terms increases, the sum of the series continues to grow. The sequence of partial sums does not approach a fixed value. Therefore, the sum of this series cannot be calculated. This series is said to be a **divergent series**.

divergent series

- a series with an infinite number of terms, in which the sequence of partial sums does not approach a fixed value
- for example,
  $2 + 4 + 8 + 16 + \cdots$

Infinite Geometric Series

The formula for the sum of a geometric series is

$$S_n = \frac{t_1(1 - r^n)}{1 - r}.$$

As n gets very large, the value of the r^n approaches 0, for values of r between -1 and 1.

So, as n gets large, the partial sum S_n approaches $\dfrac{t_1}{1 - r}$.

Therefore, the sum of an infinite geometric series is

$$S_\infty = \frac{t_1}{1 - r}, \text{ where } -1 < r < 1.$$

The *sum* of an infinite geometric series, where $-1 < r < 1$, can be determined using the formula

$$S_\infty = \frac{t_1}{1 - r}$$

where t_1 is the first term of the series

r is the common ratio

S_∞ represents the sum of an infinite number of terms

Applying the formula to the series $4 + 2 + 1 + 0.5 + 0.25 + \cdots$

$$S_\infty = \frac{t_1}{1 - r}, \text{ where } -1 < r < 1,$$

$$S_\infty = \frac{4}{1 - 0.5}$$

$$S_\infty = \frac{4}{0.5}$$

$$S_\infty = 8$$

Example 1
Sum of an Infinite Geometric Series

Decide whether each infinite geometric series is convergent or divergent.
State the sum of the series, if it exists.

a) $1 - \frac{1}{3} + \frac{1}{9} - \cdots$ **b)** $2 - 4 + 8 - \cdots$

Solution

a) $t_1 = 1, r = -\frac{1}{3}$

Since $-1 < r < 1$, the series is convergent.
Use the formula for the sum of an infinite geometric series.

$$S_\infty = \frac{t_1}{1 - r}, \text{ where } -1 < r < 1,$$

$$S_\infty = \frac{1}{1 - \left(-\frac{1}{3}\right)}$$

$$S_\infty = \frac{1}{\frac{4}{3}}$$

$$S_\infty = (1)\left(\frac{3}{4}\right)$$

$$S_\infty = \frac{3}{4}$$

b) $t_1 = 2, r = -2$
Since $r < -1$, the series is divergent and has no sum.

Your Turn

Determine whether each infinite geometric series converges or diverges.
Calculate the sum, if it exists.

a) $1 + \frac{1}{5} + \frac{1}{25} + \cdots$ **b)** $4 + 8 + 16 + \cdots$

Example 2

Apply the Sum of an Infinite Geometric Series

Assume that each shaded square represents $\frac{1}{4}$ of the area of the larger square bordering two of its adjacent sides and that the shading continues indefinitely in the indicated manner.

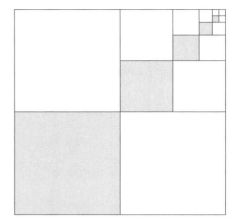

a) Write the series of terms that would represent this situation.

b) How much of the total area of the largest square is shaded?

Solution

a) The sequence of shaded regions generates an infinite geometric sequence. The series of terms that represents this situation is

$$\frac{1}{4} + \frac{1}{16} + \frac{1}{64} + \cdots$$

b) To determine the total area shaded, you need to determine the sum of all the shaded regions within the largest square.

For this series,

First term $\qquad t_1 = \frac{1}{4}$

Common ratio $\quad r = \frac{1}{4}$

Use the formula for the sum of an infinite geometric series.

$$S_\infty = \frac{t_1}{1 - r}, \text{ where } -1 < r < 1,$$

$$S_\infty = \frac{\frac{1}{4}}{1 - \frac{1}{4}}$$

$$S_\infty = \frac{\frac{1}{4}}{\frac{3}{4}}$$

$$S_\infty = \left(\frac{1}{4}\right)\left(\frac{4}{3}\right)$$

$$S_\infty = \frac{1}{3}$$

A total area of $\frac{1}{3}$ of the largest square is shaded.

Your Turn

You can express $0.\overline{584}$ as an infinite geometric series.

$0.\overline{584} = 0.584\,584\,584\ldots$

$\qquad\quad = 0.584 + 0.000\,584 + 0.000\,000\,584 + \cdots$

Determine the sum of the series.

Key Ideas

- An infinite geometric series is a geometric series that has an infinite number of terms; that is, the series has no last term.

- An infinite series is said to be convergent if its sequence of partial sums approaches a finite number. This number is the sum of the infinite series. An infinite series that is not convergent is said to be divergent.

- An infinite geometric series has a sum when $-1 < r < 1$ and the sum is given by

$$S_\infty = \frac{t_1}{1 - r}.$$

Check Your Understanding

Practise

1. State whether each infinite geometric series is convergent or divergent.

a) $t_1 = -3, r = 4$

b) $t_1 = 4, r = -\frac{1}{4}$

c) $125 + 25 + 5 + \cdots$

d) $(-2) + (-4) + (-8) + \cdots$

e) $\frac{243}{3125} - \frac{81}{625} + \frac{27}{25} - \frac{9}{5} + \cdots$

2. Determine the sum of each infinite geometric series, if it exists.

a) $t_1 = 8, r = -\frac{1}{4}$

b) $t_1 = 3, r = \frac{4}{3}$

c) $t_1 = 5, r = 1$

d) $1 + 0.5 + 0.25 + \cdots$

e) $4 - \frac{12}{5} + \frac{36}{25} - \frac{108}{125} + \cdots$

3. Express each of the following as an infinite geometric series. Determine the sum of the series.

a) $0.\overline{87}$

b) $0.\overline{437}$

4. Does 0.999… = 1? Support your answer.

5. What is the sum of each infinite geometric series?

a) $5 + 5\left(\frac{2}{3}\right) + 5\left(\frac{2}{3}\right)^2 + 5\left(\frac{2}{3}\right)^3 + \cdots$

b) $1 + \left(-\frac{1}{4}\right) + \left(-\frac{1}{4}\right)^2 + \left(-\frac{1}{4}\right)^3 + \cdots$

c) $7 + 7\left(\frac{1}{2}\right) + 7\left(\frac{1}{2}\right)^2 + 7\left(\frac{1}{2}\right)^3 + \cdots$

Apply

6. The sum of an infinite geometric series is 81, and its common ratio is $\frac{2}{3}$. What is the value of the first term? Write the first three terms of the series.

7. The first term of an infinite geometric series is -8, and its sum is $-\frac{40}{3}$. What is the common ratio? Write the first four terms of the series.

8. In its first month, an oil well near Virden, Manitoba produced 24 000 barrels of crude. Every month after that, it produced 94% of the previous month's production.

a) If this trend continued, what would be the lifetime production of this well?

b) What assumption are you making? Is your assumption reasonable?

9. The infinite series given by
$1 + 3x + 9x^2 + 27x^3 + \cdots$ has a sum
of 4. What is the value of x? List the
first four terms of the series.

10. The sum of an infinite series is twice
its first term. Determine the value of the
common ratio.

11. Each of the following represents an infinite
geometric series. For what values of x will
each series be convergent?

   a) $5 + 5x + 5x^2 + 5x^3 + \cdots$

   b) $1 + \frac{x}{3} + \frac{x^2}{9} + \frac{x^3}{27} + \cdots$

   c) $2 + 4x + 8x^2 + 16x^3 + \cdots$

12. Each side of an equilateral triangle has
length of 1 cm. The midpoints of the sides
are joined to form an inscribed equilateral
triangle. Then, the midpoints of the sides
of that triangle are joined to form another
triangle. If this process continues forever,
what is the sum of the perimeters of the
triangles?

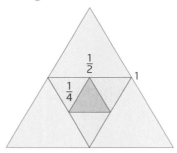

13. The length of the initial swing of a
pendulum is 50 cm. Each successive swing
is 0.8 times the length of the previous
swing. If this process continues forever,
how far will the pendulum swing?

14. Andrew uses the formula for the
sum of an infinite geometric series to
evaluate $1 + 1.1 + 1.21 + 1.331 + \cdots$. He
calculates the sum of the series to be 10. Is
Andrew's answer reasonable? Explain.

15. A ball is dropped from a height of 16 m.
The ball rebounds to one half of its
previous height each time it bounces. If
the ball keeps bouncing, what is the total
vertical distance the ball travels?

16. A pile driver pounds a metal post into
the ground. With the first impact, the post
moves 30 cm; with the second impact it
moves 27 cm. Predict the total distance that
the post will be driven into the ground if

   a) the distances form a geometric sequence
   and the post is pounded 8 times

   b) the distances form a geometric sequence
   and the post is pounded indefinitely

17. Dominique and Rita are discussing the
series $-\frac{1}{3} + \frac{4}{9} - \frac{16}{27} + \cdots$. Dominique says
that the sum of the series is $-\frac{1}{7}$. Rita says
that the series is divergent and has no sum.

   a) Who is correct?

   b) Explain your reasoning.

18. A hot air balloon rises 25 m
in its first minute of
flight. Suppose that
in each succeeding
minute the balloon
rises only 80%
as high as in the
previous minute.
What would be
the balloon's
maximum
altitude?

Hot air balloon rising over Calgary.

Extend

19. A square piece of paper with a side length
of 24 cm is cut into four small squares,
each with side lengths of 12 cm. Three of
these squares are placed side by side. The
remaining square is cut into four smaller
squares, each with side lengths of 6 cm.
Three of these squares are placed side by
side with the bigger squares. The fourth
square is cut into four smaller squares and
three of these squares are placed side by
side with the bigger squares. Suppose this
process continues indefinitely. What is the
length of the arrangement of squares?

20. The sum of the series

$0.98 + 0.98^2 + 0.98^3 + \cdots + 0.98^n = 49$.

The sum of the series

$0.02 + 0.0004 + 0.000\,008 + \cdots = \dfrac{1}{49}$.

The common ratio in the first series is 0.98 and the common ratio in the second series is 0.02. The sum of these ratios is equal to 1. Suppose that $\dfrac{1}{z} = x + x^2 + x^3 + \cdots$,

where z is an integer and $x = \dfrac{1}{z+1}$.

a) Create another pair of series that would follow this pattern, where the sum of the common ratios of the two series is 1.

b) Determine the sum of each series using the formula for the sum of an infinite series.

Create Connections

21. Under what circumstances will an infinite geometric series converge?

22. The first two terms of a series are 1 and $\dfrac{1}{4}$. Determine a formula for the sum of n terms if the series is

a) an arithmetic series

b) a geometric series

c) an infinite geometric series

23. MINI LAB Work in a group of three.

Step 1 Begin with a large sheet of grid paper and draw a square. Assume that the area of this square is 1.

Step 2 Cut the square into 4 equal parts. Distribute one part to each member of your group. Cut the remaining part into 4 equal parts. Again distribute one part to each group member. Subdivide the remaining part into 4 equal parts. Suppose you could continue this pattern indefinitely.

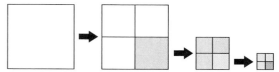

Step 3 Write a sequence for the fraction of the original square that each student received at each stage.

n	1	2	3	4
Fraction of Paper				

Step 4 Write the total area of paper each student has as a series of partial sums. What do you expect the sum to be?

Project Corner   Petroleum

- The Athabasca Oil Sands have estimated oil reserves in excess of that of the rest of the world. These reserves are estimated to be 1.6 trillion barrels.

- Canada is the seventh largest oil producing country in the world. In 2008, Canada produced an average of 438 000 m³ per day of crude oil, crude bitumen, and natural gas.

- As Alberta's reserves of light crude oil began to deplete, so did production. By 1997, Alberta's light crude oil production totalled 37.3 million cubic metres. This production has continued to decline each year since, falling to just over half of its 1990 total at 21.7 million cubic metres in 2005.

Chapter 1 Review

1.1 Arithmetic Sequences, pages 6–21

1. Determine whether each of the following sequences is arithmetic. If it is arithmetic, state the common difference.

   a) 36, 40, 44, 48, …

   b) −35, −40, −45, −50, …

   c) 1, 2, 4, 8, …

   d) 8.3, 4.3, 0.3, −3, −3.7, …

2. Match the equation for the nth term of an arithmetic sequence to the correct sequence.

   a) 18, 30, 42, 54, 66, …   **A** $t_n = 3n + 1$

   b) 7, 12, 17, 22, …   **B** $t_n = -4(n + 1)$

   c) 2, 4, 6, 8, …   **C** $t_n = 12n + 6$

   d) −8, −12, −16, −20, …   **D** $t_n = 5n + 2$

   e) 4, 7, 10, 13, …   **E** $t_n = 2n$

3. Consider the sequence 7, 14, 21, 28, …. Determine whether each of the following numbers is a term of this sequence. Justify your answer. If the number is a term of the sequence, determine the value of n for that term.

   a) 98   b) 110

   c) 378   d) 575

4. Two sequences are given:
   Sequence 1 is 2, 9, 16, 23, …
   Sequence 2 is 4, 10, 16, 22, …

   a) Which of the following statements is correct?

   A t_{17} is greater in sequence 1.

   B t_{17} is greater in sequence 2.

   C t_{17} is equal in both sequences.

   b) On a grid, sketch a graph of each sequence. Does the graph support your answer in part a)? Explain.

5. Determine the tenth term of the arithmetic sequence in which the first term is 5 and the fourth term is 17.

6. The Gardiner Dam, located 100 km south of Saskatoon, Saskatchewan, is the largest earth-filled dam in the world. Upon its opening in 1967, engineers discovered that the pressure from Lake Diefenbaker had moved the clay-based structure 200 cm downstream. Since then, the dam has been moving at a rate of 2 cm per year. Determine the distance the dam will have moved downstream by the year 2020.

1.2 Arithmetic Series, pages 22–31

7. Determine the indicated sum for each of the following arithmetic series

   a) $6 + 9 + 12 + \cdots (S_{10})$

   b) $4.5 + 8 + 11.5 + \cdots (S_{12})$

   c) $6 + 3 + 0 + \cdots (S_{10})$

   d) $60 + 70 + 80 + \cdots (S_{20})$

8. The sum of the first 12 terms of an arithmetic series is 186, and the 20th term is 83. What is the sum of the first 40 terms?

9. You have taken a job that requires being in contact with all the people in your neighbourhood. On the first day, you are able to contact only one person. On the second day, you contact two more people than you did on the first day. On day three, you contact two more people than you did on the previous day. Assume that the pattern continues.

   a) How many people would you contact on the 15th day?

   b) Determine the total number of people you would have been in contact with by the end of the 15th day.

c) How many days would you need to contact the 625 people in your neighbourhood?

10. A new set of designs is created by the addition of squares to the previous pattern.

Step 1   Step 2

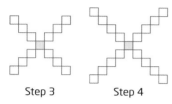

Step 3   Step 4

a) Determine the total number of squares in the 15th step of this design.

b) Determine the total number of squares required to build all 15 steps.

11. A concert hall has 10 seats in the first row. The second row has 12 seats. If each row has 2 seats more than the row before it and there are 30 rows of seats, how many seats are in the entire concert hall?

1.3 Geometric Sequences, pages 32–45

12. Determine whether each of the following sequences is geometric. If it is geometric, determine the common ratio, r, the first term, t_1, and the general term of the sequence.

a) 3, 6, 10, 15, …

b) 1, −2, 4, −8, …

c) $1, \frac{1}{2}, \frac{1}{4}, \frac{1}{8}, …$

d) $\frac{16}{9}, -\frac{3}{4}, 1, …$

13. A culture initially has 5000 bacteria, and the number increases by 8% every hour.

a) How many bacteria are present at the end of 5 h?

b) Determine a formula for the number of bacteria present after n hours.

14. In the Mickey Mouse fractal shown below, the original diagram has a radius of 81 cm. Each successive circle has a radius $\frac{1}{3}$ of the previous radius. What is the circumference of the smallest circle in the 4th stage?

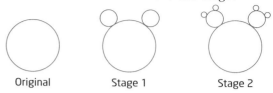

Original   Stage 1   Stage 2

15. Use the following flowcharts to describe what you know about arithmetic and geometric sequences.

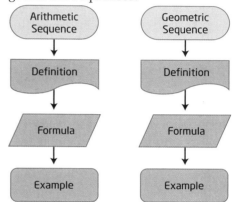

1.4 Geometric Series, pages 46–57

16. Decide whether each of the following statements relates to an arithmetic series or a geometric series.

a) A sum of terms in which the difference between consecutive terms is constant.

b) A sum of terms in which the ratio of consecutive terms is constant.

c) $S_n = \dfrac{t_1(r^n - 1)}{r - 1}, r \neq 1$

d) $S_n = \dfrac{n[2t_1 + (n - 1)d]}{2}$

e) $\dfrac{1}{4} + \dfrac{1}{2} + \dfrac{3}{4} + 1 + \cdots$

f) $\dfrac{1}{4} + \dfrac{1}{6} + \dfrac{1}{9} + \dfrac{2}{27} + \cdots$

17. Determine the sum indicated for each of the following geometric series.

a) $6 + 9 + 13.5 + \cdots (S_{10})$

b) $18 + 9 + 4.5 + \cdots (S_{12})$

c) $6000 + 600 + 60 + \cdots (S_{20})$

d) $80 + 20 + 5 + \cdots (S_{9})$

18. A student programs a computer to draw a series of straight lines with each line beginning at the end of the previous line and at right angles to it. The first line is 4 mm long. Each subsequent line is 25% longer than the previous one, so that a spiral shape is formed as shown.

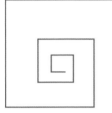

a) What is the length, in millimetres, of the eighth straight line drawn by the program? Express your answer to the nearest tenth of a millimetre.

b) Determine the total length of the spiral, in metres, when 20 straight lines have been drawn. Express your answer to the nearest hundredth of a metre.

1.5 Infinite Geometric Series, pages 58–65

19. Determine the sum of each of the following infinite geometric series.

a) $5 + 5\left(\dfrac{2}{3}\right) + 5\left(\dfrac{2}{3}\right)^2 + 5\left(\dfrac{2}{3}\right)^3 + \cdots$

b) $1 + \left(-\dfrac{1}{3}\right) + \left(-\dfrac{1}{3}\right)^2 + \left(-\dfrac{1}{3}\right)^3 + \cdots$

20. For each of the following series, state whether it is convergent or divergent. For those that are convergent, determine the sum.

a) $8 + 4 + 2 + 1 + \cdots$

b) $8 + 12 + 27 + 40.5 + \cdots$

c) $-42 + 21 - 10.5 + 5.25 - \cdots$

d) $\dfrac{3}{4} + \dfrac{3}{8} + \dfrac{3}{16} + \dfrac{3}{32} + \cdots$

21. Given the infinite geometric series:
$7 - 2.8 + 1.12 - 0.448 + \cdots$

a) What is the common ratio, r?

b) Determine S_1, S_2, S_3, S_4, and S_5.

c) What is the particular value that the sums are approaching?

d) What is the sum of the series?

22. Draw four squares adjacent to each other. The first square has a side length of 1 unit, the second has a side length of $\dfrac{1}{2}$ unit, the third has a side length of $\dfrac{1}{4}$ unit, and the fourth has a side length of $\dfrac{1}{8}$ unit.

a) Calculate the area of each square. Do the areas form a geometric sequence? Justify your answer.

b) What is the total area of the four squares?

c) If the process of adding squares with half the side length of the previous square continued indefinitely, what would the total area of all the squares be?

23. a) Copy and complete each of the following statements.

- A series is geometric if there is a common ratio r such that ▬▬▬.
- An infinite geometric series converges if ▬▬▬.
- An infinite geometric series diverges if ▬▬▬.

b) Give two examples of convergent infinite geometric series one with positive common ratio and one with negative common ratio. Determine the sum of each of your series.

Chapter 1 Practice Test

Multiple Choice

For # 1 to #5, choose the best answer.

1. What are the missing terms of the arithmetic sequence ■, 3, 9, ■, ■?

   A 1, 27, 81 **B** 9, 3, 9

   C −6, 12, 17 **D** −3, 15, 21

2. Marc has set up in his father's grocery store a display of cans as shown in the diagram. The top row (Row 1) has 1 can and each successive row has 3 more cans than the previous row. Which expression would represent the number of cans in row n?

   A $S_n = 3n + 1$ **B** $t_n = 3n - 2$

   C $t_n = 3n + 2$ **D** $S_n = 3n - 3$

3. What is the sum of the first five terms of the geometric series $16\,807 - 2401 + 343 - \cdots$?

   A 19 607 **B** 14 707

   C 16 807.29 **D** 14 706.25

4. The numbers represented by a, b, and c are the first three terms of an arithmetic sequence. The number c, when expressed in terms of a and b, would be represented by

   A $a + b$ **B** $2b - a$

   C $a + (n - 1)b$ **D** $2a + b$

5. The 20th term of a geometric sequence is 524 288 and the 14th term is 8192. The value of the third term could be

   A 4 only **B** 8 only

   C +4 or −4 **D** +8 or −8

Short Answer

6. A set of hemispherical bowls are made so they can be nested for easy storage. The largest bowl has a radius of 30 cm and each successive bowl has a radius 90% of the preceding one. What is the radius of the tenth bowl?

7. Use the following graphs to compare and contrast an arithmetic and a geometric sequence.

   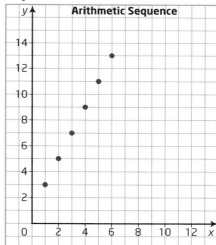

   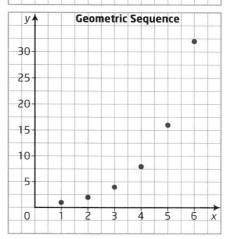

8. If 3, A, 27 is an arithmetic sequence and 3, B, 27 is a geometric sequence where $B > 0$, then what are the values of A and B?

9. Josephine Mandamin, an Anishinabe elder from Thunder Bay, Ontario, set out to walk around the Great Lakes to raise awareness about the quality of water in the lakes. In six years, she walked 17 000 km. If Josephine increased the number of kilometres walked per week by 2% every week, how many kilometres did she walk in the first week?

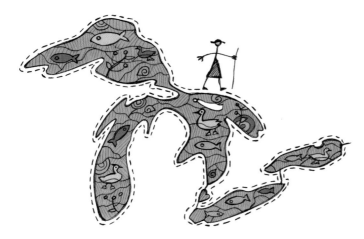

10. Consider the sequence 5, ■, ■, ■, ■, 160.

a) Assume the sequence is arithmetic. Determine the unknown terms of the sequence.

b) What is the general term of the arithmetic sequence?

c) Assume the sequence is geometric. Determine the unknown terms of the sequence.

d) What is the general term of the geometric sequence?

Extended Response

11. Scientists have been measuring the continental drift between Europe and North America for about 25 years. The data collected show that the continents are moving apart at a steady rate of about 17 mm per year.

a) According to the Pangaea theory, Europe and North America were connected at one time. Assuming this theory is correct, write an arithmetic sequence that describes how far apart the continents were at the end of each of the first five years after separation.

b) Determine the general term that describes the arithmetic sequence.

c) Approximately how many years did it take to separate to the current distance of 6000 km? Express your answer to the nearest million years.

d) What assumptions did you make in part c)?

12. Photodynamic therapy is used in patients with certain types of disease. A doctor injects a patient with a drug that is attracted to the diseased cells. The diseased cells are then exposed to red light from a laser. This procedure targets and destroys diseased cells while limiting damage to surrounding healthy tissue. The drug remains in the normal cells of the body and must be bleached out by exposure to the sun. A patient must be exposed to the sun for 30 s on the first day, and then increase the exposure by 30 s every day until a total of 30 min is reached.

a) Write the first five terms of the sequence of sun exposure times.

b) Is the sequence arithmetic or geometric?

c) How many days are required to reach the goal of 30 min of exposure to the sun?

d) What is the total number of minutes of sun exposure when a patient reaches the 30 min goal?

Canada's Natural Resources

Canada is the source of more than 60 mineral commodities, including metals, non-metals, structural materials, and mineral fuels.

Quarrying and mining are among the oldest industries in Canada. In 1672, coal was discovered on Cape Breton Island.

In the 1850s, gold discoveries in British Columbia, oil finds in Ontario, and increased production of Cape Breton coal marked a turning point in Canadian mineral history.

In 1896, gold was found in the Klondike District of what became Yukon Territory, giving rise to one of the world's most spectacular gold rushes.

In the late 1800s, large deposits of coal and oil sands were evident in part of the North-West Territories that later became Alberta.

In the post-war era there were many major mineral discoveries: deposits of nickel in Manitoba; zinc-lead, copper, and molybdenum in British Columbia; and base metals and asbestos in Québec, Ontario, Manitoba, Newfoundland, Yukon Territory, and British Columbia.

The discovery of the famous Leduc oil field in Alberta in 1947 was followed by a great expansion of Canada's petroleum industry.

In the late 1940s and early 1950s, uranium was discovered in Saskatchewan and Ontario. In fact, Canada is now the world's largest uranium producer.

Canada's first diamond-mining operation began production in October 1998 at the Ekati mine in Lac de Gras, Northwest Territories, followed by the Diavik mine in 2002.

Chapter 1 Task

Choose a natural resource that you would like to research. You may wish to look at some of the information presented in the Project Corner boxes throughout Chapter 1 for ideas. Research your chosen resource.

- List interesting facts about your chosen resource, including what it is, how it is produced, where it is exported, how much is exported, and so on.

- Look for data that would support using a sequence or series in discussing or describing your resource. List the terms for the sequence or series you include.

- Use the information you have gathered in a sequence or series to predict possible trends in the use or production of the resource over a ten-year period.

- Describe any effects the production of the natural resource has on the community.

CHAPTER 2

Trigonometry

Trigonometry has many applications. Bridge builders require an understanding of forces acting at different angles. Many bridges are supported by triangles. Trigonometry is used to design bridge side lengths and angles for maximum strength and safety.

Global positioning systems (GPSs) are used in many aspects of our lives, from cellphones and cars to mining and excavation. A GPS receiver uses satellites to triangulate a position, locating that position in terms of its latitude and longitude. Land surveying, energy conservation, and solar panel placement all require knowledge of angles and an understanding of trigonometry.

Using either the applications mentioned here or the photographs, describe three situations in which trigonometry could be used.

You may think of trigonometry as the study of acute angles and right triangles. In this chapter, you will extend your study of trigonometry to angles greater than 90° and to non-right triangles.

Did You Know?

Euclid defined an angle in his textbook *The Elements* as follows:

A plane angle is the inclination to one another of two lines in a plane which meet one another and do not lie in a straight line.

–Euclid, *The Elements*, Definition 8

Key Terms

initial arm	exact value
terminal arm	quadrantal angle
angle in standard position	sine law
reference angle	ambiguous case
	cosine law

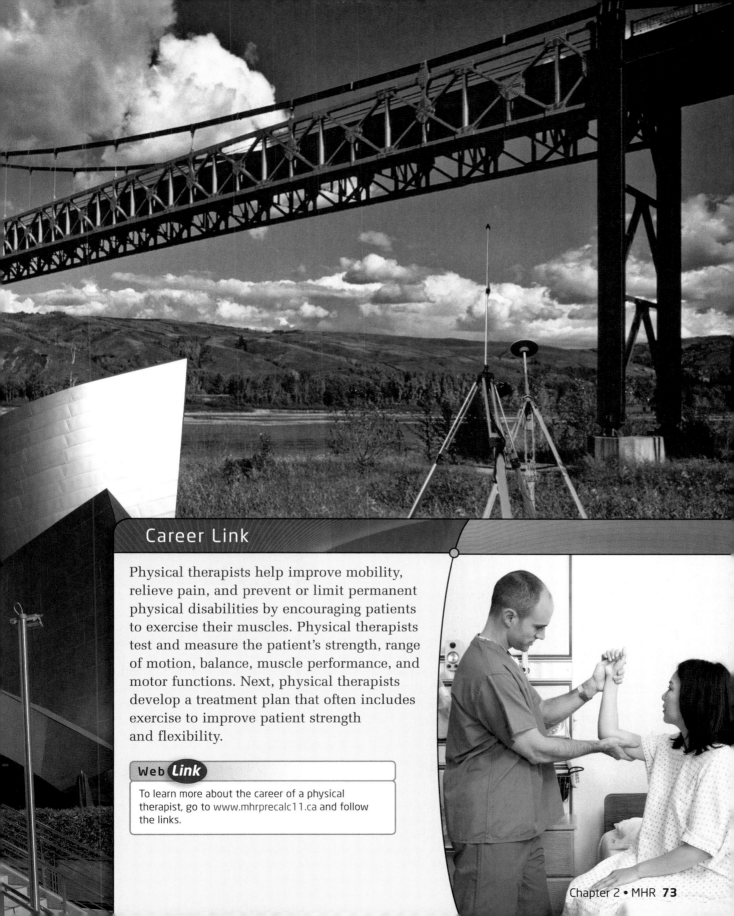

Career Link

Physical therapists help improve mobility, relieve pain, and prevent or limit permanent physical disabilities by encouraging patients to exercise their muscles. Physical therapists test and measure the patient's strength, range of motion, balance, muscle performance, and motor functions. Next, physical therapists develop a treatment plan that often includes exercise to improve patient strength and flexibility.

Web Link

To learn more about the career of a physical therapist, go to www.mhrprecalc11.ca and follow the links.

Angles in Standard Position

Focus on...

- sketching an angle from 0° to 360° in standard position and determining its reference angle
- determining the quadrant in which an angle in standard position terminates
- determining the exact values of the sine, cosine, and tangent ratios of a given angle with reference angle 30°, 45°, or 60°
- solving problems involving trigonometric ratios

Do you think angles are only used in geometry? Angles occur in many everyday situations, such as driving: when you recline a car seat to a comfortable level, when you turn a wheel to ensure a safe turn around the corner, and when you angle a mirror to get the best view of vehicles behind you.

In architecture, angles are used to create more interesting and intriguing buildings. The use of angles in art is unlimited.

In sports, estimating angles is important in passing a hockey puck, shooting a basketball, and punting a football.

Look around you. How many angles can you identify in the objects in your classroom?

Jazz by Henri Matisse

Investigate Exact Values and Angles in Standard Position

In geometry, an angle is formed by two rays with a common endpoint. In trigonometry, angles are often interpreted as rotations of a ray. The starting position and the final position are called the initial arm and the terminal arm of the angle, respectively. If the angle of rotation is counterclockwise, then the angle is positive. In this chapter, all angles will be positive.

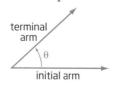

Part A: Angles in Standard Position

Work with a partner.

1. The diagrams in Group A show angles in standard position. The angles in Group B are not in standard position. How are the angles in Group A different from those in Group B? What characteristics do angles in standard position have?

Group A:

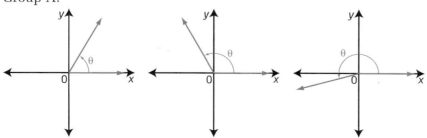

Group B:

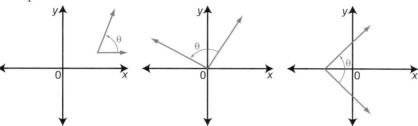

2. Which diagram shows an angle of 70° in standard position? Explain your choice.

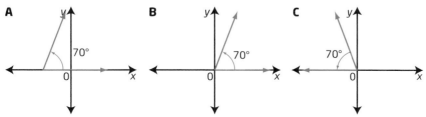

3. On grid paper, draw coordinate axes. Then, use a protractor to draw angles in standard position with each of the following measures. Explain how you drew these angles. In which quadrant does the terminal arm of each angle lie?

a) 75°   **b)** 105°   **c)** 225°   **d)** 320°

Reflect and Respond

4. Consider the angles that you have drawn. How might you define an angle in standard position?

5. Explore and explain two ways to use a protractor to draw each angle in standard position.

a) 290°   **b)** 200°   **c)** 130°   **d)** 325°

Part B: Create a 30°-60°-90° Triangle

6. Begin with an $8\frac{1}{2}'' \times 11''$ sheet of paper. Fold the paper in half lengthwise and make a crease down the middle.

7. Unfold the paper. In Figure 1, the corners are labelled A, B, C, and D.

Figure 1

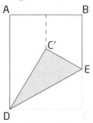
Figure 2

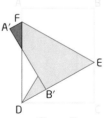
Figure 3

   a) Take corner C to the centre fold line and make a crease, DE. See Figure 2.

   b) Fold corner B so that BE lies on the edge of segment DE. The fold will be along line segment C'E. Fold the overlap (the grey-shaded region) under to complete the equilateral triangle (△DEF). See Figure 3.

8. For this activity, assume that the equilateral triangle has side lengths of 2 units.

   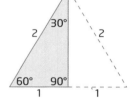

   a) To obtain a 30°-60°-90° triangle, fold the triangle in half, as shown.

   b) Label the angles in the triangle as 30°, 60°, and 90°.

   c) Use the Pythagorean Theorem to determine the exact measure of the third side of the triangle.

9. a) Write exact values for sin 30°, cos 30°, and tan 30°.

   b) Write exact values for sin 60°, cos 60°, and tan 60°.

   c) Can you use this triangle to determine the sine, cosine, and tangent ratios of 90°? Explain.

10. a) On a full sheet of grid paper, draw a set of coordinate axes.

    b) Place your 30°-60°-90° triangle on the grid so that the vertex of the 60° angle is at the origin and the 90° angle sits in quadrant I as a perpendicular on the *x*-axis. What angle in standard position is modelled?

11. a) Reflect your triangle in the *y*-axis. What angle in standard position is modelled?

    b) Reflect your original triangle in the *x*-axis. What angle in standard position is modelled?

    c) Reflect your original triangle in the *y*-axis and then in the *x*-axis. What angle in standard position is modelled?

12. Repeat steps 10 and 11 with the 30° angle at the origin.

13. When the triangle was reflected in an axis, what method did you use to determine the angle in standard position? Would this work for any angle?

14. As the triangle is reflected in an axis, how do you think that the values of the sine, cosine, and tangent ratios might change? Explain.

15. a) Do all 30°-60°-90° triangles have the side relationship of $1 : \sqrt{3} : 2$? Explain why or why not.

   b) Use a ruler to measure the side lengths of your 30°-60°-90° triangle. Do the side lengths follow the relationship $1 : \sqrt{3} : 2$? How do you know?

16. How can you create a 45°-45°-90° triangle by paper folding? What is the exact value of tan 45°? sin 45°? cos 45°?

Link the Ideas

Angles in Standard Position, 0° ≤ θ < 360°

On a Cartesian plane, you can generate an angle by rotating a ray about the origin. The starting position of the ray, along the positive x-axis, is the **initial arm** of the angle. The final position, after a rotation about the origin, is the **terminal arm** of the angle.

An angle is said to be an **angle in standard position** if its vertex is at the origin of a coordinate grid and its initial arm coincides with the positive x-axis.

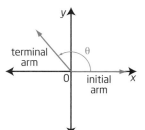 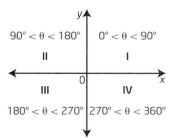

Angles in standard position are always shown on the Cartesian plane. The x-axis and the y-axis divide the plane into four quadrants.

initial arm

• the arm of an angle in standard position that lies on the x-axis

terminal arm

• the arm of an angle in standard position that meets the initial arm at the origin to form an angle

angle in standard position

• the position of an angle when its initial arm is on the positive x-axis and its vertex is at the origin

Reference Angles

For each angle in standard position, there is a corresponding acute angle called the **reference angle**. The reference angle is the acute angle formed between the terminal arm and the x-axis. The reference angle is always positive and measures between 0° and 90°. The trigonometric ratios of an angle in standard position are the same as the trigonometric ratios of its reference angle except that they may differ in sign. The right triangle that contains the reference angle and has one leg on the x-axis is known as the reference triangle.

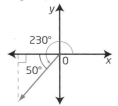
The reference angle, θ_R, is illustrated for angles, θ, in standard position where $0° \leq \theta < 360°$.

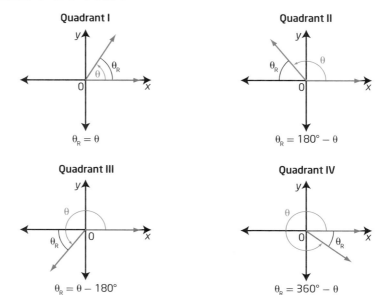

The angles in standard position with a reference angle of 20° are 20°, 160°, 200°, and 340°.

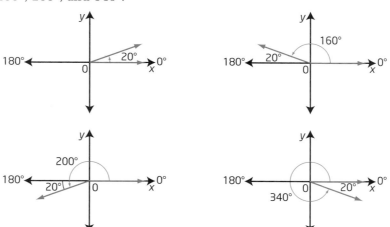

Special Right Triangles

For angles of 30°, 45°, and 60°, you can determine the **exact values** of trigonometric ratios.

Drawing the diagonal of a square with a side length of 1 unit gives a 45°-45°-90° triangle. This is an isosceles right triangle.

Use the Pythagorean Theorem to find the length of the hypotenuse.

$c^2 = a^2 + b^2$
$c^2 = 1^2 + 1^2$
$c^2 = 2$
$c = \sqrt{2}$

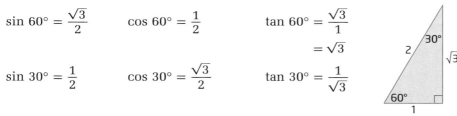

$$\sin \theta = \frac{\text{opposite}}{\text{hypotenuse}} \qquad \cos \theta = \frac{\text{adjacent}}{\text{hypotenuse}} \qquad \tan \theta = \frac{\text{opposite}}{\text{adjacent}}$$

$$\sin 45° = \frac{1}{\sqrt{2}} \qquad \cos 45° = \frac{1}{\sqrt{2}} \qquad \tan 45° = \frac{1}{1}$$

$$\tan 45° = 1$$

Drawing the altitude of an equilateral triangle with a side length of 2 units gives a 30°-60°-90° triangle.

Using the Pythagorean Theorem, the length of the altitude is $\sqrt{3}$ units.

$$\sin 60° = \frac{\sqrt{3}}{2} \qquad \cos 60° = \frac{1}{2} \qquad \tan 60° = \frac{\sqrt{3}}{1}$$
$$= \sqrt{3}$$

$$\sin 30° = \frac{1}{2} \qquad \cos 30° = \frac{\sqrt{3}}{2} \qquad \tan 30° = \frac{1}{\sqrt{3}}$$

> **exact value**
>
> - answers involving radicals are exact, unlike approximated decimal values
> - fractions such as $\frac{1}{3}$ are exact, but an approximation of $\frac{1}{3}$ such as 0.333 is not

> What are the three primary trigonometric ratios for the other acute angle in this triangle?

> Which trigonometric ratios for 30° have exact decimal values? Which are irrational numbers?

Example 1

Sketch an Angle in Standard Position, 0° ≤ θ < 360°

Sketch each angle in standard position. State the quadrant in which the terminal arm lies.

a) 36°   **b)** 210°   **c)** 315°

Solution

a) θ = 36°
  Since 0° < θ < 90°, the terminal arm of θ lies in quadrant I.

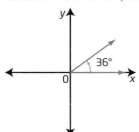

b) $\theta = 210°$

Since $180° < \theta < 270°$, the terminal arm of θ lies in quadrant III.

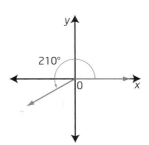

c) $\theta = 315°$

Since $270° < \theta < 360°$, the terminal arm of θ lies in quadrant IV.

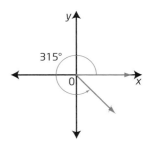

Your Turn

Sketch each angle in standard position. State the quadrant in which the terminal arm lies.

a) $150°$ **b)** $60°$ **c)** $240°$

Example 2

Determine a Reference Angle

Determine the reference angle θ_R for each angle θ. Sketch θ in standard position and label the reference angle θ_R.

a) $\theta = 130°$ **b)** $\theta = 300°$

Solution

a) $\theta_R = 180° - 130°$
$\theta_R = 50°$

b) $\theta_R = 360° - 300°$
$\theta_R = 60°$

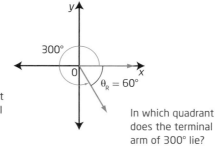

In which quadrant does the terminal arm of 130° lie?

In which quadrant does the terminal arm of 300° lie?

Your Turn

Determine the reference angle θ_R for each angle θ. Sketch θ and θ_R in standard position.

a) $\theta = 75°$ **b)** $\theta = 240°$

Example 3

Determine the Angle in Standard Position

Determine the angle in standard position when an angle of 40° is reflected
a) in the *y*-axis
b) in the *x*-axis
c) in the *y*-axis and then in the *x*-axis

Solution

a) Reflecting an angle of 40° in the *y*-axis
will result in a reference angle of 40° in
quadrant II.

The measure of the angle in
standard position for quadrant II is
$180° - 40° = 140°$.

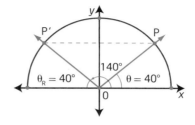

b) Reflecting an angle of 40° in the *x*-axis
will result in a reference angle of 40° in
quadrant IV.

The measure of the angle in standard
position for quadrant IV is
$360° - 40° = 320°$.

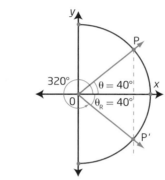

c) Reflecting an angle of 40° in the
y-axis and then in the *x*-axis will
result in a reference angle of 40° in
quadrant III.

The measure of the angle in standard
position for quadrant III is
$180° + 40° = 220°$.

What angle of rotation of the
original terminal arm would
give the same terminal arm
as this reflection?

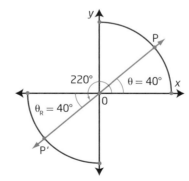

Your Turn

Determine the angle in standard position when an angle of 60° is reflected
a) in the *y*-axis
b) in the *x*-axis
c) in the *y*-axis and then in the *x*-axis

Example 4

Find an Exact Distance

Allie is learning to play the piano. Her teacher uses a metronome to help her keep time. The pendulum arm of the metronome is 10 cm long. For one particular tempo, the setting results in the arm moving back and forth from a start position of 60° to 120°. What horizontal distance does the tip of the arm move in one beat? Give an exact answer.

Solution

Draw a diagram to model the information.

OA represents the start position and OB the end position of the metronome arm for one beat. The tip of the arm moves a horizontal distance equal to a to reach the vertical position.

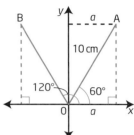

Find the horizontal distance a:

$$\cos 60° = \frac{\text{adjacent}}{\text{hypotenuse}}$$
$$\frac{1}{2} = \frac{a}{10}$$
$$10\left(\frac{1}{2}\right) = a$$
$$5 = a$$

Why is $\frac{1}{2}$ substituted for cos 60°?

Because the reference angle for 120° is 60°, the tip moves the same horizontal distance past the vertical position to reach B.

The exact horizontal distance travelled by the tip of the arm in one beat is 2(5) or 10 cm.

Your Turn

The tempo is adjusted so that the arm of the metronome swings from 45° to 135°. What exact horizontal distance does the tip of the arm travel in one beat?

Key Ideas

- An angle, θ, in standard position has its initial arm on the positive x-axis and its vertex at the origin. If the angle of rotation is counterclockwise, then the angle is positive.

- The reference angle is the acute angle whose vertex is the origin and whose arms are the x-axis and the terminal arm of θ.

- You can determine exact trigonometric ratios for angles of 30°, 45°, and 60° using special triangles.

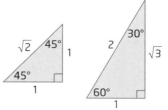

Practise

1. Is each angle, θ, in standard position?
Explain.

a)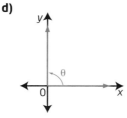

b)

c)

d)

2. Without measuring, match each angle
with a diagram of the angle in standard
position.

a) 150°   **b)** 180°

c) 45°   **d)** 320°

e) 215°   **f)** 270°

A 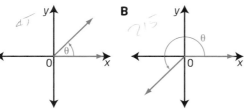   **B**

C 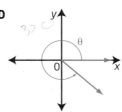   **D**

E 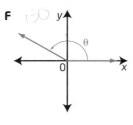   **F**

3. In which quadrant does the terminal arm
of each angle in standard position lie?

a) 48° A   **b)** 300° D

c) 185° C   **d)** 75° A

e) 220° C   **f)** 160° B

4. Sketch an angle in standard position
with each given measure.

a) 70°   **b)** 310°

c) 225°   **d)** 165°

5. What is the reference angle for each angle
in standard position?

a) 170°   **b)** 345°

c) 72°   **d)** 215°

6. Determine the measure of the three other
angles in standard position, 0° < θ < 360°,
that have a reference angle of

a) 45°   **b)** 60°

c) 30°   **d)** 75°

7. Copy and complete the table. Determine
the measure of each angle in standard
position given its reference angle and the
quadrant in which the terminal arm lies.

	Reference Angle	Quadrant	Angle in Standard Position
a)	72°	IV	
b)	56°	II	
c)	18°	III	
d)	35°	IV	

8. Copy and complete the table without
using a calculator. Express each ratio
using exact values.

θ	sin θ	cos θ	tan θ
30°			
45°			
60°			

Apply

9. A digital protractor is used in woodworking. State the measure of the angle in standard position when the protractor has a reading of 20.4°.

10. Paul and Gail decide to use a Cartesian plane to design a landscape plan for their yard. Each grid mark represents a distance of 10 m. Their home is centred at the origin. There is a red maple tree at the point (3.5, 2). They will plant a flowering dogwood at a point that is a reflection in the y-axis of the position of the red maple. A white pine will be planted so that it is a reflection in the x-axis of the position of the red maple. A river birch will be planted so that it is a reflection in both the x-axis and the y-axis of the position of the red maple.

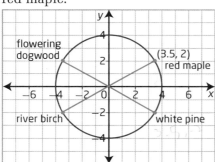

a) Determine the coordinates of the trees that Paul and Gail wish to plant.

b) Determine the angles in standard position if the lines drawn from the house to each of the trees are terminal arms. Express your answers to the nearest degree.

c) What is the actual distance between the red maple and the white pine?

11. A windshield wiper has a length of 50 cm. The wiper rotates from its resting position at 30°, in standard position, to 150°. Determine the exact horizontal distance that the tip of the wiper travels in one swipe.

12. Suppose A(x, y) is a point on the terminal arm of ∠AOC in standard position.

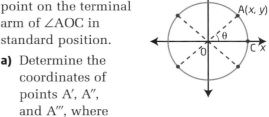

a) Determine the coordinates of points A′, A″, and A‴, where

- A′ is the image of A reflected in the x-axis
- A″ is the image of A reflected in the y-axis
- A‴ is the image of A reflected in both the x-axis and the y-axis

b) Assume that each angle is in standard position and ∠AOC = θ. What are the measures, in terms of θ, of the angles that have A′, A″, and A‴ on their terminal arms?

13. A 10-m boom lifts material onto a roof in need of repair. Determine the exact vertical displacement of the end of the boom when the operator lowers it from 60° to 30°.

14. Engineers use a bevel protractor to measure the angle and the depth of holes, slots, and other internal features. A bevel protractor is set to measure an angle of 72°. What is the measure of the angle in standard position of the lower half of the ruler, used for measuring the depth of an object?

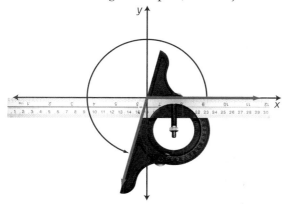

15. Researcher Mohd Abubakr developed a circular periodic table. He claims that his model gives a better idea of the size of the elements. Joshua and Andrea decided to make a spinner for the circular periodic table to help them study the elements for a quiz. They will spin the arm and then name the elements that the spinner lands on. Suppose the spinner lands so that it forms an angle in standard position of 110°. Name one of the elements it may have landed on.

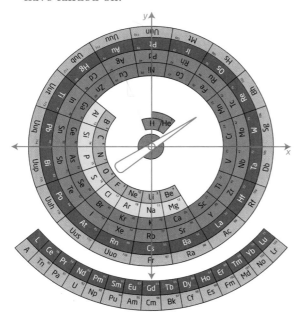

16. The Aztec people of pre-Columbian Mexico used the Aztec Calendar. It consisted of a 365-day calendar cycle and a 260-day ritual cycle. In the stone carving of the calendar, the second ring from the centre showed the days of the month, numbered from one to 20.

Suppose the Aztec Calendar was placed on a Cartesian plane, as shown.

Aztec Calendar–
Stone of the Sun

a) The blue angle marks the passing of 12 days. Determine the measure of the angle.

b) How many days would have passed if the angle had been drawn in quadrant II, using the same reference angle as in part a)?

c) Keeping the same reference angle, how many days would have passed if the angle had been drawn in quadrant IV?

17. Express each direction as an angle in standard position. Sketch each angle.

a) N20°E   **b)** S50°W

c) N80°W   **d)** S15°E

Did You Know?

Directions are defined as a measure either east or west from north and south, measured in degrees. N40°W means to start from north and measure 40° toward the west.

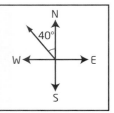

Extend

18. You can use trigonometric ratios to design robotic arms. A robotic arm is motorized so that the angle, θ, increases at a constant rate of 10° per second from an initial angle of 0°. The arm is kept at a constant length of 45 cm to the tip of the fingers.

a) Let h represent the height of the robotic arm, measured at its fingertips. When θ = 0°, h is 12 cm. Construct a table, using increments of 15°, that lists the angle, θ, and the height, h, for 0° ≤ θ ≤ 90°.

b) Does a constant increase in the angle produce a constant increase in the height? Justify your answer.

c) What conjecture would you make if θ were extended beyond 90°?

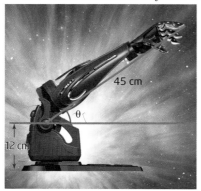

45 cm

θ

12 cm

Web Link

To learn about Beal's Conjecture and prize, go to www.mhrprecalc11.ca and follow the links.

19. Suppose two angles in standard position are supplementary and have terminal arms that are perpendicular. What are the measures of the angles?

20. Carl and a friend are on the Antique Ferris Wheel Ride at Calaway Park in Calgary. The ride stops to unload the riders. Carl's seat forms an angle of 72° with a horizontal axis running through the centre of the Ferris wheel.

a) If the radius of the Ferris wheel is 9 m and the centre of the wheel is 11 m above the ground, determine the height of Carl's seat above the ground.

b) Suppose the Ferris wheel travels at four revolutions per minute and the operator stops the ride in 5 s.

i) Determine the angle in standard position of the seat that Carl is on at this second stop. Consider the horizontal central axis to be the x-axis.

ii) Determine the height of Carl's seat at the second stop.

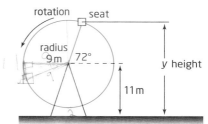

21. An angle in standard position is shown. Suppose the radius of the circle is 1 unit.

a) Which distance represents sin θ?

   A OD   **B** CD   **C** OC   **D** BA

b) Which distance represents tan θ?

   A OD   **B** CD   **C** OC   **D** BA

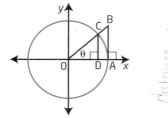

Create Connections

22. A point P(x, y) lies on the terminal arm of an angle θ. The distance from P to the origin is r units. Create a formula that links x, y, and r.

23. a) Copy and complete the table. Use a calculator and round ratios to four decimal places.

θ	20°	40°	60°	80°
$\sin \theta$				
$\sin (180° - \theta)$				
$\sin (180° + \theta)$				
$\sin (360° - \theta)$				

b) Make a conjecture about the relationships between $\sin \theta$, $\sin (180° - \theta)$, $\sin (180° + \theta)$, and $\sin (360° - \theta)$.

c) Would your conjecture hold true for values of cosine and tangent? Explain your reasoning.

24. Daria purchased a new golf club. She wants to know the distance that she will be able to hit the ball with this club. She recalls from her physics class that the distance, d, a ball travels can be modelled by the formula $d = \dfrac{V^2 \cos \theta \sin \theta}{16}$, where V is the initial velocity, in feet per second, and θ is the angle of elevation.

a) The radar unit at the practice range indicates that the initial velocity is 110 ft/s and that the ball is hit at an angle of 30° to the ground. Determine the exact distance that Daria hit the ball with this driver.

b) To get a longer hit than that in part a), should Daria increase or decrease the angle of the hit? Explain.

c) What angle of elevation do you think would produce a hit that travels the greatest distance? Explain your reasoning.

Project Corner   Prospecting

- Prospecting is exploring an area for natural resources, such as oil, gas, minerals, precious metals, and mineral specimens. Prospectors travel through the countryside, often through creek beds and along ridgelines and hilltops, in search of natural resources.

Web Link

To search for locations of various minerals in Canada, go to www.mhrprecalc11.ca and follow the links.

Trigonometric Ratios of Any Angle

Focus on...

- determining the distance from the origin to a point (x, y) on the terminal arm of an angle
- determining the value of sin θ, cos θ, or tan θ given any point (x, y) on the terminal arm of angle θ
- determining the value of sin θ, cos θ, or tan θ for θ = 0°, 90°, 180°, 270°, or 360°
- solving for all values of θ in an equation involving sine, cosine, and tangent
- solving a problem involving trigonometric ratios

The Athabasca Oil Sands are located 40 km north of Fort McMurray, AB. They are the world's largest source of synthetic crude from oil sands, and the greatest single source in Canada. Since the beginning of the first oil sands production in 1967, technological advances have allowed for a tremendous increase in production and safety.

Massive machinery has been developed specifically for the excavation of the oil sands. Power shovels are equipped with a global positioning system (GPS) to make digging more exact. The operator must understand the angles necessary to operate the massive shovel. The design of power shovels uses the laws of trigonometry.

Did You Know?

Many Canadian companies are very aware of and sensitive to concerns about the impact of mining on the environment. The companies consult with local Aboriginal people on issues such as the re-establishment of native tree species, like low-bush cranberry and buffalo berry.

Investigate Trigonometric Ratios for Angles Greater Than 90°

Materials

- grid paper
- protractor

1. On grid paper, draw a set of coordinate axes.

    a) Plot the point A(3, 4). In which quadrant does the point A lie?

    b) Draw the angle in standard position with terminal arm passing through point A.

2. Draw a line perpendicular to the x-axis through point A. Label the intersection of this line and the x-axis as point B. This point is on the initial arm of ∠AOB.

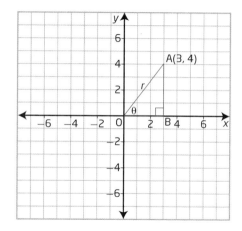

   a) Use the Pythagorean Theorem to determine the length of the hypotenuse, r.

   b) Write the primary trigonometric ratios for θ.

   c) Determine the measure of θ, to the nearest degree.

3. How is each primary trigonometric ratio related to the coordinates of point A and the radius r?

4. a) Reflect point A in the y-axis to obtain point C. Draw a line segment from point C to the origin. What are the coordinates of point C?

   b) Draw a line perpendicular to the x-axis through point C to create the reference triangle. Label the intersection of this line and the x-axis as point D. Use your answers from step 3 to write the primary trigonometric ratios for ∠COB.

5. a) What is the measure of ∠COB, to the nearest degree?

   b) How are ∠COD and ∠COB related?

Reflect and Respond

6. a) Compare the trigonometric ratios for ∠AOB and ∠COB. What are the similarities and what are the differences?

   b) Explain why some trigonometric ratios are positive and some are negative.

7. a) Reflect point C in the x-axis to obtain point E. Which trigonometric ratios would you expect to be positive? Which ones would you expect to be negative? Explain your reasoning.

   b) Use the coordinates of point E and your definitions from step 3 to confirm your prediction.

   c) Extend this investigation into quadrant IV.

8. Make a table showing the signs of the sine, cosine, and tangent ratios of an angle, θ, in each of the four quadrants. Do you notice a pattern? How could you recognize the sign (positive or negative) of the trigonometric ratios in the various quadrants?

Finding the Trigonometric Ratios of Any Angle θ, where 0° ≤ θ < 360°

Suppose θ is any angle in standard position, and P(x, y) is any point on its terminal arm, at a distance r from the origin. Then, by the Pythagorean Theorem, $r = \sqrt{x^2 + y^2}$.

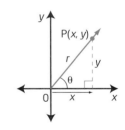

You can use a reference triangle to determine the three primary trigonometric ratios in terms of x, y, and r.

$$\sin \theta = \frac{\text{opposite}}{\text{hypotenuse}} \qquad \cos \theta = \frac{\text{adjacent}}{\text{hypotenuse}} \qquad \tan \theta = \frac{\text{opposite}}{\text{adjacent}}$$

$$\sin \theta = \frac{y}{r} \qquad\qquad\qquad \cos \theta = \frac{x}{r} \qquad\qquad\qquad \tan \theta = \frac{y}{x}$$

The chart below summarizes the signs of the trigonometric ratios in each quadrant. In each, the horizontal and vertical lengths are considered as directed distances.

Quadrant II
90° < θ < 180°

$$\sin \theta = \frac{y}{r} \qquad \cos \theta = \frac{-x}{r} \qquad \tan \theta = \frac{y}{-x}$$

$$\sin \theta > 0 \qquad \cos \theta < 0 \qquad \tan \theta < 0$$

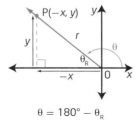

$$\theta = 180° - \theta_R$$

Quadrant I
0° < θ < 90°

$$\sin \theta = \frac{y}{r} \qquad \cos \theta = \frac{x}{r} \qquad \tan \theta = \frac{y}{x}$$

$$\sin \theta > 0 \qquad \cos \theta > 0 \qquad \tan \theta > 0$$

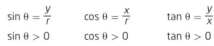
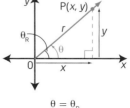

Why is r always positive?

$$\theta = \theta_R$$

Quadrant III
180° < θ < 270°

$$\sin \theta = \frac{-y}{r} \qquad \cos \theta = \frac{-x}{r} \qquad \tan \theta = \frac{-y}{-x}$$

$$\sin \theta < 0 \qquad \cos \theta < 0 \qquad \tan \theta > 0$$

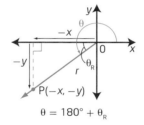

$$\theta = 180° + \theta_R$$

Quadrant IV
270° < θ < 360°

$$\sin \theta = \frac{-y}{r} \qquad \cos \theta = \frac{x}{r} \qquad \tan \theta = \frac{-y}{x}$$

$$\sin \theta < 0 \qquad \cos \theta > 0 \qquad \tan \theta < 0$$

$$\theta = 360° - \theta_R$$

Example 1

Write Trigonometric Ratios for Angles in Any Quadrant

The point P(−8, 15) lies on the terminal arm of an angle, θ, in standard position. Determine the exact trigonometric ratios for sin θ, cos θ, and tan θ.

Solution

Sketch the reference triangle by drawing a line perpendicular to the x-axis through the point (−8, 15). The point P(−8, 15) is in quadrant II, so the terminal arm is in quadrant II.

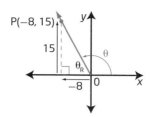

Use the Pythagorean Theorem to determine the distance, r, from P(−8, 15) to the origin, (0, 0).

$r = \sqrt{x^2 + y^2}$
$r = \sqrt{(-8)^2 + (15)^2}$
$r = \sqrt{289}$
$r = 17$

The trigonometric ratios for θ can be written as follows:

$\sin θ = \dfrac{y}{r}$ $\cos θ = \dfrac{x}{r}$ $\tan θ = \dfrac{y}{x}$

$\sin θ = \dfrac{15}{17}$ $\cos θ = \dfrac{-8}{17}$ $\tan θ = \dfrac{15}{-8}$

               $\cos θ = -\dfrac{8}{17}$ $\tan θ = -\dfrac{15}{8}$

Your Turn

The point P(−5, −12) lies on the terminal arm of an angle, θ, in standard position. Determine the exact trigonometric ratios for sin θ, cos θ, and tan θ.

Example 2

Determine the Exact Value of a Trigonometric Ratio

Determine the exact value of cos 135°.

Solution

The terminal arm of 135° lies in quadrant II. The reference angle is 180° − 135°, or 45°. The cosine ratio is negative in quadrant II.

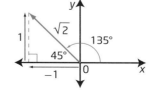

Why are side lengths 1, 1, and √2 used?

$\cos 135° = -\dfrac{1}{\sqrt{2}}$

Your Turn

Determine the exact value of sin 240°.

Example 3

Determine Trigonometric Ratios

Suppose θ is an angle in standard position with terminal arm in quadrant III, and $\cos \theta = -\dfrac{3}{4}$. What are the exact values of $\sin \theta$ and $\tan \theta$?

Solution

Sketch a diagram.

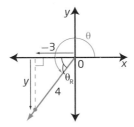

Use the definition of cosine to find the exact values of x and r.

$\cos \theta = \dfrac{x}{r}$

$\cos \theta = -\dfrac{3}{4}$

Since the terminal arm is in quadrant III, x is negative. r is always positive. So, $x = -3$ and $r = 4$.

Use $x = -3$, $r = 4$ and the Pythagorean Theorem to find y.

$\begin{aligned} x^2 + y^2 &= r^2 \\ (-3)^2 + y^2 &= 4^2 \\ 9 + y^2 &= 16 \\ y^2 &= 16 - 9 \\ y^2 &= 7 \\ y &= \pm\sqrt{7} \end{aligned}$

$y = \sqrt{7}$ is a solution for $y^2 = 7$ because $(\sqrt{7})(\sqrt{7}) = 7$
$y = -\sqrt{7}$ is also a solution because $(-\sqrt{7})(-\sqrt{7}) = 7$

Use $x = -3$, $y = -\sqrt{7}$, and $r = 4$ to write $\sin \theta$ and $\tan \theta$.

Why is $-\sqrt{7}$ used for y here?

$\sin \theta = \dfrac{y}{r}$ $\tan \theta = \dfrac{y}{x}$

$\sin \theta = \dfrac{-\sqrt{7}}{4}$ $\tan \theta = \dfrac{-\sqrt{7}}{-3}$

$\sin \theta = -\dfrac{\sqrt{7}}{4}$ $\tan \theta = \dfrac{\sqrt{7}}{3}$

Your Turn

Suppose θ is an angle in standard position with terminal arm in quadrant III, and $\tan \theta = \dfrac{1}{5}$. Determine the exact values of $\sin \theta$ and $\cos \theta$.

Example 4

Determine Trigonometric Ratios of Quadrantal Angles

Determine the values of sin θ, cos θ, and tan θ when the terminal arm of **quadrantal angle** θ coincides with the positive *y*-axis, θ = 90°.

> **quadrantal angle**
> - an angle in standard position whose terminal arm lies on one of the axes
> - examples are 0°, 90°, 180°, 270°, and 360°

Solution

Let P(*x*, *y*) be any point on the positive *y*-axis. Then, *x* = 0 and *r* = *y*.

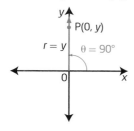

The trigonometric ratios can be written as follows.

$\sin 90° = \dfrac{y}{r}$ $\cos 90° = \dfrac{x}{r}$ $\tan 90° = \dfrac{y}{x}$

$\sin 90° = \dfrac{y}{y}$ $\cos 90° = \dfrac{0}{y}$ $\tan 90° = \dfrac{y}{0}$

$\sin 90° = 1$ $\cos 90° = 0$ $\tan 90°$ is undefined

Why is tan 90° undefined?

Your Turn

Use the diagram to determine the values of sin θ, cos θ, and tan θ for quadrantal angles of 0°, 180°, and 270°. Organize your answers in a table as shown below.

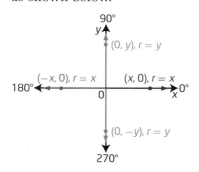

	0°	90°	180°	270°
sin θ		1		
cos θ		0		
tan θ		undefined		

Solving for Angles Given Their Sine, Cosine, or Tangent

Step 1 Determine which quadrants the solution(s) will be in by looking at the sign (+ or −) of the given ratio.

Step 2 Solve for the reference angle.

Why are the trigonometric ratios for the reference angle always positive?

Step 3 Sketch the reference angle in the appropriate quadrant. Use the diagram to determine the measure of the related angle in standard position.

Example 5

Solve for an Angle Given Its Exact Sine, Cosine, or Tangent Value

Solve for θ.

a) $\sin \theta = 0.5$, $0° \le \theta < 360°$

b) $\cos \theta = -\dfrac{\sqrt{3}}{2}$, $0° \le \theta < 180°$

Solution

a) Since the ratio for $\sin \theta$ is positive, the terminal arm lies in either quadrant I or quadrant II.

$\sin \theta_R = 0.5$
$\theta_R = 30°$

How do you know $\theta_R = 30°$?

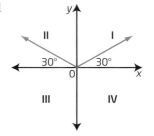

In quadrant I, $\theta = 30°$.
In quadrant II, $\theta = 180° - 30°$
$\theta = 150°$

The solution to the equation $\sin \theta = 0.5$, $0 \le \theta < 360°$, is $\theta = 30°$ or $\theta = 150°$.

b) Since the cosine ratio is negative, the terminal arm must lie in quadrant II or quadrant III. Given the restriction $0° \le \theta < 180°$, the terminal arm must lie in quadrant II.

Use a 30°-60°-90° triangle to determine the reference angle, θ_R.

$\cos \theta_R = \dfrac{\sqrt{3}}{2}$
$\theta_R = 30°$

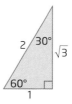

Using the reference angle of 30° in quadrant II, the measure of θ is $180° - 30° = 150°$.

The solution to the equation $\cos \theta = -\dfrac{\sqrt{3}}{2}$, $0 \le \theta < 180°$, is $\theta = 150°$.

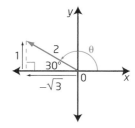

Your Turn

Solve $\sin \theta = -\dfrac{1}{\sqrt{2}}$, $0° \le \theta < 360°$.

Example 6

Solve for an Angle Given Its Approximate Sine, Cosine, or Tangent Value

Given $\cos \theta = -0.6753$, where $0° \leq \theta < 360°$, determine the measure of θ, to the nearest tenth of a degree.

Solution

The cosine ratio is negative, so the angles in standard position lie in quadrant II and quadrant III.

Use a calculator to determine the angle that has $\cos \theta_R = 0.6753$.
$\theta_R = \cos^{-1}(0.6753)$ Why is $\cos^{-1}(0.6753)$ the reference angle?
$\theta_R \approx 47.5°$

With a reference angle of $47.5°$, the measures of θ are as follows:

In quadrant II:	In quadrant III:
$\theta = 180° - 47.5°$	$\theta = 180° + 47.5°$
$\theta = 132.5°$	$\theta = 227.5°$

Your Turn

Determine the measure of θ, to the nearest degree, given $\sin \theta = -0.8090$, where $0° \leq \theta < 360°$.

Key Ideas

- The primary trigonometric ratios for an angle, θ, in standard position that has a point $P(x, y)$ on its terminal arm are
  $\sin \theta = \dfrac{y}{r}$, $\cos \theta = \dfrac{x}{r}$, and $\tan \theta = \dfrac{y}{x}$, where $r = \sqrt{x^2 + y^2}$.

- The table show the signs of the primary trigonometric ratios for an angle, θ, in standard position with the terminal arm in the given quadrant.

Ratio	Quadrant			
	I	II	III	IV
$\sin \theta$	+	+	−	−
$\cos \theta$	+	−	−	+
$\tan \theta$	+	−	+	−

- If the terminal arm of an angle, θ, in standard position lies on one of the axes, θ is called a quadrantal angle. The quadrantal angles are $0°$, $90°$, $180°$, $270°$, and $360°$, $0° \leq \theta \leq 360°$.

Practise

1. Sketch an angle in standard position so that the terminal arm passes through each point.

a) $(2, 6)$ **b)** $(-4, 2)$

c) $(-5, -2)$ **d)** $(-1, 0)$

2. Determine the exact values of the sine, cosine, and tangent ratios for each angle.

a)

b)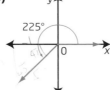

c)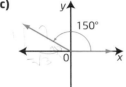

d)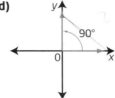

3. The coordinates of a point P on the terminal arm of each angle are shown. Write the exact trigonometric ratios $\sin \theta$, $\cos \theta$, and $\tan \theta$ for each.

a)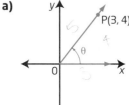

b)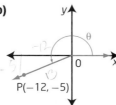

c)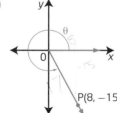

d)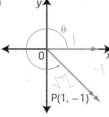

4. For each description, in which quadrant does the terminal arm of angle θ lie?

a) $\cos \theta < 0$ and $\sin \theta > 0$ cos − sin +

b) $\cos \theta > 0$ and $\tan \theta > 0$ cos + tan +

c) $\sin \theta < 0$ and $\cos \theta < 0$ sin − cos −

d) $\tan \theta < 0$ and $\cos \theta > 0$ tan − cos +

5. Determine the exact values of $\sin \theta$, $\cos \theta$, and $\tan \theta$ if the terminal arm of an angle in standard position passes through the given point.

a) $P(-5, 12)$

b) $P(5, -3)$

c) $P(6, 3)$

d) $P(-24, -10)$

6. Without using a calculator, state whether each ratio is positive or negative.

a) $\sin 155°$ +

b) $\cos 320°$ +

c) $\tan 120°$ −

d) $\cos 220°$ −

7. An angle is in standard position such that $\sin \theta = \dfrac{5}{13}$.

a) Sketch a diagram to show the two possible positions of the angle.

b) Determine the possible values of θ, to the nearest degree, if $0° \le \theta < 360°$.

8. An angle in standard position has its terminal arm in the stated quadrant. Determine the exact values for the other two primary trigonometric ratios for each.

	Ratio Value	Quadrant
a)	$\cos \theta = -\dfrac{2}{3}$	II
b)	$\sin \theta = \dfrac{3}{5}$	I
c)	$\tan \theta = -\dfrac{4}{5}$	IV
d)	$\sin \theta = -\dfrac{1}{3}$	III
e)	$\tan \theta = 1$	III

9. Solve each equation, for $0° \le \theta < 360°$, using a diagram involving a special right triangle.

a) $\cos \theta = \dfrac{1}{2}$

b) $\cos \theta = -\dfrac{1}{\sqrt{2}}$

c) $\tan \theta = -\dfrac{1}{\sqrt{3}}$

d) $\sin \theta = -\dfrac{\sqrt{3}}{2}$

e) $\tan \theta = \sqrt{3}$

f) $\tan \theta = -1$

10. Copy and complete the table using the coordinates of a point on the terminal arm.

θ	sin θ	cos θ	tan θ
0°	0	1	0
90°	1	0	un
180°	0	-1	0
270°	-1	0	un
360°	0	1	0

11. Determine the values of x, y, r, $\sin \theta$, $\cos \theta$, and $\tan \theta$ in each.

a)

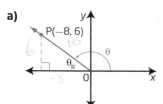

b)

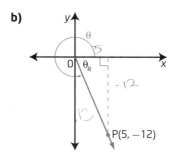

Apply

12. Point $P(-9, 4)$ is on the terminal arm of an angle θ.

a) Sketch the angle in standard position.

b) What is the measure of the reference angle, to the nearest degree?

c) What is the measure of θ, to the nearest degree?

13. Point $P(7, -24)$ is on the terminal arm of an angle, θ.

a) Sketch the angle in standard position.

b) What is the measure of the reference angle, to the nearest degree?

c) What is the measure of θ, to the nearest degree?

14. a) Determine $\sin \theta$ when the terminal arm of an angle in standard position passes through the point $P(2, 4)$.

b) Extend the terminal arm to include the point $Q(4, 8)$. Determine $\sin \theta$ for the angle in standard position whose terminal arm passes through point Q.

c) Extend the terminal arm to include the point $R(8, 16)$. Determine $\sin \theta$ for the angle in standard position whose terminal arm passes through point R.

d) Explain your results from parts a), b), and c). What do you notice? Why does this happen?

15. The point $P(k, 24)$ is 25 units from the origin. If P lies on the terminal arm of an angle, θ, in standard position, $0° \le \theta < 360°$, determine

a) the measure(s) of θ

b) the sine, cosine, and tangent ratios for θ

16. If $\cos \theta = \dfrac{1}{5}$ and $\tan \theta = 2\sqrt{6}$, determine the exact value of $\sin \theta$.

17. The angle between the horizontal and Earth's magnetic field is called the angle of dip. Some migratory birds may be capable of detecting changes in the angle of dip, which helps them navigate. The angle of dip at the magnetic equator is 0°, while the angle at the North and South Poles is 90°. Determine the exact values of $\sin \theta$, $\cos \theta$, and $\tan \theta$ for the angles of dip at the magnetic equator and the North and South Poles.

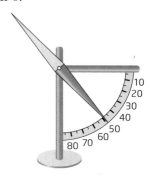

18. Without using technology, determine whether each statement is true or false. Justify your answer.

    a) $\sin 151° = \sin 29°$ ✓

    b) $\cos 135° = \sin 225°$ ✓

    c) $\tan 135° = \tan 225°$

    d) $\sin 60° = \cos 330°$

    e) $\sin 270° = \cos 180°$

19. Copy and complete the table. Use exact values. Extend the table to include the primary trigonometric ratios for all angles in standard position, $90° \le \theta \le 360°$, that have the same reference angle as those listed for quadrant I.

θ	sin θ	cos θ	tan θ
0°	0	1	0
30°	$\frac{1}{2}$	$\frac{\sqrt{3}}{2}$	$\frac{1}{\sqrt{3}}$
45°	$\frac{1}{\sqrt{2}}$	$\frac{1}{\sqrt{2}}$	1
60°	$\frac{\sqrt{3}}{2}$	$\frac{1}{2}$	$\sqrt{3}$
90°	1	0	un

20. Alberta Aboriginal Tourism designed a circular icon that represents both the Métis and First Nations communities of Alberta. The centre of the icon represents the collection of all peoples' perspectives and points of view relating to Aboriginal history, touching every quadrant and direction.

    a) Suppose the icon is placed on a coordinate plane with a reference angle of 45° for points A, B, C, and D. Determine the measure of the angles in standard position for points A, B, C, and D.

    b) If the radius of the circle is 1 unit, determine the coordinates of points A, B, C, and D.

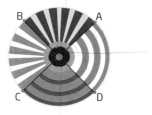

21. Explore patterns in the sine, cosine, and tangent ratios.

    a) Copy and complete the table started below. List the sine, cosine, and tangent ratios for θ in increments of 15° for $0° \le \theta \le 180°$. Where necessary, round values to four decimal places.

Angle	Sine	Cosine	Tangent
0°			
15°			
30°			
45°			
60°			

    b) What do you observe about the sine, cosine, and tangent ratios as θ increases?

    c) What comparisons can you make between the sine and cosine ratios?

    d) Determine the signs of the ratios as you move from quadrant I to quadrant II.

    e) Describe what you expect will happen if you expand the table to include quadrant III and quadrant IV.

Extend

22. a) The line $y = 6x$, for $x \ge 0$, creates an acute angle, θ, with the x-axis. Determine the sine, cosine, and tangent ratios for θ.

    b) If the terminal arm of an angle, θ, lies on the line $4y + 3x = 0$, for $x \ge 0$, determine the exact value of $\tan \theta + \cos \theta$.

23. Consider an angle in standard position with $r = 12$ cm. Describe how the measures of x, y, $\sin \theta$, $\cos \theta$, and $\tan \theta$ change as θ increases continuously from 0° to 90°.

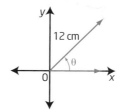

24. Suppose θ is a positive acute angle and cos θ = *a*. Write an expression for tan θ in terms of *a*.

25. Consider an angle of 60° in standard position in a circle of radius 1 unit. Points A, B, and C lie on the circumference, as shown. Show that the lengths of the sides of △ABC satisfy the Pythagorean Theorem and that ∠CAB = 90°.

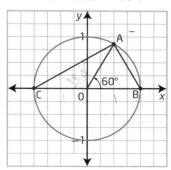

Create Connections

26. Explain how you can use reference angles to determine the trigonometric ratios of any angle, θ.

27. Point P(−5, −9) is on the terminal arm of an angle, θ, in standard position. Explain the role of the reference triangle and the reference angle in determining the value of θ.

28. Explain why there are exactly two non-quadrantal angles between 0° and 360° that have the same sine ratio.

29. Suppose that θ is an angle in standard position with cos θ = $-\frac{1}{2}$ and sin θ = $-\frac{\sqrt{3}}{2}$, 0° ≤ θ < 360°. Determine the measure of θ. Explain your reasoning, including diagrams.

30. MINI LAB Use dynamic geometry software to explore the trigonometric ratios.

Step 1 **a)** Draw a circle with a radius of 5 units and centre at the origin.

　　　b) Plot a point A on the circle in quadrant I. Join point A and the origin by constructing a line segment. Label this distance *r*.

Step 2 **a)** Record the *x*-coordinate and the *y*-coordinate for point A.

　　　b) Construct a formula to calculate the sine ratio of the angle in standard position whose terminal arm passes through point A. Use the measure and calculate features of your software to determine the sine ratio of this angle.

　　　c) Repeat step b) to determine the cosine ratio and tangent ratio of the angle in standard position whose terminal arm passes through point A.

Step 3 Animate point A. Use the motion controller to slow the animation. Pause the animation to observe the ratios at points along the circle.

Step 4 **a)** What observations can you make about the sine, cosine, and tangent ratios as point A moves around the circle?

　　　b) Record where the sine and cosine ratios are equal. What is the measure of the angle at these points?

　　　c) What do you notice about the signs of the ratios as point A moves around the circle? Explain.

　　　d) For several choices for point A, divide the sine ratio by the cosine ratio. What do you notice about this calculation? Is it true for all angles as A moves around the circle?

The Sine Law

Focus on...

- using the primary trigonometric ratios to solve problems involving triangles that are not right triangles
- recognizing when to use the sine law to solve a given problem
- sketching a diagram to represent a problem involving the sine law
- explaining a proof of the sine law
- solving problems using the sine law
- solving problems involving the ambiguous case of the sine law

How is an airplane pilot able to make precise landings even at night or in poor visibility? Airplanes have instrument landing systems that allow pilots to receive precise lateral and vertical guidance on approach and landing. Since 1994, airplanes have used the global positioning system (GPS) to provide the pilot with data on an approach. To understand the GPS, a pilot must understand the trigonometry of triangulation.

You can use right-triangle trigonometry to solve problems involving right triangles. However, many interesting problems involve oblique triangles. Oblique triangles are any triangles that do not contain a right angle. In this section, you will use right-triangle trigonometry to develop the sine law. You can use the sine law to solve some problems involving non-right triangles.

Investigate the Sine Law

Materials

- protractor

1. In an oblique triangle, the ratio of the sine of an angle to the length of its opposite side is constant. Demonstrate that this is true by drawing and measuring any oblique triangle. Compare your results with those of other students.

2. Draw an oblique triangle. Label its vertices A, B, and C and its side lengths a, b, and c. Draw an altitude from B to AC and let its height be h.

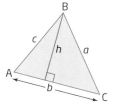

3. Use the two right triangles formed. Write a trigonometric ratio for sin A. Repeat for sin C. How are the two equations alike?

4. Rearrange each equation from step 3, expressing h in terms of the side and the sine of the angle.

5. a) Relate the two equations from step 4 to eliminate h and form one equation.

    b) Divide both sides of the equation by ac.

Reflect and Respond

6. The steps so far have led you to a partial equation for the sine law.

    a) Describe what measures in a triangle the sine law connects.

    b) What components do you need to be able to use the sine law?

7. Demonstrate how you could expand the ratios from step 5 to include the third ratio, $\dfrac{\sin B}{b}$.

8. Together, steps 5 and 7 form the sine law. Write out the sine law that you have derived and state it in words.

9. Can you solve all oblique triangles using the sine law? If not, give an example where the sine law does not allow you to solve for unknown angle(s) or side(s).

Link the Ideas

You have previously encountered problems involving right triangles that you could solve using the Pythagorean Theorem and the primary trigonometric ratios. However, a triangle that models a situation with unknown distances or angles may not be a right triangle. One method of solving an oblique triangle is to use the sine law. To prove the sine law, you need to extend your earlier skills with trigonometry.

Did You Know?

Nasir al-Din al-Tusi, born in the year 1201 c.e., began his career as an astronomer in Baghdad. In *On the Sector Figure*, he derived the sine law.

The Sine Law

The **sine law** is a relationship between the sides and angles in any triangle. Let △ABC be any triangle, where a, b, and c represent the measures of the sides opposite ∠A, ∠B, and ∠C, respectively. Then,

$$\frac{a}{\sin A} = \frac{b}{\sin B} = \frac{c}{\sin C}$$

or

$$\frac{\sin A}{a} = \frac{\sin B}{b} = \frac{\sin C}{c}$$

Proof

In △ABC, draw an altitude AD ⊥ BC.
Let AD = h.

The symbol ⊥ means "perpendicular to."

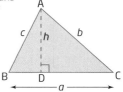

In △ABD:

$$\sin B = \frac{h}{c}$$
$$h = c \sin B$$

In △ACD:

$$\sin C = \frac{h}{b}$$
$$h = b \sin C$$

Relate these two equations, because both equal h:

$c \sin B = b \sin C$ → Divide both sides by sin B sin C.

$$\frac{c}{\sin C} = \frac{b}{\sin B}$$

This is part of the sine law.

By drawing the altitude from C and using similar steps, you can show that

$$\frac{a}{\sin A} = \frac{b}{\sin B}$$

Therefore,

$$\frac{a}{\sin A} = \frac{b}{\sin B} = \frac{c}{\sin C}$$

or

$$\frac{\sin A}{a} = \frac{\sin B}{b} = \frac{\sin C}{c}$$

Example 1

Determine an Unknown Side Length

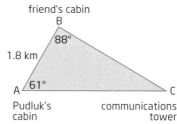

Pudluk's family and his friend own cabins on the Kalit River in Nunavut. Pudluk and his friend wish to determine the distance from Pudluk's cabin to the store on the edge of town. They know that the distance between their cabins is 1.8 km. Using a transit, they estimate the measures of the angles between their cabins and the communications tower near the store, as shown in the diagram. Determine the distance from Pudluk's cabin to the store, to the nearest tenth of a kilometre.

Solution

Method 1: Use Primary Trigonometric Ratios

Calculate the measure of ∠C.

$$\angle C = 180° - 88° - 61°$$
$$\angle C = 31°$$

What relationship exists for the sum of the interior angles of any triangle?

Draw the altitude of the triangle from B to intersect AC at point D. Label the altitude h.

The distance from Pudluk's cabin to the store is the sum of the distances AD and DC.

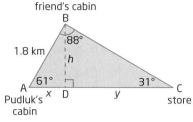

friend's cabin
1.8 km
Pudluk's cabin
store

From △ABD, determine h.

$$\sin 61° = \frac{\text{opposite}}{\text{hypotenuse}}$$

$$\sin 61° = \frac{h}{1.8}$$

$$h = 1.8 \sin 61°$$

Check that your calculator is in degree mode.

From △ABD, determine x.

$$\cos 61° = \frac{\text{adjacent}}{\text{hypotenuse}}$$

$$\cos 61° = \frac{x}{1.8}$$

$$x = 1.8 \cos 61°$$

$$x = 0.872...$$

From △BDC, determine y.

$$\tan 31° = \frac{\text{opposite}}{\text{adjacent}}$$

$$\tan 31° = \frac{h}{y}$$

$$y = \frac{1.8 \sin 61°}{\tan 31°}$$

$$y = 2.620...$$

Then, AC = $x + y$, or 3.492....
The distance from Pudluk's cabin to the store is approximately 3.5 km.

Method 2: Use the Sine Law

Calculate the measure of ∠C.

$$\angle C = 180° - 88° - 61°$$
$$\angle C = 31°$$

What is the sum of the interior angles of any triangle?

List the measures.

∠A = 61°	$a = \blacksquare$
∠B = 88°	$b = \blacksquare$
∠C = 31°	$c = 1.8$ km

Which pairs of ratios from the sine law would you use to solve for b?

$$\frac{b}{\sin B} = \frac{c}{\sin C}$$

Why is this form of the sine law used?

$$\frac{b}{\sin 88°} = \frac{1.8}{\sin 31°}$$

What do you do to each side to isolate b?

$$b = \frac{1.8 \sin 88°}{\sin 31°}$$

$$b = 3.492...$$

Compare the two methods. Which do you prefer and why?

The distance from Pudluk's cabin to the store is approximately 3.5 km.

Your Turn

Determine the distance from Pudluk's friend's cabin to the store.

Example 2

Determine an Unknown Angle Measure

In $\triangle$PQR, $\angle$P = 36°, $p = 24.8$ m, and $q = 23.4$ m. Determine the measure of $\angle$R, to the nearest degree.

Solution

Sketch a diagram of the triangle. List the measures.

$\angle$P = 36° $p = 24.8$
$\angle$Q = ■ $q = 23.4$
$\angle$R = ■ $r = $ ■

Which ratios would you use?

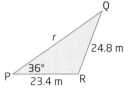

Since $p > q$, there is only one possible triangle.

Use the sine law to determine $\angle$Q.

Why do you need to determine $\angle$Q?

$$\frac{\sin Q}{q} = \frac{\sin P}{p}$$

$$\frac{\sin Q}{23.4} = \frac{\sin 36°}{24.8}$$

$$\sin Q = \frac{23.4 \sin 36°}{24.8}$$

$$\angle Q = \sin^{-1}\left(\frac{23.4 \sin 36°}{24.8}\right)$$

$$\angle Q = 33.68\ldots$$

Thus, $\angle$Q is 34°, to the nearest degree.

Use the angle sum of a triangle to determine $\angle$R.
$\angle$R = 180° − 34° − 36°
$\angle$R = 110°
The measure of $\angle$R is 110°, to the nearest degree.

Your Turn

In $\triangle$LMN, $\angle$L = 64°, $l = 25.2$ cm, and $m = 16.5$ cm. Determine the measure of $\angle$N, to the nearest degree.

The Ambiguous Case

When solving a triangle, you must analyse the given information to determine if a solution exists. If you are given the measures of two angles and one side (ASA), then the triangle is uniquely defined. However, if you are given two sides and an angle opposite one of those sides (SSA), the **ambiguous case** may occur. In the ambiguous case, there are three possible outcomes:

ambiguous case

- from the given information the solution for the triangle is not clear: there might be one triangle, two triangles, or no triangle

- no triangle exists that has the given measures; there is no solution

- one triangle exists that has the given measures; there is one solution

- two distinct triangles exist that have the given measures; there are two distinct solutions

These possibilities are summarized in the diagrams below.

Suppose you are given the measures of side b and $\angle A$ of $\triangle ABC$. You can find the height of the triangle by using $h = b \sin A$.

Why can you use this equation to find the height?

In $\triangle ABC$, $\angle A$ and side b are constant because they are given. Consider different possible lengths of side a.

For an acute $\angle A$, the four possible lengths of side a result in four different cases.

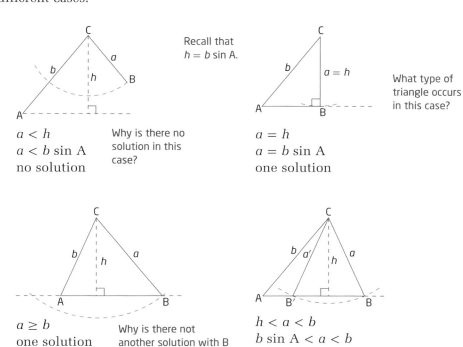

Recall that $h = b \sin A$.

What type of triangle occurs in this case?

Why is there no solution in this case?

$a < h$
$a < b \sin A$
no solution

$a = h$
$a = b \sin A$
one solution

$a \geq b$
one solution

Why is there not another solution with B on the left side of A?

$h < a < b$
$b \sin A < a < b$
two solutions

For an obtuse $\angle A$, three cases can occur.

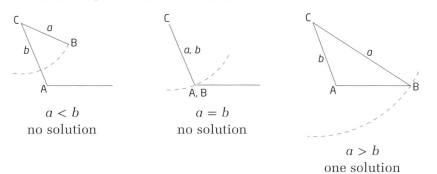

$a < b$
no solution

$a = b$
no solution

$a > b$
one solution

Example 3

Use the Sine Law in an Ambiguous Case

In $\triangle$ABC, $\angle$A = 30°, a = 24 cm, and b = 42 cm. Determine the measures of the other side and angles. Round your answers to the nearest unit.

Solution

List the measures.

$\angle$A = 30° $\quad$ a = 24 cm
$\angle$B = ■ $\quad\quad$ b = 42 cm
$\angle$C = ■ $\quad\quad$ c = ■

Because two sides and an angle opposite one of the sides are known, it is possible that this triangle may have two different solutions, one solution, or no solution. $\angle$A is acute and $a < b$, so check which condition is true.

$a < b \sin A$: no solution $\qquad$ *Why is the value of $b \sin A$ so important?*
$a = b \sin A$: one solution
$a > b \sin A$: two solutions

Sketch a possible diagram. $\qquad$ *Where does the length of CB actually fit?*

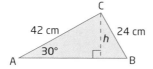

Determine the height of the triangle.

$\sin A = \dfrac{h}{b}$

$\quad h = b \sin A$
$\quad h = 42 \sin 30°$ $\qquad$ *How do you know the value of sin 30°?*
$\quad h = 21$

Since 24 > 21, the case $a > b \sin A$ occurs.

Therefore, two triangles are possible. The second solution will give an obtuse angle for $\angle$B.

Solve for $\angle$B using the sine law.

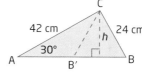

$\dfrac{\sin B}{b} = \dfrac{\sin A}{a}$

$\dfrac{\sin B}{42} = \dfrac{\sin 30°}{24}$

$\quad \sin B = \dfrac{42 \sin 30°}{24}$

$\quad\quad \angle B = \sin^{-1}\left(\dfrac{42 \sin 30°}{24}\right)$

$\quad\quad \angle B = 61.044...$

To the nearest degree, $\angle$B = 61°.

To find the second possible measure of $\angle$B, use 61° as the reference angle in quadrant II. Then, $\angle$B = 180° − 61° or $\angle$B = 119°.

Case 1: $\angle B = 61°$
$\angle C = 180° - (61° + 30°)$
$\angle C = 89°$

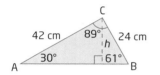

$$\frac{c}{\sin 89°} = \frac{24}{\sin 30°}$$
$$c = \frac{24 \sin 89°}{\sin 30°}$$
$$c = 47.992\ldots$$

Case 2: $\angle B = 119°$
$\angle C = 180° - (119° + 30°)$
$\angle C = 31°$

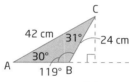

$$\frac{c}{\sin 31°} = \frac{24}{\sin 30°}$$
$$c = \frac{24 \sin 31°}{\sin 30°}$$
$$c = 24.721\ldots$$

Use the sine law to determine the measure of side c in each case.

The two possible triangles are as follows:
acute $\triangle ABC$: $\angle A = 30°$, $\angle B = 61°$, $\angle C = 89°$,
$a = 24$ cm, $b = 42$ cm, $c = 48$ cm
obtuse $\triangle ABC$: $\angle A = 30°$, $\angle B = 119°$, $\angle C = 31°$,
$a = 24$ cm, $b = 42$ cm, $c = 25$ cm

Compare the ratios $\frac{a}{\sin A}$, $\frac{b}{\sin B}$, and $\frac{c}{\sin C}$ to check your answers.

Your Turn

In $\triangle ABC$, $\angle A = 39°$, $a = 14$ cm, and $b = 10$ cm. Determine the measures of the other side and angles. Express your answers to the nearest unit.

Key Ideas

- You can use the sine law to find the measures of sides and angles in a triangle.

- For $\triangle ABC$, state the sine law as $\dfrac{a}{\sin A} = \dfrac{b}{\sin B} = \dfrac{c}{\sin C}$ or $\dfrac{\sin A}{a} = \dfrac{\sin B}{b} = \dfrac{\sin C}{c}$.

- Use the sine law to solve a triangle when you are given the measures of
  - two angles and one side
  - two sides and an angle that is opposite one of the given sides

- The ambiguous case of the sine law may occur when you are given two sides and an angle opposite one of the sides.

- For the ambiguous case in $\triangle ABC$, when $\angle A$ is an acute angle:
  - $a \geq b$ one solution
  - $a = h$ one solution $h = b \sin A$
  - $a < h$ no solution
  - $b \sin A < a < b$ two solutions

- For the ambiguous case in $\triangle ABC$, when $\angle A$ is an obtuse angle:
  - $a \leq b$ no solution
  - $a > b$ one solution

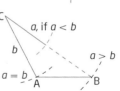

Practise

Where necessary, round lengths to the nearest tenth of a unit and angle measures to the nearest degree.

1. Solve for the unknown side or angle in each.

   a) $\dfrac{a}{\sin 35°} = \dfrac{10}{\sin 40°}$

   b) $\dfrac{b}{\sin 48°} = \dfrac{65}{\sin 75°}$

   c) $\dfrac{\sin \theta}{12} = \dfrac{\sin 50°}{65}$

   d) $\dfrac{\sin A}{25} = \dfrac{\sin 62°}{32}$

2. Determine the length of AB in each.

   a)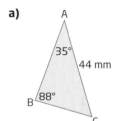

   b)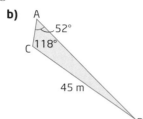

3. Determine the value of the marked unknown angle in each.

   a)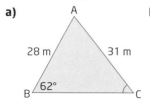

   b)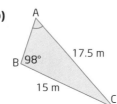

4. Determining the lengths of all three sides and the measures of all three angles is called solving a triangle. Solve each triangle.

   a)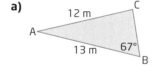

   b)

   c)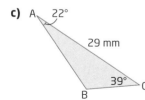

   d)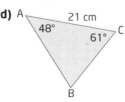

5. Sketch each triangle. Determine the measure of the indicated side.

   a) In $\triangle ABC$, $\angle A = 57°$, $\angle B = 73°$, and AB = 24 cm. Find the length of AC.

   b) In $\triangle ABC$, $\angle B = 38°$, $\angle C = 56°$, and BC = 63 cm. Find the length of AB.

   c) In $\triangle ABC$, $\angle A = 50°$, $\angle B = 50°$, and AC = 27 m. Find the length of AB.

   d) In $\triangle ABC$, $\angle A = 23°$, $\angle C = 78°$, and AB = 15 cm. Find the length of BC.

6. For each triangle, determine whether there is no solution, one solution, or two solutions.

   a) In $\triangle ABC$, $\angle A = 39°$, $a = 10$ cm, and $b = 14$ cm.

   b) In $\triangle ABC$, $\angle A = 123°$, $a = 23$ cm, and $b = 12$ cm.

   c) In $\triangle ABC$, $\angle A = 145°$, $a = 18$ cm, and $b = 10$ cm.

   d) In $\triangle ABC$, $\angle A = 124°$, $a = 1$ cm, and $b = 2$ cm.

7. In each diagram, h is an altitude. Describe how $\angle A$, sides a and b, and h are related in each diagram.

   a)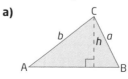

   b)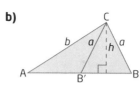

   c)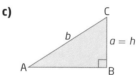

   d)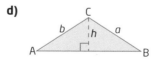

8. Determine the unknown side and angles in each triangle. If two solutions are possible, give both.

   a) In $\triangle$ABC, $\angle$C = 31°, a = 5.6 cm, and c = 3.9 cm.

   b) In $\triangle$PQR, $\angle$Q = 43°, p = 20 cm, and q = 15 cm.

   c) In $\triangle$XYZ, $\angle$X = 53°, x = 8.5 cm, and z = 12.3 cm.

9. In $\triangle$ABC, $\angle$A = 26° and b = 120 cm. Determine the range of values of a for which there is

   a) one oblique triangle

   b) one right triangle

   c) two oblique triangles

   d) no triangle

Apply

10. A hot-air balloon is flying above BC Place Stadium. Maria is standing due north of the stadium and can see the balloon at an angle of inclination of 64°. Roy is due south of the stadium and can see the balloon at an angle of inclination of 49°. The horizontal distance between Maria and Roy is 500 m.

   a) Sketch a diagram to represent the given information.

   b) Determine the distance that the hot air balloon is from Maria.

11. The Canadian Coast Guard Pacific Region is responsible for more than 27 000 km of coastline. The rotating spotlight from the Coast Guard ship can illuminate up to a distance of 250 m. An observer on the shore is 500 m from the ship. His line of sight to the ship makes an angle of 20° with the shoreline. What length of shoreline is illuminated by the spotlight?

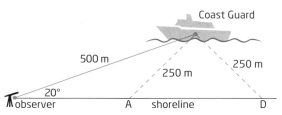

12. A chandelier is suspended from a horizontal beam by two support chains. One of the chains is 3.6 m long and forms an angle of 62° with the beam. The second chain is 4.8 m long. What angle does the second chain make with the beam?

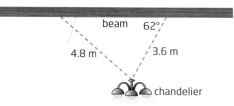

13. Nicolina wants to approximate the height of the Francophone Monument in Edmonton. From the low wall surrounding the statue, she measures the angle of elevation to the top of the monument to be 40°. She measures a distance 3.9 m farther away from the monument and measures the angle of elevation to be 26°. Determine the height of the Francophone Monument.

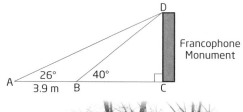

Did You Know?

The Francophone Monument located at the Legislature Grounds in Edmonton represents the union of the fleur de lis and the wild rose. This monument celebrates the contribution of francophones to Alberta's heritage.

14. From the window of his hotel in Saskatoon, Max can see statues of Chief Whitecap of the Whitecap First Nation and John Lake, leader of the Temperance Colonists, who founded Saskatoon. The angle formed by Max's lines of sight to the top and to the foot of the statue of Chief Whitecap is 3°. The angle of depression of Max's line of sight to the top of the statue is 21°. The horizontal distance between Max and the front of the statue is 66 m.

a) Sketch a diagram to represent this problem.

b) Determine the height of the statue of Chief Whitecap.

c) Determine the line-of-sight distance from where Max is standing at the window to the foot of the statue.

15. The chemical formula for water, H_2O, tells you that one molecule of water is made up of two atoms of hydrogen and one atom of oxygen bonded together. The nuclei of the atoms are separated by the distance shown, in angstroms. An angstrom is a unit of length used in chemistry.

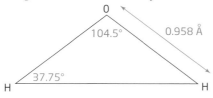

a) Determine the distance, in angstroms (Å), between the two hydrogen atoms.

b) Given that 1 Å = 0.01 mm, what is the distance between the two hydrogen atoms, in millimetres?

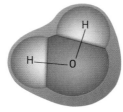

16. A hang-glider is a triangular parachute made of nylon or Dacron fabric. The pilot of a hang-glider flies through the air by finding updrafts and wind currents. The nose angle for a hang-glider may vary. The nose angle for the T2 high-performance glider ranges from 127° to 132°. If the length of the wing is 5.1 m, determine the greatest and least wingspans of the T2 glider.

Did You Know?

Cochrane, Alberta, located 22 km west of Calgary, is considered to be the perfect location for hang-gliding. The prevailing winds are heated as they cross the prairie. Then they are forced upward by hills, creating powerful thermals that produce the long flights so desired by flyers.

The Canadian record for the longest hang-gliding flight is a distance of 332.8 km, flown from east of Beiseker, Alberta, to northwest of Westlock, in May 1989, by Willi Muller.

17. On his trip to Somerset Island, Nunavut, Armand joined an informative tour near Fort Ross. During the group's first stop, Armand spotted a cairn at the top of a hill, a distance of 500 m away. The group made a second stop at the bottom of the hill. From this point, the cairn is 360 m away. The angle between the cairn, Armand's first stop, and his second stop is 35°.

a) Explain why there are two possible locations for Armand's second stop.

b) Sketch a diagram to illustrate each possible location.

c) Determine the possible distances between Armand's first and second stops.

Did You Know?

A cairn is a pile of stones placed as a memorial, tomb, or landmark.

18. Radio towers, designed to support broadcasting and telecommunications, are among the tallest non-natural structures. Construction and maintenance of radio towers is rated as one of the most dangerous jobs in the world. To change the antenna of one of these towers, a crew sets up a system of pulleys. The diagram models the machinery and cable set-up. Suppose the height of the antenna is 30 m. Determine the total height of the structure.

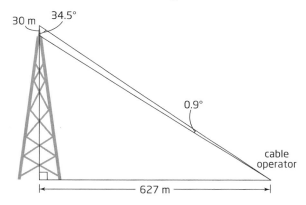

19. Given an obtuse △ABC, copy and complete the table. Indicate the reasons for each step for the proof of the sine law.

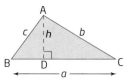

Statements	Reasons
$\sin C = \dfrac{h}{b}$ $\sin B = \dfrac{h}{c}$	
$h = b \sin C$ $h = c \sin B$	
$b \sin C = c \sin B$	
$\dfrac{\sin C}{c} = \dfrac{\sin B}{b}$	

Extend

20. Use the sine law to prove that if the measures of two angles of a triangle are equal, then the lengths of the sides opposite those angles are equal. Use a sketch in your explanation.

21. There are about 12 reported oil spills of 4000 L or more each day in Canada. Oil spills, such as occurred after the train derailment near Wabamun Lake, Alberta, can cause long-term ecological damage. To contain the spilled oil, floating booms are placed in the water. Suppose for the cleanup of the 734 000 L of oil at Wabamun, the floating booms used approximated an oblique triangle with the measurements shown. Determine the area of the oil spill at Wabamun.

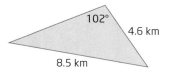

22. For each of the following, include a diagram in your solution.

    a) Determine the range of values side a can have so that △ABC has two solutions if ∠A = 40° and $b = 50.0$ cm.

    b) Determine the range of values side a can have so that △ABC has no solutions if ∠A = 56° and $b = 125.7$ cm.

    c) △ABC has exactly one solution. If ∠A = 57° and $b = 73.7$ cm, what are the values of side a for which this is possible?

23. Shawna takes a pathway through Nose Hill Park in her Calgary neighbourhood. Street lights are placed 50 m apart on the main road, as shown. The light from each streetlight illuminates a distance along the ground of up to 60 m. Determine the distance from A to the farthest point on the pathway that is lit.

Create Connections

24. Explain why the sine law cannot be used to solve each triangle.

a)
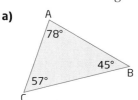

b)
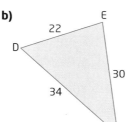

c)
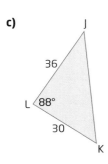

d)
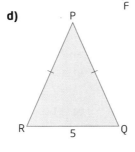

25. Explain how you could use a right △ABC to partially develop the sine law.

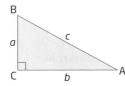

26. A golden triangle is an isosceles triangle in which the ratio of the length of the longer side to the length of the shorter side is the golden ratio, $\dfrac{\sqrt{5} + 1}{2}:1$. The golden ratio is found in art, in math, and in architecture. In golden triangles, the vertex angle measures 36° and the two base angles measure 72°.

a) The triangle in Figure 1 is a golden triangle. The base measures 8 cm. Use the sine law to determine the length of the two equal sides of the triangle.

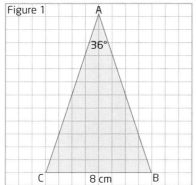

b) Use the golden ratio to determine the exact lengths of the two equal sides.

c) If you bisect one base angle of a golden triangle, you create another golden triangle similar to the first, as in Figure 2. Determine the length of side CD.

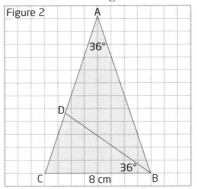

d) This pattern may be repeated, as in Figure 3. Determine the length of DE.

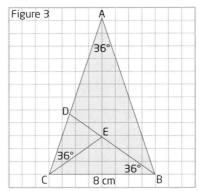

e) Describe how the spiral in Figure 4 is created.

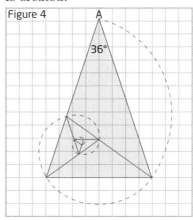

27. Complete a concept map to show the conditions necessary to be able to use the sine law to solve triangles.

28. MINI LAB Work with a partner to explore conditions for the ambiguous case of the sine law.

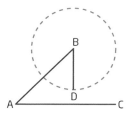

Materials

• ruler
• compass
• string
• scissors

Step 1 Draw a line segment AC. Draw a second line segment AB that forms an acute angle at A. Draw a circle, using point B as the centre, such that the circle does not touch the line segment AC. Draw a radius and label the point intersecting the circle D.

Step 2 Cut a piece of string that is the length of the radius BD. Hold one end at the centre of the circle and turn the other end through the arc of the circle.

a) Can a triangle be formed under these conditions?

b) Make a conjecture about the number of triangles formed and the conditions necessary for this situation.

Step 3 Extend the circle so that it just touches the line segment AC at point D. Cut a piece of string that is the length of the radius.

Hold one end at the centre of the circle and turn the other end through the arc of the circle.

a) Can a triangle be formed under these conditions?

b) Make a conjecture about the number of triangles formed and the conditions necessary for this situation.

Step 4 Extend the circle so that it intersects line segment AC at two distinct points. Cut a piece of string that is the length of the radius. Hold one end at the centre of the circle and turn the other end through the arc of the circle.

a) Can a triangle be formed under these conditions?

b) Make a conjecture about the number of triangles formed and the conditions necessary for this situation.

Step 5 Cut a piece of string that is longer than the segment AB. Hold one end at B and turn the other end through the arc of a circle.

a) Can a triangle be formed under these conditions?

b) Make a conjecture about the number of triangles formed and the conditions necessary for this situation.

Step 6 Explain how varying the measure of ∠A would affect your conjectures.

Project Corner | Triangulation

• Triangulation is a method of determining your exact location based on your position relative to three other established locations using angle measures or bearings.

• Bearings are angles measured in degrees from the north line in a clockwise direction. A bearing usually has three digits. For instance, north is 000°, east is 090°, south is 180°, and southwest is 225°.

• A bearing of 045° is the same as N45°E.

• How could you use triangulation to help you determine the location of your resource?

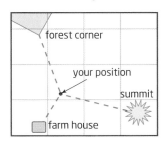

The Cosine Law

Focus on...

- sketching a diagram and solving a problem using the cosine law
- recognizing when to use the cosine law to solve a given problem
- explaining the steps in the given proof of the cosine law

The Canadarm2, one of the three components of the Mobile Servicing System, is a major part of the Canadian space robotic system. It completed its first official construction job on the International Space Station in July 2001. The robotic arm can move equipment and assist astronauts working in space. The robotic manipulator is operated by controlling the angles of its joints. The final position of the arm can be calculated by using the trigonometric ratios of those angles.

Investigate the Cosine Law

Materials

- ruler
- protractor

1. a) Draw $\triangle ABC$, where $a = 3$ cm, $b = 4$ cm, and $c = 5$ cm.

b) Determine the values of a^2, b^2, and c^2.

c) Compare the values of $a^2 + b^2$ and c^2. Which of the following is true?
- $a^2 + b^2 = c^2$
- $a^2 + b^2 > c^2$
- $a^2 + b^2 < c^2$

d) What is the measure of $\angle C$?

2. a) Draw an acute $\triangle ABC$.

b) Measure the lengths of sides a, b, and c.

c) Determine the values of a^2, b^2, and c^2.

d) Compare the values of $a^2 + b^2$ and c^2. Which of the following is true?
- $a^2 + b^2 > c^2$
- $a^2 + b^2 < c^2$

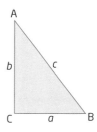

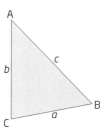

The cosine law relates the lengths of the sides of a given triangle to the cosine of one of its angles.

3. a) For △ABC given in step 1, determine the value of $2ab \cos C$.

b) Determine the value of $2ab \cos C$ for △ABC from step 2.

c) Copy and complete a table like the one started below. Record your results and collect data for the triangle drawn in step 2 from at least three other people.

Triangle Side Lengths (cm)	c^2	$a^2 + b^2$	$2ab \cos C$
$a = 3, b = 4, c = 5$			
$a = \blacksquare, b = \blacksquare, c = \blacksquare$			

4. Consider the inequality you found to be true in step 2, for the relationship between the values of c^2 and $a^2 + b^2$. Explain how your results from step 3 might be used to turn the inequality into an equation. This relationship is known as the cosine law.

5. Draw △ABC in which ∠C is obtuse. Measure its side lengths. Determine whether or not your equation from step 4 holds.

Reflect and Respond

6. The cosine law relates the lengths of the sides of a given triangle to the cosine of one of its angles. Under what conditions would you use the cosine law to solve a triangle?

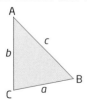

7. Consider the triangle shown.

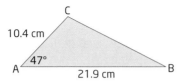

a) Is it possible to determine the length of side a using the sine law? Explain why or why not.

b) Describe how you could solve for side a.

8. How are the cosine law and the Pythagorean Theorem related?

The Cosine Law

cosine law

- if a, b, c are the sides of a triangle and C is the angle opposite c, the cosine law is
$c^2 = a^2 + b^2 - 2ab \cos C$

The **cosine law** describes the relationship between the cosine of an angle and the lengths of the three sides of any triangle.

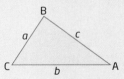

For any $\triangle ABC$, where a, b, and c are the lengths of the sides opposite to $\angle A$, $\angle B$, and $\angle C$, respectively, the cosine law states that
$c^2 = a^2 + b^2 - 2ab \cos C$

You can express the formula in different forms to find the lengths of the other sides of the triangle.
$a^2 = b^2 + c^2 - 2bc \cos A$
$b^2 = a^2 + c^2 - 2ac \cos B$

What patterns do you notice?

Proof

In $\triangle ABC$, draw an altitude h.

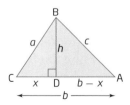

In $\triangle BCD$:
$\cos C = \dfrac{x}{a}$ $\qquad a^2 = h^2 + x^2$
$\qquad x = a \cos C$

In $\triangle ABD$, using the Pythagorean Theorem:
$c^2 = h^2 + (b - x)^2$
$c^2 = h^2 + b^2 - 2bx + x^2$ $\qquad$ Expand the binomial.
$c^2 = h^2 + x^2 + b^2 - 2bx$ $\qquad$ Why are the terms rearranged?
$c^2 = a^2 + b^2 - 2b(a \cos C)$ $\qquad$ Explain the substitutions.
$c^2 = a^2 + b^2 - 2ab \cos C$

Example 1

Determine a Distance

A surveyor needs to find the length of a swampy area near Fishing Lake, Manitoba. The surveyor sets up her transit at a point A. She measures the distance to one end of the swamp as 468.2 m, the distance to the opposite end of the swamp as 692.6 m, and the angle of sight between the two as 78.6°. Determine the length of the swampy area, to the nearest tenth of a metre.

Solution

Sketch a diagram to illustrate the problem.

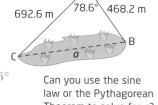

Use the cosine law.

$a^2 = b^2 + c^2 - 2bc \cos A$

$a^2 = 692.6^2 + 468.2^2 - 2(692.6)(468.2)\cos 78.6°$

$a^2 = 570\ 715.205...$

$a = \sqrt{570\ 715.205...}$

$a = 755.456...$

The length of the swampy area is 755.5 m, to the nearest tenth of a metre.

Can you use the sine law or the Pythagorean Theorem to solve for a? Why or why not?

Your Turn

Nina wants to find the distance between two points, A and B, on opposite sides of a pond. She locates a point C that is 35.5 m from A and 48.8 m from B. If the angle at C is 54°, determine the distance AB, to the nearest tenth of a metre.

Example 2

Determine an Angle

The Lions' Gate Bridge has been a Vancouver landmark since it opened in 1938. It is the longest suspension bridge in Western Canada. The bridge is strengthened by triangular braces. Suppose one brace has side lengths 14 m, 19 m, and 12.2 m. Determine the measure of the angle opposite the 14-m side, to the nearest degree.

Solution

Sketch a diagram to illustrate the situation.

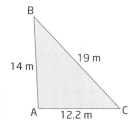

Use the cosine law: $c^2 = a^2 + b^2 - 2ab \cos C$

Method 1: Substitute Directly

$c^2 = a^2 + b^2 - 2ab \cos C$

$14^2 = 19^2 + 12.2^2 - 2(19)(12.2) \cos C$

$196 = 361 + 148.84 - 463.6 \cos C$

$196 = 509.84 - 463.6 \cos C$

$196 - 509.84 = -463.6 \cos C$

$-313.84 = -463.6 \cos C$

$\dfrac{-313.84}{-463.6} = \cos C$

$\cos^{-1}\left(\dfrac{313.84}{463.6}\right) = \angle C$

$47.393... = \angle C$

The measure of the angle opposite the 14-m side is approximately 47°.

Method 2: Rearrange the Formula to Solve for cos C

$$c^2 = a^2 + b^2 - 2ab \cos C$$
$$2ab \cos C = a^2 + b^2 - c^2$$
$$\cos C = \frac{a^2 + b^2 - c^2}{2ab}$$

How can you write a similar formula for $\angle A$ or $\angle B$?

$$\cos C = \frac{19^2 + 12.2^2 - 14^2}{2(19)(12.2)}$$
$$\angle C = \cos^{-1}\left(\frac{19^2 + 12.2^2 - 14^2}{2(19)(12.2)}\right)$$
$$\angle C = 47.393\ldots$$

The measure of the angle opposite the 14-m side is approximately $47°$.

Your Turn

A triangular brace has side lengths 14 m, 18 m, and 22 m. Determine the measure of the angle opposite the 18-m side, to the nearest degree.

Example 3

Solve a Triangle

In $\triangle ABC$, $a = 11$, $b = 5$, and $\angle C = 20°$. Sketch a diagram and determine the length of the unknown side and the measures of the unknown angles, to the nearest tenth.

Solution

Sketch a diagram of the triangle.
List the measures.

$$\angle A = \blacksquare \qquad a = 11$$
$$\angle B = \blacksquare \qquad b = 5$$
$$\angle C = 20° \qquad c = \blacksquare$$

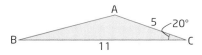

Use the cosine law to solve for c.

$$c^2 = a^2 + b^2 - 2ab \cos C$$
$$c^2 = 11^2 + 5^2 - 2(11)(5) \cos 20°$$
$$c^2 = 42.633\ldots$$
$$c = 6.529\ldots$$

Could you use the sine law? Explain.

To solve for the angles, you could use either the cosine law or the sine law.
For $\angle A$:

$$\cos A = \frac{b^2 + c^2 - a^2}{2bc}$$
$$\cos A = \frac{5^2 + (6.529\ldots)^2 - 11^2}{2(5)(6.529\ldots)}$$
$$\angle A = \cos^{-1}\left(\frac{5^2 + (6.529\ldots)^2 - 11^2}{2(5)(6.529\ldots)}\right)$$
$$\angle A = 144.816\ldots$$

For c, use your calculator value.

The measure of $\angle A$ is approximately $144.8°$.

Use the angle sum of a triangle to determine $\angle C$.
$$\angle C = 180° - (20° + 144.8°)$$
$$\angle C = 15.2°$$

Could you find the measure of $\angle A$ or $\angle C$ using the sine law? If so, which is better to find first?

The six parts of the triangle are as follows:

$\angle A = 144.8°$ $a = 11$
$\angle B = 15.2°$ $b = 5$
$\angle C = 20°$ $c = 6.5$

Your Turn

In $\triangle ABC$, $a = 9$, $b = 7$, and $\angle C = 33.6°$. Sketch a diagram and determine the length of the unknown side and the measures of the unknown angles, to the nearest tenth.

Key Ideas

- Use the cosine law to find the length of an unknown side of any triangle when you know the lengths of two sides and the measure of the angle between them.

- The cosine law states that for any $\triangle ABC$, the following relationships exist:
  $a^2 = b^2 + c^2 - 2bc \cos A$
  $b^2 = a^2 + c^2 - 2ac \cos B$
  $c^2 = a^2 + b^2 - 2ab \cos C$

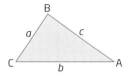

- Use the cosine law to find the measure of an unknown angle of any triangle when the lengths of three sides are known.

- Rearrange the cosine law to solve for a particular angle.
  For example, $\cos A = \dfrac{a^2 - b^2 - c^2}{-2bc}$ or $\cos A = \dfrac{b^2 + c^2 - a^2}{2bc}$.

- Use the cosine law in conjunction with the sine law to solve a triangle.

Check Your Understanding

Practise

Where necessary, round lengths to the nearest tenth of a unit and angles to the nearest degree, unless otherwise stated.

1. Determine the length of the third side of each triangle.

a)
b)

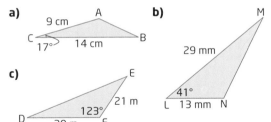

c)

2. Determine the measure of the indicated angle.

a) $\angle J$
b) $\angle L$

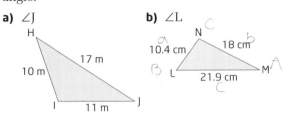

c) $\angle P$
d) $\angle C$

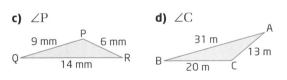

3. Determine the lengths of the unknown sides and the measures of the unknown angles.

a)

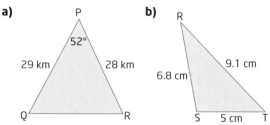

b)

4. Make a sketch to show the given information for each △ABC. Then, determine the indicated value.

   a) AB = 24 cm, AC = 34 cm, and ∠A = 67°. Determine the length of BC.

   b) AB = 15 m, BC = 8 m, and ∠B = 24°. Determine the length of AC.

   c) AC = 10 cm, BC = 9 cm, and ∠C = 48°. Determine the length of AB.

   d) AB = 9 m, AC = 12 m, and BC = 15 m. Determine the measure of ∠B.

   e) AB = 18.4 m, BC = 9.6 m, and AC = 10.8 m. Determine the measure of ∠A.

   f) AB = 4.6 m, BC = 3.2 m, and AC = 2.5 m. Determine the measure of ∠C.

Apply

5. Would you use the sine law or the cosine law to determine each indicated side length or angle measure? Give reasons for your choice.

   a) ∠F

   b) *p*

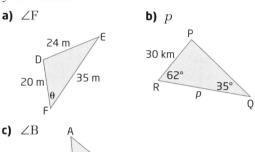

   c) ∠B

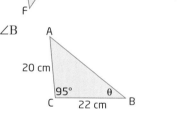

6. Determine the length of side *c* in each △ABC, to the nearest tenth.

   a) B

   b)

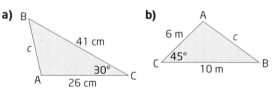

7. In a parallelogram, the measure of the obtuse angle is 116°. The adjacent sides, containing the angle, measure 40 cm and 22 cm, respectively. Determine the length of the longest diagonal.

8. The longest tunnel in North America could be built through the mountains of the Kicking Horse Canyon, near Golden, British Columbia. The tunnel would be on the Trans-Canada highway connecting the Prairies with the west coast. Suppose the surveying team selected a point A, 3000 m away from the proposed tunnel entrance and 2000 m from the tunnel exit. If ∠A is measured as 67.7°, determine the length of the tunnel, to the nearest metre.

> **Web Link**
>
> To learn more about the history of the Kicking Horse Pass and proposed plans for a new tunnel, go to www.mhrprecalc11.ca and follow the links.

9. Thousands of Canadians are active in sailing clubs. In the Paralympic Games, there are competitions in the single-handed, double-handed, and three-person categories. A sailing race course often follows a triangular route around three buoys. Suppose the distances between the buoys of a triangular course are 8.56 km, 5.93 km, and 10.24 km. Determine the measure of the angle at each of the buoys.

> **Did You Know?**
>
> Single-handed sailing means that one person sails the boat. Double-handed refers to two people. Buoys are floating markers, anchored to keep them in place. The oldest record of buoys being used to warn of rock hazards is in the thirteenth century on the Guadalquivir River near Seville in Spain.

10. The Canadian women's national ice hockey team has won numerous international competitions, including gold medals at the 2002, 2006, and 2010 Winter Olympics. A player on the blue line shoots a puck toward the 1.83-m-wide net from a point 20.3 m from one goal post and 21.3 m from the other. Within what angle must she shoot to hit the net? Answer to the nearest tenth of a degree.

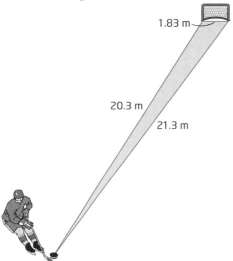

11. One of the best populated sea-run brook trout areas in Canada is Lac Guillaume-Delisle in northern Québec. Also known as Richmond Gulf, it is a large triangular-shaped lake. Suppose the sides forming the northern tip of the lake are 65 km and 85 km in length, and the angle at the northern tip is 7.8°. Determine the width of the lake at its base.

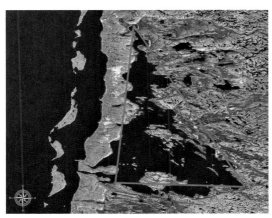

12. An aircraft-tracking station determines the distances from a helicopter to two aircraft as 50 km and 72 km. The angle between these two distances is 49°. Determine the distance between the two aircraft.

13. Tony Smith was born in 1912 in South Orange, New Jersey. As a child, Tony suffered from tuberculosis. He spent his time playing and creating with medicine boxes. His sculpture, Moondog, consists of several equilateral and isosceles triangles that combine art and math. Use the information provided on the diagram to determine the maximum width of Moondog.

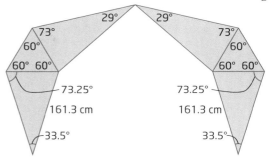

Moondog by Tony Smith

14. Julia and Isaac are backpacking in Banff National Park. They walk 8 km from their base camp heading N42°E. After lunch, they change direction to a bearing of 137° and walk another 5 km.

a) Sketch a diagram of their route.

b) How far are Julia and Isaac from their base camp?

c) At what bearing must they travel to return to their base camp?

15. A spotlight is 8 m away from a mirror on the floor. A beam of light shines into the mirror, forming an angle of 80° with the reflected light.

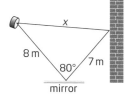

The light is reflected a distance of 7 m to shine onto a wall. Determine the distance from the spotlight to the point where the light is reflected onto the wall.

16. Erica created this design for part of a company logo. She needs to determine the accuracy of the side lengths. Explain how you could use the cosine law to verify that the side lengths shown are correct.

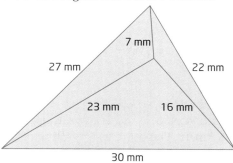

17. The sport of mountain biking became popular in the 1970s. The mountain bike was designed for off-road cycling. The geometry of the mountain bike contains two triangles designed for the safety of the rider. The seat angle and the head tube angle are critical angles that affect the position of the rider and the performance of the bike. Calculate the interior angles of the frame of the mountain bike shown.

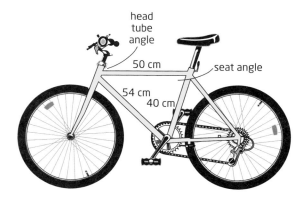

18. Distances in the throwing events at the Olympic games, traditionally measured with a tape measure, are now found with a piece of equipment called the Total Station. This instrument measures the angles and distances for events such as the shot put, the discus, and the javelin. Use the measurements shown to determine the distance, to the nearest hundredth of a metre, of the world record for the javelin throw set by Barbora Špotáková of the Czech Republic in September 2008.

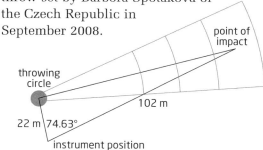

19. The Bermuda Triangle is an unmarked area in the Atlantic Ocean where there have been reports of unexplained disappearances of boats and planes and problems with radio communications. The triangle is an isosceles triangle with vertices at Miami, Florida, San Juan, Puerto Rico, and at the island of Bermuda. Miami is approximately 1660 km from both Bermuda and San Juan. If the angle formed by the sides of the triangle connecting Miami to Bermuda and Miami to San Juan is 55.5°, determine the distance from Bermuda to San Juan. Express your answer to the nearest kilometre.

20. Della Falls in Strathcona Provincial Park on Vancouver Island is the highest waterfall in Canada. A surveyor measures the angle to the top of the falls to be 61°. He then moves in a direct line toward the falls a distance of 92 m. From this closer point, the angle to the top of the falls is 71°. Determine the height of Della Falls.

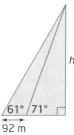

21. The floor of the Winnipeg Art Gallery is in the shape of a triangle with sides measuring 343.7 ft, 375 ft, and 200 ft. Determine the measures of the interior angles of the building.

22. Justify each step of the proof of the cosine law.

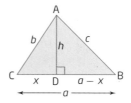

Statement	Reason
$c^2 = (a - x)^2 + h^2$	
$c^2 = a^2 - 2ax + x^2 + h^2$	
$b^2 = x^2 + h^2$	
$c^2 = a^2 - 2ax + b^2$	
$\cos C = \dfrac{x}{b}$	
$x = b \cos C$	
$c^2 = a^2 - 2a(b \cos C) + b^2$	
$c^2 = a^2 + b^2 - 2ab \cos C$	

Extend

23. Two ships leave port at 4 p.m. One is headed N38°E and is travelling at 11.5 km/h. The other is travelling at 13 km/h, with heading S47°E. How far apart are the two ships at 6 p.m.?

24. Is it possible to draw a triangle with side lengths 7 cm, 8 cm, and 16 cm? Explain why or why not. What happens when you use the cosine law with these numbers?

25. The hour and minute hands of a clock have lengths of 7.5 cm and 15.2 cm, respectively. Determine the straight-line distance between the tips of the hands at 1:30 p.m., if the hour hand travels 0.5° per minute and the minute hand travels 6° per minute.

26. Graph A(−5, −4), B(8, 2), and C(2, 7) on a coordinate grid. Extend BC to intersect the y-axis at D. Find the measure of the interior angle ∠ABC and the measure of the exterior angle ∠ACD.

27. Researchers at Queen's University use a combination of genetics, bear tracks, and feces to estimate the numbers of polar bears in an area and gather information about their health, gender, size, and age. Researchers plan to set up hair traps around King William Island, Nunavut. The hair traps, which look like fences, will collect polar bear hair samples for analysis. Suppose the hair traps are set up in the form of $\triangle ABC$, where $\angle B = 40°$, $c = 40.4$ km, and $a = 45.9$ km. Determine the area of the region.

28. If the sides of a triangle have lengths 2 m, 3 m, and 4 m, what is the radius of the circle circumscribing the triangle?

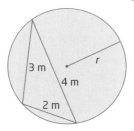

29. $\triangle ABC$ is placed on a Cartesian grid with $\angle BCA$ in standard position. Point B has coordinates $(-x, y)$. Use primary trigonometric ratios and the Pythagorean Theorem to prove the cosine law.

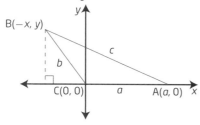

Create Connections

30. The Delta Regina Hotel is the tallest building in Saskatchewan. From the window of her room on the top floor, at a height of 70 m above the ground, Rian observes a car moving toward the hotel. If the angle of depression of the car changes from 18° to 35° during the time Rian is observing it, determine the distance the car has travelled.

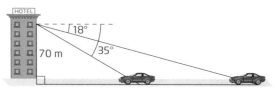

31. Given $\triangle ABC$ where $\angle C = 90°$, $a = 12.2$ cm, $b = 8.9$ cm, complete the following.

   a) Use the cosine law to find c^2.

   b) Use the Pythagorean Theorem to find c^2.

   c) Compare and contrast the cosine law with the Pythagorean Theorem.

   d) Explain why the two formulas are the same in a right triangle.

32. When solving triangles, the first step is choosing which method is best to begin with. Copy and complete the following table. Place the letter of the method beside the information given. There may be more than one answer.

   A primary trigonometric ratios

   B sine law

   C cosine law

   D none of the above

Concept Summary for Solving a Triangle	
Given	**Begin by Using the Method of**
Right triangle	
Two angles and any side	
Three sides	
Three angles	
Two sides and the included angle	
Two sides and the angle opposite one of them	

33. MINI LAB

Materials
- ruler
- protractor
- compasses

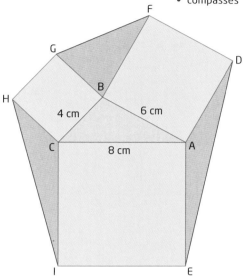

H

4 cm

6 cm

C   8 cm   A

I   E

Step 1 a) Construct △ABC with side lengths $a = 4$ cm, $b = 8$ cm, and $c = 6$ cm.

b) On each side of the triangle, construct a square.

c) Join the outside corners of the squares to form three new triangles.

Step 2 a) In △ABC, determine the measures of ∠A, ∠B, and ∠C.

b) Explain why pairs of angles, such as ∠ABC and ∠GBF, have a sum of 180°. Determine the measures of ∠GBF, ∠HCI, and ∠DAE.

c) Determine the lengths of the third sides, GF, DE, and HI, of △BGF, △ADE, and △CHI.

Step 3 For each of the four triangles, draw an altitude.

a) Use the sine ratio to determine the measure of each altitude.

b) Determine the area of each triangle.

Step 4 What do you notice about the areas of the triangles? Explain why you think this happens. Will the result be true for any △ABC?

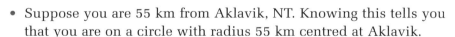

Project Corner   **Trilateration**

- GPS receivers work on the principle of trilateration. The satellites circling Earth use 3-D trilateration to pinpoint locations. You can use 2-D trilateration to see how the principle works.

- Suppose you are 55 km from Aklavik, NT. Knowing this tells you that you are on a circle with radius 55 km centred at Aklavik.

- If you also know that you are 127 km from Tuktoyuktuk, you have two circles that intersect and you must be at one of these intersection points.

- If you are told that you are 132 km from Tsiigehtchic, a third circle will intersect with one of the other two points of intersection, telling you that your location is at Inuvik.

- How can you use the method of trilateration to pinpoint the location of your resource?

If you know the angle at Inuvik, how can you determine the distance between Tuktoyuktuk and Tsiigehtchic?

Where necessary, express lengths to the nearest tenth and angles to the nearest degree.

2.1 Angles in Standard Position, pages 74–87

1. Match each term with its definition from the choices below.

a) angle in standard position

b) reference angle

c) exact value

d) sine law

e) cosine law

f) terminal arm

g) ambiguous case

A a formula that relates the lengths of the sides of a triangle to the sine values of its angles

B a value that is not an approximation and may involve a radical

C the final position of the rotating arm of an angle in standard position

D the acute angle formed by the terminal arm and the *x*-axis

E an angle whose vertex is at the origin and whose arms are the *x*-axis and the terminal arm

F a formula that relates the lengths of the sides of a triangle to the cosine value of one of its angles

G a situation that is open to two or more interpretations

2. Sketch each angle in standard position. State which quadrant the angle terminates in and the measure of the reference angle.

a) 200°

b) 130°

c) 20°

d) 330°

3. A heat lamp is placed above a patient's arm to relieve muscle pain. According to the diagram, would you consider the reference angle of the lamp to be 30°? Explain your answer.

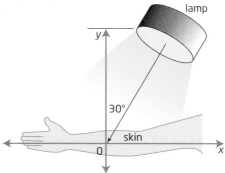

4. Explain how to determine the measure of all angles in standard position, $0° \leq \theta < 360°$, that have 35° for their reference angle.

5. Determine the exact values of the sine, cosine, and tangent ratios for each angle.

a) 225°

b) 120°

c) 330°

d) 135°

2.2 Trigonometric Ratios of Any Angle, pages 88–99

6. The point Q(−3, 6) is on the terminal arm of an angle, θ.

a) Draw this angle in standard position.

b) Determine the exact distance from the origin to point Q.

c) Determine the exact values for sin θ, cos θ, and tan θ.

d) Determine the value of θ.

7. A reference angle has a terminal arm that passes through the point P(2, −5). Identify the coordinates of a corresponding point on the terminal arm of three angles in standard position that have the same reference angle.

8. Determine the values of the primary trigonometric ratios of θ in each case.

a)

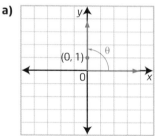

b)

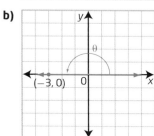

9. Determine the exact value of the other two primary trigonometric ratios given each of the following.

a) $\sin \theta = -\dfrac{3}{5}$, $\cos \theta < 0$

b) $\cos \theta = \dfrac{1}{3}$, $\tan \theta < 0$

c) $\tan \theta = \dfrac{12}{5}$, $\sin \theta > 0$

10. Solve for all values of θ, $0° \leq \theta < 360°$, given each trigonometric ratio value.

a) $\tan \theta = -1.1918$

b) $\sin \theta = -0.3420$

c) $\cos \theta = 0.3420$

2.3 The Sine Law, pages 100–113

11. Does each triangle contain sufficient information for you to determine the unknown variable using the sine law? Explain why or why not.

a) **b)**

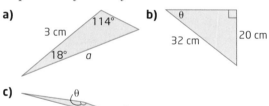

c)

12. Determine the length(s) of the indicated side(s) and the measure(s) of the indicated angle(s) in each triangle.

a) **b)**

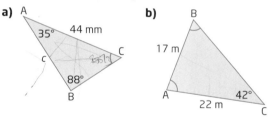

13. In △PQR, $\angle P = 63.5°$, $\angle Q = 51.2°$, and $r = 6.3$ cm. Sketch a diagram and find the measures of the unknown sides and angle.

14. In travelling to Jasper from Edmonton, you notice a mountain directly in front of you. The angle of elevation to the peak is 4.1°. When you are 21 km closer to the mountain, the angle of elevation is 8.7°. Determine the approximate height of the mountain.

15. Sarah runs a deep-sea-fishing charter. On one of her expeditions, she has travelled 40 km from port when engine trouble occurs. There are two Search and Rescue (SAR) ships, as shown below.

a) Which ship is closer to Sarah? Use the sine law to determine her distance from that ship.

b) Verify your answer in part a) by using primary trigonometric ratios.

16. Given the measure of ∠A and the length of side b in △ABC, explain the restrictions on the lengths of sides a and b for the problem to have no solution, one solution, and two solutions.

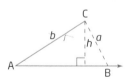

17. A passenger jet is at cruising altitude heading east at 720 km/h. The pilot, wishing to avoid a thunderstorm, changes course by heading N70°E. The plane travels in this direction for 1 h, before turning to head toward the original path. After 30 min, the jet makes another turn onto its original path.

a) Sketch a diagram to represent the distances travelled by the jet to avoid the thunderstorm.

b) What heading, east of south, did the plane take, after avoiding the storm, to head back toward the original flight path?

c) At what distance, east of the point where it changed course, did the jet resume its original path?

2.4 The Cosine Law, pages 114–125

18. Explain why each set of information does not describe a triangle that can be solved.

a) $a = 7$, $b = 2$, $c = 4$

b) $\angle A = 85°$, $b = 10$, $\angle C = 98°$

c) $a = 12$, $b = 20$, $c = 8$

d) $\angle A = 65°$, $\angle B = 82°$, $\angle C = 35°$

19. Would you use the sine law or the cosine law to find each indicated side length? Explain your reasoning.

a)

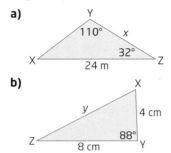

b)

20. Determine the value of the indicated variable.

a)

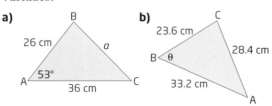

b)

21. The 12th hole at a golf course is a 375-yd straightaway par 4. When Darla tees off, the ball travels 20° to the left of the line from the tee to the hole. The ball stops 240 yd from the tee (point B). Determine how far the ball is from the centre of the hole.

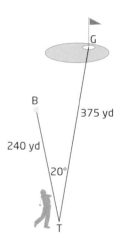

22. Sketch a diagram of each triangle and solve for the indicated value(s).

a) In △ABC, AB = 18.4 m, BC = 9.6 m, and AC = 10.8 m. Determine the measure of ∠A.

b) In △ABC, AC = 10 cm, BC = 9 cm, and ∠C = 48°. Determine the length of AB.

c) Solve △ABC, given that AB = 15 m, BC = 8 m, and ∠B = 24°.

23. Two boats leave a dock at the same time. Each travels in a straight line but in different directions. The angle between their courses measures 54°. One boat travels at 48 km/h and the other travels at 53.6 km/h.

a) Sketch a diagram to represent the situation.

b) How far apart are the two boats after 4 h?

24. The sides of a parallelogram are 4 cm and 6 cm in length. One angle of the parallelogram is 58° and a second angle is 122°.

a) Sketch a diagram to show the given information.

b) Determine the lengths of the two diagonals of the parallelogram.

Multiple Choice

For #1 to #5, choose the best answer.

1. Which angle in standard position has a different reference angle than all the others?

   A 125° **B** 155°

   C 205° **D** 335°

2. Which angle in standard position does not have a reference angle of 55°?

   A 35° **B** 125°

   C 235° **D** 305°

3. Which is the exact value of cos 150°?

   A $\dfrac{1}{2}$ **B** $\dfrac{\sqrt{3}}{2}$

   C $-\dfrac{\sqrt{3}}{2}$ **D** $-\dfrac{1}{2}$

4. The equation that could be used to determine the measure of angle θ is

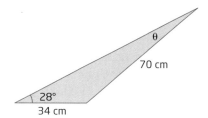

   A $\dfrac{\sin \theta}{70} = \dfrac{\sin 28°}{34}$

   B $\dfrac{\sin \theta}{34} = \dfrac{\sin 28°}{70}$

   C $\cos \theta = \dfrac{70^2 + 34^2 - 28^2}{2(70)(34)}$

   D $\theta^2 = 34^2 + 70^2 - 2(34)(70)\cos 28°$

5. For which of these triangles must you consider the ambiguous case?

   A In $\triangle ABC$, $a = 16$ cm, $b = 12$ cm, and $c = 5$ cm.

   B In $\triangle DEF$, $\angle D = 112°$, $e = 110$ km, and $f = 65$ km.

   C In $\triangle ABC$, $\angle B = 35°$, $a = 27$ m, and $b = 21$ m.

   D In $\triangle DEF$, $\angle D = 108°$, $\angle E = 52°$, and $f = 15$ cm.

Short Answer

6. The point P(2, b) is on the terminal arm of an angle, θ, in standard position. If $\cos \theta = \dfrac{1}{\sqrt{10}}$ and tan θ is negative, what is the value of b?

7. Oak Bay in Victoria, is in the direction of N57°E from Ross Bay. A sailboat leaves Ross Bay in the direction of N79°E. After sailing for 1.9 km, the sailboat turns and travels 1.1 km to reach Oak Bay.

   a) Sketch a diagram to represent the situation.

   b) What is the distance between Ross Bay and Oak Bay?

8. In $\triangle ABC$, $a = 10$, $b = 16$, and $\angle A = 30°$.

   a) How many distinct triangles can be drawn given these measurements?

   b) Determine the unknown measures in $\triangle ABC$.

9. Rudy is 20 ft from each goal post when he shoots the puck along the ice toward the goal. The goal is 6 ft wide. Within what angle must he fire the puck to have a hope of scoring a goal?

10. In $\triangle PQR$, $\angle P = 56°$, $p = 10$ cm, and $q = 12$ cm.

    a) Sketch a diagram of the triangle.

    b) Determine the length of the unknown side and the measures of the unknown angles.

11. In △ABC, M is a point on BC such that BM = 5 cm and MC = 6 cm. If AM = 3 cm and AB = 7 cm, determine the length of AC.

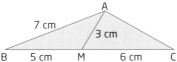

12. A fence that is 1.4 m tall has started to lean and now makes an angle of 80° with the ground. A 2.0-m board is jammed between the top of the fence and the ground to prop the fence up.

a) What angle, to the nearest degree, does the board make with the ground?

b) What angle, to the nearest degree, does the board make with the top of the fence?

c) How far, to the nearest tenth of a metre, is the bottom of the board from the base of the fence?

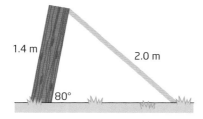

Extended Response

13. Explain, using examples, how to determine all angles $0° \leq \theta < 360°$ with a given reference angle θ_R.

14. A softball diamond is a square measuring 70 ft on each side, with home plate and the three bases as vertices. The centre of the pitcher's mound is located 50 ft from home plate on a direct line from home to second base.

a) Sketch a diagram to represent the given information.

b) Show that first base and second base are not the same distance from the pitcher's mound.

15. Describe when to use the sine law and when to use the cosine law to solve a given problem.

16. As part of her landscaping course at the Northern Alberta Institute of Technology, Justine spends a summer redesigning her aunt's backyard. She chooses triangular shapes for her theme. Justine knows some of the measurements she needs in her design. Determine the unknown side lengths in each triangle.

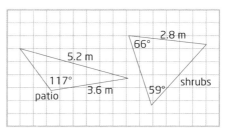

17. The North Shore Rescue (NSR) is a mountain search and rescue team based in Vancouver. On one of their training exercises, the team splits up into two groups. From their starting point, the groups head off at an angle of 129° to each other. The Alpha group walks east for 3.8 km before losing radio contact with the Beta group. If their two-way radios have a range of 6.2 km, how far could the Beta group walk before losing radio contact with the Alpha group?

Canada's Natural Resources

The emphasis of the Chapter 2 Task is the location of your resource. You will describe the route of discovery of the resource and the planned area of the resource.

Chapter 2 Task

The Journey to Locate the Resource

- Use the map provided. Include a brief log of the journey leading to your discovery. The exploration map is the route that you followed to discover your chosen resource.

- With your exploration map, determine the total distance of your route, to the nearest tenth of a kilometre. Begin your journey at point A and conclude at point J. Include the height of the Sawback Ridge and the width of Crow River in your calculations.

Developing the Area of Your Planned Resource

- Your job as a resource development officer for the company is to present a possible area of development. You are restricted by land boundaries to the triangular shape shown, with side AB of 3.9 km, side AC of 3.4 km, and ∠B = 60°.

- Determine all measures of the triangular region that your company could develop.

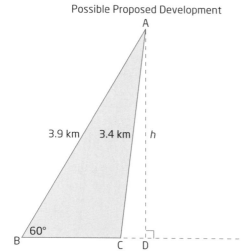

Possible Proposed Development

Web Link

To obtain a copy of an exploration map, go to www.mhrprecalc11.ca and follow the links.

Canada's Natural Resources

You need investment capital to develop your resource. Prepare a presentation to make to your investors to encourage them to invest in your project. You can use a written or visual presentation, a brochure, a video production, a computer slide show presentation, or an interactive whiteboard presentation.

Your presentation should include the following:

- Actual data taken from Canadian sources on the production of your chosen resource. Use sequences and series to show how production has increased or decreased over time, and to predict future production and sales.

- A fictitious account of a recent discovery of your resource, including a map of the area showing the accompanying distances.

- A proposal for how the resource area will be developed over the next few years

Chapter 1 Sequences and Series

1. Match each term to the correct expression.

   a) arithmetic sequence

   b) geometric sequence

   c) arithmetic series

   d) geometric series

   e) convergent series

   A 3, 7, 11, 15, 19, …

   B $5 + 1 + \frac{1}{5} + \frac{1}{25} + \cdots$

   C $1 + 2 + 4 + 8 + 16 + \cdots$

   D 1, 3, 9, 27, 81, …

   E $2 + 5 + 8 + 11 + 14 + \cdots$

2. Classify each sequence as arithmetic or geometric. State the value of the common difference or common ratio. Then, write the next three terms in each sequence.

   a) 27, 18, 12, 8, …

   b) 17, 14, 11, 8, …

   c) −21, −16, −11, −6, …

   d) 3, −6, 12, −24, …

3. For each arithmetic sequence, determine the general term. Express your answer in simplified form.

   a) 18, 15, 12, 9, …

   b) $1, \frac{5}{2}, 4, \frac{11}{2}, \ldots$

4. Use the general term to determine t_{20} in the geometric sequence 2, −4, 8, −16, ….

5. a) What is S_{12} for the arithmetic series with a common difference of 3 and $t_{12} = 31$?

   b) What is S_5 for a geometric series where $t_1 = 4$ and $t_{10} = 78\ 732$?

6. Phytoplankton, or algae, is a nutritional supplement used in natural health programs. Canadian Pacific Phytoplankton Ltd. is located in Nanaimo, British Columbia. The company can grow 10 t of marine phytoplankton on a regular 11-day cycle. Assume this cycle continues.

   a) Create a graph showing the amount of phytoplankton produced for the first five cycles of production.

   b) Write the general term for the sequence produced.

   c) How does the general term relate to the characteristics of the linear function described by the graph?

7. The Living Shangri-La is the tallest building in Metro Vancouver. The ground floor of the building is 5.8 m high, and each floor above the ground floor is 3.2 m high. There are 62 floors altogether, including the ground floor. How tall is the building?

8. Tristan and Julie are preparing a math display for the school open house. Both students create posters to debate the following question:

Does 0.999... = 1?

Julie's Poster

> **0.999... ≠ 1**
> **0.999... = 0.999 999 999 999 9...**
>
> **The decimal will continue to infinity and will never reach exactly one.**

Tristan's Poster

> **0.999... = 1**
> **Rewrite 0.999... in expanded form.**
> $$\frac{9}{10} + \frac{9}{100} + \frac{9}{1000} + \cdots$$
> **This can be written as a geometric series where** $t_1 = \frac{9}{10}$ **and** $r =$

a) Finish Tristan's poster by determining the value of the common ratio and then finding the sum of the infinite geometric series.

b) Which student do you think correctly answered the question?

Chapter 2 Trigonometry

9. Determine the exact distance, in simplified form, from the origin to a point $P(-2, 4)$ on the terminal arm of an angle.

10. Point $P(15, 8)$ is on the terminal arm of angle θ. Determine the exact values for $\sin \theta$, $\cos \theta$, and $\tan \theta$.

11. Sketch each angle in standard position and determine the measure of the reference angle.

a) 40°

b) 120°

c) 225°

d) 300°

12. The clock tower on the post office in Battleford, Saskatchewan, demonstrates the distinctive Romanesque Revival style of public buildings designed in the early decades of the twentieth century. The Battleford Post Office is similar in design to the post offices in Humboldt and Melfort. These three buildings are the only surviving post offices of this type in the Prairie Provinces.

a) What is the measure of the angle, θ, created between the hands of the clock when it reads 3 o'clock?

b) If the length of the minute hand is 2 ft, sketch a diagram to represent the clock face on a coordinate grid with the centre at the origin. Label the coordinates represented by the tip of the minute hand.

c) What are the exact values for $\sin \theta$, $\cos \theta$, and $\tan \theta$ at 3 o'clock?

Battleford post office

13. Determine the exact value of each trigonometric ratio.

a) sin 405° b) cos 330°

c) tan 225° d) cos 180°

e) tan 150° f) sin 270°

14. Radio collars are used to track polar bears by sending signals via GPS to receiving stations. Two receiving stations are 9 km apart along a straight road. At station A, the signal from one of the collars comes from a direction of 49° from the road. At station B, the signal from the same collar comes from a direction of 65° from the road. Determine the distance the polar bear is from each of the stations.

15. The Arctic Wind Riders is a program developed to introduce youth in the communities of Northern Canada to the unique sport of Paraski. This sport allows participants to sail over frozen bays, rivers, and snowy tundra using wind power. The program has been offered to close to 700 students and young adults. A typical Paraski is shown below. Determine the measure of angle θ, to the nearest tenth of a degree.

16. Waterton Lakes National Park in Alberta is a popular site for birdwatching, with over 250 species of birds recorded. Chelsea spots a rare pileated woodpecker in a tree at an angle of elevation of 52°. After walking 16 m closer to the tree, she determines the new angle of elevation to be 70°.

a) Sketch and label a diagram to represent the situation.

b) What is the closest distance that Chelsea is from the bird, to the nearest tenth of a metre?

17. In △RST, RT = 2 m, ST = 1.4 m, and ∠R = 30°. Determine the measure of obtuse ∠S to the nearest tenth of a degree.

4.88 m

29.85 m

29.85 m

θ

Clara Akulukjuk, Pangnirtung, Nunavut, learning to Paraski.

Unit 1 Test

Multiple Choice

For #1 to #5, choose the best answer.

1. Which of the following expressions could represent the general term of the sequence 8, 4, 0, …?

   A $t_n = 8 + (n - 1)4$

   B $t_n = 8 - (n - 1)4$

   C $t_n = 4n + 4$

   D $t_n = 8(-2)^{n-1}$

2. The expression for the 14th term of the geometric sequence $x, x^3, x^5, …$ is

   A x^{13}

   B x^{14}

   C x^{27}

   D x^{29}

3. The sum of the series $6 + 18 + 54 + \cdots$ to n terms is 2184. How many terms are in the series?

   A 5

   B 7

   C 8

   D 6

4. Which angle has a reference angle of 55°?

   A 35°

   B 135°

   C 235°

   D 255°

5. Given the point $P(x, \sqrt{5})$ on the terminal arm of angle θ, where $\sin \theta = \dfrac{\sqrt{5}}{5}$ and $90° \le \theta \le 180°$, what is the exact value of $\cos \theta$?

   A $\dfrac{3}{5}$

   B $-\dfrac{3}{\sqrt{5}}$

   C $\dfrac{2}{\sqrt{5}}$

   D $-\dfrac{2\sqrt{5}}{5}$

Numerical Response

Complete the statements in #6 to #8.

6. A coffee shop is holding its annual fundraiser to help send a local child to summer camp. The coffee shop plans to donate a portion of the profit for every cup of coffee served. At the beginning of the day, the owner buys the first cup of coffee and donates $20 to the fundraiser. If the coffee shop regularly serves another 2200 cups of coffee in one day, they must collect $■ per cup to raise $350.

7. An angle of 315° drawn in standard position has a reference angle of ■°.

8. The terminal arm of an angle, θ, in standard position lies in quadrant IV, and it is known that $\sin \theta = -\dfrac{\sqrt{3}}{2}$. The measure of θ is ■.

Written Response

9. Jacques Chenier is one of Manitoba's premier children's entertainers. Jacques was a Juno Award Nominee for his album *Walking in the Sun*. He has performed in over 600 school fairs and festivals across the country. Suppose there were 150 people in the audience for his first performance. If this number increased by 5 for each of the next 14 performances, what total number of people attended the first 15 of Jacques Chenier's performances?

10. The third term in an arithmetic sequence is 4 and the seventh term in the sequence is 24.

    a) Determine the value of the common difference.

    b) What is the value of t_1?

    c) Write the general term of the sequence.

    d) What is the sum of the first 10 terms of the corresponding series?

11. A new car that is worth $35 000 depreciates 20% in the first year and 10% every year after that. About how much will the car be worth 7 years after it is purchased?

12. The Multiple Sclerosis Walk is a significant contributor to the Multiple Sclerosis Society's fundraising efforts to support research. One walker was sponsored $100 plus $5 for the first kilometre, $10 for the second kilometre, $15 for the third kilometre, and so on. How far would this walker need to walk to earn $150?

13. Les Jeux de la Francophonie Canadienne are held each summer to celebrate sport, leadership, and French culture. Badminton is one of the popular events at the games. There are 64 entrants in the boys' singles tournament. There are two players per game, and only the winner advances to the next round. The number of players in each round models a geometric sequence.

a) Write the first four terms of the geometric sequence.

b) Write the general term that could be used to determine the number of players in any round of the tournament.

c) How many games must be played altogether to determine the winner of the boys' singles tournament?

14. A right triangle with a reference angle of 60° is drawn in standard position on a coordinate grid.

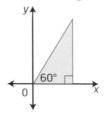

a) Apply consecutive rotations of 60° counterclockwise to complete one 360° revolution about the origin.

b) Write the sequence that represents the measures of the angles in standard position formed by the rotations.

c) Write the general term for the sequence.

15. A circular water sprinkler in a backyard sprays a radius of 5 m. The sprinkler is placed 8 m from the corner of the lot.

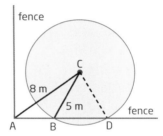

a) If the measure of ∠CAB is 32°, what is the measure of ∠CDA?

b) What length of fence, to the nearest tenth of a metre, would get wet from the sprinkler?

16. A triangle has sides that measure 61 cm, 38 cm, and 43 cm. Determine the measure of the smallest angle in the triangle.

Unit 2

Quadratics

Quadratic functions and their applications can model a large part of the world around us. Consider the path of a basketball after it leaves the shooter's hand. Think about how experts determine when and where the explosive shells used in avalanche control will land, as they attempt to make snowy areas safe for everyone. Why do satellite dishes and suspension bridges have the particular shapes that they do? You can model these and many other everyday situations mathematically with quadratic functions. In this unit, you will investigate the nature of quadratic equations and quadratic functions. You will also apply them to model real-world situations and solve problems.

Looking Ahead

In this unit, you will solve problems involving...

- equations and graphs of quadratic functions
- quadratic equations

Unit 2 Project — Quadratic Functions in Everyday Life

In this project, you will explore quadratic functions that occur in everyday life such as sports, science, art, architecture, and nature.

In Chapter 3, you will find information and make notes about quadratic functions in familiar situations. In Chapter 4, you will focus specifically on the subject of avalanche control.

At the end of the unit, you will choose between two options:
• You may choose to examine real-world situations that you can model using quadratic functions. For this option, you will mathematically determine the accuracy of your model. You will also investigate reasons for the quadratic nature of the situation.
• You may choose to apply the skills you have learned in this unit to the subject of projectile motion and the use of mathematics in avalanche control.

For either option, you will showcase what you have learned about quadratic relationships by modelling and analysing real situations involving quadratic functions or equations. You will also prepare a written summary of your observations.

CHAPTER 3

Quadratic Functions

Digital images are everywhere—on computer screens, digital cameras, televisions, mobile phones, and more. Digital images are composed of many individual *pixels*, or *picture elements*. Each pixel is a single dot or square of colour. The total number of pixels in a two-dimensional image is related to its dimensions. The more pixels an image has, the greater the quality of the image and the higher the resolution.

If the image is a square with a side length of x pixels, then you can represent the total number of pixels, p, by the function $p(x) = x^2$. This is the simplest example of a quadratic function. The word *quadratic* comes from the word *quadratum*, a Latin word meaning *square*. The term *quadratic* is used because a term like x^2 represents the area of a square of side length x.

Quadratic functions occur in a wide variety of real-world situations. In this chapter, you will investigate quadratic functions and use them in mathematical modelling and problem solving.

Did You Know?

The word *pixel* comes from combining *pix* for picture and *el* for element.

The term *megapixel* is used to refer to one million pixels. Possible dimensions for a one-megapixel image could be 1000 pixels by 1000 pixels or 800 pixels by 1250 pixels—in both cases the total number of pixels is 1 million. Digital cameras often give a value in megapixels to indicate the maximum resolution of an image.

1000 pixels

1 000 000 pixels
or
1 megapixel

1000 pixels

Key Terms

quadratic function
parabola
vertex (of a parabola)
minimum value
maximum value
axis of symmetry

vertex form (of a
  quadratic function)
standard form (of a
  quadratic function)
completing the square

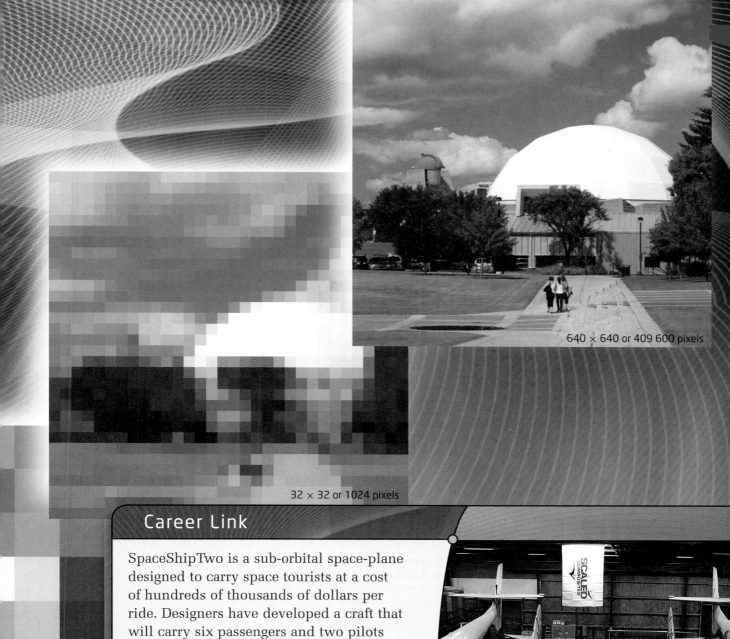

640 × 640 or 409 600 pixels

32 × 32 or 1024 pixels

8 × 8 or 64 pixels

Career Link

SpaceShipTwo is a sub-orbital space-plane designed to carry space tourists at a cost of hundreds of thousands of dollars per ride. Designers have developed a craft that will carry six passengers and two pilots to a height of 110 km above Earth and reach speeds of 4200 km/h. Engineers use quadratic functions to optimize the vehicle's storage capacity, create re-entry simulations, and help develop the structural design of the space-plane itself. Flights are due to begin no earlier than 2011.

Web Link

To learn more about aerospace design, go to www.mhrprecalc11.ca and follow the links.

Investigating Quadratic Functions in Vertex Form

Focus on...

• identifying quadratic functions in vertex form
• determining the effect of a, p, and q on the graph of $y = a(x - p)^2 + q$
• analysing and graphing quadratic functions using transformations

The Bonneville Salt Flats is a large area in Utah, in the United States, that is a remnant of an ancient lake from glacial times. The surface is extremely flat, smooth, and hard, making it an ideal place for researchers, racing enthusiasts, and automakers to test high-speed vehicles in a safer manner than on a paved track. Recently, the salt flats have become the site of an annual time-trial event for alternative-fuel vehicles. At the 2007 event, one major automaker achieved a top speed of 335 km/h with a hydrogen-powered fuel-cell car, the highest-ever recorded land speed at the time for any fuel-cell-powered vehicle.

Suppose three vehicles are involved in speed tests. The first sits waiting at the start line in one test lane, while a second sits 200 m ahead in a second test lane. These two cars start accelerating constantly at the same time. The third car leaves 5 s later from the start line in a third lane.

The graph shows a function for the distance travelled from the start line for each of the three vehicles. How are the algebraic forms of these functions related to each other?

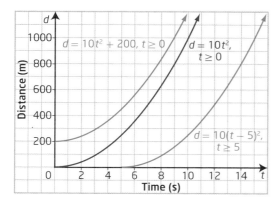

Did You Know?

The fuel cells used in this vehicle are manufactured by Ballard Power Systems, based in Burnaby, British Columbia. They have been developing hydrogen fuel cells for over 20 years.

Web Link

For more information about the Bonneville Salt Flats and about fuel-cell-powered vehicles, go to www.mhrprecalc11.ca and follow the links.

Part A: Compare the Graphs of $f(x) = x^2$ and $f(x) = ax^2$, $a \neq 0$

1. a) Graph the following functions on the same set of coordinate axes, with or without technology.

$f(x) = x^2$
$f(x) = 2x^2$
$f(x) = \frac{1}{2}x^2$

$f(x) = -x^2$
$f(x) = -2x^2$
$f(x) = -\frac{1}{2}x^2$

b) Describe how the graph of each function compares to the graph of $f(x) = x^2$, using terms such as *narrower*, *wider*, and *reflection*.

c) What relationship do you observe between the parameter, a, and the shape of the corresponding graph?

2. a) Using a variety of values of a, write several of your own functions of the form $f(x) = ax^2$. Include both positive and negative values.

b) Predict how the graphs of these functions will compare to the graph of $f(x) = x^2$. Test your prediction.

Reflect and Respond

3. Develop a rule that describes how the value of a in $f(x) = ax^2$ changes the graph of $f(x) = x^2$ when a is

a) a positive number greater than 1

b) a positive number less than 1

c) a negative number

Part B: Compare the Graphs of $f(x) = x^2$ and $f(x) = x^2 + q$

4. a) Graph the following functions on the same set of coordinate axes, with or without technology.

$f(x) = x^2$
$f(x) = x^2 + 4$
$f(x) = x^2 - 3$

b) Describe how the graph of each function compares to the graph of $f(x) = x^2$.

c) What relationship do you observe between the parameter, q, and the location of the corresponding graph?

5. a) Using a variety of values of q, write several of your own functions of the form $f(x) = x^2 + q$. Include both positive and negative values.

b) Predict how these functions will compare to $f(x) = x^2$. Test your prediction.

Reflect and Respond

6. Develop a rule that describes how the value of q in $f(x) = x^2 + q$ changes the graph of $f(x) = x^2$ when q is

a) a positive number   **b)** a negative number

Materials

- grid paper or graphing technology

Part C: Compare the Graphs of $f(x) = x^2$ and $f(x) = (x - p)^2$

7. a) Graph the following functions on the same set of coordinate axes, with or without technology.

$f(x) = x^2$
$f(x) = (x - 2)^2$
$f(x) = (x + 1)^2$

b) Describe how the graph of each function compares to the graph of $f(x) = x^2$.

c) What relationship do you observe between the parameter, p, and the location of the corresponding graph?

8. a) Using a variety of values of p, write several of your own functions of the form $f(x) = (x - p)^2$. Include both positive and negative values.

b) Predict how these functions will compare to $f(x) = x^2$. Test your prediction.

Reflect and Respond

9. Develop a rule that describes how the value of p in $f(x) = (x - p)^2$ changes the graph of $f(x) = x^2$ when p is

a) a positive number   **b)** a negative number

Link the Ideas

quadratic function

- a function f whose value $f(x)$ at x is given by a polynomial of degree two
- for example, $f(x) = x^2$ is the simplest form of a quadratic function

parabola

- the symmetrical curve of the graph of a quadratic function

vertex (of a parabola)

- the lowest point of the graph (if the graph opens upward) or the highest point of the graph (if the graph opens downward)

The graph of a **quadratic function** is a **parabola**.

When the graph opens upward, the **vertex** is the lowest point on the graph. When the graph opens downward, the vertex is the highest point on the graph.

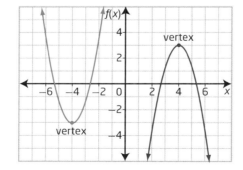

When using function notation, the values for $f(x)$ are often considered the same as the values for y.

The *y*-coordinate of the vertex is called the **minimum value** if the parabola opens upward or the **maximum value** if the parabola opens downward

The parabola is symmetric about a line called the **axis of symmetry**. This line divides the function graph into two parts so that the graph on one side is the mirror image of the graph on the other side. This means that if you know a point on one side of the parabola, you can determine a corresponding point on the other side based on the axis of symmetry.

The axis of symmetry intersects the parabola at the vertex.

The *x*-coordinate of the vertex corresponds to the equation of the axis of symmetry.

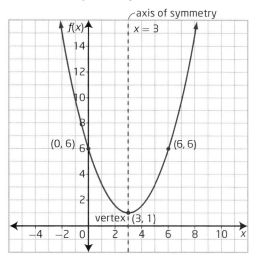

Quadratic functions written in **vertex form**, $f(x) = a(x - p)^2 + q$, are useful when graphing the function. The vertex form tells you the location of the vertex (p, q) as well as the shape of the parabola and the direction of the opening.

You can examine the parameters a, p, and q to determine information about the graph.

minimum value (of a function)

• the least value in the range of a function

• for a quadratic function that opens upward, the *y*-coordinate of the vertex

maximum value (of a function)

• the greatest value in the range of a function

• for a quadratic function that opens downward, the *y*-coordinate of the vertex

axis of symmetry

• a line through the vertex that divides the graph of a quadratic function into two congruent halves

• the *x*-coordinate of the vertex defines the equation of the axis of symmetry

vertex form (of a quadratic function)

• the form $y = a(x - p)^2 + q$, or $f(x) = a(x - p)^2 + q$, where a, p, and q are constants and $a \neq 0$

The Effect of Parameter a in $f(x) = ax^2$ on the Graph of $f(x) = x^2$

Consider the graphs of the following functions:

$f(x) = x^2$

$f(x) = 0.5x^2$ The parabola is wider in relation to the y-axis than $f(x) = x^2$ and opens upward.

$f(x) = -3x^2$ The parabola is narrower in relation to the y-axis than $f(x) = x^2$ and opens downward.

- Parameter a determines the orientation and shape of the parabola.
- The graph opens upward if $a > 0$ and downward if $a < 0$.
- If $-1 < a < 1$, the parabola is wider compared to the graph of $f(x) = x^2$.
- If $a > 1$ or $a < -1$, the parabola is narrower compared to the graph of $f(x) = x^2$.

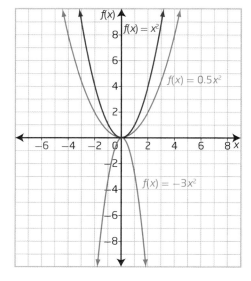

The Effect of Parameter q in $f(x) = x^2 + q$ on the Graph of $f(x) = x^2$

Consider the graphs of the following functions:

$f(x) = x^2$

$f(x) = x^2 + 5$ The graph is translated 5 units up.

$f(x) = x^2 - 4$ The graph is translated 4 units down.

- Parameter q translates the parabola vertically q units relative to the graph of $f(x) = x^2$.
- The y-coordinate of the parabola's vertex is q.

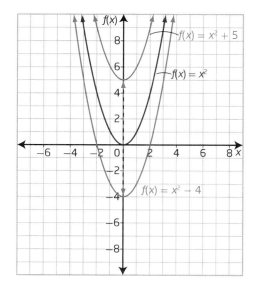

The Effect of Parameter p in $f(x) = (x - p)^2$ on the Graph of $f(x) = x^2$

Consider the graphs of the following functions:

$f(x) = x^2$

$f(x) = (x - 1)^2$ Since $p = +1$, the graph is translated 1 unit right.

$f(x) = (x + 3)^2$ Since $p = -3$, the graph is translated 3 units left.

- Parameter p translates the parabola horizontally p units relative to the graph of $f(x) = x^2$.
- The x-coordinate of the parabola's vertex is p.
- The equation of the axis of symmetry is $x - p = 0$ or $x = p$.

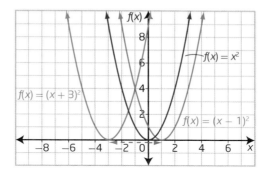

Combining Transformations

Consider the graphs of the following functions:

$f(x) = x^2$

$f(x) = -2(x - 3)^2 + 1$

- The parameter $a = -2$ determines that the parabola opens downward and is narrower than $f(x) = x^2$.
- The vertex of the parabola is located at $(3, 1)$ and represents a horizontal translation of 3 units right and a vertical translation of 1 unit up relative to the graph of $f(x) = x^2$.
- The equation of the axis of symmetry is $x - 3 = 0$ or $x = 3$.

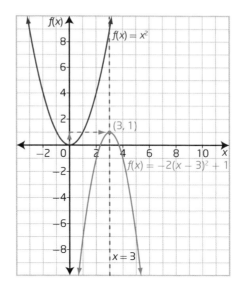

In general:
- The sign of a defines the direction of opening of the parabola. When $a > 0$, the graph opens upward, and when $a < 0$, the graph opens downward.
- The parameter a also determines how wide or narrow the graph is compared to the graph of $f(x) = x^2$.
- The point (p, q) defines the vertex of the parabola.
- The equation $x = p$ defines the axis of symmetry.

Example 1

Sketch Graphs of Quadratic Functions in Vertex Form

Determine the following characteristics for each function.
- the vertex
- the domain and range
- the direction of opening
- the equation of the axis of symmetry

Then, sketch each graph.

a) $y = 2(x + 1)^2 - 3$ **b)** $y = -\dfrac{1}{4}(x - 4)^2 + 1$

Solution

a) Use the values of a, p, and q to determine some characteristics of $y = 2(x + 1)^2 - 3$ and sketch the graph.

$$y = 2(x + 1)^2 - 3$$

$$a = 2 \qquad p = -1 \qquad q = -3$$

Since $p = -1$ and $q = -3$, the vertex is located at $(-1, -3)$.
Since $a > 0$, the graph opens upward. Since $a > 1$, the parabola is narrower compared to the graph of $y = x^2$.
Since $q = -3$, the range is $\{y \mid y \geq -3, y \in \text{R}\}$.
The domain is $\{x \mid x \in \text{R}\}$.
Since $p = -1$, the equation of the axis of symmetry is $x = -1$.

Method 1: Sketch Using Transformations
Sketch the graph of $y = 2(x + 1)^2 - 3$ by transforming the graph of $y = x^2$.
- Use the points $(0, 0)$, $(1, 1)$, and $(-1, 1)$ to sketch the graph of $y = x^2$.
- Apply the change in width.

> When using transformations to sketch the graph, you should deal with parameter a first, since its reference for wider or narrower is relative to the y-axis.

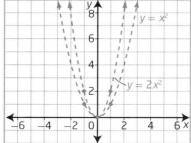

- Translate the graph.

> How are p and q related to the direction of the translations and the location of the vertex?

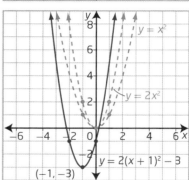

Method 2: Sketch Using Points and Symmetry
- Plot the coordinates of the vertex, $(-1, -3)$, and draw the axis of symmetry, $x = -1$.
- Determine the coordinates of one other point on the parabola.

The y-intercept is a good choice for another point.
Let $x = 0$.
$y = 2(0 + 1)^2 - 3$
$y = 2(1)^2 - 3$
$y = -1$
The point is $(0, -1)$.

For any point other than the vertex, there is a corresponding point that is equidistant from the axis of symmetry. In this case, the corresponding point for $(0, -1)$ is $(-2, -1)$.

Plot these two additional points and complete the sketch of the parabola.

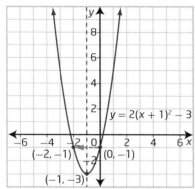

b) For the quadratic function $y = -\frac{1}{4}(x - 4)^2 + 1$, $a = -\frac{1}{4}$, $p = 4$, and $q = 1$.
The vertex is located at $(4, 1)$.
The graph opens downward and is wider than the graph $y = x^2$.
The range is $\{y \mid y \leq 1, y \in R\}$.
The domain is $\{x \mid x \in R\}$.
The equation of the axis of symmetry is $x = 4$.

Sketch the graph of $y = -\frac{1}{4}(x - 4)^2 + 1$ by using the information from the vertex form of the function.

- Plot the vertex at (4, 1).
- Determine a point on the graph. For example, determine the
  y-intercept by substituting $x = 0$ into the function.

$y = -\frac{1}{4}(0 - 4)^2 + 1$

$y = -\frac{1}{4}(-4)^2 + 1$

$y = -4 + 1$

$y = -3$

The point $(0, -3)$ is on the graph.

For any point other than the vertex, there is a corresponding point
that is equidistant from the axis of symmetry. In this case, the
corresponding point of $(0, -3)$ is $(7, -3)$.

Plot these two additional points and complete the sketch of the
parabola.

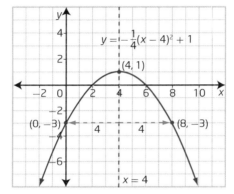

How are the values of y affected when a
is $-\frac{1}{4}$?

How are p and q related to the direction
of the translations and location of the
vertex?

How is the shape of the curve related to
the value of a?

Your Turn

Determine the following characteristics for each function.
- the vertex
- the domain and range
- the direction of opening
- the equations of the axis of symmetry

Then, sketch each graph.

a) $y = \frac{1}{2}(x - 2)^2 - 4$

b) $y = -3(x + 1)^2 + 3$

Example 2

Determine a Quadratic Function in Vertex Form Given Its Graph

Determine a quadratic function in vertex form for each graph.

a)

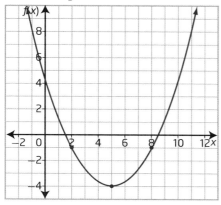

b)

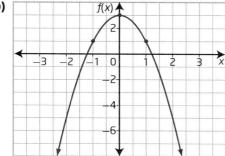

Solution

a) Method 1: Use Points and Substitution

You can determine the equation of the function using the coordinates of the vertex and one other point.

The vertex is located at $(5, -4)$, so $p = 5$ and $q = -4$. The graph opens upward, so the value of a is greater than 0.

Express the function as
$$f(x) = a(x - p)^2 + q$$
$$f(x) = a(x - 5)^2 + (-4)$$
$$f(x) = a(x - 5)^2 - 4$$

Choose one other point on the graph, such as $(2, -1)$. Substitute the values of x and y into the function and solve for a.
$$f(x) = a(x - 5)^2 - 4$$
$$-1 = a(2 - 5)^2 - 4$$
$$-1 = a(-3)^2 - 4$$
$$-1 = a(9) - 4$$
$$-1 = 9a - 4$$
$$3 = 9a$$
$$\frac{1}{3} = a$$

The quadratic function in vertex form is $f(x) = \frac{1}{3}(x - 5)^2 - 4$.

Method 2: Compare With the Graph of $f(x) = x^2$

The vertex is located at $(5, -4)$, so $p = 5$ and $q = -4$. The graph involves a translation of 5 units to the right and 4 units down.

The graph opens upward, so the value of a is greater than 0.

To determine the value of a, undo the translations and compare the vertical distances of points on the non-translated parabola relative to those on the graph of $f(x) = x^2$.

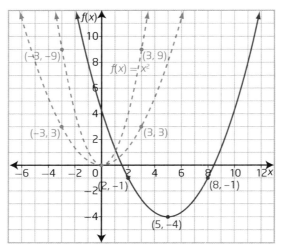

How are the y-coordinates of the corresponding points on the two parabolas with a vertex at (0, 0) related?

Since the vertical distances are one third as much, the value of a is $\frac{1}{3}$. The red graph of $f(x) = \frac{1}{3}x^2$ has been stretched vertically by a factor of $\frac{1}{3}$ compared to the graph of $f(x) = x^2$.

Substitute the values $a = \frac{1}{3}$, $p = 5$, and $q = -4$ into the vertex form, $f(x) = a(x + p)^2 + q$.

The quadratic function in vertex form is $f(x) = \frac{1}{3}(x - 5)^2 - 4$.

b) You can determine the equation of the function using the coordinates of the vertex and one other point.

The vertex is located at $(0, 3)$, so $p = 0$ and $q = 3$. The graph opens downward, so the value of a is less than 0.

Express the function as
$$f(x) = a(x - p)^2 + q$$
$$f(x) = a(x - 0)^2 + 3$$
$$f(x) = ax^2 + 3$$

Choose one other point on the graph, such as $(1, 1)$. Substitute the values of x and y into the function and solve for a.
$$f(x) = ax^2 + 3$$
$$1 = a(1)^2 + 3$$
$$1 = a + 3$$
$$-2 = a$$

The quadratic function in vertex form is $f(x) = -2x^2 + 3$.

Your Turn

Determine a quadratic function in vertex form for each graph.

a)

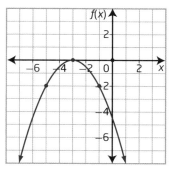

b)

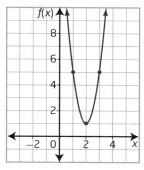

Example 3

Determine the Number of x-Intercepts Using *a* and *q*

Determine the number of x-intercepts for each quadratic function.

a) $f(x) = 0.8x^2 - 3$ **b)** $f(x) = 2(x - 1)^2$ **c)** $f(x) = -3(x + 2)^2 - 1$

Solution

You can determine the number of x-intercepts if you know the location of the vertex and direction of opening. Visualize the general position and shape of the graph based on the values of *a* and *q*.

Determine the number of x-intercepts a quadratic function has by examining
- the value of *a* to determine if the graph opens upward or downward
- the value of *q* to determine if the vertex is above, below, or on the x-axis

a) $f(x) = 0.8x^2 - 3$

Value of *a*	Value of *q*	Visualize the Graph	Number of x-Intercepts
$a > 0$ the graph opens upward	$q < 0$ the vertex is below the x-axis	(graph of upward parabola with vertex below x-axis)	2 crosses the x-axis *twice*, since it opens *upward* from a vertex *below* the x-axis

b) $f(x) = 2(x - 1)^2$

Value of *a*	Value of *q*	Visualize the Graph	Number of x-Intercepts
$a > 0$ the graph opens upward	$q = 0$ the vertex is on the x-axis	(graph of upward parabola with vertex on x-axis)	1 touches the x-axis *once*, since the vertex is *on* the x-axis

If you know that *q* is 0, does it matter what the value of *a* is?

Where on the parabola is the x-intercept in this case?

c) $f(x) = -3(x + 2)^2 - 1$

Value of a	Value of q	Visualize the Graph	Number of x-Intercepts
$a < 0$ the graph opens downward	$q < 0$ the vertex is below the x-axis		0 does not cross the x-axis, since it opens *down* from a vertex *below* the x-axis

Why does the value of p not affect the number of x-intercepts?

Your Turn

Determine the number of x-intercepts for each quadratic function without graphing.

a) $f(x) = 0.5x^2 - 7$ **b)** $f(x) = -2(x + 1)^2$ **c)** $f(x) = -\dfrac{1}{6}(x - 5)^2 - 11$

Example 4

Model Problems Using Quadratic Functions in Vertex Form

Did You Know?

The Lions' Gate Bridge carries over 60 000 vehicles per day on average. In 2009, the lights on the Lions' Gate Bridge were replaced with a new LED lighting system. The change is expected to reduce the power consumption on the bridge by 90% and significantly cut down on maintenance.

The deck of the Lions' Gate Bridge in Vancouver is suspended from two main cables attached to the tops of two supporting towers. Between the towers, the main cables take the shape of a parabola as they support the weight of the deck. The towers are 111 m tall relative to the water's surface and are 472 m apart. The lowest point of the cables is approximately 67 m above the water's surface.

a) Model the shape of the cables with a quadratic function in vertex form.

b) Determine the height above the surface of the water of a point on the cables that is 90 m horizontally from one of the towers. Express your answer to the nearest tenth of a metre.

Lion's Gate Bridge, Vancouver

Solution

a) Draw a diagram and label it with the given information.

Let the vertex of the parabolic shape be at the low point of the cables. Consider this point to be the origin.

Why is this point the simplest to use as the origin?

Draw a set of axes. Let x and y represent the horizontal and vertical distances from the low point of the cables, respectively.

You can write a quadratic function if you know the coordinates of the vertex and one other point. The vertex is (0, 0), since it is the origin. Determine the coordinates of the point at the top of each tower from the given distances.

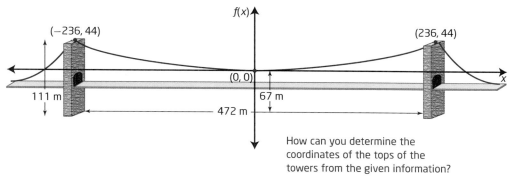

How can you determine the coordinates of the tops of the towers from the given information?

Since the vertex is located at the origin, (0, 0), no horizontal or vertical translation is necessary, and p and q are both zero. Therefore, the quadratic function is of the form $f(x) = ax^2$.

Substitute the coordinates of the top of one of the towers, (236, 44), into the equation $f(x) = ax^2$ and solve for a.

What other point could you use?

$$f(x) = ax^2$$
$$44 = a(236)^2$$
$$44 = a(55\ 696)$$
$$44 = 55\ 696a$$
$$\frac{44}{55\ 696} = a$$

a is $\dfrac{11}{13\ 924}$ in lowest terms.

Represent the shape of the cables with the following quadratic function.

$$f(x) = \frac{11}{13\ 924}x^2$$

What would the quadratic function be if the origin were placed at the water's surface directly below the lowest point of the cables?

What would it be if the origin were at water level at the base of one of the towers?

b) A point 90 m from one tower is $236 - 90$, or 146 m horizontally from the vertex. Substitute 146 for x and determine the value of $f(146)$.

$$f(x) = \frac{11}{13\ 924}x^2$$
$$f(146) = \frac{11}{13\ 924}(146)^2$$
$$= \frac{11}{13\ 924}(21\ 316)$$
$$= 16.839\ldots$$

This is approximately 16.8 m above the low point in the cables, which are approximately 67 m above the water.

The height above the water is approximately $67 + 16.8$, or 83.8 m.

Your Turn

Suppose a parabolic archway has a width of 280 cm and a height of 216 cm at its highest point above the floor.

a) Write a quadratic function in vertex form that models the shape of this archway.

b) Determine the height of the archway at a point that is 50 cm from its outer edge.

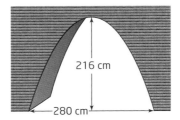

216 cm

280 cm

Key Ideas

- For a quadratic function in vertex form, $f(x) = a(x - p)^2 + q$, $a \neq 0$, the graph:
  - has the shape of a parabola
  - has its vertex at (p, q)
  - has an axis of symmetry with equation $x = p$
  - is congruent to $f(x) = ax^2$ translated horizontally by p units and vertically by q units

- Sketch the graph of $f(x) = a(x - p)^2 + q$ by transforming the graph of $f(x) = x^2$.
  - The graph opens upward if $a > 0$.
  - If $a < 0$, the parabola is reflected in the x-axis; it opens downward.
  - If $-1 < a < 1$, the parabola is wider compared to the graph of $f(x) = x^2$.
  - If $a > 1$ or $a < -1$, the parabola is narrower compared to the graph of $f(x) = x^2$.

  - The parameter q determines the vertical position of the parabola.
  - If $q > 0$, then the graph is translated q units up.
  - If $q < 0$, then the graph is translated q units down.

  - The parameter p determines the horizontal position of the parabola.
  - If $p > 0$, then the graph is translated p units to the right.
  - If $p < 0$, then the graph is translated p units to the left.

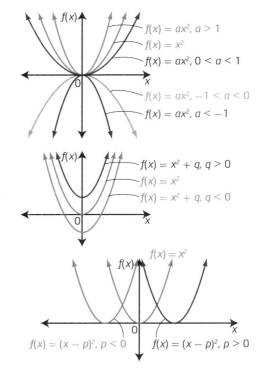

- You can determine a quadratic function in vertex form if you know the coordinates of the vertex and at least one other point.

- You can determine the number of x-intercepts of the graph of a quadratic function using the value of a to determine if the graph opens upward or downward and the value of q to determine if the vertex is above, below, or on the x-axis.

Practise

1. Describe how you can obtain the graph of each function from the graph of $f(x) = x^2$. State the direction of opening, whether it has a maximum or a minimum value, and the range for each.

   a) $f(x) = 7x^2$

   b) $f(x) = \frac{1}{6}x^2$

   c) $f(x) = -4x^2$

   d) $f(x) = -0.2x^2$

2. Describe how the graphs of the functions in each pair are related. Then, sketch the graph of the second function in each pair, and determine the vertex, the equation of the axis of symmetry, the domain and range, and any intercepts.

   a) $y = x^2$ and $y = x^2 + 1$

   b) $y = x^2$ and $y = (x - 2)^2$

   c) $y = x^2$ and $y = x^2 - 4$

   d) $y = x^2$ and $y = (x + 3)^2$

3. Describe how to sketch the graph of each function using transformations.

   a) $f(x) = (x + 5)^2 + 11$

   b) $f(x) = -3x^2 - 10$

   c) $f(x) = 5(x + 20)^2 - 21$

   d) $f(x) = -\frac{1}{8}(x - 5.6)^2 + 13.8$

4. Sketch the graph of each function. Identify the vertex, the axis of symmetry, the direction of opening, the maximum or minimum value, the domain and range, and any intercepts.

   a) $y = -(x - 3)^2 + 9$

   b) $y = 0.25(x + 4)^2 + 1$

   c) $y = -3(x - 1)^2 + 12$

   d) $y = \frac{1}{2}(x - 2)^2 - 2$

5. **a)** Write a quadratic function in vertex form for each parabola in the graph.

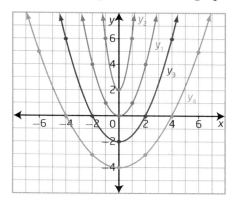

   b) Suppose four new parabolas open downward instead of upward but have the same shape and vertex as each parabola in the graph. Write a quadratic function in vertex form for each new parabola.

   c) Write the quadratic functions in vertex form of four parabolas that are identical to the four in the graph but translated 4 units to the left.

   d) Suppose the four parabolas in the graph are translated 2 units down. Write a quadratic function in vertex form for each new parabola.

6. For the function $f(x) = 5(x - 15)^2 - 100$, explain how you can identify each of the following without graphing.

   a) the coordinates of the vertex

   b) the equation of the axis of symmetry

   c) the direction of opening

   d) whether the function has a maximum or minimum value, and what that value is

   e) the domain and range

   f) the number of x-intercepts

7. Without graphing, identify the location of the vertex and the axis of symmetry, the direction of opening and the maximum or minimum value, the domain and range, and the number of x-intercepts for each function.

a) $y = -4x^2 + 14$

b) $y = (x + 18)^2 - 8$

c) $y = 6(x - 7)^2$

d) $y = -\dfrac{1}{9}(x + 4)^2 - 36$

8. Determine the quadratic function in vertex form for each parabola.

a)

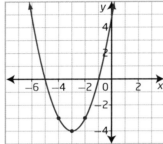

b)

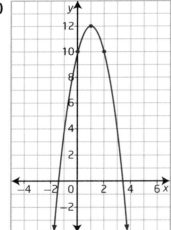

c)

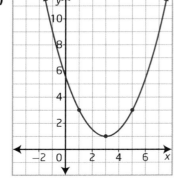

d)

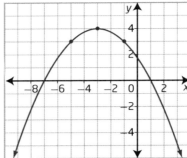

9. Determine a quadratic function in vertex form that has the given characteristics.

a) vertex at $(0, 0)$, passing through the point $(6, -9)$

b) vertex at $(0, -6)$, passing through the point $(3, 21)$

c) vertex at $(2, 5)$, passing through the point $(4, -11)$

d) vertex at $(-3, -10)$, passing through the point $(2, -5)$

Apply

10. The point $(4, 16)$ is on the graph of $f(x) = x^2$. Describe what happens to the point when each of the following sets of transformations is performed in the order listed. Identify the corresponding point on the transformed graph.

a) a horizontal translation of 5 units to the left and then a vertical translation of 8 units up

b) a multiplication of the y-values by a factor of $\dfrac{1}{4}$ and then a reflection in the x-axis

c) a reflection in the x-axis and then a horizontal translation of 10 units to the right

d) a multiplication of the y-values by a factor of 3 and then a vertical translation of 8 units down

11. Describe how to obtain the graph of $y = 20 - 5x^2$ using transformations on the graph of $y = x^2$.

12. Quadratic functions do not all have the same number of x-intercepts. Is the same true about y-intercepts? Explain.

13. A parabolic mirror was used to ignite the Olympic torch for the 2010 Winter Olympics in Vancouver and Whistler, British Columbia. Suppose its diameter is 60 cm and its depth is 30 cm.

a) Determine the quadratic function that represents its cross-sectional shape if the lowest point in the centre of the mirror is considered to be the origin, as shown.

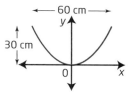

b) How would the quadratic function be different if the outer edge of the mirror were considered the origin? Explain why there is a difference.

> **Did You Know?**
>
> Before the 2010 Winter Olympics began in Vancouver and Whistler, the Olympic torch was carried over 45 000 km for 106 days through every province and territory in Canada. The torch was initially lit in Olympia, Greece, the site of the ancient Olympic Games, before beginning its journey in Canada. The flame was lit using a special bowl-shaped reflector called a parabolic mirror that focuses the Sun's rays to a single point, concentrating enough heat to ignite the torch.

14. The finance team at an advertising company is using the quadratic function $N(x) = -2.5(x - 36)^2 + 20\ 000$ to predict the effectiveness of a TV commercial for a certain product, where N is the predicted number of people who buy the product if the commercial is aired x times per week.

a) Explain how you could sketch the graph of the function, and identify its characteristics.

b) According to this model, what is the optimum number of times the commercial should be aired?

c) What is the maximum number of people that this model predicts will buy the product?

15. When two liquids that do not mix are put together in a container and rotated around a central axis, the surface created between them takes on a parabolic shape as they rotate. Suppose the diameter at the top of such a surface is 40 cm, and the maximum depth of the surface is 12 cm. Choose a location for the origin and write the function that models the cross-sectional shape of the surface.

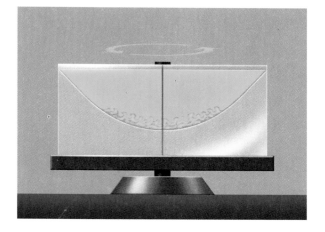

17. During a game of tennis, Natalie hits the tennis ball into the air along a parabolic trajectory. Her initial point of contact with the tennis ball is 1 m above the ground. The ball reaches a maximum height of 10 m before falling toward the ground. The ball is again 1 m above the ground when it is 22 m away from where she hit it. Write a quadratic function to represent the trajectory of the tennis ball if the origin is on the ground directly below the spot from which the ball was hit.

Did You Know?

Tennis originated from a twelfth-century French game called *jeu de paume*, meaning game of palm (of the hand). It was a court game where players hit the ball with their hands. Over time, gloves covered bare hands and, finally, racquets became the standard equipment. In 1873, Major Walter Wingfield invented a game called *sphairistike* (Greek for *playing ball*), from which modern outdoor tennis evolved.

16. The main section of the suspension bridge in Parc de la Gorge de Coaticook, Québec, has cables in the shape of a parabola. Suppose that the points on the tops of the towers where the cables are attached are 168 m apart and 24 m vertically above the minimum height of the cables.

a) Determine the quadratic function in vertex form that represents the shape of the cables. Identify the origin you used.

b) Choose two other locations for the origin. Write the corresponding quadratic function for the shape of the cables for each.

c) Use each quadratic function to determine the vertical height of the cables above the minimum at a point that is 35 m horizontally from one of the towers. Are your answers the same using each of your functions? Explain.

Did You Know?

The suspension bridge in Parc de la Gorge de Coaticook in Québec claims to be the longest pedestrian suspension bridge in the world.

18. Water is spraying from a nozzle in a fountain, forming a parabolic path as it travels through the air. The nozzle is 10 cm above the surface of the water. The water achieves a maximum height of 100 cm above the water's surface and lands in the pool. The water spray is again 10 cm above the surface of the water when it is 120 cm horizontally from the nozzle. Write the quadratic function in vertex form to represent the path of the water if the origin is at the surface of the water directly below the nozzle.

19. The function $y = x^2 + 4$ represents a translation of 4 units up, which is in the positive direction. The function $y = (x + 4)^2$ represents a translation of 4 units to the left, which is in the negative direction. How can you explain this difference?

20. In the movie, *Apollo 13*, starring Tom Hanks, scenes were filmed involving weightlessness. Weightlessness can be simulated using a plane to fly a special manoeuvre. The plane follows a specific inverted parabolic arc followed by an upward-facing recovery arc. Suppose the parabolic arc starts when the plane is at 7200 m and takes it up to 10 000 m and then back down to 7200 m again. It covers approximately 16 000 m of horizontal distance in total.

a) Determine the quadratic function that represents the shape of the parabolic path followed by the plane if the origin is at ground level directly below where the plane starts the parabolic arc.

b) Identify the domain and range in this situation.

20° Nose Low

45° Nose High

Did You Know?

Passengers can experience the feeling of *zero-g*, or weightlessness, for approximately 30 s during each inverted parabolic manoeuvre made. During the recovery arc, passengers feel almost *two-g*, or almost twice the sensation of gravity. In addition to achieving weightlessness, planes such as these are also able to fly parabolic arcs designed to simulate the gravity on the moon (one sixth of Earth's) or on Mars (one third of Earth's).

21. Determine a quadratic function in vertex form given each set of characteristics. Explain your reasoning.

a) vertex (6, 30) and a y-intercept of -24

b) minimum value of -24 and x-intercepts at -21 and -5

Extend

22. a) Write quadratic functions in vertex form that represent three different trajectories the basketball shown can follow and pass directly through the hoop without hitting the backboard.

b) Which of your three quadratic functions do you think represents the most realistic trajectory for an actual shot? Explain your thoughts.

c) What do you think are a reasonable domain and range in this situation?

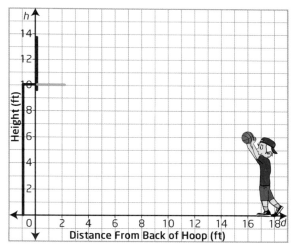

23. If the point (m, n) is on the graph of $f(x) = x^2$, determine expressions for the coordinates of the corresponding point on the graph of $f(x) = a(x - p)^2 + q$.

Create Connections

24. a) Write a quadratic function that is related to $f(x) = x^2$ by a change in width, a reflection, a horizontal translation, and a vertical translation.

b) Explain your personal strategy for accurately sketching the function.

25. Create your own specific examples of functions to explain how to determine the number of x-intercepts for quadratic functions of the form $f(x) = a(x - p)^2 + q$ without graphing.

26. MINI LAB Graphing a function like $y = -x^2 + 9$ will produce a curve that extends indefinitely. If only a portion of the curve is desired, you can state the function with a restriction on the domain. For example, to draw only the portion of the graph of $y = -x^2 + 9$ between the points where $x = -2$ and $x = 3$, write $y = -x^2 + 9$, $\{x \mid -2 \le x \le 3, x \in \mathbb{R}\}$.

Materials
- 0.5-cm grid paper

Create a line-art illustration of an object or design using quadratic and/or linear functions with restricted domains.

Step 1 Use a piece of 0.5-cm grid paper. Draw axes vertically and horizontally through the centre of the grid. Label the axes with a scale.

Step 2 Plan out a line-art drawing that you can draw using portions of the graphs of quadratic and linear functions. As you create your illustration, keep a record of the functions you use. Add appropriate restrictions to the domain to indicate the portion of the graph you want.

Step 3 Use your records to make a detailed and accurate list of instructions/ functions (including restrictions) that someone else could use to recreate your illustration.

Step 4 Trade your functions/instructions list with a partner. See if you can recreate each other's illustration using only the list as a guide.

Project Corner **Parabolic Shape**

- Many suspension bridge cables, the arches of bridges, satellite dishes, reflectors in headlights and spotlights, and other physical objects often appear to have parabolic shape.

- You can try to model a possible quadratic relationship by drawing a set of axes on an image of a physical object that appears to be quadratic in nature, and using one or more points on the curve.

- What images or objects can you find that might be quadratic?

Investigating Quadratic Functions in Standard Form

Focus on...

- identifying quadratic functions in standard form
- determining the vertex, domain and range, axis of symmetry, maximum or minimum value, and *x*-intercepts and *y*-intercept for quadratic functions in standard form
- graphing and analysing quadratic functions in applied situations

When a player kicks or punts a football into the air, it reaches a maximum height before falling back to the ground. The moment it leaves the punter's foot to the moment it is caught or hits the ground is called the *hang time* of the punt. A punter attempts to kick the football so there is a longer hang time to allow teammates to run downfield to tackle an opponent who catches the ball. The punter may think about exactly where or how far downfield the football will land. How can you mathematically model the path of a football through the air after it is punted?

Did You Know?

The Grey Cup has been the championship trophy for the Canadian Football League (CFL) since 1954. Earl Grey, the Governor General of Canada at the time, donated the trophy in 1909 for the Rugby Football Championship of Canada. Two Grey Cups won have been on the last play of the game: Saskatchewan in 1989 and Montreal in 2009.

Materials

- grid paper

Part A: Model the Path of a Football

Depending upon the situation, the punter may kick the football so that it will follow a specific path.

1. Work with a partner. Draw a coordinate grid on a sheet of grid paper. Label the x-axis as horizontal distance downfield and the y-axis as height. How do the horizontal distance and height relate to the kicking of a football?

2. On the same grid, sketch out three possible flight paths of the football.

3. Describe the shape of your graphs. Are these shapes similar to other students' graphs?

4. Describe the common characteristics of your graphs.

Reflect and Respond

5. How would you describe the maximum or minimum heights of each of your graphs?

6. Describe any type of symmetry that you see in your graphs.

7. State the domain and range for each of your graphs.

8. How do the domain and range relate to the punting of the football?

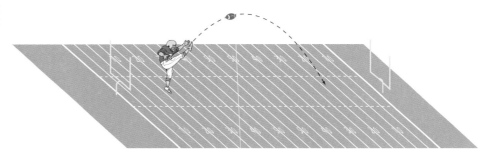

Part B: Investigate a Quadratic Function of the Form $f(x) = ax^2 + bx + c$

The path of a football through the air is just one of many real-life phenomena that can be represented by a quadratic function. A quadratic function of the form $f(x) = ax^2 + bx + c$ is written in **standard form**.

9. Using technology, graph the quadratic function $f(x) = -x^2 + 4x + 5$.

10. Describe any symmetry that the graph has.

11. Does the function have a maximum y-value? Does it have a minimum y-value? Explain.

standard form (of a quadratic function)

- the form $f(x) = ax^2 + bx + c$ or $y = ax^2 + bx + c$, where a, b, and c are real numbers and $a \neq 0$

12. Using technology, graph on a Cartesian plane the functions that result from substituting the following c-values into the function $f(x) = -x^2 + 4x + c$.

10
0
−5

13. Using technology, graph on a Cartesian plane the functions that result from substituting the following a-values into the function $f(x) = ax^2 + 4x + 5$.

−4
−2
1
2

14. Using technology, graph on a Cartesian plane the functions that result from substituting the following b-values into the function $f(x) = -x^2 + bx + 5$.

2
0
−2
−4

Reflect and Respond

15. What do your graphs show about how the function $f(x) = ax^2 + bx + c$ is affected by changing the parameter c?

16. How is the function affected when the value of a is changed? How is the graph different when a is a positive number?

17. What effect does changing the value of b have on the graph of the function?

Do any of the parameters affect the *position* of the graph?

Do any affect the *shape* of the graph?

Link the Ideas

The standard form of a quadratic function is $f(x) = ax^2 + bx + c$ or $y = ax^2 + bx + c$, where a, b, and c are real numbers with $a \neq 0$.

- a determines the shape and whether the graph opens upward (positive a) or downward (negative a)
- b influences the position of the graph
- c determines the y-intercept of the graph

You can expand $f(x) = a(x - p)^2 + q$ and compare the resulting coefficients with the standard form $f(x) = ax^2 + bx + c$, to see the relationship between the parameters of the two forms of a quadratic function.

$f(x) = a(x - p)^2 + q$
$f(x) = a(x^2 - 2xp + p^2) + q$
$f(x) = ax^2 - 2axp + ap^2 + q$
$f(x) = ax^2 + (-2ap)x + (ap^2 + q)$
$f(x) = ax^2 + bx + c$

By comparing the two forms, you can see that

$b = -2ap$ or $p = \dfrac{-b}{2a}$ and $c = ap^2 + q$ or $q = c - ap^2$.

Recall that to determine the x-coordinate of the vertex, you can use the equation $x = p$. So, the x-coordinate of the vertex is $x = -\dfrac{b}{2a}$.

Example 1

Identify Characteristics of a Quadratic Function in Standard Form

For each graph of a quadratic function, identify the following:
• the direction of opening
• the coordinates of the vertex
• the maximum or minimum value
• the equation of the axis of symmetry
• the x-intercepts and y-intercept
• the domain and range

a) $f(x) = x^2$

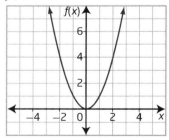

b) $f(x) = x^2 - 2x$

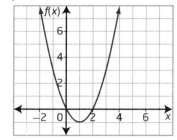

c) $f(x) = -x^2 + 2x + 8$

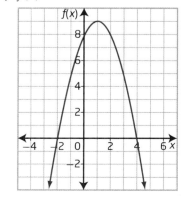

d) $f(x) = 2x^2 - 12x + 25$

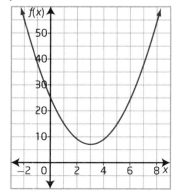

Solution

a) $f(x) = x^2$

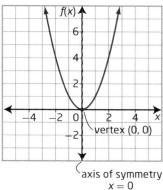

- opens upward
- vertex: (0, 0)
- minimum value of y of 0 when $x = 0$
- axis of symmetry: $x = 0$
- y-intercept occurs at (0, 0) and has a value of 0
- x-intercept occurs at (0, 0) and has a value of 0
- domain: all real numbers, or $\{x \mid x \in R\}$
- range: all real numbers greater than or equal to 0, or $\{y \mid y \geq 0, y \in R\}$

b) $f(x) = x^2 - 2x$

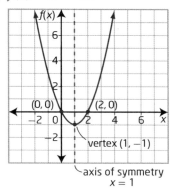

- opens upward
- vertex: (1, −1)
- minimum value of y of −1 when $x = 1$
- axis of symmetry: $x = 1$
- y-intercept occurs at (0, 0) and has a value of 0
- x-intercepts occur at (0, 0) and (2, 0) and have values of 0 and 2
- domain: all real numbers, or $\{x \mid x \in R\}$
- range: all real numbers greater than or equal to −1, or $\{y \mid y \geq -1, y \in R\}$

c) $f(x) = -x^2 + 2x + 8$

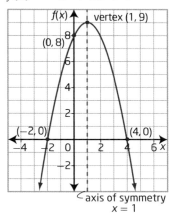

- opens downward
- vertex: (1, 9)
- maximum value of y of 9 when $x = 1$
- axis of symmetry: $x = 1$
- y-intercept occurs at (0, 8) and has a value of 8
- x-intercepts occur at (−2, 0) and (4, 0) and have values of −2 and 4
- domain: all real numbers, or $\{x \mid x \in R\}$
- range: all real numbers less than or equal to 9, or $\{y \mid y \leq 9, y \in R\}$

d) $f(x) = 2x^2 - 12x + 25$

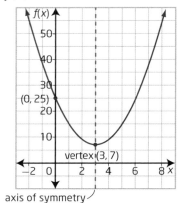

- opens upward
- vertex: $(3, 7)$
- minimum value of y of 7 when $x = 3$
- axis of symmetry: $x = 3$
- y-intercept occurs at $(0, 25)$ and has a value of 25
- no x-intercepts
- domain: all real numbers, or $\{x \mid x \in R\}$
- range: all real numbers greater than or equal to 7, or $\{y \mid y \geq 7, y \in R\}$

Your Turn

For each quadratic function, identify the following:
- the direction of opening
- the coordinates of the vertex
- the maximum or minimum value
- the equation of the axis of symmetry
- the x-intercepts and y-intercept
- the domain and range

a) $y = x^2 + 6x + 5$

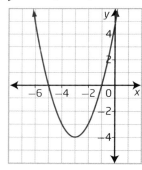

b) $y = -x^2 + 2x + 3$

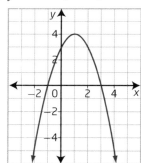

Example 2

Analysing a Quadratic Function

A frog sitting on a rock jumps into a pond. The height, h, in centimetres, of the frog above the surface of the water as a function of time, t, in seconds, since it jumped can be modelled by the function $h(t) = -490t^2 + 150t + 25$. Where appropriate, answer the following questions to the nearest tenth.

a) Graph the function.

b) What is the y-intercept? What does it represent in this situation?

c) What maximum height does the frog reach? When does it reach that height?

d) When does the frog hit the surface of the water?

e) What are the domain and range in this situation?

f) How high is the frog 0.25 s after it jumps?

Solution

a) Method 1: Use a Graphing Calculator

Enter the function and adjust the dimensions of the graph until the vertex and intercepts are visible.

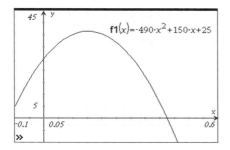

Why is it not necessary to show the negative x-intercept?

The shape of the graph might appear to resemble the path the frog follows through the air, but it is important to realize that the graph compares height to time rather than height to horizontal distance.

Method 2: Use a Spreadsheet

You can generate a table of values using a spreadsheet. From these values, you can create a graph.

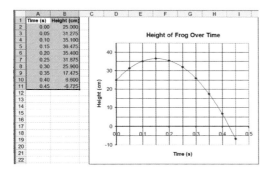

How is the pattern in the heights connected to shape of the graph?

b) The graph shows that the y-intercept is 25. This is the value of h at $t = 0$. It represents the initial height, 25 cm, from which the frog jumped.

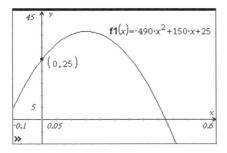

The y-intercept of the graph of $h(t) = -490t^2 + 150t + 25$ is equal to the value of the constant term, 25.

c) The coordinates of the vertex represent the time and height of the frog at its maximum point during the jump. The graph shows that after approximately 0.2 s, the frog achieves a maximum height of approximately 36.5 cm.

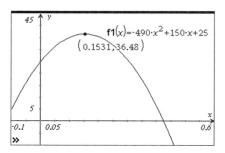

d) The positive x-intercept represents the time at which the height is 0 cm, or when the frog hits the water. The graph shows that the frog hits the water after approximately 0.4 s.

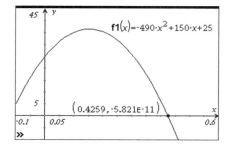

e) The domain is the set of all possible values of the independent variable, or time.

The range is the set of all possible values of the dependent variable, or height.

The values of time and height cannot be negative in this situation.

The domain is the set of all real numbers from 0 to approximately 0.4, or $\{t \mid 0 \leq t \leq 0.4, t \in \mathbb{R}\}$.

The range is the set of all real numbers from 0 to approximately 36.5, or $\{h \mid 0 \leq h \leq 36.5, h \in \mathbb{R}\}$.

f) The height of the frog after 0.25 s is the h-coordinate when t is 0.25. The graph shows that after 0.25 s, the height of the frog is approximately 31.9 cm.

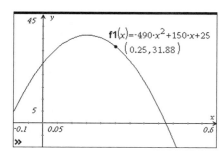

You can also determine the height after 0.25 s by substituting 0.25 for t in $h(t) = -490t^2 + 150t + 25$.

$$h(t) = -490t^2 + 150t + 25$$
$$h(0.25) = -490(0.25)^2 + 150(0.25) + 25$$
$$h(0.25) = -30.625 + 37.5 + 25$$
$$h(0.25) = 31.875$$

The height of the frog after 0.25 s is approximately 31.9 cm.

Your Turn

A diver jumps from a 3-m springboard with an initial vertical velocity of 6.8 m/s. Her height, h, in metres, above the water t seconds after leaving the diving board can be modelled by the function $h(t) = -4.9t^2 + 6.8t + 3$.

a) Graph the function.
b) What does the y-intercept represent?
c) What maximum height does the diver reach? When does she reach that height?
d) How long does it take before the diver hits the water?
e) What domain and range are appropriate in this situation?
f) What is the height of the diver 0.6 s after leaving the board?

Example 3

Write a Quadratic Function to Model a Situation

A rancher has 100 m of fencing available to build a rectangular corral.

a) Write a quadratic function in standard form to represent the area of the corral.
b) What are the coordinates of the vertex? What does the vertex represent in this situation?
c) Sketch the graph for the function you determined in part a).
d) Determine the domain and range for this situation.
e) Identify any assumptions you made in modelling this situation mathematically.

Solution

a) Let l represent the length, w represent the width, and A represent the area of the corral.

$A = lw$ w

The formula $A = lw$ has three variables. To create a function for the area in terms of the width alone, you can use an expression for the length in terms of the width to eliminate the length. The formula for the perimeter of the corral is $P = 2l + 2w$, which gives the equation $2l + 2w = 100$. Solving for l gives $l = 50 - w$.

$A = lw$
$A = (50 - w)(w)$
$A = 50w - w^2$

$A = 50w - w^2$ w

How could you write a similar function using the length instead of the width?

$50 - w$

b) Use the equation $x = p$ to determine the x-coordinate of the vertex.

$$x = \frac{-b}{2a}$$

$$x = \frac{-50}{2(-1)}$$

$$x = 25$$

Substitute the x-coordinate of the vertex into the function to determine the y-coordinate.

$$y = 50x - x^2$$
$$y = 50(25) - (25)^2$$
$$y = 625$$

The vertex is located at (25, 625). The y-coordinate of the vertex represents the maximum area of the rectangle. The x-coordinate represents the width when this occurs.

c) For the function $f(x) = 50x - x^2$, the y-intercept is the point (0, 0). Using the axis of symmetry, a point symmetric to the y-intercept is (50, 0). Sketch the parabola through these points and the vertex (25, 625).

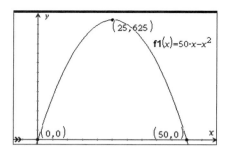

d) Negative widths, lengths, and areas do not have any meaning in this situation, so the domain and range are restricted.

The width is any real number from 0 to 50. The domain is $\{w \mid 0 \le w \le 50, w \in R\}$.

The area is any real number from 0 to 625. The range is $\{A \mid 0 \le A \le 625, A \in R\}$.

> Although 0 and 50 are theoretically possible, can they really be used as dimensions?

e) The quadratic function written in part a) assumes that the rancher will use all of the fencing to make the corral. It also assumes that any width or length from 0 m to 50 m is possible. In reality, there may be other limitations on the dimensions of the corral, such as the available area and landscape of the location on the rancher's property.

Your Turn

At a children's music festival, the organizers are roping off a rectangular area for stroller parking. There is 160 m of rope available to create the perimeter.

a) Write a quadratic function in standard form to represent the area for the stroller parking.

b) What are the coordinates of the vertex? What does the vertex represent in this situation?

c) Sketch the graph for the function you determined in part a).

d) Determine the domain and range for this situation.

e) Identify any assumptions you made.

- The standard form of a quadratic function is $f(x) = ax^2 + bx + c$ or $y = ax^2 + bx + c$, where $a \neq 0$.

- The graph of a quadratic function is a parabola that
  - is symmetric about a vertical line, called the axis of symmetry, that passes through the vertex
  - opens upward and has a minimum value if $a > 0$
  - opens downward and has a maximum value if $a < 0$
  - has a y-intercept at $(0, c)$ that has a value of c

- You can determine the vertex, domain and range, direction of opening, axis of symmetry, x-intercepts and y-intercept, and maximum or minimum value from the graph of a quadratic function.

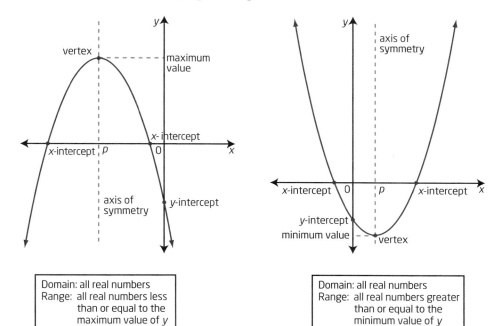

Domain: all real numbers
Range: all real numbers less than or equal to the maximum value of y

Domain: all real numbers
Range: all real numbers greater than or equal to the minimum value of y

- For any quadratic function in standard form, the x-coordinate of the vertex is given by $x = -\dfrac{b}{2a}$.

- For quadratic functions in applied situations,
  - the y-intercept represents the value of the function when the independent variable is 0
  - the x-intercept(s) represent(s) the value(s) of the independent variable for which the function has a value of 0
  - the vertex represents the point at which the function reaches its maximum or minimum
  - the domain and range may need to be restricted based on the values that are actually possible in the situation

Practise

1. Which functions are quadratic? Explain.

   a) $f(x) = 2x^2 + 3x$

   b) $f(x) = 5 - 3x$

   c) $f(x) = x(x + 2)(4x - 1)$

   d) $f(x) = (2x - 5)(3x - 2)$

2. For each graph, identify the following:
   • the coordinates of the vertex
   • the equation of the axis of symmetry
   • the x-intercepts and y-intercept
   • the maximum or minimum value and how it is related to the direction of opening
   • the domain and range

   a)
   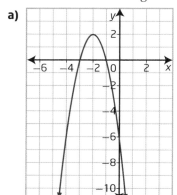

   b)
   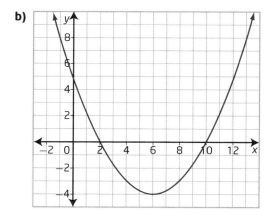

   c)
   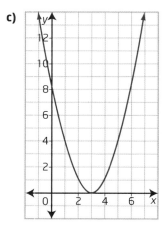

3. Show that each function fits the definition of a quadratic function by writing it in standard form.

   a) $f(x) = 5x(10 - 2x)$

   b) $f(x) = (10 - 3x)(4 - 5x)$

4. Create a table of values and then sketch the graph of each function. Determine the vertex, the axis of symmetry, the direction of opening, the maximum or minimum value, the domain and range, and any intercepts.

   a) $f(x) = x^2 - 2x - 3$

   b) $f(x) = -x^2 + 16$

   c) $p(x) = x^2 + 6x$

   d) $g(x) = -2x^2 + 8x - 10$

5. Use technology to graph each function. Identify the vertex, the axis of symmetry, the direction of opening, the maximum or minimum value, the domain and range, and any intercepts. Round values to the nearest tenth, if necessary.

   a) $y = 3x^2 + 7x - 6$

   b) $y = -2x^2 + 5x + 3$

   c) $y = 50x - 4x^2$

   d) $y = 1.2x^2 + 7.7x + 24.3$

6. The x-coordinate of the vertex is given by $x = \dfrac{-b}{2a}$. Use this information to determine the vertex of each quadratic function.

   a) $y = x^2 + 6x + 2$

   b) $y = 3x^2 - 12x + 5$

   c) $y = -x^2 + 8x - 11$

7. A siksik, an Arctic ground squirrel, jumps from a rock, travels through the air, and then lands on the tundra. The graph shows the height of its jump as a function of time. Use the graph to answer each of the following, and identify which characteristic(s) of the graph you used in each case.

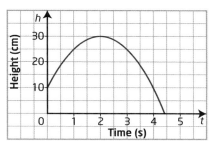

   a) What is the height of the rock that the siksik jumped from?

   b) What is the maximum height of the siksik? When did it reach that height?

   c) How long was the siksik in the air?

   d) What are the domain and range in this situation?

   e) Would this type of motion be possible for a siksik in real life? Use your answers to parts a) to d) to explain why or why not.

Did You Know?

The *siksik* is named because of the sound it makes.

8. How many x-intercepts does each function have? Explain how you know. Then, determine whether each intercept is positive, negative, or zero.

   a) a quadratic function with an axis of symmetry of $x = 0$ and a maximum value of 8

   b) a quadratic function with a vertex at $(3, 1)$, passing through the point $(1, -3)$

   c) a quadratic function with a range of $y \geq 1$

   d) a quadratic function with a y-intercept of 0 and an axis of symmetry of $x = -1$

9. Consider the function $f(x) = -16x^2 + 64x + 4$.

   a) Determine the domain and range of the function.

   b) Suppose this function represents the height, in feet, of a football kicked into the air as a function of time, in seconds. What are the domain and range in this case?

   c) Explain why the domain and range are different in parts a) and b).

Apply

10. Sketch the graph of a quadratic function that has the characteristics described in each part. Label the coordinates of three points that you know are on the curve.

   a) x-intercepts at -1 and 3 and a range of $y \geq -4$

   b) one of its x-intercepts at -5 and vertex at $(-3, -4)$

   c) axis of symmetry of $x = 1$, minimum value of 2, and passing through $(-1, 6)$

   d) vertex at $(2, 5)$ and y-intercept of 1

11. Satellite dish antennas have the shape of a parabola. Consider a satellite dish that is 80 cm across. Its cross-sectional shape can be described by the function $d(x) = 0.0125x^2 - x$, where d is the depth, in centimetres, of the dish at a horizontal distance of x centimetres from one edge of the dish.

a) What is the domain of this function?

b) Graph the function to show the cross-sectional shape of the satellite dish.

c) What is the maximum depth of the dish? Does this correspond to the maximum value of the function? Explain.

d) What is the range of the function?

e) How deep is the dish at a point 25 cm from the edge of the dish?

12. A jumping spider jumps from a log onto the ground below. Its height, h, in centimetres, as a function of time, t, in seconds, since it jumped can be modelled by the function $h(t) = -490t^2 + 75t + 12$. Where appropriate, answer the following questions to the nearest tenth.

a) Graph the function.

b) What does the h-intercept represent?

c) When does the spider reach its maximum height? What is its maximum height?

d) When does the spider land on the ground?

e) What domain and range are appropriate in this situation?

f) What is the height of the spider 0.05 s after it jumps?

Did You Know?

There are an estimated 1400 spider species in Canada. About 110 of these are jumping spiders. British Columbia has the greatest diversity of jumping spiders. Although jumping spiders are relatively small (3 mm to 10 mm in length), they can jump horizontal distances of up to 16 cm.

13. A quadratic function can model the relationship between the speed of a moving object and the wind resistance, or drag force, it experiences. For a typical car travelling on a highway, the relationship between speed and drag can be approximated with the function $f(v) = 0.002v^2$, where f is the drag force, in newtons, and v is the speed of the vehicle, in kilometres per hour.

a) What domain do you think is appropriate in this situation?

b) Considering your answer to part a), create a table of values and a graph to represent the function.

c) How can you tell from your graph that the function is not a linear function? How can you tell from your table?

d) What happens to the values of the drag force when the speed of the vehicle doubles? Does the drag force also double?

e) Why do you think a driver might be interested in understanding the relationship between the drag force and the speed of the vehicle?

Did You Know?

A *newton* (abbreviated N) is a unit of measure of force. One newton is equal to the force required to accelerate a mass of one kilogram at a rate of one metre per second squared.

14. Assume that you are an advisor to business owners who want to analyse their production costs. The production costs, C, to produce n thousand units of their product can be modelled by the function $C(n) = 0.3n^2 - 48.6n + 13\ 500$.

a) Graph the function and identify the important characteristics of the graph.

b) Write a short explanation of what the graph and each piece of information you determined in part a) shows about the production costs.

15. a) Write a function to represent the area of the rectangle. Show that the function fits the definition of a quadratic function.

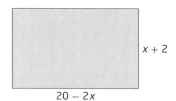

$x + 2$

$20 - 2x$

b) Graph the function.

c) What do the x-intercepts represent in this situation? How do they relate to the dimensions of the rectangle?

d) What information does the vertex give about this situation?

e) What are the domain and range? What do they represent in this situation?

f) Does the function have a maximum value in this situation? Does it have a minimum value?

g) If you graph the function you wrote in part a) with the domain being the set of all real numbers, does it have a minimum value? Explain.

16. Does the function $f(x) = 4x^2 - 3x + 2x(3 - 2x) + 1$ represent a quadratic function? Show why or why not using several different methods.

17. Maria lives on a farm. She is planning to build an enclosure for her animals that is divided into three equal-sized sections, as shown in the diagram. She has 280 m of fencing to use.

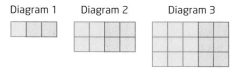

a) Write a function that represents the area of the entire enclosure in terms of its width. How do you know that it fits the definition of a quadratic function?

b) Graph the function.

c) What are the coordinates of the vertex? What do they represent?

d) What are the domain and range in this situation?

e) Does the function have a maximum value? Does it have a minimum value? Explain.

f) What assumptions did you make in your analysis of this situation?

18. a) Consider the pattern shown in the sequence of diagrams. The area of each small square is 1 square unit.

Diagram 1   Diagram 2   Diagram 3

a) Draw the next three diagrams in the sequence. What is the total area of each diagram?

b) Write a function to model the total area, A, of each diagram in terms of the diagram number, n.

c) Is the function linear or quadratic? Explain why in terms of the diagrams as well as the function.

d) If the sequence of diagrams continues, what is the domain? Are the values in the domain continuous or discrete? Explain.

e) Considering your answer to part b), graph the function to show the relationship between A and n.

19. a) Write a function for the area, A, of a circle, in terms of its radius, r.

b) What domain and range are appropriate for this function?

c) Considering your answer to part b), graph the function.

d) What are the intercepts of the graph? What meaning do they have in this situation?

e) Does this graph have an axis of symmetry? Explain.

20. The stopping distance of a vehicle is the distance travelled between the time a driver notices a need to stop and the time when the vehicle actually stops. This includes the reaction time before applying the brakes and the time it takes to stop once the brakes are applied. The stopping distance, d, in metres, for a certain vehicle can be approximated using the formula $d(t) = \dfrac{vt}{3.6} + \dfrac{v^2}{130}$, where v is the speed of the vehicle, in kilometres per hour, before braking, and t is the reaction time, in seconds, before the driver applies the brakes.

a) Suppose the driver of this vehicle has a reaction time of 1.5 s. Write a function to model the stopping distance, d, for the vehicle and driver as a function of the pre-braking speed, v.

b) Create a table of values and graph the function using a domain of $0 \le v \le 200$.

c) When the speed of the vehicle doubles, does the stopping distance also double? Use your table and graph to explain.

d) Assume that you are writing a newspaper or magazine article about safe driving. Write an argument aimed at convincing drivers to slow down. Use your graphs and other results to support your case.

Extend

21. A *family* of functions is a set of functions that are related to each other in some way.

a) Write a set of functions for part of the family defined by $f(x) = k(x^2 + 4x + 3)$ if $k = 1, 2, 3$. Simplify each equation so that it is in standard form.

b) Graph the functions on the same grid using the restricted domain of $\{x \mid 0 \le x \le 4, x \in \mathbb{R}\}$.

c) Describe how the graphs are related to each other. How are the values of y related for points on each graph for the same value of x?

d) Predict what the graph would look like if $k = 4$ and if $k = 0.5$. Sketch the graph in each case to test your prediction.

e) Predict what the graphs would look like for negative values of k. Test your prediction.

f) What does the graph look like if $k = 0$?

g) Explain how the members of the family of functions defined by $f(x) = k(x^2 + 4x + 3)$ for all values of k are related.

22. Milos said, "The a in the quadratic function $f(x) = ax^2 + bx + c$ is like the 'steepness' of the graph, just like it is for the a in $f(x) = ax + b$." In what ways might this statement be a reasonable comparison? In what ways is it not completely accurate? Explain, using examples.

23. a) The point $(-2, 1)$ is on the graph of the quadratic function $f(x) = -x^2 + bx + 11$. Determine the value of b.

b) If the points $(-1, 6)$ and $(2, 3)$ are on the graph of the quadratic function $f(x) = 2x^2 + bx + c$, determine the values of b and c.

24. How would projectile motion be different on the moon? Consider the following situations:

- an object launched from an initial height of 35 m above ground with an initial vertical velocity of 20 m/s
- a flare that is shot into the air with an initial velocity of 800 ft/s from ground level
- a rock that breaks loose from the top of a 100-m-high cliff and starts to fall straight down

a) Write a pair of functions for each situation, one representing the motion if the situation occurred on Earth and one if on the moon.

b) Graph each pair of functions.

c) Identify the similarities and differences in the various characteristics for each pair of graphs.

d) What do your graphs show about the differences between projectile motion on Earth and the moon? Explain.

> **Did You Know?**
>
> You can create a function representing the height of any projectile over time using the formula $h(t) = -0.5gt^2 + v_0t + h_0$, where g is the acceleration due to gravity, v_0 is the initial vertical velocity, and h_0 is the initial height.
>
> The *acceleration due to gravity* is a measure of how much gravity slows down an object fired upward or speeds up an object dropped or thrown downward. On the surface of Earth, the acceleration due to gravity is 9.81 m/s² in metric units or 32 ft/s² in imperial units. On the surface of the moon, the acceleration due to gravity is much less than on Earth, only 1.63 m/s² or 5.38 ft/s².

25. Determine an expression for the coordinates of each missing point described below. Explain your reasoning.

a) A quadratic function has a vertex at (m, n) and a y-intercept of r. Identify one other point on the graph.

b) A quadratic function has an axis of symmetry of $x = j$ and passes through the point $(4j, k)$. Identify one other point on the graph.

c) A quadratic function has a range of $y \geq d$ and x-intercepts of s and t. What are the coordinates of the vertex?

Create Connections

26. For the graph of a given quadratic function, how are the range, direction of opening, and location of the vertex, axis of symmetry, and x-intercepts connected?

27. MINI LAB Use computer or graphing calculator technology to investigate how the values of a, b, and c affect the graph of the function that corresponds to $y = ax^2 + bx + c$. If you are using graphing/geometry software, you may be able to use it to make sliders to change the values of a, b, and c. The will allow you to dynamically see the effect each parameter has.

For each step below, sketch one or more graphs to illustrate your findings.

Step 1 Change the values of a, b, and c, one at a time. Observe any changes that occur in the graph as a, b, or c is
- increased or decreased
- made positive or negative

Step 2 How is the y-intercept affected by the values of a, b, and c? Do all the values affect its location?

Step 3 Explore how the location of the axis of symmetry is affected by the values. Which values are involved, and how?

Step 4 Explore how the values affect the steepness of the curve as it crosses the y-axis. Do they all have an effect on this aspect?

Step 5 Observe whether any other aspects of the graph are affected by changes in a, b, and c. Explain your findings.

Completing the Square

Focus on...

- converting quadratic functions from standard to vertex form
- analysing quadratic functions of the form $y = ax^2 + bx + c$
- writing quadratic functions to model situations

Every year, staff and students hold a craft fair as a fundraiser. Sellers are charged a fee for a table at the fair. As sellers prepare for the fair, they consider what price to set for the items they sell. If items are priced too high, few people may buy them. If the prices are set too low, sellers may not take in much revenue even though many items sell. The key is to find the optimum price. How can you determine the price at which to sell items that will give the maximum revenue?

Investigate Completing the Square

Materials

- grid paper or graphing technology

Part A: Comparing Different Forms of a Quadratic Function

1. Suppose that Adine is considering pricing for the mukluks she sells at a craft fair. Last year, she sold mukluks for $400 per pair, and she sold 14 pairs. She predicts that for every $40 increase in price, she will sell one fewer pair. The revenue from the mukluk sales, $R(x)$, is (Number of Mukluks Sold)(Cost Per Mukluk).

   Copy and complete the table to model how Adine's total revenue this year might change for each price increase or decrease of $40. Continue the table to see what will happen to the total revenue if the price continues to increase or decrease.

Number of Mukluks Sold	Cost Per Mukluk ($)	Revenue, $R(x)$ ($)
14	400	5600
13	440	5720

2. What pattern do you notice in the revenue as the price changes? Why do you think that this pattern occurs?

3. Let x represent the number of $40 increases. Develop an algebraic function to model Adine's total revenue.

a) Determine an expression to represent the cost of the mukluks.

b) Determine an expression to represent the number of mukluks sold.

c) Determine the revenue function, $R(x)$, where
$R(x)$ = (Number of Mukluks Sold)(Cost Per Mukluk).

d) Expand $R(x)$ to give a quadratic function in standard form.

4. a) Graph the revenue as a function of the number of price changes.

b) What maximum possible revenue can Adine expect?

c) What price would give her the maximum possible revenue?

5. A friend of Adine's determined a function in the form
$R(x) = -40(x - 2)^2 + 5760$ where x represents the number of price decreases.

a) Expand this function and compare it to Adine's function. What do you notice?

b) Which quadratic function allows you to determine the best price and maximum revenue without graphing or creating a table of values? Explain.

Reflect and Respond

6. a) Consider the shape of your graph in step 4. Why is a quadratic function a good model to use in this situation? Why is a linear function not appropriate to relate revenue to price change?

b) What assumptions did you make in using this model to predict Adine's sales? Why might her actual sales at the fair not exactly follow the predictions made by this model?

Did You Know?

Mukluks are soft winter boots traditionally made from animal fur and hide by Arctic Aboriginal peoples. The Inuit have long worn and continue to wear this type of boot and refer to them as *kamik*.

Part B: Completing the Square

The quadratic function developed in step 3 in Part A is in standard form. The function used in step 5 is in vertex form. These quadratic functions are equivalent and can provide different information. You can convert from vertex to standard form by expanding the vertex form. How can you convert from standard to vertex form?

7. a) Select algebra tiles to represent the expression $x^2 + 6x$. Arrange them into an incomplete square as shown.

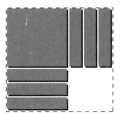

  b) What tiles must you add to complete the square?

  c) What trinomial represents the new completed square?

  d) How can you rewrite this trinomial in factored form as the square of a binomial?

8. a) Repeat the activity in step 7 using each expression in the list. Record your results in an organized fashion. Include a diagram of the tiles for each expression.

  $x^2 + 2x$
  $x^2 + 4x$
  $x^2 + 8x$
  $x^2 + 10x$

  What tiles must you add to each expression to make a complete square?

  b) Continue to model expressions until you can clearly describe the pattern that emerges. What relationship is there between the original expression and the tiles necessary to complete the square? Explain.

9. Repeat the activity, but this time model expressions that have a negative x-term, such as $x^2 - 2x$, $x^2 - 4x$, $x^2 - 6x$, and so on.

10. a) Without using algebra tiles, predict what value you need to add to the expression $x^2 + 32x$ to represent it as a completed square. What trinomial represents this completed square?

  b) How can you rewrite the trinomial in factored form as the square of a binomial?

Reflect and Respond

11. a) How are the tiles you need to complete each square related to the original expression?

  b) Does it matter whether the x-term in the original expression is positive or negative? Explain.

  c) Is it possible to complete the square for an expression with an x-term with an odd coefficient? Explain your thinking.

12. The expressions $x^2 + \blacksquare x + \blacktriangle$ and $(x + \bullet)^2$ both represent the same perfect square. Describe how the missing values are related to each other.

You can express a quadratic function in standard form, $f(x) = ax^2 + bx + c$, or in vertex form, $f(x) = a(x - p)^2 + q$. You can determine the shape of the graph and direction of opening from the value of a in either form. The vertex form has the advantage that you can identify the coordinates of the vertex as (p, q) directly from the algebraic form. It is useful to be able to determine the coordinates of the vertex algebraically when using quadratic functions to model problem situations involving maximum and minimum values.

How can you use the values of a, p, and q to determine whether a function has a maximum or minimum value, what that value is, and where it occurs?

You can convert a quadratic function in standard form to vertex form using an algebraic process called **completing the square**. Completing the square involves adding a value to and subtracting a value from a quadratic polynomial so that it contains a perfect square trinomial. You can then rewrite this trinomial as the square of a binomial.

completing the square

• an algebraic process used to write a quadratic polynomial in the form $a(x - p)^2 + q$.

$y = x^2 - 8x + 5$	
$y = (x^2 - 8x) + 5$	Group the first two terms.
$y = (x^2 - 8x + 16 - 16) + 5$	Add and subtract the square of half the coefficient of the x-term.
$y = (x^2 - 8x + 16) - 16 + 5$	Group the perfect square trinomial.
$y = (x - 4)^2 - 16 + 5$	Rewrite as the square of a binomial.
$y = (x - 4)^2 - 11$	Simplify.

In the above example, both the standard form, $y = x^2 - 8x + 5$, and the vertex form, $y = (x - 4)^2 - 11$, represent the same quadratic function. You can use both forms to determine that the graph of the function will open up, since $a = 1$. However, the vertex form also reveals without graphing that the vertex is at $(4, -11)$, so this function has a minimum value of -11 when $x = 4$.

x	y
0	5
2	-7
4	-11
6	-7
8	5

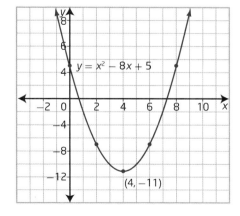

$y = x^2 - 8x + 5$

$(4, -11)$

Example 1

Convert From Standard Form to Vertex Form

Rewrite each function in vertex form by completing the square.

a) $f(x) = x^2 + 6x + 5$

b) $f(x) = 3x^2 - 12x - 9$

c) $f(x) = -5x^2 - 70x$

Solution

a) Method 1: Model with Algebra Tiles

Select algebra tiles to represent the quadratic polynomial $x^2 + 6x + 5$.

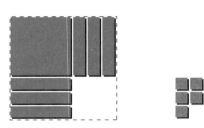

Using the x^2-tile and x-tiles, create an incomplete square to represent the first two terms. Leave the unit tiles aside for now.

How is the side length of the incomplete square related to the number of x-tiles in the original expression?

How is the number of unit tiles needed to complete the square related to the number of x-tiles in the original expression?

To complete the square, add nine zero pairs. The nine positive unit tiles complete the square and the nine negative unit tiles are necessary to maintain an expression equivalent to the original.

Why is it necessary to add the same number of red and white tiles?

Why are the positive unit tiles used to complete the square rather than the negative ones?

Simplify the expression by removing zero pairs.

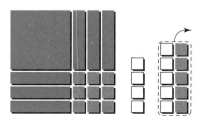

You can express the completed square in expanded form as $x^2 + 6x + 9$, but also as the square of a binomial as $(x + 3)^2$. The vertex form of the function is $y = (x + 3)^2 - 4$.

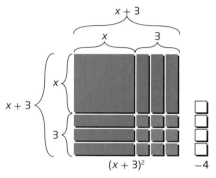

$(x + 3)^2$ -4

How are the tiles in this arrangement equivalent to the original group of tiles?

Method 2: Use an Algebraic Method

For the function $y = x^2 + 6x + 5$, the value of a is 1. To complete the square,

- group the first two terms
- inside the brackets, add and subtract the square of half the coefficient of the x-term
- group the perfect square trinomial
- rewrite the perfect square trinomial as the square of a binomial
- simplify

$y = x^2 + 6x + 5$
$y = (x^2 + 6x) + 5$
$y = (x^2 + 6x + 9 - 9) + 5$ Why is the value 9 used here? Why is 9 also subtracted?
$y = (x^2 + 6x + 9) - 9 + 5$ Why are the first three terms grouped together?
$y = (x + 3)^2 - 9 + 5$ How is the 3 inside the brackets related to the original function? How is the 3 related to the 9 that was used earlier?

$y = (x + 3)^2 - 4$ How could you check that this is equivalent to the original expression?

b) **Method 1: Use Algebra Tiles**

Select algebra tiles to represent the quadratic expression $3x^2 - 12x - 9$. Use the x^2-tiles and x-tiles to create three incomplete squares as shown. Leave the unit tiles aside for now.

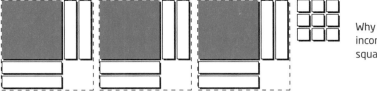

Why are three incomplete squares created?

Add enough positive unit tiles to complete each square, as well as an equal number of negative unit tiles.

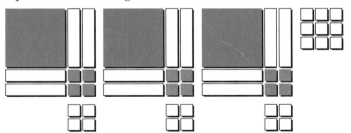

Why do positive tiles complete each square even though the x-tiles are negative?

Simplify by combining the negative unit tiles.

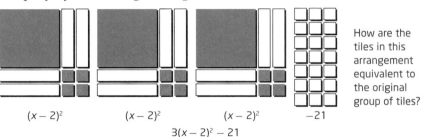

How are the tiles in this arrangement equivalent to the original group of tiles?

$(x-2)^2$ $(x-2)^2$ $(x-2)^2$ -21

$3(x-2)^2 - 21$

You can express each completed square as $x^2 - 4x + 4$, but also as $(x-2)^2$. Since there are three of these squares and 21 extra negative unit tiles, the vertex form of the function is $y = 3(x-2)^2 - 21$.

Method 2: Use an Algebraic Method

To complete the square when the leading coefficient, a, is not 1,
- group the first two terms and factor out the leading coefficient
- inside the brackets, add and subtract the square of half of the coefficient of the x-term
- group the perfect square trinomial
- rewrite the perfect square trinomial as the square of a binomial
- expand the square brackets and simplify

$y = 3x^2 - 12x - 9$
$y = 3(x^2 - 4x) - 9$ Why does 3 need to be factored from the first two terms?

$y = 3(x^2 - 4x + 4 - 4) - 9$ Why is the value 4 used inside the brackets?
$y = 3[(x^2 - 4x + 4) - 4] - 9$
$y = 3[(x - 2)^2 - 4] - 9$
$y = 3(x - 2)^2 - 12 - 9$ What happens to the square brackets? Why are the brackets still needed?

$y = 3(x - 2)^2 - 21$ Why is the constant term, -21, 12 less than at the start, when only 4 was added inside the brackets?

c) Use the process of completing the square to convert to vertex form.

$y = -5x^2 - 70x$ What happens to the x-term when a negative number is factored?
$y = -5(x^2 + 14x)$
$y = -5(x^2 + 14x + 49 - 49)$ How does a leading coefficient that is negative affect the process? How would the result be different if it had been positive?
$y = -5[(x^2 + 14x + 49) - 49]$
$y = -5[(x + 7)^2 - 49]$
$y = -5(x + 7)^2 + 245$ Why would algebra tiles not be suitable to use for this function?

Your Turn

Rewrite each function in vertex form by completing the square.

a) $y = x^2 + 8x - 7$
b) $y = 2x^2 - 20x$
c) $y = -3x^2 - 18x - 24$

Example 2

Convert to Vertex Form and Verify

a) Convert the function $y = 4x^2 - 28x - 23$ to vertex form.
b) Verify that the two forms are equivalent.

Solution

a) Complete the square to convert to vertex form.

Method 1: Use Fractions

$y = 4x^2 - 28x - 23$
$y = 4(x^2 - 7x) - 23$
$y = 4\left[x^2 - 7x + \left(\dfrac{7}{2}\right)^2 - \left(\dfrac{7}{2}\right)^2\right] - 23$
$y = 4\left(x^2 - 7x + \dfrac{49}{4} - \dfrac{49}{4}\right) - 23$
$y = 4\left[\left(x^2 - 7x + \dfrac{49}{4}\right) - \dfrac{49}{4}\right] - 23$
$y = 4\left[\left(x - \dfrac{7}{2}\right)^2 - \dfrac{49}{4}\right] - 23$
$y = 4\left(x - \dfrac{7}{2}\right)^2 - 4\left(\dfrac{49}{4}\right) - 23$
$y = 4\left(x - \dfrac{7}{2}\right)^2 - 49 - 23$
$y = 4\left(x - \dfrac{7}{2}\right)^2 - 72$

> Why is the number being added and subtracted inside the brackets not a whole number in this case?

Method 2: Use Decimals

$y = 4x^2 - 28x - 23$
$y = 4(x^2 - 7x) - 23$
$y = 4[x^2 - 7x + (3.5)^2 - (3.5)^2] - 23$
$y = 4(x^2 - 7x + 12.25 - 12.25) - 23$
$y = 4[(x^2 - 7x + 12.25) - 12.25] - 23$
$y = 4[(x - 3.5)^2 - 12.25] - 23$
$y = 4(x - 3.5)^2 - 4(12.25) - 23$
$y = 4(x - 3.5)^2 - 49 - 23$
$y = 4(x - 3.5)^2 - 72$

> Do you find it easier to complete the square using fractions or decimals? Why?

b) Method 1: Work Backward

$y = 4(x - 3.5)^2 - 72$
$y = 4(x^2 - 7x + 12.25) - 72$
$y = 4x^2 - 28x + 49 - 72$
$y = 4x^2 - 28x - 23$

Since the result is the original function, the two forms are equivalent.

> Expand the binomial square expression.
> Eliminate the brackets by distributing.
> Combine like terms to simplify.

> How are these steps related to the steps used to complete the square in part a)?

Method 2: Use Technology

Use graphing technology to graph both functions together or separately using identical window settings.

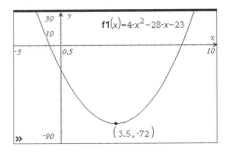 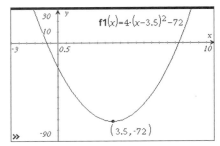

Since the graphs are identical, the two forms are equivalent.

Your Turn

a) Convert the function $y = -3x^2 - 27x + 13$ to vertex form.

b) Verify that the two forms are equivalent.

Example 3

Determine the Vertex of a Quadratic Function by Completing the Square

Consider the function $y = 5x^2 + 30x + 41$.

a) Complete the square to determine the vertex and the maximum or minimum value of the function.

b) Use the process of completing the square to verify the relationship between the value of p in vertex form and the values of a and b in standard form.

c) Use the relationship from part b) to determine the vertex of the function. Compare with your answer from part a).

Solution

a) $y = 5x^2 + 30x + 41$

$y = 5(x^2 + 6x) + 41$

$y = 5(x^2 + 6x + 9 - 9) + 41$

$y = 5[(x^2 + 6x + 9) - 9] + 41$

$y = 5[(x + 3)^2 - 9] + 41$

$y = 5(x + 3)^2 - 45 + 41$

$y = 5(x + 3)^2 - 4$

The vertex form of the function, $y = a(x - p)^2 + q$, reveals characteristics of the graph.

The vertex is located at the point (p, q). For the function $y = 5(x + 3)^2 - 4$, $p = -3$ and $q = -4$. So, the vertex is located at $(-3, -4)$. The graph opens upward since a is positive. Since the graph opens upward from the vertex, the function has a minimum value of -4 when $x = -3$.

b) Look back at the steps in completing the square.

$y = ax^2 + bx + 41$
$y = 5x^2 + 30x + 41$ *b* divided by *a* gives the coefficient of *x* inside the brackets.
$y = 5(x^2 + 6x) + 41$ 6 is $\frac{30}{5}$, or $\frac{b}{a}$.
$\vdots$

$y = 5(x + 3)^2 - 4$ Half the coefficient of *x* inside the brackets gives the value
$y = 5(x - p)^2 - 4$ of *p* in the vertex form.

3 is half of 6, or half of $\frac{b}{a}$, or $\frac{b}{2a}$.

Considering the steps in completing the square, the value of p in vertex form is equal to $-\dfrac{b}{2a}$. For any quadratic function in standard form, the equation of the axis of symmetry is $x = -\dfrac{b}{2a}$.

c) Determine the *x*-coordinate of the vertex using $x = -\dfrac{b}{2a}$.

$x = -\dfrac{30}{2(5)}$

$x = -\dfrac{30}{10}$

$x = -3$

Determine the *y*-coordinate by substituting the *x*-coordinate into the function.

$y = 5(-3)2 + 30(-3) + 41$
$y = 5(9) - 90 + 41$
$y = 45 - 90 + 41$
$y = -4$

The vertex is $(-3, -4)$.
This is the same as the coordinates for the vertex determined in part a).

Your Turn

Consider the function $y = 3x^2 + 30x + 41$.

a) Complete the square to determine the vertex of the graph of the function.

b) Use $x = -\dfrac{b}{2a}$ and the standard form of the quadratic function to determine the vertex. Compare with your answer from part a).

Example 4

Write a Quadratic Model Function

The student council at a high school is planning a
fundraising event with a professional
photographer taking portraits
of individuals or groups.
The student council
gets to charge and
keep a session
fee for each
individual or
group photo
session. Last
year, they charged
a $10 session fee
and 400 sessions were
booked. In considering what
price they should charge this year,
student council members estimate that for every
$1 increase in the price, they expect to have 20 fewer
sessions booked.

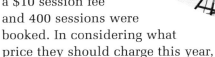

a) Write a function to model this situation.
b) What is the maximum revenue they can expect based on these
estimates. What session fee will give that maximum?
c) How can you verify the solution?
d) What assumptions did you make in creating and using this
model function?

Solution

a) The starting price is $10/session and the price increases are in
$1 increments.

Let n represent the number of price increases. The new price is $10
plus the number of price increases times $1, or $10 + 1n$ or, more
simply, $10 + n$.

The original number of sessions booked is 400. The new number
of sessions is 400 minus the number of price increases times 20, or
$400 - 20n$.

Let R represent the expected revenue, in dollars. The revenue is
calculated as the product of the price per session and the number
of sessions.

Revenue = (price)(number of sessions)
$R = (10 + n)(400 - 20n)$
$R = 4000 + 200n - 20n^2$
$R = -20n^2 + 200n + 4000$

b) Complete the square to determine the maximum revenue and the price that gives that revenue.

$R = -20n^2 + 200n + 4000$

$R = -20(n^2 - 10n) + 4000$

$R = -20(n^2 - 10n + 25 - 25) + 4000$

$R = -20[(n^2 - 10n + 25) - 25] + 4000$

$R = -20[(n - 5)^2 - 25] + 4000$

$R = -20(n - 5)^2 + 500 + 4000$

$R = -20(n - 5)^2 + 4500$

Why does changing to vertex form help solve the problem?

What other methods could you use to find the maximum revenue and the price that gives that revenue?

The vertex form of the function shows that the vertex is at (5, 4500).

The revenue, R, will be at its maximum value of $4500 when $n = 5$, or when there are five price increases of $1. So, the price per session, or session fee, should be $10 + 5$, or $15.

c) You can verify the solution using technology by graphing the function expressed in standard form.

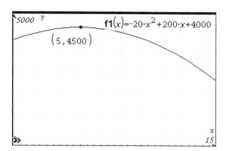

The vertex of the graph is located at (5, 4500). This verifies that the maximum revenue is $4500 with five price increases, or a session fee of $15.

You can also verify the solution numerically by examining the function table. The table shows that a maximum revenue of $4500 occurs with five price increases, or a session fee of $15.

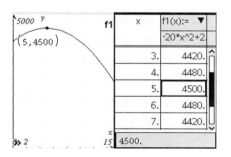

A function table is a table of values generated using a given function.

d) The price the student council sets will affect their revenue from this fundraiser, as they have predicted in using this model.

This model assumes that the price affects the revenue. The revenue function in this situation was based on information about the number of sessions booked last year and predictions on how price changes might affect revenue. However, other factors might affect revenue this year, such as
- how happy people were with their photos last year and whether they tell others or not
- whether the student council advertises the event more this year
- whether the photographer is the same or different from last year
- the date, time, and duration chosen for the event

Your Turn

A sporting goods store sells reusable sports water bottles for $8. At this price their weekly sales are approximately 100 items. Research says that for every $2 increase in price, the manager can expect the store to sell five fewer water bottles.

a) Represent this situation with a quadratic function.
b) Determine the maximum revenue the manager can expect based on these estimates. What selling price will give that maximum revenue?
c) Verify your solution.
d) Explain any assumptions you made in using a quadratic function in this situation.

Key Ideas

- You can convert a quadratic function from standard form to vertex form by completing the square.

$y = 5x^2 - 30x + 7$	← standard form
$y = 5(x^2 - 6x) + 7$	Group the first two terms. Factor out the leading coefficient if $a \neq 1$.
$y = 5(x^2 - 6x + 9 - 9) + 7$	Add and then subtract the square of half the coefficient of the x-term.
$y = 5[(x^2 - 6x + 9) - 9] + 7$	Group the perfect square trinomial.
$y = 5[(x - 3)^2 - 9] + 7$	Rewrite using the square of a binomial.
$y = 5(x - 3)^2 - 45 + 7$	Simplify.
$y = 5(x - 3)^2 - 38$	← vertex form

- Converting a quadratic function to vertex form, $y = a(x - p)^2 + q$, reveals the coordinates of the vertex, (p, q).

- You can use information derived from the vertex form to solve problems such as those involving maximum and minimum values.

Check Your Understanding

Practise

1. Use a model to determine the value of c that makes each trinomial expression a perfect square. What is the equivalent binomial square expression for each?

a) $x^2 + 6x + c$

b) $x^2 - 4x + c$

c) $x^2 + 14x + c$

d) $x^2 - 2x + c$

2. Write each function in vertex form by completing the square. Use your answer to identify the vertex of the function.

a) $y = x^2 + 8x$

b) $y = x^2 - 18x - 59$

c) $y = x^2 - 10x + 31$

d) $y = x^2 + 32x - 120$

3. Convert each function to the form $y = a(x - p)^2 + q$ by completing the square. Verify each answer with or without technology.

a) $y = 2x^2 - 12x$

b) $y = 6x^2 + 24x + 17$

c) $y = 10x^2 - 160x + 80$

d) $y = 3x^2 + 42x - 96$

4. Convert each function to vertex form algebraically, and verify your answer.

a) $f(x) = -4x^2 + 16x$

b) $f(x) = -20x^2 - 400x - 243$

c) $f(x) = -x^2 - 42x + 500$

d) $f(x) = -7x^2 + 182x - 70$

5. Verify, in at least two different ways, that the two algebraic forms in each pair represent the same function.

a) $y = x^2 - 22x + 13$
and
$y = (x - 11)^2 - 108$

b) $y = 4x^2 + 120x$
and
$y = 4(x + 15)^2 - 900$

c) $y = 9x^2 - 54x - 10$
and
$y = 9(x - 3)^2 - 91$

d) $y = -4x^2 - 8x + 2$
and
$y = -4(x + 1)^2 + 6$

6. Determine the maximum or minimum value of each function and the value of x at which it occurs.

a) $y = x^2 + 6x - 2$

b) $y = 3x^2 - 12x + 1$

c) $y = -x^2 - 10x$

d) $y = -2x^2 + 8x - 3$

7. For each quadratic function, determine the maximum or minimum value.

a) $f(x) = x^2 + 5x + 3$

b) $f(x) = 2x^2 - 2x + 1$

c) $f(x) = -0.5x^2 + 10x - 3$

d) $f(x) = 3x^2 - 4.8x$

e) $f(x) = -0.2x^2 + 3.4x + 4.5$

f) $f(x) = -2x^2 + 5.8x - 3$

8. Convert each function to vertex form.

a) $y = x^2 + \dfrac{3}{2}x - 7$

b) $y = -x^2 - \dfrac{3}{8}x$

c) $y = 2x^2 - \dfrac{5}{6}x + 1$

Apply

9. a) Convert the quadratic function $f(x) = -2x^2 + 12x - 10$ to vertex form by completing the square.

b) The graph of $f(x) = -2x^2 + 12x - 10$ is shown. Explain how you can use the graph to verify your answer.

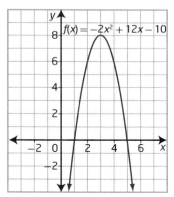

10. a) For the quadratic function $y = -4x^2 + 20x + 37$, determine the maximum or minimum value and domain and range without making a table of values or graphing.

b) Explain the strategy you used in part a).

11. Determine the vertex of the graph of $f(x) = 12x^2 - 78x + 126$. Explain the method you used.

12. Identify, explain, and correct the error(s) in the following examples of completing the square.

a) $y = x^2 + 8x + 30$
$y = (x^2 + 4x + 4) + 30$
$y = (x + 2)^2 + 30$

b) $f(x) = 2x^2 - 9x - 55$
$f(x) = 2(x^2 - 4.5x + 20.25 - 20.25) - 55$
$f(x) = 2[(x^2 - 4.5x + 20.25) - 20.25] - 55$
$f(x) = 2[(x - 4.5)^2 - 20.25] - 55$
$f(x) = 2(x - 4.5)^2 - 40.5 - 55$
$f(x) = (x - 4.5)^2 - 95.5$

c) $y = 8x^2 + 16x - 13$
$y = 8(x^2 + 2x) - 13$
$y = 8(x^2 + 2x + 4 - 4) - 13$
$y = 8[(x^2 + 2x + 4) - 4] - 13$
$y = 8[(x + 2)^2 - 4] - 13$
$y = 8(x + 2)^2 - 32 - 13$
$y = 8(x + 2)^2 - 45$

d) $f(x) = -3x^2 - 6x$
$f(x) = -3(x^2 - 6x - 9 + 9)$
$f(x) = -3[(x^2 - 6x - 9) + 9]$
$f(x) = -3[(x - 3)^2 + 9]$
$f(x) = -3(x - 3)^2 + 27$

13. The managers of a business are examining costs. It is more cost-effective for them to produce more items. However, if too many items are produced, their costs will rise because of factors such as storage and overstock. Suppose that they model the cost, C, of producing n thousand items with the function $C(n) = 75n^2 - 1800n + 60\ 000$. Determine the number of items produced that will minimize their costs.

14. A gymnast is jumping on a trampoline. His height, h, in metres, above the floor on each jump is roughly approximated by the function $h(t) = -5t^2 + 10t + 4$, where t represents the time, in seconds, since he left the trampoline. Determine algebraically his maximum height on each jump.

15. Sandra is practising at an archery club. The height, h, in feet, of the arrow on one of her shots can be modelled as a function of time, t, in seconds, since it was fired using the function $h(t) = -16t^2 + 10t + 4$.

a) What is the maximum height of the arrow, in feet, and when does it reach that height?

b) Verify your solution in two different ways.

16. Austin and Yuri were asked to convert the function $y = -6x^2 + 72x - 20$ to vertex form. Their solutions are shown.

Austin's solution:
$y = -6x^2 + 72x - 20$
$y = -6(x^2 + 12x) - 20$
$y = -6(x^2 + 12x + 36 - 36) - 20$
$y = -6[(x^2 + 12x + 36) - 36] - 20$
$y = -6[(x + 6) - 36] - 20$
$y = -6(x + 6) + 216 - 20$
$y = -6(x + 6) + 196$

Yuri's solution:

$y = -6x^2 + 72x - 20$

$y = -6(x^2 - 12x) - 20$

$y = -6(x^2 - 12x + 36 - 36) - 20$

$y = -6[(x^2 - 12x + 36) - 36] - 20$

$y = -6[(x - 6)^2 - 36] - 20$

$y = -6(x - 6)^2 - 216 - 20$

$y = -6(x - 6)^2 + 236$

a) Identify, explain, and correct any errors in their solutions.

b) Neither Austin nor Yuri verified their answers. Show several methods that they could have used to verify their solutions. Identify how each method would have pointed out if their solutions were incorrect.

17. A parabolic microphone collects and focuses sound waves to detect sounds from a distance. This type of microphone is useful in situations such as nature audio recording and sports broadcasting. Suppose a particular parabolic microphone has a cross-sectional shape that can be described by the function $d(x) = 0.03125x^2 - 1.5x$, where d is the depth, in centimetres, of the microphone's dish at a horizontal distance of x centimetres from one edge of the dish. Use an algebraic method to determine the depth of the dish, in centimetres, at its centre.

18. A concert promoter is planning the ticket price for an upcoming concert for a certain band. At the last concert, she charged $70 per ticket and sold 2000 tickets. After conducting a survey, the promoter has determined that for every $1 decrease in ticket price, she might expect to sell 50 more tickets.

a) What maximum revenue can the promoter expect? What ticket price will give that revenue?

b) How many tickets can the promoter expect to sell at that price?

c) Explain any assumptions the concert promoter is making in using this quadratic function to predict revenues.

Digging Roots, a First Nations band, from Barriere, British Columbia

19. The manager of a bike store is setting the price for a new model. Based on past sales history, he predicts that if he sets the price at $360, he can expect to sell 280 bikes this season. He also predicts that for every $10 increase in the price, he expects to sell five fewer bikes.

a) Write a function to model this situation.

b) What maximum revenue can the manager expect? What price will give that maximum?

c) Explain any assumptions involved in using this model.

20. A gardener is planting peas in a field. He knows that if he spaces the rows of pea plants closer together, he will have more rows in the field, but fewer peas will be produced by the plants in each row. Last year he planted the field with 30 rows of plants. At this spacing. he got an average of 4000 g of peas per row. He estimates that for every additional row, he will get 100 g less per row.

a) Write a quadratic function to model this situation.

b) What is the maximum number of kilograms of peas that the field can produce? What number of rows gives that maximum?

c) What assumptions are being made in using this model to predict the production of the field?

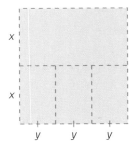

21. A holding pen is being built alongside a long building. The pen requires only three fenced sides, with the building forming the fourth side. There is enough material for 90 m of fencing.

a) Predict what dimensions will give the maximum area of the pen.

b) Write a function to model the area.

c) Determine the maximum possible area.

d) Verify your solution in several ways, with or without technology. How does the solution compare to your prediction?

e) Identify any assumptions you made in using the model function that you wrote.

22. A set of fenced-in areas, as shown in the diagram, is being planned on an open field. A total of 900 m of fencing is available. What measurements will maximize the overall area of the entire enclosure?

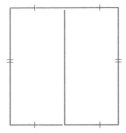

23. Use a quadratic function model to solve each problem.

a) Two numbers have a sum of 29 and a product that is a maximum. Determine the two numbers and the maximum product.

b) Two numbers have a difference of 13 and a product that is a minimum. Determine the two numbers and the minimum product.

24. What is the maximum total area that 450 cm of string can enclose if it is used to form the perimeters of two adjoining rectangles as shown?

Extend

25. Write $f(x) = -\frac{3}{4}x^2 + \frac{9}{8}x + \frac{5}{16}$ in vertex form.

26. a) Show the process of completing the square for the function $y = ax^2 + bx + c$.

b) Express the coordinates of the vertex in terms of a, b, and c.

c) How can you use this information to solve problems involving quadratic functions in standard form?

27. The vertex of a quadratic function in standard form is $\left(\dfrac{-b}{2a}, f\left(\dfrac{-b}{2a}\right)\right)$.

a) Given the function $f(x) = 2x^2 - 12x + 22$ in standard form, determine the vertex.

b) Determine the vertex by converting the function to vertex form.

c) Show the relationship between the parameters a, b, and c in standard form and the parameters a, p, and q in vertex form.

28. A Norman window has the shape of a rectangle with a semicircle on the top. Consider a Norman window with a perimeter of 6 m.

a) Write a function to approximate the area of the window as a function of its width.

b) Complete the square to approximate the maximum possible area of the window and the width that gives that area.

c) Verify your answer to part b) using technology.

d) Determine the other dimensions and draw a scale diagram of the window. Does its appearance match your expectations?

Create Connections

29. a) Is the quadratic function $f(x) = 4x^2 + 24$ written in vertex or in standard form? Discuss with a partner.

b) Could you complete the square for this function? Explain.

30. Martine's teacher asks her to complete the square for the function $y = -4x^2 + 24x + 5$. After looking at her solution, the teacher says that she made four errors in her work. Identify, explain, and correct her errors.

Martine's solution:
$y = -4x^2 + 24x + 5$
$y = -4(x^2 + 6x) + 5$
$y = -4(x^2 + 6x + 36 - 36) + 5$
$y = -4[(x^2 + 6x + 36) - 36] + 5$
$y = -4[(x + 6)^2 - 36] + 5$
$y = -4(x + 6)^2 - 216 + 5$
$y = -4(x + 6)^2 - 211$

31. A local store sells T-shirts for $10. At this price, the store sells an average of 100 shirts each month. Market research says that for every $1 increase in the price, the manager of the store can expect to sell five fewer shirts each month.

a) Write a quadratic function to model the revenue in terms of the increase in price.

b) What information can you determine about this situation by completing the square?

c) What assumptions have you made in using this quadratic function to predict revenue?

Project Corner — Quadratic Functions in Motion

- Quadratic functions appear in the shapes of various types of stationary objects, along with situations involving moving ones. You can use a video clip to show the motion of a person, animal, or object that appears to create a quadratic model function using a suitably placed set of coordinate axes.

- What situations involving motion could you model using quadratic functions?

Chapter 3 Review

3.1 Investigating Quadratic Functions in Vertex Form, pages 142–162

1. Use transformations to explain how the graph of each quadratic function compares to the graph of $f(x) = x^2$. Identify the vertex, the axis of symmetry, the direction of opening, the maximum or minimum value, and the domain and range without graphing.

   a) $f(x) = (x + 6)^2 - 14$

   b) $f(x) = -2x^2 + 19$

   c) $f(x) = \frac{1}{5}(x - 10)^2 + 100$

   d) $f(x) = -6(x - 4)^2$

2. Sketch the graph of each quadratic function using transformations. Identify the vertex, the axis of symmetry, the maximum or minimum value, the domain and range, and any intercepts.

   a) $f(x) = 2(x + 1)^2 - 8$

   b) $f(x) = -0.5(x - 2)^2 + 2$

3. Is it possible to determine the number of x-intercepts in each case without graphing? Explain why or why not.

   a) $y = -3(x - 5)^2 + 20$

   b) a parabola with a domain of all real numbers and a range of $\{y \mid y \geq 0, y \in R\}$

   c) $y = 9 + 3x^2$

   d) a parabola with a vertex at $(-4, -6)$

4. Determine a quadratic function with each set of characteristics.

   a) vertex at $(0, 0)$, passing through the point $(20, -150)$

   b) vertex at $(8, 0)$, passing through the point $(2, 54)$

   c) minimum value of 12 at $x = -4$ and y-intercept of 60

   d) x-intercepts of 2 and 7 and maximum value of 25

5. Write a quadratic function in vertex form for each graph.

   a)
   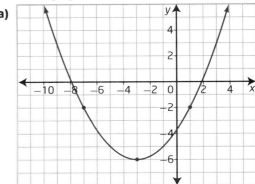

   b)
   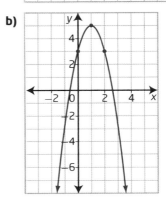

6. A parabolic trough is a solar-energy collector. It consists of a long mirror with a cross-section in the shape of a parabola. It works by focusing the Sun's rays onto a central axis running down the length of the trough. Suppose a particular solar trough has width 180 cm and depth 56 cm. Determine the quadratic function that represents the cross-sectional shape of the mirror.

7. The main span of the suspension bridge over the Peace River in Dunvegan, Alberta, has supporting cables in the shape of a parabola. The distance between the towers is 274 m. Suppose that the ends of the cables are attached to the tops of the two supporting towers at a height of 52 m above the surface of the water, and the lowest point of the cables is 30 m above the water's surface.

a) Determine a quadratic function that represents the shape of the cables if the origin is at

  i) the minimum point on the cables

  ii) a point on the water's surface directly below the minimum point of the cables

  iii) the base of the tower on the left

b) Would the quadratic function change over the course of the year as the seasons change? Explain.

8. A flea jumps from the ground to a height of 30 cm and travels 15 cm horizontally from where it started. Suppose the origin is located at the point from which the flea jumped. Determine a quadratic function in vertex form to model the height of the flea compared to the horizontal distance travelled.

Did You Know?

The average flea can pull 160 000 times its own mass and can jump 200 times its own length. This is equivalent to a human being pulling 24 million pounds and jumping nearly 1000 ft!

3.2 Investigating Quadratic Functions in Standard Form, pages 163–179

9. For each graph, identify the vertex, axis of symmetry, maximum or minimum value, direction of opening, domain and range, and any intercepts.

a)

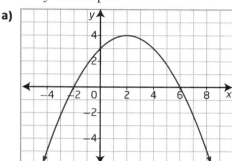

b)

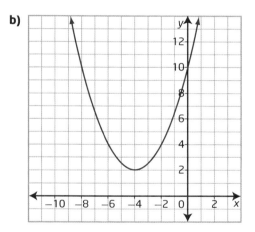

10. Show why each function fits the definition of a quadratic function.

  a) $y = 7(x + 3)^2 - 41$

  b) $y = (2x + 7)(10 - 3x)$

11. a) Sketch the graph of the function $f(x) = -2x^2 + 3x + 5$. Identify the vertex, the axis of symmetry, the direction of opening, the maximum or minimum value, the domain and range, and any intercepts.

b) Explain how each feature can be identified from the graph.

12. A goaltender kicks a soccer ball through the air to players downfield. The trajectory of the ball can be modelled by the function $h(d) = -0.032d^2 + 1.6d$, where d is the horizontal distance, in metres, from the person kicking the ball and h is the height at that distance, in metres.

  a) Represent the function with a graph, showing all important characteristics.

  b) What is the maximum height of the ball? How far downfield is the ball when it reaches that height?

  c) How far downfield does the ball hit the ground?

  d) What are the domain and range in this situation?

13. a) Write a function to represent the area of the rectangle.

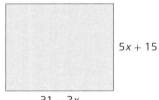

5x + 15

31 − 2x

  b) Graph the function.

  c) What do the x-intercepts represent in this situation?

  d) Does the function have a maximum value in this situation? Does it have a minimum value?

  e) What information does the vertex give about this situation?

  f) What are the domain and range?

3.3 Completing the Square, pages 180–197

14. Write each function in vertex form, and verify your answer.

  a) $y = x^2 - 24x + 10$

  b) $y = 5x^2 + 40x - 27$

  c) $y = -2x^2 + 8x$

  d) $y = -30x^2 - 60x + 105$

15. Without graphing, state the vertex, the axis of symmetry, the maximum or minimum value, and the domain and range of the function $f(x) = 4x^2 - 10x + 3$.

16. Amy tried to convert the function $y = -22x^2 - 77x + 132$ to vertex form.

  Amy's solution:
  $y = -22x^2 - 77x + 132$
  $y = -22(x^2 - 3.5x) + 132$
  $y = -22(x^2 - 3.5x - 12.25 + 12.25) + 132$
  $y = -22(x^2 - 3.5x - 12.25) - 269.5 + 132$
  $y = -22(x - 3.5)^2 - 137.5$

  a) Identify, explain, and correct the errors.

  b) Verify your correct solution in several different ways, both with and without technology.

17. The manager of a clothing company is analysing its costs, revenues, and profits to plan for the upcoming year. Last year, a certain type of children's winter coat was priced at $40, and the company sold 10 000 of them. Market research says that for every $2 decrease in the price, the manager can expect the company to sell 500 more coats.

  a) Model the expected revenue as a function of the number of price decreases.

  b) Without graphing, determine the maximum revenue and the price that will achieve that revenue.

  c) Graph the function to confirm your answer.

  d) What does the y-intercept represent in this situation? What do the x-intercepts represent?

  e) What are the domain and range in this situation?

  f) Explain some of the assumptions that the manager is making in using this function to model the expected revenue.

Multiple Choice

For #1 to #6, choose the best answer.

1. Which function is NOT a quadratic function?

A $f(x) = 2(x + 1)^2 - 7$

B $f(x) = (x - 3)(2x + 5)$

C $f(x) = 5x^2 - 20$

D $f(x) = 3(x - 9) + 6$

2. Which quadratic function represents the parabola shown?

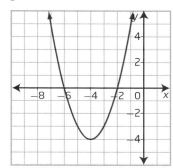

A $y = (x + 4)^2 + 4$

B $y = (x - 4)^2 + 4$

C $y = (x + 4)^2 - 4$

D $y = (x - 4)^2 - 4$

3. Identify the range for the function $y = -6(x - 6)^2 + 6$.

A $\{y \mid y \le 6, y \in R\}$

B $\{y \mid y \ge 6, y \in R\}$

C $\{y \mid y \le -6, y \in R\}$

D $\{y \mid y \ge -6, y \in R\}$

4. Which quadratic function in vertex form is equivalent to $y = x^2 - 2x - 5$?

A $y = (x - 2)^2 - 1$

B $y = (x - 2)^2 - 9$

C $y = (x - 1)^2 - 4$

D $y = (x - 1)^2 - 6$

5. Which graph shows the function $y = 1 + ax^2$ if $a < 0$?

A

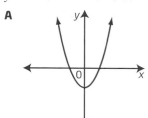

B

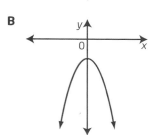

C

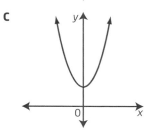

D

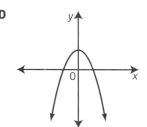

6. What conditions on a and q will give the function $f(x) = a(x - p)^2 + q$ no x-intercepts?

A $a > 0$ and $q > 0$

B $a < 0$ and $q > 0$

C $a > 0$ and $q = 0$

D $a < 0$ and $q = 0$

Short Answer

7. Write each quadratic function in vertex form by completing the square.

   a) $y = x^2 - 18x - 27$

   b) $y = 3x^2 + 36x + 13$

   c) $y = -10x^2 - 40x$

8. a) For the graph shown, give the coordinates of the vertex, the equation of the axis of symmetry, the minimum or maximum value, the domain and range, and the x-intercepts.

   b) Determine a quadratic function in vertex form for the graph.

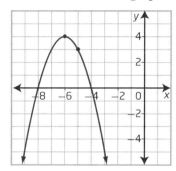

9. a) Identify the transformation(s) on the graph of $f(x) = x^2$ that could be used to graph each function.

   i) $f(x) = 5x^2$

   ii) $f(x) = x^2 - 20$

   iii) $f(x) = (x + 11)^2$

   iv) $f(x) = -\dfrac{1}{7}x^2$

   b) For each function in part a), state which of the following would be different as compared to $f(x) = x^2$ as a result of the transformation(s) involved, and explain why.

   i) vertex

   ii) axis of symmetry

   iii) range

10. Sketch the graph of the function $y = 2(x - 1)^2 - 8$ using transformations. Then, copy and complete the table.

Vertex	
Axis of Symmetry	
Direction of Opening	
Domain	
Range	
x-Intercepts	
y-Intercept	

11. The first three steps in completing the square below contain one or more errors.

$$y = 2x^2 - 8x + 9$$
$$y = 2(x^2 - 8x) + 9$$
$$y = 2(x^2 - 8x - 64 + 64) + 9$$

   a) Identify and correct the errors.

   b) Complete the process to determine the vertex form of the function.

   c) Verify your correct solution in several different ways.

12. The fuel consumption for a vehicle is related to the speed that it is driven and is usually given in litres per one hundred kilometres. Engines are generally more efficient at higher speeds than at lower speeds. For a particular type of car driving at a constant speed, the fuel consumption, C, in litres per one hundred kilometres, is related to the average driving speed, v, in kilometres per hour, by the function $C(v) = 0.004v^2 - 0.62v + 30$.

   a) Without graphing, determine the most efficient speed at which this car should be driven. Explain/show the strategy you use.

   b) Describe any characteristics of the graph that you can identify without actually graphing, and explain how you know.

13. The height, h, in metres, of a flare t seconds after it is fired into the air can be modelled by the function $h(t) = -4.9t^2 + 61.25t$.

a) At what height is the flare at its maximum? How many seconds after being shot does this occur?

b) Verify your solution both with and without technology.

Extended Response

14. Three rectangular areas are being enclosed along the side of a building, as shown. There is enough material to make 24 m of fencing.

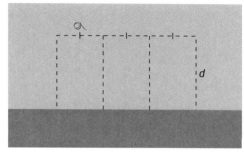

a) Write the function that represents the total area in terms of the distance from the wall.

b) Show that the function fits the definition of a quadratic function.

c) Graph the function. Explain the strategy you used.

d) What are the coordinates of the vertex? What do they represent?

e) What domain and range does the function have in this situation? Explain.

f) Does the function have a maximum value? Does it have a minimum value? Explain.

g) What assumptions are made in using this quadratic function model?

15. A stone bridge has the shape of a parabolic arch, as shown. Determine a quadratic function to represent the shape of the arch if the origin

a) is at the top of the opening under the bridge

b) is on the ground at the midpoint of the opening

c) is at the base of the bridge on the right side of the opening

d) is on the left side at the top surface of the bridge

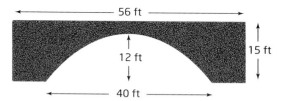

16. A store sells energy bars for $2.25. At this price, the store sold an average of 120 bars per month last year. The manager has been told that for every 5¢ decrease in price, he can expect the store to sell eight more bars monthly.

a) What quadratic function can you use to model this situation?

b) Use an algebraic method to determine the maximum revenue the manager can expect the store to achieve. What price will give that maximum?

c) What assumptions are made in this situation?

CHAPTER 4

Quadratic Equations

What do water fountains, fireworks, satellite dishes, bridges, and model rockets have in common? They all involve a parabolic shape. You can develop and use quadratic equations to solve problems involving these parabolic shapes. Quadratic equations are also used in other situations such as avalanche control, setting the best ticket prices for concerts, designing roller coasters, and planning gardens.

In this chapter, you will relate quadratic equations to the graphs of quadratic functions, and solve problems by determining and analysing quadratic equations.

Did You Know?

Apollonius, also known as the "The Greek Geometer" (c. 210 B.C.E.), was the first mathematician to study parabolas in depth.

Key Terms

quadratic equation	extraneous root
root(s) of an equation	quadratic formula
zero(s) of a function	discriminant

Career Link

Robotics engineering is a sub-field of mechanical engineering. A robotics engineer designs, maintains, and develops new applications for robots. These applications range from production line robots to those used in the medical and military fields, and from aerospace and mining to walking machines and tele-operators controlled by microchips.

A visionary robotics engineer could work on designing mobile robots, cars that drive themselves, and parts of space probes.

Web Link

To learn more about robotics engineering, go to www.mhrprecalc11.ca and follow the links.

Graphical Solutions of Quadratic Equations

Focus on...

- describing the relationships between the roots of a quadratic equation, the zeros of the corresponding quadratic function, and the x-intercepts of the graph of the quadratic function
- solving quadratic equations by graphing the corresponding quadratic function

Water fountains are usually designed to give a specific visual effect. For example, the water fountain shown consists of individual jets of water that each arch up in the shape of a parabola. Notice how the jets of water are designed to land precisely on the underwater spotlights.

How can you design a water fountain to do this? Where must you place the underwater lights so the jets of water land on them? What are some of the factors to consider when designing a water fountain? How do these factors affect the shape of the water fountain?

Investigate Solving Quadratic Equations by Graphing

Materials

- grid paper or graphing technology

1. Each water fountain jet creates a parabolic stream of water. You can represent this curve by the quadratic function $h(x) = -6(x - 1)^2 + 6$, where h is the height of the jet of water and x is the horizontal distance of the jet of water from the nozzle, both in metres.

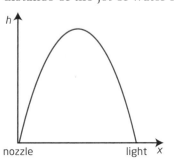

a) Graph the quadratic function $h(x) = -6(x - 1)^2 + 6$.

b) How far from the nozzle should the underwater lights be placed? Explain your reasoning.

2. You can control the height and horizontal distance of the jet of water by changing the water pressure. Suppose that the quadratic function $h(x) = -x^2 + 12x$ models the path of a jet of water at maximum pressure. The quadratic function $h(x) = -3x^2 + 12x$ models the path of the same jet of water at a lower pressure.

a) Graph these two functions on the same set of axes as in step 1.

b) Describe what you notice about the x-intercepts and height of the two graphs compared to the graph in step 1.

c) Why do you think the x-intercepts of the graph are called the zeros of the function?

Reflect and Respond

3. a) If the water pressure in the fountain must remain constant, how else could you control the path of the jets of water?

b) Could two jets of water at constant water pressure with different parabolic paths land on the same spot? Explain your reasoning.

Did You Know?

The Dubai Fountain at the Burj Khalifa in Dubai is the largest in the world. It can shoot about 22 000 gal of water about 500 ft into the air and features over 6600 lights and 25 colour projectors.

---

quadratic equation

- a second-degree equation with standard form $ax^2 + bx + c = 0$, where $a \neq 0$
- for example, $2x^2 + 12x + 16 = 0$

root(s) of an equation

- the solution(s) to an equation

zero(s) of a function

- the value(s) of x for which $f(x) = 0$
- related to the x-intercept(s) of the graph of a function, $f(x)$

You can solve a **quadratic equation** of the form $ax^2 + bx + c = 0$ by graphing the corresponding quadratic function, $f(x) = ax^2 + bx + c$. The solutions to a quadratic equation are called the **roots** of the equation. You can find the roots of a quadratic equation by determining the x-intercepts of the graph, or the **zeros** of the corresponding quadratic function.

For example, you can solve the quadratic equation $2x^2 + 2x - 12 = 0$ by graphing the corresponding quadratic function, $f(x) = 2x^2 + 2x - 12$. The graph shows that the x-intercepts occur at $(-3, 0)$ and $(2, 0)$ and have values of -3 and 2. The zeros of the function occur when $f(x) = 0$. So, the zeros of the function are -3 and 2. Therefore, the roots of the equation are -3 and 2.

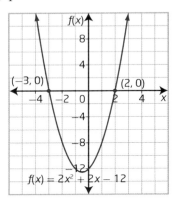

Example 1

Quadratic Equations With One Real Root

What are the roots of the equation $-x^2 + 8x - 16 = 0$?

Solution

To solve the equation, graph the corresponding quadratic function, $f(x) = -x^2 + 8x - 16$, and determine the x-intercepts.

Method 1: Use Paper and Pencil
Create a table of values. Plot the coordinate pairs and use them to sketch the graph of the function.

Why were these values of x chosen?

x	$f(x)$
-2	-36
-1	-25
0	-16
1	-9
2	-4
3	-1
4	0
5	-1
6	-4
7	-9
8	-16
9	-25
10	-36

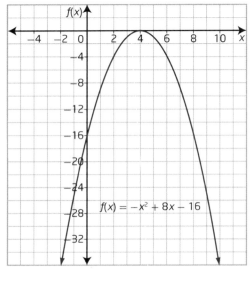

How do you know that there is only one root for this quadratic equation?

The graph meets the x-axis at the point $(4, 0)$, the vertex of the corresponding quadratic function.
The x-intercept of the graph occurs at $(4, 0)$ and has a value of 4.
The zero of the function is 4.
Therefore, the root of the equation is 4.

Method 2: Use a Spreadsheet

In a spreadsheet, enter the table of values shown. Then, use the spreadsheet's graphing features.

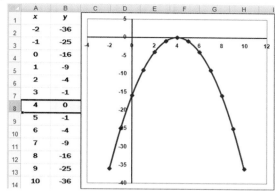

The x-intercept of the graph occurs at $(4, 0)$ and has a value of 4.

The zero of the function is 4.

Therefore, the root of the equation is 4.

Method 3: Use a Graphing Calculator

Graph the function using a graphing calculator. Then, use the trace or zero function to identify the x-intercept.

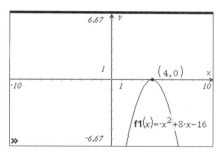

Compare the three methods. Which do you prefer? Why?

The x-intercept of the graph occurs at $(4, 0)$ and has a value of 4.
The zero of the function is 4.
Therefore, the root of the equation is 4.

Check for Methods 1, 2, and 3:
Substitute $x = 4$ into the equation $-x^2 + 8x - 16 = 0$.

Left Side $\qquad\qquad$ Right Side
$\quad -x^2 + 8x - 16 \qquad\quad$ 0
$= -(4)^2 + 8(4) - 16$
$= -16 + 32 - 16$
$= 0$
$\qquad$ Left Side = Right Side

The solution is correct.

Your Turn

Determine the roots of the quadratic equation $x^2 - 6x + 9 = 0$.

Example 2

Quadratic Equations With Two Distinct Real Roots

The manager of Jasmine's Fine Fashions is investigating the effect that raising or lowering dress prices has on the daily revenue from dress sales. The function $R(x) = 100 + 15x - x^2$ gives the store's revenue R, in dollars, from dress sales, where x is the price change, in dollars. What price changes will result in no revenue?

Solution

When there is no revenue, $R(x) = 0$. To determine the price changes that result in no revenue, solve the quadratic equation $0 = 100 + 15x - x^2$.

Graph the corresponding revenue function. On the graph, the x-intercepts will correspond to the price changes that result in no revenue.

What do the values of x that are not the x-intercepts represent?

Method 1: Use Paper and Pencil
Create a table of values. Plot the coordinate pairs and use them to sketch the graph of the function.

Why do the values of x in the table begin with negative values?

Price Change, x	Revenue, $R(x)$
−10	−150
−8	−84
−6	−26
−4	24
−2	66
0	100
2	126
4	144
6	154
8	156
10	150
12	136
14	114
16	84
18	46
20	0
22	−54

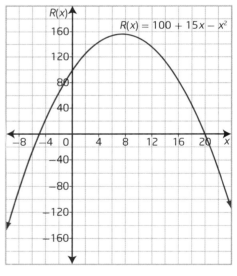

How effective is graphing by hand in this situation?

How do you know there are two roots for this quadratic equation?

The graph appears to cross the x-axis at the points $(-5, 0)$ and $(20, 0)$. The x-intercepts of the graph, or zeros of the function, are -5 and 20. Therefore, the roots of the equation are -5 and 20.

Why do the roots of the equation result in no revenue?

Method 2: Use a Spreadsheet

In a spreadsheet, enter the table of values shown.
Then, use the spreadsheet's graphing features.

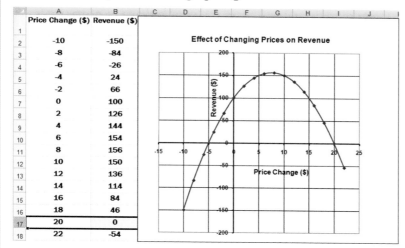

	A	B
	Price Change ($)	Revenue ($)
1		
2	-10	-150
3	-8	-84
4	-6	-26
5	-4	24
6	-2	66
7	0	100
8	2	126
9	4	144
10	6	154
11	8	156
12	10	150
13	12	136
14	14	114
15	16	84
16	18	46
17	20	0
18	22	-54

The graph crosses the x-axis at the points $(-5, 0)$ and $(20, 0)$. The x-intercepts of the graph, or zeros of the function, are -5 and 20. Therefore, the roots of the equation are -5 and 20.

Method 3: Use a Graphing Calculator

Graph the revenue function using a graphing calculator. Adjust the window settings of the graph until you see the vertex of the parabola and the x-intercepts. Use the trace or zero function to identify the x-intercepts of the graph.

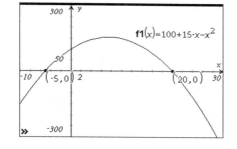

The graph crosses the x-axis at the points $(-5, 0)$ and $(20, 0)$.
The x-intercepts of the graph, or zeros of the function, are -5 and 20.
Therefore, the roots of the equation are -5 and 20.

Check for Methods 1, 2, and 3:
Substitute the values $x = -5$ and $x = 20$ into the equation
$0 = 100 + 15x - x^2$.

Left Side	Right Side
0	$100 + 15x - x^2$
	$= 100 + 15(-5) - (-5)^2$
	$= 100 - 75 - 25$
	$= 0$

Left Side = Right Side

Left Side	Right Side
0	$100 + 15x - x^2$
	$= 100 + 15(20) - (20)^2$
	$= 100 + 300 - 400$
	$= 0$

Left Side = Right Side

Both solutions are correct. A dress price increase of $20 or a decrease of $5 will result in no revenue from dress sales.

Why is one price change an increase and the other a decrease? Do both price changes make sense? Why or why not?

Your Turn

The manager at Suzie's Fashion Store has determined that the function $R(x) = 600 - 6x^2$ models the expected weekly revenue, R, in dollars, from sweatshirts as the price changes, where x is the change in price, in dollars. What price increase or decrease will result in no revenue?

Example 3

Quadratic Equations With No Real Roots

Solve $2x^2 + x = -2$ by graphing.

Solution

Rewrite the equation in the form $ax^2 + bx + c = 0$.

$2x^2 + x + 2 = 0$ Why do you rewrite the equation in the form $ax^2 + bx + c = 0$?

Graph the corresponding quadratic function $f(x) = 2x^2 + x + 2$.

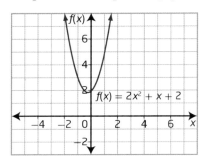

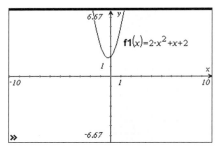

The graph does not intersect the x-axis.
There are no zeros for this function.

Therefore, the quadratic equation has no real roots.

Your Turn

Solve $3m^2 - m = -2$ by graphing.

Example 4

Solve a Problem Involving Quadratic Equations

The curve of a suspension bridge cable attached between the tops of two towers can be modelled by the function $h(d) = 0.0025(d - 100)^2 - 10$, where h is the vertical distance from the top of a tower to the cable and d is the horizontal distance from the left end of the bridge, both in metres. What is the horizontal distance between the two towers? Express your answer to the nearest tenth of a metre.

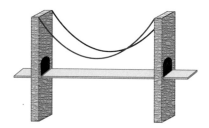

Solution

At the tops of the towers, $h(d) = 0$. To determine the locations of the two towers, solve the quadratic equation $0 = 0.0025(d - 100)^2 - 10$. Graph the cable function using graphing technology. Adjust the dimensions of the graph until you see the vertex of the parabola and the x-intercepts. Use the trace or zero function to identify the x-intercepts of the graph.

The x-intercepts of the graph occur at approximately (36.8, 0) and (163.2, 0). The zeros of the function are approximately 36.8 and 163.2. Therefore, the roots of the equation are approximately 36.8 and 163.2.

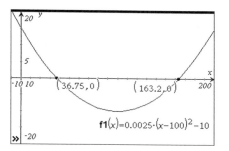

What does the x-axis represent?

The first tower is located approximately 36.8 m from the left end of the bridge.

The second tower is located approximately 163.2 m from the left end of the bridge.

Subtract to determine the distance between the two towers.
$163.2 - 36.8 = 126.4$

The horizontal distance between the two towers is approximately 126.4 m.

Your Turn

Suppose the cable of the suspension bridge in Example 4 is modelled by the function $h(d) = 0.0025(d - 100)^2 - 12$. What is the horizontal distance between the two towers? Express your answer to the nearest tenth of a metre.

- One approach to solving a quadratic equation of the form $ax^2 + bx + c = 0$, $a \neq 0$, is to graph the corresponding quadratic function, $f(x) = ax^2 + bx + c$. Then, determine the x-intercepts of the graph.

- The x-intercepts of the graph, or the zeros of the quadratic function, correspond to the solutions, or roots, of the quadratic equation.

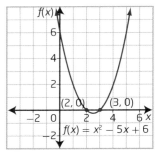

For example, you can solve $x^2 - 5x + 6 = 0$ by graphing the corresponding function, $f(x) = x^2 - 5x + 6$, and determining the x-intercepts.

The x-intercepts of the graph and the zeros of the function are 2 and 3. So, the roots of the equation are 2 and 3.

Check:
Substitute the values $x = 2$ and $x = 3$ into the equation $x^2 - 5x + 6 = 0$.

Left Side	Right Side		Left Side	Right Side
$x^2 - 5x + 6$	0		$x^2 - 5x + 6$	0
$= (2)^2 - 5(2) + 6$			$= (3)^2 - 5(3) + 6$	
$= 4 - 10 + 6$			$= 9 - 15 + 6$	
$= 0$			$= 0$	

    Left Side = Right Side   Left Side = Right Side

Both solutions are correct.

- The graph of a quadratic function can have zero, one, or two real x-intercepts. Therefore, the quadratic function has zero, one, or two real zeros, and correspondingly the quadratic equation has zero, one, or two real roots.

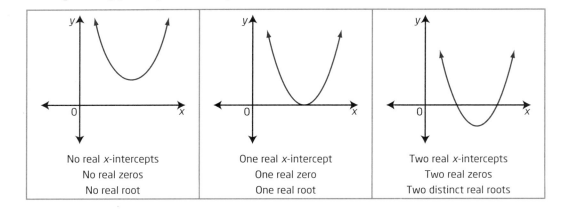

Practise

1. How many x-intercepts does each quadratic function graph have?

a)

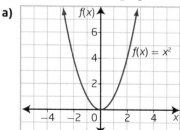

b)

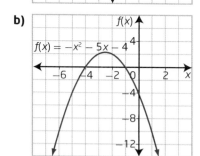

c)

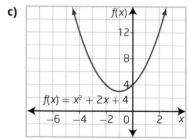

d)

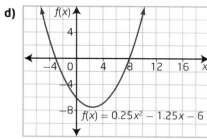

2. What are the roots of the corresponding quadratic equations represented by the graphs of the functions shown in #1? Verify your answers.

3. Solve each equation by graphing the corresponding function.

a) $0 = x^2 - 5x - 24$

b) $0 = -2r^2 - 6r$

c) $h^2 + 2h + 5 = 0$

d) $5x^2 - 5x = 30$

e) $-z^2 + 4z = 4$

f) $0 = t^2 + 4t + 10$

4. What are the roots of each quadratic equation? Where integral roots cannot be found, estimate the roots to the nearest tenth.

a) $n^2 - 10 = 0$

b) $0 = 3x^2 + 9x - 12$

c) $0 = -w^2 + 4w - 3$

d) $0 = 2d^2 + 20d + 32$

e) $0 = v^2 + 6v + 6$

f) $m^2 - 10m = -21$

Apply

5. In a Canadian Football League game, the path of the football at one particular kick-off can be modelled using the function $h(d) = -0.02d^2 + 2.6d - 66.5$, where h is the height of the ball and d is the horizontal distance from the kicking team's goal line, both in yards. A value of $h(d) = 0$ represents the height of the ball at ground level. What horizontal distance does the ball travel before it hits the ground?

6. Two numbers have a sum of 9 and a product of 20.

a) What single-variable quadratic equation in the form $ax^2 + bx + c = 0$ can be used to represent the product of the two numbers?

b) Determine the two numbers by graphing the corresponding quadratic function.

7. Two consecutive even integers have a product of 168.

a) What single-variable quadratic equation in the form $ax^2 + bx + c = 0$ can be used to represent the product of the two numbers?

b) Determine the two numbers by graphing the corresponding quadratic function.

8. The path of the stream of water coming out of a fire hose can be approximated using the function $h(x) = -0.09x^2 + x + 1.2$, where h is the height of the water stream and x is the horizontal distance from the firefighter holding the nozzle, both in metres.

a) What does the equation $-0.09x^2 + x + 1.2 = 0$ represent in this situation?

b) At what maximum distance from the building could a firefighter stand and still reach the base of the fire with the water? Express your answer to the nearest tenth of a metre.

c) What assumptions did you make when solving this problem?

9. The HSBC Celebration of Light is an annual pyro-musical fireworks competition that takes place over English Bay in Vancouver. The fireworks are set off from a barge so they land on the water. The path of a particular fireworks rocket is modelled by the function $h(t) = -4.9(t - 3)^2 + 47$, where h is the rocket's height above the water, in metres, at time, t, in seconds.

a) What does the equation $0 = -4.9(t - 3)^2 + 47$ represent in this situation?

b) The fireworks rocket stays lit until it hits the water. For how long is it lit, to the nearest tenth of a second?

10. A skateboarder jumps off a ledge at a skateboard park. His path is modelled by the function $h(d) = -0.75d^2 + 0.9d + 1.5$, where h is the height above ground and d is the horizontal distance the skateboarder travels from the ledge, both in metres.

a) Write a quadratic equation to represent the situation when the skateboarder lands.

b) At what distance from the base of the ledge will the skateboarder land? Express your answer to the nearest tenth of a metre.

11. Émilie Heymans is a three-time Canadian Olympic diving medallist. Suppose that for a dive off the 10-m tower, her height, h, in metres, above the surface of the water is given by the function $h(d) = -2d^2 + 3d + 10$, where d is the horizontal distance from the end of the tower platform, in metres.

a) Write a quadratic equation to represent the situation when Émilie enters the water.

b) What is Émilie's horizontal distance from the end of the tower platform when she enters the water? Express your answer to the nearest tenth of a metre.

Did You Know?

Émilie Heymans, from Montréal, Québec, is only the fifth Canadian to win medals at three consecutive Olympic Games.

12. Matthew is investigating the old Borden Bridge, which spans the North Saskatchewan River about 50 km west of Saskatoon. The three parabolic arches of the bridge can be modelled using quadratic functions, where h is the height of the arch above the bridge deck and x is the horizontal distance of the bridge deck from the beginning of the first arch, both in metres.

First arch:
$$h(x) = -0.01x^2 + 0.84x$$
Second arch:
$$h(x) = -0.01x^2 + 2.52x - 141.12$$
Third arch:
$$h(x) = -0.01x^2 + 4.2x - 423.36$$

a) What are the zeros of each quadratic function?

b) What is the significance of the zeros in this situation?

c) What is the total span of the Borden Bridge?

Extend

13. For what values of k does the equation $x^2 + 6x + k = 0$ have

a) one real root?

b) two distinct real roots?

c) no real roots?

14. The height of a circular arch is represented by $4h^2 - 8hr + s^2 = 0$, where h is the height, r is the radius, and s is the span of the arch, all in feet.

a) How high must an arch be to have a span of 64 ft and a radius of 40 ft?

b) How would this equation change if all the measurements were in metres? Explain.

15. Two new hybrid vehicles accelerate at different rates. The Ultra Range's acceleration can be modelled by the function $d(t) = 1.5t^2$, while the Edison's can be modelled by the function $d(t) = 5.4t^2$, where d is the distance, in metres, and t is the time, in seconds. The Ultra Range starts the race at 0 s. At what time should the Edison start so that both cars are at the same point 5 s after the race starts? Express your answer to the nearest tenth of a second.

> **Did You Know?**
>
> A hybrid vehicle uses two or more distinct power sources. The most common hybrid uses a combination of an internal combustion engine and an electric motor. These are called hybrid electric vehicles or HEVs.

Create Connections

16. Suppose the value of a quadratic function is negative when $x = 1$ and positive when $x = 2$. Explain why it is reasonable to assume that the related equation has a root between 1 and 2.

17. The equation of the axis of symmetry of a quadratic function is $x = 0$ and one of the x-intercepts is -4. What is the other x-intercept? Explain using a diagram.

18. The roots of the quadratic equation $0 = x^2 - 4x - 12$ are 6 and -2. How can you use the roots to determine the vertex of the graph of the corresponding function?

Factoring Quadratic Equations

Focus on...

- factoring a variety of quadratic expressions
- factoring to solve quadratic equations
- solving problems involving quadratic equations

Football, soccer, basketball, and volleyball are just a few examples of sports that involve throwing, kicking, or striking a ball. Each time a ball or projectile sails through the air, it follows a trajectory that can be modelled with a quadratic function.

Each of these sports is played on a rectangular playing area. The playing area for each sport can be modelled by a quadratic equation.

Investigate Solving Quadratic Equations by Factoring

Materials

- grid paper or graphing technology

1. For women's indoor competition, the length of the volleyball court is twice its width. If x represents the width, then $2x$ represents the length. The area of the court is 162 m².

    a) Write a quadratic equation in standard form, $A(x) = 0$, to represent the area of the court.

    b) Graph the corresponding quadratic function. How many x-intercepts are there? What are they?

    c) From your graph, what are the roots of the quadratic equation you wrote in part a)? How do you know these are the roots of the equation?

    d) In this context, are all the roots acceptable? Explain.

2. a) Factor the left side of the quadratic equation you wrote in step 1a).

    b) Graph the corresponding quadratic function in factored form. Compare your graph to the graph you created in step 1b).

    c) How is the factored form of the equation related to the x-intercepts of the graph?

    d) How can you use the x-intercepts of a graph, $x = r$ and $x = s$, to write a quadratic equation in standard form?

3. For men's sitting volleyball, a Paralympic sport, the length of the court is 4 m more than the width. The area of the court is 60 m².

   a) If x represents the width, write a quadratic equation in standard form to represent the area of the court.

   b) Graph the corresponding quadratic function. How many x-intercepts are there? What are they?

4. a) Use the x-intercepts, $x = r$ and $x = s$, of your graph in step 3 to write the quadratic equation $(x - r)(x - s) = 0$.

   b) Graph the corresponding quadratic function. Compare your graph to the graph you created in step 3.

Reflect and Respond

5. How does the factored form of a quadratic equation relate to the x-intercepts of the graph, the zeros of the quadratic function, and the roots of the equation?

6. Describe how you can factor the quadratic equation $0 = x^2 - 5x - 6$ to find the roots.

7. The roots of a quadratic equation are 3 and -5. What is a possible equation?

Did You Know?

Volleyball is the world's number two participation sport. Which sport do you think is number one?

Link the Ideas

Factoring Quadratic Expressions

To factor a trinomial of the form $ax^2 + bx + c$, where $a \neq 0$, first factor out common factors, if possible.

For example,
$$4x^2 - 2x - 12 = 2(2x^2 - x - 6)$$
$$= 2(2x^2 - 4x + 3x - 6)$$
$$= 2[2x(x - 2) + 3(x - 2)]$$
$$= 2(x - 2)(2x + 3)$$

You can factor perfect square trinomials of the forms $(ax)^2 + 2abx + b^2$ and $(ax)^2 - 2abx + b^2$ into $(ax + b)^2$ and $(ax - b)^2$, respectively.

For example,
$$4x^2 + 12x + 9 = (2x + 3)(2x + 3) \qquad 9x^2 - 24x + 16 = (3x - 4)(3x - 4)$$
$$= (2x + 3)^2 \qquad\qquad\qquad = (3x - 4)^2$$

You can factor a difference of squares, $(ax)^2 - (by)^2$, into $(ax - by)(ax + by)$.

For example,
$$\frac{4}{9}x^2 - 16y^2 = \left(\frac{2}{3}x - 4y\right)\left(\frac{2}{3}x + 4y\right)$$

Factoring Polynomials Having a Quadratic Pattern

You can extend the patterns established for factoring trinomials and a difference of squares to factor polynomials in quadratic form. You can factor a polynomial of the form $a(P)^2 + b(P) + c$, where P is any expression, as follows:
- Treat the expression P as a single variable, say r, by letting $r = P$.
- Factor as you have done before.
- Replace the substituted variable r with the expression P.
- Simplify the expression.

For example, in $3(x + 2)^2 - 13(x + 2) + 12$, substitute r for $x + 2$ and factor the resulting expression, $3r^2 - 13r + 12$.

$$3r^2 - 13r + 12 = (3r - 4)(r - 3)$$

Once the expression in r is factored, you can substitute $x + 2$ back in for r.

The resulting expression is
$$[3(x + 2) - 4](x + 2 - 3) = (3x + 6 - 4)(x - 1)$$
$$= (3x + 2)(x - 1)$$

You can factor a polynomial in the form of a difference of squares, as $P^2 - Q^2 = (P - Q)(P + Q)$ where P and Q are any expressions.

For example,
$$(3x + 1)^2 - (2x - 3)^2 = [(3x + 1) - (2x - 3)][(3x + 1) + (2x - 3)]$$
$$= (3x + 1 - 2x + 3)(3x + 1 + 2x - 3)$$
$$= (x + 4)(5x - 2)$$

Example 1

Factor Quadratic Expressions

Factor.

a) $2x^2 - 2x - 12$

b) $\frac{1}{4}x^2 - x - 3$

c) $9x^2 - 0.64y^2$

Solution

a) Method 1: Remove the Common Factor First
Factor out the common factor of 2.
$$2x^2 - 2x - 12 = 2(x^2 - x - 6)$$
Find two integers with a product of -6 and a sum of -1.

Factors of -6	Product	Sum
1, -6	-6	-5
2, -3	-6	-1
3, -2	-6	1
6, -1	-6	5

The factors are $x + 2$ and $x - 3$.
$$2x^2 - 2x - 12 = 2(x^2 - x - 6)$$
$$= 2(x + 2)(x - 3)$$

Method 2: Factor the Trinomial First by Grouping
To factor, $2x^2 - 2x - 12$, find two integers with
- a product of $(2)(-12) = -24$
- a sum of -2

The two integers are -6 and 4.
Write $-2x$ as the sum $-6x + 4x$.
Then, factor by grouping.

$$2x^2 - 2x - 12 = 2x^2 - 6x + 4x - 12$$
$$= 2x(x - 3) + 4(x - 3)$$
$$= (2x + 4)(x - 3)$$
$$= 2(x + 2)(x - 3)$$

Factor out the common factor of 2.

b) Factor out the common factor of $\frac{1}{4}$ first.

$$\frac{1}{4}x^2 - x - 3 = \frac{1}{4}(x^2 - 4x - 12)$$
$$= \frac{1}{4}(x + 2)(x - 6)$$

How does factoring out the common factor of $\frac{1}{4}$ help you?

How can you determine the factors for the trinomial $x^2 - 4x - 12$?

c) The binomial $9x^2 - 0.64y^2$ is a difference of squares.

The first term is a perfect square: $(3x)^2$
The second term is a perfect square: $(0.8y)^2$
$$9x^2 - 0.64y^2 = (3x)^2 - (0.8y)^2$$
$$= (3x - 0.8y)(3x + 0.8y)$$

Your Turn

Factor.

a) $3x^2 + 3x - 6$

b) $\frac{1}{2}x^2 - x - 4$

c) $0.49j^2 - 36k^2$

Did You Know?

When the leading coefficient of a quadratic polynomial is not an integer, you can factor out the rational number as a common factor.

For example,
$$\frac{1}{2}x^2 - 5x + 1$$
$$= \frac{1}{2}(x^2 - 10x + 2)$$

What do you need to multiply $\frac{1}{2}$ by to get 5?

What do you need to multiply $\frac{1}{2}$ by to get 1?

Example 2

Factor Polynomials of Quadratic Form

Factor each polynomial.

a) $12(x + 2)^2 + 24(x + 2) + 9$

b) $9(2t + 1)^2 - 4(s - 2)^2$

Solution

a) $12(x + 2)^2 + 24(x + 2) + 9$

Treat the term $x + 2$ as a single variable.
Substitute $r = x + 2$ into the quadratic expression and factor as usual.

$$12(x + 2)^2 + 24(x + 2) + 9 \qquad \text{Substitute } r \text{ for } x + 2.$$
$$= 12r^2 + 24r + 9$$
$$= 3(4r^2 + 8r + 3) \qquad \text{Factor out the common factor of 3.}$$
$$= 3(4r^2 + 2r + 6r + 3) \qquad \text{Find two integers with a product of } (4)(3) = 12$$
$$\qquad\qquad\qquad\qquad\qquad\quad \text{and a sum of 8. The integers 2 and 6 work.}$$
$$= 3[(4r^2 + 2r) + (6r + 3)] \qquad \text{Factor by grouping.}$$
$$= 3[2r(2r + 1) + 3(2r + 1)]$$
$$= 3(2r + 1)(2r + 3)$$
$$= 3[2(x + 2) + 1][2(x + 2) + 3] \qquad \text{Replace } r \text{ with } x + 2.$$
$$= 3(2x + 4 + 1)(2x + 4 + 3) \qquad \text{Simplify.}$$
$$= 3(2x + 5)(2x + 7)$$

The expression $12(x + 2)^2 + 24(x + 2) + 9$ in factored form is $3(2x + 5)(2x + 7)$.

b) $9(2t + 1)^2 - 4(s - 2)^2$

Each term of the polynomial is a perfect square.
Therefore, this is a difference of squares of the form
$P^2 - Q^2 = (P - Q)(P + Q)$ where P represents $3(2t + 1)$ and
Q represents $2(s - 2)$.

Use the pattern for factoring a difference of squares.
$$9(2t + 1)^2 - 4(s - 2)^2$$
$$= [3(2t + 1) - 2(s - 2)][3(2t + 1) + 2(s - 2)]$$
$$= (6t + 3 - 2s + 4)(6t + 3 + 2s - 4)$$
$$= (6t - 2s + 7)(6t + 2s - 1)$$

The expression $9(2t + 1)^2 - 4(s - 2)^2$ in factored form is
$(6t - 2s + 7)(6t + 2s - 1)$.

Your Turn

Factor each polynomial.

a) $-2(n + 3)^2 + 12(n + 3) + 14$

b) $4(x - 2)^2 - 0.25(y - 4)^2$

Solving Quadratic Equations by Factoring

Some quadratic equations that have real-number solutions can be factored easily.

The *zero product property* states that if the product of two real numbers is zero, then one or both of the numbers must be zero. This means that if $de = 0$, then at least one of d and e is 0.

The roots of a quadratic equation occur when the product of the factors is equal to zero. To solve a quadratic equation of the form $ax^2 + bx + c = 0$, $a \neq 0$, factor the expression and then set either factor equal to zero. The solutions are the roots of the equation.

For example, rewrite the quadratic equation $3x^2 - 2x - 5 = 0$ in factored form.

$$3x^2 - 2x - 5 = 0$$
$$(3x - 5)(x + 1) = 0$$

$$3x - 5 = 0 \quad \text{or} \quad x + 1 = 0$$
$$x = \frac{5}{3} \qquad\qquad x = -1$$

The roots are $\frac{5}{3}$ and -1.

Example 3

Solve Quadratic Equations by Factoring

Determine the roots of each quadratic equation. Verify your solutions.

a) $x^2 + 6x + 9 = 0$ **b)** $x^2 + 4x - 21 = 0$ **c)** $2x^2 - 9x - 5 = 0$

Solution

a) To solve $x^2 + 6x + 9 = 0$, determine the factors and then solve for x.
$$x^2 + 6x + 9 = 0 \qquad \text{This is a perfect square trinomial.}$$
$$(x + 3)(x + 3) = 0$$

$$(x + 3) = 0 \quad \text{or} \quad (x + 3) = 0 \qquad \text{For the quadratic equation to equal 0, one of}$$
$$x = -3 \qquad\qquad x = -3 \qquad \text{the factors must equal 0.}$$

This equation has two equal real roots. Since both roots are equal, the roots may be viewed as one distinct real root. Check by substituting the solution into the original quadratic equation.

For $x = -3$:

Left Side   Right Side
$x^2 + 6x + 9$ 0
$= (-3)^2 + 6(-3) + 9$
$= 9 - 18 + 9$
$= 0$

Left Side $=$ Right Side

The solution is correct. The roots of the equation are -3 and -3, or just -3.

b) To solve $x^2 + 4x - 21 = 0$, first determine the factors, and then solve for x.

$$x^2 + 4x - 21 = 0$$
$$(x - 3)(x + 7) = 0$$

Two integers with a product of -21 and a sum of 4 are -3 and 7.

Set each factor equal to zero and solve for x.

$$x - 3 = 0 \quad \text{or} \quad x + 7 = 0$$
$$x = 3 \qquad\qquad x = -7$$

The equation has two distinct real roots. Check by substituting each solution into the original quadratic equation.

For $x = 3$:

Left Side	Right Side
$x^2 + 4x - 21$	0
$= 3^2 + 4(3) - 21$	
$= 9 + 12 - 21$	
$= 0$	

Left Side = Right Side

For $x = -7$:

Left Side	Right Side
$x^2 + 4x - 21$	0
$= (-7)^2 + 4(-7) - 21$	
$= 49 - 28 - 21$	
$= 0$	

Left Side = Right Side

Both solutions are correct. The roots of the quadratic equation are 3 and -7.

c) To solve $2x^2 - 9x - 5 = 0$, first determine the factors, and then solve for x.

Method 1: Factor by Inspection

$2x^2$ is the product of the first terms, and -5 is the product of the second terms.

$$2x^2 - 9x - 5 = (2x + \blacksquare)(x + \blacksquare)$$

The last term, -5, is negative. So, one factor of -5 must be negative. Try factor pairs of -5 until the sum of the products of the outer and inner terms is $-9x$.

Factors of -5	Product	Middle Term
$-5, 1$	$(2x - 5)(x + 1) = 2x^2 + 2x - 5x - 5$ $= 2x^2 - 3x - 5$	$-3x$ is not the correct middle term.
$1, -5$	$(2x + 1)(x - 5) = 2x^2 - 10x + 1x - 5$ $= 2x^2 - 9x - 5$	Correct.

Therefore, $2x^2 - 9x - 5 = (2x + 1)(x - 5)$.

$$2x^2 - 9x - 5 = 0$$
$$(2x + 1)(x - 5) = 0$$

Set each factor equal to zero and solve for x.

$$2x + 1 = 0 \quad \text{or} \quad x - 5 = 0$$
$$2x = -1 \qquad\qquad x = 5$$
$$x = -\frac{1}{2}$$

The roots are $-\dfrac{1}{2}$ and 5.

Method 2: Factor by Grouping

Find two integers with a product of $(2)(-5) = -10$ and a sum of -9.

Factors of −10	Product	Sum
1, −10	−10	−9
2, −5	−10	−3
5, −2	−10	3
10, −1	−10	9

Write $-9x$ as $x - 10x$. Then, factor by grouping.

$$2x^2 - 9x - 5 = 0$$
$$2x^2 + x - 10x - 5 = 0$$
$$(2x^2 + x) + (-10x - 5) = 0$$
$$x(2x + 1) - 5(2x + 1) = 0$$
$$(2x + 1)(x - 5) = 0$$

Set each factor equal to zero and solve for x.

$$2x + 1 = 0 \quad \text{or} \quad x - 5 = 0$$
$$2x = -1 \qquad\qquad x = 5$$
$$x = -\frac{1}{2}$$

The roots are $-\frac{1}{2}$ and 5.

Check for both Methods 1 and 2:
The equation has two distinct real roots. Check by substituting each root into the original quadratic equation.

For $x = -\frac{1}{2}$:

Left Side	Right Side
$2x^2 - 9x - 5$	0

$$= 2\left(-\frac{1}{2}\right)^2 - 9\left(-\frac{1}{2}\right) - 5$$
$$= 2\left(\frac{1}{4}\right) + \frac{9}{2} - 5$$
$$= \frac{1}{2} + \frac{9}{2} - \frac{10}{2}$$
$$= 0$$

Left Side = Right Side

For $x = 5$:

Left Side	Right Side
$2x^2 - 9x - 5$	0

$$= 2(5)^2 - 9(5) - 5$$
$$= 50 - 45 - 5$$
$$= 0$$

Left Side = Right Side

Both solutions are correct.

The roots of the quadratic equation are $-\frac{1}{2}$ and 5.

Your Turn

Determine the roots of each quadratic equation.

a) $x^2 - 10x + 25 = 0$

b) $x^2 - 16 = 0$

c) $3x^2 - 2x - 8 = 0$

Example 4

Apply Quadratic Equations

Did You Know?

Dock jumping competitions started in 2000 and have spread throughout the world, with events in Canada, United States, Great Britain, Japan, Australia, and Germany. The current world record holder jumped 29 ft 1 in. (8.86 m).

Dock jumping is an exciting dog event in which dogs compete for the longest jumping distance from a dock into a body of water. The path of a Jack Russell terrier on a particular jump can be approximated by the quadratic function $h(d) = -\frac{3}{10}d^2 + \frac{11}{10}d + 2$, where h is the height above the surface of the water and d is the horizontal distance the dog travels from the base of the dock, both in feet. All measurements are taken from the base of the dog's tail. Determine the horizontal distance of the jump.

Solution

When the dog lands in the water, the dog's height above the surface is 0 m. To solve this problem, determine the roots of the quadratic equation $-\frac{3}{10}d^2 + \frac{11}{10}d + 2 = 0$.

$$-\frac{3}{10}d^2 + \frac{11}{10}d + 2 = 0$$

$$-\frac{1}{10}(3d^2 - 11d - 20) = 0 \qquad \text{Factor out the common factor of } -\frac{1}{10}.$$

$$-\frac{1}{10}(3d + 4)(d - 5) = 0$$

$3d + 4 = 0 \quad$ or $\quad d - 5 = 0 \qquad$ Solve for d to determine the roots of the equation.

$\qquad 3d = -4 \qquad\qquad d = 5 \qquad$ Why does the factor $-\frac{1}{10}$ neither result in a root nor

$\qquad\quad d = -\frac{4}{3} \qquad\qquad\qquad\quad$ affect the other roots of the equation?

Since d represents the horizontal distance of the dog from the base of the dock, it cannot be negative.

So, reject the root $-\dfrac{4}{3}$.

Check the solution by substituting $d = 5$ into the original quadratic equation.

For $d = 5$:

Left Side

$$-\dfrac{3}{10}d^2 + \dfrac{11}{10}d + 2$$

$$= -\dfrac{3}{10}(5)^2 + \dfrac{11}{10}(5) + 2$$

$$= -\dfrac{15}{2} + \dfrac{11}{2} + \dfrac{4}{2}$$

$$= 0$$

Right Side

0

Left Side = Right Side

The solution is correct.

The dog travels a horizontal distance of 5 ft.

Your Turn

A waterslide ends with the slider dropping into a deep pool of water. The path of the slider after leaving the lower end of the slide can be approximated by the quadratic function $h(d) = -\dfrac{1}{6}d^2 - \dfrac{1}{6}d + 2$, where h is the height above the surface of the pool and d is the horizontal distance the slider travels from the lower end of the slide, both in feet. What is the horizontal distance the slider travels before dropping into the pool after leaving the lower end of the slide?

Example 5

Write and Solve a Quadratic Equation

The length of an outdoor lacrosse field is 10 m less than twice the width. The area of the field is 6600 m². Determine the dimensions of an outdoor lacrosse field.

Solution

Let w represent the width of the field.
Then, the length of the field is $2w - 10$.

Use the area formula.
$$A = lw$$
$$6600 = (2w - 10)(w)$$
$$6600 = 2w^2 - 10w$$
$$0 = 2w^2 - 10w - 6600$$
$$0 = 2(w^2 - 5w - 3300)$$
$$0 = w^2 - 5w - 3300$$
$$0 = (w - 60)(w + 55)$$

$w - 60 = 0$ or $w + 55 = 0$
$w = 60$ $\qquad$ $w = -55$

Since the width of the field cannot be negative, $w = -55$ is rejected. The width of the field is 60 m. The length of the field is $2(60) - 10$ or 110 m.

Check:
The area of the field is $(60)(110)$ or 6600 m².

Your Turn

The area of a rectangular Ping-Pong table is 45 ft². The length is 4 ft more than the width. What are the dimensions of the table?

Key Ideas

- You can solve some quadratic equations by factoring.

- If two factors of a quadratic equation have a product of zero, then by the zero product property one of the factors must be equal to zero.

- To solve a quadratic equation by factoring, first write the equation in the form $ax^2 + bx + c = 0$, and then factor the left side. Next, set each factor equal to zero, and solve for the unknown.

  For example,
  $$x^2 + 8x = -12$$
  $$x^2 + 8x + 12 = 0$$
  $$(x + 2)(x + 6) = 0$$
  $$x + 2 = 0 \quad \text{or} \quad x + 6 = 0$$
  $$x = -2 \qquad\qquad x = -6$$

- The solutions to a quadratic equation are called the roots of the equation.

- You can factor polynomials in quadratic form.

  - Factor trinomials of the form $a(P)^2 + b(P) + c$, where $a \neq 0$ and P is any expression, by replacing the expression for P with a single variable. Then substitute the expression for P back into the factored expression. Simplify the final factors, if possible.

    For example, factor $2(x + 3)^2 - 11(x + 3) + 15$ by letting $r = x + 3$.
    $$\begin{aligned}
    2(x + 3)^2 - 11(x + 3) + 15 &= 2r^2 - 11r + 15 \\
    &= 2r^2 - 5r - 6r + 15 \\
    &= (2r^2 - 5r) + (-6r + 15) \\
    &= r(2r - 5) - 3(2r - 5) \\
    &= (2r - 5)(r - 3) \\
    &= [2(x + 3) - 5][(x + 3) - 3] \\
    &= (2x + 1)(x) \\
    &= x(2x + 1)
    \end{aligned}$$

  - Factor a difference of squares, $P^2 - Q^2$, where P and Q are any expressions, as $[P - Q][P + Q]$.

Check Your Understanding

Practise

1. Factor completely.

a) $x^2 + 7x + 10$

b) $5z^2 + 40z + 60$

c) $0.2d^2 - 2.2d + 5.6$

2. Factor completely.

a) $3y^2 + 4y - 7$

b) $8k^2 - 6k - 5$

c) $0.4m^2 + 0.6m - 1.8$

3. Factor completely.

a) $x^2 + x - 20$

b) $x^2 - 12x + 36$

c) $\frac{1}{4}x^2 + 2x + 3$

d) $2x^2 + 12x + 18$

4. Factor each expression.

a) $4y^2 - 9x^2$

b) $0.36p^2 - 0.49q^2$

c) $\frac{1}{4}s^2 - \frac{9}{25}t^2$

d) $0.16t^2 - 16s^2$

5. Factor each expression.

a) $(x + 2)^2 - (x + 2) - 42$

b) $6(x^2 - 4x + 4)^2 + (x^2 - 4x + 4) - 1$

c) $(4j - 2)^2 - (2 + 4j)^2$

6. What are the factors of each expression?

a) $4(5b - 3)^2 + 10(5b - 3) - 6$

b) $16(x^2 + 1)^2 - 4(2x)^2$

c) $-\frac{1}{4}(2x)^2 + 25(2y^3)^2$

7. Solve each factored equation.

a) $(x + 3)(x + 4) = 0$

b) $(x - 2)\left(x + \frac{1}{2}\right) = 0$

c) $(x + 7)(x - 8) = 0$

d) $x(x + 5) = 0$

e) $(3x + 1)(5x - 4) = 0$

f) $2(x - 4)(7 - 2x) = 0$

8. Solve each quadratic equation by factoring. Check your answers.

a) $10n^2 - 40 = 0$

b) $\frac{1}{4}x^2 + \frac{5}{4}x + 1 = 0$

c) $3w^2 + 28w + 9 = 0$

d) $8y^2 - 22y + 15 = 0$

e) $d^2 + \frac{5}{2}d + \frac{3}{2} = 0$

f) $4x^2 - 12x + 9 = 0$

9. Determine the roots of each quadratic equation. Verify your answers.

a) $k^2 - 5k = 0$

b) $9x^2 = x + 8$

c) $\frac{8}{3}t + 5 = -\frac{1}{3}t^2$

d) $\frac{25}{49}y^2 - 9 = 0$

e) $2s^2 - 4s = 70$

f) $4q^2 - 28q = -49$

10. Solve each equation.

a) $42 = x^2 - x$

b) $g^2 = 30 - 7g$

c) $y^2 + 4y = 21$

d) $3 = 6p^2 - 7p$

e) $3x^2 + 9x = 30$

f) $2z^2 = 3 - 5z$

Apply

11. A rectangle has dimensions $x + 10$ and $2x - 3$, where x is in centimetres. The area of the rectangle is 54 cm².

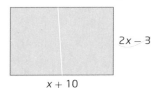

$2x - 3$

$x + 10$

a) What equation could you use to determine the value of x?

b) What is the value of x?

12. An osprey, a fish-eating bird of prey, dives toward the water to catch a salmon. The height, h, in metres, of the osprey above the water t seconds after it begins its dive can be approximated by the function $h(t) = 5t^2 - 30t + 45$.

a) Determine the time it takes for the osprey to reach a height of 20 m.

b) What assumptions did you make? Are your assumptions reasonable? Explain.

13. A flare is launched from a boat. The height, h, in metres, of the flare above the water is approximately modelled by the function $h(t) = 150t - 5t^2$, where t is the number of seconds after the flare is launched.

a) What equation could you use to determine the time it takes for the flare to return to the water?

b) How many seconds will it take for the flare to return to the water?

14. The product of two consecutive even integers is 16 more than 8 times the smaller integer. Determine the integers.

15. The area of a square is tripled by adding 10 cm to one dimension and 12 cm to the other. Determine the side length of the square.

16. Ted popped a baseball straight up with an initial upward velocity of 48 ft/s. The height, h, in feet, of the ball above the ground is modelled by the function $h(t) = 3 + 48t - 16t^2$. How long was the ball in the air if the catcher catches the ball 3 ft above the ground? Is your answer reasonable in this situation? Explain.

Did You Know?

Many Canadians have made a positive impact on Major League Baseball. Players such as Larry Walker of Maple Ridge, British Columbia, Jason Bay of Trail, British Columbia, and Justin Morneau of Westminster, British Columbia have had very successful careers in baseball's highest league.

17. A rectangle with area of 35 cm² is formed by cutting off strips of equal width from a rectangular piece of paper.

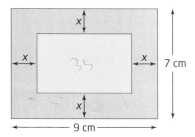

a) What is the width of each strip?

b) What are the dimensions of the new rectangle?

18. Without factoring, state if the binomial is a factor of the trinomial. Explain why or why not.

　　a) $x^2 - 5x - 36$, $x - 5$

　　b) $x^2 - 2x - 15$, $x + 3$

　　c) $6x^2 + 11x + 4$, $4x + 1$

　　d) $4x^2 + 4x - 3$, $2x - 1$

19. Solve each equation.

　　a) $x(2x - 3) - 2(3 + 2x) = -4(x + 1)$

　　b) $3(x - 2)(x + 1) - 4 = 2(x - 1)^2$

20. The hypotenuse of a right triangle measures 29 cm. One leg is 1 cm shorter than the other. What are the lengths of the legs?

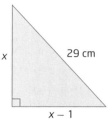

21. A field is in the shape of a right triangle. The fence around the perimeter of the field measures 40 m. If the length of the hypotenuse is 17 m, find the length of the other two sides.

22. The width of the top of a notebook computer is 7 cm less than the length. The surface area of the top of the notebook is 690 cm².

　　a) Write an equation to represent the surface area of the top of the notebook computer.

　　b) What are the dimensions of the top of the computer?

23. Stephan plans to build a uniform walkway around a rectangular flower bed that is 20 m by 40 m. There is enough material to make a walkway that has a total area of 700 m². What is the width of the walkway?

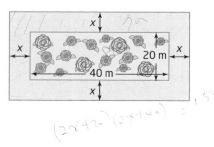

24. An 18-m-tall tree is broken during a severe storm, as shown. The distance from the base of the trunk to the point where the tip touches the ground is 12 m. At what height did the tree break?

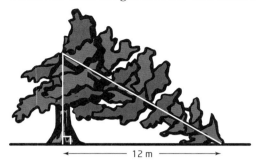

25. The pressure difference, P, in newtons per square metre, above and below an airplane wing is described by the formula $P = \left(\frac{1}{2}d\right)(v_1)^2 - \left(\frac{1}{2}d\right)(v_2)^2$, where d is the density of the air, in kilograms per cubic metre; v_1 is the velocity, in metres per second, of the air passing above; and v_2 is the velocity, in metres per second, of the air passing below. Write this formula in factored form.

26. Carlos was asked to factor the trinomial $6x^2 - 16x + 8$ completely. His work is shown below.

　　Carlos's solution:
$$6x^2 - 16x + 8$$
$$= 6x^2 - 12x - 4x + 8$$
$$= 6x(x - 2) - 4(x - 2)$$
$$= (x - 2)(6x - 4)$$

　　Is Carlos correct? Explain.

27. Factor each expression.

　　a) $3(2z + 3)^2 - 9(2z + 3) - 30$

　　b) $16(m^2 - 4)^2 - 4(3n)^2$

　　c) $\frac{1}{9}y^2 - \frac{1}{3}yx + \frac{1}{4}x^2$

　　d) $-28\left(w + \frac{2}{3}\right)^2 + 7\left(3w - \frac{1}{3}\right)^2$

Extend

28. A square has an area of $(9x^2 + 30xy + 25y^2)$ square centimetres. What is an expression for the perimeter of the square?

29. Angela opened a surf shop in Tofino, British Columbia. Her accountant models her profit, P, in dollars, with the function $P(t) = 1125(t - 1)^2 - 10\ 125$, where t is the number of years of operation. Use graphing or factoring to determine how long it will take for the shop to start making a profit.

Pete Devries

Did You Know?

Pete Devries was the first Canadian to win an international surfing competition. In 2009, he outperformed over 110 world-class surfers to win the O'Neill Cold Water Classic Canada held in Tofino, British Columbia.

Create Connections

30. Write a quadratic equation in standard form with the given root(s).

a) −3 and 3

b) 2

c) $\frac{2}{3}$ and 4

d) $\frac{3}{5}$ and $-\frac{1}{2}$

31. Create an example of a quadratic equation that cannot be solved by factoring. Explain why it cannot be factored. Show the graph of the corresponding quadratic function and show where the roots are located.

32. You can use the difference of squares pattern to perform certain mental math shortcuts. For example,

$$81 - 36 = (9 - 6)(9 + 6)$$
$$= (3)(15)$$
$$= 45$$

a) Explain how this strategy works. When can you use it?

b) Create two examples to illustrate the strategy.

Project Corner   Avalanche Safety

- Experts use avalanche control all over the world above highways, ski resorts, railroads, mining operations, and utility companies, and anywhere else that may be threatened by avalanches.

- Avalanche control is the intentional triggering of avalanches. People are cleared away to a safe distance, then experts produce more frequent, but smaller, avalanches at controlled times.

- Because avalanches tend to occur in the same zones and under certain conditions, avalanche experts can predict when avalanches are likely to occur.

- Charges are delivered by launchers, thrown out of helicopters, or delivered above the avalanche starting zones by an avalanche control expert on skis.

- What precautions would avalanche control experts need to take to ensure public safety?

Solving Quadratic Equations by Completing the Square

Focus on...

- solving quadratic equations by completing the square

Rogers Pass gets up to 15 m of snow per year. Because of the steep mountains, over 130 avalanche paths must be monitored during the winter. To keep the Trans-Canada Highway open, the Royal Canadian Artillery uses 105-mm howitzers to create controlled avalanches. The Artillery must aim the howitzer accurately to operate it safely. Suppose that the quadratic function that approximates the trajectory of a shell fired by a howitzer at an angle of 45° is $h(x) = -\frac{1}{5}x^2 + 2x + \frac{1}{20}$, where h is the height of the shell and x is the horizontal distance from the howitzer to where the shell lands, both in kilometres. How can this function be used to determine where to place the howitzer to fire at a specific spot on the mountainside?

Investigate Solving Quadratic Equations by Completing the Square

Materials

- grid paper, graphing calculator, or computer with graphing software

Sometimes factoring quadratic equations is not practical. In Chapter 3, you learned how to complete the square to analyse and graph quadratic functions. You can complete the square to help solve quadratic equations such as $-\frac{1}{5}x^2 + 2x + \frac{1}{20} = 0$.

1. Graph the function $f(x) = -\frac{1}{5}x^2 + 2x + \frac{1}{20}$.

2. What are the x-intercepts of the graph? How accurate are your answers? Why might it be important to determine more accurate zeros for the function?

3. a) Rewrite the function in the form $h(x) = a(x - p)^2 + q$ by completing the square.

b) Set $h(x)$ equal to zero. Solve for x. Express your answers as exact values.

Reflect and Respond

4. What are the two roots of the quadratic equation for projectile motion, $0 = -\frac{1}{5}x^2 + 2x + \frac{1}{20}$? What do the roots represent in this situation?

5. To initiate an avalanche, the howitzer crew must aim the shell up the slope of the mountain. The shot from the howitzer lands 750 m above where the howitzer is located. How could the crew determine the horizontal distance from the point of impact at which the howitzer must be located? Explain your reasoning. Calculate the horizontal distances involved in this scenario. Include a sketch of the path of the projectile.

6. At which horizontal distance from the point of impact would you locate the howitzer if you were in charge of setting off a controlled avalanche? Explain your reasoning.

> **Did You Know?**
>
> Parks Canada operates the world's largest mobile avalanche control program to keep the Trans-Canada Highway and the Canadian Pacific Railway operating through Rogers Pass.

Taking slope angle measurement.

Link the Ideas

You can solve quadratic equations of the form $ax^2 + bx + c = 0$, where $b = 0$, or of the form $a(x - p)^2 + q = 0$, where $a \neq 0$, that have real-number solutions by isolating the squared term and taking the square root of both sides. The square root of a positive real number can be positive or negative, so there are two possible solutions to these equations.

To solve $x^2 = 9$, take the square root of both sides.

$$x^2 = 9$$
$$\pm\sqrt{x^2} = \pm\sqrt{9}$$ Read $\pm$ as "plus or minus."   3 is a solution to the equation because $(3)(3) = 9$.
$$x = \pm 3$$ -3 is a solution to the equation because $(-3)(-3) = 9$.

To solve $(x - 1)^2 - 49 = 0$, isolate the squared term and take the square root of both sides.

$$(x - 1)^2 - 49 = 0$$
$$(x - 1)^2 = 49$$
$$x - 1 = \pm 7$$
$$x = 1 \pm 7$$

$x = 1 + 7$ or $x = 1 - 7$
$x = 8$ $x = -6$

> **Did You Know?**
>
> Around 830 c.e., Abu Ja'far Muhammad ibn Musa al-Khwarizmi wrote *Hisab al-jabr w'al-muqabala.* The word *al-jabr* from this title is the basis of the word we use today, *algebra.* In his book, al-Khwarizmi describes how to solve a quadratic equation by completing the square.

> **Web Link**
>
> To learn more about al-Khwarizmi, go to www.mhrprecalc11.ca and follow the links.

Check:
Substitute $x = 8$ and $x = -6$ into the original equation.

Left Side	Right Side	Left Side	Right Side
$(x - 1)^2 - 49$	0	$(x - 1)^2 - 49$	0
$= (8 - 1)^2 - 49$		$= (-6 - 1)^2 - 49$	
$= 7^2 - 49$		$= (-7)^2 - 49$	
$= 49 - 49$		$= 49 - 49$	
$= 0$		$= 0$	

     Left Side = Right Side   Left Side = Right Side

Both solutions are correct. The roots are 8 and -6.

Many quadratic equations cannot be solved by factoring. In addition, graphing the corresponding functions may not result in exact solutions. You can write a quadratic function expressed in standard form, $y = ax^2 + bx + c$, in vertex form, $y = a(x - p)^2 + q$, by completing the square. You can also use the process of completing the square to determine exact solutions to quadratic equations.

Example 1

Write and Solve a Quadratic Equation by Taking the Square Root

A wide-screen television has a diagonal measure of 42 in. The width of the screen is 16 in. more than the height. Determine the dimensions of the screen, to the nearest tenth of an inch.

Solution

Draw a diagram. Let h represent the height of the screen. Then, $h + 16$ represents the width of the screen.

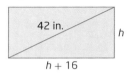

Use the Pythagorean Theorem.

$$h^2 + (h + 16)^2 = 42^2$$
$$h^2 + (h^2 + 32h + 256) = 1764$$
$$2h^2 + 32h + 256 = 1764$$
$$2h^2 + 32h = 1508$$
$$h^2 + 16h = 754 \qquad \text{Isolate the variable terms on the left side.}$$
$$h^2 + 16h + 64 = 754 + 64 \qquad \text{Add the square of half the coefficient of } h \text{ to both sides.}$$
$$(h + 8)^2 = 818 \qquad \text{Factor the perfect square trinomial on the left side.}$$
$$h + 8 = \pm\sqrt{818} \qquad \text{Take the square root of both sides.}$$
$$h = -8 \pm \sqrt{818}$$

$$h = -8 + \sqrt{818} \quad \text{or} \quad h = -8 - \sqrt{818}$$
$$h \approx 20.6 \qquad\qquad\qquad h \approx -36.6$$

Since the height of the screen cannot be negative, $h = -36.6$ is an **extraneous root**.

extraneous root

• a number obtained in solving an equation, which does not satisfy the initial restrictions on the variable

Thus, the height of the screen is approximately 20.6 in., and the width of the screen is approximately $20.6 + 16$ or 36.6 in..

Hence, the dimensions of a 42-in. television are approximately 20.6 in. by 36.6 in..

Check:
$20.6^2 + 36.6^2$ is 1763.92, and $\sqrt{1763.92}$ is approximately 42, the diagonal of the television, in inches.

Your Turn

The circular Canadian two-dollar coin consists of an aluminum and bronze core and a nickel outer ring. If the radius of the inner core is 0.84 cm and the area of the circular face of the coin is 1.96π cm², what is the width of the outer ring?

Example 2

Solve a Quadratic Equation by Completing the Square When $a = 1$

Solve $x^2 - 21 = -10x$ by completing the square. Express your answers to the nearest tenth.

Can you solve this equation by factoring? Explain.

Solution

$$x^2 - 21 = -10x$$
$$x^2 + 10x = 21$$
$$x^2 + 10x + 25 = 21 + 25$$
$$(x + 5)^2 = 46$$
$$x + 5 = \pm\sqrt{46}$$

Solve for x.

$$x + 5 = \sqrt{46} \qquad \text{or} \qquad x + 5 = -\sqrt{46}$$
$$x = -5 + \sqrt{46} \qquad\qquad x = -5 - \sqrt{46}$$
$$x = 1.7823... \qquad\qquad\quad x = -11.7823...$$

The exact roots are $-5 + \sqrt{46}$ and $-5 - \sqrt{46}$.
The roots are 1.8 and -11.8, to the nearest tenth.

You can also see the solutions to this equation graphically as the x-intercepts of the graph of the function $f(x) = x^2 + 10x - 21$.

These occur at approximately $(-11.8, 0)$ and $(1.8, 0)$ and have values of -11.8 and 1.8, respectively.

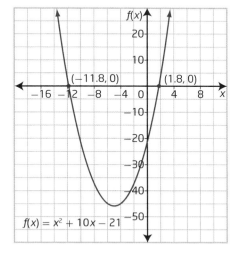

Your Turn

Solve $p^2 - 4p = 11$ by completing the square. Express your answers to the nearest tenth.

Example 3

Solve a Quadratic Equation by Completing the Square When $a \neq 1$

Determine the roots of $-2x^2 - 3x + 7 = 0$, to the nearest hundredth. Then, use technology to verify your answers.

Solution

$-2x^2 - 3x + 7 = 0$

$$x^2 + \frac{3}{2}x - \frac{7}{2} = 0 \qquad \text{Divide both sides by a factor of } -2.$$

$$x^2 + \frac{3}{2}x = \frac{7}{2} \qquad \text{Isolate the variable terms on the left side.}$$

$$x^2 + \frac{3}{2}x + \frac{9}{16} = \frac{7}{2} + \frac{9}{16} \qquad \text{Why is } \frac{9}{16} \text{ added to both sides?}$$

$$\left(x + \frac{3}{4}\right)^2 = \frac{65}{16}$$

$$x + \frac{3}{4} = \pm\sqrt{\frac{65}{16}} \qquad \text{Solve for } x.$$

$$x = -\frac{3}{4} \pm \frac{\sqrt{65}}{4}$$

$$x = \frac{-3 \pm \sqrt{65}}{4}$$

The exact roots are $\dfrac{-3 + \sqrt{65}}{4}$ and $\dfrac{-3 - \sqrt{65}}{4}$.

The roots are 1.27 and -2.77, to the nearest hundredth.

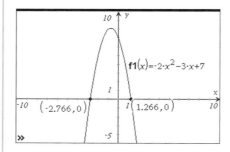

Your Turn

Determine the roots of the equation $-2x^2 - 5x + 2 = 0$, to the nearest hundredth. Verify your solutions using technology.

Example 4

Apply Completing the Square

A defender kicks a soccer ball away from her own goal. The path of the kicked soccer ball can be approximated by the quadratic function $h(x) = -0.06x^2 + 3.168x - 35.34$, where x is the horizontal distance travelled, in metres, from the goal line and h is the height, in metres.

a) You can determine the distance the soccer ball is from the goal line by solving the corresponding equation, $-0.06x^2 + 3.168x - 35.34 = 0$. How far is the soccer ball from the goal line when it is kicked? Express your answer to the nearest tenth of a metre.

b) How far does the soccer ball travel before it hits the ground?

Solution

a) Solve the equation $-0.06x^2 + 3.168x - 35.34 = 0$ by completing the square.

$$-0.06x^2 + 3.168x - 35.34 = 0$$

$$x^2 - 52.8x + 589 = 0 \qquad \text{Divide both sides by a common factor of } -0.06.$$

$$x^2 - 52.8x = -589 \qquad \text{Isolate the variable terms on the left side.}$$

$$x^2 - 52.8x + \left(\frac{52.8}{2}\right)^2 = -589 + \left(\frac{52.8}{2}\right)^2 \qquad \text{Complete the square on the left side.}$$

$$x^2 - 52.8x + 696.96 = -589 + 696.96$$

$$(x - 26.4)^2 = 107.96$$

$$x - 26.4 = \pm\sqrt{107.96} \qquad \text{Take the square root of both sides.}$$

$$
\begin{array}{lll}
x - 26.4 = \sqrt{107.96} & \text{or} \quad x - 26.4 = -\sqrt{107.96} & \text{Solve for } x. \\
\quad x = 26.4 + \sqrt{107.96} & \qquad x = 26.4 - \sqrt{107.96} & \\
\quad x = 36.7903\ldots & \qquad x = 16.0096\ldots &
\end{array}
$$

The roots of the equation are approximately 36.8 and 16.0. The ball is kicked approximately 16.0 m from the goal line.

b) From part a), the soccer ball is kicked approximately 16.0 m from the goal line. The ball lands approximately 36.8 m from the goal line. Therefore, the soccer ball travels $36.8 - 16.0$, or 20.8 m, before it hits the ground.

Your Turn

How far does the soccer ball in Example 4 travel if the function that models its trajectory is $h(x) = -0.016x^2 + 1.152x - 15.2$?

Key Ideas

- Completing the square is the process of rewriting a quadratic polynomial from the standard form, $ax^2 + bx + c$, to the vertex form, $a(x - p)^2 + q$.

- You can use completing the square to determine the roots of a quadratic equation in standard form.

For example,

$2x^2 - 4x - 2 = 0$

$x^2 - 2x - 1 = 0$ Divide both sides by a common factor of 2.

$x^2 - 2x = 1$ Isolate the variable terms on the left side.

$x^2 - 2x + 1 = 1 + 1$ Complete the square on the left side.

$(x - 1)^2 = 2$

$x - 1 = \pm\sqrt{2}$ Take the square root of both sides.

$x - 1 = \sqrt{2}$ or $x - 1 = -\sqrt{2}$ Solve for x.

$\quad x = 1 + \sqrt{2} \qquad\qquad x = 1 - \sqrt{2}$

$\quad x \approx 2.41 \qquad\qquad\quad x \approx -0.41$

- Express roots of quadratic equations as exact roots or as decimal approximations.

Check Your Understanding

Practise

1. What value of c makes each expression a perfect square?

a) $x^2 + x + c$

b) $x^2 - 5x + c$

c) $x^2 - 0.5x + c$

d) $x^2 + 0.2x + c$

e) $x^2 + 15x + c$

f) $x^2 - 9x + c$

2. Complete the square to write each quadratic equation in the form $(x + p)^2 = q$.

a) $2x^2 + 8x + 4 = 0$

b) $-3x^2 - 12x + 5 = 0$

c) $\frac{1}{2}x^2 - 3x + 5 = 0$

3. Write each equation in the form $a(x - p)^2 + q = 0$.

a) $x^2 - 12x + 9 = 0$

b) $5x^2 - 20x - 1 = 0$

c) $-2x^2 + x - 1 = 0$

d) $0.5x^2 + 2.1x + 3.6 = 0$

e) $-1.2x^2 - 5.1x - 7.4 = 0$

f) $\frac{1}{2}x^2 + 3x - 6 = 0$

4. Solve each quadratic equation. Express your answers as exact roots.

a) $x^2 = 64$

b) $2s^2 - 8 = 0$

c) $\frac{1}{3}t^2 - 1 = 11$

d) $-y^2 + 5 = -6$

5. Solve. Express your answers as exact roots.

a) $(x - 3)^2 = 4$

b) $(x + 2)^2 = 9$

c) $\left(d + \dfrac{1}{2}\right)^2 = 1$

d) $\left(h - \dfrac{3}{4}\right)^2 = \dfrac{7}{16}$

e) $(s + 6)^2 = \dfrac{3}{4}$

f) $(x + 4)^2 = 18$

6. Solve each quadratic equation by completing the square. Express your answers as exact roots.

a) $x^2 + 10x + 4 = 0$

b) $x^2 - 8x + 13 = 0$

c) $3x^2 + 6x + 1 = 0$

d) $-2x^2 + 4x + 3 = 0$

e) $-0.1x^2 - 0.6x + 0.4 = 0$

f) $0.5x^2 - 4x - 6 = 0$

7. Solve each quadratic equation by completing the square. Express your answers to the nearest tenth.

a) $x^2 - 8x - 4 = 0$

b) $-3x^2 + 4x + 5 = 0$

c) $\dfrac{1}{2}x^2 - 6x - 5 = 0$

d) $0.2x^2 + 0.12x - 11 = 0$

e) $-\dfrac{2}{3}x^2 - x + 2 = 0$

f) $\dfrac{3}{4}x^2 + 6x + 1 = 0$

Apply

8. Dinahi's rectangular dog kennel measures 4 ft by 10 ft. She plans to double the area of the kennel by extending each side by an equal amount.

a) Sketch and label a diagram to represent this situation.

b) Write the equation to model the new area.

c) What are the dimensions of the new dog kennel, to the nearest tenth of a foot?

9. Evan passes a flying disc to a teammate during a competition at the Flatland Ultimate and Cups Tournament in Winnipeg. The flying disc follows the path $h(d) = -0.02d^2 + 0.4d + 1$, where h is the height, in metres, and d is the horizontal distance, in metres, that the flying disc has travelled from the thrower. If no one catches the flying disc, the height of the disc above the ground when it lands can be modelled by $h(d) = 0$.

a) What quadratic equation can you use to determine how far the disc will travel if no one catches it?

b) How far will the disc travel if no one catches it? Express your answer to the nearest tenth of a metre.

Did You Know?

Each August, teams compete in the Canadian Ultimate Championships for the national title in five different divisions: juniors, masters, mixed, open, and women's. This tournament also determines who will represent Canada at the next world championships.

10. A model rocket is launched from a platform. Its trajectory can be approximated by the function $h(d) = -0.01d^2 + 2d + 1$, where h is the height, in metres, of the rocket and d is the horizontal distance, in metres, the rocket travels. How far does the rocket land from its launch position? Express your answer to the nearest tenth of a metre.

11. Brian is placing a photograph behind a 12-in. by 12-in. piece of matting. He positions the photograph so the matting is twice as wide at the top and bottom as it is at the sides.

The visible area of the photograph is 54 sq. in. What are the dimensions of the photograph?

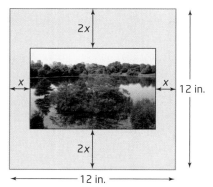

12. The path of debris from fireworks when the wind is about 25 km/h can be modelled by the quadratic function $h(x) = -0.04x^2 + 2x + 8$, where h is the height and x is the horizontal distance travelled, both measured in metres. How far away from the launch site will the debris land? Express your answer to the nearest tenth of a metre.

Extend

13. Write a quadratic equation with the given roots.

a) $\sqrt{7}$ and $-\sqrt{7}$

b) $1 + \sqrt{3}$ and $1 - \sqrt{3}$

c) $\dfrac{5 + \sqrt{11}}{2}$ and $\dfrac{5 - \sqrt{11}}{2}$

14. Solve each equation for x by completing the square.

a) $x^2 + 2x = k$

b) $kx^2 - 2x = k$

c) $x^2 = kx + 1$

15. Determine the roots of $ax^2 + bx + c = 0$ by completing the square. Can you use this result to solve any quadratic equation? Explain.

16. The sum of the first n terms, S_n, of an arithmetic series can be found using the formula

$S_n = \dfrac{n}{2}[2t_1 + (n - 1)d]$, where t_1 is the first term and d is the common difference.

a) The sum of the first n terms in the arithmetic series
$6 + 10 + 14 + \cdots$ is 3870. Determine the value of n.

b) The sum of the first n consecutive natural numbers is 780. Determine the value of n.

17. A machinist in a fabrication shop needs to bend a metal rod at an angle of 60° at a point 4 m from one end of the rod so that the ends of the rod are 12 m apart, as shown.

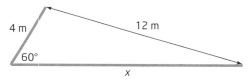

a) Using the cosine law, write a quadratic equation to represent this situation.

b) Solve the quadratic equation. How long is the rod, to the nearest tenth of a metre?

Create Connections

18. The solution to $x^2 = 9$ is $x = \pm3$. The solution to the equation $x = \sqrt{9}$ is $x = 3$. Explain why the solutions to the two equations are different.

19. Allison completed the square to determine the vertex form of the quadratic function $y = x^2 - 6x - 27$. Her method is shown.

Allison's method:

$y = x^2 - 6x - 27$
$y = (x^2 - 6x) - 27$
$y = (x^2 - 6x + 9 - 9) - 27$
$y = [(x - 3)^2 - 9] - 27$
$y = (x - 3)^2 - 36$

Riley completed the square to begin to solve the quadratic equation $0 = x^2 - 6x - 27$. His method is shown.

Riley's method:

$0 = x^2 - 6x - 27$
$27 = x^2 - 6x$
$27 + 9 = x^2 - 6x + 9$
$36 = (x - 3)^2$
$\pm 6 = x - 3$

Describe the similarities and differences between the two uses of the method of completing the square.

20. Compare and contrast the following strategies for solving $x^2 - 5x - 6 = 0$.
- completing the square
- graphing the corresponding function
- factoring

21. Write a quadratic function in the form $y = a(x - p)^2 + q$ satisfying each of the following descriptions. Then, write the corresponding quadratic equation in the form $0 = ax^2 + bx + c$. Use graphing technology to verify that your equation also satisfies the description.

a) two distinct real roots

b) one distinct real root, or two equal real roots

c) no real roots

Project Corner   Avalanche Blasting

- An avalauncher is a two-chambered compressed-gas cannon used in avalanche control work. It fires projectiles with trajectories that can be varied by altering the firing angle and the nitrogen pressure.

- The main disadvantages of avalaunchers, compared to powerful artillery such as the howitzer, are that they have a short range and poor accuracy in strong winds.

- Which would you use if you were an expert initiating a controlled avalanche near a ski resort, a howitzer or an avalauncher? Why?

Howitzer

Avalauncher

The Quadratic Formula

Focus on...

- developing the quadratic formula
- solving quadratic equations using the quadratic formula
- using the discriminant to determine the nature of the roots of a quadratic equation
- selecting an appropriate method for solving a quadratic equation
- solving problems involving quadratic equations

You can solve quadratic equations graphically, by factoring, by determining the square root, and by completing the square. Are there other ways? The Greek mathematicians Pythagoras (500 B.C.E.) and Euclid (300 B.C.E.) both derived geometric solutions to a quadratic equation. A general solution for quadratic equations using numbers was derived in about 700 C.E. by the Hindu mathematician Brahmagupta. The general formula used today was derived in about 1100 C.E. by another Hindu mathematician, Bhaskara. He was also the first to recognize that any positive number has two square roots, one positive and one negative.

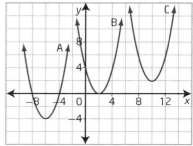

For each parabola shown, how many roots does the related quadratic equation have?

Investigate the Quadratic Formula

By completing the square, you can develop a formula that allows you to solve any quadratic equation in standard form.

quadratic formula

- a formula for determining the roots of a quadratic equation of the form $ax^2 + bx + c = 0, a \neq 0$
- $x = \dfrac{-b \pm \sqrt{b^2 - 4ac}}{2a}$

1. Copy the calculations. Describe the steps in the following example of the **quadratic formula**.

$$2x^2 + 7x + 1 = 0$$

$$x^2 + \frac{7}{2}x + \frac{1}{2} = 0$$

$$x^2 + \frac{7}{2}x = -\frac{1}{2}$$

$$x^2 + \frac{7}{2}x + \left(\frac{7}{4}\right)^2 = -\frac{1}{2} + \left(\frac{7}{4}\right)^2$$

$$\left(x + \frac{7}{4}\right)^2 = -\frac{8}{16} + \frac{49}{16}$$

$$\left(x + \frac{7}{4}\right)^2 = \frac{41}{16}$$

$$x + \frac{7}{4} = \pm\sqrt{\frac{41}{16}}$$

$$x = -\frac{7}{4} \pm \frac{\sqrt{41}}{4}$$

$$x = \frac{-7 \pm \sqrt{41}}{4}$$

2. Repeat the steps using the general quadratic equation in standard form $ax^2 + bx + c = 0$.

Reflect and Respond

3. a) Will the quadratic formula work for any quadratic equation written in any form?

b) When do you think it is appropriate to use the quadratic formula to solve a quadratic equation?

c) When is it appropriate to use a different method, such as graphing the corresponding function, factoring, determining the square root, or completing the square? Explain.

4. What is the maximum number of roots the quadratic formula will give? How do you know this?

5. Describe the conditions for a, b, and c that are necessary for the quadratic formula, $x = \dfrac{-b \pm \sqrt{b^2 - 4ac}}{2a}$, to result in only one possible root.

6. Is there a condition relating a, b, and c that will result in no real solution to a quadratic equation? Explain.

Link the Ideas

You can solve quadratic equations of the form $ax^2 + bx + c = 0$, $a \neq 0$, using the quadratic formula, $x = \dfrac{-b \pm \sqrt{b^2 - 4ac}}{2a}$.

For example, in the quadratic equation $3x^2 + 5x - 2 = 0$, $a = 3$, $b = 5$, and $c = -2$.

Substitute these values into the quadratic formula.

$$x = \frac{-b \pm \sqrt{b^2 - 4ac}}{2a}$$

$$x = \frac{-5 \pm \sqrt{5^2 - 4(3)(-2)}}{2(3)}$$

$$x = \frac{-5 \pm \sqrt{25 + 24}}{6}$$

$$x = \frac{-5 \pm \sqrt{49}}{6}$$

$$x = \frac{-5 \pm 7}{6}$$

Determine the two roots.

$$x = \frac{-5 + 7}{6} \quad \text{or} \quad x = \frac{-5 - 7}{6}$$

$$x = \frac{1}{3} \qquad\qquad x = \frac{-12}{6}$$

$$\qquad\qquad\qquad\qquad x = -2$$

The roots are $\dfrac{1}{3}$ and -2.

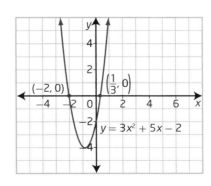

Check:

Substitute $x = \frac{1}{3}$ and $x = -2$ into the original equation.

Left Side	Right Side
$3x^2 + 5x - 2$	0

$$= 3\left(\frac{1}{3}\right)^2 + 5\left(\frac{1}{3}\right) - 2$$

$$= \frac{1}{3} + \frac{5}{3} - \frac{6}{3}$$

$$= 0$$

Left Side = Right Side

Left Side	Right Side
$3x^2 + 5x - 2$	0

$$= 3(-2)^2 + 5(-2) - 2$$

$$= 12 - 10 - 2$$

$$= 0$$

Left Side = Right Side

Both solutions are correct. The roots of the equation are $\frac{1}{3}$ and -2.

You can determine the nature of the roots for a quadratic equation by the value of the **discriminant**.

discriminant

- the expression $b^2 - 4ac$ located under the radical sign in the quadratic formula
- use its value to determine the nature of the roots for a quadratic equation $ax^2 + bx + c = 0, a \neq 0$

- When the value of the discriminant is positive, $b^2 - 4ac > 0$, there are two distinct real roots.

- When the value of the discriminant is zero, $b^2 - 4ac = 0$, there is one distinct real root, or two equal real roots.

- When the value of the discriminant is negative, $b^2 - 4ac < 0$, there are no real roots.

You can see that this is true by testing the three different types of values of the discriminant in the quadratic formula.

Example 1

Use the Discriminant to Determine the Nature of the Roots

Use the discriminant to determine the nature of the roots for each quadratic equation. Check by graphing.

a) $-2x^2 + 3x + 8 = 0$

b) $3x^2 - 5x = -9$

c) $\frac{1}{4}x^2 - 3x + 9 = 0$

Solution

To determine the nature of the roots for each equation, substitute the corresponding values for a, b, and c into the discriminant expression, $b^2 - 4ac$.

a) For $-2x^2 + 3x + 8 = 0$, $a = -2$, $b = 3$, and $c = 8$.

$$b^2 - 4ac = 3^2 - 4(-2)(8)$$
$$b^2 - 4ac = 9 + 64$$
$$b^2 - 4ac = 73$$

Since the value of the discriminant is positive, there are two distinct real roots.

The graph of the corresponding quadratic function, $y = -2x^2 + 3x + 8$, confirms that there are two distinct x-intercepts.

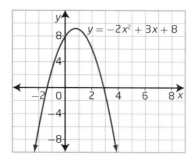

b) First, rewrite $3x^2 - 5x = -9$ in the form $ax^2 + bx + c = 0$.

$3x^2 - 5x + 9 = 0$

For $3x^2 - 5x + 9 = 0$, $a = 3$, $b = -5$, and $c = 9$.

$b^2 - 4ac = (-5)^2 - 4(3)(9)$

$b^2 - 4ac = 25 - 108$

$b^2 - 4ac = -83$

Since the value of the discriminant is negative, there are no real roots. The square root of a negative number does not result in a real number.

The graph of the corresponding quadratic function, $y = 3x^2 - 5x + 9$, shows that there are no x-intercepts.

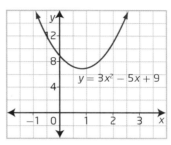

c) For $\frac{1}{4}x^2 - 3x + 9 = 0$, $a = \frac{1}{4}$, $b = -3$, and $c = 9$.

$b^2 - 4ac = (-3)^2 - 4\left(\frac{1}{4}\right)(9)$

$b^2 - 4ac = 9 - 9$

$b^2 - 4ac = 0$

Since the value of the discriminant is zero, there is one distinct real root, or two equal real roots.

The graph of the corresponding quadratic function, $y = \frac{1}{4}x^2 - 3x + 9$, confirms that there is only one x-intercept because it touches the x-axis but does not cross it.

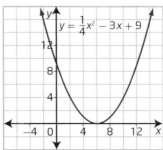

Your Turn

Use the discriminant to determine the nature of the roots for each quadratic equation. Check by graphing.

a) $x^2 - 5x + 4 = 0$ b) $3x^2 + 4x + \frac{4}{3} = 0$ c) $2x^2 - 8x = -9$

Example 2

Use the Quadratic Formula to Solve Quadratic Equations

Use the quadratic formula to solve each quadratic equation. Express your answers to the nearest hundredth.

a) $9x^2 + 12x = -4$

b) $5x^2 - 7x - 1 = 0$

Solution

a) First, write $9x^2 + 12x = -4$ in the form $ax^2 + bx + c = 0$.

$$9x^2 + 12x + 4 = 0$$

For $9x^2 + 12x + 4 = 0$, $a = 9$, $b = 12$, and $c = 4$.

$$x = \frac{-b \pm \sqrt{b^2 - 4ac}}{2a}$$

$$x = \frac{-12 \pm \sqrt{12^2 - 4(9)(4)}}{2(9)}$$

$$x = \frac{-12 \pm \sqrt{144 - 144}}{18}$$

$$x = \frac{-12 \pm \sqrt{0}}{18}$$

Since the value of the discriminant is zero, there is only one distinct real root, or two equal real roots.

$$x = \frac{-12}{18}$$

$$x = -\frac{2}{3}$$

Check:

Substitute $x = -\frac{2}{3}$ into the original equation.

Left Side   Right Side

$9x^2 + 12x$ -4

$$= 9\left(-\frac{2}{3}\right)^2 + 12\left(-\frac{2}{3}\right)$$

$$= 9\left(\frac{4}{9}\right) - 8$$

How could you use technology to check your solution graphically?

$$= 4 - 8$$

$$= -4$$

Left Side = Right Side

The root is $-\frac{2}{3}$, or approximately -0.67.

b) For $5x^2 - 7x - 1 = 0$, $a = 5$, $b = -7$, and $c = -1$.

$$x = \frac{-b \pm \sqrt{b^2 - 4ac}}{2a}$$

$$x = \frac{-(-7) \pm \sqrt{(-7)^2 - 4(5)(-1)}}{2(5)}$$

$$x = \frac{7 \pm \sqrt{49 + 20}}{10}$$

$$x = \frac{7 \pm \sqrt{69}}{10} \qquad \text{Since the value of the discriminant is positive,}$$
$$\text{there are two distinct real roots.}$$

$$x = \frac{7 + \sqrt{69}}{10} \quad \text{or} \quad x = \frac{7 - \sqrt{69}}{10}$$

$$x = 1.5306... \qquad\qquad x = -0.1306...$$

The roots are $\dfrac{7 + \sqrt{69}}{10}$ and $\dfrac{7 - \sqrt{69}}{10}$, or approximately 1.53 and -0.13.

Check:
The graph of the corresponding function, $y = 5x^2 - 7x - 1$, shows the zeros at approximately $(-0.13, 0)$ and $(1.53, 0)$.

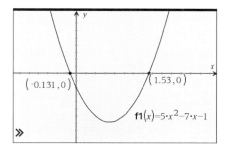

Therefore, both solutions are correct.

Your Turn

Determine the roots for each quadratic equation. Express your answers to the nearest hundredth.

a) $3x^2 + 5x - 2 = 0$

b) $\dfrac{t^2}{2} - t - \dfrac{5}{2} = 0$

Example 3

Select a Strategy to Solve a Quadratic Equation

a) Solve $6x^2 - 14x + 8 = 0$ by

    i) graphing the corresponding function

    ii) factoring the equation

    iii) completing the square

    iv) using the quadratic formula

b) Which strategy do you prefer? Justify your reasoning.

> **Solution**

a) **i)** Graph the function
$f(x) = 6x^2 - 14x + 8$, and then
determine the x-intercepts.
The x-intercepts are 1
and approximately 1.33.
Therefore, the roots are 1 and
approximately 1.33.

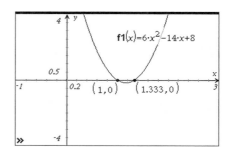

    ii) Factor the equation.
$$6x^2 - 14x + 8 = 0$$
$$3x^2 - 7x + 4 = 0$$
$$(3x - 4)(x - 1) = 0$$

By inspection, $3x^2 - 7x + 4 = (3x - \blacksquare)(x - \blacksquare)$.
What factors of 4 give the correct middle term?

$$3x - 4 = 0 \quad \text{or} \quad x - 1 = 0$$
$$3x = 4 \qquad\qquad x = 1$$
$$x = \frac{4}{3}$$

    iii) Complete the square.
$$6x^2 - 14x + 8 = 0$$
$$x^2 - \frac{7}{3}x + \frac{4}{3} = 0$$
$$x^2 - \frac{7}{3}x = -\frac{4}{3}$$
$$x^2 - \frac{7}{3}x + \frac{49}{36} = -\frac{4}{3} + \frac{49}{36}$$
$$\left(x - \frac{7}{6}\right)^2 = \frac{1}{36}$$
$$x - \frac{7}{6} = \pm\sqrt{\frac{1}{36}}$$
$$x = \frac{7}{6} \pm \frac{1}{6}$$

$$x = \frac{7}{6} + \frac{1}{6} \quad \text{or} \quad x = \frac{7}{6} - \frac{1}{6}$$
$$x = \frac{8}{6} \qquad\qquad x = \frac{6}{6}$$
$$x = \frac{4}{3} \qquad\qquad x = 1$$

iv) Use the quadratic formula. For $6x^2 - 14x + 8 = 0$, $a = 6$, $b = -14$, and $c = 8$.

$$x = \frac{-b \pm \sqrt{b^2 - 4ac}}{2a}$$

$$x = \frac{-(-14) \pm \sqrt{(-14)^2 - 4(6)(8)}}{2(6)}$$

$$x = \frac{14 \pm \sqrt{196 - 192}}{12}$$

$$x = \frac{14 \pm \sqrt{4}}{12}$$

$$x = \frac{14 \pm 2}{12}$$

$$x = \frac{14 + 2}{12} \quad \text{or} \quad x = \frac{14 - 2}{12}$$

$$x = \frac{16}{12} \qquad\qquad x = \frac{12}{12}$$

$$x = \frac{4}{3} \qquad\qquad x = 1$$

Check for methods ii), iii), and iv):

Substitute $x = \frac{4}{3}$ and $x = 1$ into the equation $6x^2 - 14x + 8 = 0$.

For $x = \frac{4}{3}$:

Left Side	Right Side
$6x^2 - 14x + 8$	0

$$= 6\left(\frac{4}{3}\right)^2 - 14\left(\frac{4}{3}\right) + 8$$

$$= 6\left(\frac{16}{9}\right) - \frac{56}{3} + \frac{24}{3}$$

$$= \frac{32}{3} - \frac{56}{3} + \frac{24}{3}$$

$$= -\frac{24}{3} + \frac{24}{3}$$

$$= 0$$

Left Side = Right Side

For $x = 1$:

Left Side	Right Side
$6x^2 - 14x + 8$	0

$$= 6(1)^2 - 14(1) + 8$$

$$= 6 - 14 + 8$$

$$= -8 + 8$$

$$= 0$$

Left Side = Right Side

Both solutions are correct. The roots are $\frac{4}{3}$ and 1.

b) While all four methods produce the same solutions, factoring is probably the most efficient strategy for this question, since the quadratic equation is not difficult to factor. If the quadratic equation could not be factored, either graphing using technology or using the quadratic formula would be preferred. Using the quadratic formula will always produce an exact answer.

Your Turn

Which method would you use to solve $0.57x^2 - 3.7x - 2.5 = 0$? Justify your choice. Then, solve the equation, expressing your answers to the nearest hundredth.

Example 4

Apply the Quadratic Formula

Leah wants to frame an oil original painted on canvas measuring 50 cm by 60 cm. Before framing, she places the painting on a rectangular mat so that a uniform strip of the mat shows on all sides of the painting. The area of the mat is twice the area of the painting. How wide is the strip of exposed mat showing on all sides of the painting, to the nearest tenth of a centimetre?

Solution

Draw a diagram.

Let x represent the width of the strip of exposed mat showing on all sides of the painting. Then, the length of the mat is $2x + 60$ and the width of the mat is $2x + 50$.

Round Bale by Jill Moloy
Lethbridge, Alberta

Use the area formula.
Let A represent the area of the mat.

$$A = lw$$
$$2(60)(50) = (2x + 60)(2x + 50)$$
$$6000 = 4x^2 + 220x + 3000$$
$$0 = 4x^2 + 220x - 3000$$
$$0 = 4(x^2 + 55x - 750)$$
$$0 = x^2 + 55x - 750$$

Substitute into the quadratic formula.

$$x = \frac{-b \pm \sqrt{b^2 - 4ac}}{2a}$$

$$x = \frac{-(55) \pm \sqrt{(55)^2 - 4(1)(-750)}}{2(1)}$$

$$x = \frac{-55 \pm \sqrt{6025}}{2}$$

$$x = \frac{-55 + \sqrt{6025}}{2} \quad \text{or} \quad x = \frac{-55 - \sqrt{6025}}{2}$$

$$x = 11.310\ldots \qquad\qquad x = -66.310\ldots$$

So, $x \approx 11.3$ or $x \approx -66.3$.

Since $x > 0$, reject $x \approx -66.3$. Therefore, the width of the strip of exposed mat is approximately 11.3 cm. The approximate dimensions of the mat are $2(11.3) + 60$ by $2(11.3) + 50$ or 82.6 cm by 72.6 cm. The approximate area of the mat is 82.6×72.6 or 5996.76 cm², which is about 6000 cm², twice the area of the painting.

Your Turn

A picture measures 30 cm by 21 cm. You crop the picture by removing strips of the same width from the top and one side of the picture. This reduces the area to 40% of the original area. Determine the width of the removed strips.

Key Ideas

- You can solve a quadratic equation of the form $ax^2 + bx + c = 0$, $a \neq 0$,

  for x using the quadratic formula $x = \dfrac{-b \pm \sqrt{b^2 - 4ac}}{2a}$.

- Use the discriminant to determine the nature of the roots of a quadratic equation.

  - When $b^2 - 4ac > 0$, there are two distinct real roots. The graph of the corresponding function has two different x-intercepts.

    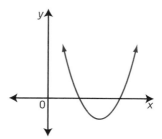

  - When $b^2 - 4ac = 0$, there is one distinct real root, or two equal real roots. The graph of the corresponding function has one x-intercept.

    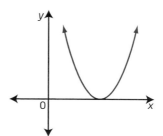

  - When $b^2 - 4ac < 0$, there are no real roots. The graph of the corresponding function has no x-intercepts.

    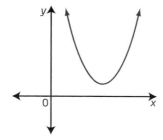

- You can solve quadratic equations in a variety of ways. You may prefer some methods over others depending on the circumstances.

Practise

1. Use the discriminant to determine the nature of the roots for each equation. Do not solve the equations. Check your answers graphically.

a) $x^2 - 7x + 4 = 0$

b) $s^2 + 3s - 2 = 0$

c) $r^2 + 9r + 6 = 0$

d) $n^2 - 2n + 1 = 0$

e) $7y^2 + 3y + 2 = 0$

f) $4t^2 + 12t + 9 = 0$

2. Without graphing, determine the number of zeros for each function.

a) $f(x) = x^2 - 2x - 14$

b) $g(x) = -3x^2 + 0.06x + 4$

c) $f(x) = \frac{1}{4}x^2 - 3x + 9$

d) $f(v) = -v^2 + 2v - 1$

e) $f(x) = \frac{1}{2}x^2 - x + \frac{5}{2}$

f) $g(y) = -6y^2 + 5y - 1$

3. Use the quadratic formula to solve each quadratic equation. Express your answers as exact roots.

a) $7x^2 + 24x + 9 = 0$

b) $4p^2 - 12p - 9 = 0$

c) $3q^2 + 5q = 1$

d) $2m^2 + 4m - 7 = 0$

e) $2j^2 - 7j = -4$

f) $16g^2 + 24g = -9$ $16g^2 + 24g + 9 = 0$

4. Use the quadratic formula to solve each equation. Express your answers to the nearest hundredth.

a) $3z^2 + 14z + 5 = 0$

b) $4c^2 - 7c - 1 = 0$

c) $-5u^2 + 16u - 2 = 0$

d) $8b^2 + 12b = -1$

e) $10w^2 - 45w = 7$

f) $-6k^2 + 17k + 5 = 0$

5. Determine the roots of each quadratic equation. Express your answers as exact values and to the nearest hundredth.

a) $3x^2 + 6x + 1 = 0$

b) $h^2 + \frac{h}{6} - \frac{1}{2} = 0$

c) $0.2m^2 = -0.3m + 0.1$

d) $4y^2 + 7 - 12y = 0$

e) $\frac{x}{2} + 1 = \frac{7x^2}{2}$

f) $2z^2 = 6z - 1$

6. Marge claims that the most efficient way to solve all quadratic equations is to use the quadratic formula. Do you agree with her? Explain with examples.

7. Solve using an appropriate method. Justify your choice of method.

a) $n^2 + 2n - 2 = 0$

b) $-y^2 + 6y - 9 = 0$

c) $-2u^2 + 16 = 0$

d) $\frac{x^2}{2} - \frac{x}{3} = 1$

e) $x^2 - 4x + 8 = 0$

Apply

8. To save materials, Choma decides to build a horse corral using the barn for one side. He has 30 m of fencing materials and wants the corral to have an area of 100 m². What are the dimensions of the corral?

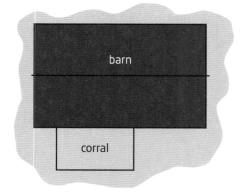

9. A mural is being painted on an outside wall that is 15 m wide and 12 m tall. A border of uniform width surrounds the mural. The mural covers 75% of the area of the wall. How wide is the border? Express your answer to the nearest hundredth of a metre.

10. Subtracting a number from half its square gives a result of 11. What is the number? Express your answers as exact values and to the nearest hundredth.

11. The mural *Northern Tradition and Transition*, located in the Saskatchewan Legislature, was painted by Métis artist Roger Jerome to honour the province of Saskatchewan's 100th anniversary in 2005. The mural includes a parabolic arch. The approximate shape of the arch can be modelled by the function $h(d) = -0.4(d - 2.5)^2 + 2.5$, where h is the height of the arch, in metres, and d is the distance, in metres, from one end of the arch. How wide is the arch at its base?

> **Did You Know?**
>
> Roger Jerome included the arch shape to symbolize the unity of northern and southern Saskatchewan.

Northern Tradition and Transition by Roger Jerome

12. An open-topped box is being made from a piece of cardboard measuring 12 in. by 30 in. The sides of the box are formed when four congruent squares are cut from the corners, as shown in the diagram. The base of the box has an area of 208 sq. in..

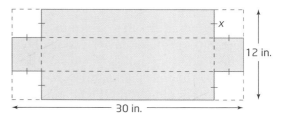

a) What equation represents the surface area of the base of the box?

b) What is the side length, x, of the square cut from each corner?

c) What are the dimensions of the box?

13. A car travelling at a speed of v kilometres per hour needs a stopping distance of d metres to stop without skidding. This relationship can be modelled by the function $d(v) = 0.0067v^2 + 0.15v$. At what speed can a car be travelling to be able to stop in each distance? Express your answer to the nearest tenth of a kilometre per hour.

a) 42 m

b) 75 m

c) 135 m

14. A study of the air quality in a particular city suggests that t years from now, the level of carbon monoxide in the air, A, in parts per million, can be modelled by the function $A(t) = 0.3t^2 + 0.1t + 4.2$.

a) What is the level, in parts per million, of carbon monoxide in the air now, at $t = 0$?

b) In how many years from now will the carbon monoxide level be 8 parts per million? Express your answer to the nearest tenth of a year.

15. A sporting goods store sells 90 ski jackets in a season for $275 each. Each $15 decrease in the price results in five more jackets being sold. What is the lowest price that would produce revenues of at least $19 600? How many jackets would be sold at this price?

16. Two guy wires are attached to the top of a telecommunications tower and anchored to the ground on opposite sides of the tower, as shown. The length of the guy wire is 20 m more than the height of the tower. The horizontal distance from the base of the tower to where the guy wire is anchored to the ground is one-half the height of the tower. How tall is the tower, to the nearest tenth of a metre?

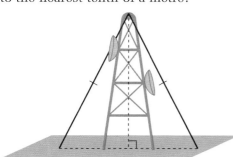

Extend

17. One root of the equation $2x^2 + bx - 24 = 0$ is -8. What are the possible values of b and the other root?

18. A cylinder has a height of 5 cm and a surface area of 100 cm². What is the radius of the cylinder, to the nearest tenth of a centimetre?

5 cm

19. In the diagram, the square has side lengths of 6 m. The square is divided into three right triangles and one acute isosceles triangle. The areas of the three right triangles are equal.

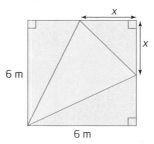

x

x

6 m

6 m

a) Determine the exact value of x.

b) What is the exact area of the acute isosceles triangle?

20. Two small private planes take off from the same airport. One plane flies north at 150 km/h. Two hours later, the second plane flies west at 200 km/h. How long after the first plane takes off will the two planes be 600 km apart? Express your answer to the nearest tenth of an hour.

Create Connections

21. Determine the error(s) in the following solution. Explain how to correct the solution.

Solve $-3x^2 - 7x + 2 = 0$.

Line 1: $x = \dfrac{-7 \pm \sqrt{(-7)^2 - 4(-3)(2)}}{2(-3)}$

Line 2: $x = \dfrac{-7 \pm \sqrt{49 - 24}}{-6}$

Line 3: $x = \dfrac{-7 \pm \sqrt{25}}{-6}$

Line 4: $x = \dfrac{-7 \pm 5}{-6}$

Line 5: So, $x = 2$ or $x = \dfrac{1}{3}$.

22. Pierre calculated the roots of a quadratic equation as $x = \dfrac{3 \pm \sqrt{25}}{2}$.

a) What are the x-intercepts of the graph of the corresponding quadratic function?

b) Describe how to use the x-intercepts to determine the equation of the axis of symmetry.

23. You have learned to solve quadratic equations by graphing the corresponding function, determining the square roots, factoring, completing the square, and applying the quadratic formula. In what circumstances would one method of solving a quadratic equation be preferred over another?

24. Create a mind map of how the concepts you have learned in Chapters 3 and 4 are connected. One is started below. Make a larger version and add any details that help you.

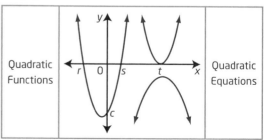

Quadratic Functions — Quadratic Equations

Project Corner | **Contour Maps**

- Contour lines are lines on a map that connect points of equal elevation.

- Contour maps show the elevations above sea level and the surface features of the land using contour lines.

- A profile view shows how the elevation changes when a line is drawn across part of a contour map.

Web Link

To explore generating a profile view, go to www.mhrprecalc11.ca and follow the links.

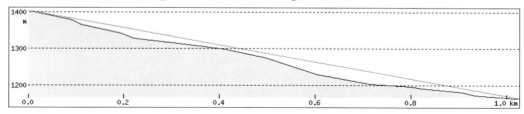

4.1 Graphical Solutions of Quadratic Equations, pages 206–217

1. Solve each quadratic equation by graphing the corresponding quadratic function.

   a) $0 = x^2 + 8x + 12$

   b) $0 = x^2 - 4x - 5$

   c) $0 = 3x^2 + 10x + 8$

   d) $0 = -x^2 - 3x$

   e) $0 = x^2 - 25$

2. Use graphing technology to determine which of the following quadratic equations has different roots from the other three.

   A $0 = 3 - 3x - 3x^2$

   B $0 = x^2 + x - 1$

   C $0 = 2(x - 1)^2 + 6x - 4$

   D $0 = 2x + 2 + 2x^2$

3. Explain what must be true about the graph of the corresponding function for a quadratic equation to have no real roots.

4. A manufacturing company produces key rings. Last year, the company collected data about the number of key rings produced per day and the corresponding profit. The data can be modelled by the function $P(k) = -2k^2 + 12k - 10$, where P is the profit, in thousands of dollars, and k is the number of key rings, in thousands.

   a) Sketch a graph of the function.

   b) Using the equation $-2k^2 + 12k - 10 = 0$, determine the number of key rings that must be produced so that there is no profit or loss. Justify your answer.

5. The path of a soccer ball can be modelled by the function $h(d) = -0.1d^2 + 0.5d + 0.6$, where h is the height of the ball and d is the horizontal distance from the kicker, both in metres.

   a) What are the zeros of the function?

   b) You can use the quadratic equation $0 = -0.1d^2 + 0.5d + 0.6$ to determine the horizontal distance that a ball travels after being kicked. How far did the ball travel downfield before it hit the ground?

4.2 Factoring Quadratic Equations, pages 218–233

6. Factor.

   a) $4x^2 - 13x + 9$

   b) $\frac{1}{2}x^2 - \frac{3}{2}x - 2$

   c) $3(v + 1)^2 + 10(v + 1) + 7$

   d) $9(a^2 - 4)^2 - 25(7b)^2$

7. Solve by factoring. Check your solutions.

   a) $0 = x^2 + 10x + 21$

   b) $\frac{1}{4}m^2 + 2m - 5 = 0$

   c) $5p^2 + 13p - 6 = 0$

   d) $0 = 6z^2 - 21z + 9$

8. Solve.

  a) $-4g^2 + 6 = -10g$

  b) $8y^2 = -5 + 14y$

  c) $30k - 25k^2 = 9$

  d) $0 = 2x^2 - 9x - 18$

9. Write a quadratic equation in standard form with the given roots.

  a) 2 and 3

  b) -1 and -5

  c) $\frac{3}{2}$ and -4

10. The path of a paper airplane can be modelled approximately by the function $h(t) = -\frac{1}{4}t^2 + t + 3$, where h is the height above the ground, in metres, and t is the time of flight, in seconds. Determine how long it takes for the paper airplane to hit the ground, $h(t) = 0$.

11. The length of the base of a rectangular prism is 2 m more than its width, and the height of the prism is 15 m.

  a) Write an algebraic expression for the volume of the rectangular prism.

  b) The volume of the prism is 2145 m³. Write an equation to model the situation.

  c) Solve the equation in part b) by factoring. What are the dimensions of the base of the rectangular prism?

12. Solve the quadratic equation $x^2 - 2x - 24 = 0$ by factoring and by graphing. Which method do you prefer to use? Explain.

4.3 Solving Quadratic Equations by Completing the Square, pages 234–243

13. Determine the value of k that makes each expression a perfect square trinomial.

  a) $x^2 + 4x + k$

  b) $x^2 + 3x + k$

14. Solve. Express your answers as exact values.

  a) $2x^2 - 98 = 0$

  b) $(x + 3)^2 = 25$

  c) $(x - 5)^2 = 24$

  d) $(x - 1)^2 = \frac{5}{9}$

15. Complete the square to determine the roots of each quadratic equation. Express your answers as exact values.

  a) $-2x^2 + 16x - 3 = 0$

  b) $5y^2 + 20y + 1 = 0$

  c) $4p^2 + 2p = -5$

16. In a simulation, the path of a new aircraft after it has achieved weightlessness can be modelled approximately by $h(t) = -5t^2 + 200t + 9750$, where h is the altitude of the aircraft, in metres, and t is the time, in seconds, after weightlessness is achieved. How long does the aircraft take to return to the ground, $h(t) = 0$? Express your answer to the nearest tenth of a second.

17. The path of a snowboarder after jumping from a ramp can be modelled by the function $h(d) = -\frac{1}{2}d^2 + 2d + 1$, where h is the height above the ground and d is the horizontal distance the snowboarder travels, both in metres.

  a) Write a quadratic equation you would solve to determine the horizontal distance the snowboarder has travelled when she lands.

  b) What horizontal distance does the snowboarder travel? Express your answer to the nearest tenth of a metre.

4.4 The Quadratic Formula, pages 244–257

18. Use the discriminant to determine the nature of the roots for each quadratic equation. Do not solve the equation.

a) $2x^2 + 11x + 5 = 0$

b) $4x^2 - 4x + 1 = 0$

c) $3p^2 + 6p + 24 = 0$

d) $4x^2 + 4x - 7 = 0$

19. Use the quadratic formula to determine the roots for each quadratic equation. Express your answers as exact values.

a) $-3x^2 - 2x + 5 = 0$

b) $5x^2 + 7x + 1 = 0$

c) $3x^2 - 4x - 1 = 0$

d) $25x^2 + 90x + 81 = 0$

20. A large fountain in a park has 35 water jets. One of the streams of water shoots out of a metal rod and follows a parabolic path. The path of the stream of water can be modelled by the function $h(x) = -2x^2 + 6x + 1$, where h is the height, in metres, at any horizontal distance x metres from its jet.

a) What quadratic equation would you solve to determine the maximum horizontal distance the water jet can reach?

b) What is the maximum horizontal distance the water jet can reach? Express your answer to the nearest tenth of a metre.

21. A ferry carries people to an island airport. It carries 2480 people per day at a cost of $3.70 per person. Surveys have indicated that for every $0.05 decrease in the fare, 40 more people will use the ferry. Use x to represent the number of decreases in the fare.

a) Write an expression to model the fare per person.

b) Write an expression to model the number of people that would use the ferry per day.

c) Determine the expression that models the revenue, R, for the ferry, which is the product of the number of people using the ferry per day and the fare per person.

d) Determine the number of fare decreases that result in a revenue of $9246.

22. Given the quadratic equation in standard form, $ax^2 + bx + c = 0$, arrange the following algebraic steps and explanations in the order necessary to derive the quadratic formula.

Algebraic Steps	Explanations
$x + \dfrac{b}{2a} = \pm\sqrt{\dfrac{b^2 - 4ac}{4a^2}}$	Complete the square.
$\left(x + \dfrac{b}{2a}\right)^2 = \dfrac{b^2 - 4ac}{4a^2}$	Solve for x.
$x^2 + \dfrac{b}{a}x = -\dfrac{c}{a}$	Subtract c from both sides.
$ax^2 + bx = -c$	Take the square root of both side.
$x^2 + \dfrac{b}{a}x + \dfrac{b^2}{4a^2} = \dfrac{b^2}{4a^2} - \dfrac{c}{a}$	Divide both sides by a.
$x = \dfrac{-b \pm \sqrt{b^2 - 4ac}}{2a}$	Factor the perfect square trinomial.

Chapter 4 Practice Test

Multiple Choice

For #1 to #5, choose the best answer.

1. What points on the graph of this quadratic function represent the locations of the zeros of the function?

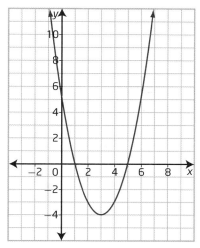

   A (0, 5) and (1, 0)

   B (0, 1) and (0, 5)

   C (1, 0) and (5, 0)

   D (5, 0) and (0, 1)

2. What is one of the factors of $x^2 - 3x - 10$?

   A $x + 5$ B $x - 5$

   C $x - 10$ D $x + 10$

3. What integral values of k will make $2x^2 + kx - 1$ factorable?

   A -1 and 2   B -2 and 2

   C -2 and 1   D -1 and 1

4. The roots, to the nearest hundredth, of $0 = -\frac{1}{2}x^2 + x + \frac{7}{2}$ are

   A 1.83 and 3.83

   B -1.83 and 3.83

   C 1.83 and -3.83

   D -1.83 and -3.83

5. The number of baseball games, G, that must be scheduled in a league with n teams can be modelled by the function $G(n) = \frac{n^2 - n}{2}$, where each team plays every other team exactly once. Suppose a league schedules 15 games. How many teams are in the league?

   A 5

   B 6

   C 7

   D 8

Short Answer

6. Determine the roots of each quadratic equation. If the quadratic equation does not have real roots, use a graph of the corresponding function to explain.

   a) $0 = x^2 - 4x + 3$

   b) $0 = 2x^2 - 7x - 15$

   c) $0 = -x^2 - 2x + 3$

7. Solve the quadratic equation $0 = 3x^2 + 5x - 1$ by completing the square. Express your answers as exact roots.

8. Use the quadratic formula to determine the roots of the equation $x^2 + 4x - 7 = 0$. Express your answers as exact roots in simplest radical form.

9. Without solving, determine the nature of the roots for each quadratic equation.

   a) $x^2 + 10x + 25 = 0$

   b) $2x^2 + x = 5$

   c) $2x^2 + 6 = 4x$

   d) $\frac{2}{3}x^2 + \frac{1}{2}x - 3 = 0$

10. The length of the hypotenuse of a right triangle is 1 cm more than triple that of the shorter leg. The length of the longer leg is 1 cm less than triple that of the shorter leg.

   a) Sketch and label a diagram with expressions for the side lengths.

   b) Write an equation to model the situation.

   c) Determine the lengths of the sides of the triangle.

Extended Response

11. A pebble is tossed upward from a scenic lookout and falls to the river below. The approximate height, h, in metres, of the pebble above the river t seconds after being tossed is modelled by the function $h(x) = -5t^2 + 10t + 35$.

   a) After how many seconds does the pebble hit the river? Express your answer to the nearest tenth of a second.

   b) How high is the scenic lookout above the river?

   c) Which method did you choose to solve the quadratic equation? Justify your choice.

12. Three rods measure 20 cm, 41 cm, and 44 cm. If the same length is cut off each piece, the remaining lengths can be formed into a right triangle. What length is cut off?

13. A rectangular piece of paper has a perimeter of 100 cm and an area of 616 cm². Determine the dimensions of the paper.

14. The parks department is planning a new flower bed. It will be rectangular with dimensions 9 m by 6 m. The flower bed will be surrounded by a grass strip of constant width with the same area as the flower bed.

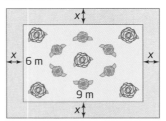

   a) Write a quadratic equation to model the situation.

   b) Solve the quadratic equation. Justify your choice of method.

   c) Calculate the perimeter of the outside of the path.

Quadratic Functions in Everyday Life

You can analyse quadratic functions and their related equations to solve problems and explore the nature of a quadratic. A quadratic can model the curve an object follows as it flies through the air. For example, consider the path of a softball, a tennis ball, a football, a baseball, a soccer ball, or a basketball. A quadratic function can also be used to design an object that has a specific curved shape needed for a project.

Quadratic equations have many practical applications. Quadratic equations may be used in the design and sales of many products found in stores. They may be used to determine the safety and the life expectancy of a product. They may also be used to determine the best price to charge to maximize revenue.

Complete one of the following two options.

Option 1 Quadratic Functions in Everyday Life

Research a real-life situation that may be modelled by a quadratic function.

- Search the Internet for two images or video clips, one related to objects in motion and one related to fixed objects. These items should show shapes or relationships that are parabolic.

- Model each image or video clip with a quadratic function, and determine how accurate the model is.

- Research the situation in each image or video clip to determine if there are reasons why it should be quadratic in nature.

- Write a one-page report to accompany your functions. Your report should include the following:
  - where quadratic functions and equations are used in your situations
  - when a quadratic function is a good model to use in a given situation
  - limitations of using a quadratic function as a model in a given situation

Option 2 Avalanche Control

Research a ski area in Western Canada that requires avalanche control.

- Determine the best location or locations to position avalanche cannons in your resort. Justify your thinking.

- Determine three different quadratic functions that can model the trajectories of avalanche control projectiles.

- Graph each function. Each graph should illustrate the specific coordinates of where the projectile will land.

- Write a one-page report to accompany your graphs. Your report should include the following:
  - the location(s) of the avalanche control cannon(s)
  - the intended path of the controlled avalanche(s)
  - the location of the landing point for each projectile

Cumulative Review, Chapters 3–4

Chapter 3 Quadratic Functions

1. Match each characteristic with the correct quadratic function.

   Characteristic

   a) vertex in quadrant III

   b) opens downward

   c) axis of symmetry: $x = 3$

   d) range: $\{y \mid y \geq 5, y \in R\}$

   Quadratic Function

   A $y = -5(x - 2)^2 - 3$

   B $y = 3(x + 3)^2 + 5$

   C $y = 2(x + 2)^2 - 3$

   D $y = 3(x - 3)^2 - 5$

2. Classify each as a quadratic function or a function that is not quadratic.

   a) $y = (x + 6) - 1$

   b) $y = -5(x + 1)^2$

   c) $y = \sqrt{(x + 2)^2} + 7$

   d) $y + 8 = x^2$

3. Sketch a possible graph for a quadratic function given each set of characteristics.

   a) axis of symmetry: $x = -2$
   range: $\{y \mid y \leq 4, y \in R\}$

   b) axis of symmetry: $x = 3$
   range: $\{y \mid y \geq 2, y \in R\}$

   c) opens upward, vertex at $(1, -3)$, one x-intercept at the point $(3, 0)$

4. Identify the vertex, domain, range, axis of symmetry, x-intercepts, and y-intercept for each quadratic function.

   a) $f(x) = (x + 4)^2 - 3$

   b) $f(x) = -(x - 2)^2 + 1$

   c) $f(x) = -2x^2 - 6$

   d) $f(x) = \frac{1}{2}(x + 8)^2 + 6$

5. Rewrite each function in the form $y = a(x - p)^2 + q$. Compare the graph of each function to the graph of $y = x^2$.

   a) $y = x^2 - 10x + 18$

   b) $y = -x^2 + 4x - 7$

   c) $y = 3x^2 - 6x + 5$

   d) $y = \frac{1}{4}x^2 + 4x + 20$

6. **a)** The approximate height, h, in metres, of an arrow shot into the air with an initial velocity of 20 m/s after t seconds can be modelled by the function $h(t) = -5t^2 + 20t + 2$. What is the maximum height reached by the arrow?

   b) From what height was the arrow shot?

   c) How long did it take for the arrow to hit the ground, to the nearest second?

Chapter 4 Quadratic Equations

7. Copy and complete the sentence, filling in the blanks with the correct terms: zeros, x-intercepts, roots.

   When solving quadratic equations, you may consider the relationship among the ▬▬▬ of a quadratic equation, the ▬▬▬ of the corresponding quadratic function, and the ▬▬▬ of the graph of the quadratic function.

8. Factor each polynomial expression.

   a) $9x^2 + 6x - 8$

   b) $16r^2 - 81s^2$

   c) $2(x + 1)^2 + 11(x + 1) + 14$

   d) $x^2y^2 - 5xy - 36$

   e) $9(3a + b)^2 - 4(2a - b)^2$

   f) $121r^2 - 400$

9. The sum of the squares of three consecutive integers is 194. What are the integers?

10. The Empress Theatre, in Fort Macleod, is Alberta's oldest continually operating theatre. Much of the theatre is the same as when it was constructed in 1912, including the 285 original seats on the main floor. The number of rows on the main floor is 4 more than the number of seats in each row. Determine the number of rows and the number of seats in each row.

11. An outdoor hot tub has a diameter of 2 m. The hot tub is surrounded by a circular wooden deck, so that the deck has a uniform width. If the top area of the deck and the hot tub is 63.6 m², how wide is deck, to the nearest tenth of a metre?

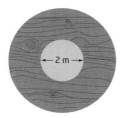

12. Dallas solves the quadratic equation $2x^2 - 12x - 7 = 0$ by completing the square. Doug solves the quadratic equation by using the quadratic formula. The solution for each student is shown. Identify the errors, if any, made by the students and determine the correct solution.

Dallas's solution:
$$2(x^2 - 12x) = 7$$
$$2(x^2 - 12x + 36) = 7 + 36$$
$$2(x - 6)^2 = 43$$
$$x = 6 \pm \sqrt{\frac{43}{2}}$$

Doug's solution:
$$x = \frac{-12 \pm \sqrt{(-12)^2 - 4(2)(-7)}}{2(2)}$$
$$x = \frac{-12 \pm \sqrt{80}}{4}$$
$$x = -3 \pm \sqrt{20}$$
$$x = -3 \pm 2\sqrt{5}$$

13. Name the method you would choose to solve each quadratic equation. Determine the roots of each equation and verify the answer.

a) $3x^2 - 6 = 0$

b) $m^2 - 15m = -26$

c) $s^2 - 2s - 35 = 0$

d) $-16x^2 + 47x + 3 = 0$

14. Use the discriminant to determine the nature of the roots for each quadratic equation.

a) $x^2 - 6x + 3 = 0$

b) $x^2 + 22x + 121 = 0$

c) $-x^2 + 3x = 5$

15. James Michels was raised in Merritt, British Columbia, and is a member of the Penticton Métis Association. James apprenticed with Coast Salish artist Joseph Campbell and now produces intricate bentwood boxes.

For one particular bentwood box, the side length of the top square piece is 1 in. longer than the side length of the bottom. Their combined area is 85 sq. in..

a) Write a quadratic equation to determine the dimensions of each square piece.

b) Select an algebraic method and solve for the roots of the quadratic equation.

c) What are the dimensions of the top and bottom of the box?

d) Explain why one of the roots from part b) is extraneous.

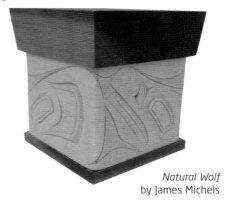

Natural Wolf
by James Michels

Unit 2 Test

Multiple Choice

For #1 to #5, choose the best answer.

1. The graph of which function is congruent to the graph of $f(x) = x^2 + 3$ but translated vertically 2 units down?

   A $f(x) = x^2 + 1$

   B $f(x) = x^2 - 1$

   C $f(x) = x^2 + 5$

   D $f(x) = (x - 2)^2 + 3$

2. The equation of the quadratic function in the form $y = a(x - p)^2 + q$ with a vertex at $(-1, -2)$ and passing through the point $(1, 6)$ is

   A $y = 4(x + 1)^2 - 2$

   B $y = 4(x - 1)^2 - 2$

   C $y = 2(x - 1)^2 - 2$

   D $y = 2(x + 1)^2 - 2$

3. The graph of $y = ax^2 + q$ intersects the x-axis in two places when

   A $a > 0, q > 0$

   B $a < 0, q < 0$

   C $a > 0, q = 0$

   D $a > 0, q < 0$

4. When $y = 2x^2 - 8x + 2$ is written in the form $y = a(x - p)^2 + q$, the values of p and q are

   A $p = -2, q = -6$

   B $p = 2, q = -6$

   C $p = 4, q = 0$

   D $p = -2, q = 6$

5. Michelle wants to complete the square to identify the vertex of the graph of the quadratic function $y = -3x^2 + 5x - 2$. Her partial work is shown.

   Step 1: $y = -3\left(x^2 + \dfrac{5}{3}x\right) - 2$

   Step 2: $y = -3\left(x^2 + \dfrac{5}{3}x + \dfrac{25}{36}\right) - 2 - \dfrac{25}{36}$

   Step 3: $y = -3\left(x + \dfrac{5}{6}\right)^2 - \dfrac{97}{36}$

   Identify the step where Michelle made her first error, as well as the correct coordinates of the vertex.

   A Step 1, vertex $\left(-\dfrac{5}{6}, -\dfrac{97}{36}\right)$

   B Step 1, vertex $\left(\dfrac{5}{6}, \dfrac{1}{12}\right)$

   C Step 2, vertex $\left(\dfrac{5}{6}, \dfrac{1}{12}\right)$

   D Step 2, vertex $\left(-\dfrac{5}{6}, -\dfrac{25}{12}\right)$

Numerical Response

Copy and complete the statements in #6 to #8.

6. The value of the discriminant for the quadratic function $y = -3x^2 - 4x + 5$ is ■.

7. The manager of an 80-unit apartment complex is trying to decide what rent to charge. At a rent of \$200 per week, all the units will be full. For each increase in rent of \$20 per week, one more unit will become vacant. The manager should charge ■ per week to maximize the revenue of the apartment complex.

8. The greater solution to the quadratic equation $9x^2 + 4x - 1 = 0$, rounded to the nearest hundredth, is ■.

Written Response

9. You create a circular piece of art for a project in art class. Your initial task is to paint a background circle entirely in blue. Suppose you have a can of blue paint that will cover 9000 cm².

   a) Determine the radius, to the nearest tenth of a centimetre, of the largest circle you can paint.

   b) If you had two cans of paint, what would be the radius of the largest circle you could paint, to the nearest tenth of a centimetre?

   c) Does the radius of the largest circle double when the amount of paint doubles?

10. Suppose Clair hits a high pop-up with an initial upward velocity of 30 m/s from a height of 1.6 m above the ground. The height, h, in metres, of the ball, t seconds after it was hit can be modelled by the function $h(t) = -4.9t^2 + 30t + 1.6$.

    a) What is the maximum height the ball reaches? Express your answer to the nearest tenth of a metre.

    b) The pitcher caught the ball at a height of 1.1 m. How long was the ball in the air? Express your answer to the nearest tenth of a second.

11. The bottom of a jewellery box is made from a square piece of cardboard by cutting 2-cm squares from each corner and turning up the sides, as shown in the figure below. The volume of the open box is 128 cm². What size of cardboard is needed?

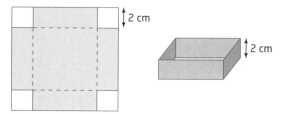

12. The side lengths of the tops of three decorative square tables can be described as three consecutive integers. The combined area of the table tops is 677 sq. in..

    a) Write a single-variable quadratic equation, in simplified form, to determine the side length of each square tabletop.

    b) Algebraically determine the roots of the quadratic equation.

    c) What are the side lengths of the tabletops?

    d) Why would you not consider both of the roots of the quadratic equation when determining a possible side length?

Unit 3

Functions and Equations

Linear relations have numerous applications in the world. However, mathematicians and scientists have found that many relationships in the natural world cannot be explained with linear models. For example, meteorology, astronomy, and population ecology require more complex mathematical relations to help understand and explain observed phenomena. Similarly, structural engineers and business people need to analyse non-linear data in their everyday working lives. In this unit, you will learn about four types of functions and equations used to model some of the most complex behaviours in our world.

Looking Ahead

In this unit, you will solve problems involving...

- radical expressions and equations
- rational expressions and equations
- absolute value functions and equations
- reciprocal functions

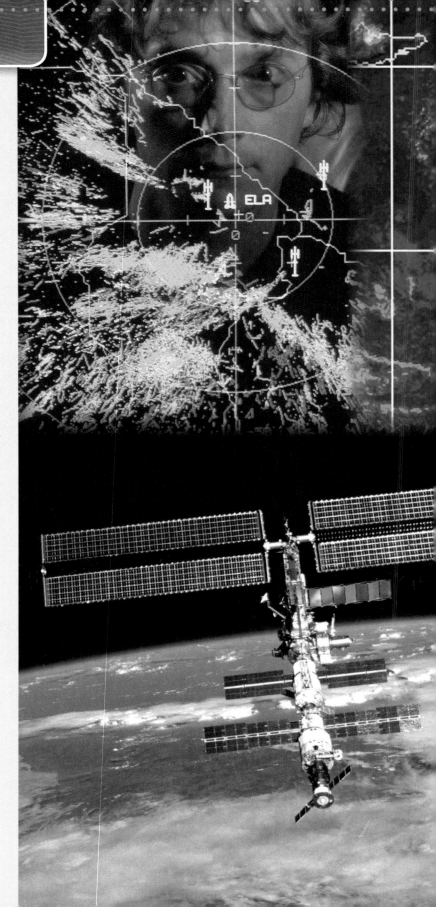

Unit 3 Project   Space: Past, Present, Future

In this project, you will explore a variety of functions and equations, including radical, rational, absolute value, and reciprocal, and how they relate to our understanding of space and its exploration.

In Chapter 5, you will gather information about our galaxy. In Chapter 6, you will gather information about peculiarities in space, such as the passage of time and black holes. In Chapter 7, you will explore space tourism.

At the end of the unit, you will choose at least one of the following three options:
• Examine an application of radicals in space or in the contributions of an astronomer. Investigate why a radical occurs in the mathematics involved in the contribution of the astronomer.
• Research an application of rational expressions in space and investigate why a rational expression models a particular situation.
• Apply the skills you have learned about absolute value functions and reciprocal functions to graphic design.

In the Project Corner box at the end of some sections, you will find information and notes about outer space. You can use this information to gather data and facts about your chosen option.

CHAPTER
5

Radical Expressions and Equations

Radical equations can be used to model a variety of relationships—from tracking storms to modelling the path of a football or a skier through the air. Radical expressions and equations allow mathematicians and scientists to work more accurately with numbers. This is important when dealing with large numbers or relations that are sensitive to small adjustments. In this chapter, you will work with a variety of radical expressions and equations including very large radicals as you analyse the cloud formations on the surface of Saturn.

Did You Know?

Weather contour graphs are 3-D graphs that show levels of atmospheric pressure, temperature, precipitation, or ocean heat. The formulas used in these graphs involve squares and square roots. Computers analyse contour graphs of the atmosphere to track weather patterns. Meteorologists use computers and satellite radar to track storms and forecast the weather.

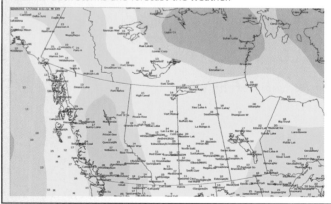

Key Terms
rationalize   radical equation
conjugates

Career Link

Meteorologists study the forces that shape weather and climate. They use formulas that may involve square roots and cube roots to help describe and predict storms and weather patterns. Atmospheric scientists are meteorologists who focus on the atmosphere and investigate the effects of human activities, such as producing pollution, on the atmosphere. Most meteorologists in Canada work for the federal government, and many study at the University of British Columbia or the University of Alberta.

Web Link

To learn more about meteorologists and atmospheric scientists, go to www.mhrprecalc11.ca and follow the links.

Working With Radicals

Focus on...

- converting between mixed radicals and entire radicals
- comparing and ordering radical expressions
- identifying restrictions on the values for a variable in a radical expression
- simplifying radical expressions using addition and subtraction

The packaging industry is huge. It involves design and production, which affect consumers. Graphic designers and packaging engineers apply mathematics skills to designing, constructing, and testing various forms of packaging. From pharmaceuticals to the automobile industry, consumer products are usually found in packages.

Investigate Radical Addition and Subtraction

Materials

- 1-cm grid paper
- scissors

Two glass vases are packaged in opposite corners of a box with a square base. A cardboard divider sits diagonally between the vases. Make a model of the box using grid paper.

1. a) Use an 8 cm by 8 cm square of 1-cm grid paper. Construct a square-based prism without a top. The side length of the base should be double the height of the sides of the box.

b) What is the exact diagonal distance across the base of the model? Explain how you determined the distance.

2. The boxes are aligned on display shelves in rows of 2, 4, and 6 boxes each. The boxes are placed corner to corner. What are the exact lengths of the possible rows? Use addition statements to represent your answers. Verify your answers.

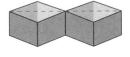

3. Suppose several classmates place three model boxes along a shelf that is $\sqrt{450}$ cm long.

a) If the boxes are placed side by side, will they fit on the shelf? If so, what distance along the shelf will be occupied? What distance will be unoccupied?

b) Will the boxes fit along the shelf if they are placed corner to corner, with the diagonals forming a straight line? If so, what distance on the shelf will be occupied? What distance will be unoccupied?

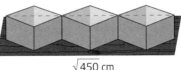

$\sqrt{450}$ cm

4. Write an addition and subtraction statement using only mixed radicals for each calculation in step 3b). A mixed radical is the product of a monomial and a radical. In $r\sqrt[n]{x}$, r is the coefficient, n is the index, and x is the radicand.

Reflect and Respond

5. Develop a general equation that represents the addition of radicals. Compare your equation and method with a classmate's. Identify any rules for using your equation.

6. Use integral values of a to verify that $\sqrt{a} + \sqrt{a} + \sqrt{a} + \sqrt{a} = 4\sqrt{a}$.

Link the Ideas

Like Radicals

Radicals with the same radicand and index are called like radicals.

Pairs of Like Radicals	Pairs of Unlike Radicals
$5\sqrt{7}$ and $-\sqrt{7}$	$2\sqrt{5}$ and $2\sqrt{3}$
$\frac{2}{3}\sqrt[3]{5x^2}$ and $\sqrt[3]{5x^2}$	$\sqrt[4]{5a}$ and $\sqrt[5]{5a}$

How are like radicals similar to like terms?

When adding and subtracting radicals, only like radicals can be combined. You may need to convert radicals to a different form (mixed or entire) before identifying like radicals.

Restrictions on Variables

If a radical represents a real number and has an even index, the radicand must be non-negative.

The radical $\sqrt{4 - x}$ has an even index. So, $4 - x$ must be greater than or equal to zero.

$$4 - x \geq 0$$
$$4 - x + x \geq 0 + x$$
$$4 \geq x$$

Isolate the variable by applying algebraic operations to both sides of the inequality symbol.

The radical $\sqrt{4 - x}$ is only defined as a real number if x is less than or equal to four. You can check this by substituting values for x that are greater than four, equal to four, and less than four.

Example 1

Convert Mixed Radicals to Entire Radicals

Express each mixed radical in entire radical form. Identify the values of the variable for which the radical represents a real number.

a) $7\sqrt{2}$ **b)** $a^4\sqrt{a}$ **c)** $5b\sqrt[3]{3b^2}$

Solution

a) Write the coefficient 7 as a square root: $7 = \sqrt{7^2}$.
Then, multiply the radicands of the square roots.
$$\begin{aligned} 7\sqrt{2} &= \sqrt{7^2}\left(\sqrt{2}\right) \\ &= \sqrt{7^2(2)} \\ &= \sqrt{49(2)} \\ &= \sqrt{98} \end{aligned}$$

How could you verify the answer?

b) Express the coefficient a^4 as a square root: $a^4 = \sqrt{(a^4)^2}$.
Multiply the radicals.
$$\begin{aligned} a^4\sqrt{a} &= \sqrt{(a^4)^2}\left(\sqrt{a}\right) \\ &= \sqrt{(a^4)^2(a)} \\ &= \sqrt{a^8(a)} \\ &= \sqrt{a^9} \end{aligned}$$

For the radical in the original expression to be a real number, the radicand must be non-negative. Therefore, a is greater than or equal to zero.

c) Write the entire coefficient, $5b$, as a cube root.
$$\begin{aligned} 5b &= \sqrt[3]{(5b)^3} \\ &= \sqrt[3]{5^3 b^3} \end{aligned}$$

Multiply the radicands of the cube roots.
$$\begin{aligned} 5b\sqrt[3]{3b^2} &= \left(\sqrt[3]{5^3 b^3}\right)\left(\sqrt[3]{3b^2}\right) \\ &= \sqrt[3]{5^3 b^3 (3b^2)} \\ &= \sqrt[3]{375 b^5} \end{aligned}$$

Since the index of the radical is an odd number, the variable, b, can be any real number.

Why can a radical with an odd index have a radicand that is positive, negative, or zero?

Your Turn

Convert each mixed radical to an entire radical. State the values of the variable for which the radical is a real number.

a) $4\sqrt{3}$ **b)** $j^3\sqrt{j}$ **c)** $2k^2\left(\sqrt[3]{4k}\right)$

Radicals in Simplest Form

A radical is in simplest form if the following are true.
- The radicand does not contain a fraction or any factor which may be removed.
- The radical is not part of the denominator of a fraction.

For example, $\sqrt{18}$ is not in simplest form because 18 has a square factor of 9, which can be removed. $\sqrt{18}$ is equivalent to the simplified form $3\sqrt{2}$.

Example 2

Express Entire Radicals as Mixed Radicals

Convert each entire radical to a mixed radical in simplest form.

a) $\sqrt{200}$ **b)** $\sqrt[4]{c^9}$ **c)** $\sqrt{48y^5}$

Solution

a) Method 1: Use the Greatest Perfect-Square Factor

The following perfect squares are factors of 200: 1, 4, 25, and 100.
Write $\sqrt{200}$ as a product using the greatest perfect-square factor.

$$\sqrt{200} = \sqrt{100(2)}$$
$$= \sqrt{100}(\sqrt{2})$$
$$= 10\sqrt{2}$$

Method 2: Use Prime Factorization

Express the radicand as a product of prime factors. The index is two.
So, combine pairs of identical factors.

$$\sqrt{200} = \sqrt{2(2)(2)(5)(5)}$$
$$= \sqrt{2^2(2)(5^2)}$$
$$= 2(5)\sqrt{2}$$
$$= 10\sqrt{2}$$

> **Did You Know?**
>
> The radical symbol represents only the *positive* square root. So, even though $(-10)^2 = 100$, $\sqrt{100} \neq \pm 10$.
> $\sqrt{100} = +10$
> $-\sqrt{100} = -10$
> In general, $\sqrt{x^2} = x$ only when x is positive.

b) Method 1: Use Prime Factorization

$$\sqrt[4]{c^9} = \sqrt[4]{c(c)(c)(c)(c)(c)(c)(c)(c)}$$
$$= \sqrt[4]{c^4(c^4)(c)}$$
$$= c(c)\sqrt[4]{c}$$
$$= c^2(\sqrt[4]{c})$$

What number tells you how many identical factors to combine?

Method 2: Use Powers

$$\sqrt[4]{c^9} = c^{\frac{9}{4}}$$
$$= c^{\frac{8}{4}+\frac{1}{4}}$$
$$= c^{\frac{8}{4}}\left(c^{\frac{1}{4}}\right)$$
$$= c^2\left(c^{\frac{1}{4}}\right)$$
$$= c^2(\sqrt[4]{c})$$

How will you decide what fractions to use for the sum?

For the radical to represent a real number, $c \geq 0$ because the index is an even number.

c) $\sqrt{48y^5}$

Determine the greatest perfect-square factors for the numerical and variable parts.

$$\sqrt{48y^5} = \sqrt{16(3)(y^4)(y)}$$
$$= 4y^2\sqrt{3y}$$

How can you determine the values of the variables for which the radical is defined as a real number?

Your Turn

Express each entire radical as a mixed radical in simplest form.
Identify any restrictions on the values for the variables.

a) $\sqrt{52}$ **b)** $\sqrt[4]{m^7}$ **c)** $\sqrt{63n^7p^4}$

Example 3

Compare and Order Radicals

Five bentwood boxes, each in the shape of a cube have the following diagonal lengths, in centimetres.

$4(13)^{\frac{1}{2}}$ $8\sqrt{3}$ 14 $\sqrt{202}$ $10\sqrt{2}$

Order the diagonal lengths from least to greatest without using a calculator.

Solution

Express the diagonal lengths as entire radicals.

$$4(13)^{\frac{1}{2}} = 4\sqrt{13} \qquad\qquad 8\sqrt{3} = \sqrt{8^2}(\sqrt{3}) \qquad\qquad 14 = \sqrt{14^2}$$
$$= \sqrt{4^2}(\sqrt{13}) \qquad\qquad\quad = \sqrt{8^2(3)} \qquad\qquad\quad = \sqrt{196}$$
$$= \sqrt{4^2(13)} \qquad\qquad\quad = \sqrt{64(3)}$$
$$= \sqrt{16(13)} \qquad\qquad\quad = \sqrt{192}$$
$$= \sqrt{208}$$

$\sqrt{202}$ is already written as an entire radical.

$$10\sqrt{2} = \sqrt{10^2}(\sqrt{2})$$
$$= \sqrt{100(2)}$$
$$= \sqrt{200}$$

Compare the five radicands and order the numbers.
$$\sqrt{192} < \sqrt{196} < \sqrt{200} < \sqrt{202} < \sqrt{208}$$

The diagonal lengths from least to greatest are $8\sqrt{3}$, 14, $10\sqrt{2}$, $\sqrt{202}$, and $4(13)^{\frac{1}{2}}$.

Your Turn

Order the following numbers from least to greatest:
$5, 3\sqrt{3}, 2\sqrt{6}, \sqrt{23}$

Example 4

Add and Subtract Radicals

Simplify radicals and combine like terms.

a) $\sqrt{50} + 3\sqrt{2}$
b) $-\sqrt{27} + 3\sqrt{5} - \sqrt{80} - 2\sqrt{12}$
c) $\sqrt{4c} - 4\sqrt{9c}, c \geq 0$

Solution

a) $\sqrt{50} + 3\sqrt{2} = \sqrt{25(2)} + 3\sqrt{2}$
$\qquad\qquad\quad = 5\sqrt{2} + 3\sqrt{2}$
$\qquad\qquad\quad = 8\sqrt{2}$

How is adding $5\sqrt{2}$ and $3\sqrt{2}$ similar to adding $5x$ and $3x$?

b) $\quad -\sqrt{27} + 3\sqrt{5} - \sqrt{80} - 2\sqrt{12}$
$= -\sqrt{3(3)(3)} + 3\sqrt{5} - \sqrt{2(2)(2)(2)(5)} - 2\sqrt{2(2)(3)}$
$= -3\sqrt{3} + 3\sqrt{5} - 4\sqrt{5} - 4\sqrt{3}$
$= -7\sqrt{3} - \sqrt{5}$

How can you identify which radicals to combine?

c) $\sqrt{4c} - 4\sqrt{9c} = \sqrt{4}(\sqrt{c}) - 4\sqrt{9}(\sqrt{c})$
$\qquad\qquad\quad = 2\sqrt{c} - 12\sqrt{c}$
$\qquad\qquad\quad = -10\sqrt{c}$

Why is $\sqrt{4}$ not equal to ± 2?
Why is $\sqrt{9}$ not equal to ± 3?

Your Turn

Simplify radicals and combine like terms.

a) $2\sqrt{7} + 13\sqrt{7}$ **b)** $\sqrt{24} - \sqrt{6}$ **c)** $\sqrt{20x} - 3\sqrt{45x},\ x \geq 0$

Example 5

Apply Addition of Radical Expressions

Consider the design shown for a skateboard ramp. What is the exact distance across the base?

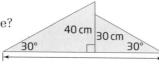

Solution

Redraw each triangle and use trigonometry to determine the lengths, x and y, of the two bases.

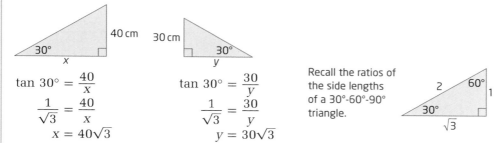

$\tan 30° = \dfrac{40}{x}$
$\dfrac{1}{\sqrt{3}} = \dfrac{40}{x}$
$x = 40\sqrt{3}$

$\tan 30° = \dfrac{30}{y}$
$\dfrac{1}{\sqrt{3}} = \dfrac{30}{y}$
$y = 30\sqrt{3}$

Recall the ratios of the side lengths of a 30°-60°-90° triangle.

Determine the total length of the bases.
$x + y = 40\sqrt{3} + 30\sqrt{3}$
$\qquad\ = 70\sqrt{3}$

The distance across the entire base is exactly $70\sqrt{3}$ cm.

Your Turn

What is the exact length of AB?

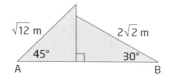

- You can compare and order radicals using a variety of strategies:
  - Convert unlike radicals to entire radicals. If the radicals have the same index, the radicands can be compared.
  - Compare the coefficients of like radicals.
  - Compare the indices of radicals with equal radicands.
- When adding or subtracting radicals, combine coefficients of like radicals. In general, $m\sqrt[r]{a} + n\sqrt[r]{a} = (m + n)\sqrt[r]{a}$, where r is a natural number, and m, n, and a are real numbers. If r is even, then $a \geq 0$.
- A radical is in simplest form if the radicand does not contain a fraction or any factor which may be removed, and the radical is not part of the denominator of a fraction.

  For example, $5\sqrt{40} = 5\sqrt{4(10)}$
  $$= 5\sqrt{4}(\sqrt{10})$$
  $$= 5(2)\sqrt{10}$$
  $$= 10\sqrt{10}$$

- When a radicand contains variables, identify the values of the variables that make the radical a real number by considering the index and the radicand:
  - If the index is an even number, the radicand must be non-negative.

    For example, in $\sqrt{3n}$, the index is even. So, the radicand must be non-negative.
    $3n \geq 0$
    $\quad n \geq 0$
  - If the index is an odd number, the radicand may be any real number.

    For example, in $\sqrt[3]{x}$, the index is odd. So, the radicand, x, can be any real number—positive, negative, or zero.

Check Your Understanding

Practise

1. Copy and complete the table.

Mixed Radical Form	Entire Radical Form
$4\sqrt{7}$	
	$\sqrt{50}$
$-11\sqrt{8}$	
	$-\sqrt{200}$

2. Express each radical as a mixed radical in simplest form.

   a) $\sqrt{56}$ b) $3\sqrt{75}$

   c) $\sqrt[3]{24}$ d) $\sqrt{c^3 d^2}$, $c \geq 0$, $d \geq 0$

3. Write each expression in simplest form. Identify the values of the variable for which the radical represents a real number.

   a) $3\sqrt{8m^4}$ b) $\sqrt[3]{24q^5}$

   c) $-2\sqrt[5]{160s^5 t^6}$

4. Copy and complete the table. State the values of the variable for which the radical represents a real number.

Mixed Radical Form	Entire Radical Form
$3n\sqrt{5}$	
	$\sqrt[3]{-432}$
$\frac{1}{2a}\sqrt[3]{7a}$	
	$\sqrt[3]{128x^4}$

5. Express each pair of terms as like radicals. Explain your strategy.

  a) $15\sqrt{5}$ and $8\sqrt{125}$

  b) $8\sqrt{112z^8}$ and $48\sqrt{7z^4}$

  c) $-35\sqrt[4]{w^2}$ and $3\sqrt[4]{81w^{10}}$

  d) $6\sqrt[3]{2}$ and $6\sqrt[3]{54}$

6. Order each set of numbers from least to greatest.

  a) $3\sqrt{6}$, 10, and $7\sqrt{2}$

  b) $-2\sqrt{3}$, -4, $-3\sqrt{2}$, and $-2\sqrt{\frac{7}{2}}$

  c) $\sqrt[3]{21}$, $3\sqrt[3]{2}$, 2.8, $2\sqrt[3]{5}$

7. Verify your answer to #6b) using a different method.

8. Simplify each expression.

  a) $-\sqrt{5} + 9\sqrt{5} - 4\sqrt{5}$

  b) $1.4\sqrt{2} + 9\sqrt{2} - 7$

  c) $\sqrt[4]{11} - 1 - 5\sqrt[4]{11} + 15$

  d) $-\sqrt{6} + \frac{9}{2}\sqrt{10} - \frac{5}{2}\sqrt{10} + \frac{1}{3}\sqrt{6}$

9. Simplify.

  a) $3\sqrt{75} - \sqrt{27}$

  b) $2\sqrt{18} + 9\sqrt{7} - \sqrt{63}$

  c) $-8\sqrt{45} + 5.1 - \sqrt{80} + 17.4$

  d) $\frac{2}{3}\sqrt[3]{81} + \frac{\sqrt[3]{375}}{4} - 4\sqrt{99} + 5\sqrt{11}$

10. Simplify each expression. Identify any restrictions on the values for the variables.

  a) $2\sqrt{a^3} + 6\sqrt{a^3}$

  b) $3\sqrt{2x} + 3\sqrt{8x} - \sqrt{x}$

  c) $-4\sqrt[3]{625r} + \sqrt[3]{40r^4}$

  d) $\frac{w}{5}\sqrt[3]{-64} + \frac{\sqrt[3]{512w^3}}{5} - \frac{2}{5}\sqrt{50w} - 4\sqrt{2w}$

Apply

11. The air pressure, p, in millibars (mbar) at the centre of a hurricane, and wind speed, w, in metres per second, of the hurricane are related by the formula $w = 6.3\sqrt{1013 - p}$. What is the exact wind speed of a hurricane if the air pressure is 965 mbar?

12. Saskatoon artist Jonathan Forrest's painting, *Clincher*, contains geometric shapes. The isosceles right triangle at the top right has legs that measure approximately 12 cm. What is the length of the hypotenuse? Express your answer as a radical in simplest form.

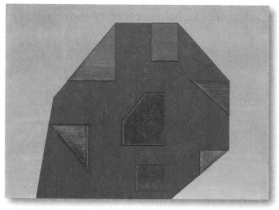

Clincher, by Jonathan Forrest Saskatoon, Saskatchewan

13. The distance, d, in millions of kilometres, between a planet and the Sun is a function of the length, n, in Earth-days, of the planet's year. The formula is $d = \sqrt[3]{25n^2}$. The length of 1 year on Mercury is 88 Earth-days, and the length of 1 year on Mars is 704 Earth-days.

Use the subtraction of radicals to determine the difference between the distances of Mercury and Mars from the Sun. Express your answer in exact form.

Planet Venus

> **Did You Know?**
>
> Distances in space are frequently measured in astronomical units (AU). The measurement 1 AU represents the average distance between the Sun and Earth during Earth's orbit. According to NASA, the average distance between Venus and Earth is 0.723 AU.

14. The speed, s, in metres per second, of a tsunami is related to the depth, d, in metres, of the water through which it travels. This relationship can be modelled with the formula $s = \sqrt{10d}$, $d \geq 0$. A tsunami has a depth of 12 m. What is the speed as a mixed radical and an approximation to the nearest metre per second?

15. A square is inscribed in a circle. The area of the circle is 38π m².

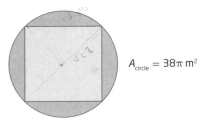

$A_{circle} = 38\pi$ m²

a) What is the exact length of the diagonal of the square?

b) Determine the exact perimeter of the square.

16. You can use Heron's formula to determine the area of a triangle given all three side lengths. The formula is $A = \sqrt{s(s-a)(s-b)(s-c)}$, where s represents the half-perimeter of the triangle and a, b, and c are the three side lengths. What is the exact area of a triangle with sides of 8 mm, 10 mm, and 12 mm? Express your answer as an entire radical and as a mixed radical.

17. Suppose an ant travels in a straight line across the Cartesian plane from (3, 4) to (6, 10). Then, it travels in a straight line from (6, 10) to (10, 18). How far does the ant travel? Express your answer in exact form.

18. Leslie's backyard is in the shape of a square. The area of her entire backyard is 98 m². The green square, which contains a tree, has an area of 8 m². What is the exact perimeter of one of the rectangular flowerbeds?

19. Kristen shows her solution to a radical problem below. Brady says that Kristen's final radical is not in simplest form. Is he correct? Explain your reasoning.

Kristen's Solution

$$y\sqrt{4y^3} + \sqrt{64y^5} = y\sqrt{4y^3} + 4y\sqrt{4y^3}$$
$$= 5y\sqrt{4y^3}$$

20. Which expression is not equivalent to $12\sqrt{6}$?

$$2\sqrt{216}, \; 3\sqrt{96}, \; 4\sqrt{58}, \; 6\sqrt{24}$$

Explain how you know without using technology.

Extend

21. A square, ABCD, has a perimeter of 4 m. △CDE is an equilateral triangle inside the square. The intersection of AC and DE occurs at point F. What is the exact length of AF?

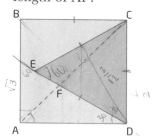

22. A large circle has centre C and diameter AB. A smaller circle has centre D and diameter BC. Chord AE is tangent to the smaller circle. If AB = 18 cm, what is the exact length of AE?

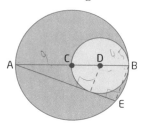

Create Connections

23. What are the exact values of the common difference and missing terms in the following arithmetic sequence? Justify your work.
$$\sqrt{27}, \blacksquare, \blacksquare, 9\sqrt{3}$$

24. Consider the following set of radicals:
$$-3\sqrt{12}, 2\sqrt{75}, -\sqrt{27}, 108^{\frac{1}{2}}$$

Explain how you could determine the answer to each question without using a calculator.

a) Using only two of the radicals, what is the greatest sum?

b) Using only two of the radicals, what is the greatest difference?

25. Support each equation using examples.

a) $(-x)^2 = x^2$

b) $\sqrt{x^2} \neq \pm x$

Project Corner — The Milky Way Galaxy

- Our solar system is located in the Milky Way galaxy, which is a spiral galaxy.

- A galaxy is a congregation of billions of stars, gases, and dust held together by gravity.

- The solar system consists of the Sun, eight planets and their satellites, and thousands of other smaller heavenly bodies such as asteroids, comets, and meteors.

- The motion of planets can be described by Kepler's three laws.

- Kepler's third law states that the ratio of the squares of the orbital periods of any two planets is equal to the ratio of the cubes of their semi-major axes. How could you express Kepler's third law using radicals? Explain this law using words and diagrams.

Multiplying and Dividing Radical Expressions

Focus on...

- performing multiple operations on radical expressions
- rationalizing the denominator
- solving problems that involve radical expressions

In the early 1980s, the Voyager spacecraft first relayed images of a special hexagonal cloud pattern at the north end of Saturn. Due to Saturn's lengthy year (26.4 Earth-years), light has not returned to its north pole until recently. The space probe Cassini has recently returned images of Saturn's north pole. Surprisingly, the hexagonal cloud feature appears to have remained in place over nearly three decades. Scientists are interested in the physics behind this unusual feature of Saturn.

Investigate Radical Multiplication and Division

Materials

- regular hexagon template or compass and ruler to construct regular hexagons
- ruler

Part A: Regular Hexagons and Equilateral Triangles

1. Divide a regular hexagon into six identical equilateral triangles.

2. Suppose the perimeter of the hexagon is 12 cm. Use trigonometry to determine the shortest distance between parallel sides of the hexagon. Express your answer as a mixed radical and an entire radical. What are the angle measures of the triangle you used? Include a labelled diagram.

3. Use another method to verify the distance in step 2.

4. The distance between parallel sides of the hexagonal cloud pattern on Saturn is $\sqrt{468\ 750\ 000}$ km. Determine the distance, in kilometres, along one edge of the cloud pattern.

Reflect and Respond

5. Verify your answer to step 4.

Part B: Isosceles Right Triangles and Rectangles

Saturn is more than nine times as far from our Sun as Earth is. At that distance, the Cassini probe is too far from the Sun (1.43 billion kilometres) to use solar panels to operate. However, some spacecrafts and some vehicles do use solar panels to generate power. The vehicle in the photograph uses solar panels and was developed at the University of Calgary.

Consider the following diagram involving rectangular solar panels and isosceles right triangular solar panels.

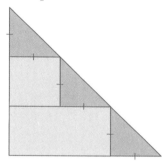

6. The legs of the three congruent isosceles triangles are $\sqrt{3}$ m long. Determine the dimensions and areas of the two rectangles.

7. What is the exact length of the hypotenuse of the large right triangle? Express your answer in mixed radical form and in entire radical form.

8. Verify your answer to step 7.

Reflect and Respond

9. Consider the two special triangles used in parts A and B. Use trigonometry to relate the angles and ratios of the exact side lengths in lowest terms?

10. Generalize a method for multiplying or dividing any two radicals. Test your method using two examples.

11. Suppose you need to show a classmate how to multiply and divide radicals. What radicals would you use in your example? Why?

Multiplying Radicals

When multiplying radicals, multiply the coefficients and multiply the radicands. You can only multiply radicals if they have the same index.

$$(2\sqrt{7})(4\sqrt{75}) = (2)(4)\sqrt{(7)(75)}$$
$$= 8\sqrt{525}$$
$$= 8\sqrt{(25)(21)} \qquad \text{Which method of simplifying a radical is being used?}$$
$$= 8(5)\sqrt{21}$$
$$= 40\sqrt{21}$$

Radicals can be simplified before multiplying:
$$(2\sqrt{7})(4\sqrt{75}) = (2\sqrt{7})\left(4\sqrt{(25)(3)}\right)$$
$$= (2\sqrt{7})\left[(4)(5)(\sqrt{3})\right]$$
$$= (2\sqrt{7})(20\sqrt{3})$$
$$= (2)(20)\sqrt{(7)(3)}$$
$$= 40\sqrt{21}$$

In general, $(m\sqrt[k]{a})(n\sqrt[k]{b}) = mn\sqrt[k]{ab}$, where k is a natural number, and m, n, a, and b are real numbers. If k is even, then $a \geq 0$ and $b \geq 0$.

Example 1

Multiply Radicals

Multiply. Simplify the products where possible.
a) $(-3\sqrt{2x})(4\sqrt{6})$, $x \geq 0$
b) $7\sqrt{3}(5\sqrt{5} - 6\sqrt{3})$
c) $(8\sqrt{2} - 5)(9\sqrt{5} + 6\sqrt{10})$
d) $9\sqrt[3]{2w}(\sqrt[3]{4w} + 7\sqrt[3]{28})$, $w \geq 0$

Solution

a) $(-3\sqrt{2x})(4\sqrt{6}) = -3(4)\sqrt{(2x)(6)}$
$$= -12\sqrt{(2x)(2)(3)}$$
$$= -12(2)\sqrt{3x}$$
$$= -24\sqrt{3x}$$

b) $7\sqrt{3}(5\sqrt{5} - 6\sqrt{3}) = 7\sqrt{3}(5\sqrt{5}) - 7\sqrt{3}(6\sqrt{3})$ Use the distributive property.
$$= 35\sqrt{15} - 42\sqrt{9}$$
$$= 35\sqrt{15} - 42(3)$$
$$= 35\sqrt{15} - 126$$

c) $(8\sqrt{2} - 5)(9\sqrt{5} + 6\sqrt{10})$
$$= 8\sqrt{2}(9\sqrt{5}) + 8\sqrt{2}(6\sqrt{10}) - 5(9\sqrt{5}) - 5(6\sqrt{10}) \qquad \text{Use the distributive property.}$$
$$= 72\sqrt{10} + 48\sqrt{20} - 45\sqrt{5} - 30\sqrt{10} \qquad \text{Simplify the radicals.}$$
$$= 72\sqrt{10} + 48\sqrt{(4)(5)} - 45\sqrt{5} - 30\sqrt{10}$$
$$= 72\sqrt{10} + 96\sqrt{5} - 45\sqrt{5} - 30\sqrt{10} \qquad \text{Collect terms with like radicals.}$$
$$= 42\sqrt{10} + 51\sqrt{5}$$

d) $9\sqrt[3]{2w}(\sqrt[3]{4w} + 7\sqrt[3]{28}) = 9\sqrt[3]{2w(4w)} + 63\sqrt[3]{2w(28)}$
$$= 9\sqrt[3]{8w^2} + 63\sqrt[3]{56w}$$
$$= 18\sqrt[3]{w^2} + 126\sqrt[3]{7w}$$

Your Turn

Multiply. Simplify where possible.

a) $5\sqrt{3}(\sqrt{6})$

b) $-2\sqrt[3]{11}(4\sqrt[3]{2} - 3\sqrt[3]{3})$

c) $(4\sqrt{2} + 3)(\sqrt{7} - 5\sqrt{14})$

d) $-2\sqrt{11c}(4\sqrt{2c^3} - 3\sqrt{3}), c \geq 0$

Example 2

Apply Radical Multiplication

An artist creates a pattern similar
to the one shown, but he frames an
equilateral triangle inside a square
instead of a circle. The area of the
square is 32 cm².

a) What is the exact perimeter of the
triangle?

b) Determine the exact height of the
triangle.

c) What is the exact area of the triangle?
Express all answers in simplest form.

Solution

Create a sketch of the problem.

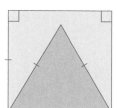

$A_{square} = 32$ cm²

a) The side length of the square is $\sqrt{32}$ cm.
Therefore, the base of the triangle is $\sqrt{32}$ cm long.

Simplify the side length.

$\sqrt{32} = \sqrt{16(2)}$
$\quad\quad = 4\sqrt{2}$

How could you determine the greatest
perfect-square factor of 32?

Determine the perimeter of the triangle.
$3(4\sqrt{2}) = 12\sqrt{2}$

The perimeter of the triangle is $12\sqrt{2}$ cm.

b) Construct the height, h, in the diagram.

Method 1: Use the Pythagorean Theorem
Since the height bisects the base of the equilateral triangle, there is a right $\triangle ABC$. The lengths of the legs are $2\sqrt{2}$ and h, and the length of the hypotenuse is $4\sqrt{2}$, all in centimetres.

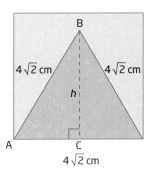

$$h^2 + (2\sqrt{2})^2 = (4\sqrt{2})^2$$
$$h^2 + 4(2) = 16(2)$$
$$h^2 + 8 = 32$$
$$h^2 = 24$$
$$h = \pm 2\sqrt{6}$$

The height of the triangle is $2\sqrt{6}$ cm.   Why is only the positive root considered?

Method 2: Use Trigonometry
Identify $\triangle ABC$ as a 30°-60°-90° triangle.

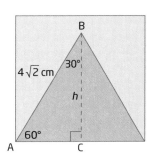

$$\sin 60° = \frac{h}{4\sqrt{2}}$$
$$\frac{\sqrt{3}}{2} = \frac{h}{4\sqrt{2}}$$
$$\frac{4\sqrt{2}(\sqrt{3})}{2} = h$$
$$2\sqrt{6} = h$$

The height of the triangle is $2\sqrt{6}$ cm.

c) Use the formula for the area of a triangle, $A = \frac{1}{2}bh$.

$$A = \frac{1}{2}(\sqrt{32})(2\sqrt{6})$$
$$A = \sqrt{(32)(6)}$$
$$A = \sqrt{192}$$
$$A = 8\sqrt{3}$$

The area of the triangle is $8\sqrt{3}$ cm².

Your Turn

An isosceles triangle has a base of $\sqrt{20}$ m. Each of the equal sides is $3\sqrt{7}$ m long. What is the exact area of the triangle?

Dividing Radicals

When dividing radicals, divide the coefficients and then divide the radicands. You can only divide radicals that have the same index.

$$\frac{4\sqrt[3]{6}}{2\sqrt[3]{3}} = 2\sqrt[3]{\frac{6}{3}}$$
$$= 2\sqrt[3]{2}$$

In general, $\dfrac{m\sqrt[k]{a}}{n\sqrt[k]{b}} = \dfrac{m}{n}\sqrt[k]{\dfrac{a}{b}}$, where k is a natural number, and m, n, a, and b are real numbers. $n \neq 0$ and $b \neq 0$. If k is even, then $a \geq 0$ and $b > 0$.

Rationalizing Denominators

To simplify an expression that has a radical in the denominator, you need to **rationalize** the denominator.

For an expression with a monomial square-root denominator, multiply the numerator and denominator by the radical term from the denominator.

$$\frac{5}{2\sqrt{3}} = \frac{5}{2\sqrt{3}}\left(\frac{\sqrt{3}}{\sqrt{3}}\right)$$

Why is this product equivalent to the original expression?

$$= \frac{5\sqrt{3}}{2\sqrt{3}(\sqrt{3})}$$

$$= \frac{5\sqrt{3}}{6}$$

For a binomial denominator that contains a square root, multiply both the numerator and denominator by a **conjugate** of the denominator.

> The product of a pair of conjugates is a difference of squares.
> $(a - b)(a + b) = a^2 - b^2$
> $(\sqrt{u} + \sqrt{v})(\sqrt{u} - \sqrt{v}) = (\sqrt{u})^2 + (\sqrt{v})(\sqrt{u}) - (\sqrt{v})(\sqrt{u}) - (\sqrt{v})^2$
> $\qquad\qquad\qquad\qquad = u - v$

In the radical expression, $\dfrac{5\sqrt{3}}{4 - \sqrt{6}}$, the conjugates of $4 - \sqrt{6}$ are $4 + \sqrt{6}$ and $-4 - \sqrt{6}$. If you multiply either of these expressions with the denominator, the product will be a rational number.

$$\frac{5\sqrt{3}}{4 - \sqrt{6}} = \left(\frac{5\sqrt{3}}{4 - \sqrt{6}}\right)\left(\frac{4 + \sqrt{6}}{4 + \sqrt{6}}\right)$$

$$= \frac{20\sqrt{3} + 5\sqrt{18}}{4^2 - (\sqrt{6})^2}$$

$$= \frac{20\sqrt{3} + 5\sqrt{9(2)}}{16 - 6}$$

$$= \frac{20\sqrt{3} + 15\sqrt{2}}{10}$$

$$= \frac{4\sqrt{3} + 3\sqrt{2}}{2}$$

Express in simplest form.

rationalize

- convert to a rational number without changing the value of the expression
- If the radical is in the denominator, both the numerator and denominator must be multiplied by a quantity that will produce a rational denominator.

conjugates

- two binomial factors whose product is the difference of two squares
- the binomials $(a + b)$ and $(a - b)$ are conjugates since their product is $a^2 - b^2$

Example 3

Divide Radicals

Simplify each expression.

a) $\dfrac{\sqrt{24x^2}}{\sqrt{3x}}, x > 0$

b) $\dfrac{4\sqrt{5n}}{3\sqrt{2}}, n \geq 0$

c) $\dfrac{11}{\sqrt{5} + 7}$

d) $\dfrac{4\sqrt{11}}{y\sqrt[3]{6}}, y \neq 0$

Solution

a)
$$\frac{\sqrt{24x^2}}{\sqrt{3x}} = \sqrt{\frac{24x^2}{3x}}$$
$$= \sqrt{8x}$$
$$= 2\sqrt{2x}$$

b)
$$\frac{4\sqrt{5n}}{3\sqrt{2}} = \frac{4\sqrt{5n}}{3\sqrt{2}}\left(\frac{\sqrt{2}}{\sqrt{2}}\right) \qquad \text{Rationalize the denominator.}$$
$$= \frac{4\sqrt{10n}}{3(2)}$$
$$= \frac{2\sqrt{10n}}{3}$$

c)
$$\frac{11}{\sqrt{5}+7} = \left(\frac{11}{\sqrt{5}+7}\right)\left(\frac{\sqrt{5}-7}{\sqrt{5}-7}\right) \qquad \text{How do you determine a conjugate of } \sqrt{5}+7?$$
$$= \frac{11(\sqrt{5}-7)}{(\sqrt{5})^2 - 7^2}$$
$$= \frac{11(\sqrt{5}-7)}{5 - 49}$$
$$= \frac{11(\sqrt{5}-7)}{-44}$$
$$= \frac{-(\sqrt{5}-7)}{4}$$
$$= \frac{7-\sqrt{5}}{4}$$

The solution can be verified using decimal approximations.

Initial expression:
$$\frac{11}{\sqrt{5}+7} \approx 1.19098$$

Final expression:
$$\frac{7-\sqrt{5}}{4} \approx 1.19098$$

d)
$$\frac{4\sqrt{11}}{y\sqrt[3]{6}} = \frac{4\sqrt{11}}{y\sqrt[3]{6}}\left(\frac{(\sqrt[3]{6})^2}{(\sqrt[3]{6})^2}\right) \qquad \text{How does the index help you determine what expression to use when rationalizing the denominator?}$$
$$= \frac{4\sqrt{11}(\sqrt[3]{6})(\sqrt[3]{6})}{y\sqrt[3]{6}(\sqrt[3]{6})(\sqrt[3]{6})}$$
$$= \frac{4\sqrt{11}(\sqrt[3]{36})}{y(6)}$$
$$= \frac{2\sqrt{11}(\sqrt[3]{36})}{3y}$$

Your Turn

Simplify each quotient. Identify the values of the variable for which the expression is a real number.

a) $\dfrac{2\sqrt{51}}{\sqrt{3}}$

b) $\dfrac{-7}{2\sqrt[3]{9p}}$

c) $\dfrac{2}{3\sqrt{5}-4}$

d) $\dfrac{6}{\sqrt{4x}+1}$

- When multiplying radicals with identical indices, multiply the coefficients and multiply the radicands:

$$(m\sqrt[k]{a})(n\sqrt[k]{b}) = mn\sqrt[k]{ab}$$

where k is a natural number, and m, n, a, and b are real numbers. If k is even, then $a \geq 0$ and $b \geq 0$.

- When dividing two radicals with identical indices, divide the coefficients and divide the radicands:

$$\frac{m\sqrt[k]{a}}{n\sqrt[k]{b}} = \frac{m}{n}\sqrt[k]{\frac{a}{b}}$$

where k is a natural number, and m, n, a, and b are real numbers. $n \neq 0$ and $b \neq 0$. If k is even, then $a \geq 0$ and $b > 0$.

- When multiplying radical expressions with more than one term, use the distributive property and then simplify.

- To rationalize a monomial denominator, multiply the numerator and denominator by an expression that produces a rational number in the denominator.

$$\frac{2}{\sqrt[5]{n}}\left(\frac{(\sqrt[5]{n})^4}{(\sqrt[5]{n})^4}\right) = \frac{2(\sqrt[5]{n})^4}{n}$$

- To simplify an expression with a square-root binomial in the denominator, rationalize the denominator using these steps:
  - Determine a conjugate of the denominator.
  - Multiply the numerator and denominator by this conjugate.
  - Express in simplest form.

Check Your Understanding

Practise

1. Multiply. Express all products in simplest form.

a) $2\sqrt{5}(7\sqrt{3})$

b) $-\sqrt{32}(7\sqrt{2})$

c) $2\sqrt[4]{48}(\sqrt[4]{5})$

d) $4\sqrt{19x}(\sqrt{2x^2})$, $x \geq 0$

e) $\sqrt[3]{54y^7}(\sqrt[3]{6y^4})$

f) $\sqrt{6t}\left(3t^2\sqrt{\frac{t}{4}}\right)$, $t \geq 0$

2. Multiply using the distributive property. Then, simplify.

a) $\sqrt{11}(3 - 4\sqrt{7})$

b) $-\sqrt{2}(14\sqrt{5} + 3\sqrt{6} - \sqrt{13})$

c) $\sqrt{y}(2\sqrt{y} + 1)$, $y \geq 0$

d) $z\sqrt{3}(z\sqrt{12} - 5z + 2)$

3. Simplify. Identify the values of the variables for which the radicals represent real numbers.

a) $-3(\sqrt{2} - 4) + 9\sqrt{2}$

b) $7(-1 - 2\sqrt{6}) + 5\sqrt{6} + 8$

c) $4\sqrt{5}(\sqrt{3j} + 8) - 3\sqrt{15j} + \sqrt{5}$

d) $3 - \sqrt[3]{4k}(12 + 2\sqrt[3]{8})$

4. Expand and simplify each expression.

   a) $(8\sqrt{7} + 2)(\sqrt{2} - 3)$

   b) $(4 - 9\sqrt{5})(4 + 9\sqrt{5})$

   c) $(\sqrt{3} + 2\sqrt{15})(\sqrt{3} - \sqrt{15})$

   d) $(6\sqrt[3]{2} - 4\sqrt{13})^2$

   e) $(-\sqrt{6} + 2)(2\sqrt{2} - 3\sqrt{5} + 1)$

5. Expand and simplify. State any restrictions on the values for the variables.

   a) $(15\sqrt{c} + 2)(\sqrt{2c} - 6)$

   b) $(1 - 10\sqrt{8x^3})(2 + 7\sqrt{5x})$

   c) $(9\sqrt{2m} - 4\sqrt{6m})^2$

   d) $(10r - 4\sqrt[3]{4r})(2\sqrt[3]{6r^2} + 3\sqrt[3]{12r})$

6. Divide. Express your answers in simplest form.

   a) $\dfrac{\sqrt{80}}{\sqrt{10}}$

   b) $\dfrac{-2\sqrt{12}}{4\sqrt{3}}$

   c) $\dfrac{3\sqrt{22}}{\sqrt{11}}$

   d) $\dfrac{3\sqrt{135m^5}}{\sqrt{21m^3}}, m > 0$

7. Simplify.

   a) $\dfrac{9\sqrt{432p^5} - 7\sqrt{27p^5}}{\sqrt{33p^4}}, p > 0$

   b) $\dfrac{6\sqrt[3]{4v^7}}{\sqrt[3]{14v}}, v > 0$

8. Rationalize each denominator. Express each radical in simplest form.

   a) $\dfrac{20}{\sqrt{10}}$

   b) $\dfrac{-\sqrt{21}}{\sqrt{7m}}, m > 0$

   c) $-\dfrac{2}{3}\sqrt{\dfrac{5}{12u}}, u > 0$

   d) $20\sqrt[3]{\dfrac{6t}{5}}$

9. Determine a conjugate for each binomial. What is the product of each pair of conjugates?

   a) $2\sqrt{3} + 1$

   b) $7 - \sqrt{11}$

   c) $8\sqrt{z} - 3\sqrt{7}, z \geq 0$

   d) $19\sqrt{h} + 4\sqrt{2h}, h \geq 0$

10. Rationalize each denominator. Simplify.

   a) $\dfrac{5}{2 - \sqrt{3}}$

   b) $\dfrac{7\sqrt{2}}{\sqrt{6} + 8}$

   c) $\dfrac{-\sqrt{7}}{\sqrt{5} - 2\sqrt{2}}$

   d) $\dfrac{\sqrt{3} + \sqrt{13}}{\sqrt{3} - \sqrt{13}}$

11. Write each fraction in simplest form. Identify the values of the variables for which each fraction is a real number.

   a) $\dfrac{4r}{\sqrt{6r} + 9}$

   b) $\dfrac{18\sqrt{3n}}{\sqrt{24n}}$

   c) $\dfrac{8}{4 - \sqrt{6t}}$

   d) $\dfrac{5\sqrt{3y}}{\sqrt{10} + 2}$

12. Use the distributive property to simplify $(c + c\sqrt{c})(c + 7\sqrt{3c}), c \geq 0$.

Apply

13. Malcolm tries to rationalize the denominator in the expression $\dfrac{4}{3 - 2\sqrt{2}}$ as shown below.

   a) Identify, explain, and correct any errors.

   b) Verify your corrected solution.

   Malcolm's solution:

   $$\dfrac{4}{3 - 2\sqrt{2}} = \left(\dfrac{4}{3 - 2\sqrt{2}}\right)\left(\dfrac{3 + 2\sqrt{2}}{3 + 2\sqrt{2}}\right)$$

   $$= \dfrac{12 + 8\sqrt{4(2)}}{9 - 8}$$

   $$= 12 + 16\sqrt{2}$$

14. In a golden rectangle, the ratio of the side dimensions is $\dfrac{2}{\sqrt{5}-1}$. Determine an equivalent expression with a rational denominator.

15. The period, T, in seconds, of a pendulum is related to its length, L, in metres. The period is the time to complete one full cycle and can be approximated with the formula $T = 2\pi\sqrt{\dfrac{L}{10}}$.

   a) Write an equivalent formula with a rational denominator.

   b) The length of the pendulum in the HSBC building in downtown Vancouver is 27 m. How long would the pendulum take to complete 3 cycles?

16. Jonasie and Iblauk are planning a skidoo race for their community of Uqsuqtuuq or Gjoa Haven, Nunavut. They sketch the triangular course on a Cartesian plane. The area of 1 grid square represents 9245 m². What is the exact length of the red track?

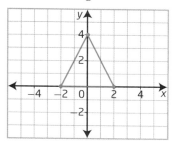

17. Simplify $\left(\dfrac{1+\sqrt{5}}{2-\sqrt{3}}\right)\left(\dfrac{1-\sqrt{5}}{2-\sqrt{3}}\right)$.

18. In a scale model of a cube, the ratio of the volume of the model to the volume of the cube is 1 : 4. Express your answers to each of the following questions as mixed radicals in simplest form.

   a) What is the edge length of the actual cube if its volume is 192 mm³?

   b) What is the edge length of the model cube?

   c) What is the ratio of the edge length of the actual cube to the edge length of the model cube?

19. Lev simplifies the expression, $\dfrac{2x\sqrt{14}}{\sqrt{3-5x}}$.

   He determines the restrictions on the values for x as follows:

$$3 - 5x > 0$$
$$-5x > -3$$
$$x > \frac{3}{5}$$

   a) Identify, explain, and correct any errors.

   b) Why do variables involved in radical expressions sometimes have restrictions on their values?

   c) Create an expression involving radicals that does not have any restrictions. Justify your response.

20. Olivia simplifies the following expression. Identify, explain, and correct any errors in her work.

$$\frac{2c - c\sqrt{25}}{\sqrt{3}} = \frac{(2c - c\sqrt{25})}{\sqrt{3}}\left(\frac{\sqrt{3}}{\sqrt{3}}\right)$$

$$= \frac{\sqrt{3}(2c - c\sqrt{25})}{3}$$

$$= \frac{\sqrt{3}(2c \pm 5c)}{3}$$

$$= \frac{\sqrt{3}(7c)}{3} \quad \text{or} \quad \frac{\sqrt{3}(-3c)}{3}$$

$$= \frac{7c\sqrt{3}}{3} \quad \text{or} \quad -c\sqrt{3}$$

21. What is the volume of the right triangular prism?

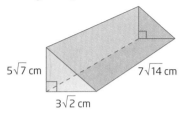

5√7 cm   7√14 cm   3√2 cm

Extend

22. A cube is inscribed in a sphere with radius 1 m. What is the surface area of the cube?

23. Line segment AB has endpoints A($\sqrt{27}$, $-\sqrt{50}$) and B($3\sqrt{48}$, $2\sqrt{98}$). What is the midpoint of AB?

24. Rationalize the denominator of $(3(\sqrt{x})^{-1} - 5)^{-2}$. Simplify the expression.

25. a) What are the exact roots of the quadratic equation $x^2 + 6x + 3 = 0$?

   b) What is the sum of the two roots from part a)?

   c) What is the product of the two roots?

   d) How are your answers from parts b) and c) related to the original equation?

26. Rationalize the denominator of $\dfrac{\sqrt[c]{a}}{\sqrt[n]{r}}$.

27. What is the exact surface area of the right triangular prism in #21?

Create Connections

28. Describe the similarities and differences between multiplying and dividing radical expressions and multiplying and dividing polynomial expressions.

29. How is rationalizing a square-root binomial denominator related to the factors of a difference of squares? Explain, using an example.

30. A snowboarder departs from a jump. The quadratic function that approximately relates height above landing area, h, in metres, and time in air, t, in seconds, is $h(t) = -5t^2 + 10t + 3$.

   a) What is the snowboarder's height above the landing area at the beginning of the jump?

   b) Complete the square of the expression on the right to express the function in vertex form. Isolate the variable t.

   c) Determine the exact height of the snowboarder halfway through the jump.

Did You Know?

Maelle Ricker from North Vancouver won a gold medal at the 2010 Vancouver Olympics in snowboard cross. She is the first Canadian woman to win a gold medal at a Canadian Olympics.

31. Are $m = \dfrac{-5 + \sqrt{13}}{6}$ and $m = \dfrac{-5 - \sqrt{13}}{6}$ solutions of the quadratic equation, $3m^2 + 5m + 1 = 0$? Explain your reasoning.

32. Two stacking bowls are in the shape of hemispheres. They have radii that can be represented by $\sqrt[3]{\dfrac{3V}{2\pi}}$ and $\sqrt[3]{\dfrac{V-1}{4\pi}}$, where V represents the volume of the bowl.

   a) What is the ratio of the larger radius to the smaller radius in simplest form?

   b) For which volumes is the ratio a real number?

33. MINI LAB

Step 1 Copy and complete the table of values for each equation using technology.

$y = \sqrt{x}$		$y = x^2$	
x	**y**	**x**	**y**
0		0	
1		1	
2		2	
3		3	
4		4	

Step 2 Describe any similarities and differences in the patterns of numbers. Compare your answers with those of a classmate.

Step 3 Plot the points for both functions. Compare the shapes of the two graphs. How are the restrictions on the variable for the radical function related to the quadratic function?

Project Corner   Space Exploration

- Earth has a diameter of about 12 800 km and a mass of about 6.0×10^{24} kg. It is about 150 000 000 km from the Sun.

- Artificial gravity is the emulation in outer space of the effects of gravity felt on a planetary surface.

- When travelling into space, it is necessary to overcome the force of gravity. A spacecraft leaving Earth must reach a gravitational escape velocity greater than 11.2 km/s. Research the formula for calculating the escape velocity. Use the formula to determine the escape velocities for the Moon and the Sun.

Radical Equations

Focus on...

- solving equations involving square roots
- determining the roots of a radical equation algebraically
- identifying restrictions on the values for the variable in a radical equation
- modelling and solving problems with radical equations

How do the length and angle of elevation of a ramp affect a skateboarder? How do these measurements affect the height at the top of a ramp? The relationships between measurements are carefully considered when determining safety standards for skate parks, playground equipment, and indoor rock-climbing walls. Architects and engineers also analyse the mathematics involved in these relationships when designing factories and structures such as bridges.

Did You Know?

Shaw Millenium Park, in Calgary, Alberta, is the largest skate park in North America. It occupies about 6000 m², which is about the same area as a CFL football field.

Investigate Radical Equations

Materials

- three metre sticks
- grid paper

1. To measure vertical distances, place a metre stick vertically against a wall. You may need to tape it in place. To measure horizontal distances, place another metre stick on the ground at the base of the first metre stick, pointing out from the wall.

2. Lean a metre stick against the vertical metre stick. Slide the top of the diagonal metre stick down the wall as the base of it moves away from the wall. Move the base a horizontal distance, h, of 10 cm away from the wall. Then, measure the vertical distance, v, that the top of the metre stick has slid down the wall.

3. Create a table and record values of v for 10-cm increments of h, up to 100 cm.

Horizontal Distance From Wall, h (cm)	Vertical Distance Down Wall, v (cm)
0	
10	
20	

4. Analyse the data in the table to determine whether the relationship between v and h is linear or non-linear. Explain how you determined your answer.

5. Refer to the diagram. If the diagonal metre stick moves v centimetres down and h centimetres away from the wall, determine the dimensions of the right triangle.

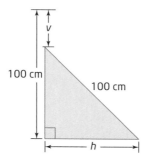

6. Write an equation describing v as a function of h. Use your equation to verify two measurements from your table in step 3.

Reflect and Respond

7. Estimate the value of h, to the nearest centimetre, when $v = 25$ cm. Verify your estimate using a metre stick.

8. As the base of the metre stick passes through the horizontal interval from $(5\sqrt{199} - 5)$ cm to $(5\sqrt{199} + 5)$ cm, what is the vertical change?

9. How is solving a **radical equation** similar to solving a linear equation and a quadratic equation? Compare your answers with those of a classmate.

radical equation

• an equation with radicals that have variables in the radicands

---

Link the Ideas

When solving a radical equation, remember to:

• identify any restrictions on the variable
• identify whether any roots are extraneous by determining whether the values satisfy the original equation

Example 1

Solve an Equation With One Radical Term

a) State the restrictions on x in $5 + \sqrt{2x - 1} = 12$ if the radical is a real number.

b) Solve $5 + \sqrt{2x - 1} = 12$.

> **Solution**

a) For the radical to be a real number, the radicand, $2x - 1$, must be greater than or equal to zero because the index is even. Isolate the variable by performing the same operations on both sides.

$$2x - 1 \geq 0$$
$$2x \geq 1$$
$$x \geq \frac{1}{2}$$

For the radical to represent a real number, the variable x must be any real number greater than or equal to $\frac{1}{2}$.

b) Isolate the radical expression. Square both sides of the equation. Then, solve for the variable.

$$5 + \sqrt{2x - 1} = 12$$
$$\sqrt{2x - 1} = 7$$
$$\left(\sqrt{2x - 1}\right)^2 = (7)^2 \qquad \text{What does squaring both sides do?}$$
$$2x - 1 = 49$$
$$2x = 50$$
$$x = 25$$

The value of x meets the restriction in part a).

Check that $x = 25$ is a solution to the original equation.

Left Side	Right Side
$5 + \sqrt{2x - 1}$	12
$= 5 + \sqrt{2(25) - 1}$	
$= 5 + \sqrt{50 - 1}$	
$= 5 + \sqrt{49}$	
$= 5 + 7$	
$= 12$	

$$\text{Left Side} = \text{Right Side}$$

Therefore, the solution is $x = 25$.

Your Turn

Identify any restrictions on y in $-8 + \sqrt{\dfrac{3y}{5}} = -2$ if the radical is a real number. Then, solve the equation.

Example 2

Radical Equation With an Extraneous Root

What are the restrictions on n if the equation $n - \sqrt{5 - n} = -7$ involves real numbers? Solve the equation.

Solution

$5 - n \geq 0$ Why must the radicand be non-negative?
$5 \geq n$

The value of n can be any real number less than or equal to five.

$n - \sqrt{5 - n} = -7$ Why, in this case, is the radical isolated
$n + 7 = \sqrt{5 - n}$ on the right side of the equal sign?
$(n + 7)^2 = (\sqrt{5 - n})^2$
$n^2 + 14n + 49 = 5 - n$
$n^2 + 15n + 44 = 0$

Select a strategy to solve the quadratic equation.

Method 1: Factor the Quadratic Equation

$n^2 + 15n + 44 = 0$
$(n + 11)(n + 4) = 0$ How can you use the zero product property?
$n + 11 = 0 \quad$ or $\quad n + 4 = 0$
$n = -11 \qquad\qquad n = -4$

Method 2: Use the Quadratic Formula, $x = \dfrac{-b \pm \sqrt{b^2 - 4ac}}{2a}$

$n = \dfrac{-15 \pm \sqrt{15^2 - 4(1)(44)}}{2(1)}$ How can you identify the values for a, b, and c?

$n = \dfrac{-15 \pm \sqrt{225 - 176}}{2}$

$n = \dfrac{-15 + 7}{2} \quad$ or $\quad n = \dfrac{-15 - 7}{2}$

$n = -4 \qquad\qquad n = -11$

Check $n = -4$ and $n = -11$ in the original equation, $n - \sqrt{5 - n} = -7$.

For $n = -4$:

Left Side	Right Side
$n - \sqrt{5 - n}$	-7
$= -4 - \sqrt{5 - (-4)}$	
$= -4 - 3$	
$= -7$	

Left Side $=$ Right Side

For $n = -11$:

Left Side	Right Side
$n - \sqrt{5 - n}$	-7
$= -11 - \sqrt{5 - (-11)}$	
$= -11 - 4$	
$= -15$	

Left Side $\neq$ Right Side

The solution is $n = -4$. The value $n = -11$ is extraneous. Extraneous roots occur because squaring both sides and solving the quadratic equation may result in roots that do not satisfy the original equation.

Your Turn

State the restrictions on the variable in $m - \sqrt{2m + 3} = 6$ if the equation involves real numbers. Then, solve the equation.

Example 3

Solve an Equation With Two Radicals

Solve $7 + \sqrt{3x} = \sqrt{5x + 4} + 5$, $x \geq 0$. Check your solution.

Solution

Isolate one radical and then square both sides.

$$7 + \sqrt{3x} = \sqrt{5x + 4} + 5$$
$$2 + \sqrt{3x} = \sqrt{5x + 4}$$
$$\left(2 + \sqrt{3x}\right)^2 = \left(\sqrt{5x + 4}\right)^2$$
$$4 + 4\sqrt{3x} + 3x = 5x + 4$$

Why is it beneficial to isolate the more complex radical first?

Isolate the remaining radical, square both sides, and solve.

$$4\sqrt{3x} = 2x$$
$$\left(4\sqrt{3x}\right)^2 = (2x)^2$$
$$16(3x) = 4x^2$$
$$48x = 4x^2$$
$$0 = 4x^2 - 48x$$
$$0 = 4x(x - 12)$$
$$4x = 0 \quad \text{or} \quad x - 12 = 0$$
$$x = 0 \qquad\qquad x = 12$$

Check $x = 0$ and $x = 12$ in the original equation.

For $x = 0$:

Left Side

$$7 + \sqrt{3x}$$
$$= 7 + \sqrt{3(0)}$$
$$= 7 + \sqrt{0}$$
$$= 7$$

Right Side

$$\sqrt{5x + 4} + 5$$
$$= \sqrt{5(0) + 4} + 5$$
$$= 2 + 5$$
$$= 7$$

Left Side = Right Side

For $x = 12$:

Left Side

$$7 + \sqrt{3x}$$
$$= 7 + \sqrt{3(12)}$$
$$= 7 + \sqrt{36}$$
$$= 13$$

Right Side

$$\sqrt{5x + 4} + 5$$
$$= \sqrt{5(12) + 4} + 5$$
$$= \sqrt{64} + 5$$
$$= 13$$

Left Side = Right Side

The solutions are $x = 0$ and $x = 12$.

Your Turn

Solve $\sqrt{3 + j} + \sqrt{2j - 1} = 5$, $j \geq \dfrac{1}{2}$.

Example 4

Solve Problems Involving Radical Equations

What is the speed, in metres per second, of a 0.4-kg football that has 28.8 J of kinetic energy? Use the kinetic energy formula, $E_k = \frac{1}{2}mv^2$, where E_k represents the kinetic energy, in joules; m represents mass, in kilograms; and v represents speed, in metres per second.

Solution

Method 1: Rearrange the Equation

$$E_k = \frac{1}{2}mv^2$$

$$\frac{2E_k}{m} = v^2$$

$$\pm\sqrt{\frac{2E_k}{m}} = v$$

Why is the symbol $\pm$ included in this step?

Substitute $m = 0.4$ and $E_k = 28.8$ into the radical equation, $v = \sqrt{\frac{2E_k}{m}}$.

$$v = \sqrt{\frac{2(28.8)}{0.4}}$$

$$v = 12$$

Why is only the positive root considered?

The speed of the football is 12 m/s.

Method 2: Substitute the Given Values and Evaluate

$$E_k = \frac{1}{2}mv^2$$

$$28.8 = \frac{1}{2}(0.4)v^2$$

$$144 = v^2$$

$$\pm12 = v$$

The speed of the football is 12 m/s.

Why is only the positive root considered?

Your Turn

Josh is shipping several small musical instruments in a cube-shaped box, including a drumstick which just fits diagonally in the box. Determine the formula for the length, d, in centimetres, of the drumstick in terms of the area, A, in square centimetres, of one face of the box. What is the area of one face of a cube-shaped box that holds a drumstick of length 23.3 cm? Express your answer to the nearest square centimetre.

Key Ideas

- You can model some real-world relationships with radical equations.
- When solving radical equations, begin by isolating one of the radical terms.
- To eliminate a square root, raise both sides of the equation to the exponent two. For example, in $3 = \sqrt{c + 5}$, square both sides.

$$3^2 = \left(\sqrt{c + 5}\right)^2$$
$$9 = c + 5$$
$$4 = c$$

- To identify whether a root is extraneous, substitute the value into the original equation. Raising both sides of an equation to an even exponent may introduce an extraneous root.
- When determining restrictions on the values for variables, consider the following:
  - Denominators cannot be equal to zero.
  - For radicals to be real numbers, radicands must be non-negative if the index is an even number.

Check Your Understanding

Practise

Determine any restrictions on the values for the variable in each radical equation, unless given.

1. Square each expression.

   a) $\sqrt{3z}$, $z \geq 0$

   b) $\sqrt{x - 4}$, $x \geq 4$

   c) $2\sqrt{x + 7}$, $x \geq -7$

   d) $-4\sqrt{9 - 2y}$, $\frac{9}{2} \geq y$

2. Describe the steps to solve the equation $\sqrt{x} + 5 = 11$, where $x \geq 0$.

3. Solve each radical equation. Verify your solutions and identify any extraneous roots.

   a) $\sqrt{2x} = 3$

   b) $\sqrt{-8x} = 4$

   c) $7 = \sqrt{5 - 2x}$

4. Solve each radical equation. Verify your solutions.

   a) $\sqrt{z} + 8 = 13$

   b) $2 - \sqrt{y} = -4$

   c) $\sqrt{3x} - 8 = -6$

   d) $-5 = 2 - \sqrt{-6m}$

5. In the solution to $k + 4 = \sqrt{-2k}$, identify whether either of the values, $k = -8$ or $k = -2$, is extraneous. Explain your reasoning.

6. Isolate each radical term. Then, solve the equation.

   a) $-3\sqrt{n - 1} + 7 = -14$, $n \geq 1$

   b) $-7 - 4\sqrt{2x - 1} = 17$, $x \geq \frac{1}{2}$

   c) $12 = -3 + 5\sqrt{8 - x}$, $x \leq 8$

7. Solve each radical equation.

a) $\sqrt{m^2 - 3} = 5$

b) $\sqrt{x^2 + 12x} = 8$

c) $\sqrt{\dfrac{q^2}{2} + 11} = q - 1$

d) $2n + 2\sqrt{n^2 - 7} = 14$

8. Solve each radical equation.

a) $5 + \sqrt{3x - 5} = x$

b) $\sqrt{x^2 + 30x} = 8$

c) $\sqrt{d + 5} = d - 1$

d) $\sqrt{\dfrac{j + 1}{3}} + 5j = 3j - 1$

9. Solve each radical equation.

a) $\sqrt{2k} = \sqrt{8}$

b) $\sqrt{-3m} = \sqrt{-7m}$

c) $5\sqrt{\dfrac{j}{2}} = \sqrt{200}$

d) $5 + \sqrt{n} = \sqrt{3n}$

10. Solve.

a) $\sqrt{z + 5} = \sqrt{2z - 1}$

b) $\sqrt{6y - 1} = \sqrt{-17 + y^2}$

c) $\sqrt{5r - 9} - 3 = \sqrt{r + 4} - 2$

d) $\sqrt{x + 19} + \sqrt{x - 2} = 7$

Apply

11. By inspection, determine which one of the following equations will have an extraneous root. Explain your reasoning.

$\sqrt{3y - 1} - 2 = 5$

$4 - \sqrt{m + 6} = -9$

$\sqrt{x + 8} + 9 = 2$

12. The following steps show how Jerry solved the equation $3 + \sqrt{x + 17} = x$. Is his work correct? Explain your reasoning and provide a correct solution if necessary.

Jerry's Solution

$3 + \sqrt{x + 17} = x$

$\sqrt{x + 17} = x - 3$

$\left(\sqrt{x + 17}\right)^2 = x^2 - 3^2$

$x + 17 = x^2 - 9$

$0 = x^2 - x - 26$

$x = \dfrac{1 \pm \sqrt{1 + 104}}{2}$

$x = \dfrac{1 \pm \sqrt{105}}{2}$

13. Collision investigators can approximate the initial velocity, v, in kilometres per hour, of a car based on the length, l, in metres, of the skid mark. The formula $v = 12.6\sqrt{l} + 8$, $l \geq 0$, models the relationship. What length of skid is expected if a car is travelling 50 km/h when the brakes are applied? Express your answer to the nearest tenth of a metre.

14. In 1805, Rear-Admiral Beaufort created a numerical scale to help sailors quickly assess the strength of the wind. The integer scale ranges from 0 to 12. The wind scale, B, is related to the wind velocity, v, in kilometres per hour, by the formula $B = 1.33\sqrt{v + 10.0} - 3.49$, $v \geq -10$.

a) Determine the wind scale for a wind velocity of 40 km/h.

b) What wind velocity results in a wind scale of 3?

Web **Link**

To learn more about the Beaufort scale, go to www.mhrprecalc11.ca and follow the links.

15. The mass, m, in kilograms, that a beam with a fixed width and length can support is related to its thickness, t, in centimetres. The formula is $t = \frac{1}{5}\sqrt{\frac{m}{3}}$, $m \geq 0$. If a beam is 4 cm thick, what mass can it support?

16. Two more than the square root of a number, n, is equal to the number. Model this situation using a radical equation. Determine the value(s) of n algebraically.

17. The speed, v, in metres per second, of water being pumped into the air to fight a fire is the square root of twice the product of the maximum height, h, in metres, and the acceleration due to gravity. At sea level, the acceleration due to gravity is 9.8 m/s².

a) Write the formula that models the relationship between the speed and the height of the water.

b) Suppose the speed of the water being pumped is 30 m/s. What expected height will the spray reach?

c) A local fire department needs to buy a pump that reaches a height of 60 m. An advertisement for a pump claims that it can project water at a speed of 35 m/s. Will this pump meet the department's requirements? Justify your answer.

18. The distance d, in kilometres, to the horizon from a height, h, in kilometres, can be modelled by the formula $d = \sqrt{2rh + h^2}$, where r represents Earth's radius, in kilometres. A spacecraft is 200 km above Earth, at point S. If the distance to the horizon from the spacecraft is 1609 km, what is the radius of Earth?

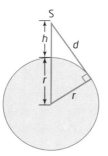

Extend

19. Solve for a in the equation $\sqrt{3x} = \sqrt{ax} + 2$, $a \geq 0$, $x > 0$.

20. Create a radical equation that results in the following types of solution. Explain how you arrived at your equation.

a) one extraneous solution and no valid solutions

b) one extraneous solution and one valid solution

21. The time, t, in seconds, for an object to fall to the ground is related to its height, h, in metres, above the ground. The formulas for determining this time are $t_m = \sqrt{\frac{h}{1.8}}$ for the moon and $t_E = \sqrt{\frac{h}{4.9}}$ for Earth. The same object is dropped from the same height on both the moon and Earth. If the difference in times for the object to reach the ground is 0.5 s, determine the height from which the object was dropped. Express your answer to the nearest tenth of a metre.

22. Refer to #18. Use the formula $d = \sqrt{2rh + h^2}$ to determine the height of a spacecraft above the moon, where the radius is 1740 km and the distance to the horizon is 610 km. Express your answer to the nearest kilometre.

23. The profit, P, in dollars, of a business can be expressed as $P = -n^2 + 200n$, where n represents the number of employees.

a) What is the maximum profit? How many employees are required for this value?

b) Rewrite the equation by isolating n.

c) What are the restrictions on the radical portion of your answer to part b)?

d) What are the domain and range for the original function? How does your answer relate to part c)?

Create Connections

24. Describe the similarities and differences between solving a quadratic equation and solving a radical equation.

25. Why are extraneous roots sometimes produced when solving radical equations? Include an example and show how the root was produced.

26. An equation to determine the annual growth rate, r, of a population of moose in Wells Gray Provincial Park, British Columbia, over a 3-year period is

$r = -1 + \sqrt[3]{\dfrac{P_f}{P_i}}$, $P_f \geq 0$, $P_i > 0$. In the

equation, P_i represents the initial population 5 years ago and P_f represents the final population after 3 years.

a) If $P_i = 320$ and $P_f = 390$, what is the annual growth rate? Express your answer as a percent to the nearest tenth.

b) Rewrite the equation by isolating P_f.

c) Determine the four populations of moose over this 3-year period.

d) What kind of sequence does the set of populations in part c) represent?

27. MINI LAB A continued radical is a series of nested radicals that may be infinite but has a finite rational result. Consider the following continued radical:

$$\sqrt{6 + \sqrt{6 + \sqrt{6 + \sqrt{6 + \cdots}}}}$$

Step 1 Using a calculator or spreadsheet software, determine a decimal approximation for the expressions in the table.

Number of Nested Radicals	Expression	Decimal Approximation
1	$\sqrt{6 + \sqrt{6}}$	
2	$\sqrt{6 + \sqrt{6 + \sqrt{6}}}$	
3	$\sqrt{6 + \sqrt{6 + \sqrt{6 + \sqrt{6}}}}$	
4		
5		
6		
7		
8		
9		

Step 2 From your table, predict the value of the expression

$$\sqrt{6 + \sqrt{6 + \sqrt{6 + \sqrt{6 + \cdots}}}} .$$

Step 3 Let $x = \sqrt{6 + \sqrt{6 + \sqrt{6 + \sqrt{6 + \cdots}}}}$. Solve the equation algebraically.

Step 4 Check your result with a classmate. Why does one of the roots need to be rejected?

Step 5 Generate another continued radical expression that will result in a finite real-number solution. Does your answer have a rational or an irrational root?

Step 6 Exchange your radical expression in step 5 with a classmate and solve their problem.

Chapter 5 Review

5.1 Working With Radicals, pages 272–281

1. Convert each mixed radical to an entire radical.

   a) $8\sqrt{5}$

   b) $-2\sqrt[5]{3}$

   c) $3y^3\sqrt{7}$

   d) $-3z(\sqrt[3]{4z})$

2. Convert each entire radical to a mixed radical in simplest form.

   a) $\sqrt{72}$

   b) $3\sqrt{40}$

   c) $\sqrt{27m^2}$, $m \geq 0$

   d) $\sqrt[3]{80x^5y^6}$

3. Simplify.

   a) $-\sqrt{13} + 2\sqrt{13}$

   b) $4\sqrt{7} - 2\sqrt{112}$

   c) $-\sqrt[3]{3} + \sqrt[3]{24}$

4. Simplify radicals and collect like terms. State any restrictions on the values for the variables.

   a) $4\sqrt{45x^3} - \sqrt{27x} + 17\sqrt{3x} - 9\sqrt{125x^3}$

   b) $\frac{2}{5}\sqrt{44a} + \sqrt{144a^3} - \frac{\sqrt{11a}}{2}$

5. Which of the following expressions is not equivalent to $8\sqrt{7}$?

   $2\sqrt{112}$, $\sqrt{448}$, $3\sqrt{42}$, $4\sqrt{28}$

   Explain how you know without using technology.

6. Order the following numbers from least to greatest: $3\sqrt{7}$, $\sqrt{65}$, $2\sqrt{17}$, 8

7. The speed, v, in kilometres per hour, of a car before a collision can be approximated from the length, d, in metres, of the skid mark left by the tire. On a dry day, one formula that approximates this speed is $v = \sqrt{169d}$, $d \geq 0$.

   a) Rewrite the formula as a mixed radical.

   b) What is the approximate speed of a car if the skid mark measures 13.4 m? Express your answer to the nearest kilometre per hour.

8. The city of Yorkton, Saskatchewan, has an area of 24.0 km². If this city were a perfect square, what would its exact perimeter be? Express your answer as a mixed radical in simplest form.

9. State whether each equation is true or false. Justify your reasoning.

   a) $-3^2 = \pm9$

   b) $(-3)^2 = 9$

   c) $\sqrt{9} = \pm3$

5.2 Multiplying and Dividing Radical Expressions, pages 282–293

10. Multiply. Express each product as a radical in simplest form.

    a) $\sqrt{2}(\sqrt{6})$

    b) $(-3f\sqrt{15})(2f^3\sqrt{5})$

    c) $(\sqrt[4]{8})(3\sqrt[4]{18})$

11. Multiply and simplify. Identify any restrictions on the values for the variable in part c).

    a) $(2 - \sqrt{5})(2 + \sqrt{5})$

    b) $(5\sqrt{3} - \sqrt{8})^2$

    c) $(a + 3\sqrt{a})(a + 7\sqrt{4a})$

12. Are $x = \dfrac{5 + \sqrt{17}}{2}$ and $x = \dfrac{5 - \sqrt{17}}{2}$ a conjugate pair? Justify your answer.

    Are they solutions of the quadratic equation $x^2 - 5x + 2 = 0$? Explain.

13. Rationalize each denominator.

a) $\dfrac{\sqrt{6}}{\sqrt{12}}$

b) $\dfrac{-1}{\sqrt[3]{25}}$

c) $-4\sqrt{\dfrac{2a^2}{9}}$, $a \geq 0$

14. Rationalize each denominator. State any restrictions on the values for the variables.

a) $\dfrac{-2}{4 - \sqrt{3}}$

b) $\dfrac{\sqrt{7}}{2\sqrt{5} - \sqrt{7}}$

c) $\dfrac{18}{6 + \sqrt{27m}}$

d) $\dfrac{a + \sqrt{b}}{a - \sqrt{b}}$

15. What is the exact perimeter of the triangle?

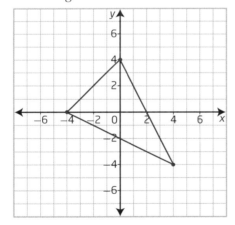

16. Simplify.

a) $\left(\dfrac{-5\sqrt{3}}{\sqrt{6}}\right)\left(\dfrac{-\sqrt{7}}{3\sqrt{21}}\right)$

b) $\left(\dfrac{2a\sqrt{a^3}}{9}\right)\left(\dfrac{12}{-\sqrt{8a}}\right)$

17. The area of a rectangle is 12 square units. The width is $(4 - \sqrt{2})$ units. Determine an expression for the length of the rectangle in simplest radical form.

5.3 Radical Equations, pages 294–303

18. Identify the values of x for which the radicals are defined. Solve for x and verify your answers.

a) $-\sqrt{x} = -7$

b) $\sqrt{4 - x} = -2$

c) $5 - \sqrt{2x} = -1$

d) $1 + \sqrt{\dfrac{7x}{3}} = 8$

19. Solve each radical equation. Determine any restrictions on the values for the variables.

a) $\sqrt{5x - 3} = \sqrt{7x - 12}$

b) $\sqrt{y - 3} = y - 3$

c) $\sqrt{7n + 25} - n = 1$

d) $\sqrt{8 - \dfrac{m}{3}} = \sqrt{3m} - 4$

e) $\sqrt[3]{3x - 1} + 7 = 3$

20. Describe the steps in your solution to #19c). Explain why one of the roots was extraneous.

21. On a calm day, the distance, d, in kilometres, that the coast guard crew on the Coast Guard cutter Vakta can see to the horizon depends on their height, h, in metres, above the water. The formula $d = \sqrt{\dfrac{3h}{2}}$, $h \geq 0$ models this relationship. What is the height of the crew above the water if the distance to the horizon is 7.1 km?

Did You Know?

The Vakta is a 16.8-m cutter used by Search and Rescue to assist in water emergencies on Lake Winnipeg. It is based in Gimli, Manitoba.

Chapter 5 Practice Test

Multiple Choice

For #1 to #6, choose the best answer.

1. What is the entire radical form of $-3(\sqrt[3]{2})$?

   A $\sqrt[3]{54}$ **B** $\sqrt[3]{-54}$

   C $\sqrt[3]{-18}$ **D** $\sqrt[3]{18}$

2. What is the condition on the variable in $2\sqrt{-7n}$ for the radicand to be a real number?

   A $n \geq 7$ **B** $n \leq -7$

   C $n \geq 0$ **D** $n \leq 0$

3. What is the simplest form of the sum $-2x\sqrt{6x} + 5x\sqrt{6x}$, $x \geq 0$?

   A $3\sqrt{6x}$ **B** $6\sqrt{12x}$

   C $3x\sqrt{6x}$ **D** $6x\sqrt{12}$

4. What is the product of $\sqrt{540}$ and $\sqrt{6y}$, $y \geq 0$, in simplest form?

   A $3y\sqrt{360}$ **B** $6y\sqrt{90}$

   C $10\sqrt{32y}$ **D** $18\sqrt{10y}$

5. Determine any root of the equation, $x + 7 = \sqrt{23 - x}$, where $x \leq 23$.

   A $x = 13$

   B $x = -2$

   C $x = 2$ and 13

   D $x = -2$ and -13

6. Suppose $\frac{5}{7}\sqrt{\frac{3}{2}}$ is written in simplest form as $a\sqrt{b}$, where a is a real number and b is an integer. What is the value of b?

   A 2 **B** 3

   C 6 **D** 14

Short Answer

7. Order the following numbers from least to greatest:

   $3\sqrt{11}, 5\sqrt{6}, 9\sqrt{2}, \sqrt{160}$

8. Express as a radical in simplest form.

$$\frac{(2\sqrt{5n})(3\sqrt{8n})}{1 - 12\sqrt{2}}, n \geq 0.$$

9. Solve $3 - x = \sqrt{x^2 - 5}$. State any extraneous roots that you found. Identify the values of x for which the radical is defined.

10. Solve $\sqrt{9y + 1} = 3 + \sqrt{4y - 2}$, $y \geq \frac{1}{2}$. Verify your solution. Justify your method. Identify any extraneous roots that you found.

11. Masoud started to simplify $\sqrt{450}$ by rewriting 450 as a product of prime factors: $\sqrt{2(3)(3)(5)(5)}$. Explain how he can convert his expression to a mixed radical.

12. For sailboats to travel into the wind, it is sometimes necessary to tack, or move in a zigzag pattern. A sailboat in Lake Winnipeg travels 4 km due north and then 4 km due west. From there the boat travels 5 km due north and then 5 km due west. How far is the boat from its starting point? Express your answer as a mixed radical.

13. You wish to rationalize the denominator in each expression. By what number will you multiply each expression? Justify your answer.

   a) $\dfrac{4}{\sqrt{6}}$

   b) $\dfrac{22}{\sqrt{y - 3}}$

   c) $\dfrac{2}{\sqrt[3]{7}}$

14. For diamonds of comparable quality, the cost, C, in dollars, is related to the mass, m, in carats, by the formula $m = \sqrt{\dfrac{C}{700}}$, $C \geq 0$. What is the cost of a 3-carat diamond?

Did You Know?

Snap Lake Mine is 220 km northeast of Yellowknife, Northwest Territories. It is the first fully underground diamond mine in Canada.

15. Teya tries to rationalize the denominator in the expression $\dfrac{5\sqrt{2} + \sqrt{3}}{4\sqrt{2} - \sqrt{3}}$. Is Teya correct? If not, identify and explain any errors she made.

Teya's Solution

$$\frac{5\sqrt{2} + \sqrt{3}}{4\sqrt{2} - \sqrt{3}} = \left(\frac{5\sqrt{2} + \sqrt{3}}{4\sqrt{2} - \sqrt{3}}\right)\left(\frac{4\sqrt{2} + \sqrt{3}}{4\sqrt{2} + \sqrt{3}}\right)$$

$$= \frac{20\sqrt{4} + 5\sqrt{6} + 4\sqrt{6} + \sqrt{9}}{32 - 3}$$

$$= \frac{40 + 9\sqrt{6} + 3}{32 - 3}$$

$$= \frac{43 + 9\sqrt{6}}{29}$$

16. A right triangle has one leg that measures 1 unit.

a) Model the length of the hypotenuse using a radical equation.

b) The length of the hypotenuse is 11 units. What is the length of the unknown leg? Express your answer as a mixed radical in simplest form.

Extended Response

17. A 100-W light bulb operates with a current of 0.5 A. The formula relating current, I, in amperes (A); power, P, in watts (W); and resistance, R, in ohms (Ω), is $I = \sqrt{\dfrac{P}{R}}$.

a) Isolate R in the formula.

b) What is the resistance in the light bulb?

18. Sylvie built a model of a cube-shaped house.

a) Express the edge length of a cube in terms of the surface area using a radical equation.

b) Suppose the surface area of the cube in Sylvie's model is 33 cm². Determine the exact edge length in simplest form.

c) If the surface area of a cube doubles, by what scale factor will the edge length change?

19. Beverley invested $3500 two years ago. The investment earned compound interest annually according to the formula $A = P(1 + i)^n$. In the formula, A represents the final amount of the investment, P represents the principal or initial amount, i represents the interest rate per compounding period, and n represents the number of compounding periods. The current amount of her investment is $3713.15.

a) Model Beverley's investment using the formula.

b) What is the interest rate? Express your answer as a percent.

CHAPTER 6

Rational Expressions and Equations

Rational expressions are used in medicine, lighting, economics, space travel, engineering, acoustics, and many other fields. For example, the rings of Saturn have puzzled astronomers since Galileo discovered them with his telescope in 1610. In October 2009, 12 years after the launch of the Cassini-Huygens project, scientists at the NASA Jet Propulsion Laboratory determined that Saturn's famous rings are neither as thin nor as flat as previously thought. Why do you think it took so long for NASA to gather and analyse this information?

In this chapter, you will learn about the algebra of rational expressions and equations. Compare the skills you learn in the chapter with those you learned in the arithmetic of fractions. They are very similar.

Did You Know?

The Cassini-Huygens project is a joint NASA and European Space Agency (ESA) robotic spacecraft mission to Saturn. The spacecraft was launched in 1997 and arrived to start its orbits around Saturn in 2004. The mission may continue until 2017.

Key Terms

rational expression
non-permissible value
rational equation

Career Link

You can use mathematical modelling to analyse problems in economics, science, medicine, urban planning, climate change, manufacturing, and space exploration. Building a mathematical model is normally a multi-stage process that involves writing equations, using them to predict what happens, experimenting to see if the prediction is correct, modifying the equations, and so on.

Marcel Tolkowsky, a 21-year-old Belgian mathematician, revolutionized the diamond-cutting industry in 1919 when he used mathematical modelling to calculate the formula for the ideal proportions in a cut diamond. By reducing the process to a mathematical formula, diamond-cutting is now more automated.

Web Link

To learn more about fields involving mathematical modelling, go to www.mhrprecalc11.ca and follow the links.

Rational Expressions

Focus on...

- determining non-permissible values for a rational expression
- simplifying a rational expression
- modelling a situation using a rational expression

Many day-to-day applications use **rational expressions**. You can determine the time it takes to travel across Canada by dividing the distance travelled, d, by the rate of speed at which you are travelling, r. Light intensity and the intensity of sound can be described mathematically as ratios in the form $\dfrac{k}{d^2}$, where k is a constant and d is the distance from the source. When would it be important to know the intensity of light or sound?

What other formulas are rational expressions?

rational expression

- an algebraic fraction with a numerator and a denominator that are polynomials
- examples are $\dfrac{1}{x}$, $\dfrac{m}{m+1}$, $\dfrac{y^2-1}{y^2+2y+1}$
- $x^2 - 4$ is a rational expression with a denominator of 1

Concert stage

Investigate Rational Expressions

Materials

- algebra tiles

1. Consider the polynomial expression $3x^2 + 12x$.

   a) Use algebra tiles to model the polynomial.

   b) Arrange the tiles in a rectangle to represent the length of each side as a polynomial.

c) Use the model from part b) to write a simplified form of the rational expression $\dfrac{3x^2 + 12x}{3x}$.

How can you verify that your answer is equivalent to the rational expression? Explain your reasoning.

d) Are these two expressions always equivalent? Why or why not?

2. Whenever you are working with algebraic fractions, it is important to determine any values that must be excluded.

a) You can write an unlimited number of arithmetic fractions, or rational numbers, of the form $\dfrac{a}{b}$, where a and b are integers. What integer cannot be used for b?

b) What happens in each of the following expressions when $x = 3$ is substituted?

i) $\dfrac{x - 7}{x - 3}$

ii) $\dfrac{x - 7}{x^2 - 9}$

iii) $\dfrac{x - 7}{x^2 - 4x + 3}$

3. What value(s) cannot be used for x in each of the following algebraic fractions?

a) $\dfrac{6 - x}{2x}$

b) $\dfrac{3}{x - 7}$

c) $\dfrac{4x - 1}{(x - 3)(2x + 1)}$

> **Did You Know?**
>
> An algebraic fraction is the quotient of two algebraic expressions. Examples of algebraic fractions are $\dfrac{-4}{x - 2}$, $\dfrac{t}{5}$, 0, $\dfrac{x^2}{3y^5}$, and $\dfrac{\sqrt{3x + 1}}{x^2}$. All rational expressions are algebraic fractions but not all algebraic fractions are rational expressions.

Reflect and Respond

4. a) What is the result when zero is divided by any non-zero number?

b) Why is division by zero undefined?

5. Write a rule that explains how to determine any values that a variable cannot be, for any algebraic fraction.

6. What operation(s) can you use when you are asked to express a rational number in lowest terms? Give examples to support your answer.

7. Describe two ways in which arithmetic fractions and algebraic fractions are similar. How do they differ?

8. a) What is the value of any rational expression in which the numerator and denominator are the same non-zero polynomials?

b) What is the value of a fraction in which the numerator and denominator are opposite integers?

c) What is the value of the rational expression $\dfrac{x - 3}{3 - x}$ for $x \neq 3$? Explain.

Non-Permissible Values

Whenever you use a rational expression, you must identify any values that must be excluded or are considered **non-permissible values**. Non-permissible values are all values that make the denominator zero.

non-permissible value

- any value for a variable that makes an expression undefined
- in a rational expression, a value that results in a denominator of zero
- in $\frac{x+2}{x-3}$, you must exclude the value for which $x - 3 = 0$, which is $x = 3$

Example 1

Determine Non-Permissible Values

For each rational expression, determine all non-permissible values.

a) $\frac{5t}{4sr^2}$ b) $\frac{3x}{x(2x-3)}$ c) $\frac{2p-1}{p^2-p-12}$

Solution

To determine non-permissible values, set the denominator equal to zero and solve.

a) $\frac{5t}{4sr^2}$

Determine the values for which $4sr^2 = 0$.

$4s = 0$ or $r^2 = 0$

$s = 0$ or $r = 0$

The non-permissible values are $s = 0$ and $r = 0$. The rational expression $\frac{5t}{4sr^2}$ is defined for all real numbers except $s = 0$ and $r = 0$.

This is written as $\frac{5t}{4sr^2}, r \neq 0, s \neq 0$.

b) $\frac{3x}{x(2x-3)}$

Determine the values for which $x(2x - 3) = 0$.

$x = 0$ or $2x - 3 = 0$

$x = \frac{3}{2}$

The non-permissible values are 0 and $\frac{3}{2}$.

> Does it matter whether the numerator becomes zero? Explain.

c) $\frac{2p-1}{p^2-p-12}$

Determine the values for which $p^2 - p - 12 = 0$.

$(p - 4)(p + 3) = 0$ Factor $p^2 - p - 12$.

$p = 4$ or $p = -3$

The non-permissible values are 4 and -3.

Your Turn

Determine the non-permissible value(s) for each rational expression.

a) $\frac{4a}{3bc}$ b) $\frac{x-1}{(x+2)(x-3)}$ c) $\frac{2y^2}{y^2-4}$

Equivalent Rational Expressions

You can multiply or divide a rational expression by 1 and not change its value. You will create an equivalent expression using this property. For example, if you multiply $\dfrac{7s}{s-2}$, $s \neq 2$, by $\dfrac{s}{s}$, you are actually multiplying by 1, provided that $s \neq 0$.

$$\left(\frac{7s}{s-2}\right)\left(\frac{s}{s}\right) = \frac{(7s)(s)}{s(s-2)}$$
$$= \frac{7s^2}{s(s-2)}, \ s \neq 0, 2$$

Why do you need to specify that $s \neq 0$?

The rational expressions $\dfrac{7s}{s-2}$, $s \neq 2$, and $\dfrac{7s^2}{s(s-2)}$, $s \neq 0, 2$, are equivalent.

Similarly, you can show that $\dfrac{7s}{s-2}$, $s \neq 2$, and $\dfrac{7s(s+2)}{(s-2)(s+2)}$, $s \neq \pm 2$, are equivalent.

What was done to the first rational expression to get the second one?

Did You Know?

Statements such as $x = 2$ and $x = -2$ can be abbreviated as $x = \pm 2$.

Simplifying Rational Expressions

Writing a rational number in lowest terms and simplifying a rational expression involve similar steps.

$$\frac{9}{12} = \frac{\overset{1}{\cancel{(3)}}(3)}{\underset{1}{\cancel{(3)}}(4)}$$
$$= \frac{3}{4}$$

How could you use models to determine the rational expression in simplest form?

$$\frac{m^3t}{m^2t^4} = \frac{\overset{1}{\cancel{(m^2)}}(m)\overset{1}{\cancel{(t)}}}{\underset{1}{\cancel{(m^2)}}\underset{1}{\cancel{(t)}}(t^3)}$$
$$= \frac{m}{t^3}, \ m \neq 0, t \neq 0$$

Why is 0 a non-permissible value for the variable m in the simplified rational expression?

To simplify a rational expression, divide both the numerator and denominator by any factors that are common to the numerator and the denominator.

Recall that $\dfrac{AB}{AC} = \left(\dfrac{A}{A}\right)\left(\dfrac{B}{C}\right)$ and $\dfrac{A}{A} = 1$.

So, $\dfrac{AB}{AC} = \dfrac{B}{C}$, where A, B, and C are polynomial factors.

When a rational expression is in simplest form, or its lowest terms, the numerator and denominator have no common factors other than 1.

Example 2

Simplify a Rational Expression

Simplify each rational expression. State the non-permissible values.

a) $\dfrac{3x - 6}{2x^2 + x - 10}$

b) $\dfrac{1 - t}{t^2 - 1}$

Solution

a) $\dfrac{3x - 6}{2x^2 + x - 10}$

Factor both the numerator and the denominator. Consider the factors of the denominator to find the non-permissible values before simplifying the expression.

Why should you determine any non-permissible values before simplifying?

$$\frac{3x - 6}{2x^2 + x - 10} = \frac{3(x - 2)}{(x - 2)(2x + 5)}$$

How do you obtain 2 and $-\dfrac{5}{2}$ as the non-permissible values?

$$= \frac{3\overset{1}{\cancel{(x - 2)}}}{\underset{1}{\cancel{(x - 2)}}(2x + 5)}$$

$$= \frac{3}{2x + 5},\ x \neq 2,\ -\frac{5}{2}$$

How could you show that the initial rational expression and the simplified version are equivalent?

b) $\dfrac{1 - t}{t^2 - 1}$

Method 1: Use Factoring −1

$$\frac{1 - t}{t^2 - 1} = \frac{1 - t}{(t - 1)(t + 1)}$$

Factor the denominator. Realize that the numerator is the opposite (additive inverse) of one of the factors in the denominator. Factor −1 from the numerator.

$$= \frac{-1(t - 1)}{(t - 1)(t + 1)}$$

$$= \frac{-1\overset{1}{\cancel{(t - 1)}}}{\underset{1}{\cancel{(t - 1)}}(t + 1)}$$

$$= \frac{-1}{t + 1},\ t \neq \pm 1$$

Method 2: Use the Property of 1

$$\frac{1-t}{t^2-1} = \frac{1-t}{(t-1)(t+1)}$$

Factor the denominator. How are the numerator and the factor $(t-1)$ in the denominator related?

$$= \frac{-1(1-t)}{-1(t-1)(t+1)}$$

Multiply the numerator and the denominator by -1.

$$= \frac{\overset{1}{\cancel{t-1}}}{-1(\underset{1}{\cancel{t-1}})(t+1)}$$

$$= \frac{1}{-1(t+1)}$$

$$= \frac{-1}{t+1}, \; t \neq \pm 1$$

Your Turn

Simplify each rational expression.
What are the non-permissible values?

a) $\dfrac{2y^2 + y - 10}{y^2 + 3y - 10}$

b) $\dfrac{6 - 2m}{m^2 - 9}$

Example 3

Rational Expressions With Pairs of Non-Permissible Values

Consider the expression $\dfrac{16x^2 - 9y^2}{8x - 6y}$.

a) What expression represents the non-permissible values for x?

b) Simplify the rational expression.

c) Evaluate the expression for $x = 2.6$ and $y = 1.2$.
Show two ways to determine the answer.

Solution

a) $\dfrac{16x^2 - 9y^2}{8x - 6y}$

Determine an expression for x for
which $8x - 6y = 0$.

$$x = \frac{6y}{8} \text{ or } \frac{3y}{4}$$

x cannot have a value of $\dfrac{3y}{4}$ or the denominator will

be zero and the expression will be undefined. The

expression for the non-permissible values of x is $x = \dfrac{3y}{4}$.

What is an expression for the non-permissible values of y?

Examples of non-permissible values include $\left(\dfrac{3}{4}, 1\right)$, $\left(\dfrac{3}{2}, 2\right)$,

$\left(\dfrac{9}{4}, 3\right)$, and so on.

b) $\dfrac{16x^2 - 9y^2}{8x - 6y} = \dfrac{(4x - 3y)(4x + 3y)}{2(4x - 3y)}$

Factor the numerator and the denominator.

$= \dfrac{(4x \overset{1}{\cancel{- 3y}})(4x + 3y)}{2(4x \underset{1}{\cancel{- 3y}})}$

What are you assuming when you divide both the numerator and the denominator by $4x - 3y$?

$= \dfrac{4x + 3y}{2}, \ x \neq \dfrac{3y}{4}$

c) First, check that the values $x = 2.6$ and $y = 1.2$ are permissible.

Left Side   Right Side
x $\dfrac{3y}{4}$
$= 2.6$ $= \dfrac{3(1.2)}{4}$
                   $= 0.9$

Left Side $\neq$ Right Side

Thus, $x \neq \dfrac{3y}{4}$ for $x = 2.6$ and $y = 1.2$, so the values are permissible.

Method 1: Substitute Into the Original Rational Expression

$\dfrac{16x^2 - 9y^2}{8x - 6y} = \dfrac{16(2.6)^2 - 9(1.2)^2}{8(2.6) - 6(1.2)}$

$= \dfrac{95.2}{13.6}$

$= 7$

Method 2: Substitute Into the Simplified Rational Expression

$\dfrac{4x + 3y}{2} = \dfrac{4(2.6) + 3(1.2)}{2}$

$= \dfrac{14}{2}$

$= 7$

The value of the expression when $x = 2.6$ and $y = 1.2$ is 7.

Your Turn

Use the rational expression $\dfrac{16x^2 - 9y^2}{8x - 6y}$ to help answer the following.

a) What is the non-permissible value for y if $x = 3$?

b) Evaluate the expression for $x = 1.5$ and $y = 2.8$.

c) Give a reason why it may be beneficial to simplify a rational expression.

- A rational expression is an algebraic fraction of the form $\frac{p}{q}$, where p and q are polynomials and $q \neq 0$.

- A non-permissible value is a value of the variable that causes an expression to be undefined. For a rational expression, this occurs when the denominator is zero.

- Rational expressions can be simplified by:
  - factoring the numerator and the denominator
  - determining non-permissible values
  - dividing both the numerator and denominator by all common factors

Check Your Understanding

Practise

1. What should replace ■ to make the expressions in each pair equivalent?

a) $\frac{3}{5}, \frac{■}{30}$

b) $\frac{2}{5}, \frac{■}{35x}, x \neq 0$

c) $\frac{4}{■}, \frac{44}{77}$

d) $\frac{x+2}{x-3}, \frac{4x+8}{■}, x \neq 3$

e) $\frac{3(6)}{■(6)}, \frac{3}{8}$

f) $\frac{1}{y-2}, \frac{■}{y^2-4}, y \neq \pm 2$

2. State the operation and quantity that must be applied to both the numerator and the denominator of the first expression to obtain the second expression.

a) $\frac{3p^2q}{pq^2}, \frac{3p}{q}$

b) $\frac{2}{x+4}, \frac{2x-8}{x^2-16}$

c) $\frac{-4(m-3)}{m^2-9}, \frac{-4}{m+3}$

d) $\frac{1}{y-1}, \frac{y^2+y}{y^3-y}$

3. What value(s) of the variable, if any, make the denominator of each expression equal zero?

a) $\frac{-4}{x}$

b) $\frac{3c-1}{c-1}$

c) $\frac{y}{y+5}$

d) $\frac{m+3}{5}$

e) $\frac{1}{d^2-1}$

f) $\frac{x-1}{x^2+1}$

4. Determine the non-permissible value(s) for each rational expression. Why are these values not permitted?

a) $\frac{3a}{4-a}$

b) $\frac{2e+8}{e}$

c) $\frac{3(y+7)}{(y-4)(y+2)}$

d) $\frac{-7(r-1)}{(r-1)(r+3)}$

e) $\frac{2k+8}{k^2}$

f) $\frac{6x-8}{(3x-4)(2x+5)}$

5. What value(s) for the variables must be excluded when working with each rational expression?

a) $\dfrac{4\pi r^2}{8\pi r^3}$

b) $\dfrac{2t + t^2}{t^2 - 1}$

c) $\dfrac{x - 2}{10 - 5x}$

d) $\dfrac{3g}{g^3 - 9g}$

6. Simplify each rational expression. State any non-permissible values for the variables.

a) $\dfrac{2c(c - 5)}{3c(c - 5)}$

b) $\dfrac{3w(2w + 3)}{2w(3w + 2)}$

c) $\dfrac{(x - 7)(x + 7)}{(2x - 1)(x - 7)}$

d) $\dfrac{5(a - 3)(a + 2)}{10(3 - a)(a + 2)}$

7. Consider the rational expression $\dfrac{x^2 - 1}{x^2 + 2x - 3}$.

a) Explain why you cannot divide out the x^2 in the numerator with the x^2 in the denominator.

b) Explain how to determine the non-permissible values. State the non-permissible values.

c) Explain how to simplify a rational expression. Simplify the rational expression.

8. Write each rational expression in simplest form. State any non-permissible values for the variables.

a) $\dfrac{6r^2 p^3}{4rp^4}$

b) $\dfrac{3x - 6}{10 - 5x}$

c) $\dfrac{b^2 + 2b - 24}{2b^2 - 72}$

d) $\dfrac{10k^2 + 55k + 75}{20k^2 - 10k - 150}$

e) $\dfrac{x - 4}{4 - x}$

f) $\dfrac{5(x^2 - y^2)}{x^2 - 2xy + y^2}$

Apply

9. Since $\dfrac{x^2 + 2x - 15}{x - 3}$ can be written as $\dfrac{(x - 3)(x + 5)}{x - 3}$, you can say that $\dfrac{x^2 + 2x - 15}{x - 3}$ and $x + 5$ are equivalent expressions. Is this statement always, sometimes, or never true? Explain.

10. Explain why 6 may not be the only non-permissible value for a rational expression that is written in simplest form as $\dfrac{y}{y - 6}$. Give examples to support your answer.

11. Mike always looks for shortcuts. He claims, "It is easy to simplify expressions such as $\dfrac{5 - x}{x - 5}$ because the top and bottom are opposites of each other and any time you divide opposites the result is -1." Is Mike correct? Explain why or why not.

12. Suppose you are tutoring a friend in simplifying rational expressions. Create three sample expressions written in the form $\dfrac{ax^2 + bx + c}{dx^2 + ex + f}$ where the numerators and denominators factor and the expressions can be simplified. Describe the process you used to create one of your expressions.

13. Shali incorrectly simplifies a rational expression as shown below.

$$\dfrac{g^2 - 4}{2g - 4} = \dfrac{(g - 2)(g + 2)}{2(g - 2)}$$
$$= \dfrac{g + 2}{2}$$
$$= g + 1$$

What is Shali's error? Explain why the step is incorrect. Show the correct solution.

14. Create a rational expression with variable p that has non-permissible values of 1 and -2.

15. The distance, d, can be determined using the formula $d = rt$, where r is the rate of speed and t is the time.

   a) If the distance is represented by $2n^2 + 11n + 12$ and the rate of speed is represented by $2n^2 - 32$, what is an expression for the time?

   b) Write your expression from part a) in simplest form. Identify any non-permissible values.

16. You have been asked to draw the largest possible circle on a square piece of paper. The side length of the piece of paper is represented by $2x$.

   a) Draw a diagram showing your circle on the piece of paper. Label your diagram.

   b) Create a rational expression comparing the area of your circle to the area of the piece of paper.

   c) Identify any non-permissible values for your rational expression.

   d) What is your rational expression in simplest form?

   e) What percent of the paper is included in your circle? Give your answer to the nearest percent.

17. A chemical company is researching the effect of a new pesticide on crop yields. Preliminary results show that the extra yield per hectare is given by the expression $\dfrac{900p}{2 + p}$, where p is the mass of pesticide, in kilograms. The extra yield is also measured in kilograms.

   a) Explain whether the non-permissible value needs to be considered in this situation.

   b) What integral value for p gives the least extra yield?

   c) Substitute several values for p and determine what seems to be the greatest extra yield possible.

18. Write an expression in simplest form for the time required to travel 100 km at each rate. Identify any non-permissible values.

   a) $2q$ kilometres per hour

   b) $(p - 4)$ kilometres per hour

19. A school art class is planning a day trip to the Glenbow Museum in Calgary. The cost of the bus is $350 and admission is $9 per student.

   a) What is the total cost for a class of 30 students?

   b) Write a rational expression that could be used to determine the cost per student if n students go on the trip.

   c) Use your expression to determine the cost per student if 30 students go.

Did You Know?

The Glenbow Museum in Calgary is one of western Canada's largest museums. It documents life in western Canada from the 1800s to the present day. Exhibits trace the traditions of the First Nations peoples as well as the hardships of ranching and farming in southern Alberta.

First Nations exhibit at Glenbow Museum

20. Terri believes that $\dfrac{5}{m + 5}$ can be expressed in simplest form as $\dfrac{1}{m + 1}$.

a) Do you agree with Terri? Explain in words.

b) Use substitution to show whether $\dfrac{5}{m + 5}$ and $\dfrac{1}{m + 1}$ are equivalent or not.

21. Sometimes it is useful to write more complicated equivalent rational expressions. For example, $\dfrac{3x}{4}$ is equivalent to $\dfrac{15x}{20}$ and to $\dfrac{3x^2 - 6x}{4x - 8}$, $x \neq 2$.

a) How can you change $\dfrac{3x}{4}$ into its equivalent form, $\dfrac{15x}{20}$?

b) What do you need to do to $\dfrac{3x}{4}$ to get $\dfrac{3x^2 - 6x}{4x - 8}$?

22. Write a rational expression equivalent to $\dfrac{x - 2}{3}$ that has

a) a denominator of 12

b) a numerator of $3x - 6$

c) a denominator of $6x + 15$

23. Write a rational expression that satisfies each set of conditions.

a) equivalent to 5, with $5b$ as the denominator

b) equivalent to $\dfrac{x + 1}{3}$, with a denominator of $12a^2b$

c) equivalent to $\dfrac{a - b}{7x}$, with a numerator of $2b - 2a$

24. The area of right $\triangle PQR$ is $(x^2 - x - 6)$ square units, and the length of side PQ is $(x - 3)$ units. Side PR is the hypotenuse.

a) Draw a diagram of $\triangle PQR$.

b) Write an expression for the length of side QR. Express your answer in simplest form.

c) What are the non-permissible values?

25. The work shown to simplify each rational expression contains at least one error. Rewrite each solution, correcting the errors.

a)
$$\dfrac{6x^2 - x - 1}{9x^2 - 1} = \dfrac{(2x + 1)(3x - 1)}{(3x + 1)(3x - 1)}$$
$$= \dfrac{2x + 1}{3x + 1}, \, x \neq -\dfrac{1}{3}$$

b)
$$\dfrac{2n^2 + n - 15}{5n - 2n^2} = \dfrac{(n + 3)(2n - 5)}{n(5 - 2n)}$$
$$= \dfrac{(n + 3)(2n - 5)}{-n(2n - 5)}$$
$$= \dfrac{n + 3}{-n}$$
$$= \dfrac{n - 3}{n}, \, n \neq 0, \dfrac{5}{2}$$

Extend

26. Write in simplest form. Identify any non-permissible values.

a) $\dfrac{(x + 2)^2 - (x + 2) - 20}{x^2 - 9}$

b) $\dfrac{4(x^2 - 9)^2 - (x + 3)^2}{x^2 + 6x + 9}$

c) $\dfrac{(x^2 - x)^2 - 8(x^2 - x) + 12}{(x^2 - 4)^2 - (x - 2)^2}$

d) $\dfrac{(x^2 + 4x + 4)^2 - 10(x^2 + 4x + 4) + 9}{(2x + 1)^2 - (x + 2)^2}$

27. Parallelogram ABFG has an area of $(16x^2 - 1)$ square units and a height of $(4x - 1)$ units. Parallelogram BCDE has an area of $(6x^2 - x - 12)$ square units and a height of $(2x - 3)$ units. What is an expression for the area of $\triangle ABC$? Leave your answer in the form $ax^2 + bx + c$. What are the non-permissible values?

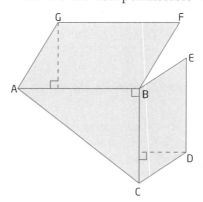

28. Carpet sellers need to know if a partial roll contains enough carpet to complete an order. Your task is to create an expression that gives the approximate length of carpet on a roll using measurements from the end of the roll.

a) Let t represent the thickness of the carpet and L the length of carpet on a roll. What is an expression for the area of the rolled edge of the carpet?

b) Draw a diagram showing the carpet rolled on a centre tube. Label the radius of the centre tube as r and the radius of the entire carpet roll as R. What is an expression for the approximate area of the edge of the carpet on the roll? Write your answer in factored form.

c) Write an expression for the length of carpet on a roll of thickness t. What conditions apply to t, L, R, and r?

Create Connections

29. Write a rational expression using one variable that satisfies the following conditions.

a) The non-permissible values are -2 and 5.

b) The non-permissible values are 1 and -3 and the expression is $\dfrac{x}{x-1}$ in simplest form. Explain how you found your expression.

30. Consider the rational expressions $\dfrac{y-3}{4}$ and $\dfrac{2y^2-5y-3}{8y+4}$, $y \neq -\dfrac{1}{2}$.

a) Substitute a value for y to show that the two expressions are equivalent.

b) Use algebra to show that the expressions are equivalent.

c) Which approach proves the two expressions are equivalent? Why?

31. Two points on a coordinate grid are represented by $A(p, 3)$ and $B(2p + 1, p - 5)$.

a) Write a rational expression for the slope of the line passing through A and B. Write your answer in simplest form.

b) Determine a value for p such that the line passing through A and B has a negative slope.

c) Describe the line through A and B for any non-permissible value of p.

32. Use examples to show how writing a fraction in lowest terms and simplifying a rational expression involve the same mathematical processes.

6.2

Multiplying and Dividing Rational Expressions

Focus on...

- comparing operations on rational expressions to the same operations on rational numbers
- identifying non-permissible values when performing operations on rational expressions
- determining the product or quotient of rational expressions in simplest form

Aboriginal House at the University of Manitoba earned gold LEED status in December 2009 for combining aboriginal values and international environmental practices. According to Elder Garry Robson, the cultural significance of the building has many layers. Elder Robson says, "Once you've learned one (layer), then you learn another and another and so on."

How does Elder Robson's observation apply in mathematics?

Aboriginal House,
University of Manitoba

Did You Know?

The Leadership in Energy and Environmental Design (LEED) rating system is a nationally accepted standard for constructing and operating green buildings. It promotes sustainability in site development, water and energy efficiency, materials selection, and indoor environmental quality.

Investigate Multiplying and Dividing Rational Expressions

Materials

- grid paper

1. Determine the product $\left(\frac{3}{4}\right)\left(\frac{1}{2}\right)$. Describe a pattern that could be used to numerically determine the answer.

2. Multiplying rational expressions follows the same pattern as multiplying rational numbers. Use your pattern from step 1 to help you multiply $\frac{x+3}{2}$ and $\frac{x+1}{4}$.

3. Determine the value of $\frac{2}{3} \div \frac{1}{6}$. Describe a pattern that could be used as a method to divide rational numbers.

4. Apply your method from step 3 to express $\dfrac{x-3}{x^2-9} \div \dfrac{x}{x+3}$ in simplest form. Do you think your method always works? Why?

5. What are the non-permissible values for x in step 4? Explain how to determine the non-permissible values.

Reflect and Respond

6. Explain how you can apply the statement "once you've learned one, then you learn another and another" to the mathematics of rational numbers and rational expressions.

7. Describe a process you could follow to find the product in simplest form when multiplying rational expressions.

8. Describe a process for dividing rational expressions and expressing the answer in simplest form. Show how your process works using an example.

9. Explain why it is important to identify all non-permissible values before simplifying when using rational expressions.

Link the Ideas

Multiplying Rational Expressions

When you multiply rational expressions, you follow procedures similar to those for multiplying rational numbers.

$$\left(\frac{5}{8}\right)\left(\frac{4}{15}\right) = \frac{(5)(4)}{(8)(15)}$$

$$= \frac{(5)(4)}{(2)(4)(3)(5)}$$

$$= \frac{\overset{1}{\cancel{(5)}}\,\overset{1}{\cancel{(4)}}}{2\underset{1}{\cancel{(4)}}(3)\underset{1}{\cancel{(5)}}}$$

$$= \frac{1}{6}$$

$$\left(\frac{4x^2}{3xy}\right)\left(\frac{y^2}{8x}\right) = \frac{(4x^2)(y^2)}{(3xy)(8x)}$$

$$= \frac{\overset{1}{\cancel{4}}\,\overset{1}{\cancel{x^2}}\,\overset{y}{\cancel{y^2}}}{\underset{6}{\cancel{24}}\,\underset{1}{\cancel{x^2}}\,\underset{1}{\cancel{y}}}$$

$$= \frac{y}{6},\ x \neq 0,\ y \neq 0$$

Values for the variables that result in any denominator of zero are non-permissible. Division by zero is not defined in the real-number system.

Example 1

Multiply Rational Expressions

Multiply. Write your answer in simplest form.
Identify all non-permissible values.

$$\frac{a^2 - a - 12}{a^2 - 9} \times \frac{a^2 - 4a + 3}{a^2 - 4a}$$

Solution

Factor each numerator and denominator.

$$\frac{a^2 - a - 12}{a^2 - 9} \times \frac{a^2 - 4a + 3}{a^2 - 4a} = \frac{(a - 4)(a + 3)}{(a - 3)(a + 3)} \times \frac{(a - 3)(a - 1)}{a(a - 4)}$$

$$= \frac{(a - 4)(a + 3)(a - 3)(a - 1)}{(a - 3)(a + 3)(a)(a - 4)}$$

$$= \frac{\overset{1}{\cancel{(a - 4)}}\overset{1}{\cancel{(a + 3)}}\overset{1}{\cancel{(a - 3)}}(a - 1)}{\underset{1}{\cancel{(a - 3)}}\underset{1}{\cancel{(a + 3)}}(a)\underset{1}{\cancel{(a - 4)}}}$$

$$= \frac{a - 1}{a}$$

The non-permissible values are $a = -3, 0, 3$, and 4, since these values give zero in the denominator of at least one fraction, and division by zero is not permitted in the real numbers.

$$\frac{a^2 - a - 12}{a^2 - 9} \times \frac{a^2 - 4a + 3}{a^2 - 4a} = \frac{a - 1}{a}, a \neq -3, 0, 3, 4$$

Where is the best place to look when identifying non-permissible values in products of rational expressions?

Your Turn

Express each product in simplest form.
What are the non-permissible values?

a) $\dfrac{d}{2\pi r} \times \dfrac{2\pi rh}{d - 2}$

b) $\dfrac{y^2 - 9}{r^3 - r} \times \dfrac{r^2 - r}{y + 3}$

Dividing Rational Expressions

Dividing rational expressions follows similar procedures to those for dividing rational numbers.

Method 1: Use a Common Denominator

$$\frac{5}{3} \div \frac{1}{6} = \frac{10}{6} \div \frac{1}{6}$$

$$= \frac{10}{1}$$

$$= 10$$

$$\frac{3x^2}{y^2} \div \frac{x}{y} = \frac{3x^2}{y^2} \div \frac{xy}{y^2}$$

$$= \frac{3x^2}{xy}$$

$$= \frac{3x}{y}, \; x \neq 0, \; y \neq 0 \quad \text{Why is } x = 0 \text{ a non-permissible value?}$$

Method 2: Multiply by the Reciprocal

$$\frac{5}{3} \div \frac{1}{6} = \frac{5}{3} \times \frac{6}{1}$$

$$= 10$$

$$\frac{3x^2}{y^2} \div \frac{x}{y} = \frac{3x^2}{y^2} \times \frac{y}{x}$$

$$= \frac{3x}{y}, \; x \neq 0, \; y \neq 0$$

Example 2

Divide Rational Expressions

Determine the quotient in simplest form. Identify all non-permissible values.

$$\frac{x^2 - 4}{x^2 - 4x} \div \frac{x^2 + x - 6}{x^2 + x - 20}$$

Did You Know?

A complex rational expression contains a fraction in both the numerator and denominator. The expression in Example 2 could also be written as the complex rational expression

$$\frac{\dfrac{x^2 - 4}{x^2 - 4x}}{\dfrac{x^2 + x - 6}{x^2 + x - 20}}$$

Solution

$$\frac{x^2 - 4}{x^2 - 4x} \div \frac{x^2 + x - 6}{x^2 + x - 20}$$

$$= \frac{(x + 2)(x - 2)}{x(x - 4)} \div \frac{(x + 3)(x - 2)}{(x + 5)(x - 4)} \qquad \text{Factor.}$$

$$= \frac{(x + 2)(x - 2)}{x(x - 4)} \times \frac{(x + 5)(x - 4)}{(x + 3)(x - 2)} \qquad \begin{array}{l}\text{Use similar procedures for dividing} \\ \text{rational expressions as for dividing} \\ \text{fractions. Recall that dividing by a} \\ \text{fraction is the same as multiplying} \\ \text{by its reciprocal.}\end{array}$$

$$= \frac{(x + 2)\cancel{(x - 2)}^{1}(x + 5)\cancel{(x - 4)}^{1}}{x\cancel{(x - 4)}_{1}(x + 3)\cancel{(x - 2)}_{1}}$$

$$= \frac{(x + 2)(x + 5)}{x(x + 3)}, \; x \neq -5, -3, 0, 2, 4 \qquad \begin{array}{l}\text{What was done to get this simpler} \\ \text{answer?}\end{array}$$

The non-permissible values for x are $-5, -3, 0, 2,$ and 4.

Which step(s) should you look at to determine non-permissible values?

Your Turn

Simplify. What are the non-permissible values?

$$\frac{c^2 - 6c - 7}{c^2 - 49} \div \frac{c^2 + 8c + 7}{c^2 + 7c}$$

Example 3

Multiply and Divide Rational Expressions

Simplify. What are the non-permissible values?

$$\frac{2m^2 - 7m - 15}{2m^2 - 10m} \div \frac{4m^2 - 9}{6} \times (3 - 2m)$$

Solution

$$\frac{2m^2 - 7m - 15}{2m^2 - 10m} \div \frac{4m^2 - 9}{6} \times (3 - 2m)$$

$$= \frac{(2m + 3)(m - 5)}{2m(m - 5)} \div \frac{(2m - 3)(2m + 3)}{6} \times (3 - 2m)$$

Apply the order of operations.

$$= \frac{(2m + 3)(m - 5)}{2m(m - 5)} \times \frac{6}{(2m - 3)(2m + 3)} \times \frac{-1(2m - 3)}{1}$$

How do you know that $3 - 2m$ and $-1(2m - 3)$ are equivalent?

$$= \frac{(2m + 3)\overset{1}{(m - 5)}\overset{3}{(6)}(-1)\overset{1}{(2m - 3)}}{2m\overset{1}{(m - 5)}\overset{1}{(2m - 3)}\overset{1}{(2m + 3)}}$$

$$= -\frac{3}{m}, \ m \neq -\frac{3}{2}, 0, 5, \frac{3}{2}$$

Where do these non-permissible values come from?

The non-permissible values for m are $\pm\frac{3}{2}$, 0, and 5.

Your Turn

Simplify. Identify all non-permissible values.

$$\frac{3x + 12}{3x^2 - 5x - 12} \div \frac{12}{3x + 4} \times \frac{2x - 6}{x + 4}$$

Key Ideas

- Multiplying rational expressions is similar to multiplying rational numbers. Factor each numerator and denominator. Identify any non-permissible values. Divide both the numerator and the denominator by any common factors to create a simplified expression.

$$\frac{2}{3} \times \frac{9}{8} = \frac{2}{3} \times \frac{(3)(3)}{2(4)}$$

$$= \frac{(2)\overset{1}{(3)}\overset{1}{(3)}}{(3)(2)(4)}$$

$$= \frac{3}{4}$$

$$\frac{2}{b - 3} \times \frac{b^2 - 9}{4b} = \frac{2}{b - 3} \times \frac{(b - 3)(b + 3)}{4b}$$

$$= \frac{\overset{1}{2}(b - 3)\overset{1}{(b + 3)}}{\underset{2}{4}b\underset{1}{(b - 3)}}$$

$$= \frac{b + 3}{2b}, \ b \neq 0, 3$$

- Dividing rational expressions is similar to dividing fractions. Convert division to multiplication by multiplying by the reciprocal of the divisor.

$$\frac{2}{3} \div \frac{4}{9} = \frac{2}{3} \times \frac{9}{4}$$

$$\frac{2(x - 1)}{3} \div \frac{(x - 1)(x + 1)}{5} = \frac{2(x - 1)}{3} \times \frac{5}{(x - 1)(x + 1)}$$

- When dividing, no denominator can equal zero. In $\frac{A}{B} \div \frac{C}{D} = \frac{A}{B} \times \frac{D}{C}$, the non-permissible values are $B = 0$, $C = 0$, and $D = 0$.

Practise

1. Simplify each product. Identify all non-permissible values.

a) $\dfrac{12m^2f}{5cf} \times \dfrac{15c}{4m}$

b) $\dfrac{3(a - b)}{(a - 1)(a + 5)} \times \dfrac{(a - 5)(a + 5)}{15(a - b)}$

c) $\dfrac{(y - 7)(y + 3)}{(2y - 3)(2y + 3)} \times \dfrac{4(2y + 3)}{(y + 3)(y - 1)}$

2. Write each product in simplest form. Determine all non-permissible values.

a) $\dfrac{d^2 - 100}{144} \times \dfrac{36}{d + 10}$

b) $\dfrac{a + 3}{a + 1} \times \dfrac{a^2 - 1}{a^2 - 9}$

c) $\dfrac{4z^2 - 25}{2z^2 - 13z + 20} \times \dfrac{z - 4}{4z + 10}$

d) $\dfrac{2p^2 + 5p - 3}{2p - 3} \times \dfrac{p^2 - 1}{6p - 3} \times \dfrac{2p - 3}{p^2 + 2p - 3}$

3. What is the reciprocal of each rational expression?

a) $\dfrac{2}{t}$

b) $\dfrac{2x - 1}{3}$

c) $\dfrac{-8}{3 - y}$

d) $\dfrac{2p - 3}{p - 3}$

4. What are the non-permissible values in each quotient?

a) $\dfrac{4t^2}{3s} \div \dfrac{2t}{s^2}$

b) $\dfrac{r^2 - 7r}{r^2 - 49} \div \dfrac{3r^2}{r + 7}$

c) $\dfrac{5}{n + 1} \div \dfrac{10}{n^2 - 1} \div (n - 1)$

5. What is the simplified product of $\dfrac{2x - 6}{x + 3}$ and $\dfrac{x + 3}{2}$? Identify any non-permissible values.

6. What is the simplified quotient of $\dfrac{y^2}{y^2 - 9}$ and $\dfrac{y}{y - 3}$? Identify any non-permissible values.

7. Show how to simplify each rational expression or product.

a) $\dfrac{3 - p}{p - 3}$

b) $\dfrac{7k - 1}{3k} \times \dfrac{1}{1 - 7k}$

8. Express each quotient in simplest form. Identify all non-permissible values.

a) $\dfrac{2w^2 - w - 6}{3w + 6} \div \dfrac{2w + 3}{w + 2}$

b) $\dfrac{v - 5}{v} \div \dfrac{v^2 - 2v - 15}{v^3}$

c) $\dfrac{9x^2 - 1}{x + 5} \div \dfrac{3x^2 - 5x - 2}{2 - x}$

d) $\dfrac{8y^2 - 2y - 3}{y^2 - 1} \div \dfrac{2y^2 - 3y - 2}{2y - 2} \div \dfrac{3 - 4y}{y + 1}$

9. Explain why the non-permissible values in the quotient $\dfrac{x - 5}{x + 3} \div \dfrac{x + 1}{x - 2}$ are -3, -1 and 2.

Apply

10. The height of a stack of plywood is represented by $\dfrac{n^2 - 4}{n + 1}$. If the number of sheets is defined by $n - 2$, what expression could be used to represent the thickness of one sheet? Express your answer in simplest form.

11. Write an expression involving a product or a quotient of rational expressions for each situation. Simplify each expression.

a) The Mennonite Heritage Village in Steinbach, Manitoba, has a working windmill. If the outer end of a windmill blade turns at a rate of $\dfrac{x-3}{5}$ metres per minute, how far does it travel in 1 h?

b) A plane travels from Victoria to Edmonton, a distance of 900 km, in $\dfrac{600}{n+1}$ hours. What is the average speed of the plane?

c) Simione is shipping his carving to a buyer in Winnipeg. He makes a rectangular box with a length of $(2x-3)$ metres and a width of $(x+1)$ metres. The volume of the box is $(x^2 + 2x + 1)$ cubic metres. What is an expression for the height of the box?

12. How does the quotient of $\dfrac{3m+1}{m-1}$ and $\dfrac{3m+1}{m^2-1}$ compare to the quotient of $\dfrac{3m+1}{m^2-1}$ and $\dfrac{3m+1}{m-1}$? Is this always true or sometimes true? Explain your thinking.

13. Simplifying a rational expression is similar to using unit analysis to convert from one unit to another. For example, to convert 68 cm to kilometres, you can use the following steps.

$$(68\text{ cm})\left(\frac{1\text{ m}}{100\text{ cm}}\right)\left(\frac{1\text{ km}}{1000\text{ m}}\right)$$
$$= (68\text{ \cancel{cm}}) \times \left(\frac{1\text{ \cancel{m}}}{100\text{ \cancel{cm}}}\right) \times \left(\frac{1\text{ km}}{1000\text{ \cancel{m}}}\right)$$
$$= \frac{68\text{ km}}{(100)(1000)}$$
$$= 0.000\ 68\text{ km}$$

Therefore, 68 cm is equivalent to 0.000 68 km. Create similar ratios that you can use to convert a measurement in yards to its equivalent in centimetres. Use 1 in. = 2.54 cm. Provide a specific example.

14. Tessa is practising for a quiz. Her work on one question is shown below.

$$\frac{c^2-36}{2c} \div \frac{c+6}{8c^2}$$
$$= \frac{2c}{(c-6)(c+6)} \times \frac{c+6}{(2c)(4c)}$$
$$= \frac{2\overset{1}{\cancel{c}}}{(c-6)\cancel{(c+6)}} \times \frac{\cancel{c+6}^{\,1}}{(2\cancel{c})(4c)}$$
$$= \frac{1}{4c(c-6)}$$

a) Identify any errors that Tessa made.

b) Complete the question correctly.

c) How does the correct answer compare with Tessa's answer? Explain.

15. Write an expression to represent the length of the rectangle. Simplify your answer.

$$A = x^2 - 9 \qquad \frac{x^2 - 2x - 3}{x+1}$$

16. What is an expression for the area of △PQR? Give your answer in simplest form.

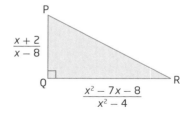

17. You can manipulate variables in a formula by substituting from one formula into another. Try this on the following. Give all answers in simplest form.

a) If $K = \dfrac{P}{2m}$ and $m = \dfrac{h}{w}$, express K in terms of P, h, and w.

b) If $y = \dfrac{2\pi}{d}$ and $x = dr$, express y in terms of π, r, and x.

c) Use the formulas $v = wr$ and $a = w^2r$ to determine a formula for a in terms of v and w.

18. The volume, V, of a gas increases or decreases with its temperature, T, according to Charles's law by the formula $\dfrac{V_1}{V_2} = \dfrac{T_1}{T_2}$. Determine V_1 if $V_2 = \dfrac{n^2 - 16}{n - 1}$, $T_1 = \dfrac{n - 1}{3}$, and $T_2 = \dfrac{n + 4}{6}$.

Express your answer in simplest form.

> **Did You Know?**
>
> Geostrophic winds are driven by pressure differences that result from temperature differences. Geostrophic winds occur at altitudes above 1000 m.

Hurricane Bonnie

Extend

19. Normally, expressions such as $x^2 - 5$ are not factored. However, you could express $x^2 - 5$ as $(x - \sqrt{5})(x + \sqrt{5})$.

a) Do you agree that $x^2 - 5$ and $(x - \sqrt{5})(x + \sqrt{5})$ are equivalent? Explain why or why not.

b) Show how factoring could be used to simplify the product $\left(\dfrac{x + \sqrt{3}}{x^2 - 3}\right)\left(\dfrac{x^2 - 7}{x - \sqrt{7}}\right)$.

c) What is the simplest form of $\dfrac{x^2 - 7}{x - \sqrt{7}}$ if you rationalize the denominator? How does this answer compare to the value of $\dfrac{x^2 - 7}{x - \sqrt{7}}$ that you obtained by factoring in part b)?

20. Fog can be cleared from airports, highways, and harbours using fog-dissipating materials. One device for fog dissipation launches canisters of dry ice to a height defined by $\dfrac{V^2 \sin x}{2g}$, where V is the exit velocity of the canister, x is the angle of elevation, and g is the acceleration due to gravity.

a) What approximate height is achieved by a canister with $V = 85$ m/s, $x = 52°$, and $g = 9.8$ m/s²?

b) What height can be achieved if $V = \dfrac{x + 3}{x - 5}$ metres per second and $x = 30°$?

Fog over Vancouver

Create Connections

21. Multiplying and dividing rational expressions is very much like multiplying and dividing rational numbers. Do you agree or disagree with this statement? Support your answer with examples.

22. Two points on a coordinate grid are represented by M($p - 1$, $2p + 3$) and N($2p - 5$, $p + 1$).

   a) What is a simplified rational expression for the slope of the line passing through M and N?

   b) Write a rational expression for the slope of any line that is perpendicular to MN.

23. Consider △ABC as shown.

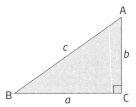

   a) What is an expression for tan B?

   b) What is an expression for $\dfrac{\sin B}{\cos B}$? Use your knowledge of rational expressions to help you write the answer in simplest form.

   c) How do your expressions for tan B and $\dfrac{\sin B}{\cos B}$ compare? What can you conclude from this exercise?

Project Corner Space Anomalies

- Time dilation is a phenomenon described by the theory of general relativity. It is the difference in the rate of the passage of time, and it can arise from the relative velocity of motion between observers and the difference in their distance from a gravitational mass.

- A planetary year is the length of time it takes a planet to revolve around the Sun. An Earth year is about 365 days long.

- There is compelling evidence that a super-massive black hole of more than 4 million solar masses is located near the Sagittarius A* region in the centre of the Milky Way galaxy.

- To predict space weather and the effects of solar activity on Earth, an understanding of both solar flares and coronal mass ejections is needed.

Black hole near Sagittarius A*

- What other types of information about the universe would be useful when predicting the future of space travel?

6.3

Adding and Subtracting Rational Expressions

Focus on...

- connecting addition and subtraction of rational expressions to the same operations with rational numbers
- identifying non-permissible values when adding and subtracting rational expressions
- determining, in simplified form, the sum or difference of rational expressions with the same denominators or with different denominators

Canada-France-Hawaii Telescope

Rational expressions are important in photography and in understanding telescopes, microscopes, and cameras. The lens equation can be written as $\frac{1}{f} = \frac{1}{u} + \frac{1}{v}$, where f is the focal length, u is the distance from the object to the lens, and v is the distance of the image from the lens. How could you simplify the expression on the right of the lens equation?

> **Did You Know?**
>
> The Canada-France-Hawaii Telescope (CFHT) is a non-profit partnership that operates a 3.6-m telescope atop Mauna Kea in Hawaii. CFHT has played an important role in studying black holes.

Investigate Adding and Subtracting Rational Expressions

1. Determine each sum or difference using diagrams or manipulatives. Describe a pattern that could be used to find the numerical answer. Give answers in lowest terms.

   a) $\frac{1}{8} + \frac{5}{8}$ **b)** $\frac{5}{6} - \frac{3}{8}$

2. Use your pattern(s) from step 1 to help you add or subtract each of the following. Express answers in simplest form. Identify any non-permissible values.

   a) $\frac{7x + 1}{x} + \frac{5x - 2}{x}$ **b)** $\frac{x}{x - 3} - \frac{3}{x - 3}$ **c)** $\frac{5}{x - 2} - \frac{3}{x + 2}$

3. Substitute numbers for x in step 2a) and c) to see if your answers are reasonable. What value(s) cannot be substituted in each case?

4. Identify similarities and differences between the processes you used in parts b) and c) in step 2.

Reflect and Respond

5. Describe a process you could use to find the answer in simplest form when adding or subtracting rational expressions.

6. Explain how adding and subtracting rational expressions is related to adding and subtracting rational numbers.

Adding or Subtracting Rational Expressions

To add or subtract rational expressions, follow procedures similar to those used in adding or subtracting rational numbers.

Case 1: Denominators Are the Same

If two rational expressions have a common denominator, add or subtract the numerators and write the answer as a rational expression with the new numerator over the common denominator.

Case 2: Denominators Are Different

To add or subtract fractions when the denominators are different, you must write equivalent fractions with the same denominator.

$$\frac{10}{3x-12} - \frac{3}{x-4} = \frac{10}{3(x-4)} - \frac{3}{x-4}$$

$$= \frac{10}{3(x-4)} - \frac{3(3)}{(x-4)(3)}$$

$$= \frac{10-9}{3(x-4)}$$

$$= \frac{1}{3(x-4)}, \; x \neq 4$$

Why is it helpful to factor each denominator?

When adding or subtracting rational expressions, you can use any equivalent common denominator. However, it is usually easier to use the lowest common denominator (LCD).

What is the LCD for $\dfrac{3}{x^2-9} + \dfrac{4}{x^2-6x+9}$?

Why is it easier to use the lowest common denominator? Try it with and without the LCD to compare.

Factor each denominator.

$$\frac{3}{(x-3)(x+3)} + \frac{4}{(x-3)(x-3)}$$

The LCD must contain the greatest number of any factor that appears in the denominator of either fraction. If a factor appears once in either or both denominators, include it only once. If a factor appears twice in any denominator, include it twice.

The LCD is $(x+3)(x-3)(x-3)$.

Example 1

Add or Subtract Rational Expressions With Common Denominators

Determine each sum or difference. Express each answer in simplest form. Identify all non-permissible values.

a) $\dfrac{2a}{b} - \dfrac{a-1}{b}$

b) $\dfrac{2x}{x+4} + \dfrac{8}{x+4}$

c) $\dfrac{x^2}{x-2} + \dfrac{3x}{x-2} - \dfrac{10}{x-2}$

Solution

a) $\dfrac{2a}{b} - \dfrac{a-1}{b} = \dfrac{2a-(a-1)}{b}$ Why is $a-1$ placed in brackets?

$\qquad\qquad = \dfrac{2a-a+1}{b}$

$\qquad\qquad = \dfrac{a+1}{b}, b \neq 0$

The non-permissible value is $b = 0$.

b) $\dfrac{2x}{x+4} + \dfrac{8}{x+4} = \dfrac{2x+8}{x+4}$

$\qquad\qquad = \dfrac{2(\overset{1}{\cancel{x+4}})}{\underset{1}{\cancel{x+4}}}$ Factor the numerator.

$\qquad\qquad = 2, x \neq -4$ How could you verify this answer?

The non-permissible value is $x = -4$.

c) $\dfrac{x^2}{x-2} + \dfrac{3x}{x-2} - \dfrac{10}{x-2} = \dfrac{x^2+3x-10}{x-2}$

$\qquad\qquad\qquad = \dfrac{(\overset{1}{\cancel{x-2}})(x+5)}{\underset{1}{\cancel{x-2}}}$

$\qquad\qquad\qquad = x+5, x \neq 2$

The non-permissible value is $x = 2$.

Your Turn

Determine each sum or difference. Express each answer in simplest form. Identify all non-permissible values.

a) $\dfrac{m}{n} - \dfrac{m+1}{n}$

b) $\dfrac{10m-1}{4m-3} - \dfrac{8-2m}{4m-3}$

c) $\dfrac{2x^2-x}{(x-3)(x+1)} + \dfrac{3-6x}{(x-3)(x+1)} - \dfrac{8}{(x-3)(x+1)}$

Example 2

Add or Subtract Rational Expressions With Unlike Denominators

Simplify. Express your answers in simplest form.

a) $\dfrac{2x}{xy} + \dfrac{4}{x^2} - 3$, $x \neq 0$, $y \neq 0$

b) $\dfrac{y^2 - 20}{y^2 - 4} + \dfrac{y - 2}{y + 2}$, $y \neq \pm 2$

c) $\dfrac{1 + \dfrac{1}{x}}{x - \dfrac{1}{x}}$, $x \neq 0$, $x \neq \pm 1$

Solution

a) The LCD is x^2y. Write each term as an equivalent rational expression with this denominator.

$$\frac{2x}{xy} + \frac{4}{x^2} - 3 = \frac{2x(x)}{xy(x)} + \frac{4(y)}{x^2(y)} - \frac{3(x^2y)}{x^2y}$$

$$= \frac{2x^2}{x^2y} + \frac{4y}{x^2y} - \frac{3x^2y}{x^2y}$$

$$= \frac{2x^2 + 4y - 3x^2y}{x^2y}$$

Therefore, $\dfrac{2x}{xy} + \dfrac{4}{x^2} - 3 = \dfrac{2x^2 + 4y - 3x^2y}{x^2y}$, $x \neq 0$, $y \neq 0$

b) Factor the first denominator, and then express each rational expression as an equivalent expression with the common denominator $(y - 2)(y + 2)$.

$$\frac{y^2 - 20}{y^2 - 4} + \frac{y - 2}{y + 2}$$

$$= \frac{y^2 - 20}{(y - 2)(y + 2)} + \frac{(y - 2)}{(y + 2)}$$

$$= \frac{y^2 - 20}{(y - 2)(y + 2)} + \frac{(y - 2)(y - 2)}{(y + 2)(y - 2)}$$

$$= \frac{y^2 - 20 + (y - 2)(y - 2)}{(y - 2)(y + 2)}$$

$$= \frac{y^2 - 20 + (y^2 - 4y + 4)}{(y - 2)(y + 2)}$$

$$= \frac{y^2 - 20 + y^2 - 4y + 4}{(y - 2)(y + 2)}$$

$$= \frac{2y^2 - 4y - 16}{(y - 2)(y + 2)}$$

$$= \frac{2(y - 4)(y \overset{1}{\cancel{+ 2}})}{(y - 2)(\underset{1}{\cancel{y + 2}})}$$

$$= \frac{2(y - 4)}{y - 2}$$

Therefore, $\dfrac{y^2 - 20}{y^2 - 4} + \dfrac{y - 2}{y + 2} = \dfrac{2(y - 4)}{y - 2}$, $y \neq \pm 2$.

c) $\dfrac{1 + \dfrac{1}{x}}{x - \dfrac{1}{x}} = \dfrac{\dfrac{x+1}{x}}{\dfrac{x^2-1}{x}}$

Find a common denominator in both the numerator and the denominator of the complex fraction.

$$= \frac{x+1}{x} \div \frac{x^2-1}{x}$$

$$= \frac{x+1}{x^2-1}$$

What was done to arrive at this rational expression?

$$= \frac{\overset{1}{\cancel{x+1}}}{(x-1)\underset{1}{\cancel{(x+1)}}}$$

$$= \frac{1}{x-1}$$

The complex rational expression could also be simplified by multiplying the numerator and the denominator by x, which is the LCD for all the rational expressions. Try this. Which approach do you prefer? Why?

Therefore, $\dfrac{1 + \dfrac{1}{x}}{x - \dfrac{1}{x}} = \dfrac{1}{x-1}$, $x \neq 0, \pm 1$.

Your Turn

Simplify. What are the non-permissible values?

a) $\dfrac{4}{p^2-1} + \dfrac{3}{p+1}$

b) $\dfrac{x-1}{x^2+x-6} - \dfrac{x-2}{x^2+4x+3}$

c) $\dfrac{2 - \dfrac{4}{y}}{y - \dfrac{4}{y}}$

Key Ideas

- You can add or subtract rational expressions with the same denominator by adding or subtracting their numerators.

$$\frac{2x-1}{x+5} - \frac{x-4}{x+5} = \frac{2x-1-(x-4)}{x+5}$$

$$= \frac{2x-1-x+4}{x+5}$$

$$= \frac{x+3}{x+5}, x \neq -5$$

- You can add or subtract rational expressions with unlike denominators after you have written each as an equivalent expression with a common denominator.

- Although more than one common denominator is always possible, it is often easier to use the lowest common denominator (LCD).

Practise

1. Add or subtract. Express answers in simplest form. Identify any non-permissible values.

a) $\dfrac{11x}{6} - \dfrac{4x}{6}$

b) $\dfrac{7}{x} + \dfrac{3}{x}$

c) $\dfrac{5t + 3}{10} + \dfrac{3t + 5}{10}$

d) $\dfrac{m^2}{m + 1} + \dfrac{m}{m + 1}$

e) $\dfrac{a^2}{a - 4} - \dfrac{a}{a - 4} - \dfrac{12}{a - 4}$

2. Show that x and $\dfrac{3x - 7}{9} + \dfrac{6x + 7}{9}$ are equivalent expressions.

3. Simplify. Identify all non-permissible values.

a) $\dfrac{1}{(x - 3)(x + 1)} - \dfrac{4}{(x + 1)}$

b) $\dfrac{x - 5}{x^2 + 8x - 20} + \dfrac{2x + 1}{x^2 - 4}$

4. Identify two common denominators for each question. What is the LCD in each case?

a) $\dfrac{x - 3}{6} - \dfrac{x - 2}{4}$

b) $\dfrac{2}{5ay^2} + \dfrac{3}{10a^2y}$

c) $\dfrac{4}{9 - x^2} - \dfrac{7}{3 + x}$

5. Add or subtract. Give answers in simplest form. Identify all non-permissible values.

a) $\dfrac{1}{3a} + \dfrac{2}{5a}$

b) $\dfrac{3}{2x} + \dfrac{1}{6}$

c) $4 - \dfrac{6}{5x}$

d) $\dfrac{4z}{xy} - \dfrac{9x}{yz}$

e) $\dfrac{2s}{5t^2} + \dfrac{1}{10t} - \dfrac{6}{15t^3}$

f) $\dfrac{6xy}{a^2b} - \dfrac{2x}{ab^2y} + 1$

6. Add or subtract. Give answers in simplest form. Identify all non-permissible values.

a) $\dfrac{8}{x^2 - 4} - \dfrac{5}{x + 2}$

b) $\dfrac{1}{x^2 - x - 12} + \dfrac{3}{x + 3}$

c) $\dfrac{3x}{x + 2} - \dfrac{x}{x - 2}$

d) $\dfrac{5}{y + 1} - \dfrac{1}{y} - \dfrac{y - 4}{y^2 + y}$

e) $\dfrac{2h}{h^2 - 9} + \dfrac{h}{h^2 + 6h + 9} - \dfrac{3}{h - 3}$

f) $\dfrac{2}{x^2 + x - 6} + \dfrac{3}{x^3 + 2x^2 - 3x}$

7. Simplify each rational expression, and then add or subtract. Express answers in simplest form. Identify all non-permissible values.

a) $\dfrac{3x + 15}{x^2 - 25} + \dfrac{4x^2 - 1}{2x^2 + 9x - 5}$

b) $\dfrac{2x}{x^3 + x^2 - 6x} - \dfrac{x - 8}{x^2 - 5x - 24}$

c) $\dfrac{n + 3}{n^2 - 5n + 6} + \dfrac{6}{n^2 - 7n + 12}$

d) $\dfrac{2w}{w^2 + 5w + 6} - \dfrac{w - 6}{w^2 + 6w + 8}$

Apply

8. Linda has made an error in simplifying the following. Identify the error and correct the answer.

$$\dfrac{6}{x - 2} + \dfrac{4}{x^2 - 4} - \dfrac{7}{x + 2}$$

$$= \dfrac{6(x + 2) + 4 - 7(x - 2)}{(x - 2)(x + 2)}$$

$$= \dfrac{6x + 12 + 4 - 7x - 14}{(x - 2)(x + 2)}$$

$$= \dfrac{-x + 2}{(x - 2)(x + 2)}$$

9. Can the rational expression $\dfrac{-x + 5}{(x - 5)(x + 5)}$ be simplified further? Explain.

10. Simplify. State any non-permissible values.

a) $\dfrac{2 - \dfrac{6}{x}}{1 - \dfrac{9}{x^2}}$

b) $\dfrac{\dfrac{3}{2} + \dfrac{3}{t}}{\dfrac{t}{t+6} - \dfrac{1}{t}}$

c) $\dfrac{\dfrac{3}{m} - \dfrac{3}{2m+3}}{\dfrac{3}{m^2} + \dfrac{1}{2m+3}}$

d) $\dfrac{\dfrac{1}{x+4} + \dfrac{1}{x-4}}{\dfrac{x}{x^2-16} + \dfrac{1}{x+4}}$

11. Calculators often perform calculations in a different way to accommodate the machine's logic. For each pair of rational expressions, show that the second expression is equivalent to the first one.

a) $\dfrac{A}{B} + \dfrac{C}{D}$; $\dfrac{\dfrac{AD}{B} + C}{D}$

b) $AB + CD + EF$; $\left[\dfrac{\left(\dfrac{AB}{D} + C\right)D}{F} + E\right]F$

12. A right triangle has legs of length $\dfrac{x}{2}$ and $\dfrac{x-1}{4}$. If all measurements are in the same units, what is a simplified expression for the length of the hypotenuse?

13. Ivan is concerned about an underweight calf. He decides to put the calf on a healthy growth program. He expects the calf to gain m kilograms per week and 200 kg in total. However, after some time on the program, Ivan finds that the calf has been gaining $(m + 4)$ kilograms per week.

a) Explain what each of the following rational expressions tells about the situation: $\dfrac{200}{m}$ and $\dfrac{200}{m+4}$.

b) Write an expression that shows the difference between the number of weeks Ivan expected to have the calf on the program and the number of weeks the calf actually took to gain 200 kg.

c) Simplify your rational expression from part b). Does your simplified expression still represent the difference between the expected and actual times the calf took to gain 200 kg? Explain how you know.

14. Suppose you can type an average of n words per minute.

a) What is an expression for the number of minutes it would take to type an assignment with 200 words?

b) Write a sum of rational expressions to represent the time it would take you to type three assignments of 200, 500, and 1000 words, respectively.

c) Simplify the sum in part b). What does the simplified rational expression tell you?

d) Suppose your typing speed decreases by 5 words per minute for each new assignment. Write a rational expression to represent how much longer it would take to type the three assignments. Express your answer in simplest form.

15. Simplify. Identify all non-permissible values.

a) $\dfrac{x - 2}{x + 5} + \dfrac{x^2 - 2x - 3}{x^2 - x - 6} \times \dfrac{x^2 + 2x}{x^2 - 4x}$

b) $\dfrac{2x^2 - x}{x^2 + 3x} \times \dfrac{x^2 - x - 12}{2x^2 - 3x + 1} - \dfrac{x - 1}{x + 2}$

c) $\dfrac{x - 2}{x + 5} - \dfrac{x^2 - 2x - 3}{x^2 - x - 6} \times \dfrac{x^2 + 2x}{x^2 - 4x}$

d) $\dfrac{x + 1}{x + 6} - \dfrac{x^2 - 4}{x^2 + 2x} \div \dfrac{2x^2 + 7x + 3}{2x^2 + x}$

16. A cyclist rode the first 20-kilometre portion of her workout at a constant speed. For the remaining 16-kilometre portion of her workout, she reduced her speed by 2 km/h. Write an algebraic expression for the total time of her bike ride.

17. Create a scenario involving two or more rational expressions. Use your expressions to create a sum or difference. Simplify. Explain what the sum or difference represents in your scenario. Exchange your work with another student in your class. Check whether your classmate's work is correct.

18. Math teachers can identify common errors that students make when adding or subtracting rational expressions. Decide whether each of the following statements is correct or incorrect. Fix each incorrect statement. Indicate how you could avoid making each error.

a) $\dfrac{a}{b} - \dfrac{b}{a} = \dfrac{a - b}{ab}$

b) $\dfrac{ca + cb}{c + cd} = \dfrac{a + b}{d}$

c) $\dfrac{a}{4} - \dfrac{6 - b}{4} = \dfrac{a - 6 - b}{4}$

d) $\dfrac{1}{1 - \dfrac{a}{b}} = \dfrac{b}{1 - a}$

e) $\dfrac{1}{a - b} = \dfrac{-1}{a + b}$

19. Keander thinks that you can split up a rational expression by reversing the process for adding or subtracting fractions with common denominators. One example is shown below.

$$\dfrac{3x - 7}{x} = \dfrac{3x}{x} - \dfrac{7}{x}$$
$$= 3 - \dfrac{7}{x}$$

a) Do you agree with Keander? Explain.

b) Keander also claims that by using this method, you can arrive at the rational expressions that were originally added or subtracted. Do you agree or disagree with Keander? Support your decision with several examples.

20. A formula for the total resistance, R, in ohms (Ω), of an electric circuit with three resistors in parallel is $R = \dfrac{1}{\dfrac{1}{R_1} + \dfrac{1}{R_2} + \dfrac{1}{R_3}}$, where R_1 is the resistance of the first resistor, R_2 is the resistance of the second resistor, and R_3 is the resistance of the third resistor, all in ohms.

a) What is the total resistance if the resistances of the three resistors are 2 Ω, 3 Ω, and 4 Ω, respectively?

b) Express the right side of the formula in simplest form.

c) Find the total resistance for part a) using your new expression from part b).

d) Which expression for R did you find easier to use? Explain.

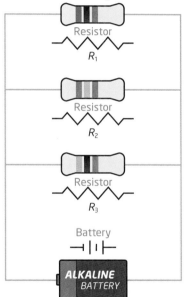

Resistor
R_1

Resistor
R_2

Resistor
R_3

Battery

ALKALINE BATTERY

Did You Know?

The English physicist James Joule (1818–1889) showed experimentally that the resistance, R, of a resistor can be calculated as $R = \dfrac{P}{I^2}$, where P is the power, in watts (W), dissipated by the resistor and I is the current, in amperes (A), flowing through the resistor. This is known as Joule's law. A resistor has a resistance of 1 Ω if it dissipates energy at the rate of 1 W when the current is 1 A.

Extend

21. Suppose that $\dfrac{a}{c} = \dfrac{b}{d}$, where a, b, c, and d are real numbers. Use both arithmetic and algebra to show that $\dfrac{a}{c} = \dfrac{a - b}{c - d}$ is true.

22. Two points on a coordinate grid are represented by $A\left(\dfrac{p - 1}{2}, \dfrac{p}{3}\right)$ and $B\left(\dfrac{p}{3}, \dfrac{2p - 3}{4}\right)$.

a) What is a simplified rational expression for the slope of the line passing through A and B?

b) What can you say about the slope of AB when $p = 3$? What does this tell you about the line through A and B?

c) Determine whether the slope of AB is positive or negative when $p < 3$ and p is an integer.

d) Predict whether the slope of AB is positive or negative when $p > 3$ and p is an integer. Check your prediction using $p = 4, 5, 6, \ldots, 10$. What did you find?

23. What is the simplified value of the following expression?

$$\left(\dfrac{p}{p - x} + \dfrac{q}{q - x} + \dfrac{r}{r - x}\right)$$
$$- \left(\dfrac{x}{p - x} + \dfrac{x}{q - x} + \dfrac{x}{r - x}\right)$$

Create Connections

24. Adding or subtracting rational expressions follows procedures that are similar to those for adding or subtracting rational numbers. Show that this statement is true for expressions with and without common denominators.

25. Two students are asked to find a fraction halfway between two given fractions. After thinking for a short time, one of the students says, "That's easy. Just find the average."

a) Show whether the student's suggestion is correct using arithmetic fractions.

b) Determine a rational expression halfway between $\frac{3}{a}$ and $\frac{7}{2a}$. Simplify your answer. Identify any non-permissible values.

26. Mila claims you can add fractions with the same numerator using a different process.

$$\frac{1}{4} + \frac{1}{3} = \frac{1}{\frac{12}{7}}$$
$$= \frac{7}{12}$$

where the denominator in the first step is calculated as $\frac{4 \times 3}{4 + 3}$.

Is Mila's method correct? Explain using arithmetic and algebraic examples.

27. An image found by a convex lens is described by the equation $\frac{1}{f} = \frac{1}{u} + \frac{1}{v}$, where f is the focal length (distance from the lens to the focus), u is the distance from the object to the lens, and v is the distance from the image to the lens. All distances are measured in centimetres.

a) Use the mathematical ideas from this section to show that $\frac{1}{f} = \frac{u + v}{uv}$.

b) What is the value of f when $u = 80$ and $v = 6.4$?

c) If you know that $\frac{1}{f} = \frac{u + v}{uv}$, what is a rational expression for f?

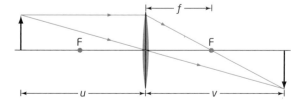

28. MINI LAB In this section, you have added and subtracted rational expressions to get a single expression. For example,

$$\frac{3}{x - 4} - \frac{2}{x - 1} = \frac{x + 5}{(x - 4)(x - 1)}.$$ What if you are given a rational expression and you want to find two expressions that can be added to get it? In other words, you are reversing the situation.

$$\frac{x + 5}{(x - 4)(x - 1)} = \frac{A}{x - 4} + \frac{B}{x - 1}$$

Step 1 To determine A, cover its denominator in the expression on the left, leaving you with $\frac{x + 5}{x - 1}$. Determine the value of $\frac{x + 5}{x - 1}$ when $x = 4$, the non-permissible value for the factor of $x - 4$.

$$\frac{x + 5}{x - 1} = \frac{4 + 5}{4 - 1} \qquad \text{You can often do this step mentally.}$$
$$= 3$$

This means $A = 3$.

Step 2 Next, cover $(x - 1)$ in the expression on the left and substitute $x = 1$ into $\frac{x + 5}{x - 4}$ to get -2. This means $B = -2$.

Step 3 Check that it works. Does

$$\frac{3}{x - 4} - \frac{2}{x - 1} = \frac{x + 5}{(x - 4)(x - 1)}?$$

Step 4 What are the values for A and B in the following?

a) $\dfrac{3x - 1}{(x - 3)(x + 1)} = \dfrac{A}{x - 3} + \dfrac{B}{x + 1}$

b) $\dfrac{6x + 15}{(x + 7)(x - 2)} = \dfrac{A}{x + 7} + \dfrac{B}{x - 2}$

Step 5 Do you believe that the method in steps 1 to 3 always works, or sometimes works? Use algebraic reasoning to show that if

$$\frac{x + 5}{(x - 4)(x - 1)} = \frac{A}{x - 4} + \frac{B}{x - 1},$$

then $A = 3$ and $B = -2$.

Rational Equations

Harbour of ancient Alexandria

Focus on...

- identifying non-permissible values in a rational equation
- determining the solution to a rational equation algebraically
- solving problems using a rational equation

Diophantus of Alexandria is often called the father of new algebra. He is best known for his *Arithmetica*, a work on solving algebraic equations and on the theory of numbers. Diophantus extended numbers to include negatives and was one of the first to describe symbols for exponents. Although it is uncertain when he was born, we can learn his age when he died from the following facts recorded about him:

> ... his boyhood lasted $\frac{1}{6}$ of his life; his beard grew after $\frac{1}{12}$ more; he married after $\frac{1}{7}$ more; his son was born 5 years later; the son lived to half his father's age and the father died 4 years later.

How many years did Diophantus live?

Investigate Rational Equations

Work with a partner on the following.

1. An equation can be used to solve the riddle about Diophantus' life. Use x to represent the number of years that he lived.

   a) Determine an expression for each unknown part of the riddle. What expression would represent his boyhood, when his beard began to grow, when he married, and so on?

   b) How could you represent 5 years later?

   c) What is an equation representing his entire life?

2. Begin to solve your equation.

   a) What number could you multiply each expression by to make each denominator 1? Perform the multiplication.

   b) Solve the resulting linear equation.

   c) How old was Diophantus when he died? Check your answer with that of a classmate.

Reflect and Respond

3. Describe a process you could use to solve an equation involving rational expressions.

4. Show similarities and differences between adding and subtracting rational expressions and your process for solving an equation involving them.

Solving Rational Equations

rational equation

- an equation containing at least one rational expression
- examples are

$x = \dfrac{x - 3}{x + 1}$ and

$\dfrac{x}{4} - \dfrac{7}{x} = 3$

Rational equations can be used to solve several different kinds of problems, such as work-related problems, where two people or machines work together at different rates to complete a task.

Working with a rational equation is similar to working with rational expressions. A significant difference occurs because in an equation, what you do to one side you must also do to the other side.

To solve a rational equation,

- factor each denominator
- identify the non-permissible values
- multiply both sides of the equation by the lowest common denominator
- solve by isolating the variable on one side of the equation
- check your answers

To solve $\dfrac{x}{4} - \dfrac{7}{x} = 3$, use the lowest common denominator to express each denominator as 1. The lowest common denominator (LCD) for this equation is $4x$. Proceed by multiplying both sides of the equation by the LCD.

$$4x\left(\dfrac{x}{4} - \dfrac{7}{x}\right) = 4x(3), \ x \neq 0$$

$$4x\left(\dfrac{x}{4}\right) - 4x\left(\dfrac{7}{x}\right) = 4x(3) \qquad \text{Multiply each term on both sides of the equation by } 4x. \text{ Simplify each term.}$$

$$x^2 - 28 = 12x$$

$$x^2 - 12x - 28 = 0$$

$$(x - 14)(x + 2) = 0$$

So, $x = 14$ or $x = -2$. 　　　　How can you check that these answers are correct?

It is important to realize that non-permissible values are identified from the original equation and that these values cannot be solutions to the final equation.

Example 1

Solve a Rational Equation

Solve the following equation. What values are non-permissible?

$$\dfrac{2}{z^2 - 4} + \dfrac{10}{6z + 12} = \dfrac{1}{z - 2}$$

Solution

$$\frac{2}{z^2 - 4} + \frac{10}{6z + 12} = \frac{1}{z - 2}$$

Factor each denominator.

$$\frac{2}{(z - 2)(z + 2)} + \frac{10}{6(z + 2)} = \frac{1}{z - 2}$$

How can you find the LCD from the factors in the denominators?

From the factors, the non-permissible values are $+2$ and -2.

$$(z - 2)(z + 2)(6)\left[\frac{2}{(z - 2)(z + 2)} + \frac{10}{6(z + 2)}\right] = (z - 2)(z + 2)(6)\left[\frac{1}{z - 2}\right]$$

$$(z - 2)(z + 2)(6)\left[\frac{2}{(z - 2)(z + 2)}\right] + (z - 2)(z + 2)(6)\left[\frac{10}{6(z + 2)}\right] = (z - 2)(z + 2)(6)\left(\frac{1}{z - 2}\right)$$

$$(6)(2) + (z - 2)(10) = (z + 2)(6)$$

$$12 + 10z - 20 = 6z + 12$$

What was done in each step?

$$4z = 20$$

$$z = 5$$

Check:
Substitute $z = 5$ into the original equation.

Left Side

$$\frac{2}{z^2 - 4} + \frac{10}{6z + 12}$$

$$= \frac{2}{5^2 - 4} + \frac{10}{6(5) + 12}$$

$$= \frac{2}{21} + \frac{10}{42}$$

$$= \frac{2}{21} + \frac{5}{21}$$

$$= \frac{7}{21}$$

$$= \frac{1}{3}$$

Right Side

$$\frac{1}{z - 2}$$

$$= \frac{1}{5 - 2}$$

$$= \frac{1}{3}$$

Left Side = Right Side

The non-permissible values are -2 and 2. The solution cannot be one of the non-permissible values. Since 5 is not one of the non-permissible values, the solution is $z = 5$.

Your Turn

Solve the equation. What are the non-permissible values?

$$\frac{9}{y - 3} - \frac{4}{y - 6} = \frac{18}{y^2 - 9y + 18}$$

Example 2

Solve a Rational Equation With an Extraneous Root

Solve the equation. What are the non-permissible values?

$$\frac{4k - 1}{k + 2} - \frac{k + 1}{k - 2} = \frac{k^2 - 4k + 24}{k^2 - 4}$$

Solution

$$\frac{4k - 1}{k + 2} - \frac{k + 1}{k - 2} = \frac{k^2 - 4k + 24}{k^2 - 4}$$

The factors in the denominators are $k + 2$ and $k - 2$.

The non-permissible values are 2 and -2.

Describe what is done in the first two steps below.

$$(k - 2)(k + 2)\left(\frac{4k - 1}{k + 2} - \frac{k + 1}{k - 2}\right) = (k - 2)(k + 2)\left[\frac{k^2 - 4k + 24}{(k - 2)(k + 2)}\right]$$

$$(k - 2)(\overset{1}{\cancel{k + 2}})\left(\frac{4k - 1}{\underset{1}{\cancel{k + 2}}}\right) - (\overset{1}{\cancel{k - 2}})(k + 2)\left(\frac{k + 1}{\underset{1}{\cancel{k - 2}}}\right) = (\overset{1}{\cancel{k - 2}})(\overset{1}{\cancel{k + 2}})\left[\frac{k^2 - 4k + 24}{(\underset{1}{\cancel{k - 2}})(\underset{1}{\cancel{k + 2}})}\right]$$

$$(k - 2)(4k - 1) - (k + 2)(k + 1) = k^2 - 4k + 24$$
$$4k^2 - 9k + 2 - (k^2 + 3k + 2) = k^2 - 4k + 24$$
$$4k^2 - 9k + 2 - k^2 - 3k - 2 = k^2 - 4k + 24$$
$$2k^2 - 8k - 24 = 0$$
$$2(k^2 - 4k - 12) = 0$$
$$2(k - 6)(k + 2) = 0$$
$$(k - 6)(k + 2) = 0$$

So, $k - 6 = 0$ or $k + 2 = 0$.
$$k = 6 \text{ or } \qquad k = -2$$

Without further checking, it appears the solutions are -2 and 6. However, -2 is a non-permissible value and is called an extraneous solution.

Check: Substitute $k = 6$ into the original equation.

Left Side

$$\frac{4k - 1}{k + 2} - \frac{k + 1}{k - 2}$$
$$= \frac{4(6) - 1}{6 + 2} - \frac{6 + 1}{6 - 2}$$
$$= \frac{23}{8} - \frac{7}{4}$$
$$= \frac{23}{8} - \frac{14}{8}$$
$$= \frac{9}{8}$$

Right Side

$$\frac{k^2 - 4k + 24}{k^2 - 4}$$
$$= \frac{6^2 - 4(6) + 24}{6^2 - 4}$$
$$= \frac{36}{32}$$
$$= \frac{9}{8}$$

Left Side = Right Side

What happens if you check using $k = -2$?

Therefore, the solution is $k = 6$.

Your Turn

Solve. What are the non-permissible values?

$$\frac{3x}{x + 2} - \frac{5}{x - 3} = \frac{-25}{x^2 - x - 6}$$

Example 3

Use a Rational Equation to Solve a Problem

Two friends share a paper route. Sheena can deliver the papers in 40 min. Jeff can cover the same route in 50 min. How long, to the nearest minute, does the paper route take if they work together?

Solution

Make a table to organize the information.

	Time to Deliver Papers (min)	Fraction of Work Done in 1 min	Fraction of Work Done in t minutes
Sheena	40	$\frac{1}{40}$	$\left(\frac{1}{40}\right)(t)$ or $\frac{t}{40}$
Jeff	50	$\frac{1}{50}$	$\frac{t}{50}$
Together	t	$\frac{1}{t}$	$\frac{t}{t}$ or 1

From the table, the equation for Sheena and Jeff to complete the work together is $\frac{t}{40} + \frac{t}{50} = 1$.

Why could this equation also be called a linear equation?

The LCD is 200.

$$200\left(\frac{t}{40}\right) + 200\left(\frac{t}{50}\right) = 200(1)$$
$$5t + 4t = 200$$
$$9t = 200$$
$$t = \frac{200}{9} \text{ or approximately } 22.2$$

Check:
Substitute $t = \frac{200}{9}$ into the original equation.

Left Side

$\frac{t}{40} + \frac{t}{50}$

$= \left(\dfrac{\frac{200}{9}}{40}\right) + \left(\dfrac{\frac{200}{9}}{50}\right)$

$= \left(\frac{200}{9}\right)\left(\frac{1}{40}\right) + \left(\frac{200}{9}\right)\left(\frac{1}{50}\right)$

$= \frac{5}{9} + \frac{4}{9}$

$= 1$

Right Side

1

Left Side = Right Side

There are no non-permissible values and the value $t = \frac{200}{9}$ checks.

Sheena and Jeff deliver the papers together in approximately 22 min.

Your Turn

Stella takes 4 h to paint a room. It takes Jose 3 h to paint the same area. How long will the paint job take if they work together?

Example 4

Use a Rational Equation to Solve a Problem

The Northern Manitoba Trapper's Festival, held in The Pas, originated in 1916. A championship dog race has always been a significant part of the festivities. In the early days, the race was non-stop from The Pas to Flin Flon and back.

In one particular race, the total distance was 140 mi. Conditions were excellent on the way to Flin Flon. However, bad weather caused the winner's average speed to decrease by 6 mph on the return trip. The total time for the trip was $8\frac{1}{2}$ h. What was the winning dog team's average speed on the way to Flin Flon?

Solution

Use the formula distance = rate × time, or time = $\dfrac{\text{distance}}{\text{rate}}$.

Let x represent the average speed, in miles per hour, on the trip from The Pas to Flin Flon.

	Distance (mi)	Rate (mph)	Time (h)
Trip to Flin Flon	70	x	$\dfrac{70}{x}$
Return from Flin Flon	70	$x - 6$	$\dfrac{70}{x-6}$
		Total	$8\frac{1}{2}$ or $\dfrac{17}{2}$

Flin Flon

$d = 70$
$r = x$
$t = \dfrac{d}{r}$
$= \dfrac{70}{x}$

The Pas

Flin Flon

$d = 70$
$r = x - 6$
$t = \dfrac{d}{r}$
$= \dfrac{70}{x-6}$

The Pas

$$\frac{70}{x} + \frac{70}{x-6} = \frac{17}{2}$$

What is the LCD for this equation?

What are the non-permissible values?

$$2(x)(x-6)\left(\frac{70}{x} + \frac{70}{x-6}\right) = 2(x)(x-6)\left(\frac{17}{2}\right)$$

$$2(\overset{1}{\cancel{x}})(x-6)\left(\frac{70}{\cancel{x}}\right) + 2(x)(\overset{1}{\cancel{x-6}})\left(\frac{70}{\cancel{x-6}}\right) = \overset{1}{\cancel{2}}(x)(x-6)\left(\frac{17}{\cancel{2}}\right)$$

$$2(x-6)(70) + 2(x)(70) = (x)(x-6)(17)$$

$$140x - 840 + 140x = 17x^2 - 102x$$

$$0 = 17x^2 - 382x + 840$$

Use the quadratic formula to solve the equation.

$$x = \frac{-b \pm \sqrt{b^2 - 4ac}}{2a}$$

$$x = \frac{-(-382) \pm \sqrt{(-382)^2 - 4(17)(840)}}{2(17)}$$

$$x = \frac{382 \pm \sqrt{88\,804}}{34}$$

$$x = \frac{382 \pm 298}{34}$$

$$x = \frac{382 + 298}{34} \quad \text{or} \quad x = \frac{382 - 298}{34}$$

$$x = 20 \quad \text{or} \quad x = \frac{42}{17}$$

How else might you have solved the quadratic equation? Explain how you know. Try it.

Check: Substitute $x = 20$ and $x = \frac{42}{17}$ into the original equation.

Left Side	Right Side	Left Side	Right Side

Left Side
$$\frac{70}{x} + \frac{70}{x - 6}$$
$$= \frac{70}{20} + \frac{70}{20 - 6}$$
$$= \frac{7}{2} + \frac{70}{14}$$
$$= 3.5 + 5$$
$$= 8.5$$

Right Side
$$\frac{17}{2} = 8.5$$

Left Side = Right Side

Left Side
$$\frac{70}{x} + \frac{70}{x - 6}$$
$$= \frac{70}{\frac{42}{17}} + \frac{70}{\frac{42}{17} - 6}$$
$$= \frac{70}{\frac{42}{17}} + \frac{70}{\frac{42}{17} - \frac{102}{17}}$$
$$= \frac{70}{\frac{42}{17}} - \frac{70}{\frac{60}{17}}$$
$$= 70\left(\frac{17}{42}\right) - 70\left(\frac{17}{60}\right)$$
$$= \frac{170}{6} - \frac{119}{6}$$
$$= 8.5$$

Right Side
$$\frac{17}{2} = 8.5$$

Left Side = Right Side

Although both solutions have been verified and both are permissible, the solution $\frac{42}{17}$ is inappropriate for this context because if this speed was reduced by 6 mph, then the speed on the return trip would be negative. Therefore, the only solution to the problem is 20 mph.

The winning dog team's average speed going to Flin Flon was 20 mph.

Your Turn

A train has a scheduled run of 160 km between two cities in Saskatchewan. If the average speed is decreased by 16 km/h, the run will take $\frac{1}{2}$ h longer. What is the average speed of the train?

Check Your Understanding

Practise

1. Use the LCD to eliminate the fractions from each equation. Do not solve.

a) $\dfrac{x-1}{3} - \dfrac{2x-5}{4} = \dfrac{5}{12} + \dfrac{x}{6}$

b) $\dfrac{2x+3}{x+5} + \dfrac{1}{2} = \dfrac{7}{2x+10}$

c) $\dfrac{4x}{x^2-9} - \dfrac{5}{x+3} = 2$

2. Solve and check each equation. Identify all non-permissible values.

a) $\dfrac{f+3}{2} - \dfrac{f-2}{3} = 2$

b) $\dfrac{3-y}{3y} + \dfrac{1}{4} = \dfrac{1}{2y}$

c) $\dfrac{9}{w-3} - \dfrac{4}{w-6} = \dfrac{18}{w^2-9w+18}$

3. Solve each rational equation. Identify all non-permissible values.

a) $\dfrac{6}{t} + \dfrac{t}{2} = 4$

b) $\dfrac{6}{c-3} = \dfrac{c+3}{c^2-9} - 5$

c) $\dfrac{d}{d+4} = \dfrac{2-d}{d^2+3d-4} + \dfrac{1}{d-1}$

d) $\dfrac{x^2+x+2}{x+1} - x = \dfrac{x^2-5}{x^2-1}$

4. Joline solved the following rational equation. She claims that the solution is $y = 1$. Do you agree? Explain.

$$\dfrac{-3y}{y-1} + 6 = \dfrac{6y-9}{y-1}$$

Apply

5. A rectangle has the dimensions shown.

a) What is an expression for the difference between the length and the width of the rectangle? Simplify your answer.

b) What is an expression for the area of the rectangle? Express the answer in simplest form.

c) If the perimeter of the rectangle is 28 cm, find the value(s) for x.

6. Solve. Round answers to the nearest hundredth.

a) $\dfrac{26}{b+5} = 1 + \dfrac{3}{b-2}$

b) $\dfrac{c}{c+2} - 3 = \dfrac{-6}{c^2-4}$

7. Experts claim that the golden rectangle is most pleasing to the eye. It has dimensions that satisfy the equation $\dfrac{l}{w} = \dfrac{l+w}{l}$, where w is the width and l is the length.

According to this relationship, how long should a rectangular picture frame be if its width is 30 cm? Give the exact answer and an approximate answer, rounded to the nearest tenth of a centimetre.

8. The sum of two numbers is 25. The sum of their reciprocals is $\dfrac{1}{4}$. Determine the two numbers.

9. Two consecutive numbers are represented by x and $x + 1$. If 6 is added to the first number and two is subtracted from the second number, the quotient of the new numbers is $\frac{9}{2}$. Determine the numbers algebraically.

10. A French club collected the same amount from each student going on a trip to Le Cercle Molière in Winnipeg. When six students could not go, each of the remaining students was charged an extra $3. If the total cost was $540, how many students went on the trip?

> **Did You Know?**
>
> Le Cercle Molière is the oldest continuously running theatre company in Canada, founded in 1925. It is located in St. Boniface, Manitoba, and moved into its new building in 2009.

11. The sum of the reciprocals of two consecutive integers is $\frac{11}{30}$. What are the integers?

12. Suppose you are running water into a tub. The tub can be filled in 2 min if only the cold tap is used. It fills in 3 min if only the hot tap is turned on. How long will it take to fill the tub if both taps are on simultaneously?

a) Will the answer be less than or greater than 2 min? Why?

b) Complete a table in your notebook similar to the one shown.

	Time to Fill Tub (min)	Fraction Filled in 1 min	Fraction Filled in x minutes
Cold Tap			
Hot Tap			
Both Taps	x	$\frac{1}{x}$	$\frac{x}{x}$ or 1

c) What is one equation that represents both taps filling the tub?

d) Solve your equation to determine the time with both taps running.

13. Two hoses together fill a pool in 2 h. If only hose A is used, the pool fills in 3 h. How long would it take to fill the pool if only hose B were used?

14. Two kayakers paddle 18 km downstream with the current in the same time it takes them to go 8 km upstream against the current. The rate of the current is 3 km/h.

a) Complete a table like the following in your notebook. Use the formula distance = rate × time.

	Distance (km)	Rate (km/h)	Time (h)
Downstream			
Upstream			

b) What equation could you use to find the rate of the kayakers in still water?

c) Solve your equation.

d) Which values are non-permissible?

> **Did You Know?**
>
> When you are travelling with the current, add the speed of the current to your rate of speed. When you are travelling against the current, subtract the speed of the current.

Kyuquot Sound, British Columbia

15. Nikita lives in Kindersley, Saskatchewan. With her old combine, she can harvest her entire wheat crop in 72 h. Her neighbour offers to help. His new combine can do the same job in 48 h. How long would it take to harvest the wheat crop with both combines working together?

16. Several cows from the Qamanirjuaq Caribou Herd took 4 days longer to travel 70 km to Forde Lake, Nunavut, than it took them to travel 60 km north beyond Forde Lake. They averaged 5 km/h less before Forde Lake because foraging was better. What was their average speed for the part beyond Forde Lake? Round your answer to the nearest tenth of a kilometre per hour.

Caribou migrating across the tundra, Hudson Bay

Did You Know?

The Qamanirjuaq (ka ma nir you ak) and Beverly barren ground caribou herds winter in the same areas of northern Manitoba, Saskatchewan, Northeast Alberta, and the Northwest Territories and migrate north in the spring into different parts of Nunavut for calving.

Web Link

This is the caribou herd that Inuit depended on in Farley Mowat's book *People of the Deer*. For more information, go to www.mhrprecalc11.ca and follow the links.

17. Ted is a long-distance driver. It took him 30 min longer to drive 275 km on the Trans-Canada Highway west of Swift Current, Saskatchewan, than it took him to drive 300 km east of Swift Current. He averaged 10 km/h less while travelling west of Swift Current due to more severe snow conditions. What was Ted's average speed for each part of the trip?

18. Two friends can paddle a canoe at a rate of 6 km/h in still water. It takes them 1 h to paddle 2 km up a river and back again. Find the speed of the current.

19. Suppose you have 21 days to read a 518-page novel. After finishing half the book, you realize that you must read 12 pages more per day to finish on time. What is your reading rate for the first half of the book? Use a table like the following to help you solve the problem.

	Reading Rate in Pages per Day	Number of Pages Read	Number of Days
First Half			
Second Half			

20. The concentration, C, of salt in a solution is determined by the formula $C = \dfrac{A}{s + w}$, where A is the constant amount of salt, s is the initial amount of solution, and w is the amount of water added.

  a) How much water must be added to a 1-L bottle of 30% salt solution to get a 10% solution?

  b) How much water must be added to a half-litre bottle of 10% salt solution to get a 2% solution?

Extend

21. If $b = \dfrac{1}{a}$ and $\dfrac{\dfrac{1}{a} - \dfrac{1}{b}}{\dfrac{1}{a} + \dfrac{1}{b}} = \dfrac{4}{5}$, solve for a.

22. A number x is the harmonic mean of a and b if $\frac{1}{x}$ is the average of $\frac{1}{a}$ and $\frac{1}{b}$.

a) Write a rational equation for the statement above. Solve for x.

b) Find two numbers that differ by 8 and have a harmonic mean of 6.

Did You Know?

The distance that a spring stretches is represented by the formula $d = km$, where d is the distance, in centimetres, m is the mass, in grams, and k is a constant.

When two springs with constants k and j are attached to one another, the new spring constant, c, can be found using the formula $\frac{1}{c} = \frac{1}{k} + \frac{1}{j}$. The new spring constant is the harmonic mean of the spring constants for the separate springs.

---

23. Sometimes is it helpful to solve for a specific variable in a formula. For example, if you solve for x in the equation $\frac{1}{x} - \frac{1}{y} = a$, the answer is $x = \dfrac{y}{ay + 1}$.

a) Show algebraically how you could solve for x if $\frac{1}{x} - \frac{1}{y} = a$. Show two different ways to get the answer.

b) In the formula $d = v_0 t + \frac{1}{2}gt^2$, solve for v_0. Simplify your answer.

c) Solve for n in the formula $I = \dfrac{E}{R + \frac{r}{n}}$.

Create Connections

24. a) Explain the difference between rational expressions and rational equations. Use examples.

b) Explain the process you would use to solve a rational equation. As a model, describe each step you would use to solve the following equation.
$$\frac{5}{x} - \frac{1}{x - 1} = \frac{1}{x - 1}$$

c) There are at least two different ways to begin solving the equation in part b). Identify a different first step from how you began your process in part b).

25. a) A laser printer prints 24 more sheets per minute than an ink-jet printer. If it takes the two printers a total of 14 min to print 490 pages, what is the printing rate of the ink-jet printer?

Did You Know?

Is a paperless office possible? According to Statistics Canada, our consumption of paper for printing and writing more than doubled between 1983 and 2003 to 91 kg, or about 20 000 pages per person per year. This is about 55 pages per person per day.

---

b) Examine the data in Did You Know? Is your paper use close to the national average? Explain.

c) We can adopt practices to conserve paper use. Work with a partner to identify eco-responsible ways you can conserve paper and ink.

26. Suppose there is a quiz in your mathematics class every week. The value of each quiz is 50 points. After the first 6 weeks, your average mark on these quizzes is 36.

a) What average mark must you receive on the next 4 quizzes so that your average is 40 on the first 10 quizzes? Use a rational equation to solve this problem.

b) There are 15 quizzes in your mathematics course. Show if it is possible to have an average of 90% on your quizzes at the end of the course if your average is 40 out of 50 on the first 10 quizzes.

27. Tyler has begun to solve a rational equation. His work is shown below.
$$\frac{2}{x - 1} - 3 = \frac{5x}{x + 1}$$
$$2(x + 1) - 3(x + 1)(x - 1) = 5x(x - 1)$$
$$2x + 2 - 3x^2 + 1 = 5x^2 - 5x$$
$$0 = 8x^2 - 7x - 3$$

a) Re-work the solution to correct any errors that Tyler made.

b) Solve for x. Give your answers as exact values.

c) What are the approximate values of x, to the nearest hundredth?

6.1 Rational Expressions, pages 310–321

1. A rational number is of the form $\frac{a}{b}$, where a and b are integers.

   a) What integer cannot be used for b? Why?

   b) How does your answer to part a) relate to rational expressions? Explain using examples.

2. You can write an unlimited number of equivalent expressions for any given rational expression. Do you agree or disagree with this statement? Explain.

3. What are the non-permissible values, if any, for each rational expression?

   a) $\dfrac{5x^2}{2y}$

   b) $\dfrac{x^2 - 1}{x + 1}$

   c) $\dfrac{27x^2 - 27}{3}$

   d) $\dfrac{7}{(a - 3)(a + 2)}$

   e) $\dfrac{-3m + 1}{2m^2 - m - 3}$

   f) $\dfrac{t + 2}{2t^2 - 8}$

4. What is the numerical value for each rational expression? Test your result using some permissible values for the variable. Identify any non-permissible values.

   a) $\dfrac{2s - 8s}{s}$

   b) $\dfrac{5x - 3}{3 - 5x}$

   c) $\dfrac{2 - b}{4b - 8}$

5. Write an expression that satisfies the given conditions in each case.

   a) equivalent to $\dfrac{x - 3}{5}$, with a denominator of $10x$

   b) equivalent to $\dfrac{x - 3}{x^2 - 9}$, with a numerator of 1

   c) equivalent to $\dfrac{c - 2d}{3f}$, with a numerator of $3c - 6d$

   d) equivalent to $\dfrac{m + 1}{m + 4}$, with non-permissible values of ± 4

6. a) Explain how to determine non-permissible values for a rational expression. Use an example in your explanation.

   b) Simplify. Determine all non-permissible values for the variables.

   i) $\dfrac{3x^2 - 13x - 10}{3x + 2}$

   ii) $\dfrac{a^2 - 3a}{a^2 - 9}$

   iii) $\dfrac{3y - 3x}{4x - 4y}$

   iv) $\dfrac{81x^2 - 36x + 4}{18x - 4}$

7. A rectangle has area $x^2 - 1$ and width $x - 1$.

   a) What is a simplified expression for the length?

   b) Identify any non-permissible values. What do they mean in this context?

6.2 Multiplying and Dividing Rational Expressions, pages 322–330

8. Explain how multiplying and dividing rational expressions is similar to multiplying and dividing fractions. Describe how they differ. Use examples to support your response.

9. Simplify each product. Determine all non-permissible values.

   a) $\dfrac{2p}{r} \times \dfrac{10q}{8p}$

   b) $4m^3 t \times \dfrac{1}{16mt^4}$

   c) $\dfrac{3a + 3b}{8} \times \dfrac{4}{a + b}$

   d) $\dfrac{x^2 - 4}{x^2 + 25} \times \dfrac{2x^2 + 10x}{x^2 + 2x}$

   e) $\dfrac{d^2 + 3d + 2}{2d + 2} \times \dfrac{2d + 6}{d^2 + 5d + 6}$

   f) $\dfrac{y^2 - 8y - 9}{y^2 - 10y + 9} \times \dfrac{y^2 - 9y + 8}{y^2 - 1} \times \dfrac{y^2 - 25}{5 - y}$

10. Divide. Express answers in simplest form. Identify any non-permissible values.

a) $2t \div \dfrac{1}{4}$

b) $\dfrac{a^3}{b^4} \div \dfrac{a^3}{b^3}$

c) $\dfrac{7}{x^2 - y^2} \div \dfrac{-35}{x - y}$

d) $\dfrac{3a + 9}{a - 3} \div \dfrac{a^2 + 6a + 9}{a - 3}$

e) $\dfrac{3x - 2}{x^3 + 3x^2 + 2x} \div \dfrac{9x^2 - 4}{3x^2 + 8x + 4} \div \dfrac{1}{x}$

f) $\dfrac{\dfrac{4 - x^2}{6}}{\dfrac{x - 2}{2}}$

11. Multiply or divide as indicated. Express answers in simplest form. Determine all non-permissible values.

a) $\dfrac{9}{2m} \div \dfrac{3}{m} \times \dfrac{m}{3}$

b) $\dfrac{x^2 - 3x + 2}{x^2 - 4} \times \dfrac{x + 3}{x^2 + 3x} \div \dfrac{1}{x + 2}$

c) $\dfrac{a - 3}{a - 4} \div \dfrac{30}{a + 3} \times \dfrac{5a - 20}{a^2 - 9}$

d) $\dfrac{3x + 12}{3x^2 - 5x - 12} \times \dfrac{x - 3}{x + 4} \div \dfrac{15}{3x + 4}$

12. The volume of a rectangular prism is $(2x^3 + 5x^2 - 12x)$ cubic centimetres. If the length of the prism is $(2x - 3)$ centimetres and its width is $(x + 4)$ centimetres, what is an expression for the height of the prism?

$(x + 4)$ centimetres
$(2x - 3)$ centimetres

6.3 Adding and Subtracting Rational Expressions, pages 331–340

13. Determine a common denominator for each sum or difference. What is the lowest common denominator (LCD) in each case? What is the advantage of using the LCD?

a) $\dfrac{4}{5x} + \dfrac{3}{10x}$

b) $\dfrac{5}{x - 2} + \dfrac{2}{x + 1} - \dfrac{1}{x - 2}$

14. Perform the indicated operations. Express answers in simplest form. Identify any non-permissible values.

a) $\dfrac{m}{5} + \dfrac{3}{5}$

b) $\dfrac{2m}{x} - \dfrac{m}{x}$

c) $\dfrac{x}{x + y} + \dfrac{y}{x + y}$

d) $\dfrac{x - 2}{3} - \dfrac{x + 1}{3}$

e) $\dfrac{x}{x^2 - y^2} - \dfrac{y}{y^2 - x^2}$

15. Add or subtract. Express answers in simplest form. Identify any non-permissible values.

a) $\dfrac{4x - 3}{6} - \dfrac{x - 2}{4}$

b) $\dfrac{2y - 1}{3y} + \dfrac{y - 2}{2y} - \dfrac{y - 8}{6y}$

c) $\dfrac{9}{x - 3} + \dfrac{7}{x^2 - 9}$

d) $\dfrac{a}{a + 3} - \dfrac{a^2 - 3a}{a^2 + a - 6}$

e) $\dfrac{a}{a - b} - \dfrac{2ab}{a^2 - b^2} + \dfrac{b}{a + b}$

f) $\dfrac{2x}{4x^2 - 9} + \dfrac{x}{2x^2 + 5x + 3} - \dfrac{1}{2x - 3}$

16. The sum of the reciprocals of two numbers will always be the same as the sum of the numbers divided by their product.

a) If the numbers are represented by a and b, translate the sentence above into an equation.

b) Use your knowledge of adding rational expressions to prove that the statement is correct by showing that the left side is equivalent to the right side.

17. Three tests and one exam are given in a course. Let a, b, and c represent the marks of the tests and d be the mark from the final exam. Each is a mark out of 100. In the final mark, the average of the three tests is worth the same amount as the exam. Write a rational expression for the final mark. Show that your expression is equivalent to $\dfrac{a + b + c + 3d}{6}$. Choose a sample of four marks and show that the simplified expression works.

18. Two sisters go to an auction sale to buy some antique chairs. They intend to pay no more than c dollars for a chair. Beth is worried she will not get the chairs. She bids $10 more per chair than she intended and spends $250. Helen is more patient and buys chairs for $10 less per chair than she intended. She spends $200 in total.

a) Explain what each of the following expressions represents from the information given about the auction sale.

i) $c + 10$ **ii)** $c - 10$

iii) $\dfrac{200}{c - 10}$ **iv)** $\dfrac{250}{c + 10}$

v) $\dfrac{200}{c - 10} + \dfrac{250}{c + 10}$

b) Determine the sum of the rational expressions in part v) and simplify the result.

6.4 Rational Equations, pages 341–351

19. What is different about the processes used to solve a rational equation from those used to add or subtract rational expressions? Explain using examples.

20. Solve each rational equation. Identify all non-permissible values.

a) $\dfrac{s - 3}{s + 3} = 2$

b) $\dfrac{x + 2}{3x + 2} = \dfrac{x + 3}{x - 1}$

c) $\dfrac{z - 2}{z} + \dfrac{1}{5} = \dfrac{-4}{5z}$

d) $\dfrac{3m}{m - 3} + 2 = \dfrac{3m - 1}{m + 3}$

e) $\dfrac{x}{x - 3} = \dfrac{3}{x - 3} - 3$

f) $\dfrac{x - 2}{2x + 1} = \dfrac{1}{2} + \dfrac{x - 3}{2x}$

g) $\dfrac{3}{x + 2} + \dfrac{5}{x - 3} = \dfrac{3x}{x^2 - x - 6} - 1$

21. The sum of two numbers is 12. The sum of their reciprocals is $\dfrac{3}{8}$. What are the numbers?

22. Matt and Elaine, working together, can paint a room in 3 h. It would take Matt 5 h to paint the room by himself. How long would it take Elaine to paint the room by herself?

23. An elevator goes directly from the ground up to the observation deck of the Calgary Tower, which is at 160 m above the ground. The elevator stops at the top for 36 s before it travels directly back down to the ground. The time for the round trip is 2.5 min. The elevator descends at 0.7 m/s faster than it goes up.

a) Determine an equation that could be used to find the rate of ascent of the elevator.

b) Simplify your equation to the form $ax^2 + bx + c = 0$, where a, b, and c are integers, and then solve.

c) What is the rate of ascent in kilometres per hour, to the nearest tenth?

Chapter 6 Practice Test

Multiple Choice

For #1 to #5, choose the best answer.

1. What are the non-permissible values for the rational expression $\dfrac{x(x + 2)}{(x - 3)(x + 1)}$?

   A 0 and -2 **B** -3 and 1

   C 0 and 2   **D** 3 and -1

2. Simplify the rational expression $\dfrac{x^2 - 7x + 6}{x^2 - 2x - 24}$ for all permissible values of x.

   A $\dfrac{x + 1}{x - 4}$ **B** $\dfrac{x - 1}{x + 4}$

   C $\dfrac{x + 1}{x + 4}$ **D** $\dfrac{x - 1}{x - 4}$

3. Simplify $\dfrac{8}{3y} + \dfrac{5y}{4} - \dfrac{5}{8}$ for all permissible values of y.

   A $\dfrac{30y^2 - 15y + 64}{24y}$ **B** $\dfrac{30y^2 + 79}{24y}$

   C $\dfrac{15y^2 + 64}{24y}$ **D** $\dfrac{5y + 3}{24y}$

4. Simplify $\dfrac{3x - 12}{9x^2} \div \dfrac{x - 4}{3x}$, $x \neq 0$ and $x \neq 4$.

   A $\dfrac{1}{x}$ **B** $\dfrac{16}{3x}$

   C x **D** $\dfrac{-12}{x - 4}$

5. Solve $\dfrac{6}{t - 3} = \dfrac{4}{t + 4}$, $t \neq 3$ and $t \neq -4$.

   A $-\dfrac{1}{2}$ **B** -1

   C -6 **D** -18

Short Answer

6. Identify all non-permissible values.
   $$\dfrac{3x - 5}{x^2 - 9} \times \dfrac{2x - 6}{3x^2 - 2x - 5} \div \dfrac{x - 3}{x + 3}$$

7. If both rational expressions are defined and equivalent, what is the value of *k*?
   $$\dfrac{2x^2 + kx - 10}{2x^2 + 7x + 6} = \dfrac{2x - 5}{2x + 3}$$

8. Add or subtract as indicated. Give your answer in simplest form.
   $$\dfrac{5y}{6} + \dfrac{1}{y - 2} - \dfrac{y + 1}{3y - 6}$$

9. Create an equation you could use to solve the following problem. Indicate what your variable represents. Do not solve your equation.

   A large auger can fill a grain bin in 5 h less time than a smaller auger. Together they fill the bin in 6 h. How long would it take the larger auger, by itself, to fill the bin?

10. List similarities and differences between the processes of adding and subtracting rational expressions and solving rational equations. Use examples.

Extended Response

11. Solve $2 - \dfrac{5}{x^2 - x - 6} = \dfrac{x + 3}{x + 2}$. Identify all non-permissible values.

12. The following rational expressions form an arithmetic sequence: $\dfrac{3 - x}{x}, \dfrac{2x - 1}{2x}, \dfrac{5x + 3}{5x}$. Use common differences to create a rational equation. Solve for *x*.

13. A plane is flying from Winnipeg to Calgary against a strong headwind of 50 km/h. The plane takes $\dfrac{1}{2}$ h longer for this flight than it would take in calm air. If the distance from Winnipeg to Calgary is 1200 km, what is the speed of the plane in calm air, to the nearest kilometre per hour?

Absolute Value and Reciprocal Functions

Suppose you and your friend each live 2 km from your school, but in opposite directions from the school. You could represent these distances as 2 km in one direction and −2 km in the other direction. However, you would both say that you live the same distance, 2 km, from your school. The *absolute value* of the distance each of you lives from your school is 2 km. Can you think of other examples where you would use an absolute value?

Currency exchange is an example of a reciprocal relationship. If 1 euro is equivalent to 1.3 Canadian dollars, what is 1 Canadian dollar worth in euros? If you take a balloon underwater, you can represent the relationship between its shrinking volume and the increasing pressure of the air inside the balloon as a reciprocal function.

Is this depth change 20 m or −20 m? Which value would you use? Why?

Depth (m)	Pressure (atm)	Air Volume (m³)	
0	1	1	
10	2	$\frac{1}{2}$	
20	3	$\frac{1}{3}$	
30	4	$\frac{1}{4}$	
40	5	$\frac{1}{5}$	

In this chapter, you will learn about absolute value and reciprocal functions. You will also learn how they are used to solve problems.

Web Link

The relationship between the pressure and the volume of a confined gas held at a constant temperature is known as Boyle's law. To learn more about Boyle's law, go to www.mhrprecalc11.ca and follow the links.

Key Terms

absolute value	absolute value equation
absolute value function	reciprocal function
piecewise function	asymptote
invariant point	

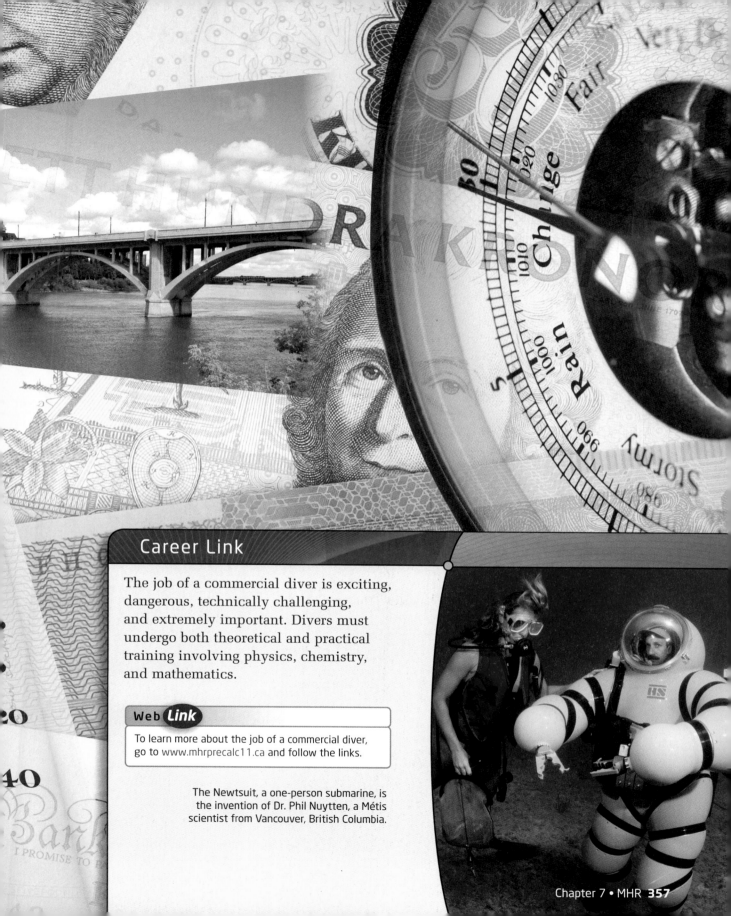

Career Link

The job of a commercial diver is exciting, dangerous, technically challenging, and extremely important. Divers must undergo both theoretical and practical training involving physics, chemistry, and mathematics.

Web **Link**

To learn more about the job of a commercial diver, go to www.mhrprecalc11.ca and follow the links.

The Newtsuit, a one-person submarine, is the invention of Dr. Phil Nuytten, a Métis scientist from Vancouver, British Columbia.

Absolute Value

Focus on...

- determining the absolute values of numbers and expressions
- explaining how the distance between two points on a number line can be expressed in terms of absolute value
- comparing and ordering the absolute values of real numbers in a given set

The hottest temperature ever recorded in Saskatoon, Saskatchewan, was 40.6 °C on June 5, 1988. The coldest temperature, −50.0 °C, was recorded on February 1, 1893. You can calculate the total temperature difference as

$$-50.0 - 40.6 = d \quad \text{or} \quad 40.6 - (-50.0) = d$$
$$-90.6 = d \qquad\qquad\qquad 90.6 = d$$

Generally, you use the positive value, 90.6 °C, when describing the difference. Why do you think this is the case? Does it matter which value you use when describing this situation? Can you describe a situation where you would use the negative value?

Delta Bessborough Hotel, Saskatoon, Saskatchewan

1. Draw a number line on grid paper that is approximately 20 units long. Label the centre of the number line as 0. Label the positive and negative values on either side of zero, as shown.

Materials

• grid paper
• ruler

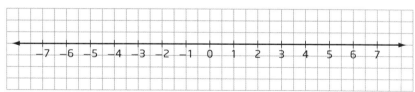

2. Mark the values +4 and −4 on your number line. Describe their distances from 0.

3. **a)** Plot two points to the right of zero. How many units are between the two points?

   b) Calculate the distance between the two points in two different ways.

4. Repeat step 3 using two points to the left of zero.

5. Repeat step 3 using one point to the right of zero and one point to the left.

6. What do you notice about the numerical values of your calculations and the number of units between each pair of points you chose in steps 3, 4, and 5?

7. What do you notice about the signs of the two calculated distances for each pair of points in steps 3, 4, and 5?

Reflect and Respond

8. Identify three different sets of points that have a distance of 5 units between them. Include one set of points that are both positive, one set of points that are both negative, and one set containing a positive and a negative value. How did you determine each set of points?

9. Explain why the distance from 0 to +3 is the same as the distance from 0 to −3. Why is the distance referred to as a positive number?

absolute value

- $|a| = \begin{cases} a, \text{ if } a \geq 0 \\ -a, \text{ if } a < 0 \end{cases}$

For a real number a, the **absolute value** is written as $|a|$ and is a positive number.

Two vertical bars around a number or expression are used to represent the absolute value of the number or expression.

For example,
- The absolute value of a positive number is the positive number.
  $|+5| = 5$
- The absolute value of zero is zero.
  $|0| = 0$
- The absolute value of a negative number is the negative of that number, resulting in the positive value of that number.
  $|-5| = -(-5)$
  $ = 5$

Absolute value can be used to represent the distance of a number from zero on a real-number line.

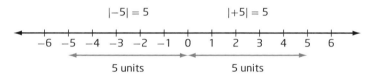

In Chapter 5, you learned that $\sqrt{x^2} = x$ only when x is positive.

How can you use this fact and the definition of absolute value to show that $\sqrt{x^2} = |x|$?

In general, the absolute value of a real number a is defined as
$$|a| = \begin{cases} a, \text{ if } a \geq 0 \\ -a, \text{ if } a < 0 \end{cases}$$

Example 1

Determining the Absolute Value of a Number

Evaluate the following.

a) $|3|$

b) $|-7|$

Solution

a) $|3| = 3$ since $|a| = a$ for $a \geq 0$.

b) $|-7| = -(-7)$
    $ = 7$
  since $|a| = -a$ for $a < 0$.

Your Turn

Evaluate the following.

a) $|9|$

b) $|-12|$

Example 2

Compare and Order Absolute Values

Write the real numbers in order from least to greatest.

$|-6.5|, 5, |4.75|, -3.4, \left|-\dfrac{12}{5}\right|, |-0.1|, -0.01, \left|-2\dfrac{1}{2}\right|$

> **Solution**

First, evaluate each number and express it in decimal form.
6.5, 5, 4.75, −3.4, 2.4, 0.1, −0.01, 2.5

Then, rearrange from least to greatest value.
−3.4, −0.01, 0.1, 2.4, 2.5, 4.75, 5, 6.5

Now, show the original numbers in order from least to greatest.
$-3.4, -0.01, |-0.1|, \left|-\dfrac{12}{5}\right|, \left|-2\dfrac{1}{2}\right|, |4.75|, 5, |-6.5|$

Your Turn

Write the real numbers in order from least to greatest.

$|3.5|, -2, |-5.75|, 1.05, \left|-\dfrac{13}{4}\right|, |-0.5|, -1.25, \left|-3\dfrac{1}{3}\right|$

Absolute value symbols should be treated in the same manner as brackets. Evaluate the absolute value of a numerical expression by first applying the order of operations inside the absolute value symbol, and then taking the absolute value of the result.

Example 3

Evaluating Absolute Value Expressions

Evaluate the following.

a) $|4| - |-6|$ **b)** $5 - 3|2 - 7|$ **c)** $|-2(5 - 7)^2 + 6|$

> **Solution**

a) $\begin{aligned}|4| - |-6| &= 4 - 6 \\ &= -2\end{aligned}$

b) $\begin{aligned}5 - 3|2 - 7| &= 5 - 3|-5| \\ &= 5 - 3(5) \\ &= 5 - 15 \\ &= -10\end{aligned}$

c) $\begin{aligned}|-2(5 - 7)^2 + 6| &= |-2(-2)^2 + 6| \\ &= |-2(4) + 6| \\ &= |-8 + 6| \\ &= |-2| \\ &= 2\end{aligned}$

Apply the order of operations to evaluate the expression inside the absolute value symbol.

Your Turn

Evaluate the following.

a) $|-4| - |-3|$ **b)** $|-12 + 8|$ **c)** $|12(-3) + 5^2|$

Example 4

Change in Stock Value

On stock markets, individual stock and bond values fluctuate a great deal, especially when the markets are volatile. A particular stock on the Toronto Stock Exchange (TSX) opened the month at $13.55 per share, dropped to $12.70, increased to $14.05, and closed the month at $13.85. Determine the total change in the value of this stock for the month. This total shows how active the stock was that month.

Solution

Represent the stock values by $V_1 = 13.55$, $V_2 = 12.70$, $V_3 = 14.05$, and $V_4 = 13.85$. Calculate each change in stock value using $|V_{i+1} - V_i|$, where $i = 1, 2, 3$.

Calculate each change in stock value and find the sum of these changes.

Does the order in which the values are subtracted matter?

$$|V_2 - V_1| + |V_3 - V_2| + |V_4 - V_3|$$
$$= |12.70 - 13.55| + |14.05 - 12.70| + |13.85 - 14.05|$$
$$= |-0.85| + |+1.35| + |-0.20|$$
$$= 0.85 + 1.35 + 0.20$$
$$= 2.40$$

The total change in stock value for the month is $2.40.

Why would an investor find the volatility of a particular stock useful when making investment decisions?

Your Turn

Wesley volunteers at a local hospital because he is interested in a career in health care. One day, he takes the elevator from the first floor up to the sixth floor to see his supervising nurse. His list of tasks for that day sends him down to the second floor to work in the gift shop, up to the fourth floor to visit with patients, and down to the first floor to greet visitors and patients. What is the total change in floors for Wesley that day?

Key Ideas

● The absolute value of a real number a is defined as

$$|a| = \begin{cases} a, \text{ if } a \geq 0 \\ -a, \text{ if } a < 0 \end{cases}$$

● Geometrically, the absolute value of a real number a, written as $|a|$, is its distance from zero on the number line, regardless of direction.

● Determine the absolute value of a numerical expression by

   ▪ evaluating the numerical expression inside the absolute value symbol using the order of operations

   ▪ taking the absolute value of the resulting expression

Check Your Understanding

Practise

1. Evaluate.

  a) $|9|$ **b)** $|0|$

  c) $|-7|$ **d)** $|-4.728|$

  e) $|6.25|$ **f)** $\left|-5\frac{1}{2}\right|$

2. Order the numbers from least to greatest.

$|0.8|, 1.1, |-2|, \left|\frac{3}{5}\right|, -0.4, \left|-1\frac{1}{4}\right|, -0.8$

3. Order the numbers from greatest to least.

$-2.4, |1.3|, \left|-\frac{7}{5}\right|, -1.9, |-0.6|, \left|1\frac{1}{10}\right|, 2.2$

4. Evaluate each expression.

  a) $|8 - 15|$ **b)** $|3| - |-8|$

  c) $|7 - (-3)|$ **d)** $|2 - 5(3)|$

5. Use absolute value symbols to write an expression for the distance between each pair of specified points on the number line. Determine the distance.

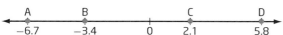

  a) A and C   **b)** B and D

  c) C and B   **d)** D and A

6. Determine the value of each absolute value expression.

  a) $2|-6 - (-11)|$

  b) $|-9.5| - |12.3|$

  c) $3\left|\frac{1}{2}\right| + 5\left|-\frac{3}{4}\right|$

  d) $|3(-2)^2 + 5(-2) + 7|$

  e) $|-4 + 13| + |6 - (-9)| - |8 - 17| + |-2|$

Apply

7. Use absolute value symbols to write an expression for the length of each horizontal or vertical line segment. Determine each length.

  a) A(8, 1) and B(3, 1)

  b) A(12, 9) and B(−8, 9)

  c) A(6, 2) and B(6, 9)

  d) A(−1, −7) and B(−1, 15)

  e) A(a, y) and B(b, y)

  f) A(x, m) and B(x, n)

8. Southern Alberta often experiences dry chinook winds in winter and spring that can change temperatures by a large amount in a short time. On a particular day in Warner, Alberta, the temperature was −11 °C in the morning. A chinook wind raised the temperature to +7 °C by afternoon. The temperature dropped to −9 °C during the night. Use absolute value symbols to write an expression for the total change in temperature that day. What is the total change in temperature for the day?

Did You Know?

A First Nations legend of the St'at'imc Nation of British Columbia says that a girl named Chinook-Wind married Glacier and moved to his country. In this foreign land, she longed for her home and sent a message to her people. They came to her first in a vision of snowflakes, then rain, and finally as a melting glacier that took her home.

9. Suppose a straight stretch of highway running west to east begins at the town of Allenby (0 km). The diagram shows the distances from Allenby east to various towns. A new grain storage facility is to be built along the highway 24 km east of Allenby. Write an expression using absolute value symbols to determine the total distance of the grain storage facility from all seven towns on the highway for this proposed location. What is the distance?

| 0 | 10 17 | 30 | 42 | 55 | 72 |

Allenby (Crawley Denford Essex Fortier Grey
Birkend Ridge

10. The Alaska Highway runs from Dawson Creek, British Columbia, to Delta Junction, Alaska. Travel guides along the highway mark historic mileposts, from mile 0 in Dawson Creek to mile 1422 in Delta Junction. The table shows the Ramsay family's trip along this highway.

	Destination	Mile Number
Starting Point	Charlie Lake campground	51
Tuesday	Liard River, British Columbia	496
Wednesday	Whitehorse, Yukon Territory	918
Thursday	Beaver Creek, Yukon Territory	1202
	Haines Junction, Yukon Territory	1016
Friday	Delta Junction, Alaska	1422

Use an expression involving absolute value symbols to determine the total distance, in miles, that the Ramsay family travelled in these four days.

Did You Know?

In 1978, the mileposts along the Canadian section were replaced with kilometre posts. Some mileposts at locations of historic significance remain, although reconstruction and rerouting mean that these markers no longer represent accurate driving distances.

11. When Vanessa checks her bank account on-line, it shows the following balances:

Date	Balance
Oct. 4	$359.22
Oct. 12	$310.45
Oct. 17	$295.78
Oct. 30	$513.65
Nov. 5	$425.59

a) Use an absolute value expression to determine the total change in Vanessa's bank balance during this period.

b) How is this different from the net change in her bank balance?

12. In physics, the amplitude of a wave is measured as the absolute value of the difference between the crest height and the trough height of the wave, divided by 2.

$$\text{Amplitude} = \frac{|\text{crest height} - \text{trough height}|}{2}$$

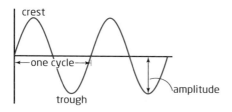

Determine the amplitude of waves with the following characteristics.

a) crest at height 17 and trough at height 2

b) crest at height 90 and trough at height −90

c) crest at height 1.25 and trough at height −0.5

13. The Festival du Voyageur is an annual Francophone winter festival held in Manitoba. One of the outdoor events at the festival is a snowshoe race. A possible trail for the race is 2 km long, with the start at 0 km; checkpoints at 500 m, 900 m, and 1600 m; and the finish at 2 km. Suppose a race organizer travels by snowmobile from the start to the 1600-m checkpoint, back to the 900-m checkpoint, then out to the finish line, and finally back to the 500-m checkpoint. Use an absolute value expression to determine the total distance travelled by the race organizer, in metres and in kilometres.

14. The Yukon Quest dog sled race runs between Fairbanks, Alaska, and Whitehorse, Yukon Territory, a distance of more than 1000 mi. It lasts for 2 weeks. The elevation at Fairbanks is 440 ft, and the elevation at Whitehorse is 2089 ft.

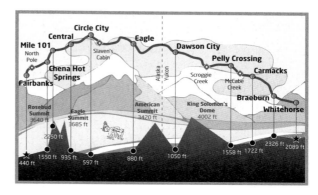

a) Determine the net change in elevation from Fairbanks to Whitehorse.

b) The race passes through Central, at an elevation of 935 ft; Circle City, whose elevation is 597 ft; and Dawson City, at an elevation of 1050 ft. What is the total change in elevation from Fairbanks to Whitehorse, passing through these cities?

Did You Know?

The Yukon Quest has run every year since 1984. The race follows the historic Gold Rush and mail delivery dog sled routes from the turn of the 20th century. In even-numbered years, the race starts in Fairbanks and ends in Whitehorse. In odd-numbered years, the race starts in Whitehorse and ends in Fairbanks.

Extend

15. A trading stock opens the day at a value of $7.65 per share, drops to $7.28 by noon, then rises to $8.10, and finally falls an unknown amount to close the trading day. If the absolute value of the total change for this stock is $1.55, determine the amount that the stock dropped in the afternoon before closing.

16. As part of a scavenger hunt, Toby collects items along a specified trail. Starting at the 2-km marker, he bicycles east to the 7-km marker, and then turns around and bicycles west back to the 3-km marker. Finally, Toby turns back east and bicycles until the total distance he has travelled is 15 km.

a) How many kilometres does Toby travel in the last interval?

b) At what kilometre marker is Toby at the end of the scavenger hunt?

17. Mikhala and Jocelyn are examining some effects of absolute value on the sum of the squares of the set of values $\{-2.5, 3, -5, 7.1\}$. Mikhala takes the absolute value of each number and then squares it. Jocelyn squares each value and then takes the absolute value.

a) What result does each student get?

b) Explain the results.

c) Is this always true? Explain.

18. a) Michel writes the expression $|x - 5|$, where x is a real number, without the absolute value symbol. His answer is shown below.

$$|x - 5| = \begin{cases} x - 5, \text{ if } x - 5 \geq 0 \\ -(x - 5), \text{ if } x - 5 < 0 \end{cases}$$

$$|x - 5| = \begin{cases} x - 5, \text{ if } x \geq 5 \\ 5 - x, \text{ if } x < 5 \end{cases}$$

Explain the steps in Michel's solution.

b) If x is a real number, then write each of the following without the absolute value symbol.

i) $|x - 7|$ **ii)** $|2x - 1|$

iii) $|3 - x|$ **iv)** $|x^2 + 4|$

19. Julia states, "To determine the absolute value of any number, change the sign of the number." Use an example to show that Julia is incorrect. In your own words, correctly complete the statement, "To determine the absolute value of a number, ..."

20. In the Millikan oil drop experiment, oil drops are electrified with either a positive or a negative charge and then sprayed between two oppositely charged metal plates. Since an individual oil drop will be attracted by one plate and repelled by the other plate, the drop will move either upward or downward toward the plate of opposite charge. If the charge on the plates is reversed, the oil drop is forced to reverse its direction and thus stay suspended indefinitely.

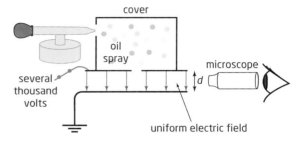

Suppose an oil drop starts out at 45 mm below the upper plate, moves to a point 67 mm below the upper plate, then to a point 32 mm from the upper plate, and finally to a point 58 mm from the upper plate. What total distance does the oil drop travel during the experiment?

Create Connections

21. Describe a situation in which the absolute value of a measurement is preferable to the actual signed value.

22. When an object is thrown into the air, it moves upward, and then changes direction as it returns to Earth. Would it be more appropriate to use signed values (+ or −) or the absolute value for the velocity of the object at any point in its flight? Why? What does the velocity of the object at the top of its flight have to be?

23. A school volleyball team has nine players. The heights of the players are 172 cm, 181 cm, 178 cm, 175 cm, 180 cm, 168 cm, 177 cm, 175 cm, and 178 cm.

a) What is the mean height of the players?

b) Determine the absolute value of the difference between each individual's height and the mean. Determine the sum of the values.

c) Divide the sum by the number of players.

d) Interpret the result in part c) in terms of the height of players on this team.

24. When writing a quadratic function in vertex form, $y = a(x - p)^2 + q$, the vertex of the graph is located at (p, q). If the function has zeros, or its graph has x-intercepts, you can find them using the equation $x = p \pm \sqrt{\left|\dfrac{q}{a}\right|}$.

a) Use this equation to find the zeros of each quadratic function.

  i) $y = 2(x + 1)^2 - 8$

  ii) $y = -(x + 2)^2 + 9$

  How could you verify that the zeros are correct?

b) What are the zeros of the function $y = 4(x - 3)^2 + 16$? Explain whether or not you could use this method to determine the zeros for all quadratic functions written in vertex form.

25. Explain, using examples, why $\sqrt{x^2} = |x|$.

Project Corner   Space Tourism

Assume the following for the future of space tourism.

- The comfort and quality of a cruise ship are available for travel in outer space.

- The space vehicle in which tourists travel is built within specified tolerances for aerodynamics, weight, payload capacity, and life-support systems, to name a few criteria.

- Each space vehicle leaves Earth within a given launch window.

- The distance of Earth from other celestial destinations changes at different times of the year.

- The quantity of fuel on board the space vehicle determines its range of travel.

- How might absolute value be involved in these design and preparation issues?

7.2

Absolute Value Functions

Focus on...

- creating a table of values for $y = |f(x)|$, given a table of values for $y = f(x)$
- sketching the graph of $y = |f(x)|$ and determining its intercept(s), domain, and range
- generalizing a rule for writing absolute value functions in piecewise notation

Stroboscopic photography involves using a flashing strobe light and a camera with an open shutter. You must take stroboscopic photographs in darkness so that every time the strobe flashes, you take a still image of a moving object at that instant. Shown here is a stroboscopic photograph following the path of a bouncing ball. To measure the total vertical distance the ball travels as it bounces over a certain time interval, use the absolute value of the function that models the height over time. What type of function would you use to model the height of this bouncing ball over time?

Investigate Absolute Value Functions

Materials

- grid paper

In this activity, you will explore the similarities and differences between linear, quadratic, and absolute value functions.

Part A: Compare Linear Functions With Corresponding Absolute Value Functions

Consider the functions $f(x) = x$ and $g(x) = |x|$.

1. Copy the table of values. Use the values of $f(x)$ to determine the values of $g(x)$ and complete the table.

What happens to the value of the functions $f(x)$ and $g(x)$ when the values of x are negative?

x	f(x)	g(x)
−3	−3	
−2	−2	
−1	−1	
0	0	
1	1	
2	2	
3	3	

2. Use the coordinate pairs to sketch graphs of the functions on the same grid.

3. Which characteristics of the two graphs are similar and which are different?

4. From the graph, explain why the absolute value relation is a function.

5. a) Describe the shape of the graph of $g(x)$.

   b) If you could sketch the graph of $g(x)$ using two linear functions, what would they be? Are there any restrictions on the domain and range of each function? If so, what are they?

Part B: Compare Quadratic Functions With Corresponding Absolute Value Functions

Consider the functions $f(x) = x^2 - 3$ and $h(x) = |x^2 - 3|$.

6. Copy the table of values. Use the values of $f(x)$ to determine the values of $h(x)$ and complete the table.

x	f(x)	h(x)
−3	6	
−2	1	
−1	−2	
0	−3	
1	−2	
2	1	
3	6	

When are the values of $f(x)$ and $h(x)$ the same and when are they different?

7. Use the coordinate pairs to sketch the graphs of $f(x)$ and $h(x)$ on the same grid.

Reflect and Respond

8. Which characteristics of the two graphs are similar and which are different?

9. a) For what values of x are the graphs of $f(x)$ and $h(x)$ the same? different?

   b) If you could sketch the graph of $h(x)$ using two quadratic functions, what would they be? Are there any restrictions on the domain and range of each function? If so, what are they?

10. Describe how the graph of a linear or quadratic function is related to its corresponding absolute value graph.

absolute value function

- a function that involves the absolute value of a variable

The vertex, (0, 0), divides the graph of this **absolute value function** $y = |x|$ into two distinct pieces.

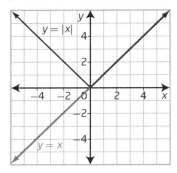

For all values of x less than zero, the y-value is $-x$. For all values of x greater than or equal to zero, the y-value is x. Since the function is defined by two different rules for each interval in the domain, you can define $y = |x|$ as the **piecewise function**

piecewise function

- a function composed of two or more separate functions or *pieces*, each with its own specific domain, that combine to define the overall function

- the absolute value function $y = |x|$ can be defined as the piecewise function
$$y = \begin{cases} x, \text{ if } x \geq 0 \\ -x, \text{ if } x < 0 \end{cases}$$

$$y = \begin{cases} x, \text{ if } x \geq 0 \\ -x, \text{ if } x < 0 \end{cases}$$

The graph shows how $y = |x|$ is related to the graph of $y = x$. Since $|x|$ cannot be negative, the part of the graph of $y = x$ that is below the x-axis is reflected in the x-axis to become the line $y = -x$ in the interval $x < 0$. The part of the graph of $y = x$ that is on or above the x-axis is zero or positive and remains unchanged as the line $y = x$ in the interval $x \geq 0$.

Example 1

Graph an Absolute Value Function of the Form $y = |ax + b|$

Consider the absolute value function $y = |2x - 3|$.
a) Determine the y-intercept and the x-intercept.
b) Sketch the graph.
c) State the domain and range.
d) Express as a piecewise function.

Solution

a) To determine the y-intercept, let $x = 0$ and solve for y.
$$y = |2x - 3|$$
$$y = |2(0) - 3|$$
$$y = |-3|$$
$$y = 3$$
The y-intercept occurs at (0, 3).

To determine the x-intercept, set $y = 0$ and solve for x.

$|2x - 3| = 0$

$2x - 3 = 0$ Since $|0| = 0$, $|2x - 3| = 0$ when $2x - 3 = 0$.

$\quad 2x = 3$

$\quad\quad x = \dfrac{3}{2}$

The x-intercept occurs at $\left(\dfrac{3}{2}, 0\right)$.

b) Method 1: Sketch Using a Table of Values

Create a table of values, using the x-intercept and values to the right and left of it.

Sketch the graph using the points in the table.

x	$y = |2x - 3|$
-1	5
0	3
$\dfrac{3}{2}$	0
3	3
4	5

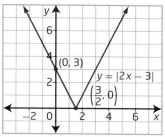

Method 2: Sketch Using the Graph of $y = 2x - 3$

Use the graph of $y = 2x - 3$ to graph $y = |2x - 3|$.

Sketch the graph of $y = 2x - 3$, which is a line with a slope of 2 and a y-intercept of -3.

The x-intercept of the original function is the x-intercept of the corresponding absolute value function. The point representing the x-intercept is an **invariant point**.

Reflect in the x-axis the part of the graph of $y = 2x - 3$ that is below the x-axis.

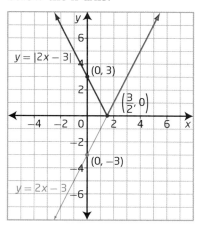

invariant point

• a point that remains unchanged when a transformation is applied to it

What other points on the graph are invariant points?

c) Since there is no *x*-value that cannot be substituted into the function $y = |2x - 3|$, the domain is all real numbers, or $\{x \mid x \in R\}$. For all values of *x*, $|2x - 3| \geq 0$. The range is $\{y \mid y \geq 0, y \in R\}$.

d) The V-shaped graph of the absolute value function $y = |2x - 3|$ is composed of two separate linear functions, each with its own domain.

- When $x \geq \dfrac{3}{2}$, the graph of $y = |2x - 3|$ is the graph of $y = 2x - 3$, which is a line with a slope of 2 and a *y*-intercept of -3.

- When $x < \dfrac{3}{2}$, the graph of $y = |2x - 3|$ is the graph of $y = 2x - 3$ reflected in the *x*-axis. The equation of the reflected graph is $y = -(2x - 3)$ or $y = -2x + 3$, which is a line with a slope of -2 and a *y*-intercept of 3.

You can combine these two linear functions with their domains to define the absolute value function $y = |2x - 3|$. Express the absolute value function $y = |2x - 3|$ as the piecewise function

$$y = \begin{cases} 2x - 3, & \text{if } x \geq \dfrac{3}{2} \\ -(2x - 3), & \text{if } x < \dfrac{3}{2} \end{cases}$$

Your Turn

Consider the absolute value function $y = |3x + 1|$.
a) Determine the *y*-intercept and the *x*-intercept.
b) Sketch the graph.
c) State the domain and range.
d) Express as a piecewise function.

Example 2

Graph an Absolute Value Function of the Form $f(x) = |ax^2 + bx + c|$

Consider the absolute value function $f(x) = |-x^2 + 2x + 8|$.
a) Determine the *y*-intercept and the *x*-intercepts.
b) Sketch the graph.
c) State the domain and range.
d) Express as a piecewise function.

Solution

a) Determine the *y*-intercept by evaluating the function at $x = 0$.
$f(x) = |-x^2 + 2x + 8|$
$f(0) = |-(0)^2 + 2(0) + 8|$
$f(0) = |8|$
$f(0) = 8$
The *y*-intercept occurs at $(0, 8)$

The *x*-intercepts are the real zeros of the function, since they correspond to the *x*-intercepts of the graph.

$$f(x) = |-x^2 + 2x + 8|$$
$$0 = -x^2 + 2x + 8$$
$$0 = -(x^2 - 2x - 8)$$
$$0 = -(x + 2)(x - 4)$$
$$x + 2 = 0 \quad \text{or} \quad x - 4 = 0$$
$$x = -2 \qquad\qquad x = 4$$

The *x*-intercepts occur at $(-2, 0)$ and $(4, 0)$.

b) Use the graph of $y = f(x)$ to graph $y = |f(x)|$.

Complete the square to convert the quadratic function $y = -x^2 + 2x + 8$ to vertex form, $y = a(x - p)^2 + q$.

$$y = -x^2 + 2x + 8$$
$$y = -(x^2 - 2x) + 8$$
$$y = -(x^2 - 2x + 1 - 1) + 8$$
$$y = -[(x^2 - 2x + 1) - 1] + 8$$
$$y = -[(x - 1)^2 - 1] + 8$$
$$y = -(x - 1)^2 - 1(-1) + 8$$
$$y = -(x - 1)^2 + 9$$

Since $p = 1$ and $q = 9$, the vertex is located at $(1, 9)$. Since $a < 0$, the parabola opens downward. Sketch the graph.

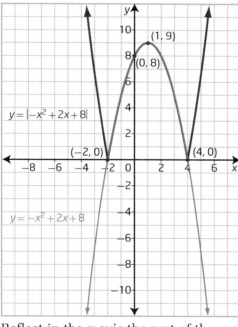

What other methods could you use to find the vertex of the quadratic function?

Reflect in the *x*-axis the part of the graph of $y = -x^2 + 2x + 8$ that lies below the *x*-axis.

c) The domain is all real numbers, or $\{x \mid x \in R\}$, and the range is all non-negative values of y, or $\{y \mid y \geq 0, y \in R\}$.

d) The graph of $y = |-x^2 + 2x + 8|$ consists of two separate quadratic functions. You can use the x-intercepts to identify each function's specific domain.

- When $-2 \leq x \leq 4$, the graph of $y = |-x^2 + 2x + 8|$ is the graph of $y = -x^2 + 2x + 8$, which is a parabola opening downward with a vertex at $(1, 9)$, a y-intercept of 8, and x-intercepts at -2 and 4.

- When $x < -2$ or $x > 4$, the graph of $y = |-x^2 + 2x + 8|$ is the graph of $y = -x^2 + 2x + 8$ reflected in the x-axis. The equation of the reflected graph is $y = -(-x^2 + 2x + 8)$ or $y = x^2 - 2x - 8$, which is a parabola opening upward with a vertex at $(1, -9)$, a y-intercept of -8, and x-intercepts at -2 and 4.

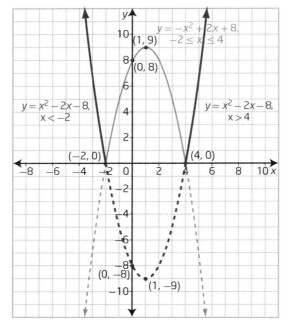

Express the absolute value function $y = |-x^2 + 2x + 8|$ as the piecewise function

$$y = \begin{cases} -x^2 + 2x + 8, & \text{if } -2 \leq x \leq 4 \\ -(-x^2 + 2x + 8), & \text{if } x < -2 \text{ or } x > 4 \end{cases}$$

Your Turn

Consider the absolute value function $f(x) = |x^2 - x - 2|$.
a) Determine the y-intercept and the x-intercepts.
b) Sketch the graph.
c) State the domain and range.
d) Express as a piecewise function.

Key Ideas

- You can analyse absolute value functions in several ways:
  - graphically, by sketching and identifying the characteristics of the graph, including the x-intercepts and the y-intercept, the minimum values, the domain, and the range
  - algebraically, by rewriting the function as a piecewise function
  - In general, you can express the absolute value function $y = |f(x)|$ as the piecewise function

  $$y = \begin{cases} f(x), \text{ if } f(x) \geq 0 \\ -f(x), \text{ if } f(x) < 0 \end{cases}$$

- The domain of an absolute value function $y = |f(x)|$ is the same as the domain of the function $y = f(x)$.

- The range of an absolute value function $y = |f(x)|$ depends on the range of the function $y = f(x)$. For the absolute value of a linear or quadratic function, the range will generally, but not always, be $\{y \mid y \geq 0, y \in \mathbb{R}\}$.

Check Your Understanding

Practise

1. Given the table of values for $y = f(x)$, create a table of values for $y = |f(x)|$.

a)

x	y = f(x)
−2	−3
−1	−1
0	1
1	3
2	5

b)

x	y = f(x)
−2	0
−1	−2
0	−2
1	0
2	4

2. The point $(-5, -8)$ is on the graph of $y = f(x)$. Identify the corresponding point on the graph of $y = |f(x)|$.

3. The graph of $y = f(x)$ has an x-intercept of 3 and a y-intercept of −4. What are the x-intercept and the y-intercept of the graph of $y = |f(x)|$?

4. The graph of $y = f(x)$ has x-intercepts of −2 and 7, and a y-intercept of $-\frac{3}{2}$. State the x-intercepts and the y-intercept of the graph of $y = |f(x)|$.

5. Copy the graph of $y = f(x)$. On the same set of axes, sketch the graph of $y = |f(x)|$.

a)

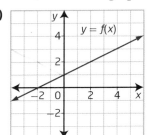

b)

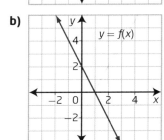

c)

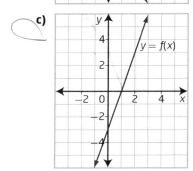

6. Sketch the graph of each absolute value function. State the intercepts and the domain and range.

a) $y = |2x - 6|$

b) $y = |x + 5|$

c) $f(x) = |-3x - 6|$

d) $g(x) = |-x - 3|$

e) $y = \left| \frac{1}{2}x - 2 \right|$

f) $h(x) = \left| \frac{1}{3}x + 3 \right|$

7. Copy the graph of $y = f(x)$. On the same set of axes, sketch the graph of $y = |f(x)|$.

a)

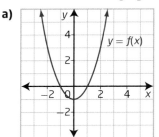

b)

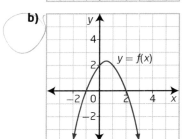

c)

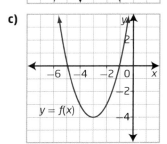

8. Sketch the graph of each function. State the intercepts and the domain and range.

a) $y = |x^2 - 4|$

b) $y = |x^2 + 5x + 6|$

c) $f(x) = |-2x^2 - 3x + 2|$

d) $y = \left| \frac{1}{4}x^2 - 9 \right|$

e) $g(x) = |(x - 3)^2 + 1|$

f) $h(x) = |-3(x + 2)^2 - 4|$

9. Write the piecewise function that represents each graph.

a)
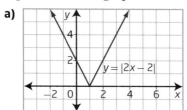
$y = |2x - 2|$

b)
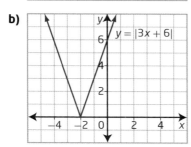
$y = |3x + 6|$

c)
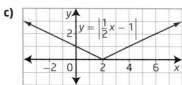
$y = \left|\frac{1}{2}x - 1\right|$

10. What piecewise function could you use to represent each graph of an absolute value function?

a)
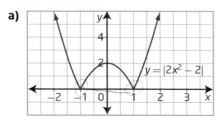
$y = |2x^2 - 2|$

b)
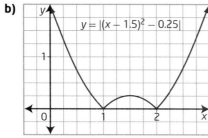
$y = |(x - 1.5)^2 - 0.25|$

c)
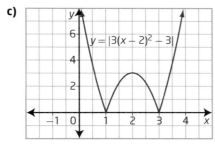
$y = |3(x - 2)^2 - 3|$

11. Express each function as a piecewise function.

    a) $y = |x - 4|$

    b) $y = |3x + 5|$

    c) $y = |-x^2 + 1|$

    d) $y = |x^2 - x - 6|$

Apply

12. Consider the function $g(x) = |6 - 2x|$.

    a) Create a table of values for the function using values of -1, 0, 2, 3, and 5 for x.

    b) Sketch the graph.

    c) Determine the domain and range for $g(x)$.

    d) Write the function in piecewise notation.

13. Consider the function $g(x) = |x^2 - 2x - 8|$.

    a) What are the y-intercept and x-intercepts of the graph of the function?

    b) Graph the function.

    c) What are the domain and range of $g(x)$?

    d) Express the function as a piecewise function.

14. Consider the function $g(x) = |3x^2 - 4x - 4|$.

    a) What are the intercepts of the graph?

    b) Graph the function.

    c) What are the domain and range of $g(x)$?

    d) What is the piecewise notation form of the function?

15. Raza and Michael are discussing the functions $p(x) = 2x^2 - 9x + 10$ and $q(x) = |2x^2 - 9x + 10|$. Raza says that the two functions have identical graphs. Michael says that the absolute value changes the graph so that $q(x)$ has a different range and a different graph from $p(x)$. Who is correct? Explain your answer.

16. Air hockey is a table game where two players try to score points by hitting a puck into the other player's goal. The diameter of the puck is 8.26 cm. Suppose a Cartesian plane is superimposed over the playing surface of an air hockey table so that opposite corners have the coordinates (0, 114) and (236, 0), as shown. The path of the puck hit by a player is given by $y = |0.475x - 55.1|$.

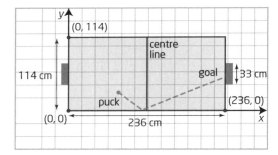

a) Graph the function.

b) At what point does the puck ricochet off the side of the table?

c) If the other player does not touch the puck, verify whether or not the puck goes into the goal.

17. The velocity, v, in metres per second, of a go-cart at a given time, t, in seconds, is modelled by the function $v(t) = -2t + 4$. The distance travelled, in metres, can be determined by calculating the area between the graph of $v(t) = |-2t + 4|$ and the x-axis. What is the distance travelled in the first 5 s?

18. a) Graph $f(x) = |3x - 2|$ and $g(x) = |-3x + 2|$. What do you notice about the two graphs? Explain why.

b) Graph $f(x) = |4x + 3|$. Write a different absolute value function of the form $g(x) = |ax + b|$ that has the same graph.

19. Graph $f(x) = |x^2 - 6x + 5|$. Write a different absolute value function of the form $g(x) = |ax^2 + bx + c|$ that has the same graph as $f(x) = |x^2 - 6x + 5|$.

20. An absolute value function has the form $f(x) = |ax + b|$, where $a \neq 0$, $b \neq 0$, and $a, b \in R$. If the function $f(x)$ has a domain of $\{x \mid x \in R\}$, a range of $\{y \mid y \geq 0, y \in R\}$, an x-intercept occurring at $\left(\frac{3}{2}, 0\right)$, and a y-intercept occurring at (0, 6), what are the values of a and b?

21. An absolute value function has the form $f(x) = |x^2 + bx + c|$, where $b \neq 0$, $c \neq 0$, and $b, c \in R$. If the function $f(x)$ has a domain of $\{x \mid x \in R\}$, a range of $\{y \mid y \geq 0, y \in R\}$, x-intercepts occurring at (−6, 0) and (2, 0), and a y-intercept occurring at (0, 12), determine the values of b and c.

22. Explain why the graphs of $y = |x^2|$ and $y = x^2$ are identical.

Extend

23. Is the following statement true for all $x, y \in R$? Justify your answer.

$$|x| + |y| = |x + y|$$

24. Draw the graph of $|x| + |y| = 5$.

25. Use the piecewise definition of $y = |x|$ to prove that for all $x, y \in R$, $|x|(|y|) = |xy|$.

26. Compare the graphs of $f(x) = |3x - 6|$ and $g(x) = |3x| - 6$. Discuss the similarities and differences.

Create Connections

27. Explain how to use a piecewise function to graph an absolute value function.

28. Consider the quadratic function $y = ax^2 + bx + c$, where a, b, and c are real numbers and $a \neq 0$. Describe the nature of the discriminant, $b^2 - 4ac$, for the graphs of $y = ax^2 + bx + c$ and $y = |ax^2 + bx + c|$ to be identical.

29. MINI LAB In Section 7.1, you solved the following problem:

Suppose a straight stretch of highway running west to east begins at the town of Allenby (0 km). The diagram shows the distances from Allenby east along the highway to various towns. A new grain storage facility is to be built along the highway 24 km from Allenby. Find the total distance of the grain storage facility from all of the seven towns on the highway for this proposed location.

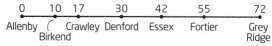

Step 1 Rather than building the facility at a point 24 km east of Allenby, as was originally planned, there may be a more suitable location along the highway that would minimize the total distance of the grain storage facility from all of the towns. Do you think that point exists? If so, predict its location.

Step 2 Let the location of the grain storage facility be at point x (x kilometres east of Allenby). Then, the absolute value of the distance of the facility from Allenby is $|x|$ and from Birkend is $|x - 10|$. Why do you need to use absolute value?

Continue this process to write absolute value expressions for the distance of the storage facility from each of the seven towns. Then, combine them to create a function for the total of the absolute value distances from the different towns to point x.

Step 3 Graph the combined function using a graphing calculator. Set an appropriate window to view the graph. What are the window settings?

Step 4 a) What does the graph indicate about placing the point x at different locations along the highway?

b) What are the coordinates of the minimum point on the graph?

c) Interpret this point with respect to the location of the grain storage facility.

30. Each set of transformations is applied to the graph of $f(x) = x^2$ in the order listed. Write the function of each transformed graph.

a) a horizontal translation of 3 units to the right, a vertical translation of 7 units up, and then take its absolute value

b) a change in the width by a factor of $\frac{4}{5}$, a horizontal translation of 3 units to the left, and then take its absolute value

c) a reflection in the x-axis, a vertical translation of 6 units down, and then take its absolute value

d) a change in the width by a factor of 5, a horizontal translation of 3 units to the left, a vertical translation of 3 units up, and then take its absolute value

Absolute Value Equations

Focus on...

- solving an absolute value equation graphically, with or without technology
- algebraically solving an equation with a single absolute value and verifying the solution
- explaining why the absolute value equation $|f(x)| = b$ for $b < 0$ has no solution

Is the speed of light the maximum velocity possible? According to Albert Einstein's theory of relativity, an object travelling near the speed of light, approximately 300 000 km/s, will move more slowly and shorten in length from the point of view of an observer on Earth. On the television show *Star Trek*, the speed of light was called Warp 1 and the spaceship *USS Enterprise* was able to travel at much greater speeds. Is this possible or just a fantasy?

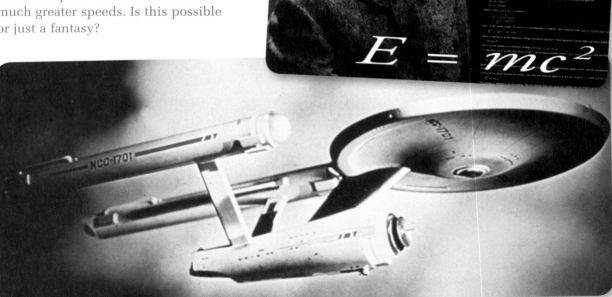

Did You Know?

The town of Vulcan, Alberta, has been using the *Star Trek* connection since the debut of the television series and now receives more than 12 000 visitors per year. There is a replica of the *USS Enterprise* in Vulcan, and the tourism centre is designed as a landing craft. Every year, in June, Vulcan hosts Galaxyfest-Spock Days.

Investigate Absolute Value Equations

1. Consider the absolute value equation $|x| = 10$.

2. Use the number line to geometrically solve the equation. How many solutions are there?

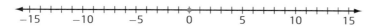

3. How many solutions are there for the equation $|x| = 15$? for $|x| = 5$? for $|x| = b$, $b \neq 0$? What are the solutions?

4. Make a conjecture about the number of solutions for an absolute value equation.

5. Solve the absolute value equation $|x| = 0$.

Reflect and Respond

6. Is it possible to have an absolute value equation that has no solutions? Under what conditions would this happen?

7. Discuss how to use the following definition of absolute value to solve absolute value equations.

$$|x| = \begin{cases} x \text{ if } x \geq 0 \\ -x \text{ if } x < 0 \end{cases}$$

8. a) From the definition of absolute value in step 7, give a general rule for solving $|A| = b$, $b \geq 0$, for A, where A is an algebraic expression.

b) State a general rule for solving the equation $|A| = b$, $b < 0$, for A.

Link the Ideas

Use the definition of absolute value when solving **absolute value equations** algebraically.

There are two cases to consider.

Case 1: The expression inside the absolute value symbol is positive or zero.

Case 2: The expression inside the absolute value symbol is negative.

absolute value equation

- an equation that includes the absolute value of an expression involving a variable

Example 1

Solve an Absolute Value Equation

Solve $|x - 3| = 7$.

Solution

Method 1: Use Algebra

Using the definition of absolute value,

$$|x - 3| = \begin{cases} x - 3, \text{ if } x \geq 3 \\ -(x - 3), \text{ if } x < 3 \end{cases}$$

Case 1

The expression $|x - 3|$ equals $x - 3$ when $x - 3 \geq 0$, or when $x \geq 3$.

$x - 3 = 7$

$\quad x = 10$

The value 10 satisfies the condition $x \geq 3$.

Case 2

The expression $|x - 3|$ equals $-(x - 3)$ when $x - 3 < 0$, or when $x < 3$.

$-(x - 3) = 7$

$\quad x - 3 = -7$

$\quad\quad x = -4$

The value -4 satisfies the condition $x < 3$.

Verify the solutions algebraically by substitution.

For $x = 10$:

Left Side	Right Side
$\quad|x - 3|$	7
$= |10 - 3|$	
$= |7|$	
$= 7$	

Left Side = Right Side

For $x = -4$:

Left Side	Right Side
$\quad|x - 3|$	7
$= |-4 - 3|$	
$= |-7|$	
$= 7$	

Left Side = Right Side

The solution is $x = 10$ or $x = -4$.

Method 2: Use a Graph

Graph the functions $f(x) = |x - 3|$ and $g(x) = 7$ on the same coordinate grid to see where they intersect.

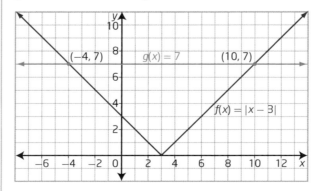

Why were these two functions chosen for $f(x)$ and $g(x)$?

The graphs intersect at $(-4, 7)$ and $(10, 7)$. This means that $x = -4$ and $x = 10$ are solutions to the equation $|x - 3| = 7$.

You can verify the solutions using technology. Input the function $f(x) = |x - 3|$ and display the table of values to confirm the solutions you found graphically.

From the table of values, the solution is $x = -4$ or $x = 10$.

x	f1(x):= ▼
	abs(x-3)
-5.	8.
-4.	7.
-3.	6.
-2.	5.
-1.	4.

x	f1(x):= ▼
	abs(x-3)
7.	4.
8.	5.
9.	6.
10.	7.
11.	8.

Your Turn

Solve $|6 - x| = 2$ graphically and algebraically.

Example 2

Solve an Absolute Value Problem

A computerized process controls the amount of batter used to produce cookies in a factory. If the computer program sets the ideal mass before baking at 55 g but allows a tolerance of ± 2.5 g, solve an absolute value equation for the maximum and minimum mass, m, of batter for cookies at this factory.

Solution

Model the situation by the equation $|m - 55| = 2.5$.

Method 1: Use a Number Line
The absolute value equation $|m - 55| = 2.5$ means that the distance between m and 55 is 2.5 units. To find m on a number line, start at 55 and move 2.5 units in either direction.

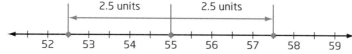

The distance from 55 to 52.5 is 2.5 units.   The distance from 55 to 57.5 is 2.5 units.

The maximum mass is 57.5 g and the minimum mass is 52.5 g.

Method 2: Use an Algebraic Method

Using the definition of absolute value,

$$|m - 55| = \begin{cases} m - 55, \text{ if } m \geq 55 \\ -(m - 55), \text{ if } m < 55 \end{cases}$$

Case 1

$$m - 55 = 2.5$$
$$m = 57.5$$

Case 2

$$-(m - 55) = 2.5$$
$$m - 55 = -2.5$$
$$m = 52.5$$

The maximum mass is 57.5 g and the minimum mass is 52.5 g.

Your Turn

A computerized process controls the amount of fish that is packaged in a specific size of can. The computer program sets the ideal mass at 170 g but allows a tolerance of ± 6 g. Solve an absolute value equation for the maximum and minimum mass, m, of fish in this size of can.

Example 3

Absolute Value Equation With an Extraneous Solution

Solve $|2x - 5| = 5 - 3x$.

Solution

Using the definition of absolute value,

How do you determine the restrictions on the domain in this example?

$$|2x - 5| = \begin{cases} 2x - 5, \text{ if } x \geq \dfrac{5}{2} \\ -(2x - 5), \text{ if } x < \dfrac{5}{2} \end{cases}$$

So, $|2x - 5| = 5 - 3x$ means $2x - 5 = 5 - 3x$ when $x \geq \dfrac{5}{2}$

or $-(2x - 5) = 5 - 3x$ when $x < \dfrac{5}{2}$.

Case 1

$$2x - 5 = 5 - 3x$$
$$5x = 10$$
$$x = 2$$

The value 2 does not satisfy the condition $x \geq \dfrac{5}{2}$, so it is an extraneous solution.

Case 2

$$-(2x - 5) = 5 - 3x$$
$$-2x + 5 = 5 - 3x$$
$$x = 0$$

The value 0 does satisfy the condition $x < \dfrac{5}{2}$.

Verify the solutions.

For $x = 2$:

Left Side	Right Side
$\lvert 2x - 5 \rvert$	$5 - 3x$
$= \lvert 2(2) - 5 \rvert$	$= 5 - 3(2)$
$= \lvert 4 - 5 \rvert$	$= 5 - 6$
$= \lvert -1 \rvert$	$= -1$
$= 1$	

Left Side $\neq$ Right Side

For $x = 0$:

Left Side	Right Side
$\lvert 2x - 5 \rvert$	$5 - 3x$
$= \lvert 2(0) - 5 \rvert$	$= 5 - 3(0)$
$= \lvert 0 - 5 \rvert$	$= 5 - 0$
$= \lvert -5 \rvert$	$= 5$
$= 5$	

Left Side $=$ Right Side

The solution is $x = 0$.

Some absolute value equations may have extraneous roots. Verify potential solutions by substituting them into the original equation.

Your Turn

Solve $\lvert x + 5 \rvert = 4x - 1$.

Example 4

Absolute Value Equation With No Solution

Solve $\lvert 3x - 4 \rvert + 12 = 9$.

Solution

$\lvert 3x - 4 \rvert + 12 = 9$ Isolate the absolute value expression.

$\quad\lvert 3x - 4 \rvert = -3$ This statement is never true.

Since the absolute value of a number is always greater than or equal to zero, by inspection this equation has no solution.

The solution set for this type of equation is the empty set.

Your Turn

Solve $\lvert 4x - 5 \rvert + 9 = 2$.

Did You Know?

The empty set is a set with no elements and is symbolized by {} or ø.

Example 5

Solve an Absolute Value Equation Involving a Quadratic Expression

Solve $|x^2 - 2x| = 1$.

> **Solution**

Using the definition of absolute value,

$$|x^2 - 2x| = \begin{cases} x^2 - 2x, & \text{if } x \le 0 \text{ or } x \ge 2 \\ -(x^2 - 2x), & \text{if } 0 < x < 2 \end{cases}$$

How can you use the x-intercepts of the related parabola and the direction in which it opens to determine the domain for each case?

Case 1

$$x^2 - 2x = 1$$
$$x^2 - 2x - 1 = 0$$
$$x = \frac{-b \pm \sqrt{b^2 - 4ac}}{2a}$$

Why is the quadratic formula used to solve for x?

$$x = \frac{-(-2) \pm \sqrt{(-2)^2 - 4(1)(-1)}}{2(1)}$$
$$x = \frac{2 \pm \sqrt{8}}{2}$$
$$x = \frac{2 \pm 2\sqrt{2}}{2}$$
$$x = 1 \pm \sqrt{2}$$

Determine whether $x = 1 + \sqrt{2}$ or $x = 1 - \sqrt{2}$ satisfies the original equation $|x^2 - 2x| = 1$.

For $x = 1 + \sqrt{2}$:

Left Side	Right Side
$\,|x^2 - 2x|$	1
$= \left|(1 + \sqrt{2})^2 - 2(1 + \sqrt{2})\right|$	
$= \left|1 + 2\sqrt{2} + 2 - 2 - 2\sqrt{2}\right|$	
$= |1|$	
$= 1$	

Left Side = Right Side

For $x = 1 - \sqrt{2}$:

Left Side	Right Side
$\,|x^2 - 2x|$	1
$= \left|(1 - \sqrt{2})^2 - 2(1 - \sqrt{2})\right|$	
$= \left|1 - 2\sqrt{2} + 2 - 2 + 2\sqrt{2}\right|$	
$= |1|$	
$= 1$	

Left Side = Right Side

Case 2

$$-(x^2 - 2x) = 1$$
$$x^2 - 2x = -1$$
$$x^2 - 2x + 1 = 0$$
$$(x - 1)^2 = 0$$
$$x - 1 = 0$$
$$x = 1$$

Determine whether $x = 1$ satisfies the original equation $|x^2 - 2x| = 1$.

Left Side   Right Side

$|x^2 - 2x|$ 1

$= |1^2 - 2(1)|$

$= |-1|$

$= 1$

Left Side = Right Side

The solutions are $x = 1$, $x = 1 + \sqrt{2}$, and $x = 1 - \sqrt{2}$.

You can also verify the solution graphically as $x = 1$, $x \approx 2.4$, and $x \approx -0.41$.

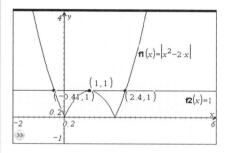

Your Turn

Solve $|x^2 - 3x| = 2$.

Example 6

Solve an Absolute Value Equation Involving Linear and Quadratic Expressions

Solve $|x - 10| = x^2 - 10x$.

Solution

Using the definition of absolute value,

$$|x - 10| = \begin{cases} x - 10, & \text{if } x \geq 10 \\ -(x - 10), & \text{if } x < 10 \end{cases}$$

Case 1

$x - 10 = x^2 - 10x$

$0 = x^2 - 11x + 10$

$0 = (x - 10)(x - 1)$

$x - 10 = 0 \quad \text{or} \quad x - 1 = 0$

$\phantom{x - 10 = 0 \quad \text{or} \quad} x = 10 \phantom{\text{or} \quad x } x = 1$

Only $x = 10$ satisfies the condition $x \geq 10$, so $x = 1$ is an extraneous root.

Case 2

$-(x - 10) = x^2 - 10x$

$-x + 10 = x^2 - 10x$

$0 = x^2 - 9x - 10$

$0 = (x - 10)(x + 1)$

$x - 10 = 0 \quad \text{or} \quad x + 1 = 0$

$\phantom{x - 10 = 0 \quad \text{or} \quad} x = 10 \phantom{\text{or} \quad x } x = -1$

Only $x = -1$ satisfies the condition $x < 10$ for this case. But $x = 10$ satisfies the condition in Case 1, so the solutions are $x = 10$ and $x = -1$.

How could you verify these solutions?

Your Turn

Solve $|x - 5| = x^2 - 8x + 15$.

Key Ideas

- You can solve absolute value equations by graphing the left side and the right side of the equation on the same set of axes and determining the points of intersection.

- To solve an absolute value equation algebraically:
  - Consider the two separate cases, corresponding to the two parts of the definition of absolute value:

  $$|x| = \begin{cases} x, \text{ if } x \geq 0 \\ -x, \text{ if } x < 0 \end{cases}$$

  - Roots that satisfy the specified condition in each case are solutions to the equation.
  - Identify and reject extraneous roots.

- Verify roots through substitution into the original equation.

- Any absolute value equation of the form $|f(x)| = a$, where $a < 0$, has no solution since by definition $|f(x)| \geq 0$.

Practise

1. Use the number line to geometrically solve each equation.

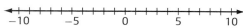

a) $|x| = 7$ **b)** $|x| + 8 = 12$

c) $|x| + 4 = 4$ **d)** $|x| = -6$

2. Solve each absolute value equation by graphing.

a) $|x - 4| = 10$ **b)** $|x + 3| = 2$

c) $6 = |x + 8|$ **d)** $|x + 9| = -3$

3. Determine an absolute value equation in the form $|ax + b| = c$ given its solutions on the number line.

a) ![number line from -10 to 10]

b) ![number line from -10 to 10]

c) ![number line from -10 to 10]

4. Solve each absolute value equation algebraically. Verify your solutions.

a) $|x + 7| = 12$

b) $|3x - 4| + 5 = 7$

c) $2|x + 6| + 12 = -4$

d) $-6|2x - 14| = -42$

5. Solve each equation.

a) $|2a + 7| = a - 4$

b) $|7 + 3x| = 11 - x$

c) $|1 - 2m| = m + 2$

d) $|3x + 3| = 2x - 5$

e) $3|2a + 7| = 3a + 12$

6. Solve each equation and verify your solutions graphically.

a) $|x| = x^2 + x - 3$

b) $|x^2 - 2x + 2| = 3x - 4$

c) $|x^2 - 9| = x^2 - 9$

d) $|x^2 - 1| = x$

e) $|x^2 - 2x - 16| = 8$

Apply

7. Bolts are manufactured at a certain factory to have a diameter of 18 mm and are rejected if they differ from this by more than 0.5 mm.

a) Write an absolute value equation in the form $|d - a| = b$ to describe the acceptance limits for the diameter, d, in millimetres, of these bolts, where a and b are real numbers.

b) Solve the resulting absolute value equation to find the maximum and minimum diameters of the bolts.

8. One experiment measured the speed of light as 299 792 456.2 m/s with a measurement uncertainty of 1.1 m/s.

a) Write an absolute value equation in the form $|c - a| = b$ to describe the measured speed of light, c, metres per second, where a and b are real numbers.

b) Solve the absolute value equation to find the maximum and minimum values for the speed of light for this experiment.

9. In communities in Nunavut, aviation fuel is stored in huge tanks at the airport. Fuel is re-supplied by ship yearly. The fuel tank in Kugaaruk holds 50 000 L. The fuel re-supply brings a volume, V, in litres, of fuel plus or minus 2000 L.

a) Write an absolute value equation in the form $|V - a| = b$ to describe the limits for the volume of fuel delivered, where a and b are real numbers.

b) Solve your absolute value equation to find the maximum and minimum volumes of fuel.

10. Consider the statement $x = 7 \pm 4.8$.

  a) Describe the values of x.

  b) Translate the statement into an equation involving absolute value.

11. When measurements are made in science, there is always a degree of error possible. Absolute error is the uncertainty of a measurement. For example, if the mass of an object is known to be 125 g, but the absolute error is said to be ± 4 g, then the measurement could be as high as 129 g and as low as 121 g.

  a) If the mass of a substance is measured once as 64 g and once as 69 g, and the absolute error is ± 2.5 g, what is the actual mass of the substance?

  b) If the volume of a liquid is measured to be 258 mL with an absolute error of ± 7 mL, what are the least and greatest possible measures of the volume?

12. The moon travels in a elliptical orbit around Earth. The distance between Earth and the moon changes as the moon travels in this orbit. The point where the moon's orbit is closest to Earth is called *perigee*, and the point when it is farthest from Earth is called *apogee*. You can use the equation $|d - 381\,550| = 25\,150$ to find these distances, d, in kilometres.

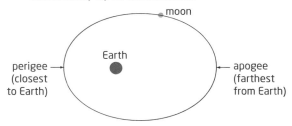

  a) Solve the equation to find the perigee and apogee of the moon's orbit of Earth.

  b) Interpret the given values 381 550 and 25 150 with respect to the distance between Earth and the moon.

Did You Know?

When a full moon is at perigee, it can appear as much as 14% larger to us than a full moon at apogee.

13. Determine whether $n \geq 0$ or $n \leq 0$ makes each equation true.

  a) $n + |-n| = 2n$ **b)** $n + |-n| = 0$

14. Solve each equation for x, where $a, b, c \in \mathrm{R}$.

  a) $|ax| - b = c$ **b)** $|x - b| = c$

15. Erin and Andrea each solve $|x - 4| + 8 = 12$. Who is correct? Explain your reasoning.

Erin's solution:
$$|x - 4| + 8 = 12$$
$$|x - 4| = 4$$
$$x + 4 = 4 \quad \text{or} \quad -x + 4 = 4$$
$$x = 0 \qquad\qquad x = 0$$

Andrea's solution:
$$|x - 4| + 8 = 12$$
$$|x - 4| = 4$$
$$x - 4 = 4 \quad \text{or} \quad -x + 4 = 4$$
$$x = 8 \qquad\qquad x = 0$$

16. Mission Creek in the Okanagan Valley of British Columbia is the site of the spawning of Kokanee salmon every September. Kokanee salmon are sensitive to water temperature. If the water is too cold, egg hatching is delayed, and if the water is too warm, the eggs die. Biologists have found that the spawning rate of the salmon is greatest when the water is at an average temperature of 11.5 °C with an absolute value difference of 2.5 °C. Write and solve an absolute value equation that determines the limits of the ideal temperature range for the Kokanee salmon to spawn.

Did You Know?

In recent years, the September temperature of Mission Creek has been rising. Scientists are considering reducing the temperature of the water by planting more vegetation along the creek banks. This would create shade, cooling the water.

17. Low-dose aspirin contains 81 mg of the active ingredient acetylsalicylic acid (ASA) per tablet. It is used to regulate and reduce heart attack risk associated with high blood pressure by thinning the blood.

a) Given a tolerance of 20% for generic brands, solve an absolute value equation for the maximum and minimum amount of ASA per tablet.

b) Which limit might the drug company tend to lean toward? Why?

Extend

18. For the launch of the Ares I-X rocket from the Kennedy Space Center in Florida in 2009, scientists at NASA indicated they had a launch window of 08:00 to 12:00 eastern time. If a launch at any time in this window is acceptable, write an absolute value equation to express the earliest and latest acceptable times for launch.

19. Determine whether each statement is sometimes true, always true, or never true, where a is a natural number. Explain your reasoning.

a) The value of $|x + 1|$ is greater than zero.

b) The solution to $|x + a| = 0$ is greater than zero.

c) The value of $|x + a| + a$ is greater than zero.

20. Write an absolute value equation with the indicated solutions or type of solution.

a) −2 and 8

b) no solution

c) one integral solution

d) two integral solutions

21. Does the absolute value equation $|ax + b| = 0$, where $a, b \in R$, always have a solution? Explain.

Create Connections

22. For each graph, an absolute value function and a linear function intersect to produce solutions to an equation composed of the two functions. Determine the equation that is being solved in each graph.

a)

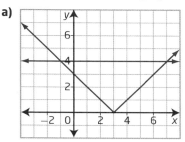

b)

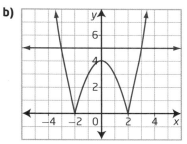

23. Explain, without solving, why the equation $|3x + 1| = -2$ has no solutions, while the equation $|3x + 1| - 4 = -2$ has solutions.

24. Why do some absolute value equations produce extraneous roots when solved algebraically? How are these roots created in the algebraic process if they are not actual solutions of the equation?

Reciprocal Functions

Focus on...

- graphing the reciprocal of a given function
- analysing the graph of the reciprocal of a given function
- comparing the graph of a function to the graph of the reciprocal of that function
- identifying the values of x for which the graph of $y = \dfrac{1}{f(x)}$ has vertical asymptotes

Isaac Newton (1643–1727) is one of the most important mathematicians and physicists in history. Besides being the co-inventor of calculus, Newton is famous for deriving the law of universal gravitation. He deduced that the forces that keep the planets in their orbits must be related reciprocally as the squares of their distances from the centres about which they revolve.

$$F_1 = F_2 = G\left(\frac{m_1 \times m_2}{r^2}\right)$$

As a result of the reciprocal relationship, as the distance, r, between two planets increases, the gravitational force, F, decreases. Similarly, as the distance decreases, the gravitational force between the planets will increase.

Did You Know?

Isaac Newton made most of his important discoveries in the 1660s. During this time he was forced to work at home because the bubonic plague resulted in the closure of all public buildings, including Cambridge University, where Newton studied.

Web Link

To learn more about Isaac Newton and his contributions to mathematics, go to www.mhrprecalc11.ca and follow the links.

Investigate Exchange Rates

Materials

- graphing calculator

Perhaps you have travelled to Mexico or to Hawaii and have exchanged Canadian dollars for pesos or U.S. dollars. Perhaps you have travelled overseas and exchanged British pounds for the Japanese yen or Swiss franc. If so, you have experienced exchange rates in action. Do you know how they work?

An exchange rate is the rate at which one currency is converted into another currency. Exchange rates are typically quoted as a ratio with either one of the currencies being set equal to one, such as 1 Australian dollar = 0.9796 Canadian dollars.

1. If the Canadian dollar is worth US$0.80, it costs C$1.25 to buy US$1. Change the values 0.80 and 1.25 to fractions in lowest terms. Can you see how these fractions are related to each other? Discuss with your classmates how you could use this relationship to determine exchange rates.

2. In step 1, the Canadian-to-U.S. dollar exchange rate is 0.80. What is the U.S.-to-Canada dollar exchange rate? How many Canadian dollars could you buy with US$1?

3. a) Copy and complete the table to determine the purchase price of US$1 for various Canadian-to-U.S. dollar exchange rates.

C$1 in US$	Purchase Price of US$1
0.65	1.54
0.70	
0.75	
0.80	
0.85	
0.90	
0.95	
1.00	
1.05	
1.10	

b) Describe your method of determining the purchase price of US$1. Would your method work for all currency exchanges?

c) Plot the ordered pairs from the table of values. Draw a smooth curve through the points. Extrapolate. Does this curve have an x-intercept? a y-intercept? Explain.

Did You Know?

For centuries, the currencies of the world were backed by gold. That is, a piece of paper currency issued by any national government represented a real amount of gold held in a vault by that government.

4. Examine the currency exchange table shown. The Japanese yen (¥) is shown as 0.0108. What does this number represent in terms of exchange rates?

CURRENCIES

Currency	In C$	Currency	In C$	Currency	In C$
Australia dollar	0.9796	Euro	1.5748	Peru sol	0.3629
Bahamas dollar	1.0525	Hong Kong dollar	0.1346	Philippine peso	0.0216
Bahrain dinar	2.7944	India rupee	0.0219	Poland zloty	0.3749
Barbados dollar	0.5287	Jamaica dollar	0.0113	Russia rouble	0.0346
Brazil real	0.6134	Japan yen	0.0108	Singapore dollar	0.7571
Chile peso	0.0020	Kenya shilling	0.0143	South Africa rand	0.1417
Chinese yuan	0.1534	S. Korea won	0.0009	Switzerland franc	1.0418
Denmark krone	0.2107	Mexico peso	0.0786	Ukraine hryvna	0.1238
Dominican peso	0.0286	New Zealand dollar	0.7801	U.A.E. dirham	0.2842
Egypt pound	0.1924	Pakistan rupee	0.0120	U.K. pound	1.7266
				U.S. dollar	1.0374

Did You Know?

A customer buys currency from a bank at a higher price and sells the same currency to a bank at a lower price. The difference between the price at which a bank sells a currency and the price at which it buys the same currency is called the spread. The spread is the cost of completing the exchange.

5. a) How many yen can you purchase with C$1? With C$200?

b) How much does it cost to purchase ¥5000?

6. Choose one other currency from the table or find current currency exchange rates on the Internet.

a) How much of that currency can be purchased with C$1?

b) How much does it cost to purchase 100 units of the foreign currency?

Reflect and Respond

7. Analyse the relationship of currency exchange between countries. For example, when you have the Canadian-to-U.S. dollar exchange rate, how do you determine the U.S.-to-Canadian dollar exchange rate? What is the relationship between the two calculations?

8. Does the relationship in step 7 always work?

Recall that the product of a number and its reciprocal is always equal to 1. For example, $\frac{3}{4}$ is the reciprocal of $\frac{4}{3}$ and $\frac{4}{3}$ is the reciprocal of $\frac{3}{4}$ because $\frac{3}{4}\left(\frac{4}{3}\right) = 1$.

So, for any non-zero real number a, the reciprocal of a is $\frac{1}{a}$ and the reciprocal of $\frac{1}{a}$ is a. For a function $f(x)$, its reciprocal is $\frac{1}{f(x)}$, provided that $f(x) \neq 0$.

Example 1

Compare the Graphs of a Function and Its Reciprocal

reciprocal function

• a function $y = \frac{1}{f(x)}$ defined by $y = \frac{1}{f(a)} = \frac{1}{b}$ if $f(a) = b$, $f(a) \neq 0$, $b \neq 0$

Sketch the graphs of $y = f(x)$ and its **reciprocal function** $y = \frac{1}{f(x)}$, where $f(x) = x$. Examine how the functions are related.

Solution

Use a table of values to graph the functions $y = x$ and $y = \frac{1}{x}$.

x	$y = x$	$y = \frac{1}{x}$
-10	-10	$-\frac{1}{10}$
-5	-5	$-\frac{1}{5}$
-2	-2	$-\frac{1}{2}$
-1	-1	-1
$-\frac{1}{2}$	$-\frac{1}{2}$	-2
$-\frac{1}{5}$	$-\frac{1}{5}$	-5
$-\frac{1}{10}$	$-\frac{1}{10}$	-10
0	0	undefined
$\frac{1}{10}$	$\frac{1}{10}$	10
$\frac{1}{5}$	$\frac{1}{5}$	5
$\frac{1}{2}$	$\frac{1}{2}$	2
1	1	1
2	2	$\frac{1}{2}$
5	5	$\frac{1}{5}$
10	10	$\frac{1}{10}$

Notice that the function values for $y = \frac{1}{x}$ can be found by taking the reciprocal of the function values for $y = x$.

What is unique about the reciprocals of -1 and 1? Why?

Why is the reciprocal of 0 undefined?

What happens to the value of the reciprocal as the absolute value of a number increases in value?

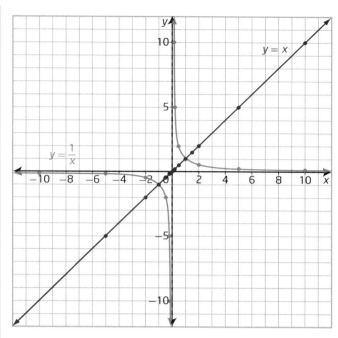

Why does the curve approach the y-axis but never touch it?

Why does the curve approach the x-axis but never touch it?

The function $y = x$ is a function of degree one, so its graph is a line.

The function $y = \frac{1}{x}$ is a rational function.

Its graph has two distinct pieces, or branches. These branches are located on either side of the **vertical asymptote**, defined by the non-permissible value of the domain of the rational function, and the **horizontal asymptote**, defined by the fact that the value 0 is not in the range of the function.

Characteristic	$y = x$	$y = \frac{1}{x}$
Domain	$\{x \mid x \in R\}$	$\{x \mid x \neq 0, x \in R\}$
Range	$\{y \mid y \in R\}$	$\{y \mid y \neq 0, y \in R\}$
End behaviour	• If $x > 0$ and $\lvert x \rvert$ is very large, then $y > 0$ and is very large. • If $x < 0$ and $\lvert x \rvert$ is very large, then $y < 0$ and $\lvert y \rvert$ is very large.	• If $x > 0$ and $\lvert x \rvert$ is very large, then $y > 0$ and is close to 0. • If $x < 0$ and $\lvert x \rvert$ is very large, then $y < 0$ and y is close to 0.
Behaviour at $x = 0$	$y = 0$	undefined, vertical asymptote at $x = 0$
Invariant points	$(-1, -1)$ and $(1, 1)$	

asymptote

• a line whose distance from a given curve approaches zero

vertical asymptote

• for reciprocal functions, occur at the non-permissible values of the function

• the line $x = a$ is a vertical asymptote if the curve approaches the line more and more closely as x approaches a, and the values of the function increase or decrease without bound as x approaches a

horizontal asymptote

• describes the behaviour of a graph when $\lvert x \rvert$ is very large

• the line $y = b$ is a horizontal asymptote if the values of the function approach b when $\lvert x \rvert$ is very large

Your Turn

Create a table of values and sketch the graphs of $y = f(x)$ and its reciprocal $y = \dfrac{1}{f(x)}$, where $f(x) = -x$. Examine how the functions are related.

Example 2

Graph the Reciprocal of a Linear Function

Consider $f(x) = 2x + 5$.

a) Determine its reciprocal function $y = \dfrac{1}{f(x)}$.

b) Determine the equation of the vertical asymptote of the reciprocal function.

c) Graph the function $y = f(x)$ and its reciprocal function $y = \dfrac{1}{f(x)}$.

Describe a strategy that could be used to sketch the graph of a reciprocal function.

Solution

a) The reciprocal function is $y = \dfrac{1}{2x + 5}$.

b) A vertical asymptote occurs at any non-permissible values of the corresponding rational expression $\dfrac{1}{2x + 5}$.

To determine non-permissible values, set the denominator equal to 0 and solve.

$2x + 5 = 0$ How are the zeros of the function $f(x) = 2x + 5$
$\quad 2x = -5$ related to the vertical asymptotes of its reciprocal
$\quad\quad x = -\dfrac{5}{2}$ function $y = \dfrac{1}{2x + 5}$?

The non-permissible value is $x = -\dfrac{5}{2}$.

In the domain of the rational expression $\dfrac{1}{2x + 5}$, $x \neq -\dfrac{5}{2}$.

The reciprocal function is undefined at this value, and its graph has a vertical asymptote with equation $x = -\dfrac{5}{2}$.

c) Method 1: Use Pencil and Paper

To sketch the graph of the function $f(x) = 2x + 5$, use the y-intercept of 5 and slope of 2.

To sketch the graph of the reciprocal of a function, consider the following characteristics:

Characteristic	Function $f(x) = 2x + 5$	Reciprocal Function $f(x) = \dfrac{1}{2x + 5}$
x-intercept and asymptotes	• The value of the function is zero at $x = -\dfrac{5}{2}$.	• The value of the reciprocal function is undefined at $x = -\dfrac{5}{2}$. A vertical asymptote exists.
Invariant points	• Solve $2x + 5 = 1$. • The value of the function is $+1$ at $(-2, 1)$.	• Solve $\dfrac{1}{2x + 5} = 1$. • The value of the reciprocal function is $+1$ at $(-2, 1)$.
	• Solve $2x + 5 = -1$. • The value of the function is -1 at $(-3, -1)$.	• Solve $\dfrac{1}{2x + 5} = -1$. • The value of the reciprocal function is -1 at $(-3, -1)$.

The graphs of $y = 2x + 5$ and $y = \dfrac{1}{2x + 5}$ are shown.

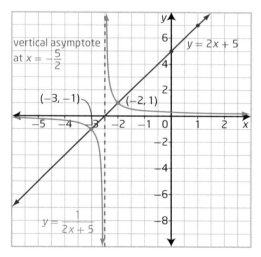

Method 2: Use a Graphing Calculator

Graph the functions using a graphing calculator.

Enter the functions as $y = 2x + 5$ and $y = \dfrac{1}{2x + 5}$ or as $y = f(x)$

and $y = \dfrac{1}{f(x)}$, where $f(x)$ has been defined as $f(x) = 2x + 5$.

Ensure that both branches of the reciprocal function are visible.

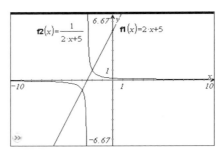

How can you determine if the window settings you chose are the most appropriate?

What are the asymptotes? How do you know?

Use the calculator's value and zero features to verify the invariant points and the y-intercept.

Use the table feature on the calculator
- to see the nature of the ordered pairs that exist when a function and its reciprocal are graphed
- to compare the two functions in terms of values remaining positive or negative or values of y increasing or decreasing
- to see what happens to the reciprocal function as the absolute values of x get very large or very small

x	f1(x):= 2*x+5	f2(x):= 1/(2*x+5)
0.	5.	0.2
1.	7.	0.142857
2.	9.	0.111111
3.	11.	0.090909
4.	13.	0.076923
5.	15.	0.066667

$f1(x):=2 \cdot x+5$

Your Turn

Consider $f(x) = 3x - 9$.

a) Determine its reciprocal function $y = \dfrac{1}{f(x)}$.

b) Determine the equation of the vertical asymptote of the reciprocal function.

c) Graph the function $y = f(x)$ and its reciprocal function $y = \dfrac{1}{f(x)}$, with and without technology. Discuss the behaviour of $y = \dfrac{1}{f(x)}$ as it nears its asymptotes.

Example 3

Graph the Reciprocal of a Quadratic Function

Consider $f(x) = x^2 - 4$.
a) What is the reciprocal function of $f(x)$?
b) State the non-permissible values of x and the equation(s) of the vertical asymptote(s) of the reciprocal function.
c) What are the x-intercepts and the y-intercept of the reciprocal function?
d) Graph the function $y = f(x)$ and its reciprocal function $y = \dfrac{1}{f(x)}$.

Solution

a) The reciprocal function is $y = \dfrac{1}{x^2 - 4}$.

b) Non-permissible values of x occur when the denominator of the corresponding rational expression is equal to 0.

$$x^2 - 4 = 0$$
$$(x - 2)(x + 2) = 0$$
$$x - 2 = 0 \quad \text{or} \quad x + 2 = 0$$
$$x = 2 \qquad\qquad x = -2$$

The non-permissible values of the corresponding rational expression are $x = 2$ and $x = -2$.

The reciprocal function is undefined at these values, so its graph has vertical asymptotes with equations $x = 2$ and $x = -2$.

c) To find the x-intercepts of the function $y = \dfrac{1}{x^2 - 4}$, let $y = 0$.

$$0 = \dfrac{1}{x^2 - 4}$$

There is no value of x that makes this equation true. Therefore, there are no x-intercepts.

To find the y-intercept, substitute 0 for x.

$$y = \dfrac{1}{0^2 - 4}$$
$$y = -\dfrac{1}{4}$$

The y-intercept is $-\dfrac{1}{4}$.

d) **Method 1: Use Pencil and Paper**
For $f(x) = x^2 - 4$, the coordinates of the vertex are $(0, -4)$.
The x-intercepts occur at $(-2, 0)$ and $(2, 0)$.

Use this information to plot the graph of $f(x)$.

To sketch the graph of the reciprocal function,
- Draw the asymptotes.
- Plot the invariant points where $f(x) = \pm 1$. The exact locations of the invariant points can be found by solving $x^2 - 4 = \pm 1$.

  Solving $x^2 - 4 = 1$ results in the points $(\sqrt{5}, 1)$ and $(-\sqrt{5}, 1)$.
  Solving $x^2 - 4 = -1$ results in the points $(\sqrt{3}, -1)$ and $(-\sqrt{3}, -1)$.

- The y-coordinates of the points on the graph of the reciprocal function are the reciprocals of the y-coordinates of the corresponding points on the graph of $f(x)$.

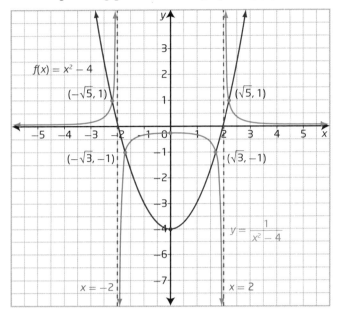

Method 2: Use a Graphing Calculator

Enter the functions $y = x^2 - 4$ and $y = \dfrac{1}{x^2 - 4}$.

Adjust the window settings so that the vertex and intercepts of $y = x^2 - 4$ are visible, if necessary.

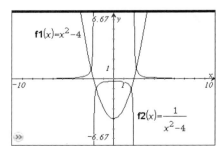

Your Turn

Consider $f(x) = x^2 + x - 6$.

a) What is the reciprocal function of $f(x)$?

b) State the non-permissible values of x and the equation(s) of the vertical asymptote(s) of the reciprocal function.

c) What are the x-intercepts and the y-intercept of the reciprocal function?

d) Sketch the graphs of $y = f(x)$ and its reciprocal function $y = \dfrac{1}{f(x)}$.

Example 4

Graph $y = f(x)$ Given the Graph of $y = \dfrac{1}{f(x)}$

The graph of a reciprocal function of the form $y = \dfrac{1}{ax + b}$, where a and b are non-zero constants, is shown.

a) Sketch the graph of the original function, $y = f(x)$.

b) Determine the original function, $y = f(x)$.

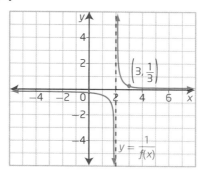

Solution

a) Since $y = \dfrac{1}{f(x)} = \dfrac{1}{ax + b}$, the original function is of the form $f(x) = ax + b$, which is a linear function. The reciprocal graph has a vertical asymptote at $x = 2$, so the graph of $y = f(x)$ has an x-intercept at $(2, 0)$. Since $\left(3, \dfrac{1}{3}\right)$ is a point on the graph of $y = \dfrac{1}{f(x)}$, the point $(3, 3)$ must be on the graph of $y = f(x)$.

Draw a line passing through $(2, 0)$ and $(3, 3)$.

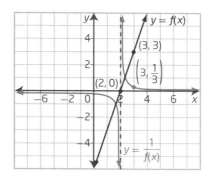

b) Method 1: Use the Slope and the y-Intercept

Write the function in the form $y = mx + b$. Use the coordinates of the two known points, $(2, 0)$ and $(3, 3)$, to determine that the slope, m, is 3. Substitute the coordinates of one of the points into $y = 3x + b$ and solve for b.

$b = -6$

The original function is $f(x) = 3x - 6$.

Method 2: Use the x-Intercept

With an x-intercept of 2, the function $f(x)$ is based on the factor $x - 2$, but it could be a multiple of that factor.

$f(x) = a(x - 2)$

Use the point $(3, 3)$ to find the value of a.

$3 = a(3 - 2)$
$3 = a$

The original function is $f(x) = 3(x - 2)$, or $f(x) = 3x - 6$.

Your Turn

The graph of a reciprocal function of the form $y = \dfrac{1}{f(x)} = \dfrac{1}{ax + b}$, where a and b are non-zero constants, is shown.

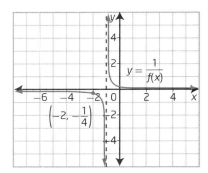

a) Sketch the graph of the original function, $y = f(x)$.

b) Determine the original function, $y = f(x)$.

Key Ideas

- If $f(x) = x$, then $\dfrac{1}{f(x)} = \dfrac{1}{x}$, where $\dfrac{1}{f(x)}$ denotes a reciprocal function.

- You can obtain the graph of $y = \dfrac{1}{f(x)}$ from the graph of $y = f(x)$ by using the following guidelines:

  - The non-permissible values of the reciprocal function are related to the position of the vertical asymptotes. These are also the non-permissible values of the corresponding rational expression, where the reciprocal function is undefined.

  - Invariant points occur when the function $f(x)$ has a value of 1 or −1. To determine the x-coordinates of the invariant points, solve the equations $f(x) = \pm 1$.

  - The y-coordinates of the points on the graph of the reciprocal function are the reciprocals of the y-coordinates of the corresponding points on the graph of $y = f(x)$.

  - As the value of x approaches a non-permissible value, the absolute value of the reciprocal function gets very large.

  - As the absolute value of x gets very large, the absolute value of the reciprocal function approaches zero.

- The domain of the reciprocal function is the same as the domain of the original function, excluding the non-permissible values.

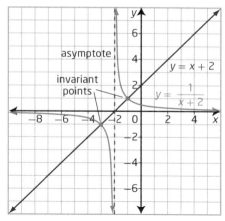

Practise

1. Given the function $y = f(x)$, write the corresponding reciprocal function.

a) $y = -x + 2$

b) $y = 3x - 5$

c) $y = x^2 - 9$

d) $y = x^2 - 7x + 10$

2. For each function,

i) state the zeros

ii) write the reciprocal function

iii) state the non-permissible values of the corresponding rational expression

iv) explain how the zeros of the original function are related to the non-permissible values of the reciprocal function

v) state the equation(s) of the vertical asymptote(s)

a) $f(x) = x + 5$ **b)** $g(x) = 2x + 1$

c) $h(x) = x^2 - 16$ **d)** $t(x) = x^2 + x - 12$

3. State the equation(s) of the vertical asymptote(s) for each function.

a) $f(x) = \dfrac{1}{5x - 10}$

b) $f(x) = \dfrac{1}{3x + 7}$

c) $f(x) = \dfrac{1}{(x - 2)(x + 4)}$

d) $f(x) = \dfrac{1}{x^2 - 9x + 20}$

4. The calculator screen gives a function table for $f(x) = \dfrac{1}{x - 3}$. Explain why there is an undefined statement.

x	f1(x):= ▼
	1/(x−3)
0.	−0.3333...
1.	−0.5
2.	−1.
3.	#UNDEF
4.	1.

5. What are the x-intercept(s) and the y-intercept of each function?

a) $f(x) = \dfrac{1}{x + 5}$

b) $f(x) = \dfrac{1}{3x - 4}$

c) $f(x) = \dfrac{1}{x^2 - 9}$

d) $f(x) = \dfrac{1}{x^2 + 7x + 12}$

6. Copy each graph of $y = f(x)$, and sketch the graph of the reciprocal function $y = \dfrac{1}{f(x)}$. Describe your method.

a)

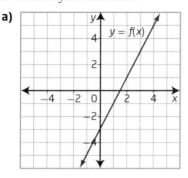

b)

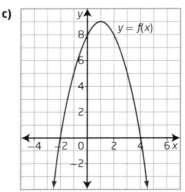

c)

7. Sketch the graphs of $y = f(x)$ and $y = \dfrac{1}{f(x)}$ on the same set of axes. Label the asymptotes, the invariant points, and the intercepts.

a) $f(x) = x - 16$

b) $f(x) = 2x + 4$

c) $f(x) = 2x - 6$

d) $f(x) = x - 1$

8. Sketch the graphs of $y = f(x)$ and $y = \dfrac{1}{f(x)}$ on the same set of axes. Label the asymptotes, the invariant points, and the intercepts.

a) $f(x) = x^2 - 16$

b) $f(x) = x^2 - 2x - 8$

c) $f(x) = x^2 - x - 2$

d) $f(x) = x^2 + 2$

9. Match the graph of the function with the graph of its reciprocal.

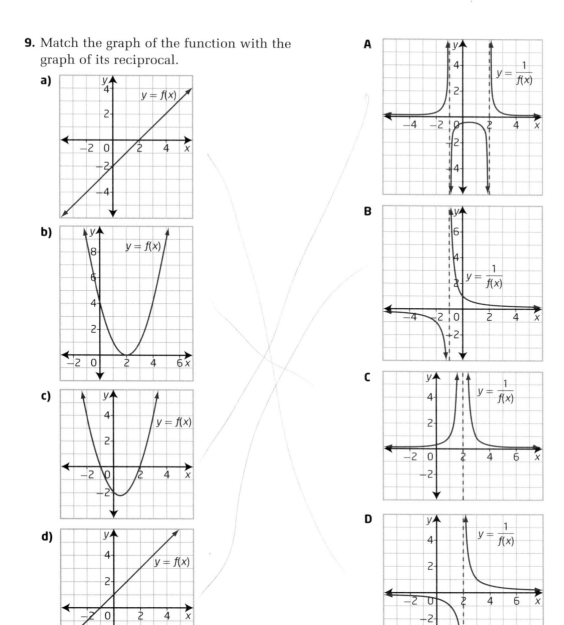

a)

b)

c)

d)

A

B

C

D

Apply

10. Each of the following is the graph of a reciprocal function, $y = \dfrac{1}{f(x)}$.

   i) Sketch the graph of the original function, $y = f(x)$.

   ii) Explain the strategies you used.

   iii) What is the original function, $y = f(x)$?

a)

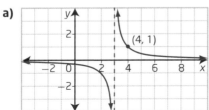

b)

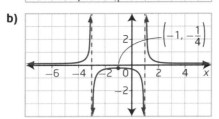

11. You can model the swinging motion of a pendulum using many mathematical rules. For example, the frequency, f, or number of vibrations per second of one swing, in hertz (Hz), equals the reciprocal of the period, T, in seconds, of the swing. The formula is $f = \dfrac{1}{T}$.

   a) Sketch the graph of the function $f = \dfrac{1}{T}$.

   b) What is the reciprocal function?

   c) Determine the frequency of a pendulum with a period of 2.5 s.

   d) What is the period of a pendulum with a frequency of 1.6 Hz?

> **Did You Know?**
>
> Much of the mathematics of pendulum motion was described by Galileo, based on his curiosity about a swinging lamp in the Cathedral of Pisa, Italy. His work led to much more accurate measurement of time on clocks.

12. The greatest amount of time, t, in minutes, that a scuba diver can take to rise toward the water surface without stopping for decompression is defined by the function

$$t = \frac{525}{d - 10},$$ where d is the depth, in metres, of the diver.

   a) Graph the function using graphing technology.

   b) Determine a suitable domain which represents this application.

   c) Determine the maximum time without stopping for a scuba diver who is 40 m deep.

   d) Graph a second function, $t = 40$. Find the intersection point of the two graphs. Interpret this point in terms of the scuba diver rising to the surface. Check this result algebraically with the original function.

   e) Does this graph have a horizontal asymptote? What does this mean with respect to the scuba diver?

> **Did You Know?**
>
> If scuba divers rise to the water surface too quickly, they may experience decompression sickness or *the bends*, which is caused by breathing nitrogen or other gases under pressure. The nitrogen bubbles are released into the bloodstream and obstruct blood flow, causing joint pain.

13. The pitch, p, in hertz (Hz), of a musical note is the reciprocal of the period, P, in seconds, of the sound wave for that note created by the air vibrations.

  a) Write a function for pitch, p, in terms of period, P.

  b) Sketch the graph of the function.

  c) What is the pitch, to the nearest 0.1 Hz, for a musical note with period 0.048 s?

14. The intensity, I, in watts per square metre (W/m²), of a sound equals 0.004 multiplied by the reciprocal of the square of the distance, d, in metres, from the source of the sound.

  a) Write a function for I in terms of d to represent this relationship.

  b) Graph this function for a domain of $d > 0$.

  c) What is the intensity of a car horn for a person standing 5 m from the car?

15. a) Describe how to find the vertex of the parabola defined by $f(x) = x^2 - 6x - 7$.

  b) Explain how knowing the vertex in part a) would help you to graph the function $g(x) = \dfrac{1}{x^2 - 6x - 7}$.

  c) Sketch the graph of $g(x) = \dfrac{1}{x^2 - 6x - 7}$.

16. The amount of time, t, to complete a large job is proportional to the reciprocal of the number of workers, n, on the job. This can be expressed as $t = k\left(\dfrac{1}{n}\right)$ or $t = \dfrac{k}{n}$, where k is a constant. For example, the Spiral Tunnels built by the Canadian Pacific Railroad in Kicking Horse Pass, British Columbia, were a major engineering feat when they opened in 1909. Building two spiral tracks each about 1 km long required 1000 workers to work about 720 days. Suppose that each worker performed a similar type of work.

  a) Substitute the given values of t and n into the formula to find the constant k.

  b) Use technology to graph the function $t = \dfrac{k}{n}$.

  c) How much time would have been required to complete the Spiral Tunnels if only 400 workers were on the job?

  d) Determine the number of workers needed if the job was to be completed in 500 days.

Did You Know?

Kicking Horse Pass is in Yoho National Park. *Yoho* is a Cree word meaning great awe or astonishment. This may be a reference to the soaring peaks, the rock walls, and the spectacular Takakkaw Falls nearby.

Extend

17. Use the summary of information to produce the graphs of both $y = f(x)$ and $y = \dfrac{1}{f(x)}$, given that $f(x)$ is a linear function.

Interval of x	$x < 3$	$x > 3$
Sign of $f(x)$	+	−
Direction of $f(x)$	decreasing	decreasing
Sign of $\dfrac{1}{f(x)}$	+	−
Direction of $\dfrac{1}{f(x)}$	increasing	increasing

18. Determine whether each statement is true or false, and explain your reasoning.

a) The graph of $y = \dfrac{1}{f(x)}$ always has a vertical asymptote.

b) A function in the form of $y = \dfrac{1}{f(x)}$ always has at least one value for which it is not defined.

c) The domain of $y = \dfrac{1}{f(x)}$ is always the same as the domain of $y = f(x)$.

Create Connections

19. Rita and Jerry are discussing how to determine the asymptotes of the reciprocal of a given function. Rita concludes that you can determine the roots of the corresponding equation, and those values will lead to the equations of the asymptotes. Jerry assumes that when the function is written in rational form, you can determine the non-permissible values. The non-permissible values will lead to the equations of the asymptotes.

a) Which student has made a correct assumption? Explain your choice.

b) Is this true for both a linear and a quadratic function?

20. The diagram shows how an object forms an inverted image on the opposite side of a convex lens, as in many cameras. Scientists discovered the relationship

$$\frac{1}{u} + \frac{1}{v} = \frac{1}{f}$$

where u is the distance from the object to the lens, v is the distance from the lens to the image, and f is the focal length of the lens being used.

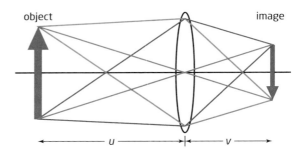

a) Determine the distance, v, between the lens and the image if the distance, u, to the object is 300 mm and the lens has a focal length, f, of 50 mm.

b) Determine the focal length of a zoom lens if an object 10 000 mm away produces an inverted image 210 mm behind the lens.

21. MINI LAB Use technology to explore the behaviour of a graph near the vertical asymptote and the end behaviour of the graph.

Consider the function
$$f(x) = \frac{1}{4x - 2}, \; x \neq \frac{1}{2}.$$

Step 1 Sketch the graph of the function $f(x) = \dfrac{1}{4x - 2}, \; x \neq \dfrac{1}{2}$, drawing in the vertical asymptote.

Step 2 a) Copy and complete the tables to show the behaviour of the function as $x \to \left(\dfrac{1}{2}\right)^{-}$ and as $x \to \left(\dfrac{1}{2}\right)^{+}$, meaning when x approaches $\dfrac{1}{2}$ from the left $(-)$ and from the right $(+)$.

As $x \to \left(\dfrac{1}{2}\right)^{-}$:   As $x \to \left(\dfrac{1}{2}\right)^{+}$:

x	f(x)
0	−0.5
0.4	
0.45	
0.47	
0.49	
0.495	
0.499	

x	f(x)
1	0.5
0.6	
0.55	
0.53	
0.51	
0.505	
0.501	

b) Describe the behaviour of the function as the value of x approaches the asymptote. Will this always happen?

Step 3 a) To explore the end behaviour of the function, the absolute value of x is made larger and larger. Copy and complete the tables for values of x that are farther and farther from zero.

As x becomes smaller:

x	f(x)
−10	$-\dfrac{1}{42}$
−100	
−1000	
−10 000	
−100 000	

As x becomes larger:

x	f(x)
10	$\dfrac{1}{38}$
100	
1 000	
10 000	
100 000	

b) Describe what happens to the graph of the reciprocal function as $|x|$ becomes very large.

22. Copy and complete the flowchart to describe the relationship between a function and its corresponding reciprocal function.

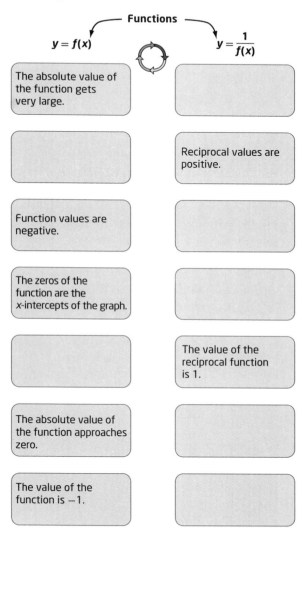

Chapter 7 Review

7.1 Absolute Value, pages 358–367

1. Evaluate.

  a) $|-5|$ **b)** $\left|2\frac{3}{4}\right|$ **c)** $|-6.7|$

2. Rearrange these numbers in order from least to greatest.

$$-4,\ \sqrt{9},\ |-3.5|,\ -2.7,\ \left|-\frac{9}{2}\right|,\ |-1.6|,\ \left|1\frac{1}{2}\right|$$

3. Evaluate each expression.

  a) $|-7 - 2|$

  b) $|-3 + 11 - 6|$

  c) $5|-3.75|$

  d) $|5^2 - 7| + |-10 + 2^3|$

4. A school group travels to Mt. Robson Provincial Park in British Columbia to hike the Berg Lake Trail. From the Robson River bridge, kilometre 0.0, they hike to Kinney Lake, kilometre 4.2, where they stop for lunch. They then trek across the suspension bridge to the campground, kilometre 10.5. The next day they hike to the shore of Berg Lake and camp, kilometre 19.6. On day three, they hike to the Alberta/British Columbia border, kilometre 21.9, and turn around and return to the campground near Emperor Falls, kilometre 15.0. On the final day, they walk back out to the trailhead, kilometre 0.0. What total distance did the school group hike?

5. Over the course of five weekdays, one mining stock on the Toronto Stock Exchange (TSX) closed at $4.28 on Monday, closed higher at $5.17 on Tuesday, finished Wednesday at $4.79, and shot up to close at $7.15 on Thursday, only to finish the week at $6.40.

  a) What is the net change in the closing value of this stock for the week?

  b) Determine the total change in the closing value of the stock.

7.2 Absolute Value Functions, pages 368–379

6. Consider the functions $f(x) = 5x + 2$ and $g(x) = |5x + 2|$.

  a) Create a table of values for each function, using values of $-2, -1, 0, 1$, and 2 for x.

  b) Plot the points and sketch the graphs of the functions on the same coordinate grid.

  c) Determine the domain and range for both $f(x)$ and $g(x)$.

  d) List the similarities and the differences between the two functions and their corresponding graphs.

7. Consider the functions $f(x) = 8 - x^2$ and $g(x) = |8 - x^2|$.

  a) Create a table of values for each function, using values of $-2, -1, 0, 1$, and 2 for x.

  b) Plot the points and sketch the graphs of the functions on the same coordinate grid.

  c) Determine the domain and range for both $f(x)$ and $g(x)$.

  d) List the similarities and the differences between the two functions and their corresponding graphs.

8. Write the piecewise function that represents each graph.

a)

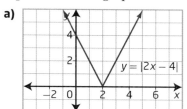

$y = |2x - 4|$

b)

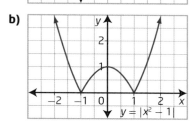

$y = |x^2 - 1|$

9. a) Explain why the functions $f(x) = 3x^2 + 7x + 2$ and $g(x) = |3x^2 + 7x + 2|$ have different graphs.

b) Explain why the functions $f(x) = 3x^2 + 4x + 2$ and $g(x) = |3x^2 + 4x + 2|$ have identical graphs.

10. An absolute value function has the form $f(x) = |ax + b|$, where $a \neq 0$, $b \neq 0$, and $a, b \in \mathbb{R}$. If the function $f(x)$ has a domain of $\{x \mid x \in \mathbb{R}\}$, a range of $\{y \mid y \geq 0, y \in \mathbb{R}\}$, an x-intercept occurring at $\left(-\frac{2}{3}, 0\right)$, and a y-intercept occurring at $(0, 10)$, what are the values of a and b?

7.3 Absolute Value Equations, pages 380–391

11. Solve each absolute value equation graphically. Express answers to the nearest tenth, when necessary.

a) $|2x - 2| = 9$

b) $|7 + 3x| = x - 1$

c) $|x^2 - 6| = 3$

d) $|m^2 - 4m| = 5$

12. Solve each equation algebraically.

a) $|q + 9| = 2$

b) $|7x - 3| = x + 1$

c) $|x^2 - 6x| = x$

d) $3x - 1 = |4x^2 - x - 4|$

13. In coastal communities, the depth, d, in metres, of water in the harbour varies during the day according to the tides. The maximum depth of the water occurs at high tide and the minimum occurs at low tide. Two low tides and two high tides will generally occur over a 24-h period. On one particular day in Prince Rupert, British Columbia, the depth of the first high tide and the first low tide can be determined using the equation $|d - 4.075| = 1.665$.

a) Find the depth of the water, in metres, at the first high tide and the first low tide in Prince Rupert on this day.

b) Suppose the low tide and high tide depths for Prince Rupert on the next day are 2.94 m, 5.71 m, 2.28 m, and 4.58 m. Determine the total change in water depth that day.

14. The mass, m, in kilograms, of a bushel of wheat depends on its moisture content. Dry wheat has moisture content as low as 5% and wet wheat has moisture content as high as 50%. The equation $|m - 35.932| = 11.152$ can be used to find the extreme masses for both a dry and a wet bushel of wheat. What are these two masses?

7.4 Reciprocal Functions, pages 392–409

15. Copy each graph of $y = f(x)$ and sketch the graph of the corresponding reciprocal function, $y = \dfrac{1}{f(x)}$. Label the asymptotes, the invariant points, and the intercepts.

a)

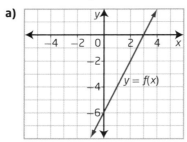

b)

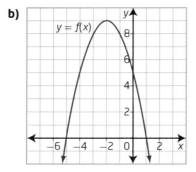

16. Sketch the graphs of $y = f(x)$ and $y = \dfrac{1}{f(x)}$ on the same set of axes. Label the asymptotes, the invariant points, and the intercepts.

a) $f(x) = 4x - 9$ **b)** $f(x) = 2x + 5$

17. For each function,

  i) determine the corresponding reciprocal function, $y = \dfrac{1}{f(x)}$

  ii) state the non-permissible values of x and the equation(s) of the vertical asymptote(s) of the reciprocal function

  iii) determine the x-intercepts and the y-intercept of the reciprocal function

  iv) sketch the graphs of $y = f(x)$ and $y = \dfrac{1}{f(x)}$ on the same set of axes

  a) $f(x) = x^2 - 25$

  b) $f(x) = x^2 - 6x + 5$

18. The force, F, in newtons (N), required to lift an object with a lever is proportional to the reciprocal of the distance, d, in metres, of the force from the fulcrum of a lever. The fulcrum is the point on which a lever pivots. Suppose this relationship can be modelled by the function $F = \dfrac{600}{d}$.

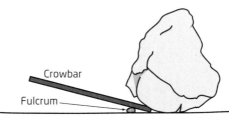

a) Determine the force required to lift an object if the force is applied 2.5 m from the fulcrum.

b) Determine the distance from the fulcrum of a 450-N force applied to lift an object.

c) How does the force needed to lift an object change if the distance from the fulcrum is doubled? tripled?

Chapter 7 Practice Test

Multiple Choice

For #1 to #5, choose the best answer.

1. The value of the expression
   $|-9 - 3| - |5 - 2^3| + |-7 + 1 - 4|$ is

   A 13

   B 19

   C 21

   D 25

2. The range of the function $f(x) = |x - 3|$ is

   A $\{y \mid y > 3, y \in R\}$

   B $\{y \mid y \geq 3, y \in R\}$

   C $\{y \mid y \geq 0, y \in R\}$

   D $\{y \mid y > 0, y \in R\}$

3. The absolute value equation $|1 - 2x| = 9$
   has solution(s)

   A $x = -4$

   B $x = 5$

   C $x = -5$ and $x = 4$

   D $x = -4$ and $x = 5$

4. The graph represents the reciprocal of
   which quadratic function?

   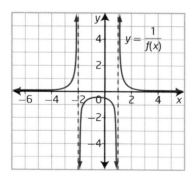

   A $f(x) = x^2 + x - 2$

   B $f(x) = x^2 - 3x + 2$

   C $f(x) = x^2 - x - 2$

   D $f(x) = x^2 + 3x + 2$

5. One of the vertical asymptotes of the graph
   of the reciprocal function $y = \dfrac{1}{x^2 - 16}$
   has equation

   A $x = 0$

   B $x = 4$

   C $x = 8$

   D $x = 16$

Short Answer

6. Consider the function $f(x) = |2x - 7|$.

   a) Sketch the graph of the function.

   b) Determine the intercepts.

   c) State the domain and range.

   d) What is the piecewise notation form of
   the function?

7. Solve the equation $|3x^2 - x| = 4x - 2$
   algebraically.

8. Solve the equation $|2w - 3| = w + 1$
   graphically.

Extended Response

9. Determine the error(s) in the following
   solution. Explain how to correct the
   solution.

   Solve $|x - 4| = x^2 + 4x$.

   Case 1

   $x + 4 = x^2 + 4x$

   $0 = x^2 + 3x - 4$

   $0 = (x + 4)(x - 1)$

   $x + 4 = 0 \quad$ or $\quad x - 1 = 0$

   $x = -4 \quad$ or $\qquad x = 1$

   Case 2

   $-x - 4 = x^2 + 4x$

   $0 = x^2 + 5x + 4$

   $0 = (x + 4)(x + 1)$

   $x + 4 = 0 \quad$ or $\quad x + 1 = 0$

   $x = -4 \quad$ or $\qquad x = -1$

   The solutions are $x = -4$, $x = -1$,
   and $x = 1$.

10. Consider the function $f(x) = 6 - 5x$.

   a) Determine its reciprocal function.

   b) State the equations of any vertical asymptotes of the reciprocal function.

   c) Graph the function $f(x)$ and its reciprocal function. Describe a strategy that could be used to sketch the graph of any reciprocal function.

11. A biologist studying Canada geese migration analysed the vee flight formation of a particular flock using a coordinate system, in metres. The centre of each bird was assigned a coordinate point. The lead bird has the coordinates $(0, 0)$, and the coordinates of two birds at the ends of each leg are $(6.2, 15.5)$ and $(-6.2, 15.5)$.

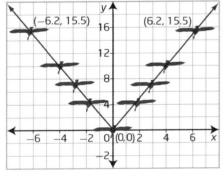

Bottom View of Flying Geese

   a) Write an absolute value function whose graph contains each leg of the vee formation.

   b) What is the angle between the legs of the vee formation, to the nearest tenth of a degree?

   c) The absolute value function $y = |2.8x|$ describes the flight pattern of a different flock of geese. What is the angle between the legs of this vee formation, to the nearest tenth of a degree?

12. Astronauts in space feel lighter because weight decreases as a person moves away from the gravitational pull of Earth. Weight, W_h, in newtons (N), at a particular height, h, in kilometres, above Earth is related to the reciprocal of that height by the formula $W_h = \dfrac{W_e}{\left(\dfrac{h}{6400} + 1\right)^2}$, where W_e is the person's weight, in newtons (N), at sea level on Earth.

Canadian astronauts Julie Payette and Bob Thirsk

   a) Sketch the graph of the function for an astronaut whose weight is 750 N at sea level.

   b) Determine this astronaut's weight at a height of
     i) 8 km   **ii)** 2000 km

   c) Determine the range of heights for which this astronaut will have a weight of less than 30 N.

Did You Know?

When people go into space, their mass remains constant but their weight decreases because of the reduced gravity.

Space: Past, Present, Future

Complete at least one of the following options.

Option 1

Research a radical equation or a formula related to space exploration or the historical contributions of an astronomer.

- Search the Internet for an equation or a formula involving radicals that is related to motion or distance in space or for an astronomer whose work led to discoveries in these areas.

- Research the formula to determine why it involves a radical, or research the mathematics behind the astronomer's discovery.

- Prepare a poster for your topic choice. Your poster should include the following:
  - background information on the astronomer or the origin of the radical equation you are presenting
  - an explanation of the mathematics involved and how the formula relates to distance or motion in space
  - sources of all materials you used in your research

Option 2

Research rational expressions related to space anomalies.

- Search the Internet for a rational expression that is related to space-time, black holes, solar activity, or another space-related topic.

- Research the topic to determine why it involves a rational expression.

- Write a one-page report on your topic choice, including the following:
  - a brief description of the space anomaly you chose and its significance
  - identification of the rational expression you are using
  - an explanation of the mathematics involved and how it helps to model the anomaly
  - sources of all research used in your report

Option 3

A company specializing in space tourism to various regions of the galaxy is sponsoring a logo design contest. The winner gets a free ticket to the destination of his or her choice.

- The company's current logo is made up of the following absolute value functions and reciprocal functions.
  - $y = -|x| + 6, -6 \le x \le 6$
  - $y = |2x|, -2 \le x \le 2$
  - $y = \dfrac{1}{x^2 - 4}, -1.95 \le x \le 1.95$
  - $y = -\dfrac{1}{x^2}, -1 \le x \le -0.5$ and $0.5 \le x \le 1$

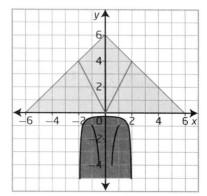

- Design a new logo for this company.

- The logo must include both reciprocal functions and absolute value functions.

- Draw your logo. List the functions you use, as well as the domains necessary for the logo.

Chapter 5 Radical Expressions and Equations

1. Express $3xy^3\sqrt{2x}$ as an entire radical.

2. Express $\sqrt{48a^3b^2c^5}$ as a simplified mixed radical.

3. Order the set of numbers from least to greatest.

$$3\sqrt{6},\ \sqrt{36},\ 2\sqrt{3},\ \sqrt{18},\ 2\sqrt{9},\ \sqrt[3]{8}$$

4. Simplify each expression. Identify any restrictions on the values for the variables.

a) $4\sqrt{2a} + 5\sqrt{2a}$

b) $10\sqrt{20x^2} - 3x\sqrt{45}$

5. Simplify. Identify any restrictions on the values of the variable in part c).

a) $2\sqrt[3]{4}(-4\sqrt[3]{6})$

b) $\sqrt{6}(\sqrt{12} - \sqrt{3})$

c) $(6\sqrt{a} + \sqrt{3})(2\sqrt{a} - \sqrt{4})$

6. Rationalize each denominator.

a) $\dfrac{\sqrt{12}}{\sqrt{4}}$

b) $\dfrac{2}{2 + \sqrt{3}}$

c) $\dfrac{\sqrt{7} + \sqrt{28}}{\sqrt{7} - \sqrt{14}}$

7. Solve the radical equation $\sqrt{x + 6} = x$. Verify your answers.

8. On a children's roller coaster ride, the speed in a loop depends on the height of the hill the car has just come down and the radius of the loop. The velocity, v, in feet per second, of a car at the top of a loop of radius, r, in feet, is given by the formula $v = \sqrt{h - 2r}$, where h is the height of the previous hill, in feet.

a) Find the height of the hill when the velocity at the top of the loop is 20 ft/s and the radius of the loop is 15 ft.

b) Would you expect the velocity of the car to increase or decrease as the radius of the loop increases? Explain your reasoning.

Chapter 6 Rational Expressions and Equations

9. Simplify each expression. Identify any non-permissible values.

a) $\dfrac{12a^3b}{48a^2b^4}$

b) $\dfrac{4 - x}{x^2 - 8x + 16}$

c) $\dfrac{(x - 3)(x + 5)}{x^2 - 1} \div \dfrac{x + 2}{x - 3}$

d) $\dfrac{5x - 10}{6x} \times \dfrac{3x}{15x - 30}$

e) $\left(\dfrac{x + 2}{x - 3}\right)\left(\dfrac{x^2 - 9}{x^2 - 4}\right) \div \left(\dfrac{x + 3}{x - 2}\right)$

10. Determine the sum or difference. Express answers in lowest terms. Identify any non-permissible values.

a) $\dfrac{10}{a + 2} + \dfrac{a - 1}{a - 7}$

b) $\dfrac{3x + 2}{x + 4} - \dfrac{x - 5}{x^2 - 4}$

c) $\dfrac{2x}{x^2 - 25} - \dfrac{3}{x^2 - 4x - 5}$

11. Sandra simplified the expression $\dfrac{(x + 2)(x + 5)}{x + 5}$ to $x + 2$. She stated that they were equivalent expressions. Do you agree or disagree with Sandra's statement? Provide a reason for your answer.

12. When two triangles are similar, you can use the proportion of corresponding sides to determine an unknown dimension. Solve the rational equation to determine the value of x.

$$\dfrac{x + 4}{4} = \dfrac{x}{3}$$

13. If a point is selected at random from a figure and is equally likely to be any point inside the figure, then the probability that a point is in the shaded region is given by

$$P = \frac{\text{area of shaded region}}{\text{area of entire figure}}$$

What is the probability that the point is in the shaded region?

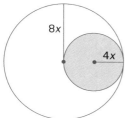

Chapter 7 Absolute Value and Reciprocal Functions

14. Order the values from least to greatest.

$|-5|$, $|4-6|$, $|2(-4)-5|$, $|8.4|$

15. Write the piecewise function that represents each graph.

a)

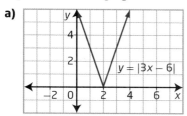

b)

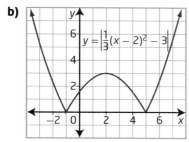

16. For each absolute value function,

i) sketch the graph

ii) determine the intercepts

iii) determine the domain and range

a) $y = |3x - 7|$ **b)** $y = |x^2 - 3x - 4|$

17. Solve algebraically. Verify your solutions.

a) $|2x - 1| = 9$ **b)** $|2x^2 - 5| = 13$

18. The area, A, of a triangle on a coordinate grid with vertices at $(0, 0)$, (a, b), and (c, d) can be calculated using the formula $A = \frac{1}{2}|ad - bc|$.

a) Why do you think absolute value must be used in the formula for area?

b) Determine the area of a triangle with vertices at $(0, 0)$, $(-5, 2)$, and $(-3, 4)$.

19. Sketch the graph of $y = f(x)$ given the graph of $y = \dfrac{1}{f(x)}$. What is the original function, $y = f(x)$?

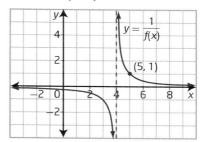

20. Copy the graph of $y = f(x)$, and sketch the graph of the reciprocal function $y = \dfrac{1}{f(x)}$. Discuss your method.

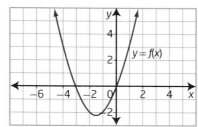

21. Sketch the graph of $y = \dfrac{1}{f(x)}$ given $f(x) = (x + 2)^2$. Label the asymptotes, the invariant points, and the intercepts.

22. Consider the function $f(x) = 3x - 1$.

a) What characteristics of the graph of $y = f(x)$ are different from those of $y = |f(x)|$?

b) Describe how the graph of $y = f(x)$ is different from the graph of $y = \dfrac{1}{f(x)}$.

Unit 3 Test

Multiple Choice

For #1 to #8, choose the best answer.

1. What is the entire radical form of $2(\sqrt[3]{-27})$?

   A $\sqrt[3]{-54}$

   B $\sqrt[3]{-108}$

   C $\sqrt[3]{-216}$

   D $\sqrt[3]{-432}$

2. What is the simplified form of $\dfrac{4\sqrt{72x^5}}{x\sqrt{8}}$, $x > 0$?

   A $\dfrac{12\sqrt{2x^3}}{\sqrt{2}}$

   B $4x\sqrt{3x}$

   C $\dfrac{6\sqrt{2x^3}}{\sqrt{2}}$

   D $12x\sqrt{x}$

3. Determine the root(s) of $x + 2 = \sqrt{x^2 + 3}$.

   A $x = -\dfrac{1}{4}$ and $x = 3$

   B $x = -\dfrac{1}{4}$

   C $x = \dfrac{1}{4}$ and $x = -3$

   D $x = \dfrac{1}{4}$

4. Simplify the rational expression $\dfrac{9x^4 - 27x^6}{3x^3}$ for all permissible values of x.

   A $3x(1 - 3x)$

   B $3x(1 - 9x^5)$

   C $3x - 9x^3$

   D $9x^3 - 9x^4$

5. Which expression could be used to determine the length of the line segment between the points $(4, -3)$ and $(-6, -3)$?

   A $-6 - 4$

   B $4 - 6$

   C $|4 - 6|$

   D $|-6 - 4|$

6. Arrange the expressions $|4 - 11|$, $\frac{1}{5}|-5|$, $\left|1 - \frac{1}{4}\right|$, and $|2| - |4|$ in order from least to greatest.

   A $|4 - 11|$, $\frac{1}{5}|-5|$, $\left|1 - \frac{1}{4}\right|$, $|2| - |4|$

   B $|2| - |4|$, $\left|1 - \frac{1}{4}\right|$, $\frac{1}{5}|-5|$, $|4 - 11|$

   C $|2| - |4|$, $\frac{1}{5}|-5|$, $\left|1 - \frac{1}{4}\right|$, $|4 - 11|$

   D $\left|1 - \frac{1}{4}\right|$, $\frac{1}{5}|-5|$, $|4 - 11|$, $|2| - |4|$

7. Which of the following statements is false?

   A $\sqrt{n}\sqrt{m} = \sqrt{mn}$

   B $\dfrac{\sqrt{18}}{\sqrt{36}} = \sqrt{\dfrac{1}{2}}$

   C $\dfrac{\sqrt{7}}{\sqrt{8n}} = \dfrac{\sqrt{14n}}{4n}$

   D $\sqrt{m^2 + n^2} = m + n$

8. The graph of $y = \dfrac{1}{f(x)}$ has vertical asymptotes at $x = -2$ and $x = 5$ and a horizontal asymptote at $y = 0$. Which of the following statements is possible?

   A $f(x) = (x + 2)(x + 5)$

   B $f(x) = x^2 - 3x - 10$

   C The domain of $f(x)$ is $\{x \mid x \neq -2, x \neq -5, x \in \mathrm{R}\}$.

   D The range of $y = \dfrac{1}{f(x)}$ is $\{y \mid y \in \mathrm{R}\}$.

Numerical Response

Copy and complete the statements in #9 to #13.

9. The radical $\sqrt{3x - 9}$ results in real numbers when $x \geq$ ■.

10. When the denominator of the expression $\dfrac{\sqrt{5}}{3\sqrt{2}}$ is rationalized, the expression becomes ■.

11. The expression $\dfrac{3x - 7}{x + 11} - \dfrac{x - k}{x + 11}$, $x \neq -11$, simplifies to $\dfrac{2x + 21}{x + 11}$ when the value of k is ■.

12. The lesser solution to the absolute value equation $|1 - 4x| = 9$ is $x = $ ■.

13. The graph of the reciprocal function $f(x) = \dfrac{1}{x^2 - 4}$ has vertical asymptotes with equations $x = $ ■ and $x = $ ■.

Written Response

14. Order the numbers from least to greatest.
$3\sqrt{7}, 4\sqrt{5}, 6\sqrt{2}, 5$

15. Consider the equation $\sqrt{3x + 4} = \sqrt{2x - 5}$.

   a) Describe a possible first step to solve the radical equation.

   b) Determine the restrictions on the values for the variable x.

   c) Algebraically determine all roots of the equation.

   d) Verify the solutions by substitution.

16. Simplify the expression
$\dfrac{4x^2 + 4x - 8}{x^2 - 5x + 4} \div \dfrac{2x^2 + 3x - 2}{4x^2 + 8x - 5}$.
List all non-permissible values for the variable.

17. The diagram shows two similar triangles.

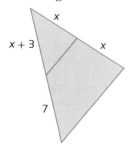

   a) Write a proportion that relates the sides of the similar triangles.

   b) Determine the non-permissible values for the rational equation.

   c) Algebraically determine the value of x that makes the triangles similar.

18. Consider the function $y = |2x - 5|$.

   a) Sketch the graph of the function.

   b) Determine the intercepts.

   c) State the domain and range.

   d) What is the piecewise notation form of the function?

19. Solve $|x^2 - 3x| = 2$. Verify your solutions graphically.

20. Consider $f(x) = x^2 + 2x - 8$. Sketch the graph of $y = f(x)$ and the graph of $y = \dfrac{1}{f(x)}$ on the same set of axes. Label the asymptotes, the invariant points, and the intercepts.

21. In the sport of curling, players measure the "weight" of their shots by timing the stone between two marked lines on the ice, usually the hog lines, which are 72 ft apart. The weight, or average speed, s, of the curling stone is proportional to the reciprocal of the time, t, it takes to travel between hog lines.

Canadian women curlers at 2010 Vancouver Olympics

   a) If $d = 72$, rewrite the formula $d = st$ as a function in terms of s.

   b) What is the weight of a stone that takes 14.5 s to travel between hog lines?

   c) How much time is required for a stone to travel between hog lines if its weight is 6.3 ft/s?

Unit 4

Systems of Equations and Inequalities

Most decisions are much easier when plenty of information is available. In some situations, linear and quadratic equations provide the facts that are needed. Linear and quadratic equations and inequalities are used by aerospace engineers to set launch schedules, by biologists to analyse and predict animal behaviour, by economists to provide advice to businesses, and by athletes to improve their performance. In this unit, you will learn methods for solving systems of linear and quadratic equations and inequalities. You will apply these skills to model and solve problems in real-world situations.

Looking Ahead

In this unit, you will model and solve problems involving...

- systems of linear-quadratic or quadratic-quadratic equations
- linear and quadratic inequalities

Unit 4 Project   Nanotechnology

Nanotechnology is the science of the very small. Scientists manipulate matter on the scale of a nanometre (one billionth of one metre, or 1×10^{-9} m) to make products that are lighter, stronger, cleaner, less expensive, and more precise. With applications in electronics, energy, health, the environment, and many aspects of modern life, nanotechnology will change how everything is designed. In Canada, the National Institute for Nanotechnology (NINT) in Edmonton, Alberta, integrates related research in physics, chemistry, engineering, biology, informatics, pharmacy, and medicine.

In this project, you will choose an object that you feel could be enhanced by nanotechnology. The object will have linear and parabolic design lines.

In Chapter 8, you will design the enhanced version of your object and determine equations that control the shape of your design.

In Chapter 9, you will complete a cost analysis on part of the construction of your object. You will compare the benefits of construction with and without nanotechnology.

At the end of your project, you will
- display your design along with the supporting equations and cost calculations as part of a nanotechnology exhibition
- participate in a gallery walk with the other members of your class

In the Project Corner boxes, you will find information about various uses of nanotechnology. Use this information to help you understand this evolving science and to spark ideas for your design object.

Systems of Equations

What causes that strange feeling in your stomach when you ride a roller coaster? Where do elite athletes get their technical information? How do aerospace engineers determine when and where a rocket will land or what its escape velocity from a planet's surface is? If you start your own business, when can you expect it to make a profit?

The solution to all these questions involves the types of equations that you will work with in this chapter. Systems of equations have applications in science, business, sports, and many other areas, and they are often used as part of a decision-making process.

Did You Know?

An object can take several different orbital paths. To leave a planet's surface, a rocket must reach escape velocity. The escape velocity is the velocity required to establish a parabolic orbit.

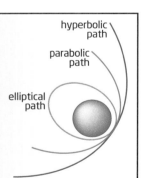

hyperbolic path

parabolic path

elliptical path

Key Terms

system of linear-quadratic equations

system of quadratic-quadratic equations

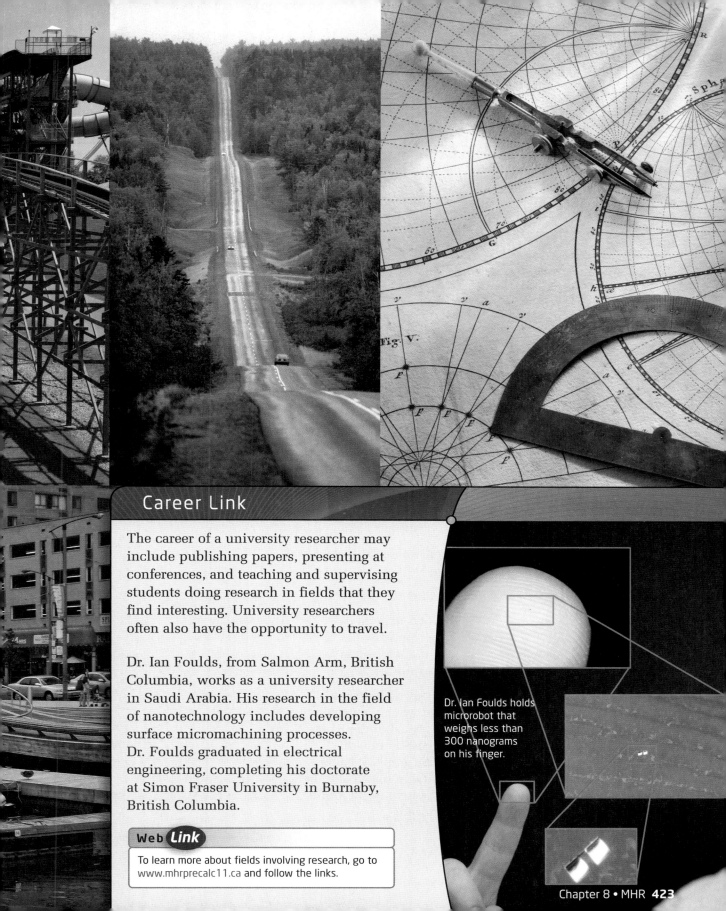

Career Link

The career of a university researcher may include publishing papers, presenting at conferences, and teaching and supervising students doing research in fields that they find interesting. University researchers often also have the opportunity to travel.

Dr. Ian Foulds, from Salmon Arm, British Columbia, works as a university researcher in Saudi Arabia. His research in the field of nanotechnology includes developing surface micromachining processes. Dr. Foulds graduated in electrical engineering, completing his doctorate at Simon Fraser University in Burnaby, British Columbia.

Dr. Ian Foulds holds microrobot that weighs less than 300 nanograms on his finger.

Web Link

To learn more about fields involving research, go to www.mhrprecalc11.ca and follow the links.

Solving Systems of Equations Graphically

Focus on...

- modelling a situation using a system of linear-quadratic or quadratic-quadratic equations
- determining the solution of a system of linear-quadratic or quadratic-quadratic equations graphically
- interpreting points of intersection and the number of solutions of a system of linear-quadratic or quadratic-quadratic equations
- solving a problem that involves a system of linear-quadratic or quadratic-quadratic equations

Companies that produce items to sell on the open market aim to make a maximum profit. When a company has no, or very few, competitors, it controls the marketplace by deciding the price of the item and the quantity sold. The graph in the Investigate below illustrates the relationship between the various aspects that a company must consider when determining the price and quantity. Notice that the curves intersect at a number of points. What do you know about points of intersection on a graph?

Investigate Solving Systems of Equations Graphically

Work with a partner to discuss your findings.

Part A: Solutions to a System

The graph shows data that a manufacturing company has collected about the business factors for one of its products.

Did You Know?

Economists often work with graphs like the one shown. The marginal cost curve shows the change in total cost as the quantity produced changes, and the marginal revenue curve shows the change in the corresponding total revenue received.

1. The company's profits are maximized when the marginal revenue is equal to the marginal cost. Locate this point on the graph. What is the quantity produced and the price of the item when profits are maximized?

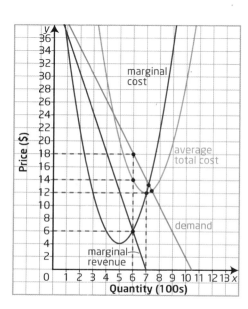

2. When the average total cost is at a minimum, it should equal the marginal cost. Is this true for the graph shown? Explain how you know.

3. A vertical line drawn to represent a production quantity of 600 items intersects all four curves on the graph. Locate the point where this vertical line intersects the demand curve. If the company produces more than 600 items, will the demand for their product increase or decrease? Explain.

Part B: Number of Possible Solutions

4. a) The manufacturing company's graph shows three examples of systems involving a parabola and a line. Identify two business factors that define one of these systems.

   b) Consider other possible systems involving one line and one parabola. Make a series of sketches to illustrate the different ways that a line and a parabola can intersect. In other words, explore the possible numbers of solutions to a **system of linear-quadratic equations** graphically.

5. a) The manufacturing company's graph shows an example of a system involving two parabolas. Identify the business factors that define this system.

   b) Consider other possible systems involving two parabolas. Make a series of sketches to illustrate the different ways that two parabolas can intersect. In other words, explore the possible numbers of solutions to a **system of quadratic-quadratic equations**.

Reflect and Respond

6. Explain how you could determine the solution(s) to a system of linear-quadratic or quadratic-quadratic equations graphically.

7. Consider the coordinates of the point of intersection of the marginal revenue curve and the marginal cost curve, (600, 6). How are the coordinates related to the equations for marginal revenue and marginal cost?

system of linear-quadratic equations
- a linear equation and a quadratic equation involving the same variables
- a graph of the system involves a line and a parabola

system of quadratic-quadratic equations
- two quadratic equations involving the same variables
- the graph involves two parabolas

Any ordered pair (x, y) that satisfies both equations in a system of linear-quadratic or quadratic-quadratic equations is a solution of the system.

For example, the point $(2, 4)$ is a solution of the system
$y = x + 2$
$y = x^2$
The coordinates $x = 2$ and $y = 4$ satisfy both equations.

A system of linear-quadratic or quadratic-quadratic equations may have no real solution, one real solution, or two real solutions. A quadratic-quadratic system of equations may also have an infinite number of real solutions.

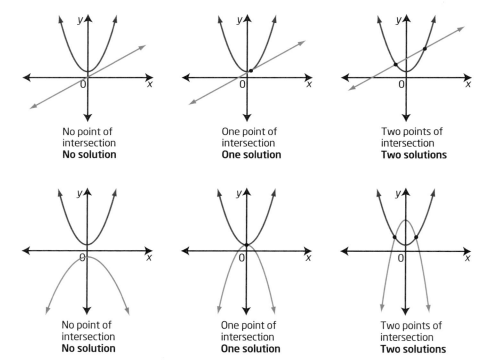

| No point of intersection **No solution** | One point of intersection **One solution** | Two points of intersection **Two solutions** |

Can two parabolas that both open downward have no points of intersection? one point? two points? Explain how.

What would the graph of a system of quadratic-quadratic equations with an infinite number of solutions look like?

| No point of intersection **No solution** | One point of intersection **One solution** | Two points of intersection **Two solutions** |

Example 1

Relate a System of Equations to a Context

Blythe Hartley, of Edmonton, Alberta, is one of Canada's best springboard divers. She is doing training dives from a 3-m springboard. Her coach uses video analysis to plot her height above the water.

a) Which system could represent the scenario? Explain your choice and why the other graphs do not model this situation.

b) Interpret the point(s) of intersection in the system you chose.

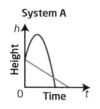 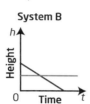 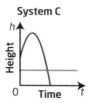 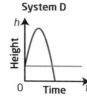

System A   System B   System C   System D

Solution

a) System D, a linear-quadratic system, represents the scenario. The board height is fixed and the diver's parabolic path makes sense relative to this height. She starts on the board, jumps to her maximum height, and then her height decreases as she heads for the water.

The springboard is fixed at a height of 3 m above the water. Its height must be modelled by a constant linear function, so eliminate System A. The path of the dive is parabolic, with the height of the diver modelled by a quadratic function, so eliminate System B. Blythe starts her dive from the 3-m board, so eliminate System C.

b) The points of intersection in System D represent the two times when Blythe's height above the water is the same as the height of the diving board.

Your Turn

Two divers start their dives at the same time. One diver jumps from a 1-m springboard and the other jumps from a 3-m springboard. Their heights above the water are plotted over time.

a) Which system could model this scenario? Explain your choice. Tell why the other graphs could not model this situation.

b) Explain why there is no point of intersection in the graph you chose.

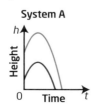 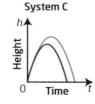 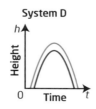

System A   System B   System C   System D

Example 2

Solve a System of Linear-Quadratic Equations Graphically

a) Solve the following system of equations graphically:
$$4x - y + 3 = 0$$
$$2x^2 + 8x - y + 3 = 0$$
b) Verify your solution.

Solution

a) Graph the corresponding functions. Adjust the dimensions of the graph so that the points of intersection are visible. Then, use the intersection feature.

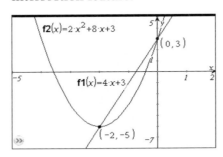

If you are using paper and pencil, it may be more convenient to write the linear equation in slope-intercept form and the quadratic equation in vertex form.

From the graph, the points of intersection are $(0, 3)$ and $(-2, -5)$.

b) Verify the solutions by substituting into the original equations.

Verify the solution $(0, 3)$:
Substitute $x = 0$, $y = 3$ into the original equations.

Left Side   Right Side
$4x - y + 3$ 0
$= 4(0) - (3) + 3$
$= 0$

        Left Side = Right Side

Left Side   Right Side
$\quad 2x^2 + 8x - y + 3$ 0
$= 2(0)^2 + 8(0) - (3) + 3$
$= 0$

        Left Side = Right Side

Verify the solution $(-2, -5)$:
Substitute $x = -2$, $y = -5$ into the original equations.

Left Side   Right Side
$4x - y + 3$ 0
$= 4(-2) - (-5) + 3$
$= -8 + 5 + 3$
$= 0$

Left Side $=$ Right Side

Left Side   Right Side
$2x^2 + 8x - y + 3$ 0
$= 2(-2)^2 + 8(-2) - (-5) + 3$
$= 8 - 16 + 5 + 3$
$= 0$

Left Side $=$ Right Side

Both solutions are correct.

The solutions to the system are $(-2, -5)$ and $(0, 3)$.

Your Turn

Solve the system graphically and verify your solution.
$x - y + 1 = 0$
$x^2 - 6x + y + 3 = 0$

Example 3

Solve a System of Quadratic-Quadratic Equations Graphically

a) Solve:
$2x^2 - 16x - y = -35$
$2x^2 - 8x - y = -11$

How many solutions do you think are possible in this situation?

b) Verify your solution.

Solution

a) Graph the corresponding functions for both equations on the same coordinate grid.

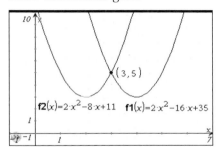

From the graph, the point of intersection is $(3, 5)$.

How do you know that the graphs do not intersect again at a greater value of y?

b) Method 1: Use Technology

$2 \cdot x^2 - 16 \cdot x - y = -35 \vert x = 3$ and $y = 5$	true
$2 \cdot x^2 - 8 \cdot x - y = -11 \vert x = 3$ and $y = 5$	true

2/99

Method 2: Use Paper and Pencil

Left Side	Right Side		Left Side	Right Side
$2x^2 - 16x - y$	-35		$2x^2 - 8x - y$	-11
$= 2(3)^2 - 16(3) - 5$			$= 2(3)^2 - 8(3) - 5$	
$= 18 - 48 - 5$			$= 18 - 24 - 5$	
$= -35$			$= -11$	
Left Side $=$ Right Side			Left Side $=$ Right Side	

Since the ordered pair (3, 5) satisfies both equations, it is the solution to the system.

Your Turn

Solve the system graphically and verify your solution.
$$2x^2 + 16x + y = -26$$
$$x^2 + 8x - y = -19$$

How many solutions do you think are possible in this situation?

Did You Know?

You can use tangent lines to draw parabolas. Draw a horizontal line segment AB. At the midpoint of AB, draw a height CD. Draw lines CA and CB (these are the first tangent lines to the parabola). Mark the same number of equally spaced points on CA and CB. Connect the point A' on CA (next to C) to the point B' on CB (next to B). Then connect A" (next to A') to B" (next to B'), and so on. Follow this pattern for successive pairs of points until all points on CB have been connected to the corresponding points on CA. This technique is the basis of most string art designs.

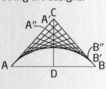

Example 4

Apply a System of Linear-Quadratic Equations

Engineers use vertical curves to improve the comfort and safety of roadways. Vertical curves are parabolic in shape and are used for transitions from one straight grade to another. Each grade line is tangent to the curve.

What does it mean for each grade line to be tangent to the curve?

There are several vertical curves on the Trans-Canada Highway through the Rocky Mountains. To construct a vertical curve, surveyors lay out a grid system and mark the location for the beginning of the curve and the end of the curve.

Suppose surveyors model the first grade line for a section of road with the linear equation $y = -0.06x + 2.6$, the second grade line with the linear equation $y = 0.09x + 2.35$, and the parabolic curve with the quadratic equation $y = 0.0045x^2 + 2.8$.

a) Write the two systems of equations that would be used to determine the coordinates of the points of tangency.

b) Using graphing technology, show the surveyor's layout of the vertical curve.

c) Determine the coordinates of the points of tangency graphically, to the nearest hundredth.

d) Interpret each point of tangency.

Solution

a) The points of tangency are where the lines touch the parabola. The two systems of equations to use are

$$y = -0.06x + 2.6 \quad \text{and} \quad y = 0.09x + 2.35$$
$$y = 0.0045x^2 + 2.8 \qquad\qquad y = 0.0045x^2 + 2.8$$

b) Graph all three equations. You may need to adjust the window to see the points of tangency.

c) Use the intersection feature to determine the coordinates of the two points of tangency.

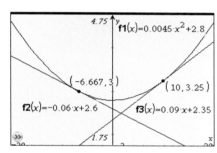

Verify using the calculator.

To the nearest hundredth, the points of tangency are $(-6.67, 3.00)$ and $(10.00, 3.25)$.

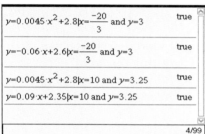

> Could this solution be found using pencil and paper? Explain.

d) This means that the vertical curve starts at the location $(-6.67, 3.00)$ on the surveyor's grid system and ends at the location $(10.00, 3.25)$.

Your Turn

Another section of road requires the curve shown in the diagram. The grade lines are modelled by the equations $y = 0.08x + 6.2$ and $y = -0.075x + 6.103\ 125$. The curve is modelled by the equation $y = -0.002x^2 + 5.4$.

a) Write the two systems of equations to use to determine the coordinates of the beginning and the end of the vertical curve on a surveyor's grid.

b) Using graphing technology, show the surveyor's layout of the vertical curve.

c) Determine the coordinates of each end of this vertical curve, to the nearest hundredth.

Example 5

Model a Situation Using a System of Equations

Suppose that in one stunt, two Cirque du Soleil performers are launched toward each other from two slightly offset seesaws. The first performer is launched, and 1 s later the second performer is launched in the opposite direction. They both perform a flip and give each other a high five in the air. Each performer is in the air for 2 s. The height above the seesaw versus time for each performer during the stunt is approximated by a parabola as shown. Their paths are shown on a coordinate grid.

Did You Know?

Cirque du Soleil is a Québec-based entertainment company that started in 1984 with 20 street performers. The company now has over 4000 employees, including 1000 performers, and performs worldwide. Their dramatic shows combine circus arts with street entertainment.

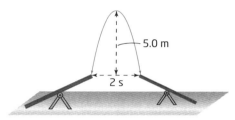

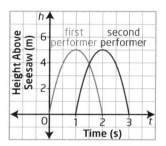

a) Determine the system of equations that models the performers' height during the stunt.

b) Solve the system graphically using technology.

c) Interpret your solution with respect to this situation.

Solution

a) For the first performer (teal parabola), the vertex of the parabola is at (1, 5).

Use the vertex form for a parabola:
$h = a(t - p)^2 + q$

Substitute the coordinates of the vertex:
$h = a(t - 1)^2 + 5$

The point (0, 0) is on the parabola. Substitute and solve for a:
$0 = a(0 - 1)^2 + 5$
$-5 = a$

The equation for the height of the first performer versus time is $h = -5(t - 1)^2 + 5$.

For the second performer (blue parabola), the vertex of the parabola is at (2, 5).

Use the vertex form for a parabola: $h = a(t - p)^2 + q$

Then, the equation with the vertex values substituted is
$h = a(t - 2)^2 + 5$

The point (1, 0) is on the parabola. Substitute and solve for a:
$0 = a(1 - 2)^2 + 5$
$-5 = a$

The equation for the height of the second performer versus time is $h = -5(t - 2)^2 + 5$.

The system of equations that models the performers' heights is
$$h = -5(t - 1)^2 + 5$$
$$h = -5(t - 2)^2 + 5$$

b) Use a graphing calculator to graph the system. Use the intersection feature to find the point of intersection.

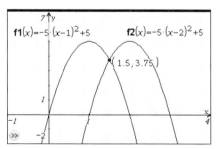

How can you verify this solution?

The system has one solution: (1.5, 3.75).

c) The solution means that the performers are at the same height, 3.75 m above the seesaw, at the same time, 1.5 s after the first performer is launched into the air. This is 0.5 s after the second performer starts the stunt. This is where they give each other a high five.

Your Turn

At another performance, the heights above the seesaw versus time for the performers during the stunt are approximated by the parabola shown. Assume again that the second performer starts 1 s after the first performer. Their paths are shown on a coordinate grid.

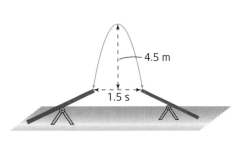

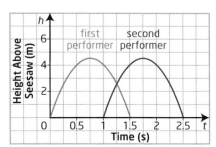

a) Determine the system of equations that models the performers' height during the stunt.
b) Solve the system graphically using technology.
c) Interpret your solution with respect to this situation.

- Any ordered pair (x, y) that satisfies both equations in a linear-quadratic system or in a quadratic-quadratic system is a solution to the system.

- The solution to a system can be found graphically by graphing both equations on the same coordinate grid and finding the point(s) of intersection.

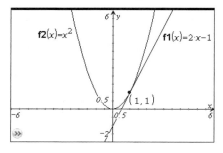
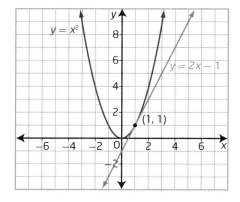

Since there is only one point of intersection, the linear-quadratic system shown has one solution, (1, 1).

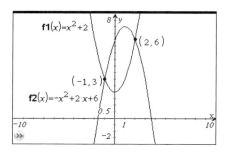
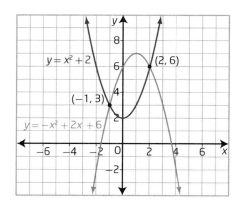

Since there are two points of intersection, the quadratic-quadratic system shown has two solutions, approximately $(-1, 3)$ and $(2, 6)$.

- Systems of linear-quadratic equations may have no real solution, one real solution, or two real solutions.

- Systems of quadratic-quadratic equations may have no real solution, one real solution, two real solutions, or an infinite number of real solutions.

Practise

Where necessary, round answers to the nearest hundredth.

1. The Canadian Arenacross Championship for motocross was held in Penticton, British Columbia, in March 2010. In the competition, riders launch their bikes off jumps and perform stunts. The height above ground level of one rider going off two different jumps at the same speed is plotted. Time is measured from the moment the rider leaves the jump. The launch height and the launch angle of each jump are different.

   a) Which system models the situation? Explain your choice. Explain why the other graphs do not model this situation.

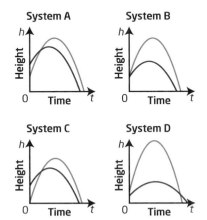

   b) Interpret the point(s) of intersection for the graph you selected.

2. Verify that $(0, -5)$ and $(3, -2)$ are solutions to the following system of equations.

   $y = -x^2 + 4x - 5$
   $y = x - 5$

3. What type of system of equations is represented in each graph? Give the solution(s) to the system.

   a)

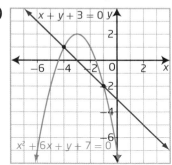

   b)

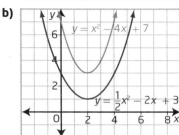

   c)

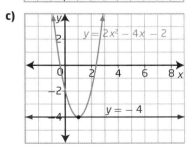

4. Solve each system by graphing. Verify your solutions.

   a) $y = x + 7$
      $y = (x + 2)^2 + 3$

   b) $f(x) = -x + 5$
      $g(x) = \frac{1}{2}(x - 4)^2 + 1$

   c) $x^2 + 16x + y = -59$
      $x - 2y = 60$

   d) $x^2 + y - 3 = 0$
      $x^2 - y + 1 = 0$

   e) $y = x^2 - 10x + 32$
      $y = 2x^2 - 32x + 137$

5. Solve each system by graphing. Verify your solutions.

a) $h = d^2 - 16d + 60$
$h = 12d - 55$

b) $p = 3q^2 - 12q + 17$
$p = -0.25q^2 + 0.5q + 1.75$

c) $2v^2 + 20v + t = -40$
$5v + 2t + 26 = 0$

d) $n^2 + 2n - 2m - 7 = 0$
$3n^2 + 12n - m + 6 = 0$

e) $0 = t^2 + 40t - h + 400$
$t^2 = h + 30t - 225$

Apply

6. Sketch the graph of a system of two quadratic equations with only one real solution. Describe the necessary conditions for this situation to occur.

7. For each situation, sketch a graph to represent a system of quadratic-quadratic equations with two real solutions, so that the two parabolas have

a) the same axis of symmetry

b) the same axis of symmetry and the same y-intercept

c) different axes of symmetry but the same y-intercept

d) the same x-intercepts

8. Given the graph of a quadratic function as shown, determine the equation of a line such that the quadratic function and the line form a system that has

a) no real solution

b) one real solution

c) two real solutions

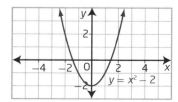

9. Every summer, the Folk on the Rocks Music Festival is held at Long Lake in Yellowknife, Northwest Territories.

Dene singer/ songwriter, Leela Gilday from Yellowknife.

Jonas has been selling shirts in the Art on the Rocks area at the festival for the past 25 years. His total costs (production of the shirts plus 15% of all sales to the festival) and the revenue he receives from sales (he has a variable pricing scheme) are shown on the graph below.

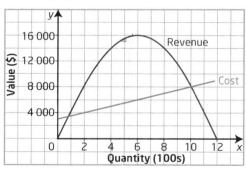

a) What are the solutions to this system? Give answers to the nearest hundred.

b) Interpret the solution and its importance to Jonas.

c) You can determine the profit using the equation Profit = Revenue − Cost. Use the graph to estimate the quantity that gives the greatest profit. Explain why this is the quantity that gives him the most profit.

10. Vertical curves are used in the construction of roller coasters. One downward-sloping grade line, modelled by the equation $y = -0.04x + 3.9$, is followed by an upward-sloping grade line modelled by the equation $y = 0.03x + 2.675$. The vertical curve between the two lines is modelled by the equation $y = 0.001x^2 - 0.04x + 3.9$. Determine the coordinates of the beginning and the end of the curve.

11. A car manufacturer does performance tests on its cars. During one test, a car starts from rest and accelerates at a constant rate for 20 s. Another car starts from rest 3 s later and accelerates at a faster constant rate. The equation that models the distance the first car travels is $d = 1.16t^2$, and the equation that models the distance the second car travels is $d = 1.74(t - 3)^2$, where t is the time, in seconds, after the first car starts the test, and d is the distance, in metres.

a) Write a system of equations that could be used to compare the distance travelled by both cars.

b) In the context, what is a suitable domain for the graph? Sketch the graph of the system of equations.

c) Graphically determine the approximate solution to the system.

d) Describe the meaning of the solution in the context.

12. Jubilee Fountain in Lost Lagoon is a popular landmark in Vancouver's Stanley Park. The streams of water shooting out of the fountain follow parabolic paths. Suppose the tallest stream in the middle is modelled by the equation $h = -0.3125d^2 + 5d$, one of the smaller streams is modelled by the equation $h = -0.85d^2 + 5.11d$, and a second smaller stream is modelled by the equation $h = -0.47d^2 + 3.2d$, where h is the height, in metres, of the water stream and d is the distance, in metres, from the central water spout.

a) Solve the system $h = -0.3125d^2 + 5d$ and $h = -0.85d^2 + 5.11d$ graphically. Interpret the solution.

b) Solve the system of equations involving the two smaller streams of water graphically. Interpret the solution.

Did You Know?

Jubilee Fountain was built in 1936 to commemorate the city of Vancouver's golden jubilee (50th birthday).

13. The sum of two integers is 21. Fifteen less than double the square of the smaller integer gives the larger integer.

a) Model this information with a system of equations.

b) Solve the system graphically. Interpret the solution.

c) Verify your solution.

14. A Cartesian plane is superimposed over a photograph of a snowboarder completing a 540° Front Indy off a jump. The blue line is the path of the jump and can be modelled by the equation $y = -x + 4$. The red parabola is the path of the snowboarder during the jump and can be modelled by the equation $y = -\frac{1}{4}x^2 + 3$. The green line is the mountainside where the snowboarder lands and can be modelled by the equation $y = \frac{3}{4}x + \frac{5}{4}$.

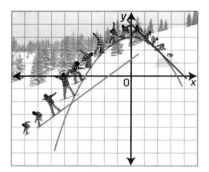

a) Determine the solutions to the linear-quadratic systems: the blue line and the parabola, and the green line and the parabola.

b) Explain the meaning of the solutions in this context.

15. A frog jumps to catch a grasshopper. The frog reaches a maximum height of 25 cm and travels a horizontal distance of 100 cm. A grasshopper, located 30 cm in front of the frog, starts to jump at the same time as the frog. The grasshopper reaches a maximum height of 36 cm and travels a horizontal distance of 48 cm. The frog and the grasshopper both jump in the same direction.

a) Consider the frog's starting position to be at the origin of a coordinate grid. Draw a diagram to model the given information.

b) Determine a quadratic equation to model the frog's height compared to the horizontal distance it travelled and a quadratic equation to model the grasshopper's height compared to the horizontal distance it travelled.

c) Solve the system of two equations.

d) Interpret your solution in the context of this problem.

Extend

16. The Greek mathematician, Menaechmus (about 380 B.C.E. to 320 B.C.E.) was one of the first to write about parabolas. His goal was to solve the problem of "doubling the cube." He used the intersection of curves to find x and y so that $\frac{a}{x} = \frac{x}{y} = \frac{y}{2a}$, where a is the side of a given cube and x is the side of a cube that has twice the volume. Doubling a cube whose side length is 1 cm is equivalent to solving $\frac{1}{x} = \frac{x}{y} = \frac{y}{2}$.

a) Use a system of equations to graphically solve $\frac{1}{x} = \frac{x}{y} = \frac{y}{2}$.

b) What is the approximate side length of a cube whose volume is twice the volume of a cube with a side length of 1 cm?

c) Verify your answer.

d) Explain how you could use the volume formula to find the side length of a cube whose volume is twice the volume of a cube with a side length of 1 cm. Why was Menaechmus unable to use this method to solve the problem?

> **Did You Know?**
>
> Duplicating the cube is a classic problem of Greek mathematics: *Given the length of an edge of a cube, construct a second cube that has double the volume of the first.* The problem was to find a ruler-and-compasses construction for the cube root of 2. Legend has it that the oracle at Delos requested that this construction be performed to appease the gods and stop a plague. This problem is sometimes referred to as the Delian problem.

17. The solution to a system of two equations is $(-1, 2)$ and $(2, 5)$.

   a) Write a linear-quadratic system of equations with these two points as its solutions.

   b) Write a quadratic-quadratic system of equations with these two points as its only solutions.

   c) Write a quadratic-quadratic system of equations with these two points as two of infinitely many solutions.

18. Determine the possible number of solutions to a system involving two quadratic functions and one linear function. Support your work with a series of sketches. Compare your work with that of a classmate.

Create Connections

19. Explain the similarities and differences between linear systems and the systems you studied in this section.

20. Without graphing, use your knowledge of linear and quadratic equations to determine whether each system has no solution, one solution, two solutions, or an infinite number of solutions. Explain how you know.

   a) $y = x^2$
   $y = x + 1$

   b) $y = 2x^2 + 3$
   $y = -2x - 5$

   c) $y = (x - 4)^2 + 1$
   $y = \frac{1}{3}(x - 4)^2 + 2$

   d) $y = 2(x + 8)^2 - 9$
   $y = -2(x + 8)^2 - 9$

   e) $y = 2(x - 3)^2 + 1$
   $y = -2(x - 3)^2 - 1$

   f) $y = (x + 5)^2 - 1$
   $y = x^2 + 10x + 24$

Project Corner — Nanotechnology

Nanotechnology has applications in a wide variety of areas.

- **Electronics:** Nanoelectronics will produce new devices that are small, require very little electricity, and produce little (if any) heat.
- **Energy:** There will be advances in solar power, hydrogen fuel cells, thermoelectricity, and insulating materials.
- **Health Care:** New drug-delivery techniques will be developed that will allow medicine to be targeted directly at a disease instead of the entire body.
- **The Environment:** Renewable energy, more efficient use of resources, new filtration systems, water purification processes, and materials that detect and clean up environmental contaminants are some of the potential eco-friendly uses.
- **Everyday Life:** Almost all areas of your life may be improved by nanotechnology: from the construction of your house, to the car you drive, to the clothes you wear.

Which applications of nanotechnology have you used?

Solving Systems of Equations Algebraically

René Descartes

Focus on...

- modelling a situation using a system of linear-quadratic or quadratic-quadratic equations
- relating a system of linear-quadratic or quadratic-quadratic equations to a problem
- determining the solution of a system of linear-quadratic or quadratic-quadratic equations algebraically
- interpreting points of intersection of a system of linear-quadratic or quadratic-quadratic equations
- solving a problem that involves a system of linear-quadratic or quadratic-quadratic equations

Many ancient civilizations, such as Egyptian, Babylonian, Greek, Hindu, Chinese, Arabic, and European, helped develop the algebra we use today. Initially problems were stated and solved verbally or geometrically without the use of symbols. The French mathematician François Viète (1540–1603) popularized using algebraic symbols, but René Descartes' (1596–1650) thoroughly thought-out symbolism for algebra led directly to the notation we use today. Do you recognize the similarities and differences between his notation and ours?

Investigate Solving Systems of Equations Algebraically

1. Solve the following system of linear-quadratic equations graphically using graphing technology.
$$y = x + 6$$
$$y = x^2$$

2. **a)** How could you use the algebraic method of elimination or substitution to solve this system of equations?

   b) What quadratic equation would you need to solve?

3. How are the roots of the quadratic equation in step 2b) related to the solution to the system of linear-quadratic equations?

4. Graph the related function for the quadratic equation from step 2b) in the same viewing window as the system of equations. Imagine a vertical line drawn through a solution to the system of equations in step 1. Where would this line intersect the equation from step 2b)? Explain this result.

5. What can you conclude about the relationship between the roots of the equation from step 2b) and the solution to the initial system of equations?

6. Consider the following system of quadratic-quadratic equations. Repeat steps 1 to 5 for this system.

$$y = 2x^2 + 3x - 3$$
$$y = x^2 + x$$

Reflect and Respond

7. Why are the x-coordinates in the solutions to the system of equations the same as the roots for the single equation you created using substitution or elimination? You may want to use sketches to help you explain.

8. Explain how you could solve a system of linear-quadratic or quadratic-quadratic equations without using any of the graphing steps in this investigation.

Link the Ideas

Recall from the previous section that systems of equations can have, depending on the type of system, 0, 1, 2, or infinite real solutions. You can apply the algebraic methods of substitution and elimination that you used to solve systems of linear equations to solve systems of linear-quadratic and quadratic-quadratic equations.

Why is it important to be able to solve systems algebraically as well as graphically?

Example 1

Solve a System of Linear-Quadratic Equations Algebraically

a) Solve the following system of equations.
$$5x - y = 10$$
$$x^2 + x - 2y = 0$$
b) Verify your solution.

Solution

a) **Method 1: Use Substitution**
Since the quadratic term is in the variable x, solve the linear equation for y.

Solve the linear equation for y.

Why is it easier to solve the first equation for y?

$$5x - y = 10$$
$$y = 5x - 10$$

Substitute $5x - 10$ for y in the quadratic equation and simplify.
$$x^2 + x - 2y = 0$$
$$x^2 + x - 2(5x - 10) = 0$$
$$x^2 - 9x + 20 = 0$$

Solve the quadratic equation by factoring.
$$(x - 4)(x - 5) = 0$$
$$x = 4 \text{ or } x = 5$$

Substitute these values into the original linear equation to determine the corresponding values of y.

When $x = 4$:

$5x - y = 10$

$5(4) - y = 10$

$y = 10$

When $x = 5$:

$5x - y = 10$

$5(5) - y = 10$

$y = 15$

> Why substitute into the linear equation rather than the quadratic?

The two solutions are (4, 10) and (5, 15).

Method 2: Use Elimination

Align the terms with the same degree.

Since the quadratic term is in the variable x, eliminate the y-term.

$5x - y = 10$ ①

$x^2 + x - 2y = 0$ ②

Multiply ① by -2 so that there is an opposite term to $-2y$ in ①.

$-2(5x - y) = -2(10)$

$-10x + 2y = -20$ ③

Add ③ and ① to eliminate the y-terms.

$$-10x + 2y = -20$$
$$\underline{x^2 + x - 2y = 0}$$
$$x^2 - 9x = -20$$

Then, solve the equation $x^2 - 9x + 20 = 0$ by factoring, as in the substitution method above, to obtain the two solutions (4, 10) and (5, 15).

> What do the two solutions tell you about the appearance of the graphs of the two equations?

b) To verify the solutions, substitute each ordered pair into the original equations.

> How could you verify the solutions using technology?

Verify the solution (4, 10):

Left Side	Right Side
$5x - y$	10
$= 5(4) - 10$	
$= 20 - 10$	
$= 10$	
Left Side $=$ Right Side	

Left Side	Right Side
$x^2 + x - 2y$	0
$= 4^2 + 4 - 2(10)$	
$= 16 + 4 - 20$	
$= 0$	
Left Side $=$ Right Side	

Verify the solution (5, 15):

Left Side	Right Side
$5x - y$	10
$= 5(5) - 15$	
$= 25 - 15$	
$= 10$	
Left Side $=$ Right Side	

Left Side	Right Side
$x^2 + x - 2y$	0
$= 5^2 + 5 - 2(15)$	
$= 25 + 5 - 30$	
$= 0$	
Left Side $=$ Right Side	

Both solutions are correct.

The two solutions are (4, 10) and (5, 15).

Your Turn

Solve the following system of equations algebraically.

$3x + y = -9$

$4x^2 - x + y = -9$

Example 2

Model a Situation With a System of Equations

Glen loves to challenge himself with puzzles. He comes across a Web site that offers online interactive puzzles, but the puzzle-makers present the following problem for entry to their site.

So you like puzzles? Well, prove your worthiness by solving this conundrum.

Determine two integers such that the sum of the smaller number and twice the larger number is 46. Also, when the square of the smaller number is decreased by three times the larger, the result is 93. In the box below, enter the smaller number followed by the larger number and you will gain access to our site.

a) Write a system of equations that relates to the problem.
b) Solve the system algebraically. What is the code that gives access to the site?

Solution

a) Let S represent the smaller number.
Let L represent the larger number.
Use these variables to write an equation to represent the first statement: "the sum of the smaller number and twice the larger number is 46."
$$S + 2L = 46$$

Next, write an equation to represent the second statement: "when the square of the smaller number is decreased by three times the larger, the result is 93."
$$S^2 - 3L = 93$$

Solving the system of equations gives the numbers that meet both sets of conditions.

b) Use the elimination method.

$S + 2L = 46$ ①

$S^2 - 3L = 93$ ②

Why was the elimination method chosen? Could you use the substitution method instead?

Multiply ① by 3 and ② by 2.

$3(S + 2L) = 3(46)$

$3S + 6L = 138$ ③

$2(S^2 - 3L) = 2(93)$

$2S^2 - 6L = 186$ ④

Add ③ and ④ to eliminate L.

$3S + 6L = 138$

$\underline{2S^2 - 6L = 186}$

$2S^2 + 3S = 324$

Why can you not eliminate the variable S?

Solve $2S^2 + 3S - 324 = 0$.

Factor.

$(2S + 27)(S - 12) = 0$

$S = -13.5$ or $S = 12$

Since the numbers are supposed to be integers, $S = 12$.

Substitute $S = 12$ into the linear equation to determine the value of L.

$S + 2L = 46$

$12 + 2L = 46$

$2L = 34$

$L = 17$

Why was ① chosen to substitute into?

The solution is (12, 17).

Verify the solution by substituting (12, 17) into the original equations:

Left Side	Right Side	Left Side	Right Side
$S + 2L$	46	$S^2 - 3L$	93
$= 12 + 2(17)$		$= 12^2 - 3(17)$	
$= 12 + 34$		$= 144 - 51$	
$= 46$		$= 93$	
Left Side = Right Side		Left Side = Right Side	

The solution is correct.

The two numbers for the code are 12 and 17. The access key is 1217.

Your Turn

Determine two integers that have the following relationships: Fourteen more than twice the first integer gives the second integer. The second integer increased by one is the square of the first integer.

a) Write a system of equations that relates to the problem.

b) Solve the system algebraically.

Example 3

Solve a Problem Involving a Linear-Quadratic System

A Canadian cargo plane drops a crate of emergency supplies to aid-workers on the ground. The crate drops freely at first before a parachute opens to bring the crate gently to the ground. The crate's height, h, in metres, above the ground t seconds after leaving the aircraft is given by the following two equations.

$h = -4.9t^2 + 700$ represents the height of the crate during free fall.

$h = -5t + 650$ represents the height of the crate with the parachute open.

a) How long after the crate leaves the aircraft does the parachute open? Express your answer to the nearest hundredth of a second.

b) What height above the ground is the crate when the parachute opens? Express your answer to the nearest metre.

c) Verify your solution.

Solution

a) The moment when the parachute opens corresponds to the point of intersection of the two heights. The coordinates can be determined by solving a system of equations.

The linear equation is written in terms of the variable h, so use the method of substitution.

Substitute $-5t + 650$ for h in the quadratic equation.
$$h = -4.9t^2 + 700$$
$$-5t + 650 = -4.9t^2 + 700$$
$$4.9t^2 - 5t - 50 = 0$$

Solve using the quadratic formula.
$$t = \frac{-b \pm \sqrt{b^2 - 4ac}}{2a}$$
$$t = \frac{-(-5) \pm \sqrt{(-5)^2 - 4(4.9)(-50)}}{2(4.9)}$$
$$t = \frac{5 \pm \sqrt{1005}}{9.8}$$
$$t = \frac{5 + \sqrt{1005}}{9.8} \quad \text{or} \quad t = \frac{5 - \sqrt{1005}}{9.8}$$

Why is $t = -2.724...$ rejected as a solution to this problem?

$$t = 3.745... \quad \text{or} \quad t = -2.724...$$

The parachute opens about 3.75 s after the crate leaves the plane.

b) To find the crate's height above the ground, substitute the value $t = 3.745\ldots$ into the linear equation.

$h = -5t + 650$

$h = -5(3.745\ldots) + 650$

$h = 631.274\ldots$

The crate is about 631 m above the ground when the parachute opens.

c) Method 1: Use Paper and Pencil

To verify the solution, substitute the answer for t into the first equation of the system.

$h = -4.9t^2 + 700$

$h = -4.9(3.745\ldots)^2 + 700$

$h = 631.274\ldots$

The solution is correct.

Method 2: Use Technology

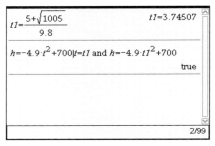

The solution is correct.

The crate is about 631 m above the ground when the parachute opens.

Your Turn

Suppose the crate's height above the ground is given by the following two equations.

$h = -4.9t^2 + 900$

$h = -4t + 500$

a) How long after the crate leaves the aircraft does the parachute open? Express your answer to the nearest hundredth of a second.

b) What height above the ground is the crate when the parachute opens? Express your answer to the nearest metre.

c) Verify your solution.

Example 4

Solve a System of Quadratic-Quadratic Equations Algebraically

a) Solve the following system of equations.

$3x^2 - x - y - 2 = 0$

$6x^2 + 4x - y = 4$

b) Verify your solution.

Solution

a) Both equations contain a single y-term, so use elimination.

$3x^2 - x - y = 2$ ①   Why can x not be eliminated?

$6x^2 + 4x - y = 4$ ②   Could this system be solved by substitution? Explain.

Subtract ① from ② to eliminate y.

$$6x^2 + 4x - y = 4$$
$$\underline{3x^2 - x - y = 2}$$
$$3x^2 + 5x = 2$$

Solve the quadratic equation.

$$3x^2 + 5x = 2$$
$$3x^2 + 5x - 2 = 0$$
$$3x^2 + 6x - x - 2 = 0$$
$$3x(x + 2) - 1(x + 2) = 0 \quad \text{Factor by grouping.}$$
$$(x + 2)(3x - 1) = 0$$
$$x = -2 \text{ or } x = \frac{1}{3}$$

Substitute these values into the equation $3x^2 - x - y = 2$ to determine the corresponding values of y.

When $x = -2$:

$$3x^2 - x - y = 2$$
$$3(-2)^2 - (-2) - y = 2$$
$$12 + 2 - y = 2$$
$$y = 12$$

When $x = \frac{1}{3}$:

$$3x^2 - x - y = 2$$
$$3\left(\frac{1}{3}\right)^2 - \frac{1}{3} - y = 2$$
$$\frac{1}{3} - \frac{1}{3} - y = 2$$
$$y = -2$$

The system has two solutions: $(-2, 12)$ and $\left(\frac{1}{3}, -2\right)$.

What do the two solutions tell you about the appearance of the graphs of the two equations?

b) To verify the solutions, substitute each ordered pair into the original equations.

Verify the solution $(-2, 12)$:

Left Side	Right Side
$3x^2 - x - y - 2$	0
$= 3(-2)^2 - (-2) - 12 - 2$	
$= 12 + 2 - 12 - 2$	
$= 0$	

Left Side = Right Side

Left Side	Right Side
$6x^2 + 4x - y$	4
$= 6(-2)^2 + 4(-2) - 12$	
$= 24 - 8 - 12$	
$= 4$	

Left Side = Right Side

Verify the solution $\left(\dfrac{1}{3}, -2\right)$:

Left Side	Right Side
$3x^2 - x - y - 2$	0
$= 3\left(\dfrac{1}{3}\right)^2 - \left(\dfrac{1}{3}\right) - (-2) - 2$	
$= \dfrac{1}{3} - \dfrac{1}{3} + 2 - 2$	
$= 0$	

Left Side = Right Side

Left Side	Right Side
$6x^2 + 4x - y$	4
$= 6\left(\dfrac{1}{3}\right)^2 + 4\left(\dfrac{1}{3}\right) - (-2)$	
$= \dfrac{2}{3} + \dfrac{4}{3} + 2$	
$= 4$	

Left Side = Right Side

Both solutions are correct.

The system has two solutions: $(-2, 12)$ and $\left(\dfrac{1}{3}, -2\right)$.

Your Turn

a) Solve the system algebraically. Explain why you chose the method that you did.
$$6x^2 - x - y = -1$$
$$4x^2 - 4x - y = -6$$

b) Verify your solution.

Example 5

Solve a Problem Involving a Quadratic-Quadratic System

During a basketball game, Ben completes an impressive "alley-oop." From one side of the hoop, his teammate Luke lobs a perfect pass toward the basket. Directly across from Luke, Ben jumps up, catches the ball and tips it into the basket. The path of the ball thrown by Luke can be modelled by the equation $d^2 - 2d + 3h = 9$, where d is the horizontal distance of the ball from the centre of the hoop, in metres, and h is the height of the ball above the floor, in metres. The path of Ben's jump can be modelled by the equation $5d^2 - 10d + h = 0$, where d is his horizontal distance from the centre of the hoop, in metres, and h is the height of his hands above the floor, in metres.

a) Solve the system of equations algebraically. Give your solution to the nearest hundredth.

b) Interpret your result. What assumptions are you making?

3 m

Solution

a) The system to solve is
$$d^2 - 2d + 3h = 9$$
$$5d^2 - 10d + h = 0$$

Solve the second equation for h since the leading coefficient of this term is 1.
$$h = -5d^2 + 10d$$

Substitute $-5d^2 + 10d$ for h in the first equation.
$$d^2 - 2d + 3h = 9$$
$$d^2 - 2d + 3(-5d^2 + 10d) = 9$$
$$d^2 - 2d - 15d^2 + 30d = 9$$
$$14d^2 - 28d + 9 = 0$$

Solve using the quadratic formula.

$$d = \frac{-b \pm \sqrt{b^2 - 4ac}}{2a}$$

$$d = \frac{-(-28) \pm \sqrt{(-28)^2 - 4(14)(9)}}{2(14)}$$

$$d = \frac{28 \pm \sqrt{280}}{28}$$

$$d = \frac{14 + \sqrt{70}}{14} \quad \text{or} \quad d = \frac{14 - \sqrt{70}}{14}$$

$$d = 1.597\ldots \qquad\qquad d = 0.402\ldots$$

Substitute these values of d into the equation $h = -5d^2 + 10d$ to find the corresponding values of h.

For $d = \dfrac{14 + \sqrt{70}}{14}$:

$$h = -5d^2 + 10d$$

$$h = -5\left(\frac{14 + \sqrt{70}}{14}\right)^2 + 10\left(\frac{14 + \sqrt{70}}{14}\right)$$

$$h = 3.214\ldots$$

For $d = \dfrac{14 - \sqrt{70}}{14}$:

$$h = -5d^2 + 10d$$

$$h = -5\left(\frac{14 - \sqrt{70}}{14}\right)^2 + 10\left(\frac{14 - \sqrt{70}}{14}\right)$$

$$h = 3.214\ldots$$

To the nearest hundredth, the solutions to the system are (0.40, 3.21) and (1.60, 3.21).

How can you verify the solutions?

b) The parabolic path of the ball and Ben's parabolic path will intersect at two locations: at a distance of 0.40 m from the basket and at a distance of 1.60 m from the basket, in both cases at a height of 3.21 m. Ben will complete the alley-oop if he catches the ball at the distance of 0.40 m from the hoop. The ball is at the same height, 3.21 m, on its upward path toward the net but it is still 1.60 m away.

Why is the solution of 1.60 m not appropriate in this context?

This will happen if you assume Ben times his jump appropriately, is physically able to make the shot, and the shot is not blocked by another player.

Your Turn

Terri makes a good hit and the baseball travels on a path modelled by $h = -0.1x^2 + 2x$. Ruth is in the outfield directly in line with the path of the ball. She runs toward the ball and jumps to try to catch it. Her jump is modelled by the equation $h = -x^2 + 39x - 378$. In both equations, x is the horizontal distance in metres from home plate and h is the height of the ball above the ground in metres.

a) Solve the system algebraically. Round your answer to the nearest hundredth.

b) Explain the meaning of the point of intersection. What assumptions are you making?

Check Your Understanding

Practise

Where necessary, round your answers to the nearest hundredth.

1. Verify that $(5, 7)$ is a solution to the following system of equations.

$$k + p = 12$$
$$4k^2 - 2p = 86$$

2. Verify that $\left(\dfrac{1}{3}, \dfrac{3}{4}\right)$ is a solution to the following system of equations.

$$18w^2 - 16z^2 = -7$$
$$144w^2 + 48z^2 = 43$$

3. Solve each system of equations by substitution, and verify your solution(s).

a) $x^2 - y + 2 = 0$
$4x = 14 - y$

b) $2x^2 - 4x + y = 3$
$4x - 2y = -7$

c) $7d^2 + 5d - t - 8 = 0$
$10d - 2t = -40$

d) $3x^2 + 4x - y - 8 = 0$
$y + 3 = 2x^2 + 4x$

e) $y + 2x = x^2 - 6$
$x + y - 3 = 2x^2$

4. Solve each system of equations by elimination, and verify your solution(s).

a) $6x^2 - 3x = 2y - 5$
$2x^2 + x = y - 4$

b) $x^2 + y = 8x + 19$
$x^2 - y = 7x - 11$

c) $2p^2 = 4p - 2m + 6$
$5m + 8 = 10p + 5p^2$ $10p + 5p^2 = 5m + A$

d) $9w^2 + 8k = -14$
$w^2 + k = -2$

e) $4h^2 - 8t = 6$
$6h^2 - 9 = 12t$

5. Solve each system algebraically. Explain why you chose the method you used.

a) $y - 1 = -\dfrac{7}{8}x$
$3x^2 + y = 8x - 1$

b) $8x^2 + 5y = 100$
$6x^2 - x - 3y = 5$

c) $x^2 - \dfrac{48}{9}x + \dfrac{1}{3}y + \dfrac{1}{3} = 0$
$-\dfrac{5}{4}x^2 - \dfrac{3}{2}x + \dfrac{1}{4}y - \dfrac{1}{2} = 0$

Apply

6. Alex and Kaela are considering the two equations $n - m^2 = 7$ and $2m^2 - 2n = -1$. Without making any calculations, they both claim that the system involving these two equations has no solution.

Alex's reasoning:
If I double every term in the first equation and then use the elimination method, both of the variables will disappear, so the system does not have a solution.

Kaela's reasoning:
If I solve the first equation for n and substitute into the second equation, I will end up with an equation without any variables, so the system does not have a solution.

a) Is each person's reasoning correct?

b) Verify the conclusion graphically.

7. Marie-Soleil solved two systems of equations using elimination. Instead of creating opposite terms and adding, she used a subtraction method. Her work for the elimination step in two different systems of equations is shown below.

First System
$$5x + 2y = 12$$
$$\underline{x^2 - 2x + 2y = 7}$$
$$-x^2 + 7x = 5$$

Second System
$$12m^2 - 4m - 8n = -3$$
$$\underline{9m^2 - m - 8n = 2}$$
$$3m^2 - 3m = -5$$

a) Study Marie-Soleil's method. Do you think this method works? Explain.

b) Redo the first step in each system by multiplying one of the equations by -1 and adding. Did you get the same results as Marie-Soleil?

c) Do you prefer to add or subtract to eliminate a variable? Explain why.

8. Determine the values of m and n if $(2, 8)$ is a solution to the following system of equations.

$$mx^2 - y = 16$$
$$mx^2 + 2y = n$$

9. The perimeter of the right triangle is 60 m. The area of the triangle is $10y$ square metres.

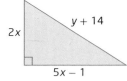

a) Write a simplified expression for the triangle's perimeter in terms of x and y.

b) Write a simplified expression for the triangle's area in terms of x and y.

c) Write a system of equations and explain how it relates to this problem.

d) Solve the system for x and y. What are the dimensions of the triangle?

e) Verify your solution.

10. Two integers have a difference of −30. When the larger integer is increased by 3 and added to the square of the smaller integer, the result is 189.

   a) Model the given information with a system of equations.

   b) Determine the value of the integers by solving the system.

   c) Verify your solution.

11. The number of centimetres in the circumference of a circle is three times the number of square centimetres in the area of the circle.

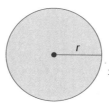

   a) Write the system of linear-quadratic equations, in two variables, that models the circle with the given property.

   b) What are the radius, circumference, and area of the circle with this property?

12. A 250-g ball is thrown into the air with an initial velocity of 22.36 m/s. The kinetic energy, E_k, of the ball is given by the equation $E_k = \frac{5}{32}(d - 20)^2$ and its potential energy, E_p, is given by the equation $E_p = -\frac{5}{32}(d - 20)^2 + 62.5$, where energy is measured in joules (J) and d is the horizontal distance travelled by the ball, in metres.

   a) At what distances does the ball have the same amount of kinetic energy as potential energy?

   b) How many joules of each type of energy does the ball have at these distances?

   c) Verify your solution by graphing.

   d) When an object is thrown into the air, the total mechanical energy of the object is the sum of its kinetic energy and its potential energy. On Earth, one of the properties of an object in motion is that the total mechanical energy is a constant. Does the graph of this system show this property? Explain how you could confirm this observation.

13. The 2015-m-tall Mount Asgard in Auyuittuq (ow you eet took) National Park, Baffin Island, Nunavut, was used in the opening scene for the James Bond movie *The Spy Who Loved Me*. A stuntman skis off the edge of the mountain, free-falls for several seconds, and then opens a parachute. The height, h, in metres, of the stuntman above the ground t seconds after leaving the edge of the mountain is given by two functions.

$h(t) = -4.9t^2 + 2015$ represents the height of the stuntman before he opens the parachute.

$h(t) = -10.5t + 980$ represents the height of the stuntman after he opens the parachute.

   a) For how many seconds does the stuntman free-fall before he opens his parachute?

   b) What height above the ground was the stuntman when he opened the parachute?

   c) Verify your solutions.

Did You Know?

Mount Asgard, named after the kingdom of the gods in Norse mythology, is known as Sivanitirutinguak (see va kneek tea goo ting goo ak) to Inuit. This name, in Inuktitut, means "shape of a bell."

14. A table of values is shown for two different quadratic functions.

First Quadratic

x	y
−1	2
0	0
1	2
2	8

Second Quadratic

x	y
−5	4
−4	1
−3	0
−2	1

a) Use paper and pencil to plot each set of ordered pairs on the same grid. Sketch the quadratic functions.

b) Estimate the solution to the system involving the two quadratic functions.

c) Determine a quadratic equation for each function and model a quadratic-quadratic system with these equations.

d) Solve the system of equations algebraically. How does your solution compare to your estimate in part b)?

15. When a volcano erupts, it sends lava fragments flying through the air. From the point where a fragment is blasted into the air, its height, h, in metres, relative to the horizontal distance travelled, x, in metres, can be approximated using the function

$$h(x) = -\frac{4.9}{(v_0 \cos \theta)^2}x^2 + (\tan \theta)x + h_0,$$

where v_0 is the initial velocity of the fragment, in metres per second; θ is the angle, in degrees, relative to the horizontal at which the fragment starts its path; and h_0 is the initial height, in metres, of the fragment.

a) The height of the summit of a volcano is 2500 m. If a lava fragment blasts out of the middle of the summit at an angle of 45° travelling at 60 m/s, confirm that the function $h(x) = -0.003x^2 + x + 2500$ approximately models the fragment's height relative to the horizontal distance travelled. Confirm that a fragment blasted out at an angle of 60° travelling at 60 m/s can be approximately modelled by the function $h(x) = -0.005x^2 + 1.732x + 2500$.

b) Solve the system

$$h(x) = -0.003x^2 + x + 2500$$
$$h(x) = -0.005x^2 + 1.732x + 2500$$

c) Interpret your solution and the conditions required for it to be true.

Did You Know?

Iceland is one of the most active volcanic areas in the world. On April 14, 2010, when Iceland's Eyjafjallajokull (ay yah fyah lah yoh kuul) volcano had a major eruption, ash was sent high into Earth's atmosphere and drifted south and east toward Europe. This large ash cloud wreaked havoc on air traffic. In fear that the airplanes' engines would be clogged by the ash, thousands of flights were cancelled for many days.

16. In western Canada, helicopter "bombing" is used for avalanche control. In high-risk areas, explosives are dropped onto the mountainside to safely start an avalanche. The function $h(x) = -\frac{5}{1600}x^2 + 200$ represents the height, h, in metres, of the explosive once it has been thrown from the helicopter, where x is the horizontal distance, in metres, from the base of the mountain. The mountainside is modelled by the function $h(x) = 1.19x$.

a) How can the following system of equations be used for this scenario?

$$h = -\frac{5}{1600}x^2 + 200$$
$$h = 1.19x$$

b) At what height up the mountain does the explosive charge land?

17. The monthly economic situation of a manufacturing firm is given by the following equations.

$$R = 5000x - 10x^2$$
$$R_M = 5000 - 20x$$
$$C = 300x + \frac{1}{12}x^2$$
$$C_M = 300 + \frac{1}{4}x^2$$

where x represents the quantity sold, R represents the firm's total revenue, R_M represents marginal revenue, C represents total cost, and C_M represents the marginal cost. All costs are in dollars.

a) Maximum profit occurs when marginal revenue is equal to marginal cost. How many items should be sold to maximize profit?

b) Profit is total revenue minus total cost. What is the firm's maximum monthly profit?

Extend

18. Kate is an industrial design engineer. She is creating the program for cutting fabric for a shade sail. The shape of a shade sail is defined by three intersecting parabolas. The equations of the parabolas are

$$y = x^2 + 8x + 16$$
$$y = x^2 - 8x + 16$$
$$y = -\frac{x^2}{8} + 2$$

where x and y are measurements in metres.

a) Use an algebraic method to determine the coordinates of the three vertices of the sail.

b) Estimate the area of material required to make the sail.

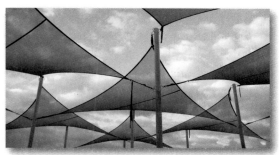

19. A normal line is a line that is perpendicular to a tangent line of a curve at the point of tangency.

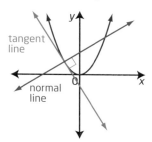

The line $y = 4x - 2$ is tangent to the curve $y = 2x^2 - 4x + 6$ at a point A.

a) What are the coordinates of point A?

b) What is the equation of the normal line to the curve $y = 2x^2 - 4x + 6$ at the point A?

c) The normal line intersects the curve again at point B, creating chord AB. Determine the length of this chord.

20. Solve the following system of equations using an algebraic method.

$$y = \frac{2x - 1}{x}$$
$$\frac{x}{x + 2} + y - 2 = 0$$

21. Determine the equations for the linear-quadratic system with the following properties. The vertex of the parabola is at $(-1, -4.5)$. The line intersects the parabola at two points. One point of intersection is on the y-axis at $(0, -4)$ and the other point of intersection is on the x-axis.

Create Connections

22. Consider graphing methods and algebraic methods for solving a system of equations. What are the advantages and the disadvantages of each method? Create your own examples to model your answer.

23. A parabola has its vertex at $(-3, -1)$ and passes through the point $(-2, 1)$. A second parabola has its vertex at $(-1, 5)$ and has y-intercept 4. What are the approximate coordinates of the point(s) at which these parabolas intersect?

24. Use algebraic reasoning to show that the graphs of $y = -\frac{1}{2}x - 2$ and $y = x^2 - 4x + 2$ do not intersect.

25. MINI LAB In this activity, you will explore the effects that varying the parameters b and m in a linear equation have on a system of linear-quadratic equations.

Step 1 Consider the system of linear-quadratic equations $y = x^2$ and $y = x + b$, where $b \in$ R. Graph the system of equations for different values of b. Experiment with changing the value of b so that for some of your values of b the parabola and the line intersect in two points, and not for others. For what value of b do the parabola and the line intersect in exactly one point? Based on your results, predict the values of b for which the system has two real solutions, one real solution, and no real solution.

Step 2 Algebraically determine the values of b for which the system has two real solutions, one real solution, and no real solution.

Step 3 Consider the system of linear-quadratic equations $y = x^2$ and $y = mx - 1$, where $m \in$ R. Graph the system of equations for different values of m. Experiment with changing the value of m. For what value of m do the parabola and the line intersect in exactly one point? Based on your results, predict the values of m for which the system has two real solutions, one real solution, and no real solution.

Step 4 Algebraically determine the values of m for which the system has two real solutions, one real solution and no real solution.

Step 5 Consider the system of linear-quadratic equations $y = x^2$ and $y = mx + b$, where $m, b \in$ R. Determine the conditions on m and b for which the system has two real solutions, one real solution, and no real solution.

Project Corner   Carbon Nanotubes and Engineering

- Carbon nanotubes are cylindrical molecules made of carbon. They have many amazing properties and, as a result, can be used in a number of different applications.

- Carbon nanotubes are up to 100 times stronger than steel and only $\frac{1}{16}$ its mass.

- Researchers mix nanotubes with plastics as reinforcers.

Nanotechnology is already being applied to sports equipment such as bicycles, golf clubs, and tennis rackets. Future uses will include things like aircraft, bridges, and cars. What are some other things that could be enhanced by this stronger and lighter product?

8.1 Solving Systems of Equations Graphically, pages 424–439

Where necessary, round your answers to the nearest hundredth.

1. Consider the tables of values for
   $y = -1.5x - 2$ and $y = -2(x - 4)^2 + 3$.

x	y
0.5	−2.75
1	−3.5
1.5	−4.25
2	−5
2.5	−5.75
3	−6.5

x	y
0.5	−21.5
1	−15
1.5	−9.5
2	−5
2.5	−1.5
3	1

   a) Use the tables to determine a solution to the system of equations
   $$y = -1.5x - 2$$
   $$y = -2(x - 4)^2 + 3$$

   b) Verify this solution by graphing.

   c) What is the other solution to the system?

2. State the number of possible solutions to each system. Include sketches to support your answers.

   a) a system involving a parabola and a horizontal line

   b) a system involving two parabolas that both open upward

   c) a system involving a parabola and a line with a positive slope

3. Solve each system of equations by graphing.

   a) $y = \frac{2}{3}x + 4$
   $y = -3(x + 6)^2$

   b) $y = x^2 - 4x + 1$
   $y = -\frac{1}{2}(x - 2)^2 + 3$

4. Adam graphed the system of quadratic equations $y = x^2 + 1$ and $y = x^2 + 3$ on a graphing calculator. He speculates that the two graphs will intersect at some large value of y. Is Adam correct? Explain.

5. Solve each system of equations by graphing.

   a) $p = \frac{1}{3}(x + 2)^2 + 2$
   $p = \frac{1}{3}(x - 1)^2 + 3$

   b) $y = -6x^2 - 4x + 7$
   $y = x^2 + 2x - 6$

   c) $t = -3d^2 - 2d + 3.25$
   $t = \frac{1}{8}d - 5$

6. An engineer constructs side-by-side parabolic arches to support a bridge over a road and a river. The arch over the road has a maximum height of 6 m and a width of 16 m. The river arch has a maximum height of 8 m, but its width is reduced by 4 m because it intersects the arch over the road. Without this intersection, the river arch would have a width of 24 m. A support footing is used at the intersection point of the arches. The engineer sketched the arches on a coordinate system. She placed the origin at the left most point of the road.

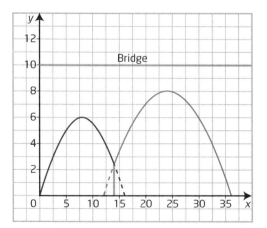

   a) Determine the equation that models each arch.

   b) Solve the system of equations.

   c) What information does the solution to the system give the engineer?

7. Caitlin is at the base of a hill with a constant slope. She kicks a ball as hard as she can up the hill.

   a) Explain how the following system models this situation.

   $$h = -0.09d^2 + 1.8d$$
   $$h = \frac{1}{2}d$$

   b) Solve the system.

   c) Interpret the point(s) of intersection in the context.

8.2 Solving Systems of Equations Algebraically, pages 440–456

8.

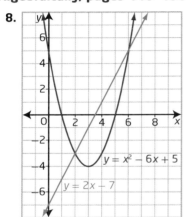

   a) Estimate the solutions to the system of equations shown in the graph.

   b) Solve the system algebraically.

9. Without solving the system $4m^2 - 3n = -2$ and $m^2 + \frac{7}{2}m + 5n = 7$, determine which solution is correct: $\left(\frac{1}{2}, 1\right)$ or $\left(\frac{1}{2}, -1\right)$.

10. Solve each system algebraically, giving exact answers. Explain why you chose the method you used.

   a) $p = 3k + 1$
   $p = 6k^2 + 10k - 4$

   b) $4x^2 + 3y = 1$
   $3x^2 + 2y = 4$

   c) $\dfrac{w^2}{2} + \dfrac{w}{4} - \dfrac{z}{2} = 3$
   $\dfrac{w^2}{3} - \dfrac{3w}{4} + \dfrac{z}{6} + \dfrac{1}{3} = 0$

   d) $2y - 1 = x^2 - x$
   $x^2 + 2x + y - 3 = 0$

11. The approximate height, h, in metres, travelled by golf balls hit with two different clubs over a horizontal distance of d metres is given by the following functions:

   seven-iron: $h(d) = -0.002d^2 + 0.3d$
   nine-iron: $h(d) = -0.004d^2 + 0.5d$

   a) At what distances is the ball at the same height when either of the clubs is used?

   b) What is this height?

12. Manitoba has many biopharmaceutical companies. Suppose scientists at one of these companies grow two different cell cultures in an identical nutrient-rich medium. The rate of increase, S, in square millimetres per hour, of the surface area of each culture after t hours is modelled by the following quadratic functions:

   First culture: $S(t) = -0.007t^2 + 0.05t$
   Second culture: $S(t) = -0.0085t^2 + 0.06t$

   a) What information would the scientists gain by solving the system of related equations?

   b) Solve the system algebraically.

   c) Interpret your solution.

Multiple Choice

For #1 to #5, choose the best answer.

1. The graph for a system of equations is shown. In which quadrant(s) is there a solution to the system?

   A I only

   B II only

   C I and II only

   D II and III only

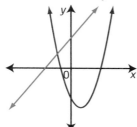

2. The system $y = \frac{1}{2}(x - 6)^2 + 2$ and $y = 2x + k$ has no solution. How many solutions does the system $y = -\frac{1}{2}(x - 6)^2 + 2$ and $y = 2x + k$ have?

   A none

   B one

   C two

   D infinitely many

3. Tables of values are shown for two different quadratic functions. What conclusion can you make about the related system of equations?

x	y		x	y
1	6		1	−6
2	−3		2	−3
3	−6		3	−2
4	−3		4	−3
5	6		5	−6

   A It does not have a solution.

   B It has at least two real solutions.

   C It has an infinite number of solutions.

   D It is quadratic-quadratic with a common vertex.

4. What is the solution to the following system of equations?

   $y = (x + 2)^2 - 2$

   $y = \frac{1}{2}(x + 2)^2$

   A no solution

   B $x = 2$

   C $x = -4$ and $x = 2$

   D $x = -4$ and $x = 0$

5. Connor used the substitution method to solve the system

   $5m - 2n = 25$

   $3m^2 - m + n = 10$

   Below is Connor's solution for m. In which line did he make an error?

   Connor's solution:
   Solve the second equation for n:

   $n = 10 - 3m^2 + m$ line 1

   Substitute into the first equation:

   $5m - 2(10 - 3m^2 + m) = 25$ line 2

   $5m - 20 + 6m^2 - 2m = 25$

   $6m^2 + 3m - 45 = 0$ line 3

   $2m^2 + m - 15 = 0$

   $(2m + 5)(m - 3) = 0$ line 4

   $m = 2.5$ or $m = -3$

   A line 1   **B** line 2

   C line 3   **D** line 4

Short Answer

Where necessary, round your answers to the nearest hundredth.

6. A student determines that one solution to a system of quadratic-quadratic equations is (2, 1). What is the value of n if the equations are

   $4x^2 - my = 10$

   $mx^2 + ny = 20$

7. Solve algebraically.

   a) $5x^2 + 3y = -3 - x$
   $2x^2 - x = -4 - 2y$

   b) $y = 7x - 11$
   $5x^2 - 3x - y = 6$

8. For a dance routine, the choreographer has arranged for two dancers to perform jeté jumps in canon. Sophie leaps first, and one count later Noah starts his jump. Sophie's jump can by modelled by the equation $h = -4.9t^2 + 5.1t$ and Noah's by the equation $h = -4.9(t - 0.5)^2 + 5.3(t - 0.5)$. In both equations, t is the time in seconds and h is the height in metres.

a) Solve the system graphically. What are the coordinates of the point(s) of intersection?

b) Interpret the solution in the context of this scenario.

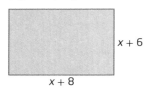

Did You Know?

Canon is a choreographic form where the dancers perform the same movement beginning at different times.

9. The perimeter of the rectangle is represented by $8y$ metres and the area is represented by $(6y + 3)$ square metres.

$x + 6$

$x + 8$

a) Write two equations in terms of x and y: one for the perimeter and one for the area of the rectangle.

b) Determine the perimeter and the area.

10. a) Determine a system of quadratic equations for the functions shown.

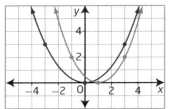

b) Solve the system algebraically.

Extended Response

11. Computer animators design game characters to have many different abilities. The double-jump mechanic allows the character to do a second jump while in mid-air and change its first trajectory to a new one.

During a double jump, the first part of the jump is modelled by the equation $h = -12.8d^2 + 6.4d$, and the second part is modelled by the equation $h = -\frac{248}{15}(d - 0.7)^2 + 2$. In both equations, d is the horizontal distance and h is the height, in centimetres.

a) Solve the system of quadratic-quadratic equations by graphing.

b) Interpret your solution.

12. The parabola $y = -x^2 + 4x + 26.5$ intersects the x-axis at points A and B. The line $y = 1.5x + 5.25$ intersects the parabola at points A and C. Determine the approximate area of $\triangle ABC$.

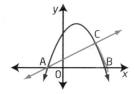

Nanotechnology

This part of your project will require you to be creative and to use your math skills. Combining your knowledge of parabolas and quadratic systems with the nanotechnology information you have gathered in this chapter, you will design a futuristic version of a every-day object. The object should have some linear and parabolic design lines.

Chapter 8 Task

Choose an object that you feel could be improved using nanotechnology. Look at the information presented in this chapter's Project Corners to give you ideas.

- Explain how the object you have chosen will be enhanced by using nanotechnology.

- Create a new design for your chosen object. Your design must include intersections of parabolic and linear design curves.

- Your design will inevitably go through a few changes as you develop it. Keep a well-documented record of the evolution of your design.

- Select a part of your design that involves an intersection of parabolas or an intersection of parabolas and lines. Determine model equations for each function involved in this part of your design.

- Using these equations, determine any points of intersection.

- What is the relevance of the points of intersection to the design of the object? How is it helpful to have model equations and to know the coordinates of the points of intersection?

Linear and Quadratic Inequalities

The solution to a problem may be not a single value, but a range of values. A chemical engineer may need a reaction to occur within a certain time frame in order to reduce undesired pollutants. An architect may design a building to deflect less than a given distance in a strong wind. A doctor may choose a dose of medication so that a safe but effective level remains in the body after a specified time.

These situations illustrate the importance of inequalities. While there may be many acceptable values in each of the scenarios above, in each case there is a lower acceptable limit, an upper acceptable limit, or both. Even though many solutions exist, we still need accurate mathematical models and methods to obtain the solutions.

Web Link

A small number of mathematicians have earned the distinction of having an inequality named for them. To learn more about these special inequalities, go to www.mhrprecalc11.ca and follow the links.

Key Terms

solution region   test point
boundary

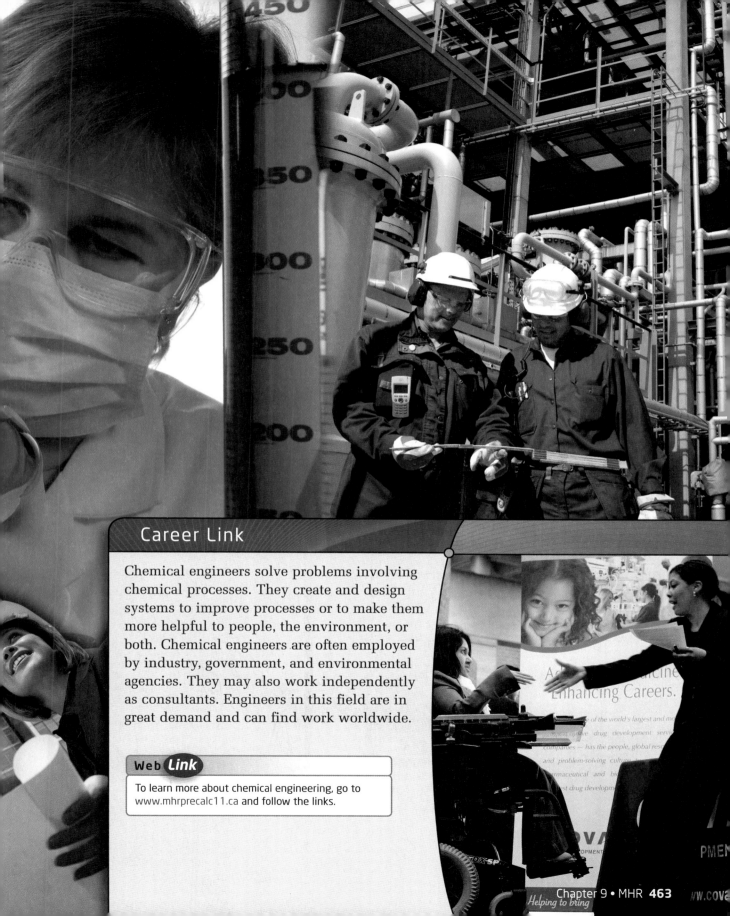

Career Link

Chemical engineers solve problems involving chemical processes. They create and design systems to improve processes or to make them more helpful to people, the environment, or both. Chemical engineers are often employed by industry, government, and environmental agencies. They may also work independently as consultants. Engineers in this field are in great demand and can find work worldwide.

Web Link

To learn more about chemical engineering, go to www.mhrprecalc11.ca and follow the links.

Linear Inequalities in Two Variables

Focus on...

- explaining when a solid or a dashed line should be used in the solution to an inequality
- explaining how to use test points to find the solution to an inequality
- sketching, with or without technology, the graph of a linear inequality
- solving a problem that involves a linear inequality

How can you choose the correct amounts of two items when both items are desirable? Suppose you want to take music lessons, but you also want to work out at a local gym. Your budget limits the amount you can spend. Solving a linear inequality can show you the alternatives that will help you meet both your musical and fitness goals and stay within your budget. Linear inequalities can model this situation and many others that require you to choose from combinations of two or more quantities.

Investigate Linear Inequalities

Materials

- grid paper
- straight edge

Suppose that you have received a gift card for a music-downloading service. The card has a value of $15. You have explored the Web site and discovered that individual songs cost $1 each and a complete album costs $5. Both prices include all taxes. Work with a partner to investigate this situation.

1. List all possible combinations of songs and albums that you can purchase if you spend all $15 of your gift card.

2. Let *x* represent the number of individual songs purchased and *y* represent the number of albums purchased. Write a linear equation in two variables to model the situation described in step 1.

3. Plot the points from step 1 that represent the coordinates of a combination of songs and albums that you can purchase for $15. On the same coordinate grid, graph the linear equation from step 2.

4. List all possible combinations of songs and albums that you can purchase for less than or equal to the total amount of your gift card.

5. Write a linear inequality in two variables to model the situation described in step 4.

6. Verify the combinations you found in step 4 by substituting the values in the inequality you wrote in step 5.

7. Compare your work with that of another pair of students to see if you agree on the possible combinations and the inequality that models the situation.

8. On the coordinate grid from step 3, plot each point that represents the coordinates of a combination of songs and albums that you can purchase for less than or equal to $15.

> **Reflect and Respond**

9. How does the graph show that it is possible to spend the entire value of the gift card?

10. Consider the inequality you wrote in step 5. Is it represented on your graph? Explain.

11. How would your graph change if the variables *x* and *y* represented quantities that could be real numbers, rather than whole numbers?

Is it convenient to find all possible combinations this way?

How is the value of the gift card reflected in your inequality?

How are the real numbers different from the whole numbers?

Web Link

Linear programming is a mathematical method of finding the best solution to a problem requiring a combination of two different items. Linear programming is part of the mathematical field of operations research. To learn more about a career as an operations researcher, go to www.mhrprecalc11.ca and follow the links.

Link the Ideas

A linear inequality in two variables may be in one of the following four forms:

- $Ax + By < C$
- $Ax + By \leq C$
- $Ax + By > C$
- $Ax + By \geq C$

where *A*, *B*, and *C* are real numbers.

An inequality in the two variables *x* and *y* describes a region in the Cartesian plane. The ordered pair (x, y) is a solution to a linear inequality if the inequality is true when the values of *x* and *y* are substituted into the inequality. The set of points that satisfy a linear inequality can be called the solution set, or **solution region**.

solution region

- all the points in the Cartesian plane that satisfy an inequality
- also known as the solution set

boundary

- a line or curve that separates the Cartesian plane into two regions
- may or may not be part of the solution region
- drawn as a solid line and included in the solution region if the inequality involves $\leq$ or $\geq$
- drawn as a dashed line and not included in the solution region if the inequality involves $<$ or $>$

The line related to the linear equality $Ax + By = C$, or **boundary**, divides the Cartesian plane into two solution regions.
- For one solution region, $Ax + By > C$ is true.
- For the other solution region, $Ax + By < C$ is true.

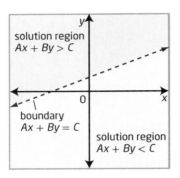

In your previous study of linear equations in two variables, the solution was all the ordered pairs located on the graph of the line. The solution to a linear inequality in two variables is a solution region that may or may not include the line, depending on the inequality.

Example 1

Graph a Linear Inequality of the Form $Ax + By \leq C$

a) Graph $2x + 3y \leq 6$.
b) Determine if the point $(-2, 4)$ is part of the solution.

Solution

a) First, determine the boundary of the graph, and then determine which region contains the solution.

There are several approaches to graphing the boundary.

Method 1: Solve for y
Solve the inequality for y in terms of x.
$$2x + 3y \leq 6$$
$$3y \leq -2x + 6$$
$$y \leq -\frac{2}{3}x + 2$$
Since the inequality symbol is $\leq$, points on the boundary are included in the solution. Use the slope of $-\frac{2}{3}$ and the y-intercept of 2 to graph the related line $y = -\frac{2}{3}x + 2$ as a solid line.

Method 2: Use the Intercepts

Since the inequality symbol is ≤, points on the boundary are included in the solution.

Use the intercepts to graph the related line $2x + 3y = 6$ as a solid line.

For $x = 0$:

$2(0) + 3y = 6$

$3y = 6$

$y = 2$

For $y = 0$:

$2x + 3(0) = 6$

$2x = 6$

$x = 3$

Locate the points $(0, 2)$ and $(3, 0)$ and draw a line passing through them.

After graphing the boundary, select a **test point** from each region to determine which contains the solution.

Why must the test point not be on the line?

For $(0, 0)$:

Left Side	Right Side
$2x + 3y$	6
$= 2(0) + 3(0)$	
$= 0$	

Left Side ≤ Right Side

For $(2, 4)$:

Left Side	Right Side
$2x + 3y$	6
$= 2(2) + 3(4)$	
$= 16$	

Left Side ≰ Right Side

test point

- a point not on the boundary of the graph of an inequality that is representative of all the points in a region
- a point that is used to determine whether the points in a region satisfy the inequality

The point $(0, 0)$ satisfies the inequality, so shade that region as the solution region.

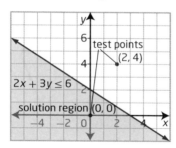

b) Determine if the point $(-2, 4)$ is in the solution region.

Left Side	Right Side
$2x + 3y$	6
$= 2(-2) + 3(4)$	
$= -4 + 12$	
$= 8$	

Left Side ≰ Right Side

The point $(-2, 4)$ is not part of the solution to the inequality $2x + 3y \leq 6$. From the graph of $2x + 3y \leq 6$, the point $(-2, 4)$ is not in the solution region.

Your Turn

a) Graph $4x + 2y \geq 10$.

b) Determine if the point $(1, 3)$ is part of the solution.

Example 2

Graph a Linear Inequality of the Form $Ax + By > C$

Graph $10x - 5y > 0$.

Solution

Solve the inequality for y in terms of x.   Is there another way to solve the inequality?

$$10x - 5y > 0$$
$$-5y > -10x$$
$$y < 2x$$ Why is the inequality symbol reversed?

Graph the related line $y = 2x$ as a broken, or dashed, line.

Use a test point from one region. Try $(-2, 3)$.

Left Side	Right Side
$10x - 5y$	0

Why is the point $(0, 0)$ not used as a test point this time?

$= 10(-2) - 5(3)$
$= -20 - 15$
$= -35$

　　　Left Side $\not>$ Right Side

The point $(-2, 3)$ does not satisfy the inequality. Shade the other region as the solution region.

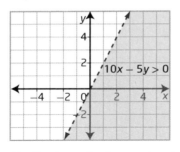

Why is the boundary graphed with a dashed line?

Verify the solution region by using a test point in the shaded region. Try $(2, -3)$.

Left Side	Right Side
$10x - 5y$	0

$= 10(2) - 5(-3)$
$= 20 + 15$
$= 35$

　　　Left Side $>$ Right Side

The graph of the solution region is correct.

Your Turn

Graph $5x - 20y < 0$.

Did You Know?

An open solution region does not include any of the points on the line that bounds it. A closed solution region includes the points on the line that bounds it.

Example 3

Write an Inequality Given Its Graph

Write an inequality to represent the graph.

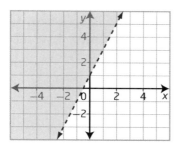

Solution

Write the equation of the boundary in slope-intercept form, $y = mx + b$.

The y-intercept is 1. So, $b = 1$.

Use the points $(0, 1)$ and $(1, 3)$ to determine that the slope, m, is 2.

$y = 2x + 1$

The boundary is a dashed line, so it is not part of the solution region.

Use a test point from the solution region to determine whether the inequality symbol is $>$ or $<$.

Try $(-2, 4)$.

Left Side   Right Side
  y $2x + 1$
$= 4$ $= 2(-2) + 1$
                  $= -3$
    Left Side $>$ Right Side

An inequality that represents the graph is $y > 2x + 1$.

Your Turn

Write an inequality to represent the graph.

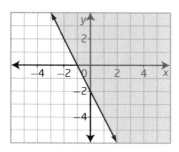

Example 4

Write and Solve an Inequality

Suppose that you are constructing a tabletop using aluminum and glass. The most that you can spend on materials is $50. Laminated safety glass costs $60/m², and aluminum costs $1.75/ft. You can choose the dimensions of the table and the amount of each material used. Find all possible combinations of materials sufficient to make the tabletop.

Solution

Let x represent the area of glass used and y represent the length of aluminum used. Then, the inequality representing this situation is

$$60x + 1.75y \leq 50$$

Solve the inequality for y in terms of x.

$$60x + 1.75y \leq 50$$
$$1.75y \leq -60x + 50$$
$$y \leq \frac{-60x}{1.75} + \frac{50}{1.75}$$

Use graphing technology to graph the related line $y = -\frac{60}{1.75}x + \frac{50}{1.75}$ as a solid line. Shade the region where a test point results in a true statement as the solution region.

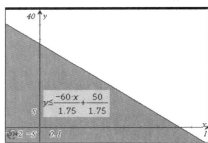

Examine the solution region.

You cannot have a negative amount of safety glass or aluminum.
Therefore, the domain and range contain only non-negative values.

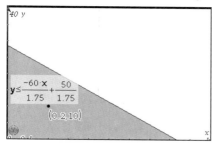

The graph shows all possible combinations of glass and aluminum that
can be used for the tabletop. One possible solution is (0.2, 10). This
represents 0.2 m² of the laminated safety glass and 10 ft of aluminum.

Your Turn

Use technology to find all possible combinations of tile and stone that
can be used to make a mosaic. Tile costs \$2.50/ft², stone costs \$6/kg, and
the budget for the mosaic is \$150.

Key Ideas

- A linear inequality in two variables describes a region of the
  Cartesian plane.

- All the points in one solution region satisfy the inequality and make
  up the solution region.

- The boundary of the solution region is the graph of the related linear
  equation.

  - When the inequality symbol is ≤ or ≥, the points on the boundary
    are included in the solution region and the line is a solid line.

  - When the inequality symbol is < or >, the points on the boundary
    are not included in the solution region and the line is a dashed line.

- Use a test point to determine which region is the solution region for
  the inequality.

Practise

1. Which of the ordered pairs are solutions to the given inequality?

   a) $y < x + 3$,
      $\{(7, 10), (-7, 10), (6, 7), (12, 9)\}$

   b) $-x + y \leq -5$,
      $\{(2, 3), (-6, -12), (4, -1), (8, -2)\}$

   c) $3x - 2y > 12$,
      $\{(6, 3), (12, -4), (-6, -3), (5, 1)\}$

   d) $2x + y \geq 6$,
      $\{(0, 0), (3, 1), (-4, -2), (6, -4)\}$

2. Which of the ordered pairs are *not* solutions to the given inequality?

   a) $y > -x + 1$,
      $\{(1, 0), (-2, 1), (4, 7), (10, 8)\}$

   b) $x + y \geq 6$,
      $\{(2, 4), (-5, 8), (4, 1), (8, 2)\}$

   c) $4x - 3y < 10$,
      $\{(1, 3), (5, 1), (-2, -3), (5, 6)\}$

   d) $5x + 2y \leq 9$,
      $\{(0, 0), (3, -1), (-4, 2), (1, -2)\}$

3. Consider each inequality.

   • Express y in terms of x, if necessary. Identify the slope and the y-intercept.

   • Indicate whether the boundary should be a solid line or a dashed line.

   a) $y \leq x + 3$

   b) $y > 3x + 5$

   c) $4x + y > 7$

   d) $2x - y \leq 10$

   e) $4x + 5y \geq 20$

   f) $x - 2y < 10$

4. Graph each inequality without using technology.

   a) $y \leq -2x + 5$

   b) $3y - x > 8$

   c) $4x + 2y - 12 \geq 0$

   d) $4x - 10y < 40$

   e) $x \geq y - 6$

5. Graph each inequality using technology.

   a) $6x - 5y \leq 18$

   b) $x + 4y < 30$

   c) $-5x + 12y - 28 > 0$

   d) $x \leq 6y + 11$

   e) $3.6x - 5.3y + 30 \geq 4$

6. Determine the solution to $-5y \leq x$.

7. Use graphing technology to determine the solution to $7x - 2y > 0$.

8. Graph each inequality. Explain your choice of graphing methods.

   a) $6x + 3y \geq 21$

   b) $10x < 2.5y$

   c) $2.5x < 10y$

   d) $4.89x + 12.79y \leq 145$

   e) $0.8x - 0.4y > 0$

9. Determine the inequality that corresponds to each graph.

   a)
   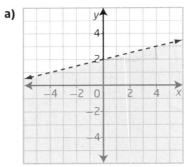

   b)
   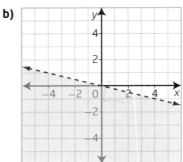

c)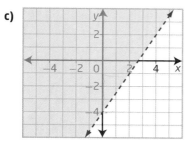

d)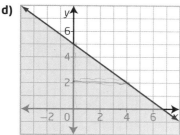

Apply

10. Express the solution to $x + 0y > 0$ graphically and in words.

11. Amaruq has a part-time job that pays her $12/h. She also sews baby moccasins and sells them for a profit of $12 each. Amaruq wants to earn at least $250/week.

a) Write an inequality that represents the number of hours that Amaruq can work and the number of baby moccasins she can sell to earn at least $250. Include any restrictions on the variables.

b) Graph the inequality.

c) List three different ordered pairs in the solution.

d) Give at least one reason that Amaruq would want to earn income from her part-time job as well as her sewing business, instead of focusing on one method only.

12. The Alberta Foundation for the Arts provides grants to support artists. The Aboriginal Arts Project Grant is one of its programs. Suppose that Camille has received a grant and is to spend at most $3000 of the grant on marketing and training combined. It costs $30/h to work with an elder in a mentorship program and $50/h for marketing assistance.

a) Write an inequality to represent the number of hours working with an elder and receiving marketing assistance that Camille can afford. Include any restrictions on the variables.

b) Graph the inequality.

Mother Eagle by Jason Carter, artist chosen to represent Alberta at the Vancouver 2010 Olympics. Jason is a member of the Little Red River Cree Nation.

Web Link

To learn more about the Alberta Foundation for the Arts, go to www.mhrprecalc11.ca and follow the links.

13. Mariya has purchased a new smart phone and is trying to decide on a service plan. Without a plan, each minute of use costs $0.30 and each megabyte of data costs $0.05. A plan that allows unlimited talk and data costs $100/month. Under which circumstances is the plan a better choice for Mariya?

14. Suppose a designer is modifying the tabletop from Example 4. The designer wants to replace the aluminum used in the table with a nanomaterial made from nanotubes. The budget for the project remains $50, the cost of glass is still $60/m², and the nanomaterial costs $45/kg. Determine all possible combinations of material available to the designer.

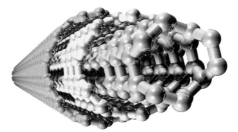

Multi-walled carbon nanotube

15. Speed skaters spend many hours training on and off the ice to improve their strength and conditioning. Suppose a team has a monthly training budget of $7000. Ice rental costs $125/h, and gym rental for strength training costs $55/h. Determine the solution region, or all possible combinations of training time that the team can afford.

Olympic gold medalist
Christine Nesbitt

Did You Know?

Canadian long-track and short-track speed skaters won 10 medals at the 2010 Olympic Winter Games in Vancouver, part of an Olympic record for the most gold medals won by a country in the history of the Winter Games.

Extend

16. Drawing a straight line is not the only way to divide a plane into two regions.

a) Determine one other relation that when graphed divides the Cartesian plane into two regions.

b) For your graph, write inequalities that describe each region of the Cartesian plane in terms of your relation. Justify your answer.

c) Does your relation satisfy the definition of a solution region? Explain.

17. Masha is a video game designer. She treats the computer screen like a grid. Each pixel on the screen is represented by a coordinate pair, with the pixel in the bottom left corner of the screen as (0, 0). For one scene in a game she is working on, she needs to have a background like the one shown.

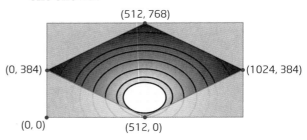

The shaded region on the screen is made up of four inequalities. What are the four inequalities?

18. **MINI LAB** Work in small groups.

In April 2008, Manitoba Hydro agreed to provide Wisconsin Public Service with up to 500 MW (megawatts) of hydroelectric power over 15 years, starting in 2018. Hydroelectric projects generate the majority of power in Manitoba; however, wind power is a method of electricity generation that may become more common. Suppose that hydroelectric power costs $60/MWh (megawatt hour) to produce, wind power costs $90/MWh, and the total budget for all power generation is $35 000/h.

Step 1 Write the inequality that represents the cost of power generation. Let x represent the number of megawatt hours of hydroelectric power produced. Let y represent the number of megawatt hours of wind power produced.

Step 2 Graph and solve the inequality for the cost of power generation given the restrictions imposed by the hydroelectric agreement. Determine the coordinates of the vertices of the solution region. Interpret the intercepts in the context of this situation.

Step 3 Suppose that Manitoba Hydro can sell the hydroelectric power for $95/MWh and the wind power for $105/MWh. The equation $R = 95x + 105y$ gives the revenue, R, in dollars, from the sale of power. Use a spreadsheet to find the revenue for a number of different points in the solution region. Is it possible to find the revenue for all possible combinations of power generation? Can you guarantee that the point giving the maximum possible revenue is shown on your spreadsheet?

	A	B	C
1	Hydroelectric (MWH)	Wind (MWH)	Revenue ($)
2	0	0	0
3	50	25	7375
4	100	50	14750
5	150	75	22125
6	200	100	29500
7			
8			

Step 4 It can be shown that the maximum revenue is always obtained from one of the vertices of the solution region. What combination of wind and hydroelectric power leads to the highest revenue?

Step 5 With your group, discuss reasons that a combination other than the one that produces the maximum revenue might be chosen.

Create Connections

19. Copy and complete the following mind map.

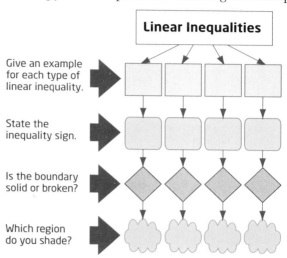

20. The graph shows the solution to a linear inequality.

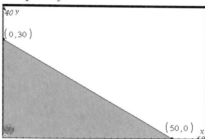

a) Write a scenario that has this region as its solution. Justify your answer.

b) Exchange your scenario with a partner. Verify that the given solution fits each scenario.

21. The inequality $2x - 3y + 24 > 0$, the positive y-axis, and the negative x-axis define a region in quadrant II.

a) Determine the area of this region.

b) How does the area of this region depend on the y-intercept of the boundary of the inequality $2x - 3y + 24 > 0$?

c) How does the area of this region depend on the slope of the boundary of the inequality $2x - 3y + 24 > 0$?

d) How would your answers to parts b) and c) change for regions with the same shape located in the other quadrants?

Quadratic Inequalities in One Variable

Focus on...

- developing strategies to solve quadratic inequalities in one variable
- modelling and solving problems using quadratic inequalities
- interpreting quadratic inequalities to determine solutions to problems

An engineer designing a roller coaster must know the minimum speed required for the cars to stay on the track. To determine this value, the engineer can solve a quadratic inequality. While infinitely many answers are possible, it is important that the engineer be sure that the speed of the car is in the solution region.

A bicycle manufacturer must know the maximum distance the rear suspension will travel when going over rough terrain. For many bicycles, the movement of the rear wheel is described by a quadratic equation, so this problem requires the solution to a quadratic inequality. Solving quadratic inequalities is important to ensure that the manufacturer can reduce warranty claims.

Investigate Quadratic Inequalities

Materials

- grid paper
- coloured pens, pencils, or markers

1. Consider the quadratic inequalities $x^2 - 3x - 4 > 0$ and $x^2 - 3x - 4 < 0$.

a) Use the graph of the corresponding function $f(x) = x^2 - 3x - 4$ to identify the zeros of the function.

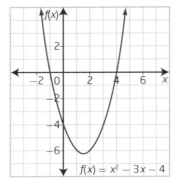

The x-axis is divided into three sections by the parabola. What are the three sections?

b) Identify the x-values for which the inequality $x^2 - 3x - 4 > 0$ is true.

c) Identify the x-values for which the inequality $x^2 - 3x - 4 < 0$ is true.

2. Consider the quadratic inequality $x^2 - x - 6 < 0$.

  a) Graph the corresponding quadratic function $f(x) = x^2 - x - 6$.

  b) How many zeros does the function have?

  c) Colour the portion of the x-axis for which the inequality $x^2 - x - 6 < 0$ is true.

  d) Write one or more inequalities to represent the values of x for which the function is negative. Show these values on a number line.

3. Consider the quadratic inequality $x^2 - 4x + 4 > 0$.

  a) Graph the corresponding quadratic function $f(x) = x^2 - 4x + 4$.

  b) How many zeros does the function have?

  c) Colour the portion of the x-axis for which the inequality $x^2 - 4x + 4 > 0$ is true.

  d) Write one or more inequalities to represent the values of x for which the function is positive. Show these values on a number line.

Reflect and Respond

4. a) Explain how you arrived at the inequalities in steps 2d) and 3d).

  b) What would you look for in the graph of the related function when solving a quadratic inequality of the form $ax^2 + bx + c > 0$ or $ax^2 + bx + c < 0$?

> **Did You Know?**
>
> Babylonian mathematicians were among the first to solve quadratics. However, they had no notation for variables, equations, or inequalities, and did not understand negative numbers. It was more than 1500 years before notation was developed.

Link the Ideas

You can write quadratic inequalities in one variable in one of the following four forms:

- $ax^2 + bx + c < 0$
- $ax^2 + bx + c \leq 0$
- $ax^2 + bx + c > 0$
- $ax^2 + bx + c \geq 0$

where a, b, and c are real numbers and $a \neq 0$.

You can solve quadratic inequalities graphically or algebraically. The solution set to a quadratic inequality in one variable can have no values, one value, or an infinite number of values.

Example 1

Solve a Quadratic Inequality of the Form $ax^2 + bx + c \leq 0$, $a > 0$

Solve $x^2 - 2x - 3 \leq 0$.

Solution

Method 1: Graph the Corresponding Function
Graph the corresponding function $f(x) = x^2 - 2x - 3$.

To determine the solution to $x^2 - 2x - 3 \leq 0$, look for the values of x for which the graph of $f(x)$ lies on or below the x-axis.

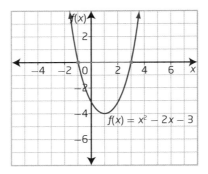

What strategies can you use to sketch the graph of a quadratic function in standard form?

The parabola lies on the x-axis at $x = -1$ and $x = 3$. The graph lies below the x-axis between these values of x. Therefore, the solution set is all real values of x between -1 and 3, inclusive, or $\{x \mid -1 \leq x \leq 3, x \in R\}$.

Method 2: Roots and Test Points
Solve the related equation $x^2 - 2x - 3 = 0$ to find the roots. Then, use a number line and test points to determine the intervals that satisfy the inequality.

$$x^2 - 2x - 3 = 0$$
$$(x + 1)(x - 3) = 0$$
$$x + 1 = 0 \quad \text{or} \quad x - 3 = 0$$
$$x = -1 \qquad x = 3$$

Plot -1 and 3 on a number line. Use closed circles since these values are solutions to the inequality.

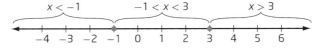

Does it matter which values you choose as test points?

Are there any values that you should not choose?

The x-axis is divided into three intervals by the roots of the equation. Choose one test point from each interval, say -2, 0, and 5. Then, substitute each value into the quadratic inequality to determine whether the result satisfies the inequality.

Use a table to organize the results.

Interval	$x < -1$	$-1 < x < 3$	$x > 3$
Test Point	-2	0	5
Substitution	$(-2)^2 - 2(-2) - 3$ $= 4 + 4 - 3$ $= 5$	$0^2 - 2(0) - 3$ $= 0 + 0 - 3$ $= -3$	$5^2 - 2(5) - 3$ $= 25 - 10 - 3$ $= 12$
Is $x^2 - 2x - 3 \le 0$?	no	yes	no

The values of x between -1 and 3 also satisfy the inequality.
The value of $x^2 - 2x - 3$ is negative in the interval $-1 < x < 3$.
The solution set is $\{x \mid -1 \le x \le 3, x \in R\}$.

Method 3: Case Analysis

Factor the quadratic expression to rewrite the inequality
as $(x + 1)(x - 3) \le 0$.

The product of two factors is negative when the factors have different
signs. There are two ways for this to happen.

Case 1: The first factor is negative and the second factor is positive.

$x + 1 \le 0$ and $x - 3 \ge 0$

Solve these inequalities to obtain $x \le -1$ and $x \ge 3$.

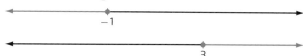

Any x-values that satisfy both conditions are part of
the solution set. There are no values that make both
of these inequalities true.

Why are there no
values that make both
inequalities true?

Case 2: The first factor is positive and the second factor is negative.

$x + 1 \ge 0$ and $x - 3 \le 0$

Solve these inequalities to obtain $x \ge -1$ and $x \le 3$.

The dashed lines indicate
that $-1 \le x \le 3$ is
common to both.

These inequalities are both true for all values
between -1 and 3, inclusive.

The solution set is $\{x \mid -1 \le x \le 3, x \in R\}$.

How would the steps in
this method change if the
original inequality were
$x^2 - 2x - 3 \ge 0$?

Your Turn

Solve $x^2 - 10x + 16 \le 0$ using two different methods.

Example 2

Solve a Quadratic Inequality of the Form $ax^2 + bx + c < 0$, $a < 0$

Solve $-x^2 + x + 12 < 0$.

> **Solution**

Method 1: Roots and Test Points

Solve the related equation $-x^2 + x + 12 = 0$ to find the roots.

$$
\begin{aligned}
-x^2 + x + 12 &= 0 \\
-1(x^2 - x - 12) &= 0 \\
-1(x + 3)(x - 4) &= 0 \\
x + 3 = 0 \quad &\text{or} \quad x - 4 = 0 \\
x = -3 \quad\quad\quad & \quad\quad x = 4
\end{aligned}
$$

Plot -3 and 4 on a number line.
Use open circles, since these values are not solutions to the inequality.

Choose a test point from each of the three intervals, say -5, 0, and 5, to determine whether the result satisfies the quadratic inequality.

Use a table to organize the results.

Interval	$x < -3$	$-3 < x < 4$	$x > 4$
Test Point	-5	0	5
Substitution	$-(-5)^2 + (-5) + 12$ $= -25 - 5 + 12$ $= -18$	$-0^2 + 0 + 12$ $= 0 + 0 + 12$ $= 12$	$-5^2 + 5 + 12$ $= -25 + 5 + 12$ $= -8$
Is $-x^2 + x + 12 < 0$?	yes	no	yes

The values of x less than -3 or greater than 4 satisfy the inequality.

The solution set is $\{x \mid x < -3 \text{ or } x > 4, x \in \mathbb{R}\}$.

Method 2: Sign Analysis

Factor the quadratic expression to rewrite the inequality as $-1(x + 3)(x - 4) < 0$.

Determine when each of the factors, $-1(x + 3)$ and $x + 4$, is positive, zero, or negative.

Since -1 is a constant factor, combine it with $(x + 3)$ to form one factor.

Substituting -4 in $-1(x + 3)$ results in a positive value (+).
$$-1(-4 + 3) = -1(-1)$$
$$= 1$$

Substituting -3 in $-1(x + 3)$ results in a value of zero (0).
$$-1(-3 + 3) = -1(0)$$
$$= 0$$

Substituting 1 in $-1(x + 3)$ results in a negative value (−).
$$-1(1 + 3) = -1(4)$$
$$= 1$$

Sketch number lines to show the results.

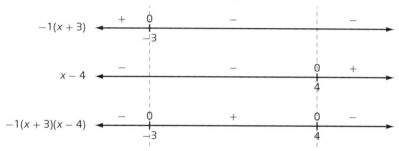

From the number line representing the product, the values of x less than -3 or greater than 4 satisfy the inequality $-1(x + 3)(x - 4) < 0$.

The solution set is $\{x \mid x < -3 \text{ or } x > 4, x \in \mathbb{R}\}$.

Your Turn

Solve $-x^2 + 3x + 10 < 0$ using two different methods.

Example 3

Solve a Quadratic Inequality in One Variable

Solve $2x^2 - 7x > 12$.

> **Solution**

Why is it important to rewrite the inequality with 0 on one side of the inequality?

Why use the quadratic formula in this case?

First, rewrite the inequality as $2x^2 - 7x - 12 > 0$.
Solve the related equation $2x^2 - 7x - 12 = 0$ to find the roots.
Use the quadratic formula with $a = 2$, $b = -7$, and $c = -12$.

$$x = \frac{-b \pm \sqrt{b^2 - 4ac}}{2a}$$

$$x = \frac{-(-7) \pm \sqrt{(-7)^2 - 4(2)(-12)}}{2(2)}$$

$$x = \frac{7 \pm \sqrt{145}}{4}$$

$$x = \frac{7 + \sqrt{145}}{4} \quad \text{or} \quad x = \frac{7 - \sqrt{145}}{4}$$

$$x \approx 4.8 \qquad\qquad\qquad x \approx -1.3$$

Use a number line and test points.

Choose a test point from each of the three intervals, say -3, 0, and 6, to determine whether the results satisfy the original quadratic inequality.

Use a table to organize the results.

Interval	$x < \dfrac{7 - \sqrt{145}}{4}$	$\dfrac{7 - \sqrt{145}}{4} < x < \dfrac{7 + \sqrt{145}}{4}$	$x > \dfrac{7 + \sqrt{145}}{4}$
Test Point	-3	0	6
Substitution	$2(-3)^2 - 7(-3)$ $= 18 + 21$ $= 39$	$2(0)^2 - 7(0)$ $= 0 + 0$ $= 0$	$2(6)^2 - 7(6)$ $= 72 - 42$ $= 30$
Is $2x^2 - 7x > 12$?	yes	no	yes

Therefore, the exact solution set is
$$\left\{ x \mid x < \frac{7 - \sqrt{145}}{4} \text{ or } x > \frac{7 + \sqrt{145}}{4}, x \in R \right\}.$$

Can you solve this inequality using sign analysis and case analysis?

Your Turn

Solve $x^2 - 4x > 10$.

Example 4

Apply Quadratic Inequalities

If a baseball is thrown at an initial speed of 15 m/s from a height of 2 m above the ground, the inequality $-4.9t^2 + 15t + 2 > 0$ models the time, t, in seconds, that the baseball is in flight. During what time interval is the baseball in flight?

Why is the quadratic expression greater than zero?

Solution

The baseball will be in flight from the time it is thrown until it lands on the ground.

Graph the corresponding quadratic function and determine the coordinates of the x-intercepts and the y-intercept.

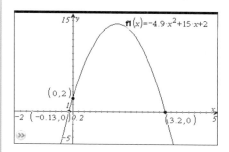

Why is it useful to know the y-intercept of the graph in this case?

The graph of the function lies on or above the x-axis for values of x between approximately -0.13 and 3.2, inclusive. However, you cannot have a negative time that the baseball will be in the air.

The solution set to the problem is $\{t \mid 0 < t < 3.2, t \in R\}$. In other words, the baseball is in flight between 0 s and approximately 3.2 s after it is thrown.

Your Turn

Suppose a baseball is thrown from a height of 1.5 m. The inequality $-4.9t^2 + 17t + 1.5 > 0$ models the time, t, in seconds, that the baseball is in flight. During what time interval is the baseball in flight?

Web Link

To learn about baseball in Canada, go to www.mhrprecalc11.ca and follow the links.

Key Ideas

- The solution to a quadratic inequality in one variable is a set of values.
- To solve a quadratic inequality, you can use one of the following strategies:
  - Graph the corresponding function, and identify the values of x for which the function lies on, above, or below the x-axis, depending on the inequality symbol.
  - Determine the roots of the related equation, and then use a number line and test points to determine the intervals that satisfy the inequality.
  - Determine when each of the factors of the quadratic expression is positive, zero, or negative, and then use the results to determine the sign of the product.
  - Consider all cases for the required product of the factors of the quadratic expression to find any x-values that satisfy both factor conditions in each case.
- For inequalities with the symbol $\geq$ or $\leq$, include the x-intercepts in the solution set.

Check Your Understanding

Practise

1. Consider the graph of the quadratic function $f(x) = x^2 - 4x + 3$.

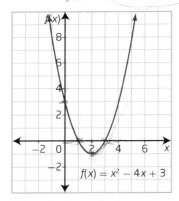

What is the solution to

a) $x^2 - 4x + 3 \leq 0$?

b) $x^2 - 4x + 3 \geq 0$?

c) $x^2 - 4x + 3 > 0$?

d) $x^2 - 4x + 3 < 0$?

2. Consider the graph of the quadratic function $g(x) = -x^2 + 4x - 4$.

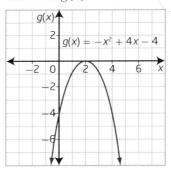

What is the solution to

a) $-x^2 + 4x - 4 \leq 0$?

b) $-x^2 + 4x - 4 \geq 0$?

c) $-x^2 + 4x - 4 > 0$?

d) $-x^2 + 4x - 4 < 0$?

3. Is the value of x a solution to the given inequality?

a) $x = 4$ for $x^2 - 3x - 10 > 0$

b) $x = 1$ for $x^2 + 3x - 4 \geq 0$

c) $x = -2$ for $x^2 + 4x + 3 < 0$

d) $x = -3$ for $-x^2 - 5x - 4 \leq 0$

4. Use roots and test points to determine the solution to each inequality.

a) $x(x + 6) \geq 40$

b) $-x^2 - 14x - 24 < 0$

c) $6x^2 > 11x + 35$

d) $8x + 5 \leq -2x^2$

5. Use sign analysis to determine the solution to each inequality.

a) $x^2 + 3x \leq 18$

b) $x^2 + 3 \geq -4x$

c) $4x^2 - 27x + 18 < 0$

d) $-6x \geq x^2 - 16$

6. Use case analysis to determine the solution to each inequality.

a) $x^2 - 2x - 15 < 0$

b) $x^2 + 13x > -12$

c) $-x^2 + 2x + 5 \leq 0$

d) $2x^2 \geq 8 - 15x$

7. Use graphing to determine the solution to each inequality.

a) $x^2 + 14x + 48 \leq 0$

b) $x^2 \geq 3x + 28$

c) $-7x^2 + x - 6 \geq 0$

d) $4x(x - 1) > 63$

8. Solve each of the following inequalities. Explain your strategy and why you chose it.

a) $x^2 - 10x + 16 < 0$

b) $12x^2 - 11x - 15 \geq 0$

c) $x^2 - 2x - 12 \leq 0$

d) $x^2 - 6x + 9 > 0$

9. Solve each inequality.

a) $x^2 - 3x + 6 \leq 10x$

b) $2x^2 + 12x - 11 > x^2 + 2x + 13$

c) $x^2 - 5x < 3x^2 - 18x + 20$

d) $-3(x^2 + 4) \leq 3x^2 - 5x - 68$

Apply

10. Each year, Dauphin, Manitoba, hosts the largest ice-fishing contest in Manitoba. Before going on any ice, it is important to know that the ice is thick enough to support the intended load. The solution to the inequality $9h^2 \geq 750$ gives the thickness, h, in centimetres, of ice that will support a vehicle of mass 750 kg.

a) Solve the inequality to determine the minimum thickness of ice that will safely support the vehicle.

b) Write a new inequality, in the form $9h^2 \geq$ mass, that you can use to find the ice thickness that will support a mass of 1500 kg.

c) Solve the inequality you wrote in part b).

d) Why is the thickness of ice required to support 1500 kg not twice the thickness needed to support 750 kg? Explain.

Did You Know?

Conservation efforts at Dauphin Lake, including habitat enhancement, stocking, and education, have resulted in sustainable fish stocks and better fishing for anglers.

11. Many farmers in Southern Alberta irrigate their crops. A centre-pivot irrigation system spreads water in a circular pattern over a crop.

a) Suppose that Murray has acquired rights to irrigate up to 63 ha (hectares) of his land. Write an inequality to model the maximum circular area, in square metres, that he can irrigate.

b) What are the possible radii of circles that Murray can irrigate? Express your answer as an exact value.

c) Express your answer in part b) to the nearest hundredth of a metre.

Did You Know?

The hectare is a unit of area defined as 10 000 m². It is primarily used as a measurement of land area.

12. Suppose that an engineer determines that she can use the formula $-t^2 + 14 \leq P$ to estimate when the price of carbon fibre will be P dollars per kilogram or less in t years from the present.

a) When will carbon fibre be available at $10/kg or less?

b) Explain why some of the values of t that satisfy the inequality do not solve the problem.

c) Write and solve a similar inequality to determine when carbon fibre prices will drop below $5/kg.

Did You Know?

Carbon fibre is prized for its high strength-to-mass ratio. Prices for carbon fibre were very high when the technology was new, but dropped as manufacturing methods improved.

13. One leg of a right triangle is 2 cm longer than the other leg. How long should the shorter leg be to ensure that the area of the triangle is greater than or equal to 4 cm²?

Extend

14. Use your knowledge of the graphs of quadratic functions and the discriminant to investigate the solutions to the quadratic inequality $ax^2 + bx + c \geq 0$.

a) Describe all cases where all real numbers satisfy the inequality.

b) Describe all cases where exactly one real number satisfies the inequality.

c) Describe all cases where infinitely many real numbers satisfy the inequality and infinitely many real numbers do not satisfy the inequality.

15. For each of the following, give an inequality that has the given solution.

a) $-2 \leq x \leq 7$

b) $x < 1$ or $x > 10$

c) $\frac{5}{3} \leq x \leq 6$

d) $x < -\frac{3}{4}$ or $x > -\frac{1}{5}$

e) $x \leq -3 - \sqrt{7}$ or $x \geq -3 + \sqrt{7}$

f) $x \in \mathbb{R}$

g) no solution

16. Solve $|x^2 - 4| \geq 2$.

17. The graph shows the solution to the inequality $-x^2 + 12x + 16 \geq -x + 28$.

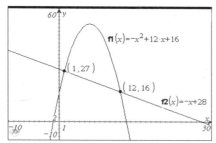

a) Why is $1 \leq x \leq 12$ the solution to the inequality?

b) Rearrange the inequality so that it has the form $q(x) \geq 0$ for a quadratic $q(x)$.

c) Solve the inequality you determined in part b).

d) How are the solutions to parts a) and c) related? Explain.

Create Connections

18. In Example 3, the first step in the solution was to rearrange the inequality $2x^2 - 7x > 12$ into $2x^2 - 7x - 12 > 0$. Which solution methods require this first step and which do not? Show the work that supports your conclusions.

19. Compare and contrast the methods of graphing, roots and test points, sign analysis, and case analysis. Explain which of the methods you prefer to use and why.

20. Devan needs to solve $x^2 + 5x + 4 \leq -2$. His solutions are shown.

Devan's solution:

> Begin by rewriting the inequality: $x^2 + 5x + 6 \geq 0$
> Factor the left side: $(x + 2)(x + 3) \geq 0$. Then, consider two cases:
>
> Case 1:
> $(x + 2) \leq 0$ and $(x + 3) \leq 0$
> Then, $x \leq -2$ and $x \leq -3$, so the solution is $x \leq -3$.
>
> Case 2:
> $(x + 2) \geq 0$ and $(x + 3) \geq 0$
> Then, $x \geq -2$ and $x \geq -3$, so the solution is $x \geq -2$.
>
> From the two cases, the solution to the inequality is $x \leq -3$ or $x \geq -2$.

a) Decide whether his solution is correct. Justify your answer.

b) Use a different method to confirm the correct answer to the inequality.

Project Corner   **Financial Considerations**

- Currently, the methods of nanotechnology in several fields are very expensive. However, as is often the case, it is expected that as technology improves, the costs will decrease. Nanotechnology seems to have the potential to decrease costs in the future. It also promises greater flexibility and greater precision in the manufacturing of goods.

- What changes in manufacturing might help lower the cost of nanotechnology?

Quadratic Inequalities in Two Variables

Focus on...

- explaining how to use test points to find the solution to an inequality
- explaining when a solid or a dashed line should be used in the solution to an inequality
- sketching, with or without technology, the graph of a quadratic inequality
- solving a problem that involves a quadratic inequality

An arch is a common way to span a doorway or window. A parabolic arch is the strongest possible arch because the arch is self-supporting. This is because the shape of the arch causes the force of gravity to hold the arch together instead of pulling the arch apart.

There are many things to consider when designing an arch. One important decision is the height of the space below the arch. To ensure that the arch is functional, the designer can set up and solve a quadratic inequality in two variables. Quadratic inequalities are applied in physics, engineering, architecture, and many other fields.

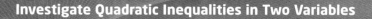

Investigate Quadratic Inequalities in Two Variables

Materials

- grid paper
- coloured pens, pencils, or markers

1. Sketch the graph of the function $y = x^2$.

2. a) Label four points on the graph and copy and complete the table for these points. One has been done for you.

x	y	Satisfies the Equation $y = x^2$?
3	9	$9 = 3^2$ Yes

b) What can you conclude about the points that lie on the parabola?

3. The parabola that you graphed in step 1 divides the Cartesian plane into two regions, one above and one below the parabola.

   a) In which of these regions do you think the solution set for $y < x^2$ lies?

   b) Plot four points in this region of the plane and create a table similar to the one in step 2, using the heading "Satisfies the Inequality $y < x^2$?" for the last column.

4. Were you correct in your thinking of which region the solution set for $y < x^2$ lies in? How do you know?

5. Shade the region containing the solution set for the inequality $y < x^2$.

6. a) In which region does the solution set for $y > x^2$ lie?

   b) Plot four points in this region of the plane and create a table similar to the one in step 2, using the heading "Satisfies the Inequality $y > x^2$?" for the last column.

7. Did the table verify the region you chose for the set of points that satisfy $y > x^2$?

8. Shade the region containing the solution set for the inequality $y > x^2$.

Reflect and Respond

9. Why is a shaded region used to represent the solution sets in steps 5 and 8?

10. Make a conjecture about how you can identify the solution region of the graph of a quadratic inequality.

11. Under what conditions would the graph of the function be part of the solution region for a quadratic inequality?

Link the Ideas

You can express a quadratic inequality in two variables in one of the following four forms:
- $y < ax^2 + bx + c$
- $y \leq ax^2 + bx + c$
- $y > ax^2 + bx + c$
- $y \geq ax^2 + bx + c$

where a, b, and c are real numbers and $a \neq 0$.

A quadratic inequality in two variables represents a region of the Cartesian plane with a parabola as the boundary. The graph of a quadratic inequality is the set of points (x, y) that are solutions to the inequality.

Consider the graph of $y < x^2 - 2x - 3$.

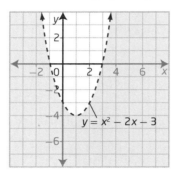

The boundary is the related parabola $y = x^2 - 2x - 3$. Since the inequality symbol is $<$, points on the boundary line are not included in the solution region, so the curve is drawn as a dashed line.

To determine which region is the solution region, choose a test point from either above or below the parabola. If the coordinates of the test point satisfy the inequality, then shade the region containing the test point. If the coordinates do not satisfy the inequality, then shade the region that does not contain the test point.

Try $(0, 0)$, which is above the parabola.

Left Side   Right Side
$$y \qquad\qquad x^2 - 2x - 3$$
$$= 0 \qquad\qquad = 0^2 - 2(0) - 3$$
$$\qquad\qquad\qquad = -3$$
Left Side $\not<$ Right Side

The point $(0, 0)$ does not satisfy the inequality. Thus, shade the region below the parabola.

Example 1

Graph a Quadratic Inequality in Two Variables With $a < 0$

a) Graph $y < -2(x - 3)^2 + 1$.
b) Determine if the point $(2, -4)$ is a solution to the inequality.

Solution

How can you use the values of a, p, and q to graph the parabola?

a) Graph the related parabola $y = -2(x - 3)^2 + 1$. Since the inequality symbol is $<$, draw the parabola as a dashed line, indicating that it is not part of the solution.

Use test points to decide which of the two regions contains the solutions to the inequality.

Choose $(0, 0)$ and $(3, -3)$.

Left Side	Right Side		Left Side	Right Side
y	$-2(x - 3)^2 + 1$		y	$-2(x - 3)^2 + 1$
$= 0$	$= -2(0 - 3)^2 + 1$		$= -3$	$= -2(3 - 3)^2 + 1$
	$= -18 + 1$			$= 0 + 1$
	$= -17$			$= 1$

Left Side $\not<$ Right Side Left Side $<$ Right Side

The point $(3, -3)$ satisfies the inequality, so shade the region below the parabola.

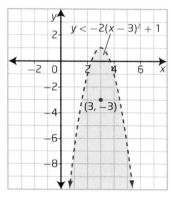

b) From the graph of $y < -2(x - 3)^2 + 1$, the point $(2, -4)$ is in the solution region. It is part of the solution to the inequality $y < -2(x - 3)^2 + 1$. Verify this by substituting in the inequality.

Left Side	Right Side
y	$-2(x - 3)^2 + 1$
$= -4$	$= -2(2 - 3)^2 + 1$
	$= -2 + 1$
	$= -1$

Left Side $<$ Right Side

Your Turn

a) Graph $y > (x - 4)^2 - 2$.

b) Determine if the point $(2, 1)$ is a solution to the inequality.

Example 2

Graph a Quadratic Inequality in Two Variables With $a > 0$

Graph $y \geq x^2 - 4x - 5$.

Solution

Graph the related parabola $y = x^2 - 4x - 5$. Since the inequality symbol is $\geq$, points on the parabola are included in the solution. Draw the parabola using a solid line.

Use a test point from one region to decide whether that region contains the solutions to the inequality.

Choose $(0, 0)$.

Left Side   Right Side
  y $x^2 - 4x - 5$
$= 0$ $= 0^2 - 4(0) - 5$
                  $= 0 - 0 - 5$
                  $= -5$
    Left Side $\geq$ Right Side

The point $(0, 0)$ satisfies the inequality, so shade the region above the parabola.

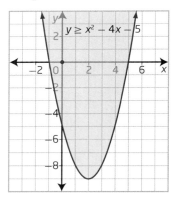

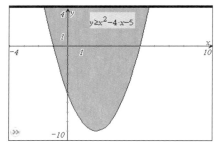

Your Turn

Graph $y \leq -x^2 + 2x + 4$.

Example 3

Determine the Quadratic Inequality That Defines a Solution Region

You can use a parabolic reflector to focus sound, light, or radio waves to a single point. A parabolic microphone has a parabolic reflector attached that directs incoming sounds to the microphone. René, a journalist, is using a parabolic microphone as he covers the Francophone Summer Festival of Vancouver. Describe the region that René can cover with his microphone if the reflector has a width of 50 cm and a maximum depth of 15 cm.

Solution

Method 1: Describe Graphically

Draw a diagram and label it with the given information.

Let the origin represent the vertex of the parabolic reflector.

Let x and y represent the horizontal and vertical distances, in centimetres, from the low point in the centre of the parabolic reflector.

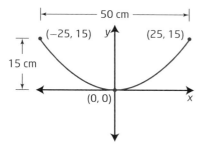

From the graph, the region covered lies between -25 cm to $+25$ cm because of the width of the microphone.

Method 2: Describe Algebraically

You can write a quadratic function to represent a parabola if you know the coordinates of the vertex and one other point.

Since the vertex is $(0, 0)$, the function is of the form $y = ax^2$.

Substitute the coordinates of the top of one edge of the parabolic reflector, $(25, 15)$, and solve to find $a = \dfrac{3}{125}$.

$$y = \frac{3}{125}x^2$$

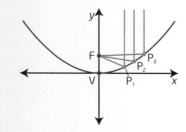

The microphone picks up sound from the space above the graph of the quadratic function. So, shade the region above the parabola.

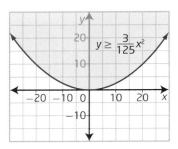

$y \geq \frac{3}{125}x^2$

Why is the reflector represented by a solid curve rather than a broken curve?

However, the maximum scope is from -25 to $+25$ because of the width of the microphone. So, the domain of the region covered by the microphone is restricted to $\{x \mid -25 \leq x \leq 25, x \in R\}$.

Use a test point from the solution region to verify the inequality symbol.

Choose the point $(5, 5)$.

Left Side   Right Side

$$y$$
$$= 5$$

$$\frac{3}{125}x^2$$
$$= \frac{3}{125}(5)^2$$
$$= \frac{3}{5}$$

Left Side $\geq$ Right Side

The region covered by the microphone can be described by the quadratic inequality $y \geq \frac{3}{125}x^2$, where $-25 \leq x \leq 25$.

Your Turn

A satellite dish is 60 cm in diameter and 20 cm deep. The dish has a parabolic cross-section. Locate the vertex of the parabolic cross-section at the origin, and sketch the parabola that represents the dish. Determine an inequality that shows the region from which the dish can receive a signal.

Example 4

Interpret the Graph of an Inequality in a Real-World Application

Samia and Jerrod want to learn the exhilarating sport of alpine rock climbing. They have enrolled in one of the summer camps at the Cascade Mountains in southern British Columbia. In the brochure, they come across an interesting fact about the manila rope that is used for rappelling down a cliff. It states that the rope can safely support a mass, M, in pounds, modelled by the inequality $M \leq 1450d^2$, where d is the diameter of the rope, in inches. Graph the inequality to examine how the mass that the rope supports is related to the diameter of the rope.

Solution

Graph the related parabola $M = 1450d^2$.

Since the inequality symbol is $\leq$, use a solid line for the parabola.

Shade the region below the parabola since the inequality is less than.

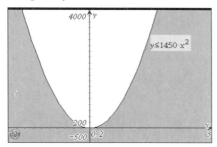

Verify the solution region using the test point $(2, 500)$.

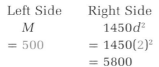

Left Side	Right Side
M	$1450d^2$
$= 500$	$= 1450(2)^2$
	$= 5800$

Left Side $\leq$ Right Side

Examine the solution.

You cannot have a negative value for the diameter of the rope or the mass. Therefore, the domain is $\{d \mid d \geq 0, d \in \mathbb{R}\}$ and the range is $\{M \mid M \geq 0, M \in \mathbb{R}\}$.

One solution is $(1.5, 1000)$. This means that a rope with a diameter of 1.5 in. will support a weight of 1000 lb.

Your Turn

Sports climbers use a rope that is longer and supports less mass than manila rope. The rope can safely support a mass, M, in pounds, modelled by the inequality $M \leq 1240(d - 2)^2$, where d is the diameter of the rope, in inches. Graph the inequality to examine how the mass that the rope supports is related to the diameter of the rope.

Key Ideas

- A quadratic inequality in two variables represents a region of the Cartesian plane containing the set of points that are solutions to the inequality.

- The graph of the related quadratic function is the boundary that divides the plane into two regions.

  - When the inequality symbol is $\leq$ or $\geq$, include the points on the boundary in the solution region and draw the boundary as a solid line.

  - When the inequality symbol is $<$ or $>$, do not include the points on the boundary in the solution region and draw the boundary as a dashed line.

- Use a test point to determine the region that contains the solutions to the inequality.

Check Your Understanding

Practise

1. Which of the ordered pairs are solutions to the inequality?

   a) $y < x^2 + 3$,
      $\{(2, 6), (4, 20), (-1, 3), (-3, 12)\}$

   b) $y \leq -x^2 + 3x - 4$,
      $\{(2, -2), (4, -1), (0, -6), (-2, -15)\}$

   c) $y > 2x^2 + 3x + 6$,
      $\{(-3, 5), (0, -6), (2, 10), (5, 40)\}$

   d) $y \geq -\frac{1}{2}x^2 - x + 5$,
      $\{(-4, 2), (-1, 5), (1, 3.5), (3, 2.5)\}$

2. Which of the ordered pairs are *not* solutions to the inequality?

   a) $y \geq 2(x - 1)^2 + 1$,
      $\{(0, 1), (1, 0), (3, 6), (-2, 15)\}$

   b) $y > -(x + 2)^2 - 3$,
      $\{(-3, 1), (-2, -3), (0, -8), (1, 2)\}$

   c) $y \leq \frac{1}{2}(x - 4)^2 + 5$,
      $\{(0, 4), (3, 1), (4, 5), (2, 9)\}$

   d) $y < -\frac{2}{3}(x + 3)^2 - 2$,
      $\{(-2, 2), (-1, -5), (-3, -2), (0, -10)\}$

3. Write an inequality to describe each graph, given the function defining the boundary parabola.

a)
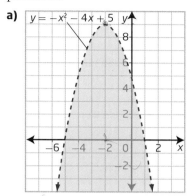

b)
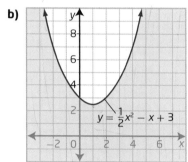

c)
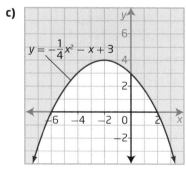

d)
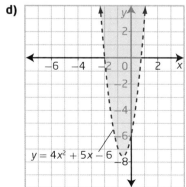

4. Graph each quadratic inequality using transformations to sketch the boundary parabola.

a) $y \geq 2(x + 3)^2 + 4$

b) $y > -\dfrac{1}{2}(x - 4)^2 - 1$

c) $y < 3(x + 1)^2 + 5$

d) $y \leq \dfrac{1}{4}(x - 7)^2 - 2$

5. Graph each quadratic inequality using points and symmetry to sketch the boundary parabola.

a) $y < -2(x - 1)^2 - 5$

b) $y > (x + 6)^2 + 1$

c) $y \geq \dfrac{2}{3}(x - 8)^2$

d) $y \leq \dfrac{1}{2}(x + 7)^2 - 4$

6. Graph each quadratic inequality.

a) $y \leq x^2 + x - 6$

b) $y > x^2 - 5x + 4$

c) $y \geq x^2 - 6x - 16$

d) $y < x^2 + 8x + 16$

7. Graph each inequality using graphing technology.

a) $y < 3x^2 + 13x + 10$

b) $y \geq -x^2 + 4x + 7$

c) $y \leq x^2 + 6$

d) $y > -2x^2 + 5x - 8$

8. Write an inequality to describe each graph.

a)
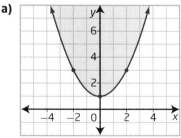

b)
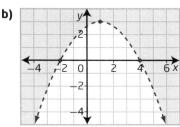

Apply

9. When a dam is built across a river, it is often constructed in the shape of a parabola. A parabola is used so that the force that the river exerts on the dam helps hold the dam together. Suppose a dam is to be built as shown in the diagram.

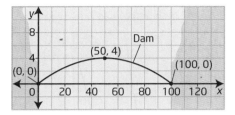

a) What is the quadratic function that models the parabolic arch of the dam?

b) Write the inequality that approximates the region below the parabolic arch of the dam.

Did You Know?

The Mica Dam, which spans the Columbia River near Revelstoke, British Columbia, is a parabolic dam that provides hydroelectric power to Canada and parts of the United States.

10. In order to get the longest possible jump, ski jumpers need to have as much lift area, L, in square metres, as possible while in the air. One of the many variables that influences the amount of lift area is the hip angle, a, in degrees, of the skier. The relationship between the two is given by $L \geq -0.000\,125a^2 + 0.040a - 2.442$.

a) Graph the quadratic inequality.

b) What is the range of hip angles that will generate lift area of at least 0.50 m²?

Canadian ski jumper
Stefan Read

11. The University Bridge in Saskatoon is supported by several parabolic arches. The diagram shows how a Cartesian plane can be applied to one arch of the bridge. The function $y = -0.03x^2 + 0.84x - 0.08$ approximates the curve of the arch, where x represents the horizontal distance from the bottom left edge and y represents the height above where the arch meets the vertical pier, both in metres.

a) Write the inequality that approximates the possible water levels below the parabolic arch of the bridge.

b) Suppose that the normal water level of the river is at most 0.2 m high, relative to the base of the arch. Write and solve an inequality to represent the normal river level below the arch.

c) What is the width of the river under the arch in the situation described in part b)?

12. In order to conduct microgravity research, the Canadian Space Agency uses a Falcon 20 jet that flies a parabolic path. As the jet nears the vertex of the parabola, the passengers in the jet experience nearly zero gravity that lasts for a short period of time. The function $h = -2.944t^2 + 191.360t + 6950.400$ models the flight of a jet on a parabolic path for time, t, in seconds, since weightlessness has been achieved and height, h, in metres.

Canadian Space Agency astronauts David Saint-Jacques and Jeremy Hansen experience microgravity during a parabolic flight as part of basic training.

a) The passengers begin to experience weightlessness when the jet climbs above 9600 m. Write an inequality to represent this information.

b) Determine the time period for which the jet is above 9600 m.

c) For how long does the microgravity exist on the flight?

13. A highway goes under a bridge formed by a parabolic arch, as shown. The highest point of the arch is 5 m high. The road is 10 m wide, and the minimum height of the bridge over the road is 4 m.

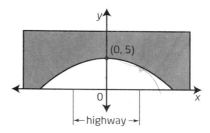

a) Determine the quadratic function that models the parabolic arch of the bridge.

b) What is the inequality that represents the space under the bridge in quadrants I and II?

Extend

14. Tavia has been adding advertisements to her Web site. Initially her revenue increased with each additional ad she included on her site. However, as she kept increasing the number of ads, her revenue began to drop. She kept track of her data as shown.

Number of Ads	0	10	15
Revenue ($)	0	100	75

a) Determine the quadratic inequality that models Tavia's revenue.

b) How many ads can Tavia include on her Web site to earn revenue of at least $50?

Did You Know?

The law of diminishing returns is a principle in economics. The law states the surprising result that when you continually increase the quantity of one input, you will eventually see a decrease in the output.

15. Oil is often recovered from a formation bounded by layers of rock that form a parabolic shape. Suppose a geologist has discovered such an oil-bearing formation. The quadratic functions that model the rock layers are $y = -0.0001x^2 - 600$ and $y = -0.0002x^2 - 700$, where x represents the horizontal distance from the centre of the formation and y represents the depth below ground level, both in metres. Write the inequality that describes the oil-bearing formation.

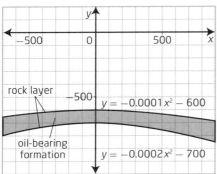

Create Connections

16. To raise money, the student council sells candy-grams each year. From past experience, they expect to sell 400 candy-grams at a price of $4 each. They have also learned from experience that each $0.50 increase in the price causes a drop in sales of 20 candy-grams.

a) Write an equality that models this situation. Define your variables.

b) Suppose the student council needs revenue of at least $1800. Solve an inequality to find all the possible prices that will achieve the fundraising goal.

c) Show how your solution would change if the student council needed to raise $1600 or more.

17. An environmentalist has been studying the methane produced by an inactive landfill. To approximate the methane produced, p, as a percent of peak output compared to time, t, in years, after the year 2000, he uses the inequality $p \leq 0.24t^2 - 8.1t + 74$.

a) For what time period is methane production below 10% of the peak production?

b) Graph the inequality used by the environmentalist. Explain why only a portion of the graph is a reasonable model for the methane output of the landfill. Which part of the graph would the environmentalist use?

c) Modify your answer to part a) to reflect your answer in part b).

d) Explain how the environmentalist can use the concept of domain to make modelling the situation with the quadratic inequality more reasonable.

18. Look back at your work in Unit 2, where you learned about quadratic functions. Working with a partner, identify the concepts and skills you learned in that unit that have helped you to understand the concepts in this unit. Decide which concept from Unit 2 was most important to your understanding in Unit 4. Find another team that chose a different concept as the most important. Set up a debate, with each team defending its choice of most important concept.

9.1 Linear Inequalities in Two Variables, pages 464–475

1. Graph each inequality without using technology.

    a) $y \leq 3x - 5$

    b) $y > -\frac{3}{4}x + 2$

    c) $3x - y \geq 6$

    d) $4x + 2y \leq 8$

    e) $10x - 4y + 3 < 11$

2. Determine the inequality that corresponds to each of the following graphs.

    a)
    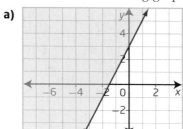

    b)
    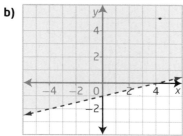

    c)
    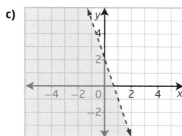

    d)
    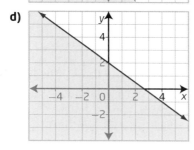

3. Graph each inequality using technology.

    a) $4x + 5y > 22$

    b) $10x - 4y + 52 \geq 0$

    c) $-3.2x + 1.1y < 8$

    d) $12.4x + 4.4y > 16.5$

    e) $\frac{3}{4}x \leq 9y$

4. Janelle has a budget of $120 for entertainment each month. She usually spends the money on a combination of movies and meals. Movie admission, with popcorn, is $15, while a meal costs $10.

    a) Write an inequality to represent the number of movies and meals that Janelle can afford with her entertainment budget.

    b) Graph the solution.

    c) Interpret your solution. Explain how the solution to the inequality relates to Janelle's situation.

5. Jodi is paid by commission as a salesperson. She earns 5% commission for each laptop computer she sells and 8% commission for each DVD player she sells. Suppose that the average price of a laptop is $600 and the average price of a DVD player is $200.

    a) What is the average amount Jodi earns for selling each item?

    b) Jodi wants to earn a minimum commission this month of $1000. Write an inequality to represent this situation.

    c) Graph the inequality. Interpret your results in the context of Jodi's earnings.

9.2 Quadratic Inequalities in One Variable, pages 476–487

6. Choose a strategy to solve each inequality. Explain your strategy and why you chose it.

  a) $x^2 - 2x - 63 > 0$

  b) $2x^2 - 7x - 30 \geq 0$

  c) $x^2 + 8x - 48 < 0$

  d) $x^2 - 6x + 4 \geq 0$

7. Solve each inequality.

  a) $x(6x + 5) \leq 4$

  b) $4x^2 < 10x - 1$

  c) $x^2 \leq 4(x + 8)$

  d) $5x^2 \geq 4 - 12x$

8. A decorative fountain shoots water in a parabolic path over a pathway. To determine the location of the pathway, the designer must solve the inequality $-\frac{3}{4}x^2 + 3x \leq 2$, where x is the horizontal distance from the water source, in metres.

  a) Solve the inequality.

  b) Interpret the solution to the inequality for the fountain designer.

9. A rectangular storage shed is to be built so that its length is twice its width. If the maximum area of the floor of the shed is 18 m², what are the possible dimensions of the shed?

10. David has learned that the light from the headlights reaches about 100 m ahead of the car he is driving. If v represents David's speed, in kilometres per hour, then the inequality $0.007v^2 + 0.22v \leq 100$ gives the speeds at which David can stop his vehicle in 100 m or less.

  a) What is the maximum speed at which David can travel and safely stop his vehicle in the 100-m distance?

  b) Modify the inequality so that it gives the speeds at which a vehicle can stop in 50 m or less.

  c) Solve the inequality you wrote in part b). Explain why your answer is not half the value of your answer for part a).

9.3 Quadratic Inequalities in Two Variables, pages 488–500

11. Write an inequality to describe each graph, given the function defining the boundary parabola.

  a)

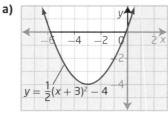

$y = \frac{1}{2}(x + 3)^2 - 4$

  b)

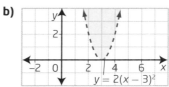

$y = 2(x - 3)^2$

12. Graph each quadratic inequality.

a) $y < x^2 + 2x - 15$

b) $y \geq -x^2 + 4$

c) $y > 6x^2 + x - 12$

d) $y \leq (x - 1)^2 - 6$

13. Write an inequality to describe each graph.

a)

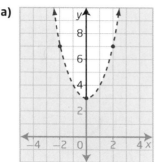

b)

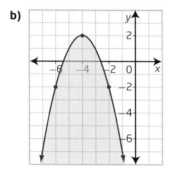

14. You can model the maximum Saskatchewan wheat production for the years 1975 to 1995 with the function $y = 0.003t^2 - 0.052t + 1.986$, where t is the time, in years, after 1975 and y is the yield, in tonnes per hectare.

a) Write and graph an inequality to model the potential wheat production during this period.

b) Write and solve an inequality to represent the years in which production is at most 2 t/ha.

> **Did You Know?**
>
> Saskatchewan has 44% of Canada's total cultivated farmland. Over 10% of the world's total exported wheat comes from this province.

15. An engineer is designing a roller coaster for an amusement park. The speed at which the roller coaster can safely complete a vertical loop is approximated by $v^2 \geq 10r$, where v is the speed, in metres per second, of the roller coaster and r is the radius, in metres, of the loop.

a) Graph the inequality to examine how the radius of the loop is related to the speed of the roller coaster.

b) A vertical loop of the roller coaster has a radius of 16 m. What are the possible safe speeds for this vertical loop?

16. The function $y = \frac{1}{20}x^2 - 4x + 90$ models the cable that supports a suspension bridge, where x is the horizontal distance, in metres, from the base of the first support and y is the height, in metres, of the cable above the bridge deck.

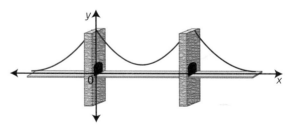

a) Write an inequality to determine the points for which the height of the cable is at least 20 m.

b) Solve the inequality. What does the solution represent?

Multiple Choice

For #1 to #5, choose the best answer.

1. An inequality that is equivalent to
$3x - 6y < 12$ is

A $y < \frac{1}{2}x - 2$

B $y > \frac{1}{2}x - 2$

C $y < 2x - 2$

D $y > 2x - 2$

2. What linear inequality does the graph show?

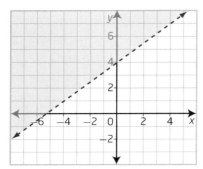

A $y > \frac{3}{4}x + 4$

B $y \geq \frac{3}{4}x + 4$

C $y < \frac{4}{3}x + 4$

D $y \leq \frac{4}{3}x + 4$

3. What is the solution set for the quadratic inequality $6x^2 - 7x - 20 < 0$?

A $\left\{ x \mid x \leq -\frac{4}{3} \text{ or } x \geq \frac{5}{2}, x \in R \right\}$

B $\left\{ x \mid -\frac{4}{3} \leq x \leq \frac{5}{2}, x \in R \right\}$

C $\left\{ x \mid -\frac{4}{3} < x < \frac{5}{2}, x \in R \right\}$

D $\left\{ x \mid x < -\frac{4}{3} \text{ or } x > \frac{5}{2}, x \in R \right\}$

4. For the quadratic function $q(x)$ shown in the graph, which of the following is true?

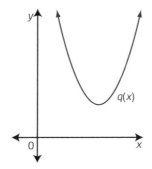

A There are no solutions to $q(x) > 0$.

B All real numbers are solutions to $q(x) \geq 0$.

C All real numbers are solutions to $q(x) \leq 0$.

D All positive real numbers are solutions to $q(x) < 0$.

5. What quadratic inequality does the graph show?

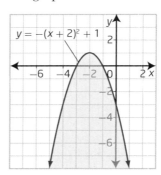

A $y < -(x + 2)^2 + 1$

B $y \geq -(x + 2)^2 + 1$

C $y \leq -(x + 2)^2 + 1$

D $y > -(x + 2)^2 + 1$

Short Answer

6. Graph $8x \geq 2(y - 5)$.

7. Solve $12x^2 < 7x + 10$.

8. Graph $y > (x - 5)^2 + 4$.

9. Stage lights often have parabolic reflectors to make it possible to focus the beam of light, as indicated by the diagram.

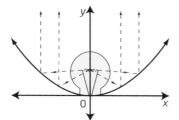

Suppose the reflector in a stage light is represented by the function $y = 0.02x^2$. What inequality can you use to model the region illuminated by the light?

10. While on vacation, Ben has $300 to spend on recreation. Scuba diving costs $25/h and sea kayaking costs $20/h. What are all the possible ways that Ben can budget his recreation money?

Extended Response

11. Malik sells his artwork for different prices depending on the type of work. Pen and ink sketches sell for $50, and watercolours sell for $80.

a) Malik needs an income of at least $1200 per month. Write an inequality to model this situation.

b) Graph the inequality. List three different ordered pairs in the solution.

c) Suppose Malik now needs at least $2400 per month. Write an inequality to represent this new situation. Predict how the answer to this inequality will be related to your answer in part b).

d) Solve the new inequality from part c) to check your prediction.

12. Let $f(x)$ represent a quadratic function.

a) State a quadratic function for which the solution set to $f(x) \leq 0$ is $\{x \mid -3 \leq x \leq 5, x \in \text{R}\}$. Justify your answer.

b) Describe all quadratics for which solutions to $f(x) \leq 0$ are of the form $m \leq x \leq n$ for some real numbers m and n.

c) For your answer in part b), explain whether it is more convenient to express quadratic functions in the form $f(x) = ax^2 + bx + c$ or $f(x) = a(x - p)^2 + q$, and why.

13. The normal systolic blood pressure, p, in millimetres of mercury (mmHg), for a woman a years old is given by $p = 0.01a^2 + 0.05a + 107$.

a) Write an inequality that expresses the ages for which you expect systolic blood pressure to be less than 120 mmHg.

b) Solve the inequality you wrote in part a).

c) Are all of the solutions to your inequality realistic answers for this problem? Explain why or why not.

Nanotechnology

The Chapter 9 Task focusses on a cost analysis of part of the construction of your object. You will compare the benefits of construction with and without nanotechnology.

Chapter 9 Task

The graph models your projected costs of production now and in the future. The linear graph represents the cost of traditional production methods, while the parabola represents the cost of nanotechnology.

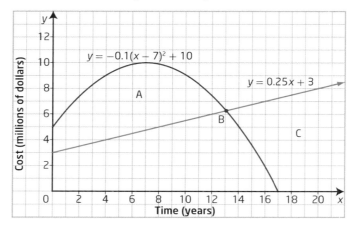

- Explain why it is reasonable to represent the costs of nanotechnology by a parabola that opens downward.
- Explain the meaning and significance of the point labelled B on the graph.
- What are the boundaries of region A? Write the inequalities that determine region A. Explain what the points in region A represent.
- What are the boundaries of region C? Write the inequalities that determine region C. Explain what the points in region C represent.
- How are regions A and C important to you as a designer and manufacturer?
- If the costs of nanotechnology decrease from their peak more quickly than anticipated, how will that change the graph and your production plans?
- The graph representing nanotechnology's cost has an x-intercept. Is this reasonable? Justify your answer.
- Is cost the only factor you would address when considering using nanotechnology to produce your product? Explain your answer.

Nanotechnology

Choose a format in which to
display your finished project that
best complements your design.
For example, you may create one
or more of the following:

- a hand-drawn illustration
- a CAD drawing
- an animation
- photographs showing your
  design from different angles
- a 3-D model of your design
- a video documenting your process and final design
- a different representation of your design

Your project should include a visual representation of the evolution of
your design. Submit the equations used when designing your project
as well as the necessary points of intersection and the answers to the
Chapter 9 Task to your teacher.

You will display your final project in a gallery walk in your classroom.
In a gallery walk, each project is posted in the classroom so that you and
your classmates can circulate and view all the projects produced, similar
to the way that you may visit an art gallery.

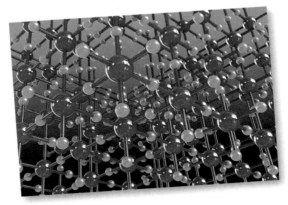

Cumulative Review, Chapters 8–9

Chapter 8 Systems of Equations

1. Examine each system of equations and match it with a possible sketch of the system. You do not need to solve the systems to match them.

A $y = x^2 + 1$
$y = -x^2 + 1$

B $y = x^2 + 1$
$y = x$

C $y = x^2 + 1$
$y = -x^2 + 4$

D $y = x^2 + 1$
$y = x + 4$

a)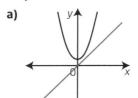

b)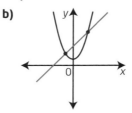

c)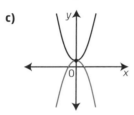

d)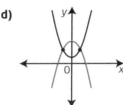

2. Solve the system of linear-quadratic equations graphically. Express your answers to the nearest tenth.

$3x + y = 4$
$y = x^2 - 3x - 1$

3. Consider the system of linear-quadratic equations

$y = -x^2 + 4x + 1$
$3x - y - 1 = 0$

a) Solve the system algebraically.

b) Explain, in graphical terms, what the ordered pairs from part a) represent.

4. Given the quadratic function $y = x^2 + 4$ and the linear function $y = x + b$, determine all the possible values of b that would result in a system of equations with

a) two solutions

b) exactly one solution

c) no solution

5. Copy and complete the flowchart for solving systems of linear-quadratic equations.

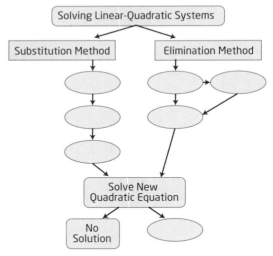

6. Copy and complete the flowchart for solving systems of quadratic-quadratic equations.

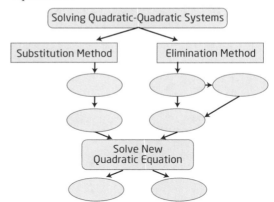

7. The price, P, in dollars, per share, of a high-tech stock has fluctuated over a 10-year period according to the equation $P = 14 + 12t - t^2$, where t is time, in years. The price of a second high-tech stock has shown a steady increase during the same time period according to the relationship $P = 2t + 30$. Algebraically determine for what values the two stock prices will be the same.

8. Explain how you could determine if the given system of quadratic-quadratic equations has zero, one, two, or an infinite number of solutions without solving or using technology.

$$y = (x - 4)^2 + 2$$
$$y = -(x + 3)^2 - 1$$

9. Solve the system of quadratic-quadratic equations graphically. Express your answers to the nearest tenth.

$$y = -2x^2 + 6x - 1$$
$$y = -4x^2 + 4x + 2$$

10. Algebraically determine the solution(s) to each system of quadratic-quadratic equations.

   a) $y = 2x^2 + 9x - 5$
   $y = 2x^2 - 4x + 8$

   b) $y = 12x^2 + 17x - 5$
   $y = -x^2 + 30x - 5$

Chapter 9 Linear and Quadratic Inequalities

11. Match each inequality with its graph.

   A $2x + y < 3$ **B** $2x - y \leq 3$

   C $2x - y \geq 3$ **D** $2x + y > 3$

   a) 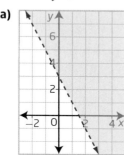   b)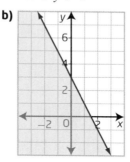

   c) 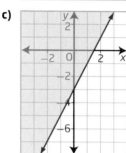   d)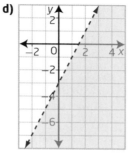

12. Write an inequality to describe each graph, given the function defining the boundary parabola.

   a)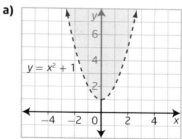

   b)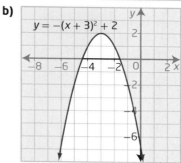

13. Explain how each test point can be used to determine the solution region that satisfies the inequality $y > x - 2$.

   a) $(0, 0)$

   b) $(2, -5)$

   c) $(-1, 1)$

14. What linear inequality is shown in the graph?

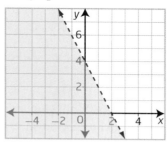

15. Sketch the graph of $y \geq x^2 - 3x - 4$. Use a test point to verify the solution region.

16. Use sign analysis to determine the solution of the quadratic inequality $2x^2 + 9x - 33 \geq 2$.

17. Suppose a rectangular area of land is to be enclosed by 1000 m of fence. If the area is to be greater than 60 000 m², what is the range of possible widths of the rectangle?

Multiple Choice

For #1 to #9, choose the best answer.

1. Which of the following ordered pairs is a solution to the system of linear-quadratic equations?

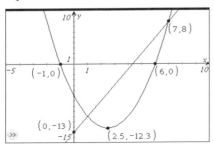

A (2.5, −12.3)   B (6, 0)

C (7, 8)   D (0, −13)

2. Kelowna, British Columbia, is one of the many places in western Canada with bicycle motocross (BMX) race tracks for teens.

Which graph models the height versus time of two of the racers travelling over one of the jumps?

A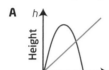

B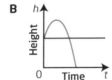

C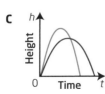

D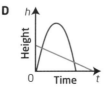

3. The ordered pairs (1, 3) and (−3, −5) are the solutions to which system of linear-quadratic equations?

A $y = 3x + 5$
$y = x^2 − 2x − 1$

B $y = 2x + 1$
$y = x^2 + 4x − 2$

C $y = x + 2$
$y = x^2 + 2$

D $y = 4x − 1$
$y = x^2 − 3x + 5$

4. How many solutions are possible for the following system of quadratic-quadratic equations?

$y − 5 = 2(x + 1)^2$
$y − 5 = −2(x + 1)^2$

A zero

B one

C two

D an infinite number

5. Which point cannot be used as a test point to determine the solution region for $4x − y ≤ 5$?

A (−1, 1)   B (2, 5)

C (3, 1)   D (2, 3)

6. Which linear inequality does the graph show?

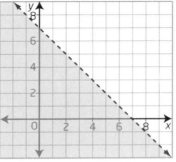

A $y ≤ −x + 7$

B $y ≥ −x + 7$

C $y > −x + 7$

D $y < −x + 7$

7. Which graph represents the quadratic inequality $y \geq 3x^2 + 10x - 8$?

A

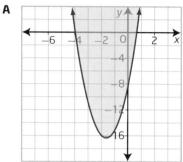

B

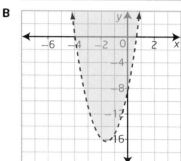

C

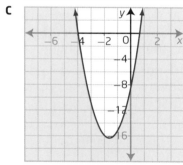

D

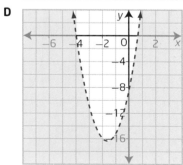

8. Determine the solution(s), to the nearest tenth, for the system of quadratic-quadratic equations.

$$y = -\frac{2}{3}x^2 + 2x + 3$$
$$y = x^2 - 4x + 5$$

A (3.2, 2.5)

B (3.2, 2.5) and (0.4, 3.7)

C (0.4, 2.5) and (2.5, 3.7)

D (0.4, 3.2)

9. What is the solution set for the quadratic inequality $-3x^2 + x + 11 < 1$?

A $\left\{ x \mid x < -\frac{5}{3} \text{ or } x > 2, x \in \mathrm{R} \right\}$

B $\left\{ x \mid x < -\frac{5}{3} \text{ or } x \geq 2, x \in \mathrm{R} \right\}$

C $\left\{ x \mid -\frac{5}{3} < x < 2, x \in \mathrm{R} \right\}$

D $\left\{ x \mid -\frac{5}{3} \leq x \leq 2, x \in \mathrm{R} \right\}$

Numerical Response

Copy and complete the statements in #10 to #12.

10. One of the solutions for the system of linear-quadratic equations $y = x^2 - 4x - 2$ and $y = x - 2$ is represented by the ordered pair $(a, 3)$, where the value of a is ■.

11. The solution of the system of quadratic-quadratic equations represented by $y = x^2 - 4x + 6$ and $y = -x^2 + 6x - 6$ with the greater coordinates is of the form (a, a), where the value of a is ■.

12. On a forward somersault dive, Laurie's height, h, in metres, above the water t seconds after she leaves the diving board is approximately modelled by $h(t) = -5t^2 + 5t + 4$. The length of time that Laurie is above 4 m is ■.

Written Response

13. Professional golfers, such as Canadian Mike Weir, make putting look easy to spectators. New technology used on a television sports channel analyses the greens conditions and predicts the path of the golf ball that the golfer should putt to put the ball in the hole. Suppose the straight line from the ball to the hole is represented by the equation $y = 2x$ and the predicted path of the ball is modelled by the equation $y = \frac{1}{4}x^2 + \frac{3}{2}x$.

a) Algebraically determine the solution to the system of linear-quadratic equations.

b) Interpret the points of intersection in this context.

14. Two quadratic functions, $f(x) = x^2 - 6x + 5$ and $g(x)$, intersect at the points $(2, -3)$ and $(7, 12)$. The graph of $g(x)$ is congruent to the graph of $f(x)$ but opens downward. Determine the equation of $g(x)$ in the form $g(x) = a(x - p)^2 + q$.

15. Algebraically determine the solutions to the system of quadratic-quadratic equations. Verify your solutions.

$$4x^2 + 8x + 9 - y = 5$$
$$3x^2 - x + 1 = y + x + 6$$

16. Dolores solved the inequality $3x^2 - 5x - 10 > 2$ using roots and test points. Her solution is shown.

$$3x^2 - 5x - 10 > 2$$
$$3x^2 - 5x - 8 > 0$$
$$3x^2 - 5x - 8 = 0$$
$$(3x - 8)(x + 1) = 0$$
$$3x - 8 = 0 \quad \text{or} \quad x + 1 = 0$$
$$3x = 8 \qquad\qquad x = -1$$
$$x = \frac{8}{3}$$

Choose test points -2, 0, and 3 from the intervals $x < -1$, $-1 < x < \frac{8}{3}$, and $x > \frac{8}{3}$, respectively.

The values of x less than -1 satisfy the inequality $3x^2 - 5x - 10 > 2$.

a) Upon verification, Dolores realized she made an error. Explain the error and provide a correct solution.

b) Use a different strategy to determine the solution to $3x^2 - 5x - 10 > 2$.

17. A scoop in field hockey occurs when a player lifts the ball off the ground with a shovel-like movement of the stick, which is placed slightly under the ball. Suppose a player passes the ball with a scoop modelled by the function $h(t) = -4.9t^2 + 10.4t$, where h is the height of the ball, in metres, and t represents time, in seconds. For what length of time, to the nearest hundredth of a second, is the ball above 3 m?

Answers

Chapter 1 Sequences and Series

1.1 Arithmetic Sequences, pages 16 to 21

1. a) arithmetic sequence: $t_1 = 16$, $d = 16$; next three terms: 96, 112, 128
   b) not arithmetic
   c) arithmetic sequence: $t_1 = -4$, $d = -3$; next three terms: $-19, -22, -25$
   d) arithmetic sequence: $t_1 = 3$, $d = -3$; next three terms: $-12, -15, -18$

2. a) 5, 8, 11, 14   **b)** $-1, -5, -9, -13$
   c) $4, \dfrac{21}{5}, \dfrac{22}{5}, \dfrac{23}{5}$ **d)** 1.25, 1.00, 0.75, 0.50

3. a) $t_1 = 11$ **b)** $t_7 = 29$ **c)** $t_{14} = 50$

4. a) 7, 11, 15, 19, 23; $t_1 = 7$, $d = 4$
   b) $6, \dfrac{9}{2}, 3, \dfrac{3}{2}$; $t_1 = 6$, $d = -\dfrac{3}{2}$
   c) 2, 4, 6, 8, 10; $t_1 = 2$, $d = 2$

5. a) 30   **b)** 82   **c)** 26   **d)** 17

6. a) $t_2 = 15$, $t_3 = 24$ **b)** $t_2 = 19$, $t_3 = 30$
   c) $t_2 = 37$, $t_3 = 32$

7. a) 5, 8, 11, 14, 17   **b)** $t_n = 3n + 2$
   c) $t_{50} = 152$, $t_{200} = 602$
   d) The general term is a linear equation of the form $y = mx + b$, where $t_n = y$ and $n = x$. Therefore, $t_n = 3n + 2$ has a slope of 3.
   e) The constant value of 2 in the general term is the y-intercept of 2.

8. A and C; both sequences have a natural-number value for n.

9. 5

10. $t_n = -3yn + 8y$; $t_{15} = -37y$

11. $x = -16$; first three terms: $-78, -116, -154$

12. $z = 2y - x$

13. a) $t_n = 6n + 4$ **b)** 58
   c) 12

14. a) 0, 8, 16, 24
   b) 32 players
   c) $t_n = 8n - 8$
   d) 12:16
   e) Example: weather, all foursomes starting on time, etc.

15. 21 square inches

16. a) $t_n = 2n - 1$ **b)** 51st day
   c) Susan continues the program until she accomplishes her goal.

17. a)

Carbon Atoms	1	2	3	4
Hydrogen Atoms	4	6	8	10

   b) $t_n = 2n + 2$ or $H = 2C + 2$
   c) 100 carbon atoms

18.

Multiples of	28	7	15
Between	1 and 1000	500 and 600	50 and 500
First Term, t_1	28	504	60
Common Difference, d	28	7	15
nth Term, t_n	980	595	495
General Term	$t_n = 28n$	$t_n = 7n + 497$	$t_n = 15n + 45$
Number of Terms	35	14	30

19. a) 14.7, 29.4, 44.1, 58.8; $t_n = 14.7n$, where n represents every increment of 30 ft in depth.
   b) 490 psi at 1000 ft and 980 psi at 2000 ft
   c)

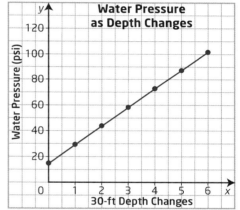

   d) 14.7 psi
   e) 14.7
   f) The y-intercept represents the first term of the sequence and the slope represents the common difference.

20. Other lengths are 6 cm, 12 cm, and 18 cm. Add the four terms to find the perimeter. Replace t_2 with $t_1 + d$, t_3 with $t_1 + 2d$, and t_4 with $t_1 + 3d$. Solve for d.

21. a) 4, 8, 12, 16, 20   **b)** $t_n = 4n$
   c) 320 min

22. -29 beekeepers

23. 5.8 million carats. This value represents the increase of diamond carats mined each year.

24. 1696.5 m

25. a) 13:54, 13:59, 14:04, 14:09, 14:14; $t_1 = 13:54$, $d = 0:05$
   b) $t_n = 0:05n + 13:49$
   c) Assume that the arithmetic sequence of times continues.
   d) 15:49

26. a) $d > 0$ **b)** $d < 0$

c) $d = 0$ **d)** t_1

e) t_n

27. Definition: An ordered list of terms in which the difference between consecutive terms is constant.

Common Difference: The difference between successive terms, $d = t_n - t_{n-1}$

Example: 12, 19, 26, …

Formula: $t_n = 7n + 5$

28. Step 1 The graph of an arithmetic sequence is always a straight line. The common difference is described by the slope of the graph. Since the common difference is always constant, the graph will be a straight line.

Step 2

a) Changing the value of the first term changes the y-intercept of the graph. The y-intercept increases as the value of the first term increases. The y-intercept decreases as the value of the first term decreases.

b) Yes, the graph keeps it shape. The slope stays the same.

Step 3

a) Changing the value of the common difference changes the slope of the graph.

b) As the common difference increases, the slope increases. As the common difference decreases, the slope decreases.

Step 4 The common difference is the slope.

Step 5 The slope of the graph represents the common difference of the general term of the sequence. The slope is the coefficient of the variable n in the general term of the sequence.

1.2 Arithmetic Series, pages 27 to 31

1. a) 493   **b)** 735

c) -1081 **d)** $\frac{301}{3} = 100.\overline{3}$

2. a) $t_1 = 1, d = 2, S_8 = 64$

b) $t_1 = 40, d = -5, S_{11} = 165$

c) $t_1 = \frac{1}{2}, d = 1, S_7 = 24.5$

d) $t_1 = -3.5, d = 2.25, S_6 = 12.75$

3. a) 344   **b)** 663

c) 195   **d)** 396

e) 133

4. a) 2   **b)** $\frac{500}{13} \approx 38.46$

c) 4   **d)** 41

5. a) 16   **b)** 10

6. a) $t_{10} = 50, S_{10} = 275$

b) $t_{10} = -17, S_{10} = -35$

c) $t_{10} = -46, S_{10} = -280$

d) $t_{10} = 7, S_{10} = 47.5$

7. a) 124 500   **b)** 82 665

8. 156 times

9. a) 2   **b)** 40   **c)** $\frac{n}{2}(1 + 3n)$

10. 8425

11. $3 + 10 + 17 + 24$

12. a) $S_n = \frac{n}{2}[2t_1 + (n-1)d]$

$S_n = \frac{n}{2}[2(5) + (n-1)10]$

$S_n = \frac{n}{2}[10 + 10n - 10]$

$S_n = \frac{n(10n)}{2}$

$S_n = \frac{10n^2}{2}$

$S_n = 5n^2$

b) $S_{100} = \frac{100}{2}[2(5) + (100-1)10]$

$S_{100} = \frac{100}{2}[10 + 990]$

$S_{100} = \frac{100}{2}(1000)$

$S_{100} = 50\ 000$

$d(100) = 5(100)^2$

$d(100) = 5(10\ 000)$

$d(100) = 50\ 000$

13. 171

14. a) the number of handshakes between six people if they each shake hands once

b) $1 + 2 + 3 + 4 + 5 + 6 + 7 + 8 + 9$

c) 435

d) Example: The number of games played in a home and away series league for n teams.

15. a) $t_1 = 6.2, d = 1.2$

b) $t_{20} = 29$

c) $S_{20} = 352$

16. 173 cm

17. a) True. Example: $2 + 4 + 6 + 8 = 20$, $4 + 8 + 12 + 16 = 40$, $40 = 2 \times 20$

b) False. Example: $2 + 4 + 6 + 8 = 20$, $2 + 4 + 6 + 8 + 10 + 12 + 14 + 16 = 72$, $72 \neq 2 \times 20$

c) True. Example: Given the sequence 2, 4, 6, 8, multiplying each term by 5 gives 10, 20, 30, 40. Both sequences are arithmetic sequences.

18. a) $7 + 11 + 15$ **b)** 250   **c)** 250

d) $S_n = \frac{n}{2}[2t_1 + (n-1)d]$

$S_n = \frac{n}{2}[2(7) + (n-1)4]$

$S_n = \frac{n}{2}[14 + 4n - 4]$

$S_n = \frac{n}{2}[4n + 10]$

$S_n = n(2n + 5)$

$S_n = 2n^2 + 5n$

19. a) $240 + 250 + 260 + \cdots + 300$
  b) $S_n = 235n + 5n^2$
  c) 1890
  d) Nathan will continue to remove an extra 10 bushels per hour.
20. $(-27) + (-22) + (-17)$
21. Jeanette and Pierre have used two different forms of the same formula. Jeanette has replaced t_n with $t_1 + (n - 1)d$.
22. a) 100
  b) $S_{\text{green}} = 1 + 2 + 3 + \cdots + 10$
  $S_{\text{blue}} = 0 + 1 + 2 + 3 + \cdots + 9$
  $S_{\text{total}} = S_{\text{green}} + S_{\text{blue}}$
  $S_{\text{total}} = \frac{10}{2}(1 + 10) + \frac{10}{2}(0 + 9)$
  $S_{\text{total}} = 5(11) + 5(9)$
  $S_{\text{total}} = 55 + 45$
  $S_{\text{total}} = 100$
23. a) 55
  b) The nth triangular number is represented by S_n.
  $S_n = \frac{n}{2}[2t_1 + (n - 1)d]$
  $S_n = \frac{n}{2}[2(1) + (n - 1)(1)]$
  $S_n = \frac{n}{2}[2 + (n - 1)]$
  $S_n = \frac{n}{2}(1 + n)$

1.3 Geometric Sequences, pages 39 to 45

1. a) geometric; $r = 2$; $t_n = 2^{n-1}$
  b) not geometric
  c) geometric; $r = -3$; $t_n = 3(-3)^{n-1}$
  d) not geometric
  e) geometric; $r = 1.5$; $t_n = 10(1.5)^{n-1}$
  f) geometric; $r = 5$; $t_n = -1(5)^{n-1}$

2.

	Geometric Sequence	Common Ratio	6th Term	10th Term
a)	6, 18, 54, …	3	1458	118 098
b)	1.28, 0.64, 0.32, …	0.5	0.04	0.0025
c)	$\frac{1}{5}, \frac{3}{5}, \frac{9}{5}, \cdots$	3	$\frac{243}{5}$	$\frac{19\,683}{5}$

3. a) $2, 6, 18, 54$　　**b)** $-3, 12, -48, 192$
  c) $4, -12, 36, -108$　　**d)** $2, 1, \frac{1}{2}, \frac{1}{4}$
4. $18.9, 44.1, 102.9$
5. a) $t_n = 3(2)^{n-1}$　　**b)** $t_n = 192\left(-\frac{1}{4}\right)^{n-1}$
  c) $t_n = \frac{5}{9}(3)^{n-1}$　　**d)** $t_n = 4(2)^{n-1}$
6. a) 4　　**b)** 7　　**c)** 5
  d) 6　　**e)** 9　　**f)** 8
7. 37
8. $16, 12, 9$; $t_n = 16\left(\frac{3}{4}\right)^{n-1}$

9. a) $t_1 = 3$; $r = 0.75$
  b) $t_n = 3(0.75)^{n-1}$
  c) approximately 53.39 cm
  d) 7
10. a) 95%
  b) $100, 95, 90.25, 85.7375$
  c) 0.95
  d) about 59.87%
  e) After 27 washings, 25% of the original colour would remain in the jeans. Example: The geometric sequence continues for each washing.
11. 1.77
12. a) $1, 2, 4, 8, 16$　　**b)** $t_n = 1(2)^{n-1}$
  c) 2^{29} or $536\,870\,912$
13. a) 1.031　　**b)** 216.3 cm
  c) 56 jumps
14. a) $1, 2, 4, 8, 16, 32$　　**b)** $t_n = 1(2)^{n-1}$
  c) 2^{25} or $33\,554\,432$
  d) All cells continue to double and all cells live.
15. 2.9%
16. 8 weeks
17. 65.2 m
18. 0.920
19. a) 76.0 mL　　**b)** 26 h
20. a)

Time, d (days)	Charge Level, C (%)
0	100
1	98
2	96.04
3	94.12

  b) $t_n = 100(0.98)^{n-1}$
  c) The formula in part b) includes the first term at $d = 0$ in the sequence. The formula $C = 100(0.98)^n$ does not consider the first term of the sequence.
  d) 81.7%
21. a) 24.14 mm　　**b)** 1107.77 mm
22. Example: If a, b, c are terms of an arithmetic sequence, then $b - a = c - b$. If 6^a, 6^b, 6^c are terms of a geometric series, then $\frac{6^b}{6^a} = \frac{6^c}{6^b}$ and $6^{b-a} = 6^{c-b}$. Therefore, $b - a = c - b$. So, when 6^a, 6^b, 6^c form a geometric sequence, then a, b, c form an arithmetic sequence.
23. $\frac{5}{3}$; $9, 15, 25$
24. a) 23.96 cm　　**b)** 19.02 cm
  c) 2.13 cm　　**d)** 2.01 cm
  e) $2.01, 1.90, 1.79$; arithmetic; $d = -0.11$ cm
25. Mala's solution is correct. Since the aquarium loses 8% of the water every day, it maintains 92% of the water every day.

26.

	$\frac{1}{500}$		$\frac{50}{3}$					
	$\frac{1}{100}$	$\frac{1}{10}$	1	10				
	$\frac{1}{20}$		2	6	18	54		
$\frac{1}{16}$	$\frac{1}{4}$	1	4			9		
	$\frac{5}{4}$		8			$\frac{3}{2}$		
	$\frac{25}{4}$		16	4	1	$\frac{1}{4}$	$\frac{1}{16}$	$\frac{1}{64}$
	$\frac{125}{4}$		32					
	$\frac{625}{4}$	100	64					

27. a) 0.86 cm²   **b)** 1.72 cm²
   c) 3.43 cm²   **d)** 109.88 cm²

1.4 Geometric Series, pages 53 to 57

1. a) geometric; $r = 6$ **b)** geometric; $r = -\frac{1}{2}$
  c) not geometric   **d)** geometric; $r = 1.1$

2. a) $t_1 = 6$, $r = 1.5$, $S_{10} = \frac{174\ 075}{256}$, $S_{10} \approx 679.98$

  b) $t_1 = 18$, $r = -0.5$, $S_{12} = \frac{12\ 285}{1024}$, $S_{12} \approx 12.00$

  c) $t_1 = 2.1$, $r = 2$, $S_9 = \frac{10\ 731}{10}$, $S_9 = 1073.10$

  d) $t_1 = 0.3$, $r = 0.01$, $S_{12} = \frac{10}{33}$, $S_{12} \approx 0.30$

3. a) 12 276   **b)** $\frac{3280}{81}$

  c) $-\frac{209\ 715}{256}$ **d)** $\frac{36\ 855}{256}$

4. a) 40.50   **b)** 0.96
  c) 109 225   **d)** 39 063

5. a) 3   **b)** 295.7

6. 7

7. a) 81   **b)** $81 + 27 + 9 + 3 + 1$

8. $t_2 = -\frac{81}{16}$; $S_6 = 7.8$

9. a) If the person in charge is included, the series is $1 + 4 + 16 + 64 + \cdots$. If the person in charge is not included, the series is $4 + 16 + 64 + \cdots$.

  b) If the person in charge is included, the sum is 349 525. If the person in charge is not included, the sum is 1 398 100.

10. 46.4 m

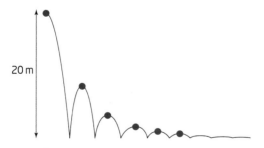

11. 794.3 km

12. b)

Stage Number	Length of Each Line Segment	Number of Line Segments	Perimeter of Snowflake
1	1	3	3
2	$\frac{1}{3}$	12	4
3	$\frac{1}{9}$	48	$\frac{16}{3}$
4	$\frac{1}{27}$	192	$\frac{64}{9}$
5	$\frac{1}{81}$	768	$\frac{256}{27}$

  c) length, $t_n = \left(\frac{1}{3}\right)^{n-1}$;

    number of line segments, $t_n = 3(4)^{n-1}$;

    perimeter, $t_n = 3\left(\frac{4}{3}\right)^{n-1}$

  d) $\frac{1024}{81} \approx 12.64$

13. 98 739

14. 91 mm

15. a) 226.9 mg   **b)** 227.3 mg

16. 8

17. $\frac{58\ 025}{48}$

18. $a = 5$, $b = 10$, $c = 20$ or $a = 20$, $b = 10$, $c = 5$

19. 15

20. $\frac{341}{4}\pi$

21.

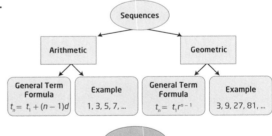

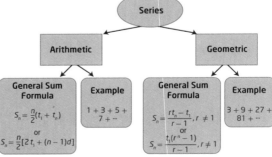

22. Examples:
  a) All butterflies produce the same number of eggs and all eggs hatch.
  b) No. Tom determined the total number of butterflies from the first to fifth generations. He should have found the fifth term, which would determine the total number of butterflies in the fifth generation only.

c) This is a reasonable estimate, but it does include all butterflies up to the fifth generation, which is 6.42×10^7 more butterflies than those produced in the fifth generation.

d) Determine $t_5 = 1(400)^4$ or 2.56×10^{10}.

1.5 Infinite Geometric Series, pages 63 to 65

1. a) divergent **b)** convergent
c) convergent **d)** divergent
e) divergent

2. a) $\frac{32}{5}$ **b)** no sum
c) no sum **d)** 2
e) 2.5

3. a) $0.87 + 0.0087 + 0.000\,087 + \cdots$;
$S_\infty = \frac{87}{99}$ or $\frac{29}{33}$

b) $0.437 + 0.000\,437 + \cdots$; $S_\infty = \frac{437}{999}$

4. Yes. The sum of the infinite series representing 0.999... is equal to 1.

5. a) 15 **b)** $\frac{4}{5}$ or 0.8
c) 14

6. $t_1 = 27$; $27 + 18 + 12 + \cdots$

7. $r = \frac{2}{5}$; $-8 - \frac{16}{5} - \frac{32}{25} - \frac{64}{125} - \cdots$

8. a) 400 000 barrels of oil
b) Determining the lifetime production assumes the oil well continues to produce at the same rate for many months. This is an unreasonable assumption because 94% is a high rate to maintain.

9. $x = \frac{1}{4}$; $1 + \frac{3}{4} + \frac{9}{16} + \frac{27}{64} + \cdots$

10. $r = \frac{1}{2}$

11. a) $-1 < x < 1$ **b)** $-3 < x < 3$
c) $-\frac{1}{2} < x < \frac{1}{2}$

12. 6 cm

13. 250 cm

14. No sum, since $r = 1.1 > 1$. Therefore, the series is divergent.

15. 48 m

16. a) approximately 170.86 cm
b) 300 cm

17. a) Rita
b) $r = -\frac{4}{3}$; therefore, $r < -1$, and the series is divergent.

18. 125 m

19. 72 cm

20. a) Example: $\frac{4}{5} + \left(\frac{4}{5}\right)^2 + \left(\frac{4}{5}\right)^3 + \cdots + \left(\frac{4}{5}\right)^n$

and $\frac{1}{5} + \left(\frac{1}{5}\right)^2 + \left(\frac{1}{5}\right)^3 + \cdots + \left(\frac{1}{5}\right)^n$

b) $S_\infty = \dfrac{t_1}{1-r} = \dfrac{\frac{4}{5}}{1-\frac{4}{5}} = \dfrac{\frac{4}{5}}{\frac{1}{5}} = 4$ and

$S_\infty = \dfrac{t_1}{1-r} = \dfrac{\frac{1}{5}}{1-\frac{1}{5}} = \dfrac{\frac{1}{5}}{\frac{4}{5}} = \frac{1}{4}$

21. Geometric series converge only when $-1 < r < 1$.

22. a) $S_n = -\frac{3}{8}n^2 + \frac{11}{8}n$

b) $S_n = \dfrac{\left(\frac{1}{4}\right)^n - 1}{-\frac{3}{4}}$

$S_n = -\frac{4}{3}\left(\frac{1}{4}\right)^n + \frac{4}{3}$

c) $S_\infty = \dfrac{1}{1-\frac{1}{4}}$

$S_\infty = \frac{4}{3}$

23. Step 3

n	1	2	3	4
Fraction of Paper	$\frac{1}{4}$	$\frac{1}{16}$	$\frac{1}{64}$	$\frac{1}{256}$

Step 4 $\frac{1}{4} + \frac{1}{16} + \frac{1}{64} + \frac{1}{256}$, Example: $S_\infty = \frac{1}{3}$

Chapter 1 Review, pages 66 to 68

1. a) arithmetic, $d = 4$ **b)** arithmetic, $d = -5$
c) not arithmetic **d)** not arithmetic

2. a) C **b)** D
c) E **d)** B
e) A

3. a) term, $n = 14$ **b)** not a term
c) term, $n = 54$ **d)** not a term

4. a) A
b)

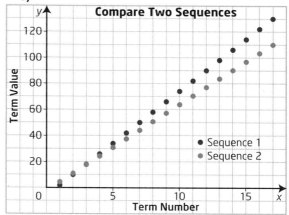

In the graph, sequence 1 has a larger positive slope than sequence 2. The value of term 17 is greater in sequence 1 than in sequence 2.

5. $t_{10} = 41$

6. 306 cm

7. a) $S_{10} = 195$ **b)** $S_{12} = 285$
   c) $S_{10} = -75$ **d)** $S_{20} = 3100$

8. $S_{40} = 3420$

9. a) 29   **b)** 225
   c) 25 days

10. a) 61   **b)** 495

11. 1170

12. a) not geometric
   b) geometric, $r = -2$, $t_1 = 1$, $t_n = (-2)^{n-1}$
   c) geometric, $r = \frac{1}{2}$, $t_1 = 1$, $t_n = \left(\frac{1}{2}\right)^{n-1}$
   d) not geometric

13. a) 7346 bacteria
   b) $t_n = 5000(1.08)^n$

14. 2π cm or approximately 6.28 cm

15.

Arithmetic Sequence	Geometric Sequence
Definition A sequence in which the difference between consecutive terms is constant	**Definition** A sequence in which the ratio between consecutive terms is constant
Formula $t_n = t_1 + (n-1)d$	**Formula** $t_n = t_1 r^{n-1}$
Example 3, 6, 9, 12, …	**Example** 4, 12, 36, 108, …

16. a) arithmetic   **b)** geometric
   c) geometric   **d)** arithmetic
   e) arithmetic   **f)** geometric

17. a) $S_{10} = \dfrac{174\ 075}{256}$, $S_{10} \approx 679.98$
   b) $S_{12} = \dfrac{36\ 855}{1024}$, $S_{12} \approx 35.99$
   c) $S_{20} = \dfrac{20\ 000}{3}$, $S_{20} \approx 6666.67$
   d) $S_{9} = \dfrac{436\ 905}{4096}$, $S_{9} \approx 106.67$

18. a) 19.1 mm   **b)** 1.37 m

19. a) $S_{\infty} = 15$ **b)** $S_{\infty} = \dfrac{3}{4}$

20. a) convergent, $S_{\infty} = 16$
   b) divergent
   c) convergent, $S_{\infty} = -28$
   d) convergent, $S_{\infty} = \dfrac{3}{2}$

21. a) $r = -0.4$
   b) $S_1 = 7$, $S_2 = 4.2$, $S_3 = 5.32$, $S_4 = 4.872$, $S_5 = 5.0512$
   c) 5
   d) $S_{\infty} = 5$

22.

   a) $1, \dfrac{1}{4}, \dfrac{1}{16}, \dfrac{1}{64}$. Yes. The areas form a geometric sequence. The common ratio is $\dfrac{1}{4}$.
   b) $1\dfrac{21}{64}$ or 1.328 125 square units
   c) $\dfrac{4}{3}$ square units

23. a) A series is geometric if there is a common ratio r such that $r \neq 1$.
An infinite geometric series converges if $-1 < r < 1$.
An infinite geometric series diverges if $r < -1$ or $r > 1$.
   b) Example:
$4 + 2 + 1 + 0.5 + \cdots$; $S_{\infty} = 8$
$21 - 10.5 + 5.25 - 2.625 + \cdots$; $S_{\infty} = 14$

Chapter 1 Practice Test, pages 69 to 70

1. D
2. B
3. B
4. B
5. C
6. 11.62 cm
7. Arithmetic sequences form straight-line graphs, where the slope is the common difference of the sequence. Geometric sequences form curved graphs.
8. $A = 15$, $B = 9$
9. 0.7 km
10. a) 5, 36, 67, 98, 129, 160
   b) $t_n = 31n - 26$
   c) 5, 10, 20, 40, 80, 160
   d) $t_n = 5(2)^{n-1}$
11. a) 17, 34, 51, 68, 85
   b) $t_n = 17n$
   c) 353 million years
   d) Assume that the continents continue to separate at the same rate every year.
12. a) 30 s, 60 s, 90 s, 120 s, 150 s
   b) arithmetic
   c) 60 days
   d) 915 min

Chapter 2 Trigonometry

2.1 Angles in Standard Position, pages 83 to 87

1. a) No; the vertex is not at the origin.
  b) Yes; the vertex is at the origin and the initial arm is on the *x*-axis.
  c) No; the initial arm is not on the *x*-axis.
  d) Yes; the vertex is at the origin and the initial arm is on the *x*-axis.

2. a) F   **b)** C   **c)** A
  d) D   **e)** B   **f)** E

3. a) I   **b)** IV   **c)** III
  d) I   **e)** III   **f)** II

4. a)

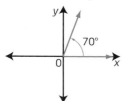

  b)

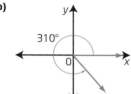

  c)

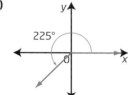

  d)

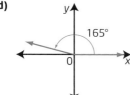

5. a) 10°   **b)** 15°   **c)** 72°   **d)** 35°
6. a) 135°, 225°, 315°   **b)** 120°, 240°, 300°
  c) 150°, 210°, 330°   **d)** 105°, 255°, 285°
7. a) 288°   **b)** 124°   **c)** 198°   **d)** 325°

8.

θ	sin θ	cos θ	tan θ
30°	$\frac{1}{2}$	$\frac{\sqrt{3}}{2}$	$\frac{1}{\sqrt{3}}$ or $\frac{\sqrt{3}}{3}$
45°	$\frac{1}{\sqrt{2}}$ or $\frac{\sqrt{2}}{2}$	$\frac{1}{\sqrt{2}}$ or $\frac{\sqrt{2}}{2}$	1
60°	$\frac{\sqrt{3}}{2}$	$\frac{1}{2}$	$\sqrt{3}$

9. 159.6°
10. a) dogwood (−3.5, 2), white pine (3.5, −2), river birch (−3.5, −2)
  b) red maple 30°, flowering dogwood 150°, river birch 210°, white pine 330°
  c) 40 m
11. $50\sqrt{3}$ cm
12. a) A′(x, −y), A″(−x, y), A‴(−x, −y)
  b) ∠A′OC = 360° − θ, ∠A″OC = 180° − θ, ∠A‴OB = 180° + θ
13. $(5\sqrt{3} − 5)$ m or $5(\sqrt{3} − 1)$ m
14. 252°
15. Cu (copper), Ag (silver), Au (gold), Uuu (unununium)
16. a) 216°   **b)** 8 days   **c)** 18 days
17. a) 70°   **b)** 220°

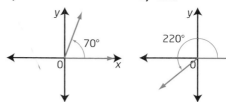

  c) 170°   **d)** 285°

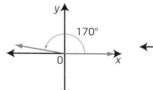 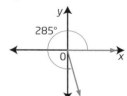

18. a)

Angle	Height (cm)
0°	12.0
15°	23.6
30°	34.5
45°	43.8
60°	51.0
75°	55.5
90°	57.0

  b) A constant increase in the angle does not produce a constant increase in the height. There is no common difference between heights for each pair of angles; for example, 23.6 cm − 12 cm = 11.6 cm, 34.5 cm − 23.6 cm = 10.9 cm.
  c) When θ extends beyond 90°, the heights decrease, with the height for 105° equal to the height for 75° and so on.
19. 45° and 135°
20. a) 19.56 m
  b) i) 192°   **ii)** 9.13 m
21. a) B   **b)** D

22. $x^2 + y^2 = r^2$

23. a)

θ	20°	40°	60°	80°
sin θ	0.3420	0.6428	0.8660	0.9848
sin (180° − θ)	0.3420	0.6428	0.8660	0.9848
sin (180° + θ)	−0.3420	−0.6428	−0.8660	−0.9848
sin (360° − θ)	−0.3420	−0.6428	−0.8660	−0.9848

b) Each angle in standard position has the same reference angle, but the sine ratio differs in sign based on the quadrant location. The sine ratio is positive in quadrants I and II and negative in quadrants III and IV.

c) The ratios would be the same as those for the reference angle for cos θ and tan θ in quadrant I but may have different signs than sin θ in each of the other quadrants.

24. a) $\dfrac{3025\sqrt{3}}{16}$ ft

b) As the angle increases to 45° the distance increases and then decreases after 45°.

c) The greatest distance occurs with an angle of 45°. The product of cos θ and sin θ has a maximum value when θ = 45°.

2.2 Trigonometric Ratios of Any Angle, pages 96 to 99

1. a)

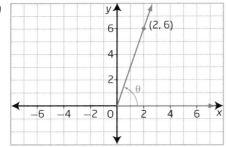

b)

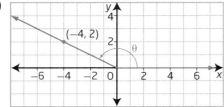

c)

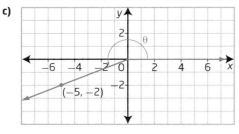

d)

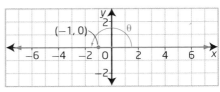

2. a) $\sin 60° = \dfrac{\sqrt{3}}{2}$, $\cos 60° = \dfrac{1}{2}$, $\tan 60° = \sqrt{3}$

b) $\sin 225° = -\dfrac{1}{\sqrt{2}}$ or $-\dfrac{\sqrt{2}}{2}$,

$\cos 225° = -\dfrac{1}{\sqrt{2}}$ or $-\dfrac{\sqrt{2}}{2}$, $\tan 225° = 1$

c) $\sin 150° = \dfrac{1}{2}$, $\cos 150° = -\dfrac{\sqrt{3}}{2}$,

$\tan 150° = -\dfrac{1}{\sqrt{3}}$ or $-\dfrac{\sqrt{3}}{3}$

d) $\sin 90° = 1$, $\cos 90° = 0$, $\tan 90°$ is undefined

3. a) $\sin θ = \dfrac{4}{5}$, $\cos θ = \dfrac{3}{5}$, $\tan θ = \dfrac{4}{3}$

b) $\sin θ = -\dfrac{5}{13}$, $\cos θ = -\dfrac{12}{13}$, $\tan θ = \dfrac{5}{12}$

c) $\sin θ = -\dfrac{15}{17}$, $\cos θ = \dfrac{8}{17}$, $\tan θ = -\dfrac{15}{8}$

d) $\sin θ = -\dfrac{1}{\sqrt{2}}$ or $-\dfrac{\sqrt{2}}{2}$, $\cos θ = \dfrac{1}{\sqrt{2}}$ or $\dfrac{\sqrt{2}}{2}$,

$\tan θ = -1$

4. a) II **b)** I **c)** III **d)** IV

5. a) $\sin θ = \dfrac{12}{13}$, $\cos θ = -\dfrac{5}{13}$, $\tan θ = -\dfrac{12}{5}$

b) $\sin θ = -\dfrac{3}{\sqrt{34}}$ or $-\dfrac{3\sqrt{34}}{34}$,

$\cos θ = \dfrac{5}{\sqrt{34}}$ or $\dfrac{5\sqrt{34}}{34}$, $\tan θ = -\dfrac{3}{5}$

c) $\sin θ = \dfrac{3}{\sqrt{45}}$ or $\dfrac{1}{\sqrt{5}}$, $\cos θ = \dfrac{6}{\sqrt{45}}$ or $\dfrac{2}{\sqrt{5}}$,

$\tan θ = \dfrac{1}{2}$

d) $\sin θ = -\dfrac{5}{13}$, $\cos θ = -\dfrac{12}{13}$, $\tan θ = \dfrac{5}{12}$

6. a) positive **b)** positive
c) negative **d)** negative

7. a)

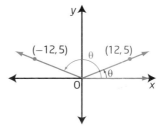

b) 23° or 157°

8. a) $\sin θ = \dfrac{\sqrt{5}}{3}$, $\tan θ = -\dfrac{\sqrt{5}}{2}$

b) $\cos θ = \dfrac{4}{5}$, $\tan θ = \dfrac{3}{4}$

c) $\sin θ = -\dfrac{4}{\sqrt{41}}$ or $-\dfrac{4\sqrt{41}}{41}$,

$\cos θ = \dfrac{5}{\sqrt{41}}$ or $\dfrac{5\sqrt{41}}{41}$

d) $\cos \theta = -\dfrac{2\sqrt{2}}{3}$, $\tan \theta = \dfrac{\sqrt{2}}{4}$

e) $\sin \theta = -\dfrac{1}{\sqrt{2}}$ or $-\dfrac{\sqrt{2}}{2}$,

$\cos \theta = -\dfrac{1}{\sqrt{2}}$ or $-\dfrac{\sqrt{2}}{2}$

9. a) 60° and 300°   **b)** 135° and 225°
c) 150° and 330°   **d)** 240° and 300°
e) 60° and 240°   **f)** 135° and 315°

10.

θ	sin θ	cos θ	tan θ
0°	0	1	0
90°	1	0	undefined
180°	0	−1	0
270°	−1	0	undefined
360°	0	1	0

11. a) $x = -8$, $y = 6$, $r = 10$, $\sin \theta = \dfrac{3}{5}$,

$\cos \theta = -\dfrac{4}{5}$, $\tan \theta = -\dfrac{3}{4}$

b) $x = 5$, $y = -12$, $r = 13$, $\sin \theta = -\dfrac{12}{13}$,

$\cos \theta = \dfrac{5}{13}$, $\tan \theta = -\dfrac{12}{5}$

12. a)

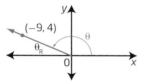

b) 24°   **c)** 156°

13. a)

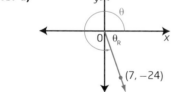

b) 74°   **c)** 286°

14. a) $\sin \theta = \dfrac{2}{\sqrt{5}}$ or $\dfrac{2\sqrt{5}}{5}$

b) $\sin \theta = \dfrac{2}{\sqrt{5}}$ or $\dfrac{2\sqrt{5}}{5}$

c) $\sin \theta = \dfrac{2}{\sqrt{5}}$ or $\dfrac{2\sqrt{5}}{5}$

d) They all have the same sine ratio. This happens because the points P, Q, and R are collinear. They are on the same terminal arm.

15. a) 74° and 106°

b) $\sin \theta = \dfrac{24}{25}$, $\cos \theta = \pm\dfrac{7}{25}$, $\tan \theta = \pm\dfrac{24}{7}$

16. $\sin \theta = \dfrac{2\sqrt{6}}{5}$

17. $\sin 0° = 0$, $\cos 0° = 1$, $\tan 0° = 0$, $\sin 90° = 1$, $\cos 90° = 0$, $\tan 90°$ is undefined

18. a) True. θ_R for 151° is 29° and is in quadrant II. The sine ratio is positive in quadrants I and II.

b) True; both sin 225° and cos 135° have a reference angle of 45° and

$\sin 45° = \cos 45° = \dfrac{1}{\sqrt{2}}$.

c) False; tan 135° is in quadrant II, where $\tan \theta < 0$, and tan 225° is in quadrant III, where $\tan \theta > 0$.

d) True; from the reference angles in a 30°-60°-90° triangle,

$\sin 60° = \cos 330° = \dfrac{\sqrt{3}}{2}$.

e) True; the terminal arms lie on the axes, passing through P(0, −1) and P(−1, 0), respectively, so sin 270° = cos 180° = −1.

19.

θ	sin θ	cos θ	tan θ
0°	0	1	0
30°	$\dfrac{1}{2}$	$\dfrac{\sqrt{3}}{2}$	$\dfrac{1}{\sqrt{3}}$ or $\dfrac{\sqrt{3}}{3}$
45°	$\dfrac{1}{\sqrt{2}}$ or $\dfrac{\sqrt{2}}{2}$	$\dfrac{1}{\sqrt{2}}$ or $\dfrac{\sqrt{2}}{2}$	1
60°	$\dfrac{\sqrt{3}}{2}$	$\dfrac{1}{2}$	$\sqrt{3}$
90°	1	0	undefined
120°	$\dfrac{\sqrt{3}}{2}$	$-\dfrac{1}{2}$	$-\sqrt{3}$
135°	$\dfrac{1}{\sqrt{2}}$ or $\dfrac{\sqrt{2}}{2}$	$-\dfrac{1}{\sqrt{2}}$ or $-\dfrac{\sqrt{2}}{2}$	−1
150°	$\dfrac{1}{2}$	$-\dfrac{\sqrt{3}}{2}$	$-\dfrac{1}{\sqrt{3}}$ or $-\dfrac{\sqrt{3}}{3}$
180°	0	−1	0
210°	$-\dfrac{1}{2}$	$-\dfrac{\sqrt{3}}{2}$	$\dfrac{1}{\sqrt{3}}$ or $\dfrac{\sqrt{3}}{3}$
225°	$-\dfrac{1}{\sqrt{2}}$ or $-\dfrac{\sqrt{2}}{2}$	$-\dfrac{1}{\sqrt{2}}$ or $-\dfrac{\sqrt{2}}{2}$	1
240°	$-\dfrac{\sqrt{3}}{2}$	$-\dfrac{1}{2}$	$\sqrt{3}$
270°	−1	0	undefined
300°	$-\dfrac{\sqrt{3}}{2}$	$\dfrac{1}{2}$	$-\sqrt{3}$
315°	$-\dfrac{1}{\sqrt{2}}$ or $-\dfrac{\sqrt{2}}{2}$	$\dfrac{1}{\sqrt{2}}$ or $\dfrac{\sqrt{2}}{2}$	−1
330°	$-\dfrac{1}{2}$	$\dfrac{\sqrt{3}}{2}$	$-\dfrac{1}{\sqrt{3}}$ or $-\dfrac{\sqrt{3}}{3}$
360°	0	1	0

20. a) $\angle A = 45°$, $\angle B = 135°$, $\angle C = 225°$, $\angle D = 315°$

b) $A\left(\dfrac{1}{\sqrt{2}}, \dfrac{1}{\sqrt{2}}\right)$, $B\left(-\dfrac{1}{\sqrt{2}}, \dfrac{1}{\sqrt{2}}\right)$,

$C\left(-\dfrac{1}{\sqrt{2}}, -\dfrac{1}{\sqrt{2}}\right)$, $D\left(\dfrac{1}{\sqrt{2}}, -\dfrac{1}{\sqrt{2}}\right)$

21. a)

Angle	Sine	Cosine	Tangent
0°	0	1	0
15°	0.2588	0.9659	0.2679
30°	0.5	0.8660	0.5774
45°	0.7071	0.7071	1
60°	0.8660	0.5	1.7321
75°	0.9659	0.2588	3.7321
90°	1	0	undefined
105°	0.9659	−0.2588	−3.7321
120°	0.8660	−0.5	−1.7321
135°	0.7071	−0.7071	−1
150°	0.5	−0.8660	−0.5774
165°	0.2588	−0.9659	−0.2679
180°	0	−1	0

b) As θ increases from 0° to 180°, $\sin\theta$ increases from a minimum of 0 to a maximum of 1 at 90° and then decreases to 0 again at 180°. $\sin\theta = \sin(180° - \theta)$. Cos θ decreases from a maximum of 1 at 0° and continues to decrease to a minimum value of −1 at 180°. $\cos\theta = -\cos(180° - \theta)$. Tan θ increases from 0 to being undefined at 90° then back to 0 again at 180°.

c) For $0° \leq \theta \leq 90°$, $\cos\theta = \sin(90° - \theta)$. For $90° \leq \theta \leq 180°$, $\cos\theta = -\sin(\theta - 90°)$.

d) Sine ratios are positive in quadrants I and II, and both the cosine and tangent ratios are positive in quadrant I and negative in quadrant II.

e) In quadrant III, the sine and cosine ratios are negative and the tangent ratios are positive. In quadrant IV, the cosine ratios are positive and the sine and tangent ratios are negative.

22. a) $\sin\theta = \dfrac{6}{\sqrt{37}}$ or $\dfrac{6\sqrt{37}}{37}$,

$\cos\theta = \dfrac{1}{\sqrt{37}}$ or $\dfrac{\sqrt{37}}{37}$, $\tan\theta = 6$

b) $\dfrac{1}{20}$

23. As θ increases from 0° to 90°, x decreases from 12 to 0, y increases from 0 to 12, $\sin\theta$ increases from 0 to 1, $\cos\theta$ decreases from 1 to 0, and $\tan\theta$ increases from 0 to undefined.

24. $\tan\theta = \dfrac{\sqrt{1 - a^2}}{a}$

25. Since $\angle BOA$ is 60°, the coordinates of point A are $\left(\dfrac{1}{2}, \dfrac{\sqrt{3}}{2}\right)$. The coordinates of point B are (1, 0) and of point C are (−1, 0). Using the Pythagorean theorem $d^2 = (x_2 - x_1)^2 + (y_2 - y_1)^2$, $d_{AB} = 1$, $d_{BC} = 2$, and $d_{AC} = \sqrt{3}$. Then, $AB^2 = 1$, $AC^2 = 3$, and $BC^2 = 4$. So, $AB^2 + AC^2 = BC^2$.

The measures satisfy the Pythagorean Theorem, so $\triangle ABC$ is a right triangle and $\angle CAB = 90°$. Alternatively, $\angle CAB$ is inscribed in a semicircle and must be a right angle. Hence, $\triangle CAB$ is a right triangle and the Pythagorean Theorem must hold true.

26. Reference angles can determine the trigonometric ratio of any angle in quadrant I. Adjust the signs of the trigonometric ratios for quadrants II, III, and IV, considering that the sine ratio is positive in quadrant II and negative in quadrants III and IV, the cosine ratio is positive in the quadrant IV but negative in quadrants II and III, and the tangent ratio is positive in quadrant III but negative in quadrants II and IV.

27. Use the reference triangle to identify the measure of the reference angle, and then adjust for the fact that P is in quadrant III. Since $\tan\theta_R = \dfrac{9}{5}$, you can find the reference angle to be 61°. Since the angle is in quadrant III, the angle is 180° + 61° or 241°.

28. Sine is the ratio of the opposite side to the hypotenuse. The hypotenuse is the same value, r, in all four quadrants. The opposite side, y, is positive in quadrants I and II and negative in quadrants III and IV. So, there will be exactly two sine ratios with the same positive values in quadrants I and II and two sine ratios with the same negative values in quadrants III and IV.

29. $\theta = 240°$. Both the sine ratio and the cosine ratio are negative, so the terminal arm must be in quadrant III. The value of the reference angle when $\sin\theta_R = \dfrac{\sqrt{3}}{2}$ is 60°. The angle in quadrant III is 180° + 60° or 240°.

30. Step 4

a) As point A moves around the circle, the sine ratio increases from 0 to 1 in quadrant I, decreases from 1 to 0 in quadrant II, decreases from 0 to −1 in quadrant III, and increases from −1 to 0 in quadrant IV. The cosine ratio decreases from 1 to 0 in quadrant I, decreases from 0 to −1 in quadrant II, increases from −1 to 0 in quadrant III, and increases from 0 to 1 in quadrant IV. The tangent ratio increases from 0 to infinity in quadrant I, is undefined for an angle of 90°, increases from negative infinity to 0 in the second quadrant, increases from 0 to positive infinity in the third quadrant, is undefined for an angle of 270°, and increases from negative infinity to 0 in quadrant IV.

b) The sine and cosine ratios are the same when A is at approximately (3.5355, 3.5355) and (−3.5355, −3.5355). This corresponds to 45° and 225°.

c) The sine ratio is positive in quadrants I and II and negative in quadrants III and IV. The cosine ratio is positive in quadrant I, negative in quadrants II and III, and positive in quadrant IV. The tangent ratio is positive in quadrant I, negative in quadrant II, positive in quadrant III, and negative in quadrant IV.

d) When the sine ratio is divided by the cosine ratio, the result is the tangent ratio. This is true for all angles as A moves around the circle.

2.3 The Sine Law, pages 108 to 113

1. a) 8.9 **b)** 50.0
 c) 8° **d)** 44°
2. a) 36.9 mm **b)** 50.4 m
3. a) 53° **b)** 58°
4. a) $\angle C = 86°$, $\angle A = 27°$, $a = 6.0$ m or
  $\angle C = 94°$, $\angle A = 19°$, $a = 4.2$ m
 b) $\angle C = 54°$, $c = 40.7$ m, $a = 33.6$ m
 c) $\angle B = 119°$, $c = 20.9$ mm, $a = 12.4$ mm
 d) $\angle B = 71°$, $c = 19.4$ cm, $a = 16.5$ cm
5. a) $AC = 30.0$ cm

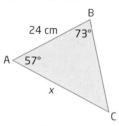

 b) $AB = 52.4$ cm

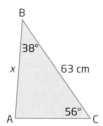

 c) $AB = 34.7$ m

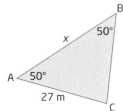

d) $BC = 6.0$ cm

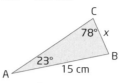

6. a) two solutions **b)** one solution
 c) one solution **d)** no solutions
7. a) $a > b \sin A$, $a > h$, $b > h$
 b) $a > b \sin A$, $a > h$, $a < b$
 c) $a = b \sin A$, $a = h$
 d) $a > b \sin A$, $a > h$, $a \geq b$
8. a) $\angle A = 48°$, $\angle B = 101°$, $b = 7.4$ cm or
  $\angle A = 132°$, $\angle B = 17°$, $b = 2.2$ cm
 b) $\angle P = 65°$, $\angle R = 72°$, $r = 20.9$ cm or
  $\angle P = 115°$, $\angle R = 22°$, $r = 8.2$ cm
 c) no solutions
9. a) $a \geq 120$ cm **b)** $a = 52.6$ cm
 c) 52.6 cm $< a <$ 120 cm
 d) $a < 52.6$ cm
10. a)

 b) 409.9 m
11. 364.7 m
12. 41°
13. 4.5 m
14. a)

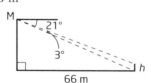

 b) 4.1 m **c)** 72.2 m
15. a) 1.51 Å **b)** 0.0151 mm
16. least wingspan 9.1 m, greatest wingspan 9.3 m
17. a) Since $a < b$ (360 < 500) and
   $a > b \sin A$ (360 > 500 sin 35°), there are
   two possible solutions for the triangle.
 b)

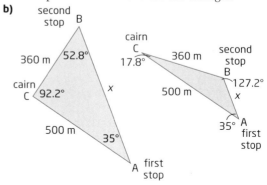

c) Armand's second stop could be either 191.9 m or 627.2 m from his first stop.

18. 911.6 m

19.

Statements	Reasons
$\sin C = \dfrac{h}{b}$ $\sin B = \dfrac{h}{c}$	sin B ratio in △ABD sin C ratio in △ACD
$h = b \sin C$ $h = c \sin B$	Solve each ratio for *h*.
$b \sin C = c \sin B$	Equivalence property or substitution
$\dfrac{\sin C}{c} = \dfrac{\sin B}{b}$	Divide both sides by *bc*.

20.

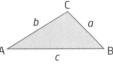

Given ∠A = ∠B, prove that side AC = BC, or *a* = *b*.
Using the sine law,
$$\frac{a}{\sin A} = \frac{b}{\sin B}$$
But ∠A = ∠B, so sin A = sin B.
Then, $\dfrac{a}{\sin A} = \dfrac{b}{\sin A}$.
So, *a* = *b*.

21. 14.1 km²

22. a) 32.1 cm < *a* < 50.0 cm

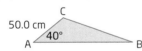

b) *a* < 104.2 cm

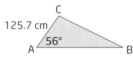

c) *a* = 61.8 cm

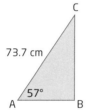

23. 166.7 m

24. a) There is no known side opposite a known angle.

b) There is no known angle opposite a known side.

c) There is no known side opposite a known angle.

d) There is no known angle and only one known side.

25.

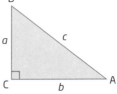

In △ABC,
$\sin A = \dfrac{a}{c}$ and $\sin B = \dfrac{b}{c}$
Thus, $c = \dfrac{a}{\sin A}$ and $c = \dfrac{b}{\sin B}$.
Then, $\dfrac{a}{\sin A} = \dfrac{b}{\sin B}$.
This is only true for a right triangle and does not show a proof for oblique triangles.

26. a) 12.9 cm

b) $(4\sqrt{5} + 4)$ cm or $4(\sqrt{5} + 1)$ cm

c) 4.9 cm

d) 3.1 cm

e) The spiral is created by connecting the 36° angle vertices for the reducing golden triangles.

27. Concept maps will vary.

28. Step 1

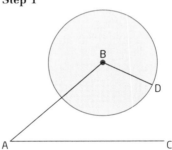

Step 2
a) No.
b) There are no triangles formed when BD is less than the distance from B to the line AC.

Step 3

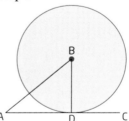

a) Yes.
b) One triangle can be formed when BD equals the distance from B to the line AC.

Step 4

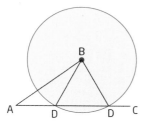

a) Yes.

b) Two triangles can be formed when BD is greater than the distance from B to the line AC.

Step 5

a) Yes.

b) One triangle is formed when BD is greater than the length AB.

Step 6 The conjectures will work so long as ∠A is an acute angle. The relationship changes when ∠A > 90°.

2.4 The Cosine Law, pages 119 to 125

1. **a)** 6.0 cm   **b)** 21.0 mm   **c)** 45.0 m
2. **a)** ∠J = 34°   **b)** ∠L = 55°
   c) ∠P = 137°   **d)** ∠C = 139°
3. **a)** ∠Q = 62°, ∠R = 66°, p = 25.0 km
   b) ∠S = 100°, ∠R = 33°, ∠T = 47°
4. **a)**

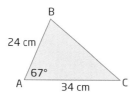

BC = 33.1 cm

b)

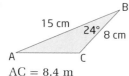

AC = 8.4 m

c)

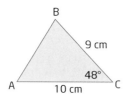

AB = 7.8 cm

d)

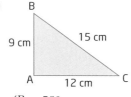

∠B = 53°

e)

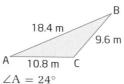

∠A = 24°

f)

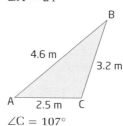

∠C = 107°

5. **a)** Use the cosine law because three sides are given (SSS). There is no given angle and opposite side to be able to use the sine law.
   b) Use the sine law because two angles and an opposite side are given.
   c) Use the cosine law to find the missing side length. Then, use the sine law to find the indicated angle.

6. **a)** 22.6 cm
   b) 7.2 m
7. 53.4 cm
8. 2906 m
9. The angles between the buoys are 35°, 88°, and 57°.
10. 4.2°
11. 22.4 km
12. 54.4 km
13. 458.5 cm
14. **a)**

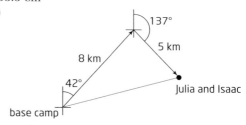

   b) 9.1 km
   c) 255°
15. 9.7 m
16. Use the cosine law in each oblique triangle to find the measure of each obtuse angle. These three angles meet at a point and should sum to 360°. The three angles are 118°, 143°, and 99°. Since 118° + 143° + 99° = 360°, the side measures are accurate.
17. The interior angles of the bike frame are 73°, 62°, and 45°.
18. 98.48 m
19. 1546 km

20. 438.1 m

21. The interior angles of the building are 65°, 32°, and 83°.

22.

Statement	Reason
$c^2 = (a - x)^2 + h^2$	Use the Pythagorean Theorem in △ABD.
$c^2 = a^2 - 2ax + x^2 + h^2$	Expand the square of a binomial.
$b^2 = x^2 + h^2$	Use the Pythagorean Theorem in △ACD.
$c^2 = a^2 - 2ax + b^2$	Substitute b^2 for $x^2 + h^2$.
$\cos C = \dfrac{x}{b}$	Use the cosine ratio in △ACD.
$x = b \cos C$	Multiply both sides by b.
$c^2 = a^2 - 2ab \cos C + b^2$	Substitute $b \cos C$ for x in step 4.
$c^2 = a^2 + b^2 - 2ab \cos C$	Rearrange.

23. 36.2 km

24. No. The three given lengths cannot be arranged to form a triangle ($a^2 + b^2 < c^2$). When using the cosine law, the cosines of the angles are either greater than 1 or less than -1, which is impossible.

25. 21.2 cm

26. $\angle ABC = 65°$, $\angle ACD = 97°$

27. 596 km^2

28. 2.1 m

29.

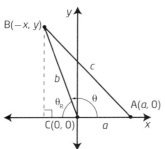

$$\cos \theta_R = -\cos \theta = -\frac{x}{\sqrt{x^2 + y^2}}$$
$$b = \sqrt{x^2 + y^2}$$
$$c = \sqrt{(a + x)^2 + y^2}$$

Prove that $c^2 = a^2 + b^2 - 2ab \cos C$:

Left Side $= \left(\sqrt{(a + x)^2 + y^2}\right)^2$
$= (a + x)^2 + y^2$
$= a^2 + 2ax + x^2 + y^2$

Right Side $= a^2 + \left(\sqrt{x^2 + y^2}\right)^2$
$\quad - 2a\left(\sqrt{x^2 + y^2}\right)\left(-\dfrac{x}{\sqrt{x^2 + y^2}}\right)$
$= a^2 + x^2 + y^2 + 2ax$
$= a^2 + 2ax + x^2 + y^2$

Left Side = Right Side
Therefore, the cosine law is true.

30. 115.5 m

31. a) 228.05 cm^2

b) 228.05 cm^2

c) These methods give the same measure when $\angle C = 90°$.

d) Since $\cos 90° = 0$, $2ab \cos 90° = 0$, so $a^2 + b^2 - 2ab \cos 90° = a^2 + b^2$. Therefore, c^2 can be found using the cosine law or the Pythagorean Theorem when there is a right triangle.

32.

Concept Summary for Solving a Triangle	
Given	Begin by Using the Method of
Right triangle	A
Two angles and any side	B
Three sides	C
Three angles	D
Two sides and the included angle	C
Two sides and the angle opposite one of them	B

33. Step 2

a) $\angle A = 29°$, $\angle B = 104°$, $\angle C = 47°$

b) The angles at each vertex of a square are 90°. Therefore,
$360° = \angle ABC + 90° + \angle GBF + 90°$
$180° = \angle ABC + \angle GBF$
$\angle GBF = 76°$, $\angle HCI = 133°$, $\angle DAE = 151°$

c) GF = 6.4 cm, ED = 13.6 cm, HI = 11.1 cm

Step 3

a) For △HCI, the altitude from C to HI is 2.1 cm. For △AED, the altitude from A to DE is 1.6 cm. For △BGF, the altitude from B to GF is 3.6 cm. For △ABC, the altitude from B to AC is 2.9 cm.

b) area of △ABC is 11.7 cm^2, area of △BGF is 11.7 cm^2, area of △AED is 11.7 cm^2, area of △HCI is 11.7 cm^2

Step 4 All four triangles have the same area. Since you use reference angles to determine the altitudes, the product of $\frac{1}{2}bh$ will determine the same area for all triangles. This works for any triangle.

Chapter 2 Review, pages 126 to 128

1. a) E   **b)** D   **c)** B   **d)** A
   e) F   **f)** C   **g)** G

2. a)

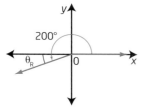

Quadrant III, $\theta_R = 20°$

b)

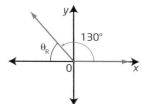

Quadrant II, $\theta_R = 50°$

c)

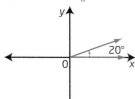

Quadrant I, $\theta_R = 20°$

d)

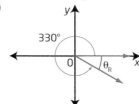

Quadrant IV, $\theta_R = 30°$

3. No. Reference angles are measured from the x-axis. The reference angle is 60°.

4. quadrant I: $\theta = 35°$, quadrant II: $\theta = 180° - 35°$ or 145°, quadrant III: $\theta = 180° + 35°$ or 215°, quadrant IV: $\theta = 360° - 35°$ or 325°

5. a) $\sin 225° = -\dfrac{1}{\sqrt{2}}$ or $-\dfrac{\sqrt{2}}{2}$,
$\cos 225° = -\dfrac{1}{\sqrt{2}}$ or $-\dfrac{\sqrt{2}}{2}$, $\tan 225° = 1$

b) $\sin 120° = \dfrac{\sqrt{3}}{2}$, $\cos 120° = -\dfrac{1}{2}$,
$\tan 120° = -\sqrt{3}$

c) $\sin 330° = -\dfrac{1}{2}$, $\cos 330° = \dfrac{\sqrt{3}}{2}$,
$\tan 330° = -\dfrac{1}{\sqrt{3}}$ or $-\dfrac{\sqrt{3}}{3}$

d) $\sin 135° = \dfrac{1}{\sqrt{2}}$ or $\dfrac{\sqrt{2}}{2}$,
$\cos 135° = -\dfrac{1}{\sqrt{2}}$ or $-\dfrac{\sqrt{2}}{2}$, $\tan 135° = -1$

6. a)

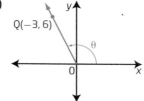

b) $\sqrt{45}$ or $3\sqrt{5}$

c) $\sin \theta = \dfrac{6}{\sqrt{45}}$ or $\dfrac{2\sqrt{5}}{5}$,
$\cos \theta = -\dfrac{3}{\sqrt{45}}$ or $-\dfrac{\sqrt{5}}{5}$, $\tan \theta = -2$

d) 117°

7. $(2, 5), (-2, 5), (-2, -5)$

8. a) $\sin 90° = 1$, $\cos 90° = 0$, $\tan 90°$ is undefined

b) $\sin 180° = 0$, $\cos 180° = -1$, $\tan 180° = 0$

9. a) $\cos \theta = -\dfrac{4}{5}$, $\tan \theta = \dfrac{3}{4}$

b) $\sin \theta = -\dfrac{\sqrt{8}}{3}$ or $-\dfrac{2\sqrt{2}}{3}$,
$\tan \theta = -\sqrt{8}$ or $-2\sqrt{2}$

c) $\sin \theta = \dfrac{12}{13}$, $\cos \theta = \dfrac{5}{13}$

10. a) 130° or 310°   **b)** 200° or 340°

c) 70° or 290°

11. a) Yes; there is a known angle $(180° - 18° - 114° = 48°)$ and a known opposite side (3 cm), plus another known angle.

b) Yes; there is a known angle (90°) and opposite side (32 cm), plus one other known side.

c) No; there is no known angle or opposite side.

12. a) $\angle C = 57°$, $c = 36.9$ mm

b) $\angle A = 78°$, $\angle B = 60°$

13.

$\angle R = 65.3°$, $q = 5.4$ cm, $p = 6.2$ cm

14. 2.8 km

15. a) Ship B, 50.0 km

b)

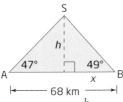

Use $\tan 49° = \dfrac{h}{x}$ and $\tan 47° = \dfrac{h}{68 - x}$.

Solve $x \tan 49° = (68 - x) \tan 47°$.

$x = 32.8$ km

Then, use $\cos 49° = \dfrac{32.8}{BS}$ and $\cos 47° = \dfrac{35.2}{AS}$

to find BS and AS.

AS = 51.6 km, BS = 50.0 km

16. no solutions if $a < b \sin A$, one solution if $a = b \sin A$ or if $a \geq b$, and two solutions if $b > a > b \sin A$

17. a)

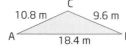

b) 47° E of S

c) 939.2 km

18. a) The three sides do not meet to form a triangle since $4 + 2 < 7$.

b) $\angle A + \angle C > 180°$

c) Sides a and c lie on top of side b, so no triangle is formed.

d) $\angle A + \angle B + \angle C < 180°$

19. a) sine law; there is a known angle and a known opposite side plus another known angle

b) cosine law; there is a known SAS (side-angle-side)

20. a) $a = 29.1$ cm

b) $\angle B = 57°$

21. 170.5 yd

22. a)

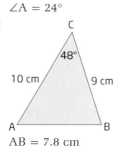

$\angle A = 24°$

b)

C

48°

10 cm   9 cm

A   B

AB = 7.8 cm

c)

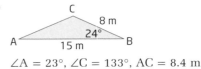

$\angle A = 23°$, $\angle C = 133°$, AC = 8.4 m

23. a)

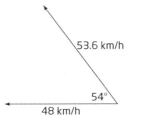

53.6 km/h

54°

48 km/h

b) 185.6 km

24. a)

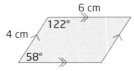

6 cm

122°

4 cm

58°

b) 8.8 cm and 5.2 cm

Chapter 2 Practice Test, pages 129 to 130

1. A

2. A

3. C

4. B

5. C

6. -6

7. a)

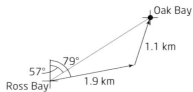

Oak Bay

1.1 km

79°

57°

Ross Bay   1.9 km

b) 2.6 km

8. a) two

b) $\angle B = 53°$, $\angle C = 97°$, $c = 19.9$ or $\angle B = 127°$, $\angle C = 23°$, $c = 7.8$

9. $\angle R = 17°$

10. a)

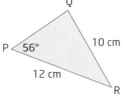

Q

10 cm

P 56°

12 cm

R

b) $\angle R = 40°$, $\angle Q = 84°$, $r = 7.8$ cm or $\angle R = 28°$, $\angle Q = 96°$, $r = 5.7$ cm

11. 5.2 cm

12. a) 44°   **b)** 56°   **c)** 1.7 m

13. quadrant I: $\theta = \theta_R$, quadrant II: $\theta = 180° - \theta_R$, quadrant III: $\theta = 180° + \theta_R$, quadrant IV: $\theta = 360° - \theta_R$

14. a)

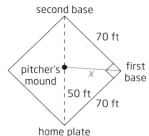

b)
$$a^2 + b^2 = c^2$$
$$70^2 + 70^2 = c^2$$
$$c = 99$$

Second base to pitcher's mound is $99 - 50$ or 49 ft.

Distance from first base to pitcher's mound is $x^2 = 50^2 + 70^2 - 2(50)(70)\cos 45°$ or 49.5 ft.

15. Use the sine law when the given information includes a known angle and a known opposite side, plus one other known side or angle. Use the cosine law when given oblique triangles with known SSS or SAS.

16. patio triangle: 38°, 25°, 2.5 m; shrubs triangle: 55°, 2.7 m, 3.0 m

17. 3.1 km

Cumulative Review, Chapters 1–2, pages 133 to 135

1. a) A **b)** D **c)** E **d)** C **e)** B

2. a) geometric, $r = \dfrac{2}{3}$; $\dfrac{16}{3}, \dfrac{32}{9}, \dfrac{64}{27}$

b) arithmetic, $d = -3$; 5, 2, -1

c) arithmetic, $d = 5$; -1, 4, 9

d) geometric, $r = -2$; 48, -96, 192

3. a) $t_n = -3n + 21$

b) $t_n = \dfrac{3}{2}n - \dfrac{1}{2}$

4. $t_n = 2(-2)^{n-1} \Rightarrow t_{20} = -2^{20}$ or $-1\,048\,576$

5. a) $S_{12} = 174$ **b)** $S_5 = 484$

6. a)

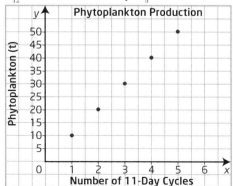

b) $t_n = 10n$

c) The general term is a linear equation with a slope of 10.

7. 201 m

8. a) $r = 0.1$, $S_{\infty} = 1$

b) Answers will vary.

9. $2\sqrt{5}$

10. $\sin \theta = \dfrac{8}{17}$, $\cos \theta = \dfrac{15}{17}$, $\tan \theta = \dfrac{8}{15}$

11. a) 40° **b)** 60°

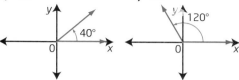

c) 45° **d)** 60°

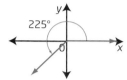

12. a) 90°

b)

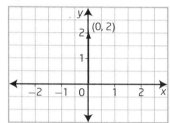

c) $\sin \theta = 1$, $\cos \theta = 0$, $\tan \theta$ is undefined

13. a) $\sin 405° = \dfrac{1}{\sqrt{2}}$ or $\dfrac{\sqrt{2}}{2}$

b) $\cos 330° = \dfrac{\sqrt{3}}{2}$

c) $\tan 225° = 1$

d) $\cos 180° = -1$

e) $\tan 150° = = -\dfrac{1}{\sqrt{3}}$ or $-\dfrac{\sqrt{3}}{3}$

f) $\sin 270° = -1$

14. The bear is 8.9 km from station A and 7.4 km from station B.

15. 9.4°

16. a)

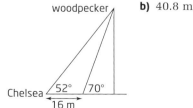

b) 40.8 m

17. 134.4°

Unit 1 Test, pages 136 to 137

1. B

2. C

3. D

4. C

5. D

6. $0.15 per cup

7. 45°

8. 300°

9. 2775

10. a) 5   **b)** −6
    c) $t_n = 5n − 11$ **d)** $S_{10} = 165$

11. $14 880.35

12. 4 km

13. a) 64, 32, 16, 8, …   **b)** $t_n = 64\left(\dfrac{1}{2}\right)^{n-1}$

    c) 63 games

14. a)

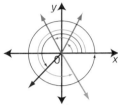

    b) 60, 120, 180, 240, 300, 360
    c) $t_n = 60n$

15. a) 58°   **b)** 5.3 m

16. 38°

Chapter 3 Quadratic Functions

3.1 Investigating Quadratic Functions in Vertex Form, pages 157 to 162

1. a) Since $a > 0$ in $f(x) = 7x^2$, the graph opens upward, has a minimum value, and has a range of $\{y \mid y \geq 0, y \in R\}$.

    b) Since $a > 0$ in $f(x) = \dfrac{1}{6}x^2$, the graph opens upward, has a minimum value, and has a range of $\{y \mid y \geq 0, y \in R\}$.

    c) Since $a < 0$ in $f(x) = -4x^2$, the graph opens downward, has a maximum value, and has a range of $\{y \mid y \leq 0, y \in R\}$.

    d) Since $a < 0$ in $f(x) = -0.2x^2$, the graph opens downward, has a maximum value, and has a range of $\{y \mid y \leq 0, y \in R\}$.

2. a) The shapes of the graphs are the same with the parabola of $y = x^2 + 1$ being one unit higher. vertex: (0, 1), axis of symmetry: $x = 0$, domain: $\{x \mid x \in R\}$, range: $\{y \mid y \geq 1, y \in R\}$, no x-intercepts, y-intercept occurs at (0, 1)

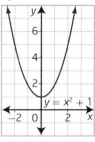

    b) The shapes of the graphs are the same with the parabola of $y = (x − 2)^2$ being two units to the right. vertex: (2, 0), axis of symmetry: $x = 2$, domain: $\{x \mid x \in R\}$, range: $\{y \mid y \geq 0, y \in R\}$, x-intercept occurs at (2, 0), y-intercept occurs at (0, 4)

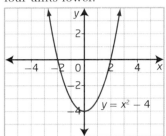

    c) The shapes of the graphs are the same with the parabola of $y = x^2 − 4$ being four units lower.

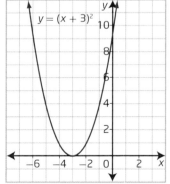

vertex: (0, −4), axis of symmetry: $x = 0$, domain: $\{x \mid x \in R\}$, range: $\{y \mid y \geq −4, y \in R\}$, x-intercepts occur at (−2, 0) and (2, 0), y-intercept occurs at (0, −4)

    d) The shapes of the graphs are the same with the parabola of $y = (x + 3)^2$ being three units to the left.

vertex: (−3, 0), axis of symmetry: $x = −3$, domain: $\{x \mid x \in R\}$, range: $\{y \mid y \geq 0, y \in R\}$, x-intercept occurs at (−3, 0), y-intercept occurs at (0, 9)

3. a) Given the graph of $y = x^2$, move the entire graph 5 units to the left and 11 units up.

b) Given the graph of $y = x^2$, apply the change in width, which is a multiplication of the y-values by a factor of 3, making it narrower, reflect it in the x-axis so it opens downward, and move the entire new graph down 10 units.

c) Given the graph of $y = x^2$, apply the change in width, which is a multiplication of the y-values by a factor of 5, making it narrower. Move the entire new graph 20 units to the left and 21 units down.

d) Given the graph of $y = x^2$, apply the change in width, which is a multiplication of the y-values by a factor of $\frac{1}{8}$, making it wider, reflect it in the x-axis so it opens downward, and move the entire new graph 5.6 units to the right and 13.8 units up.

4. a)

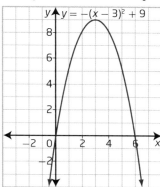

vertex: (3, 9), axis of symmetry: $x = 3$, opens downward, maximum value of 9, domain: $\{x \mid x \in R\}$, range: $\{y \mid y \le 9, y \in R\}$, x-intercepts occur at (0, 0) and (6, 0), y-intercept occurs at (0, 0)

b)

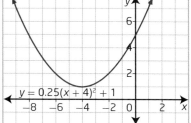

vertex: (−4, 1), axis of symmetry: $x = -4$, opens upward, minimum value of 1, domain: $\{x \mid x \in R\}$, range: $\{y \mid y \ge 1, y \in R\}$, no x-intercepts, y-intercept occurs at (0, 5)

c)

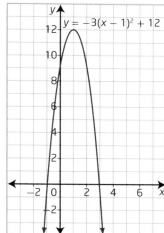

vertex: (1, 12), axis of symmetry: $x = 1$, opens downward, maximum value of 12, domain: $\{x \mid x \in R\}$, range: $\{y \mid y \le 12, y \in R\}$, x-intercepts occur at (−1, 0) and (3, 0), y-intercept occurs at (0, 9)

d)

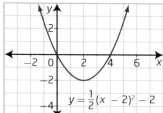

vertex: (2, −2), axis of symmetry: $x = 2$, opens upward, minimum value of −2, domain: $\{x \mid x \in R\}$, range: $\{y \mid y \ge -2, y \in R\}$, x-intercepts occur at (0, 0) and (4, 0), y-intercept occurs at (0, 0)

5. a) $y_1 = x^2$, $y_2 = 4x^2 + 2$, $y_3 = \frac{1}{2}x^2 - 2$, $y_4 = \frac{1}{4}x^2 - 4$

b) $y_1 = -x^2$, $y_2 = -4x^2 + 2$, $y_3 = -\frac{1}{2}x^2 - 2$, $y_4 = -\frac{1}{4}x^2 - 4$

c) $y_1 = (x + 4)^2$, $y_2 = 4(x + 4)^2 + 2$, $y_3 = \frac{1}{2}(x + 4)^2 - 2$, $y_4 = \frac{1}{4}(x + 4)^2 - 4$

d) $y_1 = x^2 - 2$, $y_2 = 4x^2$, $y_3 = \frac{1}{2}x^2 - 4$, $y_4 = \frac{1}{4}x^2 - 6$

6. For the function $f(x) = 5(x - 15)^2 - 100$, $a = 5$, $p = 15$, and $q = -100$.

a) The vertex is located at (p, q), or (15, −100).

b) The equation of the axis of symmetry is $x = p$, or $x = 15$.

c) Since $a > 0$, the graph opens upward.

d) Since $a > 0$, the graph has a minimum value of q, or -100.

e) The domain is $\{x \mid x \in R\}$. Since the function has a minimum value of -100, the range is $\{y \mid y \geq -100, y \in R\}$.

f) Since the graph has a minimum value of -100 and opens upward, there are two x-intercepts.

7. a) vertex: $(0, 14)$, axis of symmetry: $x = 0$, opens downward, maximum value of 14, domain: $\{x \mid x \in R\}$, range: $\{y \mid y \leq 14, y \in R\}$, two x-intercepts

b) vertex: $(-18, -8)$, axis of symmetry: $x = -18$, opens upward, minimum value of -8, domain: $\{x \mid x \in R\}$, range: $\{y \mid y \geq -8, y \in R\}$, two x-intercepts

c) vertex: $(7, 0)$, axis of symmetry: $x = 7$, opens upward, minimum value of 0, domain: $\{x \mid x \in R\}$, range: $\{y \mid y \geq 0, y \in R\}$, one x-intercept

d) vertex: $(-4, -36)$, axis of symmetry: $x = -4$, opens downward, maximum value of -36, domain: $\{x \mid x \in R\}$, range: $\{y \mid y \leq -36, y \in R\}$, no x-intercepts

8. a) $y = (x + 3)^2 - 4$ **b)** $y = -2(x - 1)^2 + 12$

c) $y = \frac{1}{2}(x - 3)^2 + 1$ **d)** $y = -\frac{1}{4}(x + 3)^2 + 4$

9. a) $y = -\frac{1}{4}x^2$ **b)** $y = 3x^2 - 6$

c) $y = -4(x - 2)^2 + 5$ **d)** $y = \frac{1}{5}(x + 3)^2 - 10$

10. a) $(4, 16) \rightarrow (-1, 16) \rightarrow (-1, 24)$

b) $(4, 16) \rightarrow (4, 4) \rightarrow (4, -4)$

c) $(4, 16) \rightarrow (4, -16) \rightarrow (14, -16)$

d) $(4, 16) \rightarrow (4, 48) \rightarrow (4, 40)$

11. Starting with the graph of $y = x^2$, apply the change in width, which is a multiplication of the y-values by a factor of 5, reflect the graph in the x-axis, and then move the entire graph up 20 units.

12. Example: Quadratic functions will always have one y-intercept. Since the graphs always open upward or downward and have a domain of $\{x \mid x \in R\}$, the parabola will always cross the y-axis. The graphs must always have a value at $x = 0$ and therefore have one y-intercept.

13. a) $y = \frac{1}{30}x^2$

b) The new function could be $y = \frac{1}{30}(x - 30)^2 - 30$ or $y = \frac{1}{30}(x + 30)^2 - 30$. Both graphs have the same size and shape, but the new function has been transformed by a horizontal translation of 30 units to the right or to the left and a vertical translation of 30 units down to represent a point on the edge as the origin.

14. a) The vertex is located at $(36, 20\ 000)$, it opens downward, and it has a change in width by a multiplication of the y-values by a factor of 2.5 of the graph $y = x^2$. The equation of the axis of symmetry is $x = 36$, and the graph has a maximum value of 20 000.

b) 36 times

c) 20 000 people

15. Examples: If the vertex is at the origin, the quadratic function will be $y = 0.03x^2$. If the edge of the rim is at the origin, the quadratic function will be $y = 0.03(x - 20)^2 - 12$.

16. a) Example: Placing the vertex at the origin, the quadratic function is $y = \frac{1}{294}x^2$ or $y \approx 0.0034x^2$.

b) Example: If the origin is at the top of the left tower, the quadratic function is $y = \frac{1}{294}(x - 84)^2 - 24$ or $y \approx 0.0034(x - 84)^2 - 24$. If the origin is at the top of the right tower, the quadratic function is $y = \frac{1}{294}(x + 84)^2 - 24$ or $y \approx 0.0034(x + 84)^2 - 24$.

c) 8.17 m; this is the same no matter which function is used.

17. $y = -\frac{9}{121}(x - 11)^2 + 9$

18. $y = -\frac{1}{40}(x - 60)^2 + 90$

19. Example: Adding q is done after squaring the x-value, so the transformation applies directly to the parabola $y = x^2$. The value of p is added or subtracted before squaring, so the shift is opposite to the sign in the bracket to get back to the original y-value for the graph of $y = x^2$.

20. a) $y = -\frac{7}{160\ 000}(x - 8000)^2 + 10\ 000$

b) domain: $\{x \mid 0 \leq x \leq 16\ 000, x \in R\}$, range: $\{y \mid 7200 \leq y \leq 10\ 000, y \in R\}$

21. a) Since the vertex is located at $(6, 30)$, $p = 6$ and $q = 30$. Substituting these values into the vertex form of a quadratic function and using the coordinates of the given point, the function is $y = -1.5(x - 6)^2 + 30$.

b) Knowing that the x-intercepts are -21 and -5, the equation of the axis of symmetry must be $x = -13$. Then, the vertex is located at $(-13, -24)$. Substituting the coordinates of the vertex and one of the x-intercepts into the vertex form, the quadratic function is $y = 0.375(x + 13)^2 - 24$.

22. a) Examples: I chose $x = 8$ as the axis of symmetry, I choose the position of the hoop to be (1, 10), and I allowed the basketball to be released at various heights (6 ft, 7 ft, and 8 ft) from a distance of 16 ft from the hoop. For each scenario, substitute the coordinates of the release point into the function $y = a(x - 8)^2 + q$ to get an expression for q. Then, substitute the expression for q and the coordinates of the hoop into the function. My three functions are
$y = -\dfrac{4}{15}(x - 8)^2 + \dfrac{346}{15}$,
$y = -\dfrac{3}{15}(x - 8)^2 + \dfrac{297}{15}$, and
$y = -\dfrac{2}{15}(x - 8)^2 + \dfrac{248}{15}$.

b) Example: $y = -\dfrac{4}{15}(x - 8)^2 + \dfrac{346}{15}$ ensures that the ball passes easily through the hoop.

c) domain: $\{x \mid 0 \le x \le 16, x \in R\}$,

range: $\left\{y \mid 0 \le y \le \dfrac{346}{15}, y \in R\right\}$

23. $(m + p, an + q)$

24. Examples:
a) $f(x) = -2(x - 1)^2 + 3$
b) Plot the vertex (1, 3). Determine a point on the curve, say the y-intercept, which occurs at (0, 1). Determine that the corresponding point of (0, 1) is (2, 1). Plot these two additional points and complete the sketch of the parabola.

25. Example: You can determine the number of x-intercepts if you know the location of the vertex and the direction of opening. Visualize the general position and shape of the graph based on the values of a and q. Consider $f(x) = 0.5(x + 1)^2 - 3$, $g(x) = 2(x - 3)^2$, and $h(x) = -2(x + 3)^2 - 4$. For $f(x)$, the parabola opens upward and the vertex is below the x-axis, so the graph has two x-intercepts. For $g(x)$, the parabola opens upward and the vertex is on the x-axis, so the graph has one x-intercept. For $h(x)$, the parabola opens downward and the vertex is below the x-axis, so the graph has no x-intercepts.

26. Answers may vary.

3.2 Investigating Quadratic Functions in Standard Form, pages 174 to 179

1. a) This is a quadratic function, since it is a polynomial of degree two.
b) This is not a quadratic function, since it is a polynomial of degree one.
c) This is not a quadratic function. Once the expression is expanded, it is a polynomial of degree three.

d) This is a quadratic function. Once the expression is expanded, it is a polynomial of degree two.

2. a) The coordinates of the vertex are (−2, 2). The equation of the axis of symmetry is $x = -2$. The x-intercepts occur at (−3, 0) and (−1, 0), and the y-intercept occurs at (0, −6). The graph opens downward, so the graph has a maximum of 2 of when $x = -2$. The domain is $\{x \mid x \in R\}$ and the range is $\{y \mid y \le 2, y \in R\}$.

b) The coordinates of the vertex are (6, −4). The equation of the axis of symmetry is $x = 6$. The x-intercepts occur at (2, 0) and (10, 0), and the y-intercept occurs at (0, 5). The graph opens upward, so the graph has a minimum of −4 when $x = 6$. The domain is $\{x \mid x \in R\}$ and the range is $\{y \mid y \ge -4, y \in R\}$.

c) The coordinates of the vertex are (3, 0). The equation of the axis of symmetry is $x = 3$. The x-intercept occurs at (3, 0), and the y-intercept occurs at (0, 8). The graph opens upward, so the graph has a minimum of 0 when $x = 3$. The domain is $\{x \mid x \in R\}$ and the range is $\{y \mid y \ge 0, y \in R\}$.

3. a) $f(x) = -10x^2 + 50x$
b) $f(x) = 15x^2 - 62x + 40$

4. a)

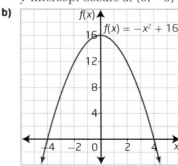

vertex is (1, −4); axis of symmetry is $x = 1$; opens upward; minimum value of −4 when $x = 1$; domain is $\{x \mid x \in R\}$, range is $\{y \mid y \ge -4, y \in R\}$; x-intercepts occur at (−1, 0) and (3, 0), y-intercept occurs at (0, −3)

b)

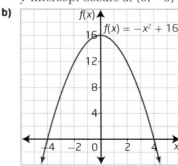

vertex is (0, 16); axis of symmetry is $x = 0$; opens downward; maximum value of 16 when $x = 0$; domain is $\{x \mid x \in R\}$, range is $\{y \mid y \le 16, y \in R\}$; x-intercepts occur at $(-4, 0)$ and $(4, 0)$, y-intercept occurs at $(0, 16)$

c)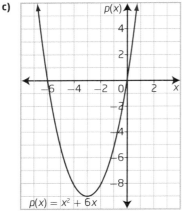

$p(x) = x^2 + 6x$

vertex is $(-3, -9)$; axis of symmetry is $x = -3$; opens upward; minimum value of -9 when $x = -3$; domain is $\{x \mid x \in R\}$, range is $\{y \mid y \ge -9, y \in R\}$; x-intercepts occur at $(-6, 0)$ and $(0, 0)$, y-intercept occurs at $(0, 0)$

d)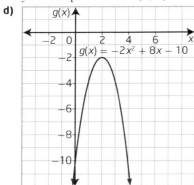

$g(x) = -2x^2 + 8x - 10$

vertex is $(2, -2)$; axis of symmetry is $x = 2$; opens downward; maximum value of -2 when $x = 2$; domain is $\{x \mid x \in R\}$, range is $\{y \mid y \le -2, y \in R\}$; no x-intercepts, y-intercept occurs at $(0, -10)$

5. a)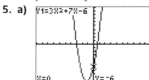

vertex is $(-1.2, -10.1)$; axis of symmetry is $x = -1.2$; opens upward; minimum value of -10.1 when $x = -1.2$; domain is $\{x \mid x \in R\}$, range is $\{y \mid y \ge -10.1, y \in R\}$; x-intercepts occur at $(-3, 0)$ and $(0.7, 0)$, y-intercept occurs at $(0, -6)$

b)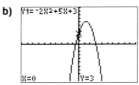

vertex is $(1.3, 6.1)$; axis of symmetry is $x = 1.3$; opens downward; maximum value of 6.1 when $x = 1.3$; domain is $\{x \mid x \in R\}$, range is $\{y \mid y \le 6.1, y \in R\}$; x-intercepts occur at $(-0.5, 0)$ and $(3, 0)$, y-intercept occurs at $(0, 3)$

c)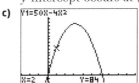

vertex is $(6.3, 156.3)$; axis of symmetry is $x = 6.3$; opens downward; maximum value of 156.3 when $x = 6.3$; domain is $\{x \mid x \in R\}$, range is $\{y \mid y \le 156.3, y \in R\}$; x-intercepts occur at $(0, 0)$ and $(12.5, 0)$, y-intercept occurs at $(0, 0)$

d)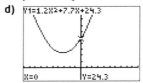

vertex is $(-3.2, 11.9)$; axis of symmetry is $x = -3.2$; opens upward; minimum value of 11.9 when $x = -3.2$; domain is $\{x \mid x \in R\}$, range is $\{y \mid y \ge 11.9, y \in R\}$; no x-intercepts, y-intercept occurs at $(0, 24.3)$

6. a) $(-3, -7)$ **b)** $(2, -7)$ **c)** $(4, 5)$

7. a) 10 cm, h-intercept of the graph
  b) 30 cm after 2 s, vertex of the parabola
  c) approximately 4.4 s, t-intercept of the graph
  d) domain: $\{t \mid 0 \le t \le 4.4, t \in R\}$, range: $\{h \mid 0 \le h \le 30, h \in R\}$
  e) Example: No, siksik cannot stay in the air for 4.4 s in real life.

8. Examples:
  a) Two; since the graph has a maximum value, it opens downward and would cross the x-axis at two different points. One x-intercept is negative and the other is positive.
  b) Two; since the vertex is at $(3, 1)$ and the graph passes through the point $(1, -3)$, it opens downward and crosses the x-axis at two different points. Both x-intercepts are positive.

c) Zero; since the graph has a minimum of 1 and opens upward, it will not cross the *x*-axis.

d) Two; since the graph has an axis of symmetry of $x = -1$ and passes through the *x*- and *y*-axes at (0, 0), the graph could open upward or downward and has another *x*-intercept at (−2, 0). One *x*-intercept is zero and the other is negative.

9. a) domain: $\{x \mid x \in R\}$, range: $\{y \mid y \le 68, y \in R\}$

b) domain: $\{x \mid 0 \le x \le 4.06, x \in R\}$, range: $\{y \mid 0 \le y \le 68, y \in R\}$

c) Example: The domain and range of algebraic functions may include all real values. For given real-world situations, the domain and range are determined by physical constraints such as time must be greater than or equal to zero and the height must be above ground, or greater than or equal to zero.

10. Examples:

a)
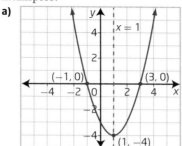

b)
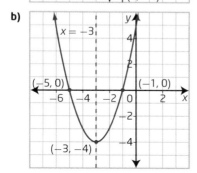

c)
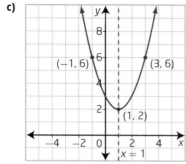

d)
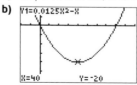

11. a) $\{x \mid 0 \le x \le 80, x \in R\}$

b)
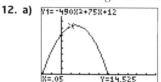

c) The maximum depth of the dish is 20 cm, which is the *y*-coordinate of the vertex (40, −20). This is not the maximum value of the function. Since the parabola opens upward, this the minimum value of the function.

d) $\{d \mid -20 \le d \le 0, d \in R\}$

e) The depth is approximately 17.19 cm, 25 cm from the edge of the dish.

12. a) Y1=-490X2+75X+12 [graph: X=.05 Y=14.525]

b) The *h*-intercept represents the height of the log.

c) 0.1 s; 14.9 cm

d) 0.3 s

e) domain: $\{t \mid 0 \le t \le 0.3, t \in R\}$, range: $\{h \mid 0 \le h \le 14.9, h \in R\}$

f) 14.5 cm

13. Examples:

a) $\{v \mid 0 \le v \le 150, v \in R\}$

b)

v	*f*
0	0
25	1.25
50	5
75	11.25
100	20
125	31.25
150	45

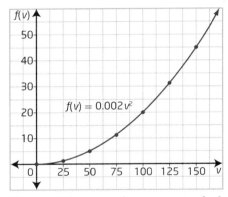

c) The graph is a smooth curve instead of a straight line. The table of values shows that the values of f are not increasing at a constant rate for equal increments in the value of v.

d) The values of the drag force increase by a value other than 2. When the speed of the vehicle doubles, the drag force quadruples.

e) The driver can use this information to improve gas consumption and fuel economy.

14. a)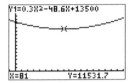

The coordinates of the vertex are (81, 11 532). The equation of the axis of symmetry is $x = 81$. There are no x-intercepts. The y-intercept occurs at (0, 13 500). The graph opens upward, so the graph has a minimum value of 11 532 when $x = 81$. The domain is $\{n \mid n \geq 0, n \in R\}$. The range is $\{C \mid C \geq 11\ 532, C \in R\}$.

b) Example: The vertex represents the minimum cost of $11 532 to produce 81 000 units. Since the vertex is above the n-axis, there are no n-intercepts, which means the cost of production is always greater than zero. The C-intercept represents the base production cost. The domain represents thousands of units produced, and the range represents the cost to produce those units.

15. a) $A = -2x^2 + 16x + 40$

b)

c) The values between the x-intercepts will produce a rectangle. The rectangle will have a width that is 2 greater than the value of x and a length that is 20 less 2 times the value of x.

d) The vertex indicates the maximum area of the rectangle.

e) domain: $\{x \mid -2 \leq x \leq 10, x \in R\}$, range: $\{A \mid 0 \leq A \leq 72, A \in R\}$; the domain represents the values for x that will produce dimensions of a rectangle. The range represents the possible values of the area of the rectangle.

f) The function has both a maximum value and a minimum value for the area of the rectangle.

g) Example: No; the function will open downward and therefore will not have a minimum value for a domain of real numbers.

16. Example: No; the simplified version of the function is $f(x) = 3x + 1$. Since this is not a polynomial of degree two, it does not represent a quadratic function. The graph of the function $f(x) = 4x^2 - 3x + 2x(3 - 2x) + 1$ is a straight line.

17. a) $A = -2x^2 + 140x$; this is a quadratic function since it is a polynomial of degree two.

b)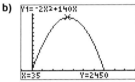

c) (35, 2450); The vertex represents the maximum area of 2450 m² when the width is 35 m.

d) domain: $\{x \mid 0 \leq x \leq 70, x \in R\}$, range: $\{A \mid 0 \leq A \leq 2450, A \in R\}$ The domain represents the possible values of the width, and the range represents the possible values of the area.

e) The function has a maximum area (value) of 2450 m² and a minimum value of 0 m². Areas cannot have negative values.

f) Example: The quadratic function assumes that Maria will use all of the fencing to make the enclosure. It also assumes that any width from 0 m to 70 m is possible.

18. a) Diagram 4   Diagram 5   Diagram 6

Diagram 4: 24 square units
Diagram 5: 35 square units
Diagram 6: 48 square units

b) $A = n^2 + 2n$

c) Quadratic; the function is a polynomial of degree two.

d) $\{n \mid n \geq 1, n \in \mathbb{N}\}$; The values of n are natural numbers. So, the function is discrete. Since the numbers of both diagrams and small squares are countable, the function is discrete.

e)

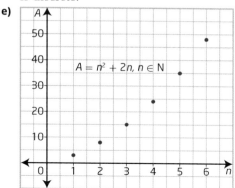

19. a) $A = \pi r^2$

b) domain: $\{r \mid r \geq 0, r \in \mathbb{R}\}$,
range: $\{A \mid A \geq 0, A \in \mathbb{R}\}$

c)

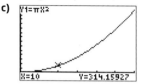

d) The x-intercept and the y-intercept occur at $(0, 0)$. They represent the minimum values of the radius and the area.

e) Example: There is no axis of symmetry within the given domain and range.

20. a) $d(v) = \dfrac{1.5v}{3.6} + \dfrac{v^2}{130}$

b)

v	d
0	0
25	15
50	40
75	75
100	119
125	172
150	236
175	308
200	391

$$d(v) = \frac{1.5v}{3.6} + \frac{v^2}{130}$$

c) No; when v doubles from 25 km/h to 50 km/h, the stopping distance increases by a factor of $\dfrac{40}{15} = 2.67$, and when the velocity doubles from 50 km/h to 100 km/h, the stopping distance increases by a factor of $\dfrac{119}{40} = 2.98$. Therefore, the stopping distance increases by a factor greater than two.

d) Example: Using the graph or table, notice that as the speed increases the stopping distances increase by a factor greater than the increase in speed. Therefore, it is important for drivers to maintain greater distances between vehicles as the speed increases to allow for increasing stopping distances.

21. a) $f(x) = x^2 + 4x + 3$, $f(x) = 2x^2 + 8x + 6$, and $f(x) = 3x^2 + 12x + 9$

b)

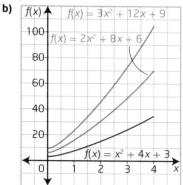

c) Example: The graphs have similar shapes, curving upward at a rate that is a multiple of the first graph. The values of y for each value of x are multiples of each other.

d) Example: If $k = 4$, the graph would start with a y-intercept 4 times as great as the first graph and increase with values of y that are 4 times as great as the values of y of the first function. If $k = 0.5$, the graph would start with a y-intercept $\dfrac{1}{2}$ of the original y-intercept and increase with values of y that are $\dfrac{1}{2}$ of the original values of y for each value of x.

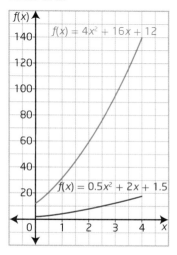

e) Example: For negative values of k, the graph would be reflected in the x-axis, with a smooth decreasing curve. Each value of y would be a negative multiple of the original value of y for each value of x.

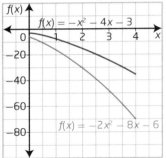

f) The graph is a line on the x-axis.

g) Example: Each member of the family of functions for $f(x) = k(x^2 + 4x + 3)$ has values of y that are multiples of the original function for each value of x.

22. Example: The value of a in the function $f(x) = ax^2 + bx + c$ indicates the steepness of the curved section of a function in that when $a > 0$, the curve will move up more steeply as a increases and when $-1 < a < 1$, the curve will move up more slowly the closer a is to 0. The sign of a is also similar in that if $a > 0$, then the graph curves up and when $a < 0$, the graph will curve down from the vertex. The value of a in the function $f(x) = ax + b$ indicates the exact steepness or slope of the line determined by the function, whereas the slope of the function $f(x) = ax^2 + bx + c$ changes as the value of x changes and is not a direct relationship for the entire graph.

23. a) $b = 3$
b) $b = -3$ and $c = 1$

24. a)

Earth	Moon
$h(t) = -4.9t^2 + 20t + 35$	$h(t) = -0.815t^2 + 20t + 35$
$h(t) = -16t^2 + 800t$	$h(t) = -2.69t^2 + 800t$
$h(t) = -4.9t^2 + 100$	$h(t) = -0.815t^2 + 100$

b)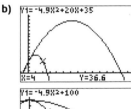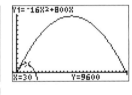

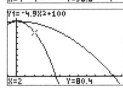

c) Example: The first two graphs have the same y-intercept at $(0, 35)$. The second two graphs pass through the origin $(0, 0)$. The last two graphs share the same y-intercept at $(0, 100)$. Each pair of graphs share the same y-intercept and share the same constant term.

d) Example: Every projectile on the moon had a higher trajectory and stayed in the air for a longer period of time.

25. Examples:

a) $(2m, r)$; apply the definition of the axis of symmetry. The horizontal distance from the y-intercept to the x-coordinate of the vertex is $m - 0$, or m. So, one other point on the graph is $(m + m, r)$, or $(2m, r)$.

b) $(-2j, k)$; apply the definition of the axis of symmetry. The horizontal distance from the given point to the axis of symmetry is $4j - j$, or $3j$. So, one other point on the graph is $(j - 3j, k)$, or $(-2j, k)$.

c) $\left(\dfrac{s + t}{2}, d\right)$; apply the definitions of the axis of symmetry and the minimum value of a function. The x-coordinate of the vertex is halfway between the x-intercepts, or $\dfrac{s + t}{2}$. The y-coordinate of the vertex is the least value of the range, or d.

26. Example: The range and direction of opening are connected and help determine the location of the vertex. If $y \geq q$, then the graph will open upward. If $y \leq q$, then the graph will open downward. The range also determines the maximum or minimum value of the function and the y-coordinate of the vertex. The equation of the axis of symmetry determines the x-coordinate of the vertex. If the vertex is above the x-axis and the graph opens upward, there will be no x-intercepts. However, if it opens downward, there will be two x-intercepts. If the vertex is on the x-axis, there will be only one x-intercept.

27. Step 2 The y-intercept is determined by the value of c. The values of a and b do not affect its location.

Step 3 The axis of symmetry is affected by the values of a and b. As the value of a increases, the value of the axis of symmetry decreases. As the value of b increases, the value of the axis of symmetry increases.

Step 4 Increasing the value of a increases the steepness of the graph.

Step 5 Changing the values of a, b, and c affects the position of the vertex, the steepness of the graph, and whether the graph opens upward ($a > 0$) or downward ($a < 0$). a affects the steepness and determines the direction of opening. b and a affect the value of the axis of symmetry, with b having a greater effect. c determines the value of the y-intercept.

3.3 Completing the Square, pages 192 to 197

1. a) $x^2 + 6x + 9$; $(x + 3)^2$
   b) $x^2 - 4x + 4$; $(x - 2)^2$
   c) $x^2 + 14x + 49$; $(x + 7)^2$
   d) $x^2 - 2x + 1$; $(x - 1)^2$
2. a) $y = (x + 4)^2 - 16$; $(-4, -16)$
   b) $y = (x - 9)^2 - 140$; $(9, -140)$
   c) $y = (x - 5)^2 + 6$; $(5, 6)$
   d) $y = (x + 16)^2 - 376$; $(-16, -376)$
3. a) $y = 2(x - 3)^2 - 18$; working backward, $y = 2(x - 3)^2 - 18$ results in the original function, $y = 2x^2 - 12x$.
   b) $y = 6(x + 2)^2 - 7$; working backward, $y = 6(x + 2)^2 - 7$ results in the original function, $y = 6x^2 + 24x + 17$.
   c) $y = 10(x - 8)^2 - 560$; working backward, $y = 10(x - 8)^2 - 560$ results in the original function, $y = 10x^2 - 160x + 80$.
   d) $y = 3(x + 7)^2 - 243$; working backward, $y = 3(x + 7)^2 - 243$ results in the original function, $y = 3x^2 + 42x - 96$.
4. a) $f(x) = -4(x - 2)^2 + 16$; working backward, $f(x) = -4(x - 2)^2 + 16$ results in the original function, $f(x) = -4x^2 + 16x$.
   b) $f(x) = -20(x + 10)^2 + 1757$; working backward, $f(x) = -20(x + 10)^2 + 1757$ results in the original function, $f(x) = -20x^2 - 400x - 243$.
   c) $f(x) = -(x + 21)^2 + 941$; working backward, $f(x) = -(x + 21)^2 + 941$ results in the original function, $f(x) = -x^2 - 42x + 500$.
   d) $f(x) = -7(x - 13)^2 + 1113$; working backward, $f(x) = -7(x - 13)^2 + 1113$ results in the original function, $f(x) = -7x^2 + 182x - 70$.
5. Verify each part by expanding the vertex form of the function and comparing with the standard form and by graphing both forms of the function.
6. a) minimum value of -11 when $x = -3$
   b) minimum value of -11 when $x = 2$
   c) maximum value of 25 when $x = -5$
   d) maximum value of 5 when $x = 2$
7. a) minimum value of $-\dfrac{13}{4}$
   b) minimum value of $\dfrac{1}{2}$

c) maximum value of 47
d) minimum value of -1.92
e) maximum value of 18.95
f) maximum value of 1.205
8. a) $y = \left(x + \dfrac{3}{4}\right)^2 - \dfrac{121}{16}$
   b) $y = -\left(x + \dfrac{3}{16}\right)^2 + \dfrac{9}{256}$
   c) $y = 2\left(x - \dfrac{5}{24}\right)^2 + \dfrac{263}{288}$
9. a) $f(x) = -2(x - 3)^2 + 8$
   b) Example: The vertex of the graph is $(3, 8)$. From the function $f(x) = -2(x - 3)^2 + 8$, $p = 3$ and $q = 8$. So, the vertex is $(3, 8)$.
10. a) maximum value of 62; domain: $\{x \mid x \in R\}$, range: $\{y \mid y \le 62, y \in R\}$
   b) Example: By changing the function to vertex form, it is possible to find the maximum value since the function opens down and $p = 62$. This also helps to determine the range of the function. The domain is all real numbers for non-restricted quadratic functions.
11. Example: By changing the function to vertex form, the vertex is $\left(\dfrac{13}{4}, -\dfrac{3}{4}\right)$ or $(3.25, -0.75)$.
12. a) There is an error in the second line of the solution. You need to add and subtract the square of half the coefficient of the x-term.
   $y = x^2 + 8x + 30$
   $y = (x^2 + 8x + 16 - 16) + 30$
   $y = (x + 4)^2 + 14$
   b) There is an error in the second line of the solution. You need to add and subtract the square of half the coefficient of the x-term. There is also an error in the last line. The factor of 2 disappeared.
   $f(x) = 2x^2 - 9x - 55$
   $f(x) = 2[x^2 - 4.5x + 5.0625 - 5.0625] - 55$
   $f(x) = 2[(x^2 - 4.5x + 5.0625) - 5.0625] - 55$
   $f(x) = 2[(x - 2.25)^2 - 5.0625] - 55$
   $f(x) = 2(x - 2.25)^2 - 10.125 - 55$
   $f(x) = 2(x - 2.25)^2 - 65.125$
   c) There is an error in the third line of the solution. You need to add and subtract the square of half the coefficient of the x-term.
   $y = 8x^2 + 16x - 13$
   $y = 8[x^2 + 2x] - 13$
   $y = 8[x^2 + 2x + 1 - 1] - 13$
   $y = 8[(x^2 + 2x + 1) - 1] - 13$
   $y = 8[(x + 1)^2 - 1] - 13$
   $y = 8(x + 1)^2 - 8 - 13$
   $y = 8(x + 1)^2 - 21$

d) There are two errors in the second line of the solution. You need to factor the leading coefficient from the first two terms and add and subtract the square of half the coefficient of the *x*-term. There is also an error in the last line. The −3 factor was not distributed correctly.

$f(x) = -3x^2 - 6x$
$f(x) = -3[x^2 + 2x + 1 - 1]$
$f(x) = -3[(x^2 + 2x + 1) - 1]$
$f(x) = -3[(x + 1)^2 - 1]$
$f(x) = -3(x + 1)^2 + 3$

13. 12 000 items

14. 9 m

15. a) 5.56 ft; 0.31 s after being shot
b) Example: Verify by graphing and finding the vertex or by changing the function to vertex form and using the values of *p* and *q* to find the maximum value and when it occurs.

16. a) Austin got +12*x* when dividing 72*x* by −6 and should have gotten −12*x*. He also forgot to square the quantity (*x* + 6). Otherwise his work was correct and his answer should be $y = -6(x - 6)^2 + 196$. Yuri got an answer of −216 when he multiplied −6 by −36. He should have gotten 216 to get the correct answer of $y = -6(x - 6)^2 + 196$.
b) Example: To verify an answer, either work backward to show the functions are equivalent or use technology to show the graphs of the functions are identical.

17. 18 cm

18. a) The maximum revenue is $151 250 when the ticket price is $55.
b) 2750 tickets
c) Example: Assume that the decrease in ticket prices determines the same increase in ticket sales as indicated by the survey.

19. a) $R(n) = -50n^2 + 1000n + 100\,800$, where *R* is the revenue of the sales and *n* is the number of $10 increases in price.
b) The maximum revenue is $105 800 when the bikes are sold for $460.
c) Example: Assume that the predictions of a decrease in sales for every increase in price holds true.

20. a) $P(n) = -0.1n^2 + n + 120$, where *P* is the production of peas, in kilograms, and *n* is the increase in plant rows.
b) The maximum production is 122.5 kg of peas when the farmer plants 35 rows of peas.
c) Example: Assume that the prediction holds true.

21. a) Answers may vary.
b) $A = -2w^2 + 90w$, where *A* is the area and *w* is the width.
c) 1012.5 m²
d) Example: Verify the solution by graphing or changing the function to vertex form, where the vertex is (22.5, 1012.5).
e) Example: Assume that the measurements can be any real number.

22. The dimensions of the large field are 75 m by 150 m, and the dimensions of the small fields are 75 m by 50 m.

23. a) The two numbers are 14.5 and 14.5, and the maximum product is 210.25.
b) The two numbers are 6.5 and −6.5, and the minimum product is −42.25.

24. 8437.5 cm²

25. $f(x) = -\dfrac{3}{4}\left(x - \dfrac{3}{4}\right)^2 + \dfrac{47}{64}$

26. a)
$$y = ax^2 + bx + c$$
$$y = a\left(x^2 + \frac{b}{a}x\right) + c$$
$$y = a\left(x^2 + \frac{b}{a}x + \left(\frac{b}{2a}\right)^2 - \left(\frac{b^2}{4a^2}\right)\right) + c$$
$$y = a\left(x + \frac{b}{2a}\right)^2 - \frac{ab^2}{4a^2} + c$$
$$y = a\left(x + \frac{b}{2a}\right)^2 + \frac{4a^2c - ab^2}{4a^2}$$
$$y = a\left(x + \frac{b}{2a}\right)^2 + \frac{a(4ac - b^2)}{4a^2}$$
$$y = a\left(x + \frac{b}{2a}\right)^2 + \frac{4ac - b^2}{4a}$$
b) $\left(-\dfrac{b}{2a}, \dfrac{4ac - b^2}{4a}\right)$
c) Example: This formula can be used to find the vertex of any quadratic function without using an algebraic method to change the function to vertex form.

27. a) (3, 4)
b) $f(x) = 2(x - 3)^2 + 4$, so the vertex is (3, 4).
c) $a = a$, $p = -\dfrac{b}{2a}$, and $q = \dfrac{4ac - b^2}{4a}$

28. a) $A = -\left(\dfrac{4 + \pi}{8}\right)w^2 + 3w$
b) maximum area of $\dfrac{18}{4 + \pi}$, or approximately 2.52 m², when the width is $\dfrac{12}{4 + \pi}$, or approximately 1.68 m
c) Verify by graphing and comparing the vertex values, $\left(\dfrac{12}{4 + \pi}, \dfrac{18}{4 + \pi}\right)$, or approximately (1.68, 2.52).
d) width: $\dfrac{12}{4 + \pi}$ or approximately 1.68 m,
length: $\dfrac{6}{4 + \pi}$ or approximately 0.84 m,
radius: $\dfrac{6}{4 + \pi}$ or approximately 0.84 m; Answers may vary.

29. Examples:
  a) The function is written in both forms; standard form is $f(x) = 4x^2 + 24$ and vertex form is $f(x) = 4(x + 0)^2 + 24$.
  b) No, since it is already in completed square form.

30. Martine's first error was that she did not correctly factor -4 from $-4x^2 + 24x$. Instead of $y = -4(x^2 + 6x) + 5$, it should have been $y = -4(x^2 - 6x) + 5$. Her second error occurred when she completed the square. Instead of $y = -4(x^2 + 6x + 36 - 36) + 5$, it should have been $y = -4(x^2 - 6x + 9 - 9) + 5$. Her third error occurred when she factored $(x^2 + 6x + 36)$. This is not a perfect square trinomial and is not factorable. Her last error occurred when she expanded the expression $-4[(x + 6)^2 - 36] + 5$. It should be $-4(x - 3)^2 + 36 + 5$ not $-4(x + 6)^2 - 216 + 5$. The final answer is $y = -4(x - 3)^2 + 41$.

31. a) $R = -5x^2 + 50x + 1000$
  b) By completing the square, you can determine the maximum revenue and price to charge to produce the maximum revenue, as well as predict the number of T-shirts that will sell.
  c) Example: Assume that the market research holds true for all sales of T-shirts.

Chapter 3 Review, pages 198 to 200

1. a) Given the graph of $f(x) = x^2$, move it 6 units to the left and 14 units down.
  vertex: $(-6, -14)$, axis of symmetry: $x = -6$, opens upward, minimum value of -14, domain: $\{x \mid x \in R\}$, range: $\{y \mid y \geq -14, y \in R\}$
  b) Given the graph of $f(x) = x^2$, change the width by multiplying the y-values by a factor of 2, reflect it in the x-axis, and move the entire graph up 19 units.
  vertex: $(0, 19)$, axis of symmetry: $x = 0$, opens downward, maximum value of 19, domain: $\{x \mid x \in R\}$, range: $\{y \mid y \leq 19, y \in R\}$
  c) Given the graph of $f(x) = x^2$, change the width by multiplying the y-values by a factor of $\frac{1}{5}$, move the entire graph 10 units to the right and 100 units up.
  vertex: $(10, 100)$, axis of symmetry: $x = 10$, opens upward, minimum value of 100, domain: $\{x \mid x \in R\}$, range: $\{y \mid y \geq 100, y \in R\}$
  d) Given the graph of $f(x) = x^2$, change the width by multiplying the y-values by a factor of 6, reflect it in the x-axis, and move the entire graph 4 units to the right.

vertex: $(4, 0)$, axis of symmetry: $x = 4$, opens downward, maximum value of 0, domain: $\{x \mid x \in R\}$, range: $\{y \mid y \leq 0, y \in R\}$

2. a)

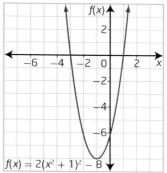

vertex: $(-1, -8)$, axis of symmetry: $x = -1$, minimum value of -8, domain: $\{x \mid x \in R\}$, range: $\{y \mid y \geq -8, y \in R\}$, x-intercepts occur at $(-3, 0)$ and $(1, 0)$, y-intercept occurs at $(0, -6)$

b)

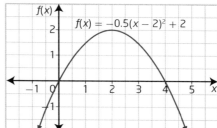

vertex: $(2, 2)$, axis of symmetry: $x = 2$, maximum value of 2, domain: $\{x \mid x \in R\}$, range: $\{y \mid y \leq 2, y \in R\}$, x-intercepts occur at $(0, 0)$ and $(4, 0)$, y-intercept occurs at $(0, 0)$

3. Examples:
  a) Yes. The vertex is $(5, 20)$, which is above the x-axis, and the parabola opens downward to produce two x-intercepts.
  b) Yes. Since $y \geq 0$, the graph touches the x-axis at only one point and has one x-intercept.
  c) Yes. The vertex of $(0, 9)$ is above the x-axis and the parabola opens upward, so the graph does not cross or touch the x-axis and has no x-intercepts.
  d) No. It is not possible to determine if the graph opens upward to produce two x-intercepts or downward to produce no x-intercepts.

4. a) $y = -0.375x^2$ **b)** $y = 1.5(x - 8)^2$
  c) $y = 3(x + 4)^2 + 12$
  d) $y = -4(x - 4.5)^2 + 25$

5. a) $y = \frac{1}{4}(x + 3)^2 - 6$ **b)** $y = -2(x - 1)^2 + 5$

6. Example: Two possible functions for the mirror are $y = 0.0069(x - 90)^2 - 56$ and $y = 0.0069x^2$.

7. a) i) $y = \dfrac{22}{18\ 769}x^2$ **ii)** $y = \dfrac{22}{18\ 769}x^2 + 30$

iii) $y = \dfrac{22}{18\ 769}(x - 137)^2 + 30$

b) Example: The function will change as the seasons change with the heat or cold changing the length of the cable and therefore the function.

8. $y = -\dfrac{8}{15}(x - 7.5)^2 + 30$ or
$y \approx -0.53(x - 7.5)^2 + 30$

9. a) vertex: $(2, 4)$, axis of symmetry: $x = 2$, maximum value of 4, opens downward, domain: $\{x \mid x \in R\}$, range: $\{y \mid y \le 4, y \in R\}$, x-intercepts occur at $(-2, 0)$ and $(6, 0)$, y-intercept occurs at $(0, 3)$

b) vertex: $(-4, 2)$, axis of symmetry: $x = -4$, maximum value of 2, opens upward, domain: $\{x \mid x \in R\}$, range: $\{y \mid y \ge 2, y \in R\}$, no x-intercepts, y-intercept occurs at $(0, 10)$

10. a) Expanding $y = 7(x + 3)^2 - 41$ gives $y = 7x^2 + 42x + 22$, which is a polynomial of degree two.

b) Expanding $y = (2x + 7)(10 - 3x)$ gives $y = -6x^2 - x + 70$, which is a polynomial of degree two.

11. a)

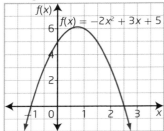

vertex: $(0.75, 6.125)$, axis of symmetry: $x = 0.75$, opens downward, maximum value of 6.125, domain: $\{x \mid x \in R\}$, range: $\{y \mid y \le 6.125, y \in R\}$, x-intercepts occur at $(-1, 0)$ and $(2.5, 0)$, y-intercept occurs at $(0, 5)$

b) Example: The vertex is the highest point on the curve. The axis of symmetry divides the graph in half and is defined by the x-coordinate of the vertex. Since $a < 0$, the graph opens downward. The maximum value is the y-coordinate of the vertex. The domain is all real numbers. The range is less than or equal to the maximum value, since the graph opens downward. The x-intercepts are where the graph crosses the x-axis, and the y-intercept is where the graph crosses the y-axis.

12. a)

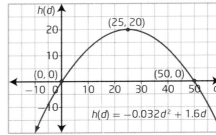

b) The maximum height of the ball is 20 m. The ball is 25 m downfield when it reaches its maximum height.

c) The ball lands downfield 50 m.

d) domain: $\{x \mid 0 \le x \le 50, x \in R\}$, range: $\{y \mid 0 \le y \le 20, y \in R\}$

13. a) $y = (5x + 15)(31 - 2x)$ or
$y = -10x^2 + 125x + 465$

b)

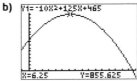

c) The values between the x-intercepts will produce a rectangle.

d) Yes; the maximum value is 855.625; the minimum value is 0.

e) The vertex represents the maximum area and the value of x that produces the maximum area.

f) domain: $\{x \mid 0 \le x \le 15.5, x \in R\}$, range: $\{y \mid 0 \le y \le 855.625, y \in R\}$

14. a) $y = (x - 12)^2 - 134$

b) $y = 5(x + 4)^2 - 107$

c) $y = -2(x - 2)^2 + 8$

d) $y = -30(x + 1)^2 + 135$

15. vertex: $\left(\dfrac{5}{4}, -\dfrac{13}{4}\right)$, axis of symmetry: $x = \dfrac{5}{4}$, minimum value of $-\dfrac{13}{4}$, domain: $\{x \mid x \in R\}$, range: $\left\{y \mid y \ge -\dfrac{13}{4}, y \in R\right\}$

16. a) In the second line, the second term should have been $+3.5x$. In the third line, Amy found the square of half of 3.5 to be 12.25; it should have been 3.0625 and this term should be added and then subtracted. The solution should be
$y = -22x^2 - 77x + 132$
$y = -22(x^2 + 3.5x) + 132$
$y = -22(x^2 + 3.5x + 3.0625 - 3.0625) + 132$
$y = -22(x^2 + 3.5x + 3.0625) + 67.375 + 132$
$y = -22(x + 1.75)^2 + 199.375$

b) Verify by expanding the vertex form to standard form and by graphing both forms to see if they produce the same graph.

17. a) $R = (40 - 2x)(10\ 000 + 500x)$ or
$R = -1000x^2 + 400\ 000$ where R is
the revenue and x is the number of
price decreases.
b) The maximum revenue is \$400 000 and the
price is \$40 per coat.
c)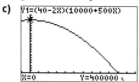

d) The y-intercept represents the sales before
changing the price. The x-intercepts indicate
the number of price increases or decreases
that will produce revenue.
e) domain: $\{x \mid -20 \le x \le 20, x \in R\}$,
range: $\{y \mid 0 \le y \le 400\ 000, y \in R\}$
f) Example: Assume that a whole number of
price increases can be used.

Chapter 3 Practice Test, pages 201 to 203

1. D
2. C
3. A
4. D
5. D
6. A
7. a) $y = (x - 9)^2 - 108$
b) $y = 3(x + 6)^2 - 95$
c) $y = -10(x + 2)^2 + 40$
8. a) vertex: $(-6, 4)$, axis of symmetry: $x = -6$,
maximum value of 4, domain: $\{x \mid x \in R\}$,
range: $\{y \mid y \le 4, y \in R\}$, x-intercepts occur
at $(-8, 0)$ and $(-4, 0)$
b) $y = -(x + 6)^2 + 4$
9. a) **i)** change in width by a multiplication of
the y-values by a factor of 5
ii) vertical translation of 20 units down
iii) horizontal translation of 11 units to
the left
iv) change in width by a multiplication
of the y-values by a factor of $\frac{1}{7}$ and a
reflection in the x-axis
b) Examples:
i) The vertex of the functions in part a) ii)
and iii) will be different as compared
to $f(x) = x^2$ because the entire graph is
translated. Instead of a vertex of $(0, 0)$,
the graph of the function in part a) ii)
will be located at $(0, -20)$ and the vertex
of the graph of the function in part a) iii)
will be located at $(-11, 0)$.

ii) The axis of symmetry of the function in
part a) iii) will be different as compared
to $f(x) = x^2$ because the entire graph is
translated horizontally. Instead of an axis
of symmetry of $x = 0$, the graph of the
function in part a) iii) will have an axis
of symmetry of $x = -11$.
iii) The range of the functions in part a) ii)
and iv) will be different as compared
to $f(x) = x^2$ because the entire graph is
either translated vertically or reflected
in the x-axis. Instead of a range of
$\{y \mid y \ge 0, y \in R\}$, the function in
part a) ii) will have a range of
$\{y \mid y \ge -20, y \in R\}$ and the function
in part a) iv) will have a range of
$\{y \mid y \le 0, y \in R\}$.

10.

Vertex	$(1, -8)$
Axis of Symmetry	$x = 1$
Direction of Opening	upward
Domain	$\{x \mid x \in R\}$
Range	$\{y \mid y \ge -8, y \in R\}$
x-Intercepts	-1 and 3
y-Intercept	-6

11. a) In the second line, the 2 was not factored
out of the second term. In the third line, you
need to add and subtract the square of half
the coefficient of the x-term. The first three
steps should be
$y = 2x^2 - 8x + 9$
$y = 2(x^2 - 4x) + 9$
$y = 2(x^2 - 4x + 4 - 4) + 9$
b) The rest of the process is shown.
$y = 2[(x^2 - 4x + 4) - 4] + 9$
$y = 2(x - 2)^2 - 8 + 9$
$y = 2(x - 2)^2 + 1$
c) The solution can be verified by expanding
the vertex form to standard form or
by graphing both functions to see that
they coincide.

12. Examples:

a) The vertex form of the function
$C(v) = 0.004v^2 - 0.62v + 30$ is
$C(v) = 0.004(v - 77.5)^2 + 5.975$. The
most efficient speed would be 77.5 km/h
and will produce a fuel consumption of
5.975 L/100 km.

b) By completing the square and
determining the vertex of the function,
you can determine the most efficient fuel
consumption and at what speed it occurs.

13. a) The maximum height of the flare is
191.406 25 m, 6.25 s after being shot.

b) Example: Complete the square to produce
the vertex form and use the value of q to
determine the maximum height and the
value of p to determine when it occurs,
or use the fact that the x-coordinate of the
vertex of a quadratic function in standard
form is $x = -\dfrac{b}{2a}$ and substitute this value
into the function to find the corresponding
y-coordinate, or graph the function to find
the vertex.

14. a) $A(d) = -4d^2 + 24d$

b) Since the function is a polynomial of
degree two, it satisfies the definition of a
quadratic function.

c)

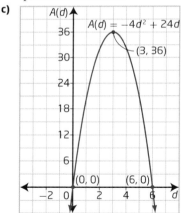

Example: By completing the square,
determine the vertex, find the y-intercept
and its corresponding point, plot the three
points, and join them with a smooth curve.

d) (3, 36); the maximum area of 36 m² happens
when the fence is extended to 3 m from
the building.

e) domain: $\{d \mid 0 \le d \le 6, d \in R\}$,
range: $\{A \mid 0 \le A \le 36, A \in R\}$; negative
distance and area do not have meaning in
this situation.

f) Yes; the maximum value is 36 when d is 3,
and the minimum value is 0 when d is 0 or 6.

g) Example: Assume that any real-number
distance can be used to build the fence.

15. a) $f(x) = -0.03x^2$

b) $f(x) = -0.03x^2 + 12$

c) $f(x) = -0.03(x + 20)^2 + 12$

d) $f(x) = -0.03(x - 28)^2 - 3$

16. a) $R = (2.25 - 0.05x)(120 + 8x)$

b) Expand and complete the square to get the
vertex form of the function. A price of $1.50
gives the maximum revenue of $360.

c) Example: Assume that any whole number of
price decreases can occur.

Chapter 4 Quadratic Equations

4.1 Graphical Solutions of Quadratic Equations, pages 215 to 217

1. a) 1   **b)** 2   **c)** 0   **d)** 2

2. a) 0   **b)** -1 and -4

   c) none   **d)** -3 and 8

3. a) $x = -3, x = 8$ **b)** $r = -3, r = 0$

   c) no real solutions   **d)** $x = 3, x = -2$

   e) $z = 2$ **f)** no real solutions

4. a) $n \approx -3.2, n \approx 3.2$ **b)** $x = -4, x = 1$

   c) $w = 1, w = 3$ **d)** $d = -8, d = -2$

   e) $v \approx -4.7, v \approx -1.3$ **f)** $m = 3, m = 7$

5. 60 yd

6. a) $-x^2 + 9x - 20 = 0$ or $x^2 - 9x + 20 = 0$

   b) 4 and 5

7. a) $x^2 + 2x - 168 = 0$

   b) $x = 12$ and $x = 14$ or $x = -12$ and $x = -14$

8. a) Example: Solving the equation leads to the
distance from the firefighter that the water
hits the ground. The negative solution is not
part of this situation.

   b) 12.2 m

   c) Example: Assume that aiming the hose
higher would not reach farther. Assume that
wind does not affect the path of the water.

9. a) Example: Solving the equation leads to the
time that the fireworks hit the ground. The
negative solution is not part of the situation.

   b) 6.1 s

10. a) $-0.75d^2 + 0.9d + 1.5 = 0$ **b)** 2.1 m

11. a) $-2d^2 + 3d + 10 = 0$ **b)** 3.1 m

12. a) first arch: $x = 0$ and $x = 84$, second arch:
$x = 84$ and $x = 168$, third arch: $x = 168$
and $x = 252$

   b) The zeros represent where the arches reach
down to the bridge deck.

   c) 252 m

13. a) $k = 9$ **b)** $k < 9$ **c)** $k > 9$

14. a) 64 ft

    b) The relationship between the height, radius, and span of the arch stays the same. Input the measures in metres and solve.

15. about 2.4 s

16. For the value of the function to change from negative to positive, it must cross the x-axis and therefore there must be an x-intercept between the two values of x.

17. The other x-intercept would have to be 4.

18. The x-coordinate of the vertex is halfway between the two roots. So, it is at 2. You can then substitute $x = 2$ into the equation to find the minimum value of -16.

4.2 Factoring Quadratic Equations, pages 229 to 233

1. a) $(x + 2)(x + 5)$ **b)** $5(z + 2)(z + 6)$
    c) $0.2(d - 4)(d - 7)$

2. a) $(y - 1)(3y + 7)$ **b)** $(4k - 5)(2k + 1)$
    c) $0.2(2m - 3)(m + 3)$

3. a) $(x + 5)(x - 4)$ **b)** $(x - 6)^2$
    c) $\frac{1}{4}(x + 2)(x + 6)$ **d)** $2(x + 3)^2$

4. a) $(2y + 3x)(2y - 3x)$
    b) $(0.6p + 0.7q)(0.6p - 0.7q)$
    c) $\left(\frac{1}{2}s + \frac{3}{5}t\right)\left(\frac{1}{2}s - \frac{3}{5}t\right)$
    d) $(0.4t + 4s)(0.4t - 4s)$

5. a) $(x + 8)(x - 5)$
    b) $(2x^2 - 8x + 9)(3x^2 - 12x + 11)$
    c) $(-4)(8j)$

6. a) $(10b)(10b - 7)$
    b) $16(x^2 - x + 1)(x^2 + x + 1)$
    c) $(10y^3 - x)(10y^3 + x)$

7. a) $x = -3, x = -4$ **b)** $x = 2, x = -\frac{1}{2}$
    c) $x = -7, x = 8$ **d)** $x = 0, x = -5$
    e) $x = -\frac{1}{3}, x = \frac{4}{5}$ **f)** $x = 4, x = \frac{7}{2}$

8. a) $n = -2, n = 2$ **b)** $x = -4, x = -1$
    c) $w = -9, x = -\frac{1}{3}$ **d)** $y = \frac{5}{4}, y = \frac{3}{2}$
    e) $d = -\frac{3}{2}, d = -1$ **f)** $x = \frac{3}{2}$

9. a) 0 and 5   **b)** $-\frac{8}{9}$ and 1
    c) -5 and -3 **d)** $-\frac{21}{5}$ and $\frac{21}{5}$
    e) -5 and 7   **f)** $\frac{7}{2}$

10. a) -6 and 7   **b)** -10 and 3
    c) -7 and 3   **d)** $-\frac{1}{3}$ and $\frac{3}{2}$
    e) -5 and 2   **f)** -3 and $\frac{1}{2}$

11. a) $(x + 10)(2x - 3) = 54$ **b)** 3.5 cm

12. a) 1 s and 5 s

    b) Assume that the mass of the fish does not affect the speed at which the osprey flies after catching the fish. This may not be a reasonable assumption for a large fish.

13. a) $150t - 5t^2 = 0$ **b)** 30 s

14. 8 and 10 or 0 and -2

15. 15 cm

16. 3 s; this seems a very long time considering the ball went up only 39 ft.

17. a) 1 cm
    b) 7 cm by 5 cm

18. a) No; $(x - 5)$ is not a factor of the expression $x^2 - 5x - 36$, since $x = 5$ does not satisfy the equation $x^2 - 5x - 36 = 0$.

    b) Yes; $(x + 3)$ is a factor of the expression $x^2 - 2x - 15$, since $x = -3$ satisfies the equation $x^2 - 2x - 15 = 0$.

    c) No; $(4x + 1)$ is not a factor of the expression $6x^2 + 11x + 4$, since $x = -\frac{1}{4}$ does not satisfy the equation $6x^2 + 11x + 4 = 0$.

    d) Yes; $(2x - 1)$ is a factor of the expression $4x^2 + 4x - 3$, since $x = \frac{1}{2}$ satisfies the equation $4x^2 + 4x - 3 = 0$.

19. a) $-\frac{1}{2}$ and 2   **b)** -4 and 3

20. 20 cm and 21 cm

21. 8 m and 15 m

22. a) $x(x - 7) = 690$ **b)** 30 cm by 23 cm

23. 5 m

24. 5 m

25. $P = \frac{1}{2}d(v_1 + v_2)(v_1 - v_2)$

26. No; the factor $6x - 4$ still has a common factor of 2.

27. a) $6(z - 1)(2z + 5)$
    b) $4(2m^2 - 8 - 3n)(2m^2 - 8 + 3n)$
    c) $\frac{1}{36}(2y - 3x)^2$
    d) $7\left(w - \frac{5}{3}\right)(5w + 1)$

28. $4(3x + 5y)$ centimetres

29. The shop will make a profit after 4 years.

30. a) $x^2 - 9 = 0$ **b)** $x^2 - 4x + 4 = 0$
    c) $3x^2 - 14x + 8 = 0$
    d) $10x^2 - x - 3 = 0$

31. Example: $x^2 - x + 1 = 0$

32. a) Instead of evaluating $81 - 36$, use the difference of squares pattern to rewrite the expression as $(9 - 6)(9 + 6)$ and then simplify. You can use this method when a question asks you to subtract a square number from a square number.

b) Examples:

$$144 - 25 = (12 - 5)(12 + 5)$$
$$= (7)(17)$$
$$= 119$$
$$256 - 49 = (16 - 7)(16 + 7)$$
$$= (9)(23)$$
$$= 207$$

4.3 Solving Quadratic Equations by Completing the Square, pages 240 to 243

1. a) $c = \dfrac{1}{4}$ **b)** $c = \dfrac{25}{4}$

c) $c = 0.0625$ **d)** $c = 0.01$

e) $c = \dfrac{225}{4}$ **f)** $c = \dfrac{81}{4}$

2. a) $(x + 2)^2 = 2$ **b)** $(x + 2)^2 = \dfrac{17}{3}$

c) $(x - 3)^2 = -1$

3. a) $(x - 6)^2 - 27 = 0$ **b)** $5(x - 2)^2 - 21 = 0$

c) $-2\left(x - \dfrac{1}{4}\right)^2 - \dfrac{7}{8} = 0$

d) $0.5(x + 2.1)^2 + 1.395 = 0$

e) $-1.2(x + 2.125)^2 - 1.981\,25 = 0$

f) $\dfrac{1}{2}(x + 3)^2 - \dfrac{21}{2} = 0$

4. a) $x = \pm 8$ **b)** $s = \pm 2$

c) $t = \pm 6$ **d)** $y = \pm\sqrt{11}$

5. a) $x = 1, x = 5$ **b)** $x = -5, x = 1$

c) $d = -\dfrac{3}{2}, d = \dfrac{1}{2}$ **d)** $h = \dfrac{3 \pm \sqrt{7}}{4}$

e) $s = \dfrac{-12 \pm \sqrt{3}}{2}$ **f)** $x = -4 \pm 3\sqrt{2}$

6. a) $x = -5 \pm \sqrt{21}$ **b)** $x = 4 \pm \sqrt{3}$

c) $x = -1 \pm\sqrt{\dfrac{2}{3}}$ or $\dfrac{-3 \pm \sqrt{6}}{3}$

d) $x = 1 \pm \sqrt{\dfrac{5}{2}}$ or $\dfrac{2 \pm \sqrt{10}}{2}$

e) $x = -3 \pm \sqrt{13}$ **f)** $x = 4 \pm 2\sqrt{7}$

7. a) $x = 8.5, x = -0.5$ **b)** $x = -0.8, x = 2.1$

c) $x = 12.8, x = -0.8$ **d)** $x = -7.7, x = 7.1$

e) $x = -2.6, x = 1.1$ **f)** $x = -7.8, x = -0.2$

8. a)

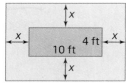

b) $4x^2 + 28x - 40 = 0$

c) 12.4 ft by 6.4 ft

9. a) $-0.02d^2 + 0.4d + 1 = 0$

b) 22.2 m

10. 200.5 m

11. 6 in. by 9 in.

12. 53.7 m

13. a) $x^2 - 7 = 0$ **b)** $x^2 - 2x - 2 = 0$

c) $4x^2 - 20x + 14 = 0$ or $2x^2 - 10x + 7 = 0$

14. a) $x = -1 \pm \sqrt{k + 1}$ **b)** $x = \dfrac{1 \pm \sqrt{k^2 + 1}}{k}$

c) $x = \dfrac{k \pm \sqrt{k^2 + 4}}{2}$

15. $x = \dfrac{-b \pm \sqrt{b^2 - 4ac}}{2a}$ No. Some will result in a negative in the radical, which means the solution(s) are not real.

16. a) $n = 43$ **b)** $n = 39$

17. a) $12^2 = 4^2 + x^2 - 2(4)(x)\cos(60°)$

b) 13.5 m

18. Example: In the first equation, you must take the square root to isolate or solve for x. This creates the $\pm$ situation. In the second equation, $\sqrt{9}$ is already present, which means the principle or positive square root only.

19. Example: Allison did all of her work on one side of the equation; Riley worked on both sides. Both end up at the same solution but by different paths.

20. Example:
- Completing the square requires operations with rational numbers, which could lead to arithmetic errors.
- Graphing the corresponding function using technology is very easy. Without technology, the manual graph could take a longer amount of time.
- Factoring should be the quickest of the methods. All of the methods lead to the same answers.

21. a) Example: $y = 2(x - 1)^2 - 3, 0 = 2x^2 - 4x - 1$

b) Example: $y = 2(x + 2)^2, 0 = 2x^2 + 8x + 8$

c) Example: $y = 3(x - 2)^2 + 1, 0 = 3x^2 - 12x + 13$

4.4 The Quadratic Formula, pages 254 to 257

1. a) two distinct real roots
b) two distinct real roots
c) two distinct real roots
d) one distinct real root
e) no real roots
f) one distinct real root

2. a) 2   **b)** 2   **c)** 1
d) 1   **e)** 0   **f)** 2

3. a) $x = -3, x = -\dfrac{3}{7}$ **b)** $p = \dfrac{3 \pm 3\sqrt{2}}{2}$

c) $q = \dfrac{-5 \pm \sqrt{37}}{6}$ **d)** $m = \dfrac{-2 \pm 3\sqrt{2}}{2}$

e) $j = \dfrac{7 \pm \sqrt{17}}{4}$ **f)** $g = -\dfrac{3}{4}$

4. a) $z = -4.28, z = -0.39$
b) $c = -0.13, c = 1.88$
c) $u = 0.13, u = 3.07$
d) $b = -1.41, b = -0.09$
e) $w = -0.15, w = 4.65$
f) $k = -0.27, k = 3.10$

5. a) $x = \dfrac{-3 \pm \sqrt{6}}{3}$, -0.18 and -1.82

b) $h = \dfrac{-1 \pm \sqrt{73}}{12}$, -0.80 and 0.63

c) $m = \dfrac{-0.3 \pm \sqrt{0.17}}{0.4}$, -1.78 and 0.28

d) $y = \dfrac{3 \pm \sqrt{2}}{2}$, 0.79 and 2.21

e) $x = \dfrac{1 \pm \sqrt{57}}{14}$, -0.47 and 0.61

f) $z = \dfrac{3 \pm \sqrt{7}}{2}$, 0.18 and 2.82

6. Example: Some are easily solved so they do not require the use of the quadratic formula. $x^2 - 9 = 0$

7. a) $n = -1 \pm \sqrt{3}$; complete the square
b) $y = 3$; factor
c) $u = \pm 2\sqrt{2}$; square root
d) $x = \dfrac{1 \pm \sqrt{19}}{3}$; quadratic formula
e) no real roots; graphing

8. 5 m by 20 m or 10 m by 10 m

9. 0.89 m

10. $1 \pm \sqrt{23}$, -3.80 and 5.80

11. 5 m

12. a) $(30 - 2x)(12 - 2x) = 208$
b) 2 in.
c) 8 in. by 26 in. by 2 in.

13. a) 68.8 km/h   **b)** 95.2 km/h
c) 131.2 km/h

14. a) 4.2 ppm   **b)** 3.4 years

15. $155, 130 jackets

16. 169.4 m

17. $b = 13$, $x = \dfrac{3}{2}$

18. 2.2 cm

19. a) $\left(-3 + 3\sqrt{5}\right)$ m   **b)** $\left(-45 + 27\sqrt{5}\right)$ m²

20. 3.5 h

21. Error in Line 1: The $-b$ would make the first number $-(-7) = 7$.
Error in Line 2: $-4(-3)(2) = +24$ not -24.
The correct solution is $x = \dfrac{-7 \pm \sqrt{73}}{6}$.

22. a) $x = -1$ and $x = 4$
b) Example: The axis of symmetry is halfway between the roots. $\dfrac{-1 + 4}{2} = \dfrac{3}{2}$. Therefore, the equation of the axis of symmetry is $x = \dfrac{3}{2}$.

23. Example: If the quadratic is easily factored, then factoring is faster. If it is not easily factored, then using the quadratic formula will yield exact answers. Graphing with technology is a quick way of finding out if there are real solutions.

24. Answers may vary.

Chapter 4 Review, pages 258 to 260

1. a) $x = -6$, $x = -2$ **b)** $x = -1$, $x = 5$
c) $x = -2$, $x = -\dfrac{4}{3}$ **d)** $x = -3$, $x = 0$
e) $x = -5$, $x = 5$

2. D

3. Example: The graph cannot cross over or touch the x-axis.

4. a) Example:

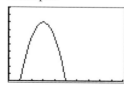

b) 1000 key rings or 5000 key rings produce no profit or loss because the value of P is 0 then.

5. a) -1 and 6   **b)** 6 m

6. a) $(x - 1)(4x - 9)$ **b)** $\dfrac{1}{2}(x + 1)(x - 4)$
c) $(3v + 10)(v + 2)$
d) $(3a^2 - 12 + 35b)(3a^2 - 12 - 35b)$

7. a) $x = -7$, $x = -3$ **b)** $m = -10$, $m = 2$
c) $p = -3$, $p = \dfrac{2}{5}$ **d)** $z = \dfrac{1}{2}$, $z = 3$

8. a) $g = 3$, $g = -\dfrac{1}{2}$ **b)** $y = \dfrac{1}{2}$, $y = \dfrac{5}{4}$
c) $k = \dfrac{3}{5}$ **d)** $x = -\dfrac{3}{2}$, $x = 6$

9. a) Example: $0 = x^2 - 5x + 6$
b) Example: $0 = x^2 + 6x + 5$
c) Example: $0 = 2x^2 + 5x - 12$

10. 6 s

11. a) $V = 15(x)(x + 2)$ **b)** $2145 = 15x(x + 2)$
c) 11 m by 13 m

12. $x = -4$ and $x = 6$. Example: Factoring is fairly easy and exact.

13. a) $k = 4$ **b)** $k = \dfrac{9}{4}$

14. a) $x = \pm 7$ **b)** $x = 2$, $x = -8$
c) $x = 5 \pm 2\sqrt{6}$ **d)** $x = \dfrac{3 \pm \sqrt{5}}{3}$

15. a) $x = 4 \pm \sqrt{\dfrac{29}{2}}$ or $\dfrac{8 \pm \sqrt{58}}{2}$
b) $y = -2 \pm \sqrt{\dfrac{19}{5}}$ or $\dfrac{-10 \pm \sqrt{95}}{5}$
c) no real solutions

16. 68.5 s

17. a) $0 = -\dfrac{1}{2}d^2 + 2d + 1$ **b)** 4.4 m

18. a) two distinct real roots
b) one distinct real root
c) no real roots
d) two distinct real roots

19. a) $x = -\dfrac{5}{3}$, $x = 1$ **b)** $x = \dfrac{-7 \pm \sqrt{29}}{10}$
c) $x = \dfrac{2 \pm \sqrt{7}}{3}$ **d)** $x = -\dfrac{9}{5}$

20. a) $0 = -2x^2 + 6x + 1$ **b)** 3.2 m
21. a) $3.7 - 0.05x$ **b)** $2480 + 40x$
  c) $R = -2x^2 + 24x + 9176$
  d) 5 or 7
22.

Algebraic Steps	Explanations
$ax^2 + bx = -c$	Subtract c from both sides.
$x^2 + \dfrac{b}{a}x = -\dfrac{c}{a}$	Divide both sides by a.
$x^2 + \dfrac{b}{a}x + \dfrac{b^2}{4a^2} = \dfrac{b^2}{4a^2} - \dfrac{c}{a}$	Complete the square.
$\left(x + \dfrac{b}{2a}\right)^2 = \dfrac{b^2 - 4ac}{4a^2}$	Factor the perfect square trinomial.
$x + \dfrac{b}{2a} = \pm\sqrt{\dfrac{b^2 - 4ac}{4a^2}}$	Take the square root of both sides.
$x = \dfrac{-b \pm \sqrt{b^2 - 4ac}}{2a}$	Solve for x.

Chapter 4 Practice Test, pages 261 to 262

1. C
2. B
3. D
4. B
5. B
6. a) $x = 3, x = 1$ **b)** $x = -\dfrac{3}{2}, x = 5$
  c) $x = -3, x = 1$
7. $x = \dfrac{-5 \pm \sqrt{37}}{6}$
8. $x = -2 \pm \sqrt{11}$
9. a) one distinct real root
  b) two distinct real roots
  c) no real roots
  d) two distinct real roots
10. a)

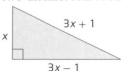

  b) $x^2 + (3x - 1)^2 = (3x + 1)^2$
  c) 12 cm, 35 cm, and 37 cm
11. a) 3.8 s
  b) 35 m
  c) Example: Choose graphing with technology so you can see the path and know which points correspond to the situation.
12. 5 cm
13. 22 cm by 28 cm
14. a) $(9 + 2x)(6 + 2x) = 108$ or
    $4x^2 + 30x - 54 = 0$
  b) $x = 1.5$
    Example: Factoring is the most efficient strategy.
  c) 42 m

Cumulative Review, Chapters 3–4, pages 264 to 265

1. a) C **b)** A **c)** D **d)** B
2. a) not quadratic **b)** quadratic
  c) not quadratic **d)** quadratic
3. a) Example: **b)** Example:

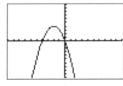 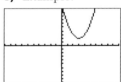

  c) Example:

4. a) vertex: $(-4, -3)$, domain: $\{x \mid x \in R\}$, range: $\{y \mid y \geq -3, y \in R\}$, axis of symmetry: $x = -4$, x-intercepts occur at approximately $(-5.7, 0)$ and $(-2.3, 0)$, y-intercept occurs at $(0, 13)$
  b) vertex: $(2, 1)$, domain: $\{x \mid x \in R\}$, range: $\{y \mid y \leq 1, y \in R\}$, axis of symmetry: $x = 2$, x-intercepts occur at $(1, 0)$ and $(3, 0)$, y-intercept occurs at $(0, -3)$
  c) vertex: $(0, -6)$, domain: $\{x \mid x \in R\}$, range: $\{y \mid y \leq -6, y \in R\}$, axis of symmetry: $x = 0$, no x-intercepts, y-intercept occurs at $(0, -6)$
  d) vertex: $(-8, 6)$, domain: $\{x \mid x \in R\}$, range: $\{y \mid y \geq 6, y \in R\}$, axis of symmetry: $x = -8$, no x-intercepts, y-intercept occurs at $(0, 38)$
5. a) $y = (x - 5)^2 - 7$; the shapes of the graphs are the same with the parabola of $y = (x - 5)^2 - 7$ being translated 5 units to the right and 7 units down.
  b) $y = -(x - 2)^2 - 3$; the shapes of the graphs are the same with the parabola of $y = -(x - 2)^2 - 3$ being reflected in the x-axis and translated 2 units to the right and 3 units down.
  c) $y = 3(x - 1)^2 + 2$; the shape of the graph of $y = 3(x - 1)^2 + 2$ is narrower by a multiplication of the y-values by a factor of 3 and translated 1 unit to the right and 2 units up.

d) $y = \frac{1}{4}(x + 8)^2 + 4$; the shape of the graph of $y = \frac{1}{4}(x + 8)^2 + 4$ is wider by a multiplication of the y-values by a factor of $\frac{1}{4}$ and translated 8 units to the left and 4 units up.

6. a) 22 m   **b)** 2 m   **c)** 4 s

7. In order: roots, zeros, x-intercepts

8. a) $(3x + 4)(3x - 2)$ **b)** $(4r - 9s)(4r + 9s)$
   c) $(x + 3)(2x + 9)$ **d)** $(xy + 4)(xy - 9)$
   e) $5(a + b)(13a + b)$ **f)** $(11r + 20)(11r - 20)$

9. 7, 8, 9 or $-9, -8, -7$

10. 15 seats per row, 19 rows

11. 3.5 m

12. Example: Dallas did not divide the 2 out of the -12 in the first line or multiply the 36 by 2 and thus add 72 to the right side instead of 36 in line two. Doug made a sign error on the -12 in the first line. He should have calculated 200 as the value in the radical, not 80. When he simplified, he took $\sqrt{80}$ divided by 4 to get $\sqrt{20}$, which is not correct.

The correct answer is $3 \pm \dfrac{5}{\sqrt{2}}$ or $\dfrac{6 \pm 5\sqrt{2}}{2}$.

13. a) Example: square root, $x = \pm\sqrt{2}$
   b) Example: factor, $m = 2$ and $m = 13$
   c) Example: factor, $s = -5$ and $s = 7$
   d) Example: use quadratic formula, $x = -\dfrac{1}{16}$ and $x = 3$

14. a) two distinct real roots
   b) one distinct real root
   c) no real roots

15. a) $85 = x^2 + (x + 1)^2$
   b) Example: factoring, $x = -7$ and $x = 6$
   c) The top is 7-in. by 7-in. and the bottom is 6-in. by 6-in.
   d) Example: Negative lengths are not possible.

Unit 2 Test, pages 266 to 267

1. A
2. D
3. D
4. B
5. B
6. 76
7. $900
8. 0.18
9. a) 53.5 cm   **b)** 75.7 cm   **c)** No
10. a) 47.5 m   **b)** 6.1 s
11. 12 cm by 12 cm
12. a) $3x^2 + 6x - 672 = 0$
   b) $x = -16$ and $x = 14$
   c) 14 in., 15 in., and 16 in.
   d) Negative lengths are not possible.

Chapter 5 Radical Expressions and Equations

5.1 Working With Radicals, pages 278 to 281

1.

Mixed Radical Form	Entire Radical Form
$4\sqrt{7}$	$\sqrt{112}$
$5\sqrt{2}$	$\sqrt{50}$
$-11\sqrt{8}$	$-\sqrt{968}$
$-10\sqrt{2}$	$-\sqrt{200}$

2. a) $2\sqrt{14}$ **b)** $15\sqrt{3}$
   c) $2\sqrt[3]{3}$ **d)** $cd\sqrt{c}$

3. a) $6m^2\sqrt{2}$, $m \in R$ **b)** $2q\sqrt[3]{3q^2}$, $q \in R$
   c) $-4st\sqrt[5]{5t}$, $s, t \in R$

4.

Mixed Radical Form	Entire Radical Form
$3n\sqrt{5}$	$\sqrt{45n^2}$, $n \geq 0$ or $-\sqrt{45n^2}$, $n < 0$
$-6\sqrt[3]{2}$	$\sqrt[3]{-432}$
$\dfrac{1}{2a}\sqrt[3]{7a}$	$\sqrt[3]{\dfrac{7}{8a^2}}$, $a \neq 0$
$4x\sqrt[3]{2x}$	$\sqrt[3]{128x^4}$

5. a) $15\sqrt{5}$ and $40\sqrt{5}$ **b)** $32z^4\sqrt{7}$ and $48z^2\sqrt{7}$
   c) $-35\sqrt[4]{w^2}$ and $9w^2(\sqrt[4]{w^2})$
   d) $6\sqrt[3]{2}$ and $18\sqrt[3]{2}$

6. a) $3\sqrt{6}, 7\sqrt{2}, 10$
   b) $-3\sqrt{2}, -4, -2\sqrt{\dfrac{7}{2}}, -2\sqrt{3}$
   c) $\sqrt[3]{21}, 2.8, 2\sqrt[3]{5}, 3\sqrt[3]{2}$

7. Example: Technology could be used.

8. a) $4\sqrt{5}$ **b)** $10.4\sqrt{2} - 7$
   c) $-4\sqrt[4]{11} + 14$ **d)** $-\dfrac{2}{3}\sqrt{6} + 2\sqrt{10}$

9. a) $12\sqrt{3}$ **b)** $6\sqrt{2} + 6\sqrt{7}$
   c) $-28\sqrt{5} + 22.5$ **d)** $\dfrac{13}{4}\sqrt[3]{3} - 7\sqrt{11}$

10. a) $8a\sqrt{a}$, $a \geq 0$ **b)** $9\sqrt{2x} - \sqrt{x}$, $x \geq 0$
   c) $2(r - 10)\sqrt[3]{5r}$, $r \in R$
   d) $\dfrac{4w}{5} - 6\sqrt{2w}$, $w \geq 0$

11. $25.2\sqrt{3}$ m/s

12. $12\sqrt{2}$ cm

13. $12\sqrt[3]{3025}$ million kilometres

14. $2\sqrt{30}$ m/s $\approx$ 11 m/s

15. a) $2\sqrt{38}$ m   **b)** $8\sqrt{19}$ m

16. $\sqrt{1575}$ mm², $15\sqrt{7}$ mm²

17. $7\sqrt{5}$ units

18. $14\sqrt{2}$ m

19. Brady is correct. The answer can be further simplified to $10y^2\sqrt{y}$.

20. $4\sqrt{58}$
Example: Simplify each radical to see which is not a like radical to $12\sqrt{6}$.

21. $\sqrt{2} - \sqrt{3}$ m

22. $12\sqrt{2}$ cm

23. $5\sqrt{3}$ and $7\sqrt{3}$

It is an arithmetic sequence with a common difference of $2\sqrt{3}$.

24. a) $2\sqrt{75}$ and $108^{\frac{1}{2}}$ Example: Write the radicals in simplest form; then, add the two radicals with the greatest coefficients.

b) $2\sqrt{75}$ and $-3\sqrt{12}$ Example: Write the radicals in simplest form; then, subtract the radical with the least coefficient from the radical with the greatest coefficient.

25. a) Example: If $x = 3$,
$(-3)^2 = (-3)(-3)$
$(-3)^2 = 9$
$(-3)^2 = 3^2$

b) Example: If $x = 3$,
$\sqrt{3^2} = \sqrt{9}$
$\sqrt{9} = 3$
$\sqrt{3^2} \neq -3$

5.2 Multiplying and Dividing Radical Expressions, pages 289 to 293

1. a) $14\sqrt{15}$ **b)** -56 **c)** $4\sqrt[4]{15}$

d) $4x\sqrt{38x}$ **e)** $3y^3\left(\sqrt[3]{12y^2}\right)$ **f)** $\frac{3t^3}{2}\sqrt{6}$

2. a) $3\sqrt{11} - 4\sqrt{77}$
b) $-14\sqrt{10} - 6\sqrt{3} + \sqrt{26}$
c) $2y + \sqrt{y}$ **d)** $6z^2 - 5z^2\sqrt{3} + 2z\sqrt{3}$

3. a) $6\sqrt{2} + 12$ **b)** $1 - 9\sqrt{6}$
c) $\sqrt{15j} + 33\sqrt{5}, j \geq 0$ **d)** $3 - 16\sqrt[3]{4k}$

4. a) $8\sqrt{14} - 24\sqrt{7} + 2\sqrt{2} - 6$
b) -389
c) $-27 + 3\sqrt{5}$
d) $36\sqrt[3]{4} - 48\sqrt{13}(\sqrt[3]{2}) + 208$
e) $-4\sqrt{3} + 3\sqrt{30} - \sqrt{6} + 4\sqrt{2} - 6\sqrt{5} + 2$

5. a) $15c\sqrt{2} - 90\sqrt{c} + 2\sqrt{2c} - 12, c \geq 0$
b) $2 + 7\sqrt{5x} - 40x\sqrt{2x} - 140x^2\sqrt{10}, x \geq 0$
c) $258m - 144m\sqrt{3}, m \geq 0$
d) $20r\sqrt[3]{6r^2} + 30r\sqrt[3]{12r} - 16r\sqrt[3]{3} - 24\sqrt[3]{6r^2}$

6. a) $2\sqrt{2}$ **b)** -1
c) $3\sqrt{2}$ **d)** $\frac{9m\sqrt{35}}{7}$

7. a) $\frac{87\sqrt{11p}}{11}$ **b)** $\frac{6v^2\sqrt[3]{98}}{7}$

8. a) $2\sqrt{10}$ **b)** $\frac{-\sqrt{3m}}{m}$
c) $\frac{-\sqrt{15u}}{9u}$ **d)** $4\sqrt[3]{150t}$

9. a) $2\sqrt{3} - 1; 11$ **b)** $7 + \sqrt{11}; 38$
c) $8\sqrt{z} + 3\sqrt{7}; 64z - 63$
d) $19\sqrt{h} - 4\sqrt{2h}; 329h$

10. a) $10 + 5\sqrt{3}$ **b)** $\frac{-7\sqrt{3} + 28\sqrt{2}}{29}$
c) $\frac{\sqrt{35} + 2\sqrt{14}}{3}$ **d)** $\frac{-8 - \sqrt{39}}{5}$

11. a) $\frac{4r^2\sqrt{6} - 36r}{6r^2 - 81}, r \neq \frac{\pm3\sqrt{6}}{2}$
b) $\frac{9\sqrt{2}}{2}, n > 0$

c) $\frac{16 + 4\sqrt{6t}}{8 - 3t}, t \neq \frac{8}{3}, t \geq 0$
d) $\frac{5\sqrt{30y} - 10\sqrt{3y}}{6}, y \geq 0$

12. $c^2 + 7c\sqrt{3c} + c^2\sqrt{c} + 7c^2\sqrt{3}$

13. a) When applying the distributive property, Malcolm distributed the 4 to both the whole number and the root. The 4 should only be distributed to the whole number. The correct answer is $12 + 8\sqrt{2}$.

b) Example: Verify using decimal approximations.
$$\frac{4}{3 - 2\sqrt{2}} \approx 23.3137$$
$$12 + 8\sqrt{2} \approx 23.3137$$

14. $\frac{\sqrt{5} + 1}{2}$

15. a) $T = \frac{\pi\sqrt{10L}}{5}$ **b)** $\frac{9\pi\sqrt{30}}{5}$ s

16. $860 + 172\sqrt{5}$ m

17. $-28 - 16\sqrt{3}$

18. a) $4\sqrt[3]{3}$ mm **b)** $2\sqrt[3]{6}$ mm **c)** $2\sqrt[3]{3} : \sqrt[3]{6}$

19. a) Lev forgot to switch the inequality sign when he divided by -5. The correct answer is $x < \frac{3}{5}$.

b) The square root of a negative number is not a real number.

c) Example: The expression cannot have a variable in the denominator or under the radical sign. $\frac{2x\sqrt{14}}{3\sqrt{5}}$

20. Olivia evaluated $\sqrt{25}$ as ±5 in the third step. The final steps should be as follows:
$$\frac{\sqrt{3}(2c - 5c)}{3} = \frac{\sqrt{3}(-3c)}{3}$$
$$= -c\sqrt{3}$$

21. 735 cm^3

22. 12 m^2

23. $\left(\frac{15\sqrt{3}}{2}, \frac{9\sqrt{2}}{2}\right)$

24. $\frac{25x^2 + 30x\sqrt{x} + 9x}{625x^2 - 450x + 81}$ or $\frac{x(25x + 30\sqrt{x} + 9)}{(25x - 9)^2}$

25. a) $-3 \pm \sqrt{6}$ **b)** -6 **c)** 3
d) Examples: The answer to part b) is the opposite value of the coefficient of the middle term. The answer to part c) is the value of the constant.

26. $\frac{(\sqrt[c]{a})(\sqrt[n-1]{r})}{r}$

27. $(15\sqrt{14} + 42\sqrt{7} + 245\sqrt{2} + 7\sqrt{2702})$ cm^2

28. Example: You cannot multiply or divide radical expressions with different indices, or algebraic expressions with different variables.

29. Examples: To rationalize the denominator you need to multiply the numerator and denominator by a conjugate. To factor a difference of squares, each factor is the conjugate of the other. If you factor $3a - 16$ as a difference of squares, the factors are $\sqrt{3a} - 4$ and $\sqrt{3a} + 4$. The factors form a conjugate pair.

30. a) 3 m

b) $h(t) = -5(t - 1)^2 + 8; t = \sqrt{\dfrac{8 - h}{5}} + 1$

c) $\dfrac{19 + 4\sqrt{10}}{4}$ m

Example: The snowboarder starts the jump at $t = 0$ and ends the jump at $t = \dfrac{5 + 2\sqrt{10}}{5}$. The snowboarder will be halfway at $t = \dfrac{5 + 2\sqrt{10}}{10}$. Substitute this value of t into the original equation to find the height at the halfway point.

31. Yes, they are. Example: using the quadratic formula

32. a) $\dfrac{\sqrt[3]{6V(V - 1)^2}}{V - 1}$

b) A volume greater than one will result in a real ratio.

33. Step 1

$y = \sqrt{x}$

x	y
0	0
1	1
4	2
9	3
16	4

$y = x^2$

x	y
0	0
1	1
2	4
3	9
4	16

Step 2 Example: The values of x and y have been interchanged.

Step 3

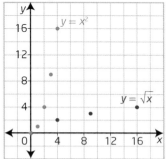

Example: The restrictions on the radical function produce the right half of the parabola.

5.3 Radical Equations, pages 300 to 303

1. a) $3z$ **b)** $x - 4$
c) $4(x + 7)$ **d)** $16(9 - 2y)$
2. Example: Isolate the radical and square both sides. $x = 36$

3. a) $x = \dfrac{9}{2}$ **b)** $x = -2$ **c)** $x = -22$
4. a) $z = 25$ **b)** $y = 36$
c) $x = \dfrac{4}{3}$ **d)** $m = -\dfrac{49}{6}$
5. $k = -8$ is an extraneous root because if -8 is substituted for k, the result is a square root that equals a negative number, which cannot be true in the real-number system.
6. a) $n = 50$ **b)** no solution **c)** $x = -1$
7. a) $m = \pm 2\sqrt{7}$ **b)** $x = -16, x = 4$
c) $q = 2 + 2\sqrt{6}$ **d)** $n = 4$
8. a) $x = 10$ **b)** $x = -32, x = 2$
c) $d = 4$ **d)** $j = -\dfrac{2}{3}$
9. a) $k = 4$ **b)** $m = 0$
c) $j = 16$ **d)** $n = \dfrac{50 + 25\sqrt{3}}{2}$
10. a) $z = 6$ **b)** $y = 8$ **c)** $r = 5$ **d)** $x = 6$
11. The equation $\sqrt{x + 8} + 9 = 2$ has an extraneous root because simplifying it further to $\sqrt{x + 8} = -7$ has no solution.
12. Example: Jerry made a mistake when he squared both sides, because he squared each term on the right side rather than squaring $(x - 3)$. The right side should have been $(x - 3)^2 = x^2 - 6x + 9$, which gives $x = 8$ as the correct solution. Jerry should have listed the restriction following the first line: $x \geq -17$.
13. 11.1 m
14. a) $B \approx 6$ **b)** about 13.8 km/h
15. 1200 kg
16. $2 + \sqrt{n} = n; n = 4$
17. a) $v = \sqrt{19.6h}, h \geq 0$ **b)** 45.9 m
c) 34.3 m/s; A pump at 35 m/s will meet the requirements.
18. 6372.2 km
19. $a = \dfrac{3x - 4\sqrt{3x} + 4}{x}$
20. a) Example: $\sqrt{4a} = -8$
b) Example: $2 + \sqrt{x + 4} = x$
21. 2.9 m
22. 104 km
23. a) The maximum profit is $10 000 and it requires 100 employees.
b) $n = 100 \pm \sqrt{10\,000 - P}$
c) $P \leq 10\,000$
d) domain: $n \geq 0, n \in W$
range: $P \leq 10\,000, P \in W$
24. Example: Both types of equations may involve rearranging. Solving a radical involves squaring both sides; using the quadratic formula involves taking a square root.
25. Example: Extraneous roots may occur because squaring both sides and solving the quadratic equation may result in roots that do not satisfy the original equation.

26. a) 6.8%
    b) $P_f = P_i(r + 1)^3$
    c) 320, 342, 365, 390
    d) geometric sequence with $r = 1.068\ldots$
27. Step 1

1	$\sqrt{6 + \sqrt{6}}$	2.906 800 603
2	$\sqrt{6 + \sqrt{6 + \sqrt{6}}}$	2.984 426 344
3	$\sqrt{6 + \sqrt{6 + \sqrt{6 + \sqrt{6}}}}$	2.997 403 267
4	$\sqrt{6 + \sqrt{6 + \sqrt{6 + \sqrt{6 + \sqrt{6}}}}}$	2.999 567 18
5	$\sqrt{6 + \sqrt{6 + \sqrt{6 + \sqrt{6 + \sqrt{6 + \sqrt{6}}}}}}$	2.999 927 862
6	$\sqrt{6 + \sqrt{6 + \sqrt{6 + \sqrt{6 + \sqrt{6 + \sqrt{6 + \sqrt{6}}}}}}}$	2.999 987 977
7	$\sqrt{6 + \sqrt{6 + \sqrt{6 + \sqrt{6 + \sqrt{6 + \sqrt{6 + \sqrt{6 + \sqrt{6}}}}}}}}$	2.999 997 996
8	$\sqrt{6 + \sqrt{6 + \sqrt{6 + \sqrt{6 + \sqrt{6 + \sqrt{6 + \sqrt{6 + \sqrt{6 + \sqrt{6}}}}}}}}}$	2.999 999 666
9	$\sqrt{6 + \sqrt{6 + \sqrt{6 + \sqrt{6 + \sqrt{6 + \sqrt{6 + \sqrt{6 + \sqrt{6 + \sqrt{6 + \sqrt{6}}}}}}}}}}$	2.999 999 944

Step 2 Example: 3.0
Step 3
$$x = \sqrt{6 + x}, \ x \geq -6$$
$$x^2 = 6 + x$$
$$(x - 3)(x + 2) = 0$$
$$x = 3 \text{ or } x = -2$$
Step 4 The value of x must be positive because it is a square root.

Chapter 5 Review, pages 304 to 305

1. a) $\sqrt{320}$ **b)** $\sqrt[5]{-96}$
   c) $\sqrt{63y^6}$ **d)** $\sqrt[3]{-108z^4}$
2. a) $6\sqrt{2}$ **b)** $6\sqrt{10}$
   c) $3m\sqrt{3}$ **d)** $2xy^2(\sqrt[3]{10x^2})$
3. a) $\sqrt{13}$ **b)** $-4\sqrt{7}$ **c)** $\sqrt[3]{3}$
4. a) $-33x\sqrt{5x} + 14\sqrt{3x}, \ x \geq 0$
   b) $\frac{3}{10}\sqrt{11a} + 12a\sqrt{a}, \ a \geq 0$
5. $3\sqrt{42}$ Example: Simplify each radical to see if it equals $8\sqrt{7}$.
6. $3\sqrt{7}, \ 8, \ \sqrt{65}, \ 2\sqrt{17}$
7. a) $v = 13\sqrt{d}$ **b)** 48 km/h
8. $8\sqrt{6}$ km
9. a) false   **b)** true   **c)** false
10. a) $2\sqrt{3}$ **b)** $-30f^4\sqrt{3}$ **c)** $6\sqrt[4]{9}$
11. a) -1 **b)** $83 - 20\sqrt{6}$
   c) $a^2 + 17a\sqrt{a} + 42a, \ a \geq 0$
12. Yes; they are conjugate pairs and the solutions to the quadratic equation.
13. a) $\frac{\sqrt{2}}{2}$ **b)** $\frac{-(\sqrt[3]{25})^2}{25}$ **c)** $\frac{-4a\sqrt{2}}{3}$
14. a) $\frac{-8 - 2\sqrt{3}}{13}$ **b)** $\frac{2\sqrt{35} + 7}{13}$
   c) $\frac{12 - 6\sqrt{3m}}{4 - 3m}, \ m \geq 0 \text{ and } m \neq \frac{4}{3}$

d) $\frac{a^2 + 2a\sqrt{b} + b}{a^2 - b}, \ b \geq 0 \text{ and } b \neq a^2$
15. $4\sqrt{2} + 8\sqrt{5}$
16. a) $\frac{5\sqrt{6}}{18}$ **b)** $\frac{-2a^2\sqrt{2}}{3}$
17. $\frac{24 + 6\sqrt{2}}{7}$ units
18. a) radical defined for $x \geq 0$; solution: $x = 49$
   b) radical defined for $x \leq 4$; no solution
   c) radical defined for $x \geq 0$; solution: $x = 18$
   d) radical defined for $x \geq 0$; solution: $x = 21$
19. a) restriction: $x \geq \frac{12}{7}$; solution: $x = \frac{9}{2}$
   b) restriction: $y \geq 3$; solution: $y = 3$ and $y = 4$
   c) restriction: $n \geq \frac{-25}{7}$; solution: $n = 8$
   d) restriction: $0 \leq m \leq 24$; solution: $m = 12$
   e) no restrictions; solution: $x = -21$
20. Example: Isolate the radical; then, square both sides. Expand and simplify. Solve the quadratic equation. $n = -3$ is an extraneous root because when it is substituted into the original equation a false statement is reached.
21. 33.6 m

Chapter 5 Practice Test, pages 306 to 307

1. B
2. D
3. C
4. D
5. B
6. C
7. $3\sqrt{11}, \ 5\sqrt{6}, \ \sqrt{160}, \ 9\sqrt{2}$
8. $\frac{-12n\sqrt{10} - 288n\sqrt{5}}{287}$
9. The radical is defined for $x \leq -\sqrt{5}$ and $x \geq \sqrt{5}$. The solution is $x = \frac{7}{3}$.
10. The solution is $\frac{102 + 6\sqrt{214}}{25}$. The extraneous root is $\frac{102 - 6\sqrt{214}}{25}$.
11. $15\sqrt{2}$
12. $9\sqrt{2}$ km
13. a) $\sqrt{6}$ **b)** $\sqrt{y - 3}$ **c)** $\sqrt[3]{49}$
14. \$6300
15. She is correct.
16. a) $\sqrt{1 + x^2}$ **b)** $2\sqrt{30}$ units
17. a) $R = \frac{P}{I^2}$ **b)** 400 Ω
18. a) $x = \sqrt{\frac{SA}{6}}$ **b)** $\frac{\sqrt{22}}{2}$ cm   **c)** $\sqrt{2}$
19. a) $3713.15 = 3500(1 + i)^2$ **b)** 3%

Chapter 6 Rational Expressions and Equations

6.1 Rational Expressions, pages 317 to 321

1. a) 18   **b)** $14x$ **c)** 7
   d) $4x - 12$ **e)** 8   **f)** $y + 2$

2. a) Divide both by pq.
   b) Multiply both by $(x - 4)$.
   c) Divide both by $(m - 3)$.
   d) Multiply both by $(y^2 + y)$.

3. a) 0   **b)** 1   **c)** -5
   d) none   **e)** ± 1 **f)** none

4. The following values are non-permissible because they would make the denominator zero, and division by zero is not defined.
   a) 4   **b)** 0   **c)** $-2, 4$
   d) $-3, 1$ **e)** 0   **f)** $\dfrac{4}{3}, -\dfrac{5}{2}$

5. a) $r \neq 0$ **b)** $t \neq \pm 1$
   c) $x \neq 2$ **d)** $g \neq 0, \pm 3$

6. a) $\dfrac{2}{3}$; $c \neq 0, 5$ **b)** $\dfrac{3(2w + 3)}{2(3w + 2)}$; $w \neq -\dfrac{2}{3}, 0$
   c) $\dfrac{x + 7}{2x - 1}$; $x \neq \dfrac{1}{2}, 7$ **d)** $-\dfrac{1}{2}$; $a \neq -2, 3$

7. a) x^2 is not a factor.
   b) Factor the denominator. Set each factor equal to zero and solve. $x \neq -3, 1$
   c) Factor the numerator and denominator. Determine the non-permissible values. Divide like factors. $\dfrac{x + 1}{x + 3}$

8. a) $\dfrac{3r}{2p}$, $r \neq 0, p \neq 0$ **b)** $-\dfrac{3}{5}$, $x \neq 2$
   c) $\dfrac{b - 4}{2(b - 6)}$, $b \neq \pm 6$ **d)** $\dfrac{k + 3}{2(k - 3)}$, $k \neq -\dfrac{5}{2}, 3$
   e) $-1, x \neq 4$ **f)** $\dfrac{5(x + y)}{x - y}$, $x \neq y$

9. Sometimes true. The statement is not true when $x = 3$.

10. There may have been another factor that divided out. For example: $\dfrac{y(y + 3)}{(y - 6)(y + 3)}$

11. yes, provided the non-permissible value, $x \neq 5$, is discussed

12. Examples: $\dfrac{x^2 + 2x + 1}{x^2 + 3x + 2}$, $\dfrac{x^2 + 4x + 4}{x^2 + 5x + 6}$, $\dfrac{2x^2 + 5x + 2}{3x^2 + 7x + 2}$
Write a rational expression in simplest form, and multiply both the numerator and the denominator by the same factor. For example, the first expression was obtained as follows: $\dfrac{x + 1}{x + 2} = \dfrac{(x + 1)(x + 1)}{(x + 2)(x + 1)}$.

13. Shali divided the term 2 in the numerator and the denominator. You may only divide by factors. The correct solution is the second step, $\dfrac{g + 2}{2}$.

14. Example: $\dfrac{2p}{p^2 + p - 2}$

15. a) $\dfrac{2n^2 + 11n + 12}{2n^2 - 32}$ **b)** $\dfrac{2n + 3}{2(n - 4)}$, $n \neq \pm 4$

16. a)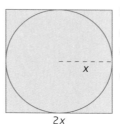
   b) $\dfrac{\pi x^2}{4x^2}$
   c) $x \neq 0$
   d) $\dfrac{\pi}{4}$
   e) 79%

17. a) The non-permissible value, -2, does not make sense in the context as the mass cannot be -2 kg.
   b) $p = 0$ **c)** 900 kg

18. a) $\dfrac{50}{q}$, $q \neq 0$ **b)** $\dfrac{100}{p - 4}$, $p \neq 4$

19. a) \$620   **b)** $\dfrac{350 + 9n}{n}$
   c) \$20.67

20. a) No; she divided by the term, 5, not a factor.
   b) Example: If $m = 5$ then $\dfrac{5}{10} \neq \dfrac{1}{6}$.

21. a) Multiply by $\dfrac{5}{5}$.   **b)** Multiply by $\dfrac{x - 2}{x - 2}$.

22. a) $\dfrac{4x - 8}{12}$ **b)** $\dfrac{3x - 6}{9}$
   c) $\dfrac{2x^2 + x - 10}{6x + 15}$

23. a) $\dfrac{25b}{5b}$ **b)** $\dfrac{4a^2bx + 4a^2b}{12a^2b}$
   c) $\dfrac{2b - 2a}{-14x}$

24. a)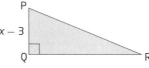
   b) $2(x + 2)$ **c)** $x \neq 3$

25. a) $\dfrac{(2x - 1)(3x + 1)}{(3x + 1)(3x - 1)} = \dfrac{(2x - 1)}{(3x - 1)}$, $x \neq \pm\dfrac{1}{3}$
   b) In the last step: $\dfrac{n + 3}{-n} = \dfrac{-n - 3}{n}$, $n \neq 0, \dfrac{5}{2}$

26. a) $\dfrac{x + 6}{x + 3}$, $x \neq \pm 3$
   b) $(2x - 7)(2x - 5)$, $x \neq -3$
   c) $\dfrac{(x - 3)(x + 2)}{(x + 3)(x - 2)}$, $x \neq -3, -1, 2$
   d) $\dfrac{(x + 5)(x + 3)}{3}$, $x \neq \pm 1$

27. $6x^2 + \dfrac{19}{2}x + 2$, $x \neq \dfrac{1}{4}, \dfrac{3}{2}$

28. a) Lt

b)

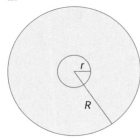

$$\pi(R - r)(R + r)$$

c) $L = \dfrac{\pi(R + r)(R - r)}{t}$, $t > 0$, $R > r$, and t, R, and r should be expressed in the same units.

29. Examples:

a) $\dfrac{2}{(x + 2)(x - 5)}$

b) $\dfrac{x^2 + 3x}{x^2 + 2x - 3}$; the given expression has a non-permissible value of -1. Multiply the numerator and denominator by a factor, $x + 3$, that has a non-permissible value of -3.

30. a) Example: if $y = 7$,

$$\dfrac{y - 3}{4} \quad \text{and} \quad \dfrac{2y^2 - 5y - 3}{8y + 4}$$

$$= \dfrac{7 - 3}{4} \qquad\qquad = \dfrac{2(7^2) - 5(7) - 3}{8(7) + 4}$$

$$= 1 \qquad\qquad\qquad = \dfrac{60}{60}$$

$$\qquad\qquad\qquad\qquad = 1$$

b) $\dfrac{2y^2 - 5y - 3}{8y + 4} = \dfrac{(2y + 1)(y - 3)}{4(2y + 1)} = \dfrac{y - 3}{4}$

c) The algebraic approach, in part b), proves that the expressions are equivalent for all values of y, except the non-permissible value.

31. a) $m = \dfrac{p - 8}{p + 1}$

b) Any value $-1 < p < 8$ will give a negative slope. Example: If $p = 0$, $m = \dfrac{-8}{1}$.

c) If $p = -1$, then the expression is undefined, and the line is vertical.

32. Example: $\dfrac{12}{15} = \dfrac{(3)(4)}{(3)(5)} = \dfrac{4}{5}$,

$$\dfrac{x^2 - 4}{x^2 + 5x + 6} = \dfrac{(x + 2)(x - 2)}{(x + 3)(x + 2)}$$

$$= \dfrac{(x - 2)}{(x + 3)}, \; x \neq -3, -2$$

6.2 Multiplying and Dividing Rational Expressions, pages 327 to 330

1. a) $9m$, $c \neq 0$, $f \neq 0$, $m \neq 0$

b) $\dfrac{a - 5}{5(a - 1)}$, $a \neq -5$, 1, $a \neq b$

c) $\dfrac{4(y - 7)}{(2y - 3)(y - 1)}$, $y \neq -3$, 1, $\pm\dfrac{3}{2}$

2. a) $\dfrac{d - 10}{4}$, $d \neq -10$ **b)** $\dfrac{a - 1}{a - 3}$, $a \neq \pm 3$, -1

c) $\dfrac{1}{2}$, $z \neq 4$, $\pm\dfrac{5}{2}$

d) $\dfrac{p + 1}{3}$, $p \neq -3$, 1, $\dfrac{3}{2}$, $\dfrac{1}{2}$

3. a) $\dfrac{t}{2}$ **b)** $\dfrac{3}{2x - 1}$

c) $\dfrac{y - 3}{8}$ **d)** $\dfrac{p - 3}{2p - 3}$

4. a) $s \neq 0$, $t \neq 0$ **b)** $r \neq \pm 7$, 0

c) $n \neq \pm 1$

5. $x - 3$, $x \neq -3$

6. $\dfrac{y}{y + 3}$, $y \neq \pm 3$, 0

7. a) $\dfrac{3 - p}{p - 3} = \dfrac{-1(p - 3)}{p - 3} = -1$, $p \neq 3$

b) $\dfrac{7k - 1}{3k} \times \dfrac{1}{1 - 7k}$

$$= \dfrac{7k - 1}{3k} \times \dfrac{1}{-1(7k - 1)}$$

$$= \dfrac{-1}{3k} \text{ or } -\dfrac{1}{3k}, \; k \neq 0, \dfrac{1}{7}$$

8. a) $\dfrac{w - 2}{3}$, $w \neq -2$, $-\dfrac{3}{2}$

b) $\dfrac{v^2}{v + 3}$, $v \neq 0$, -3, 5,

c) $\dfrac{-1(3x - 1)}{x + 5}$, $x \neq -5$, 2, $-\dfrac{1}{3}$

d) $\dfrac{-2}{y - 2}$, $y \neq \pm 1$, 2, $-\dfrac{1}{2}$, $\dfrac{3}{4}$

9. -3 and -2 are the non-permissible values of the original denominators, and -1 is the non-permissible value when the reciprocal of the divisor is created.

10. $\dfrac{n^2 - 4}{n + 1} \div (n - 2)$; $\dfrac{n + 2}{n + 1}$, $n \neq -1$, 2

11. a) $\dfrac{(x - 3)}{5}(60) = 12x - 36$ metres

b) $900 \div \dfrac{600}{n + 1} = \dfrac{3n + 3}{2}$ kilometres per hour, $n \neq -1$

c) $\dfrac{x^2 + 2x + 1}{(2x - 3)(x + 1)} = \dfrac{x + 1}{2x - 3}$ metres, $x \neq \dfrac{3}{2}$, -1

12. They are reciprocals of each other. This is always true. The divisor and dividend are interchanged.

13. Example:

$$1 \text{ yd}\left(\dfrac{3 \text{ ft}}{1 \text{ yd}}\right)\left(\dfrac{12 \text{ in.}}{1 \text{ ft}}\right)\left(\dfrac{2.54 \text{ cm}}{1 \text{ in.}}\right) = 91.44 \text{ cm}$$

14. a) Tessa took the reciprocal of the dividend, not the divisor.

b) $= \dfrac{(c + 6)(c - 6)}{2c} \times \dfrac{8c^2}{c + 6}$

$$= 4c(c - 6)$$

$$= 4c^2 - 24c, \; c \neq 0, -6$$

c) The correct answer is the reciprocal of Tessa's answer. Taking reciprocals of either factor produces reciprocal answers.

15. $(x^2 - 9) \div \dfrac{x^2 - 2x - 3}{x + 1} = x + 3;\ x \neq 3,\ x \neq -1$

16. $\left(\dfrac{1}{2}\right)\left(\dfrac{x + 2}{x - 8}\right)\left(\dfrac{x^2 - 7x - 8}{x^2 - 4}\right);\ \dfrac{x + 1}{2(x - 2)},\ x \neq \pm 2,\ 8$

17. a) $K = \dfrac{Pw}{2h},\ m \neq 0,\ w \neq 0,\ h \neq 0$

b) $y = \dfrac{2\pi r}{x},\ d \neq 0,\ x \neq 0,\ r \neq 0$

c) $a = vw,\ w \neq 0$

18. $2(n - 4),\ n \neq -4,\ 1,\ 4$

19. a) Yes; when the two binomial factors are multiplied, you get the expression $x^2 - 5$.

b) $\dfrac{x + \sqrt{7}}{x - \sqrt{3}}$

c) $x + \sqrt{7}$; it is the same.

20. a) approximately 290 m

b) $\dfrac{(x + 3)^2}{4g(x - 5)^2}$ metres

21. Agree. Example: $\left(\dfrac{2}{3}\right)\left(\dfrac{1}{5}\right) = \dfrac{(2)(1)}{(3)(5)} = \dfrac{2}{15}$,

and $\dfrac{2}{3} \div \dfrac{1}{5} = \left(\dfrac{2}{3}\right)\left(\dfrac{5}{1}\right) = \dfrac{10}{3}$

$\dfrac{(x + 2)}{(x + 3)} \times \dfrac{(x + 1)}{(x + 3)} = \dfrac{(x + 2)(x + 1)}{(x + 3)(x + 3)}$

$= \dfrac{x^2 + 3x + 2}{x^2 + 6x + 9},\ x \neq -3$

$\dfrac{(x + 2)}{(x + 3)} \div \dfrac{(x + 1)}{(x + 3)} = \dfrac{(x + 2)}{(x + 3)} \times \dfrac{(x + 3)}{(x + 1)}$

$= \dfrac{(x + 2)}{(x + 1)},\ x \neq -3, -1$

22. a) $\dfrac{p + 2}{4 - p}$ **b)** $\dfrac{p - 4}{p + 2}$

23. a) $\tan B = \dfrac{b}{a}$ **b)** $\dfrac{\frac{b}{c}}{\frac{a}{c}} = \dfrac{b}{a}$

c) They are the same; $\tan B = \dfrac{\sin B}{\cos B}$.

6.3 Adding and Subtracting Rational Expressions, pages 336 to 340

1. a) $\dfrac{7x}{6}$ **b)** $\dfrac{10}{x},\ x \neq 0$

c) $\dfrac{4t + 4}{5}$ or $\dfrac{4(t + 1)}{5}$ **d)** $m,\ m \neq -1$

e) $a + 3,\ a \neq 4$

2. $\dfrac{3x - 7}{9} + \dfrac{6x + 7}{9} = \dfrac{3x - 7 + 6x + 7}{9}$

$= \dfrac{9x}{9}$

$= x$

3. a) $\dfrac{-4x + 13}{(x - 3)(x + 1)},\ x \neq -1,\ 3$

b) $\dfrac{3x(x + 6)}{(x - 2)(x + 10)(x + 2)},\ x \neq -10,\ \pm 2$

4. a) 24, 12; LCD = 12

b) $50a^3y^3,\ 10a^2y^2$; LCD $= 10a^2y^2$

c) $(9 - x^2)(3 + x),\ 9 - x^2$; LCD $= 9 - x^2$ or $(3 - x)(3 + x)$

5. a) $\dfrac{11}{15a},\ a \neq 0$ **b)** $\dfrac{x + 9}{6x},\ x \neq 0$

c) $\dfrac{2(10x - 3)}{5x},\ x \neq 0$

d) $\dfrac{(2z - 3x)(2z + 3x)}{xyz},\ x \neq 0,\ y \neq 0,\ z \neq 0$

e) $\dfrac{4st + t^2 - 4}{10t^3},\ t \neq 0$

f) $\dfrac{6bxy^2 - 2ax + a^2b^2y}{a^2b^2y},\ a \neq 0,\ b \neq 0,\ y \neq 0$

6. a) $\dfrac{-5x + 18}{(x + 2)(x - 2)},\ x \neq \pm 2$

b) $\dfrac{3x - 11}{(x - 4)(x + 3)},\ x \neq -3,\ 4$

c) $\dfrac{2x(x - 4)}{(x - 2)(x + 2)},\ x \neq \pm 2$

d) $\dfrac{3}{y},\ y \neq -1,\ 0$

e) $\dfrac{-3(5h + 9)}{(h + 3)(h + 3)(h - 3)},\ h \neq \pm 3$

f) $\dfrac{(2x - 3)(x + 2)}{x(x - 2)(x - 1)(x + 3)},\ x \neq -3,\ 0,\ 1,\ 2$

7. a) $\dfrac{2(x^2 - 3x + 5)}{(x - 5)(x + 5)},\ x \neq \pm 5,\ \dfrac{1}{2}$

b) $\dfrac{-x + 4}{(x - 2)(x + 3)},\ x \neq -3,\ 0,\ 2,\ 8$

c) $\dfrac{n + 8}{(n - 4)(n - 2)},\ n \neq 2,\ 3,\ 4$

d) $\dfrac{w + 9}{(w + 3)(w + 4)},\ w \neq -2,\ -3,\ -4$

8. In the third line, multiplying by -7 should give $-7x + 14$. Also, she has forgotten to list the non-permissible values.

$= \dfrac{6x + 12 + 4 - 7x + 14}{(x - 2)(x + 2)}$

$= \dfrac{-x + 30}{(x - 2)(x + 2)},\ x \neq \pm 2$

9. Yes. Factor -1 from the numerator to create $-1(x - 5)$. Then, the expression simplifies to $\dfrac{-1}{x + 5}$.

10. a) $\dfrac{2x}{x + 3},\ x \neq 0,\ \pm 3$

b) $\dfrac{3(t + 6)}{2(t - 3)},\ t \neq -6,\ -2,\ 0,\ 3$

c) $\dfrac{3m}{m + 3},\ m \neq 0,\ -\dfrac{3}{2},\ -3$

d) $\dfrac{x}{x - 2},\ x \neq \pm 4,\ 2$

11. a)
$$\frac{\frac{AD}{B} + C}{D} = \left(\frac{AD + CB}{B}\right) \div D$$
$$= \left(\frac{AD + CB}{B}\right)\left(\frac{1}{D}\right)$$
$$= \frac{AD + CB}{BD}$$
$$= \frac{AD}{BD} + \frac{CB}{BD}$$
$$= \frac{A}{B} + \frac{C}{D}$$

b)
$$\left[\frac{\left(\frac{AB}{D} + C\right)D}{F} + E\right]F = \left(\frac{AB}{D} + C\right)D + EF$$
$$= AB + CD + EF$$

12. $\dfrac{\sqrt{5x^2 - 2x + 1}}{4}$

13. a) $\dfrac{200}{m}$ tells the expected number of weeks to gain 200 kg; $\dfrac{200}{m + 4}$ tells the number of weeks to gain 200 kg when the calf is on the healthy growth program.

b) $\dfrac{200}{m} - \dfrac{200}{m + 4}$

c) $\dfrac{800}{m(m + 4)}$, $m \neq 0, -4$; yes, the expressions are equivalent.

14. a) $\dfrac{200}{n}$ minutes

b) $\left(\dfrac{200}{n} + \dfrac{500}{n} + \dfrac{1000}{n}\right)$ minutes

c) $\dfrac{1700}{n}$ minutes; the time it would take to type all three assignments

d)
$$\left(\frac{200}{n} + \frac{500}{n - 5} + \frac{1000}{n - 10}\right) - \frac{1700}{n}$$
$$= \frac{12\,500n - 75\,000}{n(n - 5)(n - 10)}$$

15. a) $\dfrac{2x^2 + 13}{(x - 4)(x + 5)}$, $x \neq -5, -2, 0, 3, 4$

b) $\dfrac{-9}{(x - 1)(x + 2)}$, $x \neq -3, -2, 0, 1, \dfrac{1}{2}$

c) $\dfrac{3(1 - 4x)}{(x + 5)(x - 4)}$, $x \neq -5, -2, 0, 3, 4$

d) $\dfrac{15}{(x + 6)(x + 3)}$, $x \neq 0, -2, -3, -6, -\dfrac{1}{2}$

16. $\left(\dfrac{20}{x} + \dfrac{16}{x - 2}\right)$ hours

17. Example: In a three-person relay, Barry ran the first 12 km at a constant rate. Jim ran the second leg of 8 km at a rate 3 km/h faster, and Al ran the last leg of 5 km at a rate 2 km/h slower than Barry. The total time for the relay would be $\left(\dfrac{12}{x} + \dfrac{8}{x + 3} + \dfrac{5}{x - 2}\right)$ hours.

18. a) Incorrect: $\dfrac{a}{b} - \dfrac{b}{a} = \dfrac{a^2 - b^2}{ab}$. Find the LCD first, do not just combine pieces.

b) Incorrect: $\dfrac{ca + cb}{c + cd} = \dfrac{a + b}{1 + d}$. Factor c from the numerator and from the denominator, remembering that $c(1) = c$.

c) Incorrect: $\dfrac{a}{4} - \dfrac{6 - b}{4} = \dfrac{a - 6 + b}{4}$. Distribute the subtraction to both terms in the numerator of the second rational expression by first putting the numerator in brackets.

d) Incorrect: $\dfrac{1}{1 - \dfrac{a}{b}} = \dfrac{b}{b - a}$. Simplify the denominator first, and then divide.

e) Incorrect: $\dfrac{1}{a - b} = \dfrac{-1}{b - a}$. Multiplying both numerator and denominator by -1, which is the same as multiplying the whole expression by 1, changes every term to its opposite.

19. a) Agree. Each term in the numerator is divided by the denominator, and then can be simplified.

b) Disagree. If Keander was given the rational expression $\dfrac{3x - 7}{x}$, there are multiple original expressions that he could come up with, for example $\dfrac{2x - 1}{x} + \dfrac{x - 6}{x}$ or $\dfrac{x^2 - x + 11}{x} - \dfrac{x^2 - 4x + 18}{x}$.

20. a) $\dfrac{12}{13}$ Ω

b) $\dfrac{R_1 R_2 R_3}{R_2 R_3 + R_1 R_3 + R_1 R_2}$

c) $\dfrac{12}{13}$ Ω

d) the simplified form from part b), because with it you do not need to find the LCD first

21. Example:

Arithmetic:	Algebra:
If $\dfrac{2}{3} = \dfrac{6}{9}$, then	If $\dfrac{x}{2} = \dfrac{3x}{6}$, then
$\dfrac{2}{3} = \dfrac{2 - 6}{3 - 9}$	$\dfrac{x}{2} = \dfrac{x - 3x}{2 - 6}$
$= \dfrac{-4}{-6}$	$= \dfrac{-2x}{-4}$
$= \dfrac{2}{3}$	$= \dfrac{x}{2}$

22. a) $\dfrac{-2p + 9}{2(p - 3)}$, $p \neq 3$

b) $\dfrac{3}{0}$; the slope is undefined when $p = 3$, so this is a vertical line through A and B.

c) The slope is negative.

d) When $p = 4$, the slope is positive; from $p = 5$ to $p = 10$ the slope is always negative.

23. 3

24. Examples: $\frac{2}{5} + \frac{1}{5} = \frac{2+1}{5} = \frac{3}{5}$ and

$\frac{2}{5} + \frac{1}{3} = \frac{2(3) + 1(5)}{15} = \frac{11}{15}$

$\frac{2}{x} + \frac{1}{x} = \frac{2+1}{x} = \frac{3}{x}$ and

$\frac{2}{x} + \frac{1}{y} = \frac{2(y) + 1(x)}{xy} = \frac{2y + x}{xy}$

25. a) The student's suggestion is correct.

Example: find the average of $\frac{1}{2}$ and $\frac{3}{4}$.

$\left(\frac{1}{2} + \frac{3}{4}\right) \div 2 = \left(\frac{2+3}{4}\right) \times \left(\frac{1}{2}\right)$

$= \frac{5}{8}$

Halfway between $\frac{1}{2}$ and $\frac{3}{4}$, or $\frac{4}{8}$ and $\frac{6}{8}$, is $\frac{5}{8}$.

b) $\frac{13}{4a}$, $a \neq 0$

26. Yes. Example: $\frac{1}{2} + \frac{1}{3} = \frac{5}{6}$ and $\frac{1}{2} + \frac{1}{3} = \frac{1}{\frac{6}{5}} = \frac{5}{6}$

$\frac{1}{x} + \frac{1}{y} = \frac{x+y}{xy}$ and $\frac{1}{x} + \frac{1}{y} = \frac{1}{\frac{xy}{x+y}} = \frac{x+y}{xy}$

27. a) $\frac{1}{u} + \frac{1}{v} = \frac{u+v}{uv}$ **b)** 5.93 cm

c) $f = \frac{uv}{u+v}$

28. Step 3 Yes

Step 4 a) $A = 2$, $B = 1$

b) $A = 3$, $B = 3$

Step 5 Always:

$\frac{3}{x-4} + \frac{-2}{x-1} = \frac{3(x-1) + -2(x-4)}{(x-4)(x-1)}$

$= \frac{x+5}{(x-4)(x-1)}$

6.4 Rational Equations, pages 348 to 351

1. a) $4(x-1) - 3(2x-5) = 5 + 2x$

b) $2(2x+3) + 1(x+5) = 7$

c) $4x - 5(x-3) = 2(x+3)(x-3)$

2. a) $f = -1$ **b)** $y = 6$, $y \neq 0$

c) $w = 12$, $w \neq 3, 6$

3. a) $t = 2$ or $t = 6$, $t \neq 0$ **b)** $c = 2$, $c \neq \pm 3$

c) $d = -2$ or $d = 3$, $d \neq -4, 1$

d) $x = 3$, $x \neq \pm 1$

4. No. The solution is not a permissible value.

5. a) $\frac{3-x}{x^2} - \frac{2}{x}$, $\frac{3-3x}{x^2}$, $x > 0$

b) $\frac{3-x}{x^2} \times \frac{2}{x}$, $\frac{6-2x}{x^3}$, $x > 0$

c) $x = \frac{1}{2}$

6. a) $b = 3.44$ or $b = 16.56$

b) $c = -3.54$ or $c = 2.54$

7. $l = 15(\sqrt{5} + 1)$, 48.5 cm

8. The numbers are 5 and 20.

9. The numbers are 3 and 4.

10. 30 students

11. The integers are 5 and 6.

12. a) Less than 2 min. There is more water going in at once.

b)

	Time to Fill Tub (min)	Fraction Filled in 1 min	Fraction Filled in x minutes
Cold Tap	2	$\frac{1}{2}$	$\frac{x}{2}$
Hot Tap	3	$\frac{1}{3}$	$\frac{x}{3}$
Both Taps	x	$\frac{1}{x}$	1

c) $\frac{x}{2} + \frac{x}{3} = 1$ **d)** 1.2 min

13. 6 h

14. a)

	Distance (km)	Rate (km/h)	Time (h)
Downstream	18	$x + 3$	$\frac{18}{x+3}$
Upstream	8	$x - 3$	$\frac{8}{x-3}$

b) $\frac{18}{x+3} = \frac{8}{x-3}$ **c)** 7.8 km/h

d) $x \neq \pm 3$

15. 28.8 h

16. 5.7 km/h

17. about 50 km/h west of Swift Current, and 60 km/h east of Swift Current

18. about 3.5 km/h

19.

	Reading Rate in Pages per Day	Number of Pages Read	Number of Days
First Half	x	259	$\frac{259}{x}$
Second Half	$x + 12$	259	$\frac{259}{x+12}$

about 20 pages per day for the first half of the book

20. a) 2 L **b)** 4.5 L

21. $a = \pm \frac{1}{3}$

22. a) $\frac{\frac{1}{a} + \frac{1}{b}}{2} = \frac{1}{x}$, $x = \frac{2ab}{a+b}$

b) 4 and 12, or -6 and 2

23. a) $\frac{1}{x} - \frac{1}{y} = a$ or $\frac{1}{x} - \frac{1}{y} = a$

$y - x = axy$ $\frac{y-x}{xy} = a$

$y = axy + x$ $y - x = axy$

$y = x(ay + 1)$ $y = axy + x$

$\frac{y}{ay+1} = x$ $y = x(ay + 1)$

            $\frac{y}{ay+1} = x$

In both, $x \neq 0$, $y \neq 0$, $ay \neq -1$.

b) $\dfrac{2d - gt^2}{2t} = v_0, t \neq 0$

c) $n = \dfrac{Ir}{E - IR}, n \neq 0, R \neq -\dfrac{r}{n}, E \neq Ir, I \neq 0$

24. a) Rational expressions combine operations and variables in one or more terms. Rational equations involve rational expressions and an equal sign.

Example: $\dfrac{1}{x} + \dfrac{1}{y}$ is a rational expression, which can be simplified but not solved.

$\dfrac{1}{x} + \dfrac{1}{2x} = 5$ is a rational equation that can be solved.

b) Multiply each term by the LCD. Then, divide common factors.

$$\dfrac{5}{x} - \dfrac{1}{x - 1} = \dfrac{1}{x - 1}$$

$$x(x - 1)\left(\dfrac{5}{x}\right) - x(x - 1)\left(\dfrac{1}{x - 1}\right) = x(x - 1)\left(\dfrac{1}{x - 1}\right)$$

Simplify the remaining factors by multiplying. Solve the resulting linear equation.

$(x - 1)(5) - x(1) = x(1)$
$5x - 5 - x = x$
$3x = 5$
$x = \dfrac{5}{3}$

c) Example: Add the second term on the left to both sides, to give $\dfrac{5}{x} = \dfrac{2}{x - 1}$.

25. a) 5.5 pages per minute
b) and **c)** Answers may vary.

26. a) 46
b) $\dfrac{45}{50}$ is 90%, so $\dfrac{10(40) + 5(x)}{15} = 45$. For this equation to be true, you would need 55 on each of the remaining quizzes, which is not possible.

27. a) The third line should be
$2x + 2 - 3x^2 + 3 = 5x^2 - 5x$
$0 = 8x^2 - 7x - 5$

b) $\dfrac{7 \pm \sqrt{209}}{16}$

c) $x = 1.34$ or $x = -0.47$

Chapter 6 Review, pages 352 to 354

1. a) 0. It creates an expression that is undefined.
b) Example: Some rational expressions have non-permissible values.

For $\dfrac{2}{x - 3}$, x may not take on the value 3.

2. Agree. Example: There are an unlimited number of ways of creating equivalent expressions by multiplying the numerator and denominator by the same term; because you are actually multiplying by 1 $\left(\dfrac{X}{X} = 1\right)$.

3. a) $y \neq 0$ **b)** $x \neq -1$ **c)** none
d) $a \neq -2, 3$ **e)** $m \neq -1, \dfrac{3}{2}$ **f)** $t \neq \pm 2$

4. a) $-6; s \neq 0$ **b)** $-1; x \neq \dfrac{3}{5}$ **c)** $-\dfrac{1}{4}; b \neq 2$

5. a) $\dfrac{2x^2 - 6x}{10x}$ **b)** $\dfrac{1}{x + 3}$

c) $\dfrac{3c - 6d}{9f}$ **d)** $\dfrac{m^2 - 3m - 4}{m^2 - 16}$

6. a) Factor the denominator(s), set each factor equal to zero, and solve.

Example: Since $\dfrac{m - 4}{m^2 - 9} = \dfrac{m - 4}{(m + 3)(m - 3)}$, the non-permissible values are ± 3.

b) i) $x - 5, x \neq -\dfrac{2}{3}$ **ii)** $\dfrac{a}{a + 3}, a \neq \pm 3$

iii) $-\dfrac{3}{4}, x \neq y$ **iv)** $\dfrac{9x - 2}{2}, x \neq \dfrac{2}{9}$

7. a) $x + 1$
b) $x \neq 1$, as this would make a width of 0, and $x \neq -1$, as this would make a length of 0.

8. Example: The same processes are used for rational expressions as for fractions. Multiplying involves finding the product of the numerators and then the product of the denominators. To divide, you multiply by the reciprocal of the divisor. The differences are that rational expressions involve variables and may have non-permissible values.

$\left(\dfrac{1}{2}\right)\left(\dfrac{3}{5}\right) = \dfrac{(1)(3)}{(2)(5)}$ $= \dfrac{3}{10}$	$\dfrac{x + 2}{2} \times \dfrac{x + 3}{5} = \dfrac{(x + 2)(x + 3)}{(2)(5)}$ $= \dfrac{x^2 + 5x + 6}{10}$
$\dfrac{3}{4} \div \dfrac{1}{2} = \left(\dfrac{3}{4}\right)\left(\dfrac{2}{1}\right)$ $= \dfrac{3}{2}$	$\dfrac{x + 2}{4} \div \dfrac{x + 1}{2} = \dfrac{x + 2}{4} \times \dfrac{2}{x + 1}$ $= \dfrac{x + 2}{2(x + 1)}, x \neq -1$

9. a) $\dfrac{5q}{2r}, r \neq 0, p \neq 0$ **b)** $\dfrac{m^2}{4t^3}, m \neq 0, t \neq 0$

c) $\dfrac{3}{2}, a \neq -b$

d) $\dfrac{2(x - 2)(x + 5)}{(x^2 + 25)}, x \neq -2, 0$

e) $1, d \neq -3, -2, -1$

f) $\dfrac{-(y - 8)(y + 5)}{(y - 1)}, y \neq \pm 1, 5, 9$

10. a) $8t$ **b)** $\dfrac{1}{b}, a \neq 0, b \neq 0$

c) $\dfrac{-1}{5(x + y)}, x \neq \pm y$ **d)** $\dfrac{3}{a + 3}, a \neq \pm 3$

e) $\dfrac{1}{x + 1}, x \neq -2, -1, 0, \pm \dfrac{2}{3}$

f) $\dfrac{-(x + 2)}{3}, x \neq 2$

11. a) $\dfrac{m}{2}, m \neq 0$ **b)** $\dfrac{x - 1}{x}, x \neq -3, -2, 0, 2$

c) $\dfrac{1}{6}, a \neq \pm 3, 4$ **d)** $\dfrac{1}{5}, x \neq 3, -\dfrac{4}{3}, -4$

12. x centimetres
13. a) $10x$
b) $(x - 2)(x + 1)$
Example: The advantage is that less simplifying needs to be done.

14. a) $\dfrac{m+3}{5}$ **b)** $\dfrac{m}{x}, x \neq 0$

c) $1, x \neq -y$ **d)** -1

e) $\dfrac{1}{x-y}, x \neq \pm y$

15. a) $\dfrac{5x}{12}$ **b)** $1, y \neq 0$

c) $\dfrac{9x+34}{(x+3)(x-3)}, x \neq \pm 3$

d) $\dfrac{a}{(a+3)(a-2)}, a \neq -3, 2$

e) $1, a \neq \pm b$

f) $\dfrac{2x^2 - 6x - 3}{(x+1)(2x-3)(2x+3)}, x \neq -1, \pm\dfrac{3}{2}$

16. a) $\dfrac{1}{a} + \dfrac{1}{b} = \dfrac{a+b}{ab}$

b) Left Side $= \dfrac{1}{a} + \dfrac{1}{b}$

$= \dfrac{b}{ab} + \dfrac{a}{ab}$

$= \dfrac{a+b}{ab}$

$=$ Right Side

17. Exam mark, $d = \dfrac{a+b+c}{3}$;

Final mark $= \left(\dfrac{1}{2}\right)\left(\dfrac{a+b+c}{3}\right) + \left(\dfrac{1}{2}\right)d$

$= \dfrac{a+b+c+3d}{6}$

Example: $\dfrac{60+70+80}{3} = d$

$\dfrac{60+70+80+3(70)}{6} = 70$

18. a)   **i)** the amount that Beth spends per chair; $10 more per chair than planned

   ii) the amount that Helen spends per chair; $10 less per chair than planned

   iii) the number of chairs Helen bought

   iv) the number of chairs Beth bought

   v) the total number of chairs purchased by the two sisters

b) $\dfrac{450c - 500}{c^2 - 100}$ or $\dfrac{50(9c-10)}{(c-10)(c+10)}, c \neq \pm 10$

19. Example: When solving a rational equation, you multiply all terms by the LCD to eliminate the denominators. In addition and subtraction of rational expressions, you use an LCD to simplify by grouping terms over one denominator.

Add or subtract.	Solve.
$\dfrac{x}{3} + \dfrac{x}{2}$	$\dfrac{x}{3} + \dfrac{x}{2} = 5$
$= \dfrac{2x}{6} + \dfrac{3x}{6}$	$2x + 3x = 30$
$= \dfrac{5x}{6}$	$5x = 30$
	$x = 6$

20. a) $s = -9, s \neq -3$

b) $x = -4$ or $x = -1, x \neq 1, -\dfrac{2}{3}$

c) $z = 1, z \neq 0$

d) $m = 1$ or $m = -\dfrac{21}{2}, m \neq \pm 3$

e) no solution, $x \neq 3$

f) $x = \dfrac{\pm\sqrt{6}}{2}, x \neq 0, -\dfrac{1}{2}$

g) $x = -5$ or $x = 1, x \neq -2, 3$

21. The numbers are 4 and 8.

22. Elaine would take 7.5 h.

23. a) $\dfrac{160}{x} + 36 + \dfrac{160}{x+0.7} = 150$

b) $570x^2 - 1201x - 560 = 0, x = 2.5$ m/s.

c) The rate of ascent is 9 km/h.

Chapter 6 Practice Test, page 355

1. D

2. B

3. A

4. A

5. D

6. $x \neq -3, -1, 3, \dfrac{5}{3}$

7. $k = -1$

8. $\dfrac{5y-2}{6}, y \neq 2$

9. Let x represent the time for the smaller auger to fill the bin.

$\dfrac{6}{x} + \dfrac{6}{x-5} = 1$

10. Example: For both you use an LCD. When solving, you multiply by the LCD to eliminate the denominators, while in addition and subtraction of rational expressions, you use the LCD to group terms over a single denominator.

Add or subtract.	Solve.
$\dfrac{x}{4} - \dfrac{x}{7}$	$\dfrac{x}{5} + \dfrac{x}{3} = 16$
$= \dfrac{7x}{28} - \dfrac{4x}{28}$	$15\left(\dfrac{x}{5}\right) + 15\left(\dfrac{x}{3}\right) = 15(16)$
$= \dfrac{3x}{28}$	$3x + 5x = 240$
	$8x = 240$
	$x = 30$

11. $x = 4; x \neq -2, 3$

12. $\dfrac{5x+3}{5x} - \dfrac{2x-1}{2x} = \dfrac{2x-1}{2x} - \dfrac{3-x}{x}; x = 2.3$

13. The speed in calm air is 372 km/h.

Chapter 7 Absolute Value and Reciprocal Functions

7.1 Absolute Value, pages 363 to 367

1. a) 9   **b)** 0   **c)** 7

d) 4.728   **e)** 6.25   **f)** 5.5

2. $-0.8, -0.4, \left|\dfrac{3}{5}\right|, |0.8|, 1.1, \left|-1\dfrac{1}{4}\right|, |-2|$

3. $2.2, \left|-\dfrac{7}{5}\right|, |1.3|, \left|1\dfrac{1}{10}\right|, |-0.6|, -1.9, -2.4$

4. a) 7   **b)** −5   **c)** 10   **d)** 13

5. Examples:
- **a)** $|2.1 - (-6.7)| = 8.8$ **b)** $|5.8 - (-3.4)| = 9.2$
- **c)** $|2.1 - (-3.4)| = 5.5$ **d)** $|-6.7 - 5.8| = 12.5$

6. a) 10   **b)** −2.8   **c)** 5.25   **d)** 9   **e)** 17

7. Examples:
- **a)** $|3 - 8| = 5$ **b)** $|-8 - 12| = 20$
- **c)** $|9 - 2| = 7$ **d)** $|15 - (-7)| = 22$
- **e)** $|a - b|$ **f)** $|m - n|$

8. $|7 - (-11)| + |-9 - 7|$; 34 °C

9. Example:
$|24 - 0| + |24 - 10| + |24 - 17| + |24 - 30| +$
$|24 - 42| + |24 - 55| + |24 - 72|$; 148 km

10. 1743 miles

11. a) \$369.37
- **b)** The net change is the change from the beginning point to the end point. The total change is all the changes in between added up.

12. a) 7.5   **b)** 90   **c)** 0.875

13. 4900 m or 4.9 km

14. a) 1649 ft   **b)** 2325 ft

15. \$0.36

16. a) 6 km   **b)** 9 km

17. a) The students get the same result of 90.66.
- **b)** It does not matter the order in which you square something and take the absolute value of it.
- **c)** Yes, because the result of squaring a number is the same whether it was positive or negative.

18. a) Michel looks at both cases; the argument is either positive or negative.
- **b)** **i)** $|x - 7| = \begin{cases} x - 7 \text{ if } x \geq 7 \\ 7 - x \text{ if } x < 7 \end{cases}$

     ii) $|2x - 1| = \begin{cases} 2x - 1 \text{ if } x \geq \frac{1}{2} \\ 1 - 2x \text{ if } x < \frac{1}{2} \end{cases}$

     iii) $|3 - x| = \begin{cases} 3 - x, \text{ if } x \leq 3 \\ x - 3, \text{ if } x > 3 \end{cases}$

     iv) $x^2 + 4$

19. Example: Changing +5 to −5 is incorrect.
Example: Change the sign so that it is positive.

20. 83 mm

21. Example: when you want just the speed of something and not the velocity

22. Example: signed because you want positive for up, negative for down, and zero for the top

23. a) 176 cm
- **b)** 4; 5; 2; 1; 4; 8; 1; 1; 2; 28 is the sum
- **c)** 3.11
- **d)** It means that most of the players are within 3.11 cm of the mean.

24. a) **i)** $x = 1, x = -3$
-    **ii)** $x = 1, x = -5$; you can verify by trying them in the equation.
- **b)** It has no zeros. This method can only be used for functions that have zeros.

25. Example: Squaring a number makes it positive, while the square root returns only the positive root.

7.2 Absolute Value Functions, pages 375 to 379

1. a)

x	$y = |f(x)|$
−2	3
−1	1
0	1
1	3
2	5

b)

x	$y = |f(x)|$
−2	0
−1	2
0	2
1	0
2	4

2. $(-5, 8)$

3. x-intercept: 3; y-intercept: 4

4. x-intercepts: −2, 7; y-intercept: $\frac{3}{2}$

5. a)
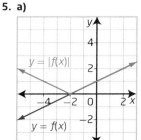
b)
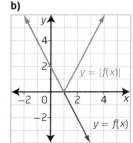

c)
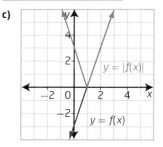

6. a) x-intercept: 3; y-intercept: 6; domain: $\{x \mid x \in R\}$; range: $\{y \mid y \geq 0, y \in R\}$

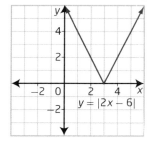

b) *x*-intercept: −5; *y*-intercept: 5;
domain: $\{x \mid x \in R\}$; range: $\{y \mid y \geq 0, y \in R\}$

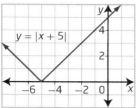

c) *x*-intercept: −2; *y*-intercept: 6;
domain: $\{x \mid x \in R\}$; range: $\{y \mid y \geq 0, y \in R\}$

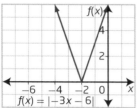

d) *x*-intercept: −3; *y*-intercept: 3;
domain: $\{x \mid x \in R\}$; range: $\{y \mid y \geq 0, y \in R\}$

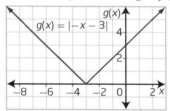

e) *x*-intercept: 4; *y*-intercept: 2;
domain: $\{x \mid x \in R\}$; range: $\{y \mid y \geq 0, y \in R\}$

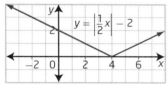

f) *x*-intercept: −9; *y*-intercept: 3;
domain $\{x \mid x \in R\}$; range $\{y \mid y \geq 0, y \in R\}$

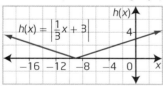

7. a)

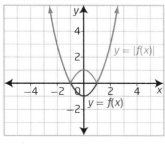

b)

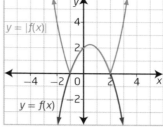

c)

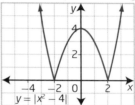

8. a) *x*-intercepts: −2, 2; *y*-intercept: 4;
domain: $\{x \mid x \in R\}$; range: $\{y \mid y \geq 0, y \in R\}$

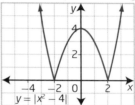

b) *x*-intercepts: −3, −2; *y*-intercept: 6;
domain: $\{x \mid x \in R\}$; range: $\{y \mid y \geq 0, y \in R\}$

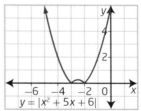

c) *x*-intercepts: −2, 0.5; *y*-intercept: 2;
domain: $\{x \mid x \in R\}$; range: $\{y \mid y \geq 0, y \in R\}$

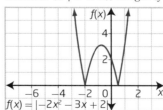

d) x-intercepts: −6, 6; y-intercept: 9;
domain: $\{x \mid x \in R\}$; range: $\{y \mid y \geq 0, y \in R\}$

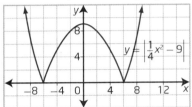

e) y-intercept: 10; domain: $\{x \mid x \in R\}$;
range: $\{y \mid y \geq 1, y \in R\}$

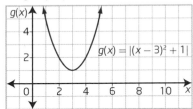

f) y-intercept: 16; domain: $\{x \mid x \in R\}$;
range: $\{y \mid y \geq 4, y \in R\}$

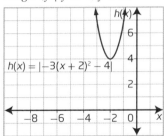

9. a) $y = 2x - 2$ if $x \geq 1$
$y = 2 - 2x$ if $x < 1$
b) $y = 3x + 6$ if $x \geq -2$
$y = -3x - 6$ if $x < -2$
c) $y = \frac{1}{2}x - 1$ if $x \geq 2$
$y = 1 - \frac{1}{2}x$ if $x < 2$

10. a) $y = 2x^2 - 2$ if $x \leq -1$ or $x \geq 1$
$y = -2x^2 + 2$ if $-1 < x < 1$
b) $y = (x - 1.5)^2 - 0.25$ if $x \leq 1$ or $x \geq 2$
$y = -(x - 1.5)^2 + 0.25$ if $1 < x < 2$
c) $y = 3(x - 2)^2 - 3$ if $x \leq 1$ or $x \geq 3$
$y = -3(x - 2)^2 + 3$ if $1 < x < 3$

11. a) $y = x - 4$ if $x \geq 4$
$y = 4 - x$, if $x < 4$
b) $y = 3x + 5$ if $x \geq -\frac{5}{3}$
$y = -3x - 5$ if $x < -\frac{5}{3}$
c) $y = -x^2 + 1$ if $-1 \leq x \leq 1$
$y = x^2 - 1$ if $x < -1$ or $x > 1$
d) $y = x^2 - x - 6$ if $x \leq -2$ or $x \geq 3$
$y = -x^2 + x + 6$ if $-2 < x < 3$

12. a)

x	g(x)
−1	8
0	6
2	2
3	0
5	4

b)

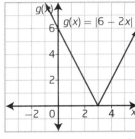

c) domain: $\{x \mid x \in R\}$; range: $\{y \mid y \geq 0, y \in R\}$
d) $y = 6 - 2x$ if $x \leq 3$
$y = 2x - 6$ if $x > 3$

13. a) y-intercept: 8; x-intercepts: −2, 4
b)

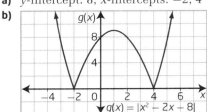

c) domain: $\{x \mid x \in R\}$; range: $\{y \mid y \geq 0, y \in R\}$
d) $y = x^2 - 2x - 8$ if $x \leq -2$ or $x \geq 4$;
$y = -x^2 + 2x + 8$ if $-2 < x < 4$

14. a) x-intercepts: $-\frac{2}{3}$, 2; y-intercept: 4
b)

c) domain: $\{x \mid x \in R\}$; range: $\{y \mid y \geq 0, y \in R\}$
d) $y = 3x^2 - 4x - 4$ if $x \leq -\frac{2}{3}$ or $x \geq 2$;
$y = -3x^2 + 4x + 4$ if $-\frac{2}{3} < x < 2$

15. Michael is right. Since the vertex of the original function is below the x-axis, the absolute value function will have a different range and a different graph.

16. a)

y-intercept graph with $y = |0.475x - 55.1|$

b) (116, 0)
c) (236, 57) is where the puck will be at the far side of the table, which is right in the middle of the goal.

17. The distance travelled is 13 m.

18. a) The two graphs are identical. They are identical because one is the negative of the other but since they are in absolute value brackets there is no change.

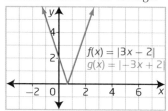

$$f(x) = |3x - 2|$$
$$g(x) = |-3x + 2|$$

b) $f(x) = |-4x - 3|$

19. $f(x) = |-x^2 + 6x - 5|$

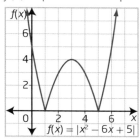

$$f(x) = |x^2 - 6x + 5|$$

20. $a = -4, b = 6$ or $a = 4, b = -6$

21. $b = 4; c = -12$

22. Example: The square of something is always positive, so taking the absolute value does nothing.

23. Example: No, it is not true for all $x, y \in R$. For instance, if x and y are of different sign the left side will not equal the right side.

24.

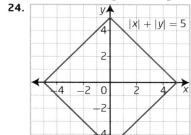

$$|x| + |y| = 5$$

25.

Case	$|x||y|$	$|xy|$
$x \geq 0, y \geq 0$	xy	xy
$x \geq 0, y < 0$	$x(-y)$	$-xy$
$x < 0, y \geq 0$	$(-x)y$	$-xy$
$x < 0, y < 0$	$(-x)(-y)$	xy

26. Example: They have the same shape but different positions.

27. Example: Graph the functions, taking care to allow them only in their specified domain.

28. If the discriminant is less than or equal to 0 and $a > 0$, then the graphs will be equivalent.

29. Examples:
Step 1 Yes.
Step 2 Absolute value is needed because the facility could be to the east or west of each town.
total $= |x| + |x - 10| + |x - 17| + |x - 30|$
$\qquad + |x - 42| + |x - 55| + |x - 72|$
Step 3 x: [0, 60, 10]
y: [−30, 300, 20]
Step 4 The point (30, 142) on the graph shows that there is a point that minimizes

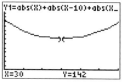

the distance to each city. The point represents a place 30 km east of Allenby and results in a total distance from all towns of 142 km.

30. a) $y = |(x - 3)^2 + 7|$ **b)** $y = \left|\frac{4}{5}(x + 3)^2\right|$

c) $y = |-x^2 - 6|$ **d)** $y = |5(x + 3)^2 + 3|$

7.3 Absolute Value Equations, pages 389 to 391

1. a) $x = -7, x = 7$ **b)** $x = -4, x = 4$
c) $x = 0$ **d)** no solution
2. a) $x = -6, x = 14$ **b)** $x = -5, x = -1$
c) $x = -14, x = -2$ **d)** no solution
3. a) $|x| = 2$ **b)** $|x - 2| = 6$
c) $|x - 4| = 5$
4. a) $x = -19, x = 5$ **b)** $x = \frac{2}{3}, x = 2$
c) no solution   **d)** $x = 3.5, x = 10.5$
5. a) no solution   **b)** $x = -9, x = 1$
c) $m = -\frac{1}{3}, m = 3$ **d)** no solution
e) $a = -\frac{11}{3}, a = -3$
6. a) $x = -3, x = \sqrt{3}$ **b)** $x = 2, x = 3$
c) $x \leq -3$ or $x \geq 3$
d) $x = \frac{1 + \sqrt{5}}{2}, x = \frac{\sqrt{5} - 1}{2}$
e) $x = -4, x = -2, x = 4, x = 6$
7. a) $|d - 18| = 0.5$
b) 17.5 mm and 18.5 mm are allowed
8. a) $|c - 299\ 792\ 456.2| = 1.1$
b) 299 792 455.1 m/s or 299 792 457.3 m/s
9. a) $|V - 50\ 000| = 2000$ **b)** 48 000 L, 52 000 L
10. a) 2.2, 11.8   **b)** $|x - 7| = 4.8$
11. a) 66.5 g   **b)** 251 mL and 265 mL
12. a) perigee: 356 400 km; apogee: 406 700 km
b) Example: The moon is usually around 381 550 km away plus or minus 25 150 km.
13. a) greater than or equal to zero
b) less than or equal to zero
14. a) $x = \frac{b + c}{a}$ if $x \geq 0$, $x = \frac{-b - c}{a}$ if $x < 0$; $b + c \geq 0, a \neq 0$
b) $x = b + c$ if $x \geq b$, $x = b - c$ if $x < b$; $c \geq 0$

15. Andrea is correct. Erin did not choose the two cases correctly.

16. $|t - 11.5| = 2.5$; $t = 9$ °C, $t = 14$ °C

17. a) $|x - 81| = 16.2$; 64.8 mg, 97.2 mg
   b) Example: They might lean toward 97.2 mg because it would provide more relief because there is more of the active ingredient.

18. $|t - 10| = 2$

19. a) sometimes true; $x \neq -1$
   b) sometimes true; if $x = -a$, then the solution is 0. For all other values of x, the solution is greater than 0.
   c) always true

20. Examples:
   a) $|x - 3| = 5$ **b)** $|x| = -2$
   c) $|x| = 0$ **d)** $|x| = 5$

21. Yes; the positive case is $ax + b = 0$, which always has a solution.

22. a) $|x - 3| = 4$ **b)** $|x^2 - 4| = 5$

23. Example: The first equation has no solution because an absolute value expression cannot equal a negative number. The second equation has two solutions because the absolute value expression equates to a positive number, so two cases are possible.

24. Example: When solving each case, the solutions generated are for the domain $\{x \mid x \in \mathbb{R}\}$. However, since each case is only valid for a specific domain, solutions outside of that domain are extraneous.

7.4 Reciprocal Functions, pages 403 to 409

1. a) $y = \dfrac{1}{2 - x}$ **b)** $y = \dfrac{1}{3x - 5}$

   c) $y = \dfrac{1}{x^2 - 9}$ **d)** $y = \dfrac{1}{x^2 - 7x + 10}$

2. a) i) $x = -5$ **ii)** $y = \dfrac{1}{x + 5}$ **iii)** $x \neq -5$
   iv) The zeros of the original function are the non-permissible values of the reciprocal function.
   v) $x = -5$

   b) i) $x = -\dfrac{1}{2}$ **ii)** $y = \dfrac{1}{2x + 1}$ **iii)** $x \neq -\dfrac{1}{2}$
   iv) The zeros of the original function are the non-permissible values of the reciprocal function.
   v) $x = -\dfrac{1}{2}$

   c) i) $x = -4$, $x = 4$ **ii)** $y = \dfrac{1}{x^2 - 16}$
   iii) $x \neq -4$, $x \neq 4$
   iv) The zeros of the original function are the non-permissible values of the reciprocal function.

   v) $x = -4$, $x = 4$
   d) i) $x = 3$, $x = -4$ **ii)** $y = \dfrac{1}{x^2 + x - 12}$
   iii) $x \neq 3$, $x \neq -4$
   iv) The zeros of the original function are the non-permissible values of the reciprocal function.
   v) $x = 3$, $x = -4$

3. a) $x = 2$ **b)** $x = -\dfrac{7}{3}$
   c) $x = 2$, $x = -4$ **d)** $x = 4$, $x = 5$

4. When $x = 3$, there is a division by zero, which is undefined.

5. a) no x-intercepts, y-intercept: $\dfrac{1}{5}$

   b) no x-intercepts, y-intercept: $-\dfrac{1}{4}$

   c) no x-intercepts, y-intercept: $-\dfrac{1}{9}$

   d) no x-intercepts, y-intercept: $\dfrac{1}{12}$

6. Example: Locate zeros and invariant points. Use these points to help sketch the graph of the reciprocal function.

   a)
   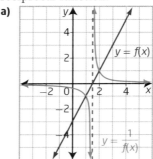

   b)
   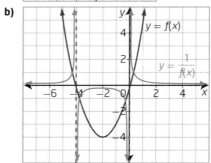

   c)
   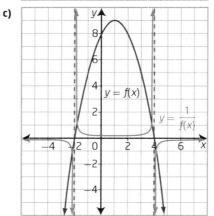

7. a)

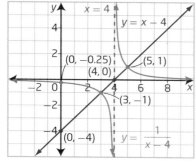

b)

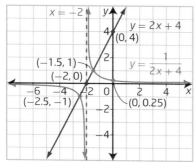

c)

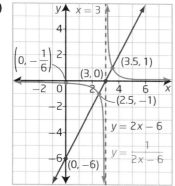

d)

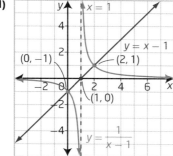

8. a)

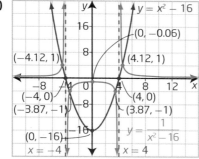

b)

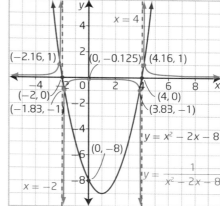

c)

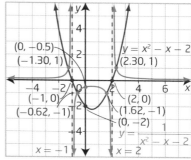

d)

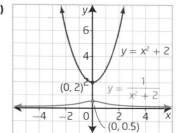

9. a) D   **b)** C   **c)** A   **d)** B

10. a) i)

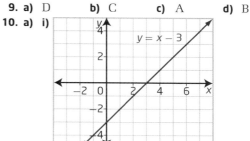

ii) Example: Use the vertical asymptote to find the zero of the function. Then, use the invariant point and the x-intercept to graph the function.

iii) $y = x - 3$

b) i)

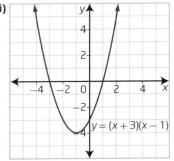

$y = (x + 3)(x - 1)$

ii) Example: Use the vertical asymptotes to find the zeros of the function. Then, use the given point to determine the vertex and then graph the function.

iii) $y = (x + 3)(x - 1)$

11. a)

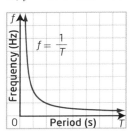

$f = \dfrac{1}{T}$

b) $y = T$

c) 0.4 Hz

d) 0.625 s

12. a)

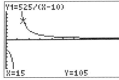

b) $\{d \mid d > 10, d \in R\}$

c) 17.5 min

d) 23.125 m; it means that the diver has a maximum of 40 min at a depth of 23.125 m.

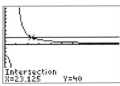

e) Yes; at large depths it is almost impossible to not stop for decompression.

13. a) $p = \dfrac{1}{P}$

b)

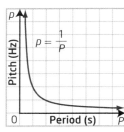

$p = \dfrac{1}{P}$

c) 20.8 Hz

14. a) $I = 0.004\dfrac{1}{d^2}$

b)

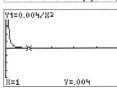

c) 0.000 16 W/m²

15. a) Example: Complete the square to change it to vertex form.

b) Example: The vertex helps with the location of the maximum for the U-shaped section of the graph of $g(x)$.

c)

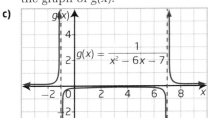

$g(x) = \dfrac{1}{x^2 - 6x - 7}$

16. a) $k = 720\ 000$ **b)**

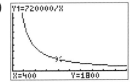

c) 1800 days

d) 1440 workers

17.

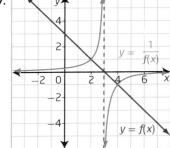

$y = \dfrac{1}{f(x)}$

$y = f(x)$

18. a) False; only if the function has a zero is this true.

b) False; only if the function has a zero is this true.

c) False; sometimes there is an undefined value.

19. a) Both students are correct. The non-permissible values are the roots of the corresponding equation.

b) Yes

20. a) $v = 60$ mm   **b)** $f = 205.68$ mm

21. Step 1

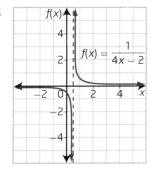

$f(x) = \dfrac{1}{4x - 2}$

Step 2

a)

x	f(x)
0	−0.5
0.4	−2.5
0.45	−5
0.47	−8.33
0.49	−25
0.495	−50
0.499	−250

x	f(x)
1	0.5
0.6	2.5
0.55	5
0.53	8.33
0.51	25
0.505	50
0.501	250

b) The function approaches infinity or negative infinity. The function will always approach infinity or negative infinity.

Step 3

a)

x	f(x)
−10	$-\dfrac{1}{42}$
−100	$-\dfrac{1}{402}$
−1000	$-\dfrac{1}{4002}$
−10 000	$-\dfrac{1}{40\ 002}$
−100 000	$-\dfrac{1}{400\ 002}$

x	f(x)
10	$\dfrac{1}{38}$
100	$\dfrac{1}{398}$
1000	$\dfrac{1}{3998}$
10 000	$\dfrac{1}{39\ 998}$
100 000	$\dfrac{1}{399\ 998}$

b) The function approaches zero.

22.

y = f(x)	$y = \dfrac{1}{f(x)}$
The absolute value of the function gets very large.	The absolute value of the function gets very small.
Function values are positive.	Reciprocal values are positive.
Function values are negative.	Reciprocal values are negative.
The zeros of the function are the x-intercepts of the graph.	The zeros of the function are the vertical asymptotes of the graph.
The value of the function is 1.	The value of the reciprocal function is 1.
The absolute value of the function approaches zero.	The absolute value of the reciprocal approaches infinity or negative infinity.
The value of the function is −1.	The value of the reciprocal function is −1.

Chapter 7 Review, pages 410 to 412

1. a) 5   **b)** 2.75   **c)** 6.7

2. $-4, -2.7, \left|1\frac{1}{2}\right|, |-1.6|, \sqrt{9}, |-3.5|, \left|-\frac{9}{2}\right|$

3. a) 9   **b)** 2   **c)** 18.75   **d)** 20

4. 43.8 km

5. a) $2.12   **b)** $4.38

6. a)

x	f(x)	g(x)
−2	−8	8
−1	−3	3
0	2	2
1	7	7
2	12	12

b)

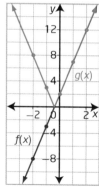

c) f(x): domain $\{x \mid x \in R\}$, range $\{y \mid y \in R\}$; g(x): domain $\{x \mid x \in R\}$, range $\{y \mid y \geq 0, y \in R\}$

d) Example: They are the same graph except the absolute value function never goes below zero; instead it reflects back over the x-axis.

7. a)

x	f(x)	g(x)
−2	4	4
−1	7	7
0	8	8
1	7	7
2	4	4

b)

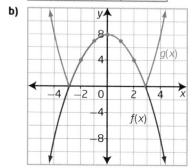

c) f(x): domain $\{x \mid x \in R\}$, range $\{y \mid y \leq 8, y \in R\}$; g(x): domain $\{x \mid x \in R\}$, range $\{y \mid y \geq 0, y \in R\}$

d) Example: They are the same graph except the absolute value function never goes below zero; instead it reflects back over the x-axis.

8. a) $y = 2x − 4$ if $x \geq 2$
$y = 4 − 2x$ if $x < 2$

b) $y = x^2 − 1$ if $x \leq −1$ or $x \geq 1$
$y = 1 − x^2$ if $−1 < x < 1$

9. a) The functions have different graphs because the initial graph goes below the x-axis. The absolute value brackets reflect anything below the x-axis above the x-axis.

b) The functions have the same graphs because the initial function is always positive.

10. $a = 15$, $b = 10$

11. a) $x = -3.5$, $x = 5.5$

b) no solution

c) $x = -3$, $x = 3$, $x \approx -1.7$, $x \approx 1.7$

d) $m = -1$, $m = 5$

12. a) $q = -11$, $q = -7$ **b)** $x = \frac{1}{4}$, $x = \frac{2}{3}$

c) $x = 0$, $x = 5$, $x = 7$

d) $x = \frac{3}{2}$, $x = \frac{-1 + \sqrt{21}}{4}$

13. a) first low tide 2.41 m; first high tide 5.74 m

b) The total change is 8.5 m.

14. The two masses are 24.78 kg and 47.084 kg.

15. a)

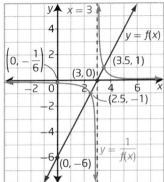

b)

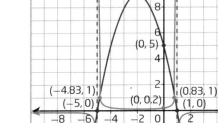
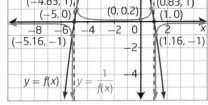

16. a)

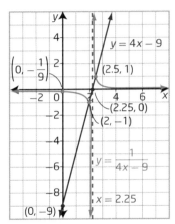

b)

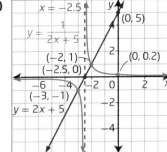

17. a) i) $y = \dfrac{1}{x^2 - 25}$

ii) The non-permissable values are $x = -5$ and $x = 5$. The equations of the vertical asymptotes are $x = -5$ and $x = 5$.

iii) no x-intercepts; y-intercept: $-\dfrac{1}{25}$

iv)

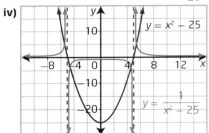

b) i) $y = \dfrac{1}{x^2 - 6x + 5}$

ii) The non-permissable values are $x = 5$ and $x = 1$. The equations of the vertical asymptotes are $x = 5$ and $x = 1$.

iii) no x-intercept; y-intercept $\dfrac{1}{5}$

iv)

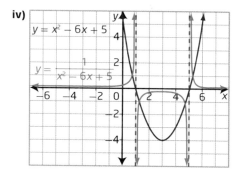

$y = x^2 - 6x + 5$

$y = \dfrac{1}{x^2 - 6x + 5}$

18. a) 240 N   **b)** 1.33 m

c) If the distance is doubled the force is halved. If the distance is tripled only a third of the force is needed.

Chapter 7 Practice Test, pages 413 to 414

1. B

2. C

3. D

4. A

5. B

6. a)

$f(x)$

$f(x) = |2x - 7|$

b) x-intercept: $\dfrac{7}{2}$; y-intercept: 7

c) domain: $\{x \mid x \in R\}$; range: $\{y \mid y \geq 0, y \in R\}$

d) $y = 2x - 7$ if $x \geq \dfrac{7}{2}$

$y = 7 - 2x$ if $x < \dfrac{7}{2}$

7. $x = 1$, $x = \dfrac{2}{3}$

8. $w = 4$, $w = \dfrac{2}{3}$

9. Example: In Case 1, the mistake is that after taking the absolute value brackets off, the inside term was incorrectly copied down. It should have been $x - 4$. Then, there are no solutions from Case 1. In Case 2, the mistake is that after taking the absolute value brackets off, the inside term was incorrectly multiplied by negative one. It should have been $-x + 4$. Then, the solutions are $x = \dfrac{-5 + \sqrt{41}}{2}$ and $x = \dfrac{-5 - \sqrt{41}}{2}$.

10. a) $y = \dfrac{1}{6 - 5x}$ **b)** $x = \dfrac{6}{5}$

c) Example: Use the asymptote already found and the invariant points to sketch the graph.

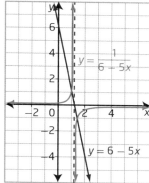

$y = \dfrac{1}{6 - 5x}$

$y = 6 - 5x$

11. a) $y = |2.5x|$ **b)** 43.6°   **c)** 39.3°

12. a)

Y1=750/(X/6400+1)²

X=1600   Y=480

b) i) 748.13 N   **ii)** 435.37 N

c) more than 25 600 km will result in a weight less than 30 N.

Cumulative Review, Chapters 5–7, pages 416 to 417

1. $\sqrt{18x^3y^6}$

2. $4abc^2\sqrt{3ac}$

3. $\sqrt[3]{8}$, $2\sqrt{3}$, $\sqrt{18}$, $\sqrt{36}$, $2\sqrt{9}$, $3\sqrt{6}$

4. a) $9\sqrt{2a}$, $a \geq 0$

b) $11x\sqrt{5}$, $x \geq 0$

5. a) $-16\sqrt[3]{3}$ **b)** $3\sqrt{2}$

c) $12a - 12\sqrt{a} + 2\sqrt{3a} - 2\sqrt{3}$, $a \geq 0$

6. a) $\sqrt{3}$ **b)** $4 - 2\sqrt{3}$

c) $-3 - 3\sqrt{2}$

7. $x = 3$

8. a) 430 ft

b) Example: The velocity would decrease with an increasing radius because of the expression $h - 2r$.

9. a) $\dfrac{a}{4b^3}$, $a \neq 0$, $b \neq 0$ **b)** $\dfrac{-1}{x - 4}$, $x \neq 4$

c) $\dfrac{(x - 3)^2(x + 5)}{(x + 2)(x + 1)(x - 1)}$, $x \neq 1, -1, -2, 3$

d) $\dfrac{1}{6}$, $x \neq 0, 2$

e) 1, $x \neq -3, -2, 2, 3$

10. a) $\dfrac{a^2 + 11a - 72}{(a + 2)(a - 7)}$, $a \neq -2, 7$

b) $\dfrac{3x^3 + x^2 - 11x + 12}{(x + 4)(x - 2)(x + 2)}$, $x \neq -4, -2, 2$

c) $\dfrac{2x^2 - x - 15}{(x - 5)(x + 5)(x + 1)}$, $x \neq -5, -1, 5$

11. Example: No; they are not equivalent because the expression should have the restriction of $x \neq -5$.

12. $x = 12$

13. $\dfrac{1}{4}$

14. $|4 - 6|$, $|-5|$, $|8.4|$, $|2(-4) - 5|$

15. a) $y = 3x - 6$ if $x \geq 2$
$y = 6 - 3x$ if $x < 2$

b) $y = \dfrac{1}{3}(x - 2)^2 - 3$ if $x \leq -1$ or $x \geq 5$
$y = -\dfrac{1}{3}(x - 2)^2 + 3$ if $-1 < x < 5$

16. a) i)

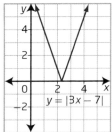

ii) x-intercept: $\dfrac{7}{3}$; y-intercept: 7

iii) domain: $\{x \mid x \in R\}$; range: $\{y \mid y \geq 0, y \in R\}$

b) i)

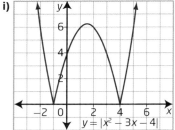

ii) x-intercepts: -1, 4; y-intercept: 4

iii) domain: $\{x \mid x \in R\}$; range: $\{y \mid y \geq 0, y \in R\}$

17. a) $x = 5$, $x = -4$ **b)** $x = 3$, $x = -3$

18. a) Example: Absolute value must be used because area is always positive.

b) Area = 7

19.

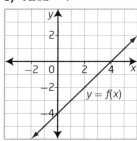

$f(x) = x - 4$

20.

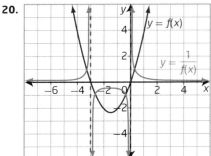

21.

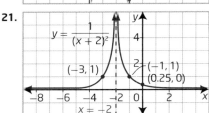

22. a) Example: The shape, range, and y-intercept will be different for $y = |f(x)|$.

b) Example: The graph of the reciprocal function has a horizontal asymptote at $y = 0$ and a vertical asymptote at $x = \dfrac{1}{3}$.

Unit 3 Test, pages 418 to 419

1. C
2. D
3. B
4. C
5. D
6. B
7. D
8. B
9. 3
10. $\dfrac{\sqrt{10}}{6}$
11. 28
12. -2
13. $-2, 2$
14. 5, $3\sqrt{7}$, $6\sqrt{2}$, $4\sqrt{5}$
15. a) Example: Square both sides.
    b) $x \geq 2.5$ **c)** There are no solutions.
16. $\dfrac{4(2x + 5)}{(x - 4)}$, $x \neq -2.5, -2, 1, 0.5, 4$
17. Example:
    a) $\dfrac{2x}{x} = \dfrac{x + 10}{x + 3}$ **b)** $x \neq -3, 0$ **c)** $x = 4$
18. a)

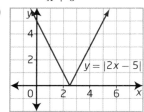

b) y-intercept: 5; x-intercept: $\dfrac{5}{2}$

c) domain: $\{x \mid x \in R\}$; range: $\{y \mid y \geq 0, y \in R\}$

d) $y = 2x - 5$ if $x \geq \dfrac{5}{2}$

$y = 5 - 2x$ if $x < \dfrac{5}{2}$

19. $x = \dfrac{3 \pm \sqrt{17}}{2}$, 1, 2

20.

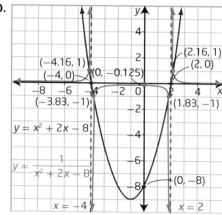

21. a) $t = \dfrac{72}{s}$ **b)** 4.97 ft/s   **c)** 11.43 s

Chapter 8 Systems of Equations

8.1 Solving Systems of Equations Graphically, pages 435 to 439

1. a) System A models the situation: to go off a ramp at different heights means two positive vertical intercepts, and in this system the launch angles are different, causing the bike with the lower trajectory to land sooner. System B is not correct because it shows both jumps starting from the same height. System C has one rider start from zero, which would mean no ramp. In System D, a steeper trajectory would mean being in the air longer but the rider is going at the same speed.

b) The rider was at the same height and at the same time after leaving the jump regardless of which ramp was chosen.

2. For $(0, -5)$: In $y = -x^2 + 4x - 5$:

Left Side   Right Side
$y = -5$ $-x^2 + 4x - 5$
                          $= -(0)^2 + 4(0) - 5$
                          $= -5$
Left Side = Right Side

In $y = x - 5$:
Left Side   Right Side
$y = -5$ $x - 5$
                          $= 0 - 5$
                          $= -5$
Left Side = Right Side

For $(3, -2)$: In $y = -x^2 + 4x - 5$:

Left Side   Right Side
$y = -2$ $-x^2 + 4x - 5$
                          $= -(3)^2 + 4(3) - 5$
                          $= -2$
Left Side = Right Side

In $y = x - 5$:
Left Side   Right Side
$y = -2$ $x - 5$
                          $= 3 - 5$
                          $= -2$
Left Side = Right Side
So, both solutions are verified.

3. a) linear-quadratic; $(-4, 1)$ and $(-1, -2)$

b) quadratic-quadratic; no solution

c) linear-quadratic; $(1, -4)$

4. a)

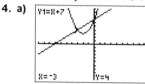 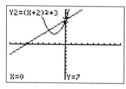

$(-3, 4)$ and $(0, 7)$

b)

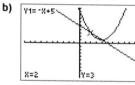 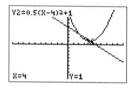

$(2, 3)$ and $(4, 1)$

c)

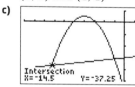 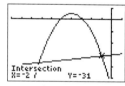

$(-14.5, -37.25)$ and $(-2, -31)$

d)

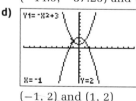 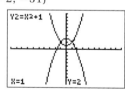

$(-1, 2)$ and $(1, 2)$

e)

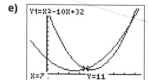 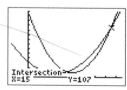

$(7, 11)$ and $(15, 107)$

5. a)

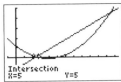

(5, 5) and (23, 221) or $d = 5$, $h = 5$ and $d = 23$, $h = 221$

b)

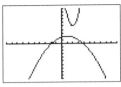

no solution

c)

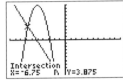 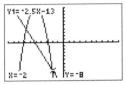

$(-6.75, 3.875)$ and $(-2, -8)$ or $v = -6.75$, $t = 3.875$ and $v = -2$, $t = -8$

d)

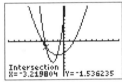 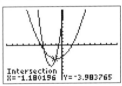

$(-3.22, -1.54)$ and $(-1.18, -3.98)$ or $n = -3.22$, $m = -1.54$ and $n = -1.18$, $m = -3.98$

e)

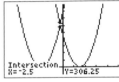

$(-2.5, 306.25)$ or $h = -2.5$, $t = 306.25$

6. The two parabolas have the same vertex, but different values of a.
Example: $y = x^2$ and $y = 2x^2$.

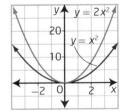

7. Examples:

a)   **b)**

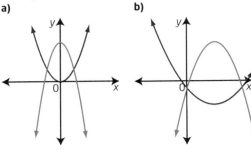

c)   **d)**

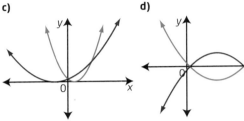

8. Examples:
  a) $y = x - 3$ **b)** $y = -2$ **c)** $y = x - 1$

9. a) (100, 3800) and (1000, 8000)
  b) When he makes and sells either 100 or 1000 shirts, Jonas makes no profit as costs equal revenue.
  c) Example: (550, 15 500). This quantity (550 shirts) has the greatest difference between cost and revenue.

10. (0, 3.9) and (35.0, 3.725)

11. a) $d = 1.16t^2$ and $d = 1.74(t - 3)^2$
  b) A suitable domain is $0 \le t \le 23$.

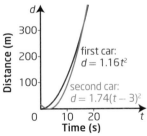

  c)

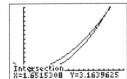 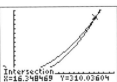

(1.65, 3.16) and (16.35, 310.04) While (1.65, 3.16) is a graphical solution to the system, it is not a solution to the problem since the second car starts 3 s after the first car.
  d) At 16.35 s after the first car starts, both cars have travelled the same distance.

12. a)

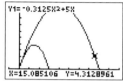

Both start at (0, 0), at the fountain, and they have one other point in common, approximately (0.2, 1.0). The tallest stream reaches higher and farther than the smaller stream.

b)

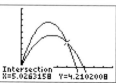

They both start at (0, 0), but the second stream passes through the other fountain's spray 5.03 m from the fountain, at a height of 4.21 m.

13. a) Let x represent the smaller integer and y the larger integer. $x + y = 21$, $2x^2 - 15 = y$.

b)

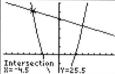 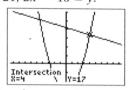

One point of intersection does not give integers. The two integers are 4 and 17.

14. a) The blue line and the parabola intersect at (2, 2). The green line and the parabola intersect at (−4.54, −2.16).

b) Example: There is one possible location to leave the jump and one location for the landing.

15. a)

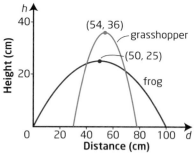

b) Frog: $y = -0.01(x - 50)^2 + 25$
Grasshopper: $y = -0.0625(x - 54)^2 + 36$

c) (40.16, 24.03) and (69.36, 21.25)

d) These are the locations where the frog and grasshopper are at the same distance and height relative to the frog's starting point. If the frog does not catch the grasshopper at the first point, there is another opportunity. However, we do not know anything about time, i.e., the speed of either one, so the grasshopper may be gone.

16. a) (0, 0) and approximately (1.26, 1.59) Since 0 is a non-permissible value for x and y, the point (0, 0) is not a solution to this system.

b) 1.26 cm

c) $V = lwh$
$V = 1.26 \times 1.26 \times 1.26$
$V = 2.000\ 376$
So, the volume is very close to 2 cm³.

d) If x represents the length of one side, then $V = x^3$. For a volume of 2 cm³, $2 = x^3$. Then, $x = \sqrt[3]{2}$ or approximately 1.26. Menaechmus did not have a calculator to find roots.

17. Examples:

a) $y = x^2 + 1$ and $y = x + 3$

b) $y = x^2 + 1$ and $y = -(x - 1)^2 + 6$

c) $y = x^2 + 1$ and $y = (x + 1)^2 - 2x$

18. Examples:

No solution: Two parabolas do not intersect and the line is between them, intersecting neither, or the parabolas are coincident and the line does not intersect them.

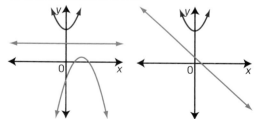

One solution: Two parabolas intersect once, with a line tangent to both curves, or the parabolas are coincident and the line is tangent.

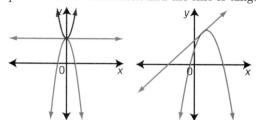

Two solutions: Two parabolas intersect twice, with a line passing through both points of intersection, or the parabolas are coincident and the line passes through two points on them.

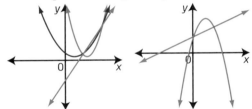

19. Example: Similarities: A different number of solutions are possible. It can be solved graphically or algebraically. Differences: Some systems involving quadratic equations cannot be solved by elimination. The systems in this section involve equations that are more difficult to solve.

20. a) Two solutions. The y-intercept of the line is above the vertex, and the parabola opens upward.
b) No solution. The parabola's vertex is at $(0, 3)$ and it opens upward, while the line has y-intercept -5 and negative slope.
c) Two solutions. One vertex is directly above the other. The upper parabola has a smaller vertical stretch factor.
d) One solution. They share the same vertex. One opens upward, the other downward.
e) No solution. The first parabola has its vertex at $(3, 1)$ and opens upward. The second parabola has it vertex at $(3, -1)$ and opens downward.
f) An infinite number of solutions. When the first equation is expanded, it is exactly the same as the second equation.

8.2 Solving Systems of Equations Algebraically, pages 451 to 456

1. In $k + p = 12$:
Left Side
$k + p$
$= 5 + 7$
$= 12$
$=$ Right Side

In $4k^2 - 2p = 86$:
Left Side
$4k^2 - 2p$
$= 4(5)^2 - 2(7)$
$= 86$
$=$ Right Side

So, $(5, 7)$ is a solution.

2. In $18w^2 - 16z^2 = -7$:

$$\text{Left Side} = 18\left(\frac{1}{3}\right)^2 - 16\left(\frac{3}{4}\right)^2$$
$$= 18\left(\frac{1}{9}\right) - 16\left(\frac{9}{16}\right)$$
$$= 2 - 9$$
$$= -7$$
$$= \text{Right Side}$$

In $144w^2 + 48z^2 = 43$:
$$\text{Left Side} = 144\left(\frac{1}{3}\right)^2 + 48\left(\frac{3}{4}\right)^2$$
$$= 16 + 27$$
$$= 43$$
$$= \text{Right Side}$$

So, $\left(\frac{1}{3}, \frac{3}{4}\right)$ is a solution.

3. a) $(-6, 38)$ and $(2, 6)$ **b)** $(0.5, 4.5)$
c) $(-2, 10)$ and $(2, 30)$
d) $(-2.24, -1.94)$ and $(2.24, 15.94)$
e) no solution

4. a) $\left(-\frac{1}{2}, 4\right)$ and $(3, 25)$
b) $(-0.5, 14.75)$ and $(8, 19)$
c) $(-1.52, -2.33)$ and $(1.52, 3.73)$
d) $(1.41, -4)$ and $(-1.41, -4)$
e) There are an infinite number of solutions.

5. a) $(2.71, -1.37)$ and $(0.25, 0.78)$
b) $(-2.41, 10.73)$ and $(2.5, 10)$
c) $(0.5, 6.25)$ and $(0.75, 9.3125)$

6. a) They are both correct.
b) Graph $n = m^2 + 7$ and $n = m^2 + 0.5$ to see that there is no point of intersection.

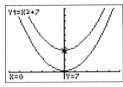

7. a) Yes. Multiplying by (-1) and then adding is equivalent to subtraction.
b) Yes.
c) Example: Adding is easier for most people. Subtracting with negative signs can be error prone.

8. $m = 6$, $n = 40$

9. a) $7x + y + 13$ **b)** $5x^2 - x$
c) $60 = 7x + y + 13$ and $10y = 5x^2 - x$. Since the perimeter and the area are both based on the same dimensions, x and y must represent the same values. You can solve the system to find the actual dimensions.
d) $(5, 12)$; the base is 24 m, the height is 10 m and the hypotenuse is 26 m.
e) A neat verification uses the Pythagorean Theorem: $24^2 + 10^2 = 676$ and $26^2 = 676$. Alternatively, in the context:
Perimeter $= 24 + 10 + 26 = 60$
Area $= \frac{1}{2}(24)(10) = 120$

10. a) $x - y = -30$ and $y + 3 + x^2 = 189$
b) $(12, 42)$ or $(-13, 17)$
c) For 12 and 42:
$12 - 42 = -30$ and
$42 + 3 + 12^2 = 189$
For -13 and 17: $-13 - 17 = -30$ and
$17 + 3 + (-13)^2 = 189$
So, both solutions check.

11. a) $C = 2\pi r$, $C = 3\pi r^2$

b) $r = \frac{2}{3}$, $C = \frac{4\pi}{3}$, $A = \frac{4\pi}{9}$

12. a) 5.86 m and 34.14 m **b)** 31.25 J

c)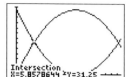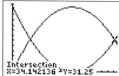

d) Find the sum of the values of E_k and E_p at several choices for d. Observe that the sum is constant, 62.5. This can be deduced from the graph because each is a reflection of the other in the horizontal line $y = 31.25$.

13. a) approximately 15.64 s

b) approximately 815.73 m

c) $h(t) = -4.9t^2 + 2015$
$$= -4.9(15.64)^2 + 2015$$
$$\approx 816.4$$
$h(t) = -10.5t + 980$
$$= -10.5(15.64) + 980$$
$$\approx 815.78$$
The solution checks. Allowing for rounding errors, the height is about 816 m when the parachute is opened after 15.64 s.

14. a)

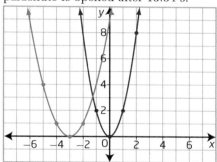

b) $(-1.3, 3)$ **c)** $y = 2x^2$ and $y = (x + 3)^2$

d) $(-1.24, 3.09)$ and $(7.24, 104.91)$ Example: The estimate was close for one point, but did not get the other.

15. a) For the first fragment, substitute $v_0 = 60$, $\theta = 45°$, and $h_0 = 2500$:
$$h(x) = -\frac{4.9}{(v_0 \cos \theta)^2}x^2 + (\tan \theta)x + h_0$$
$$h(x) = -\frac{4.9}{(60 \cos 45°)^2}x^2 + (\tan 45°)x + 2500$$
$$h(x) \approx -0.003x^2 + x + 2500$$
For the second fragment, substitute $v_0 = 60$, $\theta = 60°$, and $h_0 = 2500$:
$$h(x) = -\frac{4.9}{(v_0 \cos \theta)^2}x^2 + (\tan \theta)x + h_0$$
$$h(x) = -\frac{4.9}{(60 \cos 60°)^2}x^2 + (\tan 60°)x + 2500$$
$$h(x) \approx -0.005x^2 + 1.732x + 2500$$

b) (0, 2500) and (366, 2464.13)

c) Example: This is where the fragments are at the same height and the same distance from the summit.

16. a) The solution for the system of equations will tell the horizontal distance from and the height above the base of the mountain, where the charge lands.

b) 150.21 m

17. a) 103 items **b)** $377 125.92

18. a) $(-3.11, 0.79)$, $(3.11, 0.79)$ and $(0, 16)$

b) Example: 50 m²

19. a) $(2, 6)$ **b)** $y = -\frac{1}{4}x + \frac{13}{2}$ **c)** 2.19 units

20. $(2, 1.5)$ and $(-1, 3)$

21. $y = 0.5(x + 1)^2 - 4.5$ and $y = -x - 4$ or $y = 0.5(x + 1)^2 - 4.5$ and $y = 2x - 4$

22. Example: Graphing is relatively quick using a graphing calculator, but may be time-consuming and inaccurate using pencil and grid paper. Sometimes, rearranging the equation to enter into the calculator is a bit tricky. The algebraic methods will always give an exact answer and do not rely on having technology available. Some systems of equations may be faster to solve algebraically, especially if one variable is easily eliminated.

23. $(-3.39, -0.70)$ and $(-1.28, 4.92)$

24. Example: Express the quadratic in vertex form, $y = (x - 2)^2 - 2$. This parabola has its minimum at $(2, -2)$ and its y-intercept at 2. The linear function has its y-intercept at -2 and has a negative slope so it is never close to the parabola. Algebraically,
$$-\frac{1}{2}x - 2 = x^2 - 4x + 2$$
$$-x - 4 = 2x^2 - 8x + 4$$
$$0 = 2x^2 - 7x + 8$$
This quadratic equation has no real roots. Therefore, the graphs do not intersect.

25. Step 1: Example: In a standard viewing window, it looks like there are two solutions when $b > 0$, one solution when $b = 0$, and no solution when $b < 0$

Step 2: There are two solutions when $b > -\frac{1}{4}$, one solution when $b = -\frac{1}{4}$, and no solution when $b < -\frac{1}{4}$.

Steps 3 and 4: two solutions when $|m| > 2$, one solution when $m = \pm 2$, and no solution when $|m| < 2$

Step 5: For $m = 1$: two solutions when $b > 0$, one solution when $b = 0$, and no solution when $b < 0$; for $m = -1$: two solutions when $b < 0$, one solution when $b = 0$, and no solution when $b > 0$; two solutions when $|m| > 2b$, one solution when $m = \pm 2b$, and no solution when $|m| < 2b$

Chapter 8 Review, pages 457 to 458

1. a) $(2, -5)$

b)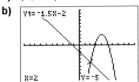

c) $(6.75, -12.125)$

2. a) no solution, one solution, two solutions

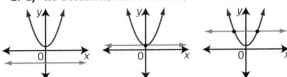

b) no solution, one solution, two solutions

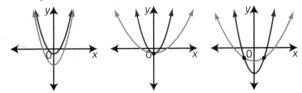

c) no solution, one solution, two solutions

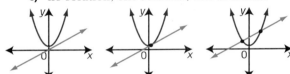

3. a)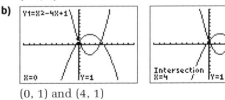

$(-6, 0)$

b)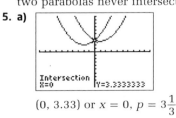

$(0, 1)$ and $(4, 1)$

4. Example: Adam is not correct. For all values of x, $x^2 + 3$ is always 2 greater than $x^2 + 1$ and the two parabolas never intersect.

5. a)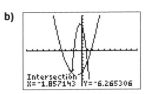

$(0, 3.33)$ or $x = 0$, $p = 3\frac{1}{3}$

b)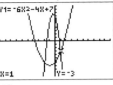

$(-1.86, -6.27)$ and $(1, -3)$

c)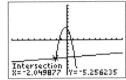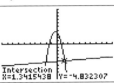

$(-2.05, -5.26)$ and $(1.34, -4.83)$ or $d = -2.05$, $t = -5.26$ and $d = -1.34$, $t = -4.83$

6. a) road arch: $y = -\dfrac{3}{32}(x - 8)^2 + 6$

river arch: $y = -\dfrac{1}{18}(x - 24)^2 + 8$

b) $(14.08, 2.53)$

c) Example: the location and height of the support footing

7. a) Example: The first equation models the horizontal distance travelled and the height of the ball; it would follow a parabolic path that opens downward. The linear equation models the profile of the hill with a constant slope.

b) $d = 0$, $h = 0$ and $d = 14.44$, $h = 7.22$

c) Example: The point $(0, 0)$ represents the starting point, where the ball was kicked. The point $(14.44, 7.22)$ is where the ball would land on the hill. The coordinates give the horizontal distance and vertical distance from the point that the ball was kicked.

8. a) Example: $(2, -3)$ and $(6, 5)$

b) $(2, -3)$ and $(6, 5)$

9. The solution $\left(\dfrac{1}{2}, 1\right)$ is correct.

10. a) $\left(\dfrac{1}{2}, \dfrac{5}{2}\right)$ and $\left(-\dfrac{5}{3}, -4\right)$; substitution, because the first equation is already solved for p

b) $(3.16, -13)$ and $(-3.16, -13)$; elimination, because it is easy to make opposite coefficients for the y-terms

c) $\left(-\dfrac{2}{3}, -\dfrac{53}{9}\right)$ and $(2, -1)$; elimination after clearing the fractions

d) $(0.88, 0.45)$ and $(-1.88, 3.22)$; substitution after isolating y in the second equation

11. a) 0 m and 100 m   **b)** 0 m and 10 m

12. a) the time when both cultures have the same rate of increase of surface area

b) $(0, 0)$ and $(6.67, 0.02)$

c) The point $(0, 0)$ represents the starting point. In 6 h 40 min, the two cultures have the same rate of increase of surface area.

Chapter 8 Practice Test, pages 459 to 460

1. C

2. C

3. B

4. D

5. D

6. $n = -4$

7. a) $\left(\dfrac{3}{4}, -\dfrac{35}{16}\right)$ and $(-2, -7)$ **b)** $(1, -4)$

8. a)

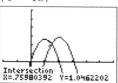

(0.76, 1.05)

b) Example: At this time, 0.76 s after Sophie starts her jump, both dancers are at the same height above the ground.

9. a) perimeter: $8y = 4x + 28$
area: $6y + 3 = x^2 + 14x + 48$

b) The perimeter is 16 m. The area is 15 m².

10. a) $y = \dfrac{1}{3}x^2$ and $y = \dfrac{1}{2}(x - 1)^2$

b) (5.45, 9.90) and (0.55, 0.10)

11. a)

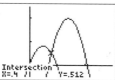

b) Example: At this point, a horizontal distance of 0.4 cm and a vertical distance of 0.512 cm from the start of the jump, the second part of the jump begins.

12. A$(-3.52, 0)$, B$(7.52, 0)$, C$(6.03, 14.29)$
area $= 78.88$ square units

Chapter 9 Linear and Quadratic Inequalities

9.1 Linear Inequalities in Two Variables, pages 472 to 475

1. a) $(6, 7)$, $(12, 9)$
b) $(-6, -12)$, $(4, -1)$, $(8, -2)$
c) $(12, -4)$, $(5, 1)$ **d)** $(3, 1)$, $(6, -4)$
2. a) $(1, 0)$, $(-2, 1)$ **b)** $(-5, 8)$, $(4, 1)$
c) $(5, 1)$ **d)** $(3, -1)$
3. a) $y \le x + 3$; slope of 1; y-intercept of 3; the boundary is a solid line.
b) $y > 3x + 5$; slope of 3; y-intercept of 5; the boundary is a dashed line.
c) $y > -4x + 7$; slope of -4; y-intercept of 7; the boundary is a dashed line.

d) $y \ge 2x - 10$; slope of 2; y-intercept of -10; the boundary is a solid line.

e) $y \ge -\dfrac{4}{5}x + 4$; slope of $-\dfrac{4}{5}$; y-intercept of 4; the boundary is a solid line.

f) $y > \dfrac{1}{2}x - 5$; slope of $\dfrac{1}{2}$; y-intercept of -5; the boundary is a dashed line.

4. a)

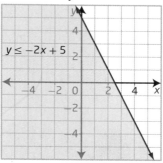

b)

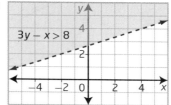

c)

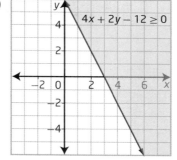

d)

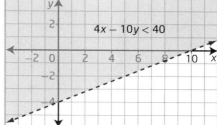

e)

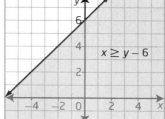

5. a) $y \geq \frac{6}{5}x - \frac{18}{5}$

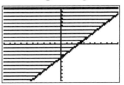

b) $y < -\frac{1}{4}x + \frac{15}{2}$

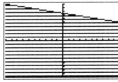

c) $y > \frac{5}{12}x + \frac{7}{3}$

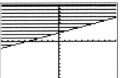

d) $y \geq \frac{1}{6}x - \frac{11}{6}$

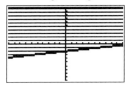

e) $y \leq \frac{36}{53}x + \frac{260}{53}$

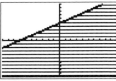

6. $y \geq -\frac{1}{5}x$

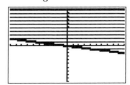

7. $y < \frac{7}{2}x$

8. Examples:
a) Graph by hand because the slope and the y-intercept are whole numbers.

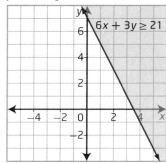

b) Graph by hand because the slope and the y-intercept are whole numbers.

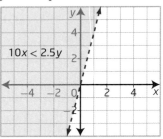

c) Graph by hand because the slope is a simple fraction and the y-intercept is 0.

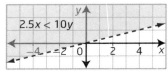

d) Graph using technology because the slope and the y-intercept are complicated fractions.

$$y \leq -\frac{489}{1279}x + \frac{14\ 500}{1279}$$

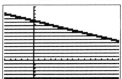

e) Graph by hand because the slope and the y-intercept are whole numbers.

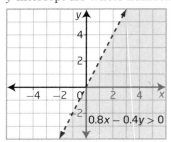

9. a) $y < \frac{1}{4}x + 2$ **b)** $y < -\frac{1}{4}x$

c) $y > \frac{3}{2}x - 4$ **d)** $y \leq -\frac{3}{4}x + 5$

10.

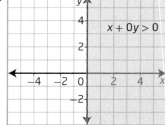

The graph of this solution is everything to the right of the y-axis.

11. a) $12x + 12y \geq 250$, where x represents the number of moccasins sold, $x \geq 0$, and y represents the hours worked, $y \geq 0$.

b)

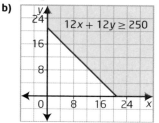

c) Example: (4, 20), (8, 16), (12, 12)

d) Example: If she loses her job, then she will still have a source of income.

12. a) $30x + 50y \leq 3000$, $x \geq 0$, $y \geq 0$, where x represents the hours of work and y represents the hours of marketing assistance.

b)

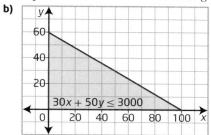

13. $0.3x + 0.05y \leq 100$, $x \geq 0$, $y \geq 0$, where x represents the number of minutes used and y represents the megabytes of data used; she should stay without a plan if her usage stays in the region described by the inequality.

14. $60x + 45y \leq 50$, $x \geq 0$, $y \geq 0$, where x represents the area of glass and y represents the mass of nanomaterial.

15. $125x + 55y \leq 7000$, $x \geq 0$, $y \geq 0$, where x represents the hours of ice rental and y represents the hours of gym rental.

16. Example:

a) $y = x^2$ **b)** $y \geq x^2$; $y < x^2$

c) This does satisfy the definition of a solution region. The boundary is a curve not a line.

17. $y \geq \frac{3}{4}x + 384$, $0 \leq x \leq 512$; $y \leq -\frac{3}{4}x + 384$,

$0 \leq x \leq 512$; $y \geq -\frac{3}{4}x + 1152$, $512 \leq x \leq 1024$;

$y \leq \frac{3}{4}x - 384$, $512 \leq x \leq 1024$

18. Step 1 $60x + 90y \leq 35\ 000$

Step 2 $y \leq -\frac{2}{3}x + \frac{3500}{9}$, $0 \leq x \leq 500$, $y \geq 0$

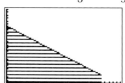

(0, 0), approximately (0, 388.9) and (500, 55.6), and (500, 0); y-intercept: the maximum number of megawatt hours of wind power that can be produced; x-intercept: the maximum number of megawatt hours of hydroelectric power that can be produced

Step 3 Example: It would be very time-consuming to attempt to find the revenue for all possible combinations of power generation. You cannot be certain that the spreadsheet gives the maximum revenue.

Step 4 The maximum revenue is $53 338, with 500 MWh of hydroelectric power and approximately 55.6 MWh of wind power.

19. Example:

	Example 1	Example 2	Example 3	Example 4
Linear Inequality	$y \geq x$	$y \leq x$	$y > x$	$y < x$
Inequality Sign	$\geq$	$\leq$	$>$	$<$
Boundary Solid/Dashed	Solid	Solid	Dashed	Dashed
Shaded Region	Above	Below	Above	Below

20. Example: Any scenario with a solution that has the form $5y + 3x \leq 150$, $x \geq 0$, $y \geq 0$ is correct.

21. a) 48 units²

b) The y-intercept is the height of the triangle. The larger it gets, the larger the area gets.

c) The slope of the inequality dictates where the x-intercept will be, which is the base of the triangle. Steeper slope gives a closer x-intercept, which gives a smaller area.

d) If you consider the magnitude, then nothing changes.

9.2 Quadratic Inequalities in One Variable, pages 484 to 487

1. a) $\{x \mid 1 \leq x \leq 3, x \in R\}$

b) $\{x \mid x \leq 1 \text{ or } x \geq 3, x \in R\}$

c) $\{x \mid x < 1 \text{ or } x > 3, x \in R\}$

d) $\{x \mid 1 < x < 3, x \in R\}$

2. a) $\{x \mid x \in R\}$ **b)** $\{x \mid x = 2, x \in R\}$

c) no solution **d)** $\{x \mid x \neq 2, x \in R\}$

3. a) not a solution **b)** solution

c) solution **d)** not a solution

4. a) $\{x \mid x \leq -10 \text{ or } x \geq 4, x \in R\}$

b) $\{x \mid x < -12 \text{ or } x > -2, x \in R\}$

c) $\left\{x \mid x < -\frac{5}{3} \text{ or } x > \frac{7}{2}, x \in R\right\}$

d) $\left\{x \mid -2 - \frac{\sqrt{6}}{2} \leq x \leq 2 + \frac{\sqrt{6}}{2}, x \in R\right\}$

5. a) $\{x \mid -6 \le x \le 3, x \in R\}$
  b) $\{x \mid x \le -3 \text{ or } x \ge -1, x \in R\}$
  c) $\left\{x \mid \dfrac{3}{4} < x < 6, x \in R\right\}$
  d) $\{x \mid -8 \le x \le 2, x \in R\}$
6. a) $\{x \mid -3 < x < 5, x \in R\}$
  b) $\{x \mid x < -12 \text{ or } x > -1, x \in R\}$
  c) $\{x \mid x \le 1 - \sqrt{6} \text{ or } x \ge 1 + \sqrt{6}, x \in R\}$
  d) $\left\{x \mid x \le -8 \text{ or } x \ge \dfrac{1}{2}, x \in R\right\}$
7. a) $\{x \mid -8 \le x \le -6, x \in R\}$
  b) $\{x \mid x \le -4 \text{ or } x \ge 7, x \in R\}$
  c) There is no solution.
  d) $\left\{x \mid x < -\dfrac{7}{2} \text{ or } x > \dfrac{9}{2}, x \in R\right\}$
8. a) $\{x \mid 2 < x < 8, x \in R\}$
    Example: Use graphing because it is a simple graph to draw.
  b) $\left\{x \mid x \le -\dfrac{3}{4} \text{ or } x \ge \dfrac{5}{3}, x \in R\right\}$
    Example: Use sign analysis because it is easy to factor.
  c) $\{x \mid 1 - \sqrt{13} \le x \le 1 + \sqrt{13}, x \in R\}$
    Example: Use test points and the zeros.
  d) $\{x \mid x \ne 3, x \in R\}$
    Example: Use case analysis because it is easy to factor and solve for the inequalities.
9. a) $\left\{x \mid \dfrac{13 - \sqrt{145}}{2} \le x \le \dfrac{13 + \sqrt{145}}{2}, x \in R\right\}$
  b) $\{x \mid x < -12 \text{ or } x > 2, x \in R\}$
  c) $\left\{x \mid x < \dfrac{5}{2} \text{ or } x > 4, x \in R\right\}$
  d) $\left\{x \mid x \le -\dfrac{8}{3} \text{ or } x \ge \dfrac{7}{2}, x \in R\right\}$
10. a) Ice equal to or thicker than $\dfrac{5\sqrt{30}}{3}$ cm, or about 9.13 cm, will support the weight of a vehicle.
  b) $9h^2 \ge 1500$
  c) Ice equal to or thicker than $\dfrac{10\sqrt{15}}{3}$ cm, or about 12.91 cm, will support the weight of a vehicle.
  d) Example: The relationship between ice strength and thickness is not linear.
11. a) $\pi x^2 \le 630\ 000$, where x represents the radius, in metres.
  b) $0 \le x \le \sqrt{\dfrac{630\ 000}{\pi}}$ **c)** $0 \text{ m} \le x \le 447.81 \text{ m}$
12. a) 2 years or more
  b) One of the solutions is negative, which does not make sense in this problem. Time cannot be negative.
  c) $-t^2 + 14 \le 5$; $t \ge 3$; 3 years or more
13. $\dfrac{x^2}{2} + x \ge 4$; the shorter leg should be greater than or equal to 2 cm.

14. a) $a > 0; b^2 - 4ac \le 0$ **b)** $a < 0; b^2 - 4ac = 0$
  c) $a \ne 0; b^2 - 4ac > 0$
15. Examples:
  a) $x^2 - 5x - 14 \le 0$ **b)** $x^2 - 11x + 10 > 0$
  c) $3x^2 - 23x + 30 \le 0$ **d)** $20x^2 + 19x + 3 > 0$
  e) $x^2 + 6x + 2 \ge 0$ **f)** $x^2 + 1 > 0$
  g) $x^2 + 1 < 0$
16. $\{x \mid x \le -\sqrt{6} \text{ or } -\sqrt{2} \le x \le \sqrt{2} \text{ or } x \ge \sqrt{6}, x \in R\}$
17. a) It is the solution because it is the set of values for which the parabola lies above the line.
  b) $-x^2 + 13x - 12 \ge 0$
  c) $\{x \mid 1 \le x \le 12, x \in R\}$
  d) They are the same solutions. The inequality was just rearranged in part c).
18. They all require this step because you need the related function to work with.
19. Answers may vary.
20. a) The solution is incorrect. He switched the inequality sign when he added 2 to both sides in the first step.
  b) $\{x \mid -3 \le x \le -2, x \in R\}$

9.3 Quadratic Inequalities in Two Variables, pages 496 to 500

1. a) $(2, 6), (-1, 3)$
  b) $(2, -2), (0, -6), (-2, -15)$
  c) None
  d) $(-4, 2), (1, 3.5), (3, 2.5)$
2. a) $(0, 1), (1, 0), (3, 6), (-2, 15)$
  b) $(-2, -3), (0, -8)$
  c) $(2, 9)$
  d) $(-2, 2), (-3, -2)$
3. a) $y < -x^2 - 4x + 5$ **b)** $y \le \dfrac{1}{2}x^2 - x + 3$
  c) $y \ge -\dfrac{1}{4}x^2 - x + 3$ **d)** $y > 4x^2 + 5x - 6$
4. a)

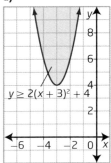

$y \ge 2(x + 3)^2 + 4$

b)

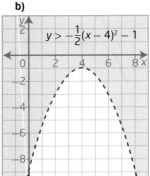

$y > -\dfrac{1}{2}(x - 4)^2 - 1$

c)

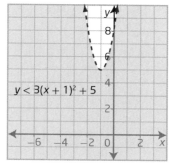

$y < 3(x + 1)^2 + 5$

d)

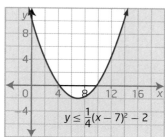

$y \leq \frac{1}{4}(x - 7)^2 - 2$

5. a)

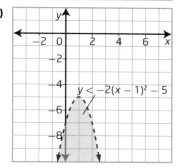

$y < -2(x - 1)^2 - 5$

b)

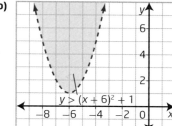

$y > (x + 6)^2 + 1$

c)

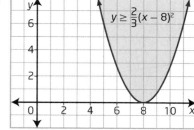

$y \geq \frac{2}{3}(x - 8)^2$

d)

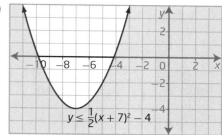

$y \leq \frac{1}{2}(x + 7)^2 - 4$

6. a)

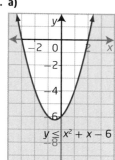

$y \leq x^2 + x - 6$

b)

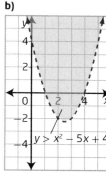

$y > x^2 - 5x + 4$

c)

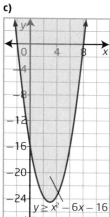

$y \geq x^2 - 6x - 16$

d)

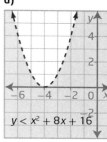

$y < x^2 + 8x + 16$

7. a) $y < 3x^2 + 13x + 10$ **b)** $y \geq -x^2 + 4x + 7$

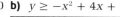

c) $y \leq x^2 + 6$ **d)** $y > -2x^2 + 5x - 8$

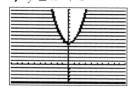

8. a) $y \geq \frac{1}{2}x^2 + 1$

    b) $y > -\frac{1}{3}(x - 1)^2 + 3$

9. a) $y = -\dfrac{1}{625}(x - 50)^2 + 4$

b) $y < -\dfrac{1}{625}(x - 50)^2 + 4, 0 \leq x \leq 100$

10. a) $L \geq -0.000\,125a^2 + 0.040a - 2.442,$
$0 \leq a \leq 180, L \geq 0$

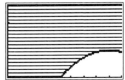

b) any angle greater than or equal to
approximately 114.6° and less than
or equal to 180°

11. a) $y < -0.03x^2 + 0.84x - 0.08$

b) $0 \leq -0.03x^2 + 0.84x - 0.28$
$\{x \mid 0.337... \leq x \leq 27.662..., x \in R\}$

c) The width of the river is 27.325 m.

12. a) $0 < -2.944t^2 + 191.360t - 2649.6$

b) Between 20 s and 45 s is when the jet is
above 9600 m.

c) 25 s

13. a) $y = -0.04x^2 + 5$ **b)** $0 \leq -0.04x^2 + 5$

14. a) $y \leq -x^2 + 20x$ or $y \leq -1(x - 10)^2 + 100$

b) $-x^2 + 20x - 50 \geq 0$; she must have between
3 and 17 ads.

15. $y \leq -0.0001x^2 - 600$ and $y \geq -0.0002x^2 - 700$

16. a) $y = (4 + 0.5x)(400 - 20x)$ or
$y = -10x^2 + 120x + 1600$; x represents the
number of $0.50 increases and y represents
the total revenue.

b) $0 \leq -10x^2 + 120x - 200$; to raise $1800 the
price has to be between $5 and $9.

c) $0 \leq -10x^2 + 120x$; to raise $1600 the price
has to be between $4 and $10.

17. a) $0 \leq 0.24x^2 - 8.1x + 64$; from approximately
12.6 years to 21.1 years after the year 2000

b) $p \leq 0.24t^2 - 8.1t + 74, t \geq 0, p \geq 0$

Only the portion of the graph from $t = 0$
to $t \approx 16.9$ and from $p = 0$ to $p = 100$ is
reasonable. This represents the years over
which the methane produced goes from a
maximum percent of 100 to a minimum
percent around 16.9 years.

c) from approximately 12.6 years to 16.9 years
after the year 2000

d) He should take only positive values of x
from 0 to 16.9, because after that the model
is no longer relevant.

18. Answers may vary.

Chapter 9 Review, pages 501 to 503

1. a)

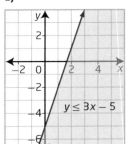

b)

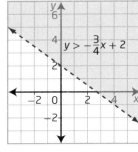

c)

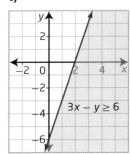

d)

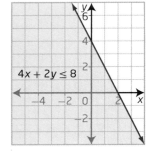

e)

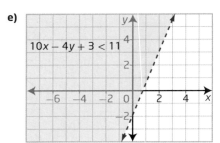

2. a) $y \geq 2x + 3$ **b)** $y > 0.25x - 1$

c) $y < -3x + 2$ **d)** $y \leq -0.75x + 2$

3. a) $y > -\dfrac{4}{5}x + \dfrac{22}{5}$ **b)** $y \leq \dfrac{5}{2}x + 13$

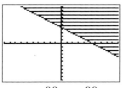
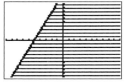

c) $y < \dfrac{32}{11}x + \dfrac{80}{11}$ **d)** $y > -\dfrac{31}{11}x + \dfrac{165}{44}$

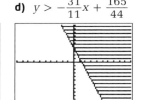

e) $y \geq \dfrac{1}{12}x$

4. a) $15x + 10y \leq 120$, where x represents the number of movies and y represents the number of meals.

b) $y \leq -1.5x + 12$

c) The region below the line in quadrant I $(x \geq 0, y \geq 0)$ shows which combinations will work for her budget. The values of x and y must be whole numbers.

5. a) $30 for a laptop and $16 for a DVD player

b) $30x + 16y \geq 1000$, where x represents the number of laptops sold and y represents the number DVD player sold.

c) $y \geq -1.875x + 62.5$
The region above the line in quadrant I shows which combinations will give the desired commission. The values of x and y must be whole numbers.

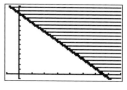

6. a) $\{x \mid x < -7 \text{ or } x > 9, x \in R\}$

b) $\{x \mid x \leq -2.5 \text{ or } x \geq 6, x \in R\}$

c) $\{x \mid -12 < x < 4, x \in R\}$

d) $\{x \mid x \leq 3 - \sqrt{5} \text{ or } x \geq 3 + \sqrt{5}, x \in R\}$

7. a) $\left\{x \mid -\dfrac{4}{3} \leq x \leq \dfrac{1}{2}, x \in R\right\}$

b) $\left\{x \mid \dfrac{5 - \sqrt{21}}{4} < x < \dfrac{5 + \sqrt{21}}{4}, x \in R\right\}$

c) $\{x \mid -4 \leq x \leq 8, x \in R\}$

d) $\left\{x \mid x \leq \dfrac{-6 - 2\sqrt{14}}{5}\right.$
or $\left. x \geq \dfrac{-6 + 2\sqrt{14}}{5}, x \in R\right\}$

8. a) $\left\{x \mid \dfrac{6 - 2\sqrt{3}}{3} \leq x \leq \dfrac{6 + 2\sqrt{3}}{3}, x \in R\right\}$

b) The path has to be between those two points to allow people up to 2 m in height to walk under the water.

9. The length can be anything up to and including 6 m. The width is just half the length, so it is a maximum of 3 m.

10. a) 104.84 km/h

b) $0.007v^2 + 0.22v \leq 50$

c) The solution to the inequality within the given context is $0 < v \leq 70.25$. The maximum stopping speed of 70.25 km/h is not half of the answer from part a) because the function is quadratic not linear.

11. a) $y \leq \dfrac{1}{2}(x + 3)^2 - 4$ **b)** $y > 2(x - 3)^2$

12. a)

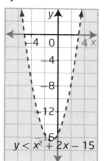

$y < x^2 + 2x - 15$

b)

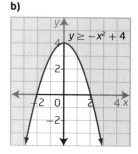

$y \geq -x^2 + 4$

c)

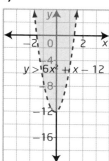

$y > 6x^2 + x - 12$

d)

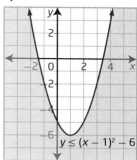

$y \leq (x - 1)^2 - 6$

13. a) $y < x^2 + 3$

b) $y \leq -(x + 4)^2 + 2$

14. a) $y \leq 0.003t^2 - 0.052t + 1.986$,
$0 \leq t \leq 20, y \geq 0$

b) $0.003t^2 - 0.052t - 0.014 \leq 0$; the years it was at most 2 t/ha were from 1975 to 1992.

15. a) $r \leq 0.1v^2$
You cannot have a negative value for the speed or the radius. Therefore, the domain is $\{v \mid v \geq 0, v \in R\}$ and the range is $\{r \mid r \geq 0, r \in R\}$.

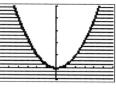

b) Any speed above 12.65 m/s will complete the loop.

16. a) $20 \leq \dfrac{1}{20}x^2 - 4x + 90$

b) $\{x \mid 0 \leq x \leq 25.86 \text{ or } 54.14 \leq x \leq 90, x \in R\}$; the solution shows where the cable is at least 20 m high.

Chapter 9 Practice Test, pages 504 to 505

1. B
2. A
3. C
4. B
5. C
6.

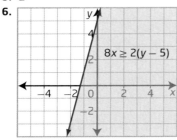

7. $\left\{x \mid -\dfrac{2}{3} < x < \dfrac{5}{4}, x \in \mathbb{R}\right\}$

8.

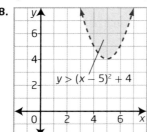

9. $y \geq 0.02x^2$

10. $25x + 20y \leq 300$, where x represents the number of hours scuba diving ($x \geq 0$) and y represents the number of hours sea kayaking ($y \geq 0$).

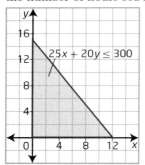

11. a) $50x + 80y \geq 1200$, where x represents the number of ink sketches sold ($x \geq 0$) and y represents the number of watercolours sold ($y \geq 0$).

b) $y \geq -\dfrac{5}{8}x + 15$,
$y \geq 0, x \geq 0$

Example: (0, 15), (2, 15), (8, 12)

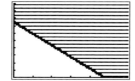

c) $50x + 80y \geq 2400$, where x represents the number of ink sketches sold ($x \geq 0$) and y represents the number of watercolours sold ($y \geq 0$); the related line is parallel to the original with a greater x-intercept and y-intercept.

d) $y \geq -\dfrac{5}{8}x + 30$,
$y \geq 0, x \geq 0$

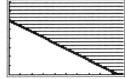

12. a) Example: $f(x) = x^2 - 2x - 15$
b) Example: any quadratic function with two real zeros and whose graph opens upward
c) Example: It is easier to express them in vertex form because you can tell if the parabola opens upward and has a vertex below the x-axis, which results in two zeros.

13. a) $0.01a^2 + 0.05a + 107 < 120$
b) $\{x \mid -38.642 < x < 33.642, x \in \mathbb{R}\}$
c) The only solutions that make sense are those where x is greater than 0. A person cannot have a negative age.

Cumulative Review, Chapters 8–9, pages 508 to 509

1. a) B **b)** D **c)** A **d)** C
2. $(-2.2, 10.7)$, $(2.2, -2.7)$
3. a) $(-1, -4)$, $(2, 5)$
b) The ordered pairs represent the points where the two functions intersect.
4. a) $b > 3.75$ **b)** $b = 3.75$ **c)** $b < 3.75$
5.

Solving Linear-Quadratic Systems		
Substitution Method	**Elimination Method**	
Determine which variable to solve for.	Determine which variable to eliminate.	Multiply the linear equation as needed.
Solve the linear equation for the chosen variable.		
Substitute the expression for the variable into the quadratic equation and simplify.	Add a new linear equation and quadratic equation.	
Solve New Quadratic Equation		
No Solution	Substitute the value(s) into the original linear equation to determine the corresponding value(s) of the other variable.	

6.

Solving Quadratic-Quadratic Systems		
Substitution Method	**Elimination Method**	
Solve one quadratic equation for the y-term.	Eliminate the y-term.	Multiply equations as needed.
Substitute the expression for the y-term into the other quadratic equation and simplify.	Add new equations.	
Solve New Quadratic Equation		
No solution.	Substitute the value(s) into an original equation to determine the corresponding value(s) of x.	

7. The two stocks will be the same price at \$34 and \$46.

8. Example: The number of solutions can be determined by the location of the vertex and the direction in which the parabola opens. The vertex of the first parabola is above the x-axis and it opens upward. The vertex of the second parabola is below the x-axis and it opens downward. The system will have no solution.

9. $(-1.8, -18.6)$, $(0.8, 2.6)$

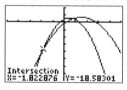 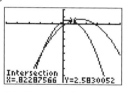

10. a) $(1, 6)$ **b)** $(0, -5)$, $(1, 24)$

11. a) D   **b)** A   **c)** B   **d)** C

12. a) $y > x^2 + 1$ **b)** $y \geq -(x + 3)^2 + 2$

13. a) Results in a true statement. Shade the region that contains the point $(0, 0)$.
   b) Results in a false statement. Shade the region that does not contain the point $(2, -5)$.
   c) The point $(-1, 1)$ cannot be used as a test point. The point is on the boundary line.

14. $y < -2x + 4$

15.

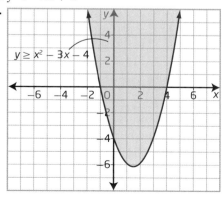

$y \geq x^2 - 3x - 4$

16. $\{x \mid x \leq -7 \text{ or } x \geq 2.5, x \in R\}$

17. The widths must be between 200 m and 300 m.

Unit 4 Test, pages 511 to 513

1. C
2. C
3. B
4. B
5. D
6. D
7. A
8. B
9. A
10. 5
11. 3
12. 1 s
13. a) $(0, 0)$, $(2, 4)$
   b) The points are where the golfer is standing and where the hole is.
14. $g(x) = -(x - 6)^2 + 13$
15. $(-9, 256)$, $(-1, 0)$
16. a) Example: In the second step, she should have subtracted 2 from both sides of the inequality. It should be $3x^2 - 5x - 12 > 0$.
   b) $\left\{x \mid x < -\dfrac{4}{3} \text{ or } x > 3, x \in R\right\}$
17. The ball is above 3 m for 1.43 s.

Glossary

A

absolute value For a real number a, the absolute value is written as $|a|$ and is a positive number.

$$|a| = \begin{cases} a, \text{ if } a \geq 0 \\ -a, \text{ if } a < 0 \end{cases}$$

absolute value equation An equation that includes the absolute value of an expression involving a variable.

absolute value function A function that involves the absolute value of a variable.

acute angle An angle that is between $0°$ and $90°$.

acute triangle A triangle in which each of the three interior angles is acute.

altitude (of a triangle) The perpendicular distance from a vertex to the opposite side of a triangle.

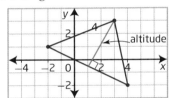

ambiguous case From the given information, the solution for the triangle is not clear: there might be one triangle, two triangles, or no triangle.

angle in standard position The position of an angle when its initial arm is on the positive x-axis and its vertex is at the origin of a coordinate grid.

arithmetic sequence A sequence in which the difference between consecutive terms is constant. An arithmetic sequence is represented by the formula for the general term $t_n = t_1 + (n - 1)d$, where t_1 is the first term, n is the number of terms, and d is the common difference.

The sequence 1, 4, 7, 10, ... is arithmetic.

arithmetic series The terms of an arithmetic sequence expressed as a sum. This sum can be determined using the formula $S_n = \frac{n}{2}[2t_1 + (n - 1)d]$ or $S_n = \frac{n}{2}(t_1 + t_n)$, where n is the number of terms, t_1 is the first term, d is the common difference, and t_n is the nth term.

asymptote A line whose distance from a given curve approaches zero.

axis of symmetry A line through the vertex that divides the graph of a quadratic function into two congruent halves. The x-coordinate of the vertex defines the equation of the axis of symmetry.

B

binomial A polynomial with two terms.

For example, $x^2 + 3$, $m^2n + 4n$, and $2x - 5y$ are binomials.

boundary A line or curve that separates the Cartesian plane into two regions and may or may not be part of the solution region. Drawn as a solid line and included in the solution region if the inequality involves $\leq$ or $\geq$. Drawn as a dashed line and not included in the solution region if the inequality involves $<$ or $>$.

C

common difference The difference between successive terms in an arithmetic sequence, which may be positive or negative. The common difference, d, is equal to $t_n - t_{n-1}$.

For the sequence 1, 4, 7, 10, ..., the common difference is 3.

common ratio The ratio of successive terms in a geometric sequence, which may be positive or negative. The common ratio, r, is equal to $\frac{t_n}{t_{n-1}}$.

For the sequence 1, 2, 4, 8, 16, ..., the common ratio is 2.

completing the square An algebraic process used to write a quadratic polynomial in the form $a(x - p)^2 + q$.

conjugates Two binomial factors whose product is the difference of two squares. The binomials $(a + b)$ and $(a - b)$ are conjugates since their product is $a^2 - b^2$.

convergent series A series with an infinite number of terms, in which the sequence of partial sums approaches a fixed value. This type of series has $-1 < r < 1$, and the fixed value can be determined using the formula $S_\infty = \dfrac{t_1}{1 - r}$.

cosine law The relationship between the cosine of an angle and the lengths of the three sides of any triangle. If a, b, c are the sides of a triangle and C is the angle opposite c, the cosine law is $c^2 = a^2 + b^2 - 2ab \cos C$.

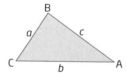

cosine ratio For an acute angle in a right triangle, the ratio of the length of the adjacent side to the length of the hypotenuse.

$$\cos A = \frac{\text{adjacent}}{\text{hypotenuse}}$$

D

degree (of a polynomial) The degree of the highest-degree term in a polynomial.

> For example, the polynomial $7a^2 - 3a$ has degree two.

difference of squares An expression of the form $a^2 - b^2$ that involves the subtraction of two squares.

> For example, $x^2 - 4$ and $(y + 1)^2 - (z + 2)^2$ are differences of squares.

discriminant The expression $b^2 - 4ac$ located under the radical sign in the quadratic formula. Its value is used to determine the nature of the roots of a quadratic equation $ax^2 + bx + c = 0$, $a \neq 0$.

divergent series A series with an infinite number of terms, in which the sequence of partial sums does not approach a fixed value. This type of series has $r > 1$ or $r < -1$.

domain The set of all possible values for the independent variable in a relation.

E

elimination method An algebraic method of solving a system of equations. Add or subtract the equations to eliminate one variable and solve for the other variable.

exact value Answers involving radicals or fractions are exact, unlike approximated decimal values.

> Fractions such as $\frac{1}{3}$ are exact, but an approximation of $\frac{1}{3}$ such as 0.333 is not.

extraneous root A number obtained in solving an equation that does not satisfy the initial restrictions on the variable.

F

factor Any number or algebraic expression that when multiplied with one or more other numbers or algebraic expressions forms a product.

> The factors of 12 are 1, 2, 3, 4, and 6.

> The factors of $4a^2 + 2ab$ are 1, 2, a, $2a$, $4a + 2b$, $2a + b$, and $4a^2 + 2ab$.

finite sequence A sequence that ends and has a final term.

> The sequence 2, 5, 8, 11, 14 is a finite sequence.

function A relation in which each value of the independent variable is associated with exactly one value of the dependent variable. For every value in the domain, there is a unique value in the range.

function notation A notation used when a relation is a function. It is written $f(x)$ and read as "f of x" or "f at x."

G

general term An expression for directly determining any term of a sequence, or the nth term. It is denoted by t_n.

> For the sequence 1, 4, 7, 10, …,
> the general term is $t_n = 3n - 2$.

geometric sequence A sequence in which the ratio of consecutive terms is constant. A geometric sequence can be represented by the formula for the general term $t_n = t_1 r^{n-1}$, where t_1 is the first term, r is the common ratio, and n is the number of terms.

> The sequence 1, 2, 4, 8, 16, … is geometric.

geometric series The terms of a geometric sequence expressed as a sum. This sum can be determined using the formula $S_n = \dfrac{t_1(r^n - 1)}{r - 1}$, where t_1 is the first term, r is the common ratio, n is the number of terms, and $r \neq 1$.

H

horizontal asymptote Describes the behaviour of a graph when $|x|$ is very large. The line $y = b$ is a horizontal asymptote if the values of the function approach b when $|x|$ is very large.

I

index Indicates which root to take.

$$\text{index} \searrow \; \sqrt[n]{x}$$

initial arm The arm of an angle in standard position that lies on the x-axis.

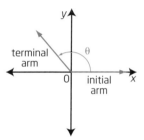

inequality A mathematical statement comparing expressions that may not be equal. These can be written using the symbols less than ($<$), greater than ($>$), less than or equal to ($\leq$), greater than or equal to ($\geq$), and not equal to ($\neq$).

infinite sequence A sequence that does not end or have a final term.

> The sequence 5, 10, 15, 20, … is an infinite sequence.

infinite geometric series A geometric series that does not end or have a final term. An infinite geometric series may be convergent or divergent.

invariant point A point that remains unchanged when a transformation is applied to it.

M

maximum value (of a function) The greatest value in the range of a function. For a quadratic function that opens downward, the y-coordinate of the vertex.

minimum value (of a function) The least value in the range of a function. For a quadratic function that opens upward, the y-coordinate of the vertex.

monomial A polynomial with one term.

> For example, 5, $2x$, $3s^2$, $-8cd$, and $\dfrac{n^4}{3}$ are monomials.

N

non-permissible value Any value for a variable that makes an expression undefined. For rational expressions, any value that results in a denominator of zero.

In $\dfrac{x + 2}{x - 3}$, you must exclude the value for which $x - 3 = 0$, giving a non-permissible value of $x = 3$.

O

oblique triangle A triangle that does not contain a right angle.

obtuse angle An angle that measures more than 90° but less than 180°.

obtuse triangle A triangle containing one obtuse angle.

P

parabola The symmetrical curve of the graph of a quadratic function.

parameter A constant that can assume different values but does not change the form of the expression or function.

In $y = mx + b$, m is a parameter that represents the slope of the line and b is a parameter that represents the y-intercept.

perfect square trinomial The result of squaring a binomial.

For example, $(x + 5)^2 = x^2 + 10x + 25$ is a perfect square trinomial.

piecewise function A function composed of two or more separate functions or *pieces*, each with its own specific domain, that combine to define the overall function. The absolute value function $y = |x|$ can be defined as the piecewise function $y = \begin{cases} x, \text{ if } x \geq 0 \\ -x, \text{ if } x < 0 \end{cases}$.

polynomial An algebraic expression formed by adding or subtracting terms that are products of whole-number powers of variables.

For example, $x + 5$, $2d - 2.4$, and $3s^2 + 5s - 6$ are polynomials.

primary trigonometric ratios The three ratios—sine, cosine, and tangent—defined in a right triangle.

Pythagorean Theorem In a right triangle, the square of the length of the hypotenuse is equal to the sum of the squares of the lengths of the other two sides.

Q

quadrant On a Cartesian plane, the x-axis and the y-axis divide the plane into four quadrants.

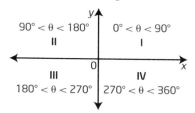

quadrantal angle An angle in standard position whose terminal arm lies on one of the axes.

Examples are 0°, 90°, 180°, 270°, and 360°.

quadratic equation A second-degree equation with standard form $ax^2 + bx + c = 0$, where $a \neq 0$.

For example, $2x^2 + 12x + 16 = 0$.

quadratic formula The formula $x = \dfrac{-b \pm \sqrt{b^2 - 4ac}}{2a}$ for determining the roots of a quadratic equation of the form $ax^2 + bx + c = 0$, $a \neq 0$.

quadratic function A function f whose value $f(x)$ is given by a polynomial of degree two.

For example, $f(x) = x^2$ is the simplest form of a quadratic function.

R

radical Consists of a root symbol, an index, and a radicand. It can be rational (for example, $\sqrt{4}$) or irrational (for example, $\sqrt{2}$).

radical equation An equation with radicals that have variables in the radicands.

radicand The quantity under the radical sign.

range The set of all possible values for the dependent variable as the independent variable takes on all possible values of the domain.

rational equation An equation containing at least one rational expression.

For example, $x = \dfrac{x - 3}{x + 1}$ and $\dfrac{x}{4} - \dfrac{7}{x} = 3$.

rational expression An algebraic fraction with a numerator and a denominator that are polynomials.

For example, $\dfrac{1}{x}$, $\dfrac{m}{m + 1}$, and $\dfrac{y^2 - 1}{y^2 + 2y + 1}$. $x^2 - 4$ is a rational expression with a denominator of 1.

rationalize A procedure for converting to a rational number without changing the value of the expression. If the radical is in the denominator, both the numerator and denominator must be multiplied by a quantity that will produce a rational denominator.

reciprocal (of a number) The multiplier of a number to give a product of 1. For example, $\dfrac{3}{4}$ is the reciprocal of $\dfrac{4}{3}$ because $\dfrac{3}{4} \times \dfrac{4}{3} = 1$.

reciprocal function A function $y = \dfrac{1}{f(x)}$ defined by $y = \dfrac{1}{f(a)} = \dfrac{1}{b}$ if $f(a) = b$, $f(a) \neq 0$, $b \neq 0$.

reference angle The acute angle whose vertex is the origin and whose arms are the terminal arm of the angle and the x-axis. The reference angle is always a positive acute angle.

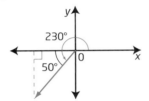

The reference angle for 230° is 50°.

reflection A transformation in which a figure is reflected over a reflection line.

root(s) of an equation The solution(s) to an equation.

S

sequence An ordered list of numbers, where a mathematical pattern or rule is used to generate the next term in the list.

sine law The relationship between the sides and angles in any triangle. The sides of a triangle are proportional to the sines of the opposite angles.

$$\dfrac{a}{\sin A} = \dfrac{b}{\sin B} = \dfrac{c}{\sin C}$$

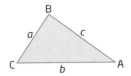

sine ratio For an acute angle in a right triangle, the ratio of the length of the opposite side to the length of the hypotenuse. $\sin A = \dfrac{\text{opposite}}{\text{hypotenuse}}$

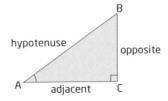

solution (of an inequality) A value or set of values that results in a true inequality statement. The solution can contain a specific value or many values.

solution region All the points in the Cartesian plane that satisfy an inequality. Also known as the solution set.

square root One of two equal factors of a number.

For example, $\sqrt{49} = \sqrt{(7)(7)}$
$= 7$

standard form (of a quadratic function) The form $f(x) = ax^2 + bx + c$ or $y = ax^2 + bx + c$, where a, b, and c are real numbers and $a \neq 0$.

substitution method An algebraic method of solving a system of equations. Solve one equation for one variable. Then, substitute that value into the other equation and solve for the other variable.

system of linear-quadratic equations A linear equation and a quadratic equation involving the same variables. A graph of the system involves a line and a parabola.

system of quadratic-quadratic equations Two quadratic equations involving the same variables. The graph involves two parabolas.

T

tangent ratio For an acute angle in a right triangle, the ratio of the length of the opposite side to the length of the adjacent side. $\tan A = \dfrac{\text{opposite}}{\text{adjacent}}$

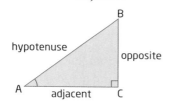

terminal arm The arm of an angle in standard position that meets the initial arm at the origin to form an angle.

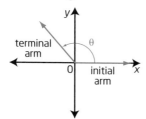

test point A point not on the boundary of the graph of an inequality that is representative of all the points in a region. A point that is used to determine whether the points in a region satisfy the inequality.

transformation A change made to a figure or a relation such that the figure or the graph of the relation is shifted or changed in shape. Examples are translations, reflections, and stretches.

translation A slide transformation that results in a shift of the original figure or graph without changing its shape.

trinomial A polynomial with three terms.

For example, $x^2 + 3x - 1$ and $2x^2 - 5xy + 10y^2$ are trinomials.

V

vertex (of a parabola) The lowest point of the graph (if the graph opens upward) or the highest point of the graph (if the graph opens downward).

vertex form (of a quadratic function) The form $y = a(x - p)^2 + q$, or $f(x) = a(x - p)^2 + q$, where a, p, and q are constants and $a \neq 0$.

vertical asymptote For reciprocal functions, vertical asymptotes occur at the non-permissible values of the function. The line $x = a$ is a vertical asymptote if the curve approaches the line more and more closely as x approaches a, and the values of the function increase or decrease without bound as x approaches a.

X

x-intercept The x-coordinate of the point where a line or curve crosses the x-axis. It is the value of x when $y = 0$.

Y

y-intercept The y-coordinate of the point where a line or curve crosses the y-axis. It is the value of y when $x = 0$.

Z

zero(s) of a function The value(s) of x for which $f(x) = 0$. These values of x are related to the x-intercept(s) of the graph of a function $f(x)$.

zero product property States that if the product of two real numbers is zero, then one or both of the numbers must be zero.

Index

A

absolute value, 356, 358–363
  comparing and ordering, 361
  defined, 360
  determining, 360
  evaluating expressions, 361
absolute value equations, 380–388
  defined, 381
  extraneous solution for,
    383–384
  linear and quadratic
    expressions, 386–387
  no solution for, 384
  problems involving, 387–388
  quadratic, 385–386
  solving, 382–383
absolute value functions, 368–375
  defined, 370
  graphing, 370–374
  invariant point, 371
  linear, 368–369
  piecewise definition, 370
  quadratic, 369
  See also functions
adding
  radicals, 276–277
  rational expressions and
    equations, 332–335
algebra
  determining terms, 13–14
  systems of equations, 440–451
ambiguous case, 104–107
angles
  cosine law, 117–118
  quadrantal angle, 93
  sine law, 104
  See also trigonometric ratios
angles (standard position), 74–82
  defined, 77
  determining, 81
  exact values, 79, 82
  initial arm, 77
  reference angle, 78, 80–81
  special right triangles, 79
  terminal arm, 77
arithmetic sequences, 6–16
  arithmetic series, 24
  common difference, 9
  defined, 9
  determining number of terms, 12

determining terms, 10–11,
  13–14
Gauss's method, 22–24
general term, 9
generating, 14–15
staircase numbers, 6–8
arithmetic series, 22–27
  defined, 24
  determining terms, 26
  determining the sum of, 25
  Gauss's method, 22–24
asymptote, 395
axis of symmetry, 145

B

boundary, 466

C

career links
  aerospace designer, 141
  biomedical engineer, 5
  chemical engineer, 463
  commercial diver, 357
  mathematical modeller, 309
  meteorologist, 271
  physical therapist, 73
  robotics engineer, 205
  university researcher, 423
common denominator, 332–333
common difference, 9
common ratio, 34
completing the square, 180–192,
  234–240
  applying, 239
  converting to vertex form,
    183–188
  defined, 183
  to find maximum values, 191
  quadratic equations, 234–240
  quadratic functions, 180–182
  solving a quadratic equation,
    236
conjugates, 287
convergent series, 60
cosine law, 114–119
  defined, 116
  determining angles, 117–118
  determining distance, 116–117
  triangles, 118–119

D

denominator, 332–335
discriminant, 246
divergent series, 60
dividing
  radical expressions, 286–288
  rational expressions, 322–326

E

exact value, 79
extraneous roots
  absolute value equations,
    383–384
  defined, 236
  radical equations, 297
  rational equations, 344

F

factoring quadratic equations. *See*
  quadratic equations (factoring)
Fibonacci sequence, 4, 32
finite sequences, 8
fractal geometry, 46–47
  See also geometric series
functions
  absolute value, 368–375
  linear, 368–369, 396–399
  maximum value of, 145
  minimum value of, 145
  quadratic, 142–146
  reciprocal, 392–403
  See also absolute value
    functions; quadratic
    functions; reciprocal
    functions

G

Gauss's method, 22–24
general term
  arithmetic sequences, 9
  geometric sequences, 34
geometric sequences, 32–39
  applying, 37
  common ratio, 34
  defined, 32
  determining terms, 34–36
  general term, 34
geometric series, 46–53
  applying, 52

system of linear-quadratic
equations, 425, 426, 427,
428–429, 430–431, 441–445
system of quadratic-quadratic
equations, 425, 429–430,
432–433, 447–450

T

terminal arm, 77
test points, 467
triangles
cosine law, 118–119
equilateral triangles, 282
isosceles right triangles, 283
special right triangles, 79
trigonometry
ambiguous case, 104–107
angle in standard position,
74–82
cosine law, 114–119

exact value, 79, 82
initial arm, 77
quadrantal angle, 93
reference angle, 78, 80–81
sine law, 100–107
special right triangles, 79
terminal arm, 77
trigonometric ratios, 88–95
trigonometric ratios, 88–95
angles greater than 90 degrees,
88–89
determining, 90–95

U

unit projects
avalanche control, 263
Canada's natural resources, 3,
71, 131–132
nanotechnology, 421, 461,
506–507

quadratic functions in
everyday life, 139, 263
space: past, present, future,
269, 415
See also project corner
unlike denominators, 332, 334–335

V

vertex (of a parabola), 144
vertex form (of a quadratic
function). *See* quadratic
functions (vertex form)

Z

Zeno's paradoxes, 58
zero(s) of a function, 208

Credits

Photo Credits

iv David Tanaka; v Kelly Funk/All Canada Photos; vi top background Karen Kasmauski/CORBIS, left David Tanaka, left bottom Keith Douglas, middle top O. Bierwagon/IVY IMAGES, right top Lloyd Sutton/Alamy, middle W.Ivy/IVY IMAGES; vii TOP top left background NASA Goddard Space Flight Center, top left Gemini Observatory, GMOS Team, lower left background Brenda Tharp/Photo Researchers Inc., left Alexander Kuzovlev/iStock, top right Nick Higham/Alamy/GetStock, middle CCL/wiki, bottom right Masterfile; LOWER top Jerry Lodriguss/Photo Researchers Inc., Science Source/Photo Researchers Inc.; viii NASA; ix middle left Bill Ivy, Diving Plongeon Canada, Clarence W. Norris/Lone Pine Photo; xi Al Harvey/The Slide Farm; pp2–3 background Karen Kasmauski/CORBIS, left David Tanaka, left bottom Keith Douglas, middle top O. Bierwagon/IVY IMAGES, right top Lloyd Sutton/Alamy; pp4–5 top left background NASA Goddard Space Flight Center, top left Gemini Observatory-GMOS Team, lower left background Brenda Tharp/Photo Researchers Inc., left Alexander Kuzovlev/iStock, top right Nick Higham/Alamy/GetStock, middle CCL/wiki, bottom Masterfile; p6 top Jerry Lodriguss/Photo Researchers Inc., Science Source/Photo Researchers Inc.; p12 Richard Sidey/iStock; p18 "Geese and Ulus" by Lucy Ango'yuaq of Baker Lake. 22"by 27" fabric, Used by permission of the artist. Photo by WarkInuit; p19 top catnap/iStock, Photo courtesy of Rio Tinto; p20 David Tanaka; p22 Bettman/Corbis; p25 Edward R. Degginger/Alamy/GetStock; p28 top "A Breach in Hunger" Photo: Dave Roels. Used by permission of The Greater Vancouver Food Bank and CANstruction Vancouver, "UnBEARable Hunger" by Butler Rogers Baskett Architects, P.C.-2008 International Jurors' Favorite. Photo: Kevin Wick. Canstruction is a trademarked Charity Competition of the Design and Construction Industry under the auspices of the Society for Design Administration; p31 top chris scredon/iStock, Ljupco Smokovsk/iStock, Reuters/Corbis; p32 Janez Habjanic/iStock; pp33, 35,40 David Tanaka; p41 top Bill Ivy, Biophoto Associates/Photo Researchers Inc.; p42 top left clockwise Courtesy of the Arctic Winter Games, Sol Neelman/Corbis, CCL/wiki, Jesper Kunuk Egede; p43 top efesan/iStock, Leslie Casals/iStock; p45 B. Lowry/IVY IMAGES; p46 top John Glover/Alamy/GetStock, David Tanaka, Manor Photography/

Alamy/GetStock; p52 David Tanaka; p55 top Bill Ivy, Jeff Greenberg/Alamy/GetStock; p57 Bill Ivy; p58 Mary Evans Picture Library/Alamy; p64 O. Bierwagon/IVY IMAGES; p66 Clarence W. Norris/Lone Pine Photo; p70 Toronto Star/GetStock; p71 top Keith Douglas, Paul A. Souders/CORBIS, Judy Waytiuk/Alamy/Get Stock; pp72–73 background J. DeVisser/IVY IMAGES, lower left Ethel Davies/Robert Harding World Imagery/Corbis, middle right Henryk Sadura/iStock, lower right Artiga Photo/Corbis; p74 Stapleton Collection/Corbis; p82 McGraw Hill Companies; p84 lower Hazlan Abdul Hakim/iStock; p85 top left David Tanaka, Don Bayley/iStock, Derivative work by Chris Buckley, UK. Original by Mohammed Abubakr, ECE, GRIET, Hyderabad, India. Used by permission; p86 Courtesy of Uncle Milton Industries. Used by permission; p88 Courtesy of Syncrude Canada Ltd.; p100 Hal Bergman/iStock; p101 CCL/wiki; p102 Bryan & Cherry Alexander/Arctic Photos; p109 Terry Melnyk; p110 left "The Founders, Chief Whitecap and John Lake" by Hans Holtkamp, Traffic Bridge, River Landing, Saskatoon 06. Wayne Shiels/Lone Pine Photo; top right Daniel Cardiff/iStock, Olivier Pitras/Sygma/Corbis; p114 NASA; p117 Cameron Whitman/iStock; p121 left NASA, "Moondog" by Tony White, National Gallery of Washington; p123 top Russ Heinl/All Canada Photos; p124 Peter J. Van Coeverden de Groot; p132 W. Ivy/IVY IMAGES; p133 Al Harvey/The Slide Farm; p134 M. Fieguth/IVY IMAGES; p135 top W. Lankinen/IVY IMAGES, Guy Laflamme/Kunoki; p137 Manitoba MS Society; pp138–139 background Ed Darack/Science Faction/Corbis, top left background clockwise Mark Herreid/iStock, Victor Kapas/iStock, James Brittain/VIEW/Corbis, Clayton Hansen/iStock, Chris Moseley/Canadian Avalanche Association; pp140–141 David Tanaka, bottom right Thierry Boccon-Gibod/Getty Images; p142 Used by permission, Ford Motor Company; p154 Arpad Benedek/iStock; p159 Orestis Panagiotou/epa/Corbis; p160 top Alan Marsh/First Light, David Keith Jones/Alamy/GetStock; p163 top Ryan Remiorz/The Canadian Press, Chuck Stoody/The Canadian Press; p169 Arco Images GmbH/Alamy; p171 Chris Harris/All Canada Photos; p175 Ron Erwin/iStock; p176 Bryan Weinstein/iStock; p180 Cliff Whittem/Alamy/GetStock; p181 Pat O'Hara/Corbis; p190 moodboard/CORBIS; p194 top Joe Gough/iStock, Lynden Pioneer Museum/Alamy/GetStock; p195 top Bill Ivy,

Technical Art

Brad Black, Tom Dart, Kim Hutchinson, and Brad Smith of First Folio Resource Group, Inc.